ASPEN PUBLISHERS

PAYMENT SYSTEMS

Second Edition

Lary Lawrence

Harriet L. Bradley Chair of Contract Law
Loyola Law School, Los Angeles

The *Emanuel Law Outlines* Series

™ Wolters Kluwer

Law & Business

AUSTIN   BOSTON   CHICAGO   NEW YORK   THE NETHERLANDS

© 2009 by Aspen Publishers, Inc.
A Wolters Kluwer Company
www.aspenpublishers.com

All rights reserved. No part of this publication may be reproduced or transmitted in any form or by any means, electronic or mechanical, including photocopy, recording, or any information storage and retrieval system, without permission in writing from the publisher. Requests for permission to make copies of any part of this publication should be mailed to:

Aspen Publishers
Attn: Permissions Department
76 Ninth Avenue, 7th Floor
New York, NY 10011-5201

To contact Customer Care, e-mail customer.care@aspenpublishers.com, call 1-800-234-1660, fax 1-800-901-9075, or mail correspondence to:

Aspen Publishers
Attn: Order Department
PO Box 990
Frederick, MD 21705

Printed in the United States of America.

1 2 3 4 5 6 7 8 9 0

ISBN 978-0-7355-7053-5

This book is intended as a general review of a legal subject. It is not intended as a source of advice for the solution of legal matters or problems. For advice on legal matters, the reader should consult an attorney.

Library of Congress Cataloging-in-Publication Data
Lawrence, Lary.
    Payment systems / Lary Lawrence. — 2nd ed.
        p. cm. — (Emanuel law outlines series)
    Includes bibliographical references and index.
    ISBN 978-0-7355-7053-5 (pbk.)
    1. Negotiable instruments — United States — Outlines, syllabi, etc. 2. Payment — United
        States — Outlines, syllabi, etc. I. Title.
KF957.L38 2009
346.73'096 — dc22

2009023590

About Wolters Kluwer Law & Business

Wolters Kluwer Law & Business is a leading provider of research information and workflow solutions in key specialty areas. The strength of the individual brands of Aspen Publishers, CCH, Kluwer Law International and Loislaw are aligned within Wolters Kluwer Law & Business to provide comprehensive, in-depth solutions and expert-authored content for the legal, professional and education markets.

CCH was founded in 1913 and has served more than four generations of business professionals and their clients. The CCH products in the Wolters Kluwer Law & Business group are highly regarded electronic and print resources for legal, securities, antitrust and trade regulation, government contracting, banking, pension, payroll, employment and labor, and healthcare reimbursement and compliance professionals.

Aspen Publishers is a leading information provider for attorneys, business professionals and law students. Written by preeminent authorities, Aspen products offer analytical and practical information in a range of specialty practice areas from securities law and intellectual property to mergers and acquisitions and pension/benefits. Aspen's trusted legal education resources provide professors and students with high-quality, up-to-date and effective resources for successful instruction and study in all areas of the law.

Kluwer Law International supplies the global business community with comprehensive English-language international legal information. Legal practitioners, corporate counsel and business executives around the world rely on the Kluwer Law International journals, loose-leafs, books and electronic products for authoritative information in many areas of international legal practice.

Loislaw is a premier provider of digitized legal content to small law firm practitioners of various specializations. Loislaw provides attorneys with the ability to quickly and efficiently find the necessary legal information they need, when and where they need it, by facilitating access to primary law as well as state-specific law, records, forms and treatises.

Wolters Kluwer Law & Business, a unit of Wolters Kluwer, is headquartered in New York and Riverwoods, Illinois. Wolters Kluwer is a leading multinational publisher and information services company.

Summary of Contents

Table of Contents vii

Preface xxv

Casebook Correlation Chart xxvii

Capsule Summary C-1

1. What Is a Negotiable Instrument? 1

2. Holder-in-Due-Course Status and Available Claims, Defenses, Claims in Recoupment, and Discharges 19

3. Nature of Liability on Instruments 67

4. Forgery, Alteration, and Other Fraudulent Activity 107

5. Payor Bank/Customer Relationship 141

6. The Bank Collection Process 161

7. Wholesale Funds Transfers 179

8. Consumer Electronic Fund Transfers 199

9. Lender Credit Cards 211

Essay Exam Questions and Answers 219

Glossary 229

Table of Cases 241

Table of Statutes 243

Subject Matter Index 253

Table of Contents

Preface xxv

Casebook Correlation Chart xxvii

Capsule Summary C-1

CHAPTER 1
WHAT IS A NEGOTIABLE INSTRUMENT?

I. What Is a Negotiable Instrument? 1
   A. Introduction 1
   B. Primary difference from ordinary contract right 1
   C. Other differences 2

II. Governing Law 2
   A. Basic governing law 2
   B. Coverage of Article 3 2
      1. Exclusions 2
   C. Coverage of Article 4 2
      1. Item 2
      2. Exclusions 2
   D. Article 4 prevails over Article 3 2
   E. Federal common law 3
      1. Basically same as Article 3 3
      2. Differences 3
      3. Not involving rights and duties of United States 3

III. Types of Negotiable Instruments 3
   A. Introduction 3
   B. Notes 3
      1. Purpose 3
      2. Diversity of form 3
      3. Certificate of deposit 3
   C. Drafts 4
      1. Purpose 4
      2. Checks 4
      3. Bank checks 4
      4. Traveler's checks 4
      5. Personal money order 5
      6. Drafts (other than checks) 5
      7. Payable through items 5
      8. Payable at items 5
      9. Remotely created consumer item 6

IV. Requirements for Negotiability 6
  A. Introduction 6
  B. Compliance with U.C.C. §3-104(a) 6
  C. Requirements for negotiability 6
  D. Instrument must be in writing 7
    1. What is a writing? 7
    2. Signed 7
  E. Promise or order 8
    1. Promise 8
    2. Order 8
  F. The promise or order must be unconditional 8
    1. Express condition 8
    2. Implied condition 8
    3. Payment out of particular fund 8
    4. Reference to separate agreement 9
  G. Fixed Amount 9
    1. Determined by reference to instrument alone 9
    2. Exceptions 10
  H. Payable in money 11
    1. Money 11
    2. Payable in either currency 11
  I. Payable to order or to bearer 11
    1. Payable to bearer 11
    2. Payable to order 11
    3. Payable to both order and bearer 12
  J. Payable on demand or at a definite time 12
    1. Payable on demand 12
    2. Payable at a definite time 12
  K. No other promises or orders 14
    1. Clauses defeating negotiability 14
    2. Permissible promises and instructions 14
    3. Limited to maker or drawer 14
    4. Conditional sales contracts 15
  L. Negotiability determined by writing itself 15
    1. Not negotiable by agreement alone 15
    2. May be treated as negotiable 15
    3. Writing "not negotiable" defeats negotiability 15

CHAPTER 2

HOLDER-IN-DUE-COURSE STATUS AND AVAILABLE CLAIMS, DEFENSES, CLAIMS IN RECOUPMENT, AND DISCHARGES

I. Introduction 19
  A. Holder-in-due-course status 19
  B. General requirements for holder-in-due-course status 19

II. Holder Status 20
  A. Introduction 20
  B. Holder need not own instrument 20
  C. Requirements for holder status 20
  D. Ways of acquiring holder status 20
    1. Issuance of instrument 20
    2. Negotiation of instrument 20
  E. Obligation must run to possessor 21
  F. Indorsement 21
    1. Types of indorsements 21
    2. Indorsement must be written on instrument 22
    3. Manner of negotiation depends on last indorsement 22
    4. To whom an instrument is payable 22
    5. When payable to account number 23
    6. Payable to agent for identified person 23
    7. Payable to office or officer 24
    8. Payable to fund or organization 24
    9. Payable to trust or estate 24
    10. Other words of description 24
    11. Two or more payees 24
  G. Depositary bank's status as holder 25
    1. No indorsement necessary 25
    2. Customer liable as indorser 25
    3. Depositary bank's warranty 25
    4. Delivered for collection 25

III. Value 25
  A. Issued or transferred for value 25
  B. Consideration vs. value 26
  C. Promise of performance as value 26
  D. Value to the extent performed 26
    1. Formula when partial performance by holder 26
  E. Security interest in instrument as value 26
    1. Security interest in instrument 26
    2. Lien on instrument 26
    3. Value only to extent of amount owed 27
  F. Payment or security for antecedent debt as value 27
  G. Negotiable instrument or irrevocable obligation as value 27
  H. Taking for value by collecting bank 28
    1. Manner of acquiring a security interest 28
    2. U.C.C. §4-210 not exclusive 28
    3. To extent credit given has been withdrawn or applied 28
    4. Applies to debt of customer 28
    5. Withdrawal as a matter of right 28
    6. Makes advance against item 28
    7. Simultaneous deposits 29
    8. Order withdrawn when deposits not simultaneous 29

IV. Good Faith 29
   A. Definition 29
   B. Subjective element 29
   C. Objective element 29

V. Notice 30
   A. Notice of infirmities 30
   B. Notice need not relate to defense or claim raised 30
   C. When notice effective 30
   D. Effect of subsequent notice 30
   E. When notice imputed to organization 30
      1. Organization 31
      2. Due diligence 31
   F. Manner of obtaining notice 32
      1. Actual knowledge 32
      2. Notification 32
      3. Reason to know 32
   G. Notice of claim or defense 33
      1. Notice not obtained from public filing 33
      2. Notice not obtained from executory promise 33
      3. Notice from defenses from other transactions 33
      4. Purchase at a discount 33
      5. Notice of breach of fiduciary duty 33
      6. Notice that an instrument is forged, altered, or otherwise
         irregular 35
      7. Notice that instrument is overdue or has been dishonored 35
      8. Notice of discharge 36

VI. Denial of Holder-in-Due-Course Status to Certain
    Classes of Purchasers 37
   A. Introduction 37
   B. Acquisition by taking over estate 37
   C. Purchase in execution, bankruptcy, or creditor's sale 37
   D. Purchase in bulk transaction 37
      1. Liquidation sale 37
      2. Organizational change 38
   E. Consumer notes 38
      1. Definitions under FTC rule 39
      2. FTC rule 39
      3. State legislation 39
      4. 2002 amendments and consumer transactions 40

VII. Defenses, Claims to the Instrument, Claims in Recoupment, and
    Discharges 40
   A. Introduction 40
   B. Defenses and claims in recoupment to which all persons take subject ... 41
      1. Defenses and claims in recoupment assertible against holder itself ... 41
      2. Real defenses 41

C. Defenses available only against a person without the rights of a holder in due course 43
    1. Ordinary defenses 43
    2. Claims in recoupment 44
    3. Defenses and claims in recoupment of other persons 45
    4. Claims to the instrument 45
D. Discharges 46
    1. Effect of discharge 46
    2. Discharge by payment 46
    3. Discharge by tender of payment 49
    4. Discharge by cancellation or renunciation 51
    5. Discharge of simple contract 52

VIII. Admissibility of Evidence Extrinsic to the Instrument 52
A. Introduction 52
B. Agreement as defense 52
C. Same transaction 52
D. The parol evidence rule 52
    1. Consistent additional terms admissible 53
    2. Conditions precedent 53
    3. Sham 53
    4. Special purpose or conditional delivery 53
    5. Defenses 53
    6. Ambiguities 53

IX. Transfer of Instrument and Shelter Provision 53
A. Introduction 53
B. What is a transfer? 54
    1. No transfer until delivery 54
    2. Intent to vest rights in transferee 54
C. Right to transferor's indorsement 54
D. The shelter provision 54
    1. Transferee acquires rights of holder in due course 54
    2. Same rights as transferor 54
    3. Exceptions to shelter provision 55
E. Reacquisition by prior holder 55
    1. Reacquisition by negotiation 55
    2. Reacquisition by transfer 56

X. Defenses and Claims to Bank Checks 56
A. Introduction 56
B. Rules not applicable if bank uses bank check 56
C. Terminology 56
D. Rules governing obligated bank's right to refuse payment on a bank check 56
    1. Penalty for wrongfully refusing to pay 57
    2. Consequential damages 57
    3. Bank's defenses to liability for expenses and consequential damages 57
    4. Third-party claims 57

XI. Federal Holder-in-Due-Course Status 58
   A. Introduction 58
   B. Federal law governs 58
   C. Federal holder-in-due-course doctrine 58
   D. D'Oench, Duhme doctrine 59

CHAPTER 3
NATURE OF LIABILITY ON INSTRUMENTS

I. Liability of Issuer, Drawer, Acceptor, and Indorser 67
   A. Introduction 67
   B. Obligation of issuer of note or cashier's check 68
   C. Obligation of drawer 68
      1. Effect of acceptance 68
      2. Disclaimer of liability 68
   D. Obligation of drawee 68
   E. The obligation of an acceptor 68
      1. Acceptance vs. payment 69
      2. Manner of acceptance 69
   F. Obligation of indorser 69
      1. What is an indorser? 69
      2. Two purposes of indorsement 69
      3. To whom obligation owed 69
      4. Indorsement without recourse 70
      5. Dishonor and notice of dishonor required 70
      6. Discharge if presentment on check delayed 70
      7. Liable in any order 70

II. Presentment, Dishonor, Notice of Dishonor 71
   A. Dishonor 71
   B. Presentment 71
      1. Manner and time of presentment 71
      2. Where presentment can be made 71
      3. Rights of party to whom presentment is made 71
      4. Effect of delay in presentment 72
      5. When presentment excused 72
   C. Dishonor 73
      1. Dishonor of demand note 73
      2. Dishonor of note not payable on demand 73
      3. Dishonor of check 73
      4. Dishonor of other demand draft 73
      5. Dishonor of draft not payable on demand 73
      6. Dishonor of accepted draft 74
   D. Notice of dishonor 74
      1. Time within which notice of dishonor must be given 74

    2. When delay in notice of dishonor excused 75

    3. When notice of dishonor excused 75

III. Transfer Warranties 75

  A. Creating transfer warranties 75

  B. Who makes the transfer warranties 75

  C. To whom transfer warranties are made 76

  D. Content of transfer warranties 76

    1. Warranty that transferor is a person entitled to enforce the instrument 76

    2. Warranty that all signatures are authentic and authorized 77

    3. Warranty of no alteration 77

    4. Warranty that transferor not subject to any defense or claim in recoupment 77

    5. Warranty of no knowledge of insolvency proceedings 78

    6. 2002 amendments 78

IV. Sureties and Accommodation Parties 78

  A. Introduction 78

  B. What is an accommodation party? 78

    1. Both surety and debtor must sign instrument 78

    2. When both do not sign same instrument 78

    3. Collection guaranteed 79

    4. Accommodation party cannot receive direct benefit from instrument 79

    5. Accommodation party liable in capacity in which she signs 79

    6. 2002 amendments 79

  C. Relationship between accommodation and accommodated parties 80

    1. Right of reimbursement 80

    2. Right of subrogation 80

    3. 2002 amendments 81

  D. Relationship between accommodation parties 81

    1. Right of contribution 81

    2. Subsuretyship 81

  E. Defenses available to accommodation party 81

    1. May not raise lack of consideration 81

    2. Right of accommodation party to raise accommodated party's defenses 81

  F. Discharge of indorsers and accommodation parties (suretyship defenses) 82

    1. Suretyship defenses 82

    2. Limited to accommodation parties and indorsers 82

    3. Release of principal obligor 83

    4. Extensions and modifications 85

    5. Extensions—extent of discharge 85

    6. Modifications—extent of discharge 87

    7. Consent and waiver 89

    8. Impairment of collateral 89

    9. When is collateral impaired? 90

    10. Extent of discharge for impairment of collateral 91

    11. Consent to impairment of collateral 92

V. Liability of Agents, Principals, and Co-Obligors 92
  A. Represented person and representative 92
  B. Liability of represented person 92
     1. Types of authority 92
     2. Manner of signing 92
  C. Liability of representative 93
     1. Unauthorized signature 93
     2. Authorized signature 93
  D. Liability of persons signing in the same capacity in the same transaction 94
     1. Right of contribution 94
     2. Liability of indorsers 95

VI. Effect of Taking Instrument on the Underlying Obligation 96
  A. Introduction 96
  B. Ordinary instruments 96
     1. Obligation suspended 96
     2. Effect of dishonor 96
     3. Effect of discharge 97
  C. Bank checks 97
     1. Only bank liable 97
     2. Party liable if indorses 97
  D. Taking instrument for underlying obligation 97

VII. Accord and Satisfaction by Use of Instrument 98
  A. Introduction 98
  B. Good faith required 98
  C. Debtor discharged even if language stricken 98
  D. Exception for lockbox accounts 98
  E. Exception for returning payment 98
  F. Limitation on exceptions 98

VIII. Procedural Issues Involving Negotiable Instruments 99
  A. Procedural differences for actions on negotiable instruments 99
  B. Persons entitled to enforce instrument 99
     1. Rights of a holder 99
     2. Owner of lost instrument 99
     3. Person from whom payment recovered 99
  C. Burden of proof in negotiable instruments cases 99
     1. Exception to producing instrument 99
     2. Proving signatures 99
     3. Burden on obligor to prove defense 100
     4. After defense proved, duty of plaintiff to prove holder-in-due-course
        status 100

IX. Enforcement of Lost, Destroyed, or Stolen Instruments 100
  A. Lost, destroyed, or stolen ordinary instruments 100
     1. Adequate protection 100
     2. Right to recover on instrument only 100
     3. What claimant must prove 100

B. Lost, destroyed, or stolen bank checks 101
    1. Who may use U.C.C. §3-312 101
    2. Manner of asserting claim 101
    3. When claim is effective 101
    4. Bank discharged by payment to claimant 102

CHAPTER 4

FORGERY, ALTERATION, AND OTHER FRAUDULENT ACTIVITY

I. Unauthorized Signatures 107
  A. Introduction 107
  B. Two consequences of unauthorized signature 107
  C. Person whose name is signed not liable 108
    1. Unauthorized signer liable 108
    2. Loss shifted 108
  D. Effect of forged indorsement in chain of title 108
    1. Person whose signature forged still owner 108
    2. Different result if precluded 108
  E. Transfer warranties 108
    1. Person entitled to enforce instrument 108
    2. All signatures are authentic 108
    3. 2002 amendments 108
  F. Presentment warranties 108
    1. Persons who make presentment warranties 109
    2. To whom presentment warranties are made 109
    3. Warranties made to drawee of unaccepted draft 109
    4. 2002 amendments 110
    5. Warranties made to other payors 110
  G. Recovery by payor of payment made by mistake 111
    1. Typical mistakes 111
    2. Protected persons under U.C.C. §3-418 111
    3. Consequences when payment is recovered 111
  H. Conversion 111
    1. When taking by transfer constitutes conversion 111
    2. When payment constitutes conversion 112
    3. When taking instrument by agent is conversion 112
    4. Taking instrument for collection 112
    5. Who may bring an action for conversion? 112
    6. Defenses to conversion action 113
    7. Measure of damages for conversion 113
    8. Statute of limitations for conversion 113
  I. Application of rules when signature of maker or acceptor unauthorized 113
    1. When payment not made 114
    2. When payment made 114

   J. Application of rules when signature of drawer unauthorized 114
      1. When drawee makes payment 114
      2. When drawee does not make payment 114
      3. 2002 amendments 115
   K. Application of rules when indorsement is unauthorized 115
      1. Allocation of loss when check not delivered to payee 115
      2. Allocation of loss after delivery to payee 115

II. Alterations and Incomplete Instruments 116
   A. What is an alteration? 116
   B. Allocation of loss in case of alteration 117
      1. Preclusion to assert alteration 117
      2. Payment by drawee 117
      3. When drawer, maker, or acceptor pays 117
      4. When instrument not paid 118
   C. Discharge of party whose obligation is affected 118
      1. Against whom discharge effective 118
      2. Alteration must be fraudulent 118
   D. Incomplete instruments 118
      1. When completion authorized 119
      2. When completion unauthorized 119

III. Grounds of Preclusion 119
   A. Introduction 119
   B. Ratification 119
   C. Estoppel 119
   D. Preclusion through negligence 119
      1. Who may assert the preclusion? 120
      2. Comparative negligence 120
      3. Failure to exercise ordinary care 120
      4. Substantially contributes 122
   E. Impostors, fictitious payees, and employer's responsibility for unauthorized
      indorsements by employees 122
      1. The impostor rule 122
      2. Fictitious payee rule 124
      3. Employer's responsibility for fraudulent indorsement by
         employee 125
   F. Customer's duty to review bank statement 127
      1. Applies to items 127
      2. No duty of bank to send statement of account to customer 127
      3. If bank sends statement of account 127
      4. Customer's duty to examine bank statement 127
      5. Duty of bank to prove loss 128
      6. Forgery or alteration by same wrongdoer 128
      7. Good faith and comparative negligence 128
      8. 1-year preclusion 128
      9. Duty of payor bank to raise defense 129

IV. Restrictive Indorsements 129
    A. Definition 129
    B. Types of restrictive indorsements 129
        1. For deposit 129
        2. Trust indorsement 129
    C. Does not limit right to negotiate 129
    D. Effect of "for deposit only" indorsement 130
        1. Payor and intermediary banks exempted 130
        2. Depositary bank liable for conversion 130
        3. Nonbank 130
    E. Effect of trust indorsement 130
        1. When taker deals directly with fiduciary 130
        2. When taker does not deal directly with fiduciary 131

CHAPTER 5
PAYOR BANK/CUSTOMER RELATIONSHIP

I. When Item Properly Payable 141
    A. Introduction 141
    B. Items creating overdrafts 142
    C. Postdated checks 142
        1. Same procedure as stop payment order 142
        2. Same damages as for payment over stop payment order 142
    D. Bank not obligated to pay stale checks 142
        1. Bank has option to pay 142
        2. Drawer remains liable 143
    E. Bank's right of set-off 143
        1. Account must belong to customer 143
        2. Debts must be matured 143
        3. Notice not required 144
        4. Limitations on consumer debts 144
    F. Death or incompetence of customer 144
        1. Effect of incompetence 144
        2. Effect of death 144

II. Variation by Agreement 145
    A. Introduction 145
    B. Limitations on agreements 145
    C. Contracts of adhesion 145
        1. Customer's actual knowledge relevant 145
        2. Against public policy 145
        3. Agreements may limit customers' rights 146

III. Wrongful Dishonor 146
    A. Introduction 146
    B. Pivotal issue is whether sufficient funds in account 146
        1. Bank may pay checks in any order 146

2. Time for determining whether sufficient funds exist 146
C. Duty owed only to customer 146
   1. Payee and other holders 146
   2. Corporate officers or partners not customers 146
D. Damages 147
   1. Loss of profits 147
   2. Damage to reputation 147
   3. Emotional distress damages 147
   4. Punitive damages 147

IV. Customer's Right to Stop Payment 147
A. Introduction 147
B. Closed accounts 147
C. More than one customer 148
D. Payable from customer's account 148
E. Effect of stop payment order 148
F. Requirements for stop payment order 148
   1. Adequate description of item 148
   2. Oral or written 149
G. Timeliness of stop payment order, legal process, notice, and set-off 149
   1. Test for determining when stop payment order or other legals come too late 149
   2. Effect of stop payment order or other legal arriving on time 150
   3. Effect of stop payment order or other legal arriving too late 151
H. Damages for payment in violation of stop payment order 151
   1. Measure of damages 151
   2. Damages also include wrongful dishonor of subsequent items 152
I. Payor bank's right of subrogation on improper payment 152
   1. What constitutes improper payment 152
   2. Payor bank subrogated to other parties' rights against drawer 152
   3. Payor bank subrogated to drawer's rights 153

V. Funds Availability Under Regulation CC 153
A. Introduction 153
B. Regulation CC 154
   1. Mandatory funds availability schedule 154
   2. Next-day availability 154
   3. Second-day and fifth-day availability 155
   4. Extensions of mandatory availability schedule 155
C. Availability under Article 4 156

CHAPTER 6

THE BANK COLLECTION PROCESS

I. Introduction to the Check Collection Process 161
A. Introduction 161
B. Bank 161
C. Branch banking 161

D. Types of banks under Article 4 162
    1. Payor bank 162
    2. Depositary bank 162
    3. Collecting bank 162
    4. Intermediary bank 162
    5. Presenting bank 162
E. Types of banks under Regulation CC 163
    1. Paying bank 163
    2. Returning bank 163
F. Clearinghouses 163

II. Law Governing the Check Collection Process 163
  A. Introduction 163

III. Variation by Agreement 164
  A. Introduction 164
  B. Limitations 164
  C. Binding on customer 164
  D. Clearinghouse rules 164

IV. Duties of Payor Bank 164
  A. Introduction 164
  B. Duty to pay or settle on day of presentment 164
    1. Exception for immediate payment over the counter 165
    2. Exception for on-us checks 165
    3. Failure to settle for demand item on day of receipt 165
    4. Means of dishonoring item 165
    5. Manner of payment 167
    6. Failure to settle or timely return of item 167
    7. Payor bank's liability on documentary drafts and items not payable on demand 168
    8. Final payment 168
    9. Duties of paying banks under Regulation CC in returning unpaid items 169

V. Duties of Collecting Banks 172
  A. Introduction 172
  B. Collecting bank's status as agent 172
    1. Intermediary and presenting banks 172
    2. Termination of agency status 172
  C. Right of chargeback 172
    1. Right to refund 172
    2. Even if collecting bank negligent 173
    3. Requirements for chargeback 173
    4. Consequences of failing to meet requirements 173
  D. Duty of collecting bank to use ordinary care in collecting and returning items 173
    1. Acting reasonably 173
    2. Delay excused 173
    3. Liable only for own negligence 173
    4. Measure of damages for failure to exercise ordinary care 174
    5. Electronic presentment 174

E. Encoding warranties   174
   1. Liability for misencoding   174

CHAPTER 7

WHOLESALE FUNDS TRANSFERS

I. What is a Funds Transfer?   179
  A. Definition of funds transfer   179
  B. Terminology of funds transfers   180
    1. Sender   180
    2. Customer   180
    3. Receiving bank   180
    4. Beneficiary   180
    5. Beneficiary's bank   180
    6. Payment order   180
    7. Originator   180
    8. Originator's bank   180
  C. What is a funds transfer   180
    1. Includes all payment orders   181
    2. One-bank funds transfer   181
    3. Intermediary bank   181
  D. Funds transfers must be between banks   181
  E. Requirements for a payment order   181
    1. Unconditional   182
    2. Reimbursed by sender   182
    3. Transmitted directly to receiving bank   182
  F. Consumer transactions excluded   182

II. Payment Obligations in Chain of Title   182
  A. Introduction   182

III. Duties and Liabilities of Receiving Bank   183
  A. Introduction   183
  B. Rejection   183
  C. Execution of order   183
    1. Execution date   183
    2. Payment date   183
    3. Duty to issue payment order   183
    4. Time when payment order can be accepted   183
    5. Damages for breach of duty by receiving bank   184
  D. Erroneous execution of payment order   184
    1. Duplicative order, order in greater amount than authorized, or to
      wrong beneficiary   184
    2. Payment in a lesser amount   185
    3. Duty of sender on receipt of notification of error   185

IV. Duties of Beneficiary's Bank   186
  A. Overview   186

B. Manner in which beneficiary's bank accepts payment order 186
   1. Payment 186
   2. Acceptance by notification 186
   3. Acceptance by receipt of payment 186
   4. By inaction 186
C. Rejection of payment order 186
   1. Time within which rejection must occur 186
   2. No rejection after acceptance 187
D. Liability for failure to make prompt payment 187
E. Duty to notify beneficiary 187

V. Effect of Acceptance on Underlying Obligation 188
A. When payment is accomplished 188

VI. Cancellation (Stopping Payment) of Payment Order 188
A. Introduction 188
B. Effect of cancellation 188
C. Right to cancel unaccepted orders 188
   1. Manner of cancellation 189
   2. Cancellation by operation of law 189
D. Cancellation of order accepted by receiving bank 189
E. Cancellation of order after acceptance by beneficiary's bank 189

VII. Liability for Authorized Payment Orders 190
A. Introduction 190

VIII. Liability for Unauthorized Payment Orders 190
A. Introduction 190
B. Security procedure 190
C. Requirements for sender's liability for verified payment orders 191
   1. First step 191
   2. Second step 191
D. Summary of when loss falls on bank 192
E. Contrary agreement prohibited 192
F. Duty of customer on receipt of notification of error 192

IX. Erroneous Payment Orders 192
A. Introduction 192
B. Allocation of loss when no security procedure in place 192
C. Allocation of loss when security procedure in place 192
D. Sender's duty on receipt of notice of acceptance 193

X. Misdescriptions 193
A. Introduction 193
B. Nonexistent or unidentifiable person or account 193
C. When beneficiary identified by both name and number 193
D. Misdescription of intermediary bank or beneficiary's bank 194
   1. Identification by number only 194
   2. Conflict between name and number 194

XI. Injunction 195
    A. Generally 195

CHAPTER 8

CONSUMER ELECTRONIC FUND TRANSFERS

I. Law Governing Consumer Electronic Fund Transfers 199
    A. Introduction 199

II. What is an Electronic Fund Transfer? 199
    A. Introduction 199
    B. Typical electronic fund transfers 200
    C. How initiated 200

III. Consumer's Liability for Unauthorized Transfers 201
    A. Introduction 201
    B. What is an unauthorized fund transfer? 201
        1. No longer authorized after notification 201
        2. Obtained through robbery or fraud 201
    C. Conditions to consumer's liability for unauthorized fund transfers 201
        1. Transfer through accepted access device 201
        2. Means to identify consumer 201
        3. Disclosures 201
    D. Limitation of consumer liability 202
    E. Failure to report loss of device 202
    F. Failure to report unauthorized transfers on periodic statement 202
    G. Combination of failure to report lost device and failure to report
       unauthorized transfers 202

IV. Stopping Payment of Electronic Fund Transfers 203
    A. Introduction 203
    B. No right to reverse ordinary fund transfer 203
        1. EFTA 203
        2. State law 203
    C. Stopping payment on preauthorized electronic fund transfers 203
        1. Manner of stopping payment 204
        2. Damages for failing to stop preauthorized fund transfer 204

V. Consumer Liability to Third Parties in the Event of System Malfunction 204
    A. Introduction 204

VI. Restrictions on Issuance of Access Devices 205
    A. Introduction 205

VII. Special Rules for Preauthorized Transfers 205
    A. Introduction 205
    B. Transfers to consumer's account 205
        1. Notice that transfer made 205

2. Notice that transfer not made 205
3. Readily available telephone line 205
C. Transfers from consumer's account 205

VIII. Documentation Requirements 206
A. Introduction 206
B. Receipts at electronic terminals 206
C. Periodic statements 206

IX. Error Resolution Procedures 206
A. Introduction 206
B. What is an "error"? 206
C. Notice of error 206
D. Bank's duty to investigate 206
1. Does not recredit 207
2. Recredits 207
E. After the bank makes its determination 207

X. Liability for Failing to Make Correct Fund Transfer 207
A. Introduction 207

XI. Civil Liability 207
A. Enforcement actions provided by EFTA 207
B. Individual consumers 207
C. Class actions 207
D. Treble damages 207
E. Defenses to liability 208
1. Bona fide error 208
2. Offers to pay damages 208

CHAPTER 9

LENDER CREDIT CARDS

I. Terminology in Credit Card Transactions 211
A. Introduction 211

II. Law Governing Credit Card Transactions 211
A. Introduction 211
B. Federal law 211
1. Primarily consumer protection 212
2. Other law 212

III. Liability for Unauthorized Use 212
A. Introduction 212
B. Conditions to liability 212
1. Accepted card 212
2. Disclosures 212
3. Merchant identification 212
C. Unauthorized use 213

D. Authorized use 213
   1. Actual authority 213
   2. Apparent authority 213

IV. Right to Refuse Payment 214
  A. Introduction 214
  B. Conditions to right to withhold payment 214
    1. Good-faith attempt to resolve dispute 214
    2. More than $50 215
    3. Purchase within same state or within 100 miles 215
  C. Exceptions 215
  D. Limited to amount of credit outstanding 215

V. Error Resolution Procedures 215
  A. Introduction 215
  B. What cardholder must do on noticing billing error 215
  C. What the card issuer must do on receipt of billing error notice ... 216
    1. If error is found 216
    2. If no error found 216
  D. Remedy 216

Essay Exam Questions and Answers 219

Glossary 229

Table of Cases 241

Table of Statutes 243

Subject Matter Index 253

Preface

Have you ever written a check to pay your bills? Have you ever used an automated teller machine (ATM) to deposit or withdraw cash? Have you used your ATM or credit card to pay for groceries or gas, or a meal at a restaurant? If so, then you already have first-hand experience with the three types of payment systems: negotiable instruments (a check), electronic fund transfers (the ATM), and credit cards. This *Emanuel Law Outline* will guide you to an understanding of the state and federal law that applies to these three types of payment systems.

Without reading your course description, it may be difficult to determine which course offered by your school teaches the law of payment systems, because the title of the course varies from school to school. It may be called *Payment Systems*, *Negotiable Instruments*, or *Commercial Paper*. Or, it may be a component of a course called *Sales and Payments* or *Commercial Law*. You will find the *Emanuel Law Outline* for Payment Systems a useful study guide in all of these courses.

Although most of the rules found in the law of payment systems are logical and understandable, the law of payment systems is quite technical. Some of the rules begin to make sense only when placed in the context of modern technology or banking practices. The law can seem disjointed unless it is carefully organized according to its basic precepts. To further complicate matters, many of the terms used in payment systems have different applications from how they are used in other areas of law. Your *Emanuel Law Outline* for Payment Systems will help you make sense of it all.

This *Emanuel Law Outline* explains—in clear, understandable language—what you need to know about banking and technology in order to understand the law of payment systems. All of the attendant terms are defined; all of the applicable rules are explained. Throughout, you will find several summaries of the law and numerous examples to help make even the most abstract terms and concepts more concrete and understandable. Those elements most likely to appear on an exam have been brought to the foreground. The examples will help you successfully attack any exam question.

The best way to understand payment systems law is to diagram the transaction in question. This book will teach you how to do just that by illustrating transactions with plenty of examples. When you understand the structure of a transaction, you are better able to identify the issues at stake: who is suing whom for what, what defense might be offered by the one being sued, and what principles and policy considerations apply to the situation. Then you will be ready to refer to the Uniform Commercial Code (U.C.C.) or federal statutory and regulatory provisions to see how that issue is handled. To aid your understanding of the U.C.C. and federal statutes and regulations, your *Emanuel Law Outline* includes many examples that show you how to work through the relevant code section. Just refer to the section that covers the material giving you difficulty.

The best way to use your *Emanuel Law Outline* is to read the relevant portions of the Capsule Summary first and then read the class assignment in your casebook. This will give you a feel for the concepts and issues you will encounter. (You can refer to the Glossary for a definition of any terms not defined in your casebook.) Then study the portions of the *Outline* that cover the topic of your assignment. This book is not intended to substitute for your casebook reading, but used as a study guide, it will be a great help as you prepare for class and exams. Good luck!

Because only five states have adopted the 2002 amendments to U.C.C. Articles 3 and 4 as of the writing of this book, the book is based on "old" Articles 3 and 4. However, references to the 2002 amendments have been made where the 2002 amendment will have an impact on the application of the law.

I would like to give my sincere thanks and appreciation to my research assistant Eric Kweon for his invaluable assistance without which this book would not be of the high quality that it is.

Lary Lawrence
Loyola Law School
May 2009

CASEBOOK CORRELATION CHART

Note: General sections of the outline are omitted from this chart.
NC = not directly covered by this textbook.

Emanuel's Payment Systems Law Outline	Warren & Walt, *Payments and Credits* (7th ed., 2007)	Mann, *Payment Systems and Other Financial Systems* (4th ed., 2008)	Rusch, *Payment Systems: Problems, Materials and Cases* (3d ed., 2007)	Whaley, *Problems and Materials on Payment Law* (8th ed., 2008)	Nickles and Matthews, *Payments Law and Commercial Paper: Learning and Teaching Materials* (2009)
CHAPTER 1 **WHAT IS A NEGOTIABLE INSTRUMENT?**					
I. What Is a Negotiable Instrument?	1-24	431-449	37-40	1-34	68-71
II. Governing Law	2-3	431-449	37-40	2	68-71, 412-414
III. Types of Negotiable Instruments	5-6	431-434	37-40	2-4	412-414
IV. Requirements for Negotiability	15-24	434-449	47-54	4-25	69
CHAPTER 2 **HOLDER-IN-DUE COURSE STATUS AND AVAILALE CLAIMS, DEFENSES, CLAIMS IN RECOUPMENT, AND DISCHARGES**					
I. Introduction	12	467	79-81	4, 35	161-167
II. Holder Status	24	467-469	81-87	35-36	161-167, 186-187
III. Value	63-76	467	81-108	36-39	162
IV. Good Faith	24-44	468	81-108	39-67	163, 187, 182-200
V. Notice	24-44	468-469	81-108	39-69	162-163
VI. Denial of Holder-in-Due Course, Status of Certain Classes of Purchasers	44, 57, 64	475-476	NC	36	NC
VII. Defenses, Claims to the Instrument, Claims in Recoupment, and Discharges	9-15	469-473	109-130	78-108	165-171
VIII. Admissibility of Evidence Extrinsic to the Instrument	NC	NC	47-50	101-107	167-171
IX. Transfer of Instrument and Shelter Provision	7-9	475-476	64, 69, 106	69-77	164, 174-180
X. Defenses and Claims to Bank Checks	89-90	NC	271	199-207	386-387
XI. Federal Holder-in-Due-Course Status	NC	NC	106	36	NC
CHAPTER 3 **NATURE OF LIABILITY ON INSTRUMENTS**					
I. Liability of Issuer, Drawer, Acceptor, and Indorser	77-83	456-458	55-63	118-122, 145-171	148-161

Emanuel's Payment Systems Law Outline	Warren & Walt, *Payments and Credits* (7th ed., 2007)	Mann, *Payment Systems and Other Financial Systems* (4th ed., 2008)	Rusch, *Payment Systems: Problems, Materials and Cases* (3d ed., 2007)	Whaley, *Problems and Materials on Payment Law* (8th ed., 2008)	Nickles and Matthews, *Payments Law and Commercial Paper: Learning and Teaching Materials* (2009)
II.　Presentment, Dishonor, Notice of Dishonor – Conditions to Drawer's and Indorser's Liability	78-83	454-455	71-79	146-156	74-76, 80-91
III.　Transfer Warranties	83-84	91, 96	166-171	262-264	326-327
IV.　Sureties and Accommodation Parties	95-104	347	118-120	122-145	NC
V.　Liability of Agents, Principals, and Co-Obligors	104-112	456-466	120-131	163-171	NC
VI.　Effect of Taking Instrument on the Underlying Obligation	86	458-459	112-116	112-118	68-71
VII.　Accord and Satisfaction by Use of Instrument	113-119	459-463	116-118	19	71-72
VIII.　Procedural Issues Involving Negotiable Instruments	8	87-89	63-71	97-100	72-74
IX.　Enforcement of Lost, Destroyed, or Stolen Instruments	90-95	134	270-271	206-207	387-389, 400-408
CHAPTER 4 **FORGERY, ALTERATION, AND OTHER FRAUDULENT ACTIVITY**					
I.　Unauthorized Signatures	257-310	89-99	237-268	259-285	272-273, 286-296
II.　Alterations and Incomplete Instruments	316-322	100	268-270	322-323	273-274
III.　Grounds of Preclusion	258-310	103-124	237-239, 247-250	285-322	277-279, 296-307
IV.　Restrictive Indorsements	322-328	453	247-250	253-254	333-336
CHAPTER 5 **PAYOR BANK/CUSTOMER RELATIONSHIP**					
I.　When Item Properly Payable	329, 364	15-21	180-183	173-177, 183-190	211-213, 237-243
II.　Variation by Agreement	362-365	18, 25, 106	NC	193	NC
III.　Wrongful Dishonor	348-359	37-45	186-198	178-183	213-218, 243-255
IV.　Customer's Right to Stop Payment	330-341	19-21	198-201	190-207	218-221, 255-261
V.　Funds Availability Under Regulation CC	166-170, 329	26-36, 67-72, 76-78	222-233	210-221	116-119, 124-147
CHAPTER 6 **THE BANK COLLECTION PROCESS**					
I.　Introduction to Check Collection Process	120	52-57	173-180, 202	211	72-74

Emanuel's Payment Systems Law Outline	Warren & Walt, *Payments and Credits* (7th ed., 2007)	Mann, *Payment Systems and Other Financial Systems* (4th ed., 2008)	Rusch, *Payment Systems: Problems, Materials and Cases* (3d ed., 2007)	Whaley, *Problems and Materials on Payment Law* (8th ed., 2008)	Nickles and Matthews, *Payments Law and Commercial Paper: Learning and Teaching Materials* (2009)
II. Law Governing the Check Collection Process	121 *et seq.*	52-83	173-180	209	72-74
III. Variation by Agreement	120	52-57	NC	193	73
IV. Duties of Payor Bank	121-151	46-51	209-216	211-221, 228-240	74-113
V. Duties of Collecting Banks	151-165	52-57	203-209, 216-222	242-251	74-113
CHAPTER 7 **WHOLESALE FUNDS TRANSFERS**					
I. What Is a Funds Transfer?	205-212	224-235, 272-287	325-327	325-326	609-612, 633-639
II. Payment Obligations in Chain of Title	206, 213-214	225-248	345-347	340-352	NC
III. Duties and Liabilities of Receiving Bank	213-236	225-241	336-341	334-365	614-616
IV. Duties of Beneficiary's Bank	236-241	235-242	341-343	334-365	614-616
V. Effect of Acceptance on Underlying Obligation	213-214	243	346-347	337-340	614-616
VI. Cancellation (Stopping Payment) or Payment Order	215-216	243-245	343-344	190-207	617-618, 633-639
VII. Liability for Authorized Payment Orders	233-236	268-271	350	364	NC
VIII. Liability for Unauthorized Payment Orders	233-236	268-271	350-352	364	618-622, 639-645
IX. Erroneous Payment Orders	225-231	256-267	352-371	351-365	NC
X. Misdescriptions	236-241	NC	352-371	351-365	622-624, 645-669
XI. Injunction	NC	NC	347	NC	NC
CHAPTER 8 **CONSUMER ELECTRONIC FUND TRANSFERS**					
I. Law Governing Consumer Electronic Fund Transfers	247-256	327-340	327-334, 336-337	325-365	670-672
II. What Is an Electronic Fund Transfer?	247-248	327	325-327	325-326	672-680, 704-709
III. Consumer's Liability for Unauthorized Transfers	248-250	300-305	334-336	326-330	686-691, 715-725
IV. Stopping Payment of Electronic Fund Transfers	215-216	NC	NC	NC	693-694
V. Consumer Liability to Third Parties in the Event of System Malfunction	231-233	271-272	NC	340-365	NC
VI. Restrictions on Issuance of Access Devices	NC	NC	NC	NC	NC

Emanuel's Payment Systems Law Outline	Warren & Walt, *Payments and Credits* (7th ed., 2007)	Mann, *Payment Systems and Other Financial Systems* (4th ed., 2008)	Rusch, *Payment Systems: Problems, Materials and Cases* (3d ed., 2007)	Whaley, *Problems and Materials on Payment Law* (8th ed., 2008)	Nickles and Matthews, *Payments Law and Commercial Paper: Learning and Teaching Materials* (2009)
VII. Special Rules for Preauthorized Transfers	NC	NC	NC	NC	691-693, 726-732
VIII. Documentation Requirements	248	205-206	NC	331	NC
IX. Error Resolution Procedures	248	249-259	NC	331	696-697
X. Liability for Failing to Make Correct Fund Transfer	NC	249-267	350	351-365	NC
XI. Civil Liability	248	NC	NC	351-365	694-696
CHAPTER 9 **LENDER CREDIT CARDS**					
I. Terminology in Credit Card Transactions	170-174	137-140	14-17	326-328	497-501
II. Law Governing Credit Card Transactions	170-204	137-140	17-20	326-328	514-519
III. Liability for Unauthorized Use	176-187	160-183	20-35	327	524-530, 550-559, 574-583
IV. Right to Refuse Payment	187-202	160-183	21-35	327-328	530-534, 583-603
V. Error Resolution Procedures	187-189	160-161, 170-171	21-35	328-329	534-538, 583-603

Capsule Summary

This Capsule Summary is intended for review at the end of the course. Reading it is not a substitute for mastering the material in the main outline. Numbers in brackets refer to the pages in the main outline where the topic is discussed.

CHAPTER 1

WHAT IS A NEGOTIABLE INSTRUMENT?

I. WHAT IS A NEGOTIABLE INSTRUMENT?

A. **Definition:** A negotiable instrument is a cross between a contract and money.

1. **Primary difference from ordinary contract right:** An assignee of an ordinary contract right takes subject to all the defenses to which his assignor took subject. A holder in due course of a negotiable instrument takes the instrument free from virtually all defenses. [1]

2. **Other differences:** Simpler to plead and prove case on a negotiable instrument. [2]

II. GOVERNING LAW

A. **The U.C.C.:** The basic law governing negotiable instruments is contained in Articles 3 and 4 of the Uniform Commercial Code. In 2002, the American Law Institute and the National Conference of Commissioners on Uniform State Laws proposed several amendments to Articles 3 and 4. However, until enacted by the particular state, these amendments will not be the law in that state. [2]

1. **Coverage of Article 3:** Article 3 governs writings meeting the requirements of U.C.C. §3-104(a). U.C.C. §3-102 specifically excludes from the scope of Article 3 the following writings that otherwise may qualify as negotiable instruments: (1) investment securities governed by Article 8, (2) money, and (3) payment orders governed by Article 4A. U.C.C. §3-102(a). [2]

2. **Coverage of Article 4:** Article 4 governs the bank collection process. The coverage of Article 4 is limited to items. Any promise or order to pay money handled by a bank for collection or payment is an item whether or not the promise or order would qualify as a negotiable instrument under Article 3. U.C.C. §4-104(a)(9). "Item" does not include payment orders governed by Article 4A or debit and credit card slips. U.C.C. §4-104(a)(9). [2]

3. **Article 4 prevails over Article 3:** When the results reached under an applicable provision of Article 4 conflict with the results reached under a provision of Article 3, Article 4 controls. U.C.C. §3-102(b); U.C.C. §4-102(a). [2-3]

4. **Federal common law:** In the absence of a federal statute or regulation, if the United States is a party to an instrument, its rights and duties are governed by federal common law and not by the Code. U.C.C. §4-102, Official Comment 1. [3]

III. TYPES OF NEGOTIABLE INSTRUMENTS

Article 3 negotiable instruments are classified into two basic categories: **Notes and drafts**. [3-6] Negotiable instruments include:

- **Notes:** A note is a promise by one party (called the "*maker*") to pay to another party (called the "payee") a sum of money. The usual purpose of a note is to evidence a debt. Notes thus primarily serve a credit rather than a payment function. [3]

- **Certificates of deposit:** A certificate of deposit is a note issued by a bank. It is defined as "an acknowledgment by a bank of the receipt of money together with an engagement by the bank to repay the money." U.C.C. §3-104(j). Certificates of deposit are the means by which banks raise money and depositors assure themselves of a good return on their money. [3-4]

- **Drafts:** A "*draft*", sometimes known as a bill of exchange, is a three-party instrument by which a person called a "*drawer*" (the person who typically signs the draft in the lower right-hand corner) orders a person called a "*drawee*" (the person named in the draft to whom the order is directed) to pay the payee. Drafts are usually payment instruments by which the drawer makes payment to the payee. [4]

- **Checks:** A check is a draft drawn on a bank (called either the "*drawee bank*" or the "*payor bank*") and payable on demand. U.C.C. §3-104(f). Because all checks are drafts, unless the Code specifically provides otherwise, checks are governed by the same rules that govern drafts. [4]

- **Bank checks (including cashier's checks, teller's checks, and certified checks):** Bank checks are treated differently from ordinary checks for several purposes including: (1) the ability of the issuing bank to refuse payment; (2) the loss or destruction of a bank check; (3) the effect of taking a bank check on the underlying obligation, and (4) the statute of limitations on bringing an action against the issuing bank. [4]

- **Traveler's checks:** To be a traveler's check, the check must require, as a condition to payment, a countersignature by the person whose specimen signature appears on the instrument. U.C.C. §3-104(i). A holder in due course does not take subject to the risk that the traveler's check was stolen and the countersignature forged. U.C.C. §3-106(c); U.C.C. §3-106, Official Comment 2. [4-5]

- **Personal money order:** A personal money order is a draft sold by the drawee to a person who typically does not have an account with the drawee. It is, in effect, a single-transaction checking account. If the drawee is a bank, the personal money order is a check; if a non-bank, a personal money order is a draft. The drawee bank is not liable on a personal money order because the bank has not signed the order. [5]

- **Time drafts:** A time draft is a draft payable at a definite time. [5]

- **Sight drafts:** A sight draft is a draft payable on demand. [5]

- **Documentary drafts:** A documentary draft is a draft, whether payable at a definite time or on demand, which is accompanied by a letter containing instructions that the draft is not to be paid unless the holder presents to the drawee certain designated documents. [5]

- **Banker's acceptances:** A banker's acceptance is a draft drawn on and accepted by a bank. By accepting the draft, the bank becomes liable to pay the draft. U.C.C. §3-413(a). [5]

- **Trade acceptances:** A trade acceptance is a draft drawn on and accepted by a person other than a bank. [5]

- **Payable through items:** The bank through which the item is payable, having no right to pay the item, is a collecting bank and not the payor bank. U.C.C. §4-106(a); U.C.C. §4-106, Official Comment 1. [5]

- **Payable at items:** Article 4 provides two alternative provisions that a state may adopt as to the manner in which instruments payable at a bank are to be treated. The first alternative provision treats a "payable at" item as a check. U.C.C. §4-106(b), Alternative A. Under the second alternative, a payable at item is treated as though it is "payable through" the designated bank. U.C.C. §4-106(b), Alternative B. [5-6]

- **Remotely created consumer item:** The 2002 amendments have added a new type of negotiable instrument. A "remotely created consumer item" is "an item drawn on a consumer account, which is not created by the payor bank and does not bear a handwritten signature purporting to be the signature of the drawer." [Rev] U.C.C. §3-103(a)(16). [6]

IV. REQUIREMENTS FOR NEGOTIABILITY

Only a writing complying with the requirements of U.C.C. §3-104(a) is a negotiable instrument under Article 3. U.C.C. §3-104, Official Comment 1. Negotiability is determined solely by reference to the four corners of the instrument. A separate agreement cannot affect the negotiability of an instrument. U.C.C. §3-104(a) sets forth the following requirements for negotiability. [6-7]

1. **A signed writing:** As long as the signer intends for it to be her signature, she may use any name, word, or mark as her signature including a fictitious name, a trade name, or the signer's first name. A signature may be in the form of printing, handwriting, typing, or even the imprinting of a thumbprint. U.C.C. §1-201, Official Comment 39; U.C.C. §3-401(b); U.C.C. §3-401, Official Comment 2. [7]

2. **An unconditional promise or order:** A promise or an order that is expressly conditioned upon the happening of a specified event is not unconditional. A promise or order is regarded as unconditional if the promise or order is subject only to an implied or constructive condition. U.C.C. §3-106(a); U.C.C. §3-106, Official Comment 1. A promise or an order is not unconditional if it states that the promise or order is subject to, or governed by, another writing or if rights of the parties are stated in another writing. U.C.C. §3-106(a)(ii) and (iii). An instrument that merely refers to the existence of another writing may be negotiable. U.C.C. §3-106(a). An instrument may retain its negotiability while referring to another writing for rights as to collateral, acceleration, or prepayment. U.C.C. §3-106(b)(i). [8-9]

3. **Principal sum must be payable in a fixed amount of money:** An instrument is not payable in a fixed amount if the terms used in the instrument to express the sum payable or any component thereof are ambiguous or if reference must be made to an outside source or writing to

determine the principal amount. Interest and other charges do not have to be payable in a fixed amount. U.C.C. §3-112, Official Comment 1. Virtually any type of provision for the payment of interest is permissible. An instrument may state the obligation to pay interest as a fixed or variable amount of money or as a fixed or variable rate or rates. The amount or rate of interest may be stated or described in the instrument in any manner and may require reference to information not contained in the instrument. U.C.C. §3-112(b); U.C.C. §3-112, Official Comment 1. Provisions for attorneys' fees and costs incurred in the collection of the instrument are permissible "other charges" even though they do not specify a particular sum. Provisions for pre-payment penalties, late payment penalties, or other penalties, discounts, or rebates are also permissible "other charges." A duty to pay taxes or to pay to insure collateral are probably not permissible other charges and, therefore, their inclusion will defeat an instrument's negotiability. An instrument is not negotiable unless it is payable in money. U.C.C. §3-104(a). [9-11]

4. **Must be payable to bearer or to order:** An instrument that is payable to bearer may take one of several forms: (a) state that it is payable "to bearer"; (b) use language indicating that the person in possession of it is entitled to payment, e.g., to "holder," to "cash," or to the "order of cash"; or (c) does not name a payee, e.g., "pay to order of _____." U.C.C. §3-109(a). An instrument is payable to order if it is payable to the "order of [an identified person]" or to an "[identified person] or order." U.C.C. §3-109(b). When an instrument is payable both to order and to bearer, the instrument is payable to bearer. U.C.C. §3-109(b); U.C.C. §3-109, Official Comment 2. Instruments containing the following designations are payable to bearer: (a) "bearer or order," (b) "order of bearer," (c) "John Doe or bearer," or (d) "order of cash." U.C.C. §3-109(a) and Official Comment 2. However, a check that meets all the requirements of U.C.C. §3-104(a), except for not being made payable to "order" or "bearer," is a negotiable instrument governed by Article 3. U.C.C. §3-104(c). [11-12]

5. **Must be payable on demand or at a definite time:** A promise or an order is payable on demand if it states that it is (a) payable on demand, on presentation, or at sight; (b) otherwise indicates that it is payable at the will of the holder; or (c) fails to state when payment is due. U.C.C. §3-108(a). An instrument otherwise payable on demand remains payable on demand even if it is postdated or antedated. U.C.C. §3-113(a). A promise or an order is payable at a definite time if it is payable (a) at a fixed date; (b) a definite period after a stated date, or; (c) on "elapse of a definite period of time after sight or acceptance." U.C.C. §3-108(b). An instrument is payable at a definite time as long as the date is readily ascertainable at the time the promise or order is issued even if the date is not specified in the instrument. A note or draft payable a fixed period "after date" that does not state a date is an incomplete instrument. Once the note or draft is completed by the addition of a date, the instrument becomes payable at a definite time. An instrument that is otherwise payable at a definite time remains so even if the time of payment is subject to acceleration. Any type of acceleration clause is permissible. U.C.C. §3-108(b)(ii). An instrument that is subject to prepayment by the obligor remains payable at a definite time. U.C.C. §3-108(b)(i). An instrument remains payable at a definite time even if the holder has the right to extend the time of payment indefinitely. U.C.C. §3-108(b)(iii); U.C.C. §3-108, Official Comment. In contrast, when the maker or the acceptor has the right to extend the time for payment or the time is automatically extended upon the occurrence of a specified event, the instrument is payable at a definite time only if the right to extend is limited to extension to a further definite time. U.C.C. §3-108(b)(iii) and (iv); U.C.C. §3-108, Official Comment. [12-14]

6. **Can contain no other undertaking or instruction by the person promising or ordering payment to do any act in addition to the payment of money:** Inclusion in an instrument of a promise, an obligation, an order, or a power not authorized by Article 3 defeats the instrument's negotiability. U.C.C. §3-104(a)(3); U.C.C. §3-104, Official Comment 1. The prohibition against additional terms is limited to undertakings and instructions given by the person promising or ordering payment. A promise by the holder does not violate this prohibition. U.C.C. §3-104(a)(3). A negotiable instrument may also contain an undertaking or a power to give, maintain, or protect collateral to secure payment. This would include provisions granting the holder a security interest in the collateral or securing both the obligation evidenced by the instrument itself and any other obligation of the obligor. A negotiable instrument may also contain an authorization or power to the holder to confess judgment or realize on, or dispose of, collateral, or a waiver of the benefit of any law intended for the advantage or protection of an obligor. U.C.C. §3-104(a)(3); U.C.C. §3-104, Official Comment 1. [14-15]

CHAPTER 2
HOLDER-IN-DUE-COURSE STATUS AND AVAILABLE CLAIMS, DEFENSES, CLAIMS IN RECOUPMENT, AND DISCHARGES

I. INTRODUCTION

To obtain holder-in-due-course status, a purchaser of an instrument must take the instrument as a holder, for value, in good faith, and without notice of certain proscribed facts. U.C.C. §3-302(a). [19-20]

II. HOLDER STATUS

A. **General rule:** For a person to qualify as the holder of an instrument, the person must have possession of the instrument, and the obligation evidenced by the instrument must run to him. [20]

B. **Ways of acquiring holder status:** A person can become a holder either through issuance or negotiation. [20-21]

1. **Issuance:** An instrument is "issued" when it is first delivered by the maker or drawer to either a holder or nonholder for the purpose of giving rights on the instrument to any person. U.C.C. §3-105(a). [20]

2. **Negotiation:** "Negotiation" is a transfer of possession of an instrument, whether voluntary or involuntary, by a person, other than the issuer (i.e., maker or drawer), to another person who thereby **becomes** its holder. U.C.C. §3-201(a). When an instrument is payable to bearer, transfer of possession alone is sufficient for its negotiation. A thief or finder of an instrument payable to bearer becomes the holder even though the transfer of possession was involuntary. U.C.C. §3-201, Official Comment 1. To negotiate an instrument payable to order, the instrument must also be indorsed to that person or to bearer. U.C.C. §3-201(b). [20-21]

C. Indorsement: An "indorsement" sufficient to negotiate an instrument must be written by or on behalf of the holder. U.C.C. §3-201(b). A forged or unauthorized indorsement is not effective to negotiate the instrument. Thus, if an indorsement in the chain of title is forged or unauthorized, no transferee subsequent to the unauthorized or forged indorsement can become a holder. [21]

1. **Types of indorsements:** Two types of indorsements can be used to negotiate an instrument. [21]

   a. **Special indorsement:** A "special indorsement" identifies the person to whom the instrument is payable. U.C.C. §3-205(a). [21]

   b. **Blank indorsement:** A "blank indorsement" is an indorsement that is not payable to an identified person. An instrument indorsed in blank becomes payable to bearer and any person who possesses the instrument becomes its holder. A blank indorsement can consist of the unaccompanied signature of the holder; the signature of the holder accompanied by such phrases as "pay to bearer," "pay to holder," "pay to bank," or "pay to cash"; or use of the words "pay to _____" with no one's name filled in. U.C.C. §3-205(b). [21]

   c. **Conversion of blank to special indorsement:** Any holder of an instrument indorsed in blank may convert the blank indorsement into a special indorsement by writing over the signature of the indorser the name of an indorsee. U.C.C. §3-205(c); U.C.C. §3-205, Official Comment 2. [22]

2. **Indorsement must be written on instrument:** An indorsement must be written on the instrument itself. However, as long as the separate piece of paper is affixed to the instrument (called an "*allonge*"), the indorsement on that separate piece of paper is sufficient to negotiate the instrument. U.C.C. §3-204(a). [22]

3. **Manner of negotiation depends on last indorsement:** An instrument becomes payable to order or payable to bearer depending on whether the last indorsement is a special or a blank indorsement. U.C.C. §3-205. [22]

4. **To whom an instrument is payable:** The basic rule is that the person to whom an instrument is initially payable is determined by the intent of the person signing the instrument as the issuer (i.e.drawer or maker), in the name of the issuer, or on behalf of the issuer whether or not that person is authorized. U.C.C. §3-110(a). [22]

   a. **Need not be real name of payee:** An instrument is payable to the person intended by the signer even if the payee is identified by a name other than her real name. U.C.C. §3-110(a). [22]

      i. **Indorsement in either name effective:** When a payee is designated in a name other than her true name, an indorsement in either the payee's true name or the name appearing on the instrument (or in both) is effective to negotiate the instrument. U.C.C. §3-204(d); U.C.C. §3-204, Official Comment 3. [22]

   b. **More than one person signing as issuer:** If an instrument is signed by more than one person as maker or drawer and each signer intends that a different person be the person designated as the payee, the instrument is payable to any person intended by any one of the signers. U.C.C. §3-110(a). [23]

   c. **Intent of forger determinative:** When the drawer's signature on the check is forged, the payee is the person to whom the forger intended that payment be made. [23]

d. **Checkwriting machine:** When the signature of the issuer is made by automated means, such as by a checkwriting machine, the identity of the payee is determined by the intent of the person who supplied the name (or other identification) of the payee, whether or not the person was an authorized agent or even connected with the issuer. U.C.C. §3-110(b). [23]

5. **Two or more payees:** An instrument payable to two or more persons is payable to them either jointly or in the alternative. [24]

   a. **Jointly:** If an instrument is payable jointly, all payees must participate in any negotiation, discharge, or enforcement of the instrument. U.C.C. §3-110(d); U.C.C. §3-110, Official Comment 4. [24]

   b. **Alternative:** An instrument payable in the alternative may be negotiated, discharged, or enforced by any payee who is in possession of the instrument. U.C.C. §3-110(d); U.C.C. §3-110, Official Comment 4. Instruments payable "to P or R," "to P and R in the alternative," or "to P/R" ("/" means either/or) are payable to P or R in the alternative. [24]

   c. **Ambiguous:** When it is unclear whether an instrument is payable alternatively or jointly, e.g., "to P and/or R," the instrument is deemed to be payable in the alternative. U.C.C. §3-110(d). [24]

D. **Depositary bank's status as holder:** If a customer delivers an item to a depositary bank for collection, whether or not the customer indorses the item, the depositary bank becomes a holder of the item at the time it receives the item if the customer, at the time of delivery, was a holder of the item. U.C.C. §4-205(1); U.C.C. §4-205, Official Comment. [25]

III. VALUE

An instrument is issued or transferred for value when it is taken for the following:

A. **Promise of performance:** The instrument is issued or transferred for a promise of performance, to the extent the promise has been performed. Any promise that would constitute consideration under contract law constitutes a "promise of performance" under Article 3. U.C.C. §3-303(a)(1). When a holder has only partially performed the agreed-on consideration, the holder has the rights of a holder in due course to the extent of the fraction of the amount payable under the instrument equal to the value of the partial performance divided by the value of the promised performance. U.C.C. §3-302(d). [26]

B. **Security interest or lien:** A holder takes for value to the extent that she acquires a security interest in, or other lien on, the instrument other than a lien obtained by judicial proceeding. [26-27]

1. **Security interest in instrument:** The holder may acquire a security interest in, or a lien on, an instrument in two ways: a voluntary transfer by the debtor, usually an Article 9 security interest, U.C.C. §3-303(a)(2); U.C.C. §3-303, Official Comment 3; or a security interest that a collecting bank automatically acquires under U.C.C. §4-210(a). A collecting bank acquires a security interest in an item and any accompanying documents or the proceeds of either the item or the documents. The collecting bank acquires a security interest only to the extent that the bank allows the customer to use the funds. A collecting bank also acquires a security interest when it applies the item in part or in full in payment of a debt owed to it by its customer. U.C.C. §4-210(a)(1). If the credit given for the item is available for withdrawal as a matter of

right, the collecting bank has a security interest in the item whether or not the credit is drawn on or there is a right of chargeback. U.C.C. §4-210(a)(2). When the bank makes an advance against the item, a security interest arises whether or not the item is deposited into the customer's account. U.C.C. §4-210(a). When credits given for several items deposited at one time, or pursuant to a single agreement, are withdrawn or applied in part, the bank's security interest applies to all the items. U.C.C. §4-210(b). Credits first given are deemed to be first drawn on. U.C.C. §4-210(b). Thus, when items are not deposited simultaneously, the security interest attaches to the items in the order in which they were deposited. [26]

   2. **Lien on instrument:** A person who has a lien on an instrument by operation of law takes the instrument for value. The most typical type of lien is a common law or statutory banker's lien. U.C.C. §3-303(a)(2); U.C.C. §3-303, Official Comment 3. In contrast, a lien acquired by judicial process, e.g., attachment, garnishment, or execution, does not constitute value. U.C.C. §3-303(a)(2); U.C.C. §3-303, Official Comment 3. [26-27]

   3. **Value only to extent of amount owed:** A lienholder or secured party takes the instrument for value only to the extent of the amount owed on the underlying debt. U.C.C. §3-302(e). [27]

C. For antecedent claim: The instrument is issued or transferred as payment of, or as security for, an antecedent claim against any person, whether or not the claim is due. [27]

D. Negotiable instrument or irrevocable commitment: An instrument is taken for value if it is issued or transferred in exchange for a negotiable instrument or for the incurring of an irrevocable commitment to a third person by the person taking the instrument. U.C.C. §3-303(a). [27]

IV. GOOD FAITH

The standard of good faith adopted by the Code is partially subjective and partially objective. [29]

   1. **Subjective element:** The subjective part of the standard is found in the requirement that the particular holder be honest in fact in the transaction. A person is honest in fact if she honestly is unaware of the claim or defense even though a reasonable person would have been aware under the circumstances. [29]

   2. **Objective element:** The objective element of good faith requires "the observance of reasonable commercial standards of fair dealing." U.C.C. §3-103(a)(4). The duty of the holder to comply with reasonable commercial standards extends only to its obligation of fair dealing. The holder has no duty to exercise due care with respect to the purchase. U.C.C. §3-103, Official Comment 4. The issue is not whether the holder was negligent in its actions but rather whether it was attempting to take advantage of the obligor. [29-30]

V. NOTICE

A. Notice of infirmity: A holder cannot become a holder in due course if it has notice of any infirmity in the instrument or in the underlying transaction in which the instrument was issued or negotiated. [30]

B. Notice need not relate to defense or claim raised: A purchaser who has notice of a proscribed fact is completely denied holder-in-due-course status and therefore takes subject to all claims, defenses, and claims in recoupment whether or not related to the defense or claim of which he has notice. [30]

C. **Effect of subsequent notice:** Once a purchaser becomes a holder in due course, notice subsequently obtained does not destroy its holder-in-due-course status. [30]

D. **When notice imputed to organization:** Notice to an organization is effective for a particular transaction from the earlier of the time the notice either: (1) is brought to the attention of the individual conducting the transaction; or (2) should have been brought to her attention had the organization exercised due diligence. U.C.C. §1-201(27); [Rev] U.C.C. §1-202(f). As long as the organization is in reasonable compliance with its established procedures, notice will not be imputed to the organization until the information actually reaches the party conducting the transaction. If there are no established procedures or if the procedures are not generally followed, notice will be effective from the moment that the information would have reached the party conducting the transaction had reasonable procedures been in place at the time. [30-31]

E. **Manner of obtaining notice:** A purchaser may obtain notice in three possible ways: [32]

1. **Actual knowledge:** A purchaser has actual knowledge of an infirmity when she is subjectively aware of the existence of the claim, defense, or claim in recoupment. [32]

2. **Notification:** A person receives a notice or notification when it comes to her attention or when it is duly delivered at the place of business through which the contract was made or at any other place held out by her as the place for receipt of such communications. U.C.C. §1-201(26); [Rev] U.C.C. §1-202(e) . Notification is effective even if the holder did not actually read the notification and thereby acquire actual knowledge of the claim, defense, or claim in recoupment. [32]

3. **Reason to know:** A purchaser may also have notice of an infirmity if, from all the facts and circumstances known to him at the time in question, he has reason to know that the infirmity exists. U.C.C. §1-201(25)(c); [Rev] U.C.C. §1-202(a)(3). [32]

   a. **Subjective element:** The standard has a subjective element in that the test is whether "from all the facts and circumstances *known to him*": the purchaser has reason to know of the infirmity. [32]

   b. **Two tests:** Two tests have been adopted by courts for determining whether a purchaser has reason to know of a claim, defense, or claim in recoupment. [32]

      i. **Inferable knowledge test:** Under the inferable knowledge test, a holder has reason to know of a claim, claim in recoupment, or defense only if the only reasonable conclusion the holder could reach from the facts known to the holder is that the claim, claim in recoupment, or defense exists. The holder has no duty to inquire into suspicious circumstances. The holder may assume an innocent explanation for a suspicious circumstance. [32-33]

      ii. **Duty to inquire test:** The duty to inquire test is whether a reasonable person, considering all the facts and circumstances known to the holder, would have further investigated and thereby discovered the existence of the claim, defense, or claim in recoupment. This test is an objective test allowing the court to determine whether the holder, as a reasonable person, should have, through the exercise of reasonable diligence, discovered the defense, claim, or claim in recoupment. The holder must investigate to determine whether the suspicious circumstances indicate that some infirmity exists in the instrument or underlying transaction. [33]

F. Notice of claim or defense: A purchaser cannot be a holder in due course if she has notice of any claim to the instrument as described in U.C.C. §3-306 or of any defense or claim in recoupment described in U.C.C. §3-305(a). U.C.C. §3-302(a)(2). [33]

1. **Notice not obtained from public filing:** Public filing or recording of a document does not, by itself, constitute notice of a defense, claim in recoupment, or claim to the instrument. U.C.C. §3-302(b); U.C.C. §9-309. [33]

2. **Notice not obtained from executory promise:** Knowledge that an instrument was issued or negotiated in return for an executory promise (a promise to perform in the future) or accompanied by a separate agreement does not give a purchaser notice of a claim, defense, or claim in recoupment. The purchaser does not have a duty to inquire as to whether the promise has been performed. The purchaser has notice of a defense or claim in recoupment only if she has notice that a breach has already occurred. [33]

3. **Notice from defenses in other transactions:** Under the *"inferable knowledge test"*, notice of a defense to the specific instrument that the holder is purchasing will not be imputed to her even if the holder knew of many complaints from the makers of other instruments purchased from the payee. Under the *"duty to inquire test"*, a court may find that the numerous prior complaints give rise to a duty on the part of the holder to investigate this specific transaction. If the investigation would have revealed a defense, the holder will be deemed to have notice of the defense. [33]

4. **Purchase at a discount:** Under the inferable knowledge test, the purchaser is not imputed with notice of a claim, defense, or claim in recoupment solely because of her knowledge that the instrument was purchased at a substantial discount. The holder has the right to assume, for example, that the large discount is a result of a substantial risk that the maker is insolvent or of the seller's urgent need for immediate cash. Under the *duty to inquire test*, a purchaser is required to investigate why the instrument is selling at such a large discount. [33]

5. **Notice of breach of fiduciary duty:** Certain conditions must be met before the purchaser will be deemed to have notice of a breach of fiduciary duty. [33-34]

   a. **Represented person must make claim to instrument:** If the fiduciary breaches his duty by negotiating the instrument for his own or for some third-party's benefit, the represented person has an equitable claim of ownership to the instrument or its proceeds. U.C.C. §3-307, Official Comment 2. A purchaser is deemed to have notice of a breach of fiduciary claim only if the represented person makes a claim to the instrument. Notice is not imputed to the purchaser if no such claim is made. U.C.C. §3-307(b)(iii). [34]

   b. **Taker must know that person with whom he is dealing is a fiduciary:** The rules for determining whether the holder has *notice* of a breach of fiduciary duty apply only when the taker of the instrument from the fiduciary *knows* that the person with whom he is dealing is a fiduciary. U.C.C. §3-307(b)(ii). [34]

c. **Three situations involving notice of breach of fiduciary duty:**

   i. **When instrument made payable to represented party or to fiduciary as such:** A taker of an instrument payable to the represented party, or to the fiduciary as such, has notice of a breach of fiduciary duty if the instrument is taken in payment of, or as security for, a debt known by the taker to be the personal debt of the fiduciary, taken in a transaction known by the taker to be for the personal benefit of the fiduciary, or deposited in an account other than that of the fiduciary as such or of the represented person. U.C.C. §3-307(b)(2). The holder is not deemed to have notice unless it knows that the value is being given for the personal benefit of the fiduciary. The fact that the holder has knowledge that a person is a fiduciary neither gives notice to nor imposes a duty on it to inquire as to the use of the instrument. [34-35]

   ii. **When instrument drawn or made by represented person or fiduciary as such to taker:** The same rules apply when an instrument is issued by the represented person or the fiduciary as such directly to the taker. U.C.C. §3-307(b)(4). [35]

   iii. **When payable to fiduciary personally:** A different rule applies when the instrument is payable to the fiduciary personally, whether drawn by the represented person or by the fiduciary himself. In these cases, the taker has notice of a breach of fiduciary duty only if it has *actual knowledge* of the breach. U.C.C. §3-307(b)(3). The holder must therefore know not only that the value is being applied for the personal benefit of the fiduciary but also that such application is a breach of her fiduciary duty. [35]

6. **Notice that an instrument is forged, altered, or otherwise irregular:** A purchaser cannot be a holder in due course if the instrument, when issued or negotiated to the holder, bears such apparent evidence of forgery or alteration or is otherwise so irregular or incomplete as to call into question its authenticity. U.C.C. §3-302(a)(1). The test is whether the instrument on its face is so suspect that a reasonable person would question its authenticity. [35]

7. **Notice that instrument is overdue or has been dishonored:** A purchaser is denied holder-in-due-course status if he has notice that an instrument is overdue or has been dishonored. U.C.C. §3-302(a)(2)(iii). [35]

   a. **When an instrument is "overdue":**

      i. **Checks:** A check is *overdue* the day after the day demand for payment is duly made or 90 days after its stated date, whichever is earlier. U.C.C. §3-304(a)(1)-(2). [36]

      ii. **Other demand instruments:** Any other instrument payable on demand becomes overdue at the earlier of either: (1) the day after the day demand for payment is duly made or (2) when the instrument has been outstanding for a period of time after its date that is unreasonably long. U.C.C. §3-304(a)(1), (3). [36]

      iii. **When date accelerated:** Once an instrument has been accelerated causing the entire principal amount to be immediately due, the instrument becomes overdue on the day after the accelerated due date. U.C.C. §3-304(b)(3). [36]

      iv. **Payable in installments:** Absent acceleration, an instrument payable in installments becomes overdue upon default for nonpayment of an installment. The instrument remains overdue until the default is cured. U.C.C. §3-304(b)(1). [36]

    v. Not payable in installments: Absent acceleration, an instrument not payable in installments is overdue on the day after its due date. U.C.C. §3-304(b)(2). [36]

    vi. Default in interest only: As long as there is no default in the payment of the principal amount, the instrument is not overdue simply because there is a default in the payment of interest. U.C.C. §3-304(c). [36]

8. Notice of discharge: Notice of the discharge of a party, other than a discharge in an insolvency proceeding, is not notice of a defense. U.C.C. §3-302(b). However, a holder who has notice of a discharge will take subject to any discharge of which he has notice. U.C.C. §3-302(b). If a taker knows that either the maker, drawer, or acceptor (the people ultimately liable on an instrument) has been discharged in insolvency proceedings, the taker is denied holder-in-due-course status. U.C.C. §3-302, Official Comment 3. [36]

VI. DENIAL OF HOLDER-IN-DUE-COURSE STATUS TO CERTAIN CLASSES OF PURCHASERS

Four categories of holders do not become holders in due course even after meeting all the requirements contained in U.C.C. §3-302(a) for holder-in-due-course status. [37]

1. Acquisition by taking over estate: A person who acquires an instrument by taking over an estate or other organization that previously held the instrument cannot, by such acquisition, become a holder in due course. U.C.C. §3-302(c)(iii). [37]

2. Purchase in execution, bankruptcy, or creditor's sale: A purchaser of an instrument in an execution, bankruptcy or creditor's sale, or similar proceeding, or under legal process, cannot become a holder in due course. U.C.C. §3-302(c). [37]

3. Purchase in bulk transaction: A person cannot become a holder in due course by purchase of an instrument as part of a bulk transaction not in the regular course of the transferor's business. U.C.C. §3-302(c)(ii). Two types of bulk transactions are prohibited. The first type is a bulk sale of instruments for the purpose of liquidating the holder's assets in preparation for the termination of its business. In contrast, a sale in the seller's ordinary course of business is not a bulk transfer. The second prohibited type of bulk transfer occurs when there is a change in the organizational structure of the holder so that, even though the same actual entity retains the instruments, there has technically been a transfer from one entity to another. U.C.C. §3-302, Official Comment 5. [37-38]

4. Consumer notes: The Federal Trade Commission and most state legislatures have enacted rules or statutes affecting the ability of a holder of an instrument, issued in a consumer transaction, to take the instrument free from the consumer's defenses. [38]

    a. FTC rule: The Federal Trade Commission promulgated a rule aimed at preventing financiers of negotiable instruments from taking instruments free from consumers' defenses. A seller in the business of selling goods to consumers must include a legend in its consumer credit contracts that provides that any assignee of the instrument takes subject to all claims and defenses the debtor could assert against the assignor of the instrument. [39]

        i. When legend omitted: A holder in due course takes free of the consumer's defenses. [39]

ii. **When legend included:** When the required language is included, the holder takes subject to the consumer's claims and defenses. The note remains negotiable, but there can be no holder in due course, thus enabling the consumer to assert any of his defenses against the holder. U.C.C. §3-106(d). Furthermore, the holder is liable to the consumer up to, but no more than, the funds received by the holder from the consumer pursuant to the instrument. [39]

b. **State legislation:** Many states have also enacted legislation that preserves, to varying degrees, the ability of a consumer to raise defenses against a holder of the note. This legislation has taken diverse forms. Under the 1969 version of the Uniform Consumer Credit Code ("UCCC"), a seller or lessor in a consumer credit sale or consumer lease may not take in payment a negotiable instrument (other than a check). A holder is not in good faith, and thus cannot qualify as a holder in due course, if it takes a negotiable instrument with notice that the instrument is issued in violation of the UCCC. Some state legislation, including those of states adopting the 1974 version of the UCCC, make an assignee of a consumer credit sale, whether or not a holder in due course, subject to all of the consumer's claims and defenses. Uniform Consumer Credit Code §3-404 (1974). Other states adopt statutory schemes that preserve the right of a consumer to raise defenses and claims against a holder in due course to the extent that the consumer gives notice of his claim or defense to the holder within a set period of time, either after his purchase or after notice of the negotiation to the holder. [39-40]

c. **2002 amendments:** The 2002 amendments have added a new rule governing the ability of consumers to raise their claims or defenses in consumer transactions. A *"consumer transaction"* is "a transaction in which an individual incurs an obligation primarily for personal, family, or household purposes." [Rev] U.C.C. §3-103(a)(3). [40]

i. **Instrument treated as if proper notice given:** In a consumer transaction, a negotiable instrument that omits the notice required by the Federal Trade Commission (or other similar legend required by any other applicable law) is to be treated as if the instrument had included the required notice. As a result, a consumer can raise the same claims and defenses that it could if the FTC language was included even though the instrument does not contain the required notice requirement. [Rev] U.C.C. §3-305(e) and Official Comment 6. [40]

ii. **Nothing in [Rev] U.C.C. §3-305 limits right of consumer to raise claims:** Thus, to the extent that a consumer protection statute gives the consumer the right to raise claims in recoupment or defenses, nothing in [Rev] U.C.C. §3-305 limits that right. In other words, [Rev] U.C.C. §3-305 is subject to any other law that establishes a different rule for consumer transactions. [Rev] U.C.C. §3-305(f) and Official Comment 7. [40]

VII. DEFENSES, CLAIMS TO THE INSTRUMENT, CLAIMS IN RECOUPMENT, AND DISCHARGES

A. **Recovering from the obligor:** Any holder or person with the rights of a holder (collectively called *a "person entitled to enforce an instrument"*) may recover from the obligor in the absence of a claim to the instrument, defense, claim in recoupment, or discharge. U.C.C. §3-308(b). [40]

B. Defenses and claims in recoupment to which all persons take subject: Any person, whether or not the person qualifies as a holder in due course, takes subject to the following defenses or claims in recoupment. [41]

1. Defenses and claims in recoupment assertible against holder itself: The person entitled to enforce the instrument takes subject to any defense or claim in recoupment assertible against the holder himself arising from the transaction out of which the instrument was issued. U.C.C. §3-305(a)(3), (b). [41]

2. Real defenses: Four defenses are known as *"real defenses"*, which all holders, even ones acquiring the status of holder in due course, take subject. [41]

a. Infancy: To the extent that the obligor's infancy is a defense to a simple contract, it is also a defense available against any party (including a holder in due course). U.C.C. §3-305(a)(1)(i). [41-42]

b. Incapacity, duress, or illegality: Legal incapacity (e.g., mental incompetency or statutory incapacity to execute the instrument arising from a corporation's exceeding its corporate powers), duress, or illegality (e.g., the use of the instrument to pay a gambling debt, as a bribe, or to purchase known stolen property), to the extent that such defenses render the obligation of the obligor a nullity, are defenses assertible against any person. U.C.C. §3-305(a)(1)(ii). Unlike infancy, these defenses are real defenses *only if statutory or case law makes the transaction void.* U.C.C. §3-305, Official Comment 1. [42]

c. Fraud in the factum: The obligor may raise against any person the defense that he has been induced by fraud to sign the instrument with neither knowledge, nor reasonable opportunity to learn, of the instrument's character or its essential terms. U.C.C. §3-305(a)(1)(iii). An obligor is ignorant of an instrument's character if he is under the impression that he is signing something other than a promise to pay money. An obligor would be ignorant of the instrument's essential terms if he believes, for example, that he is signing a note payable in 2 years when, in fact, it is payable on demand. U.C.C. §3-305, Official Comment 1. The obligor cannot raise the defense if he, under the circumstances, knew or should have discovered the character and essential terms of the instrument. If the obligor had the opportunity to, but did not, read the instrument, the defense will seldom be available. [42-43]

d. Discharge in insolvency proceeding: The obligor's discharge in insolvency proceedings is a defense assertible against any person. U.C.C. §3-305(a)(1)(iv). [43]

C. Defenses available only against a person without the rights of a holder in due course: The following defenses are available only against persons who do not have the rights of a holder in due course. All these defenses are cut off when the instrument is acquired by a holder in due course. U.C.C. §3-305(b). [43]

1. Ordinary defenses: A person not having the rights of a holder in due course takes subject to virtually any defense, including: (1) that the instrument was not issued, conditionally issued, or issued for a special purpose, U.C.C. §3-105(b); U.C.C. §3-305(b)(1)-(3); or (2) any defense that would be available to him if the obligation arose out of an ordinary contract. U.C.C. §3-305(a)(2). No consideration is necessary for an instrument given in payment of, or as security for, an antecedent obligation of any kind. U.C.C. §3-303(a)(3). [43-44]

2. **Claims in recoupment:** A claim in recoupment is assertible against any person not having the rights of a holder in due course. The claim of recoupment may be asserted against the transferee only to the extent that it reduces the amount owing on the instrument at the time the action is brought. U.C.C. §3-305(a)(3). As against the transferee, the obligor cannot raise a set-off from a transaction other than the one that gave rise to the instrument. U.C.C. §3-305, Official Comment 3. [44-45]

3. **Defenses and claims in recoupment of other persons:** With the exception of an accommodation party, an obligor may only raise his own defenses. He may not attempt to raise a defense or claim in recoupment of another party to the instrument, nor may the other party intervene in the action to raise the defense himself. U.C.C. §3-305(c); U.C.C. §3-305, Official Comment 4. [45]

4. **Claims to the instrument:** A person with the rights of a holder in due course takes free of all claims to the instrument. U.C.C. §3-306. A person who lacks the rights of a holder in due course takes the instrument subject to all valid claims of a property or possessory interest in the instrument or its proceeds, including a claim to rescind a negotiation and to recover the instrument or its proceeds. U.C.C. §3-306. This includes both legal and equitable claims of ownership as well as a secured party's claim to a security interest in the instrument. [45]

5. **Third-party claims:** When the party being sued on the instrument does not have a claim of her own, the obligor may not use a third-party claim to defeat the holder's action unless the claimant is made a party to the action and asserts her own claim to the instrument. U.C.C. §3-305(c). The obligor may, however, without the third party being a party to the action, assert a third-party claim if the obligor knows that the holder is in wrongful possession of a stolen instrument. U.C.C. §3-602(b)(2). [46]

D. **Discharges:** A discharge is effective against any person except a holder in due course who was without notice of the discharge when she took the instrument. U.C.C. §3-601(b). [46]

1. **Discharge by payment:** An instrument is discharged to the extent that payment is made by, or on behalf of, a party obliged to pay the instrument and to a person entitled to enforce the instrument. U.C.C. §3-602(a); U.C.C. §3-602, Official Comment. [46]

   a. **Payment must be made to a person entitled to enforce the instrument:** Being the person entitled to enforce the instrument, payment to a thief of an instrument payable to bearer discharges the party making the payment. In contrast, the party making payment is not discharged if she pays someone who is not a person entitled to enforce the instrument. [46]

   b. **Adverse claim to instrument:** Subject to certain exceptions, the obligor is discharged to the extent of her payment to the person entitled to enforce the instrument even though payment is made with knowledge of a claim to the instrument by the true owner. U.C.C. §3-602(a). Payment to the person entitled to enforce the instrument does not discharge the person making payment if the adverse claimant's claim is valid and enforceable against the person entitled to enforce the instrument and either: (a) the claimant obtains an injunction against payment and the obligor pays the person entitled to enforce the instrument even though she has knowledge of the injunction; or (b) the obligor accepts from the claimant indemnity against any loss resulting from the obligor's refusal to pay the person entitled to enforce the instrument. A court will not grant an injunction unless the person entitled to enforce the instrument, the claimant, and the party obliged to pay are all subject to the court's jurisdiction. When the obligor accepts indemnity from the claimant, the obligor is not discharged if she pays in spite of the indemnity. However, the obligor has no duty to accept indemnity from the claimant. Indemnification of the obligor is not effective to prevent the obligor's discharge if the instrument involved is a bank check. Even if the claimant does not obtain an injunction or supply indemnity, the obligor is not discharged if she knows that the instrument is stolen and pays the person entitled to enforce the instrument knowing that he is in wrongful possession of the instrument. U.C.C. §3-602(b)(2). Because a holder in due course takes the instrument free from all claims to the instrument, payment to a holder in due course always discharges the obligor. [47-48]

e. 2002 amendments: A new subsection (b) has been added to [Rev] U.C.C. §3-602. [49]

   i. When payment to former holder discharges note: Subject to [Rev] U.C.C. §3-602(e), a note is paid to the extent payment is made to a person that formerly was entitled to enforce the note only if, at the time of the payment, the party obliged to pay has not received adequate notification that the note has been transferred and that payment is to be made to the transferee. [Rev] U.C.C. §3-602(b) and Official Comment 2. [49]

   ii. Adequacy of notification: For the notification to be adequate, it must:

   (a) be signed by either the transferor or the transferee;

   (b) reasonably identify the transferred note; and

   (c) provide an address at which subsequent payments are to be made. [Rev] U.C.C. §3-602(b). [49]

   iii. Demand for proof of transfer: Upon request, a transferee is required to seasonably furnish reasonable proof that the note has been transferred. [49]

   iv. Effect of failure to provide proof of transfer: Unless the transferee complies with the request, a payment to the person that formerly was entitled to enforce the note results in the obligor's discharge even if the obligor has received a notification of the transfer. [Rev] U.C.C. §3-602(b). [49]

   v. Imputed notice of payment: [Rev] U.C.C. §3-602(d) provides that a transferee, or any party that has acquired rights in the instrument directly or indirectly from a transferee, is deemed to have notice of any payment that is made under [Rev] U.C.C. §3-602(b) between the date that the note is transferred to the transferee and before the party obliged to pay the note receives adequate notification of the transfer. It does not matter that the transferee is, or is not, a holder in due course. [49]

2. Discharge by tender of payment: An effective tender of payment discharges the obligation of the obligor to pay interest accruing after the due date on the amount tendered. U.C.C. §3-603(c). Upon the holder's refusal of the obligor's tender, an indorser or an accommodation party who has a right of recourse with respect to the obligation to which the tender relates is discharged to the extent of the amount tendered. U.C.C. §3-603(b); U.C.C. §3-603, Official Comment. The law governing tender of payments under a simple contract determines whether a co-maker, co-acceptor, or co-indorser is discharged to the extent of his right of contribution. The law generally provides that a co-obligor is discharged to the extent of his right of contribution. The law generally provides that a co-obligor is discharged to the extent of his right of recourse. [49-50]

3. **Discharge by cancellation or renunciation:** A person entitled to enforce an instrument may, without consideration, discharge any party to the instrument in any manner apparent on the face of the instrument or the indorsement U.C.C. §3-604(a). A person entitled to enforce the instrument may, without consideration, discharge any party to the instrument by renouncing his rights in a signed writing. U.C.C. §3-604(a)

A party is discharged upon surrender of the instrument to the party to be discharged. U.C.C. §3-604(a). A cancellation, renunciation, or surrender of an instrument is ineffective if it is unintentional, unauthorized, or procured by fraud or mistake. In determining whether a mistake vitiates the discharge, all the rules of equity come into play. For example, the holder may not assert mistake as a grounds for denying the obligor a discharge if the obligor in good faith changed his position in good faith reliance on the cancellation, renunciation, or surrender. [51]

2002 amendments: The 2002 amendments have changed the requirement of a "signed writing" to a "signed record." [Rev] U.C.C. §3-604(a). A *"record"* is "information that is inscribed on a tangible medium or that is stored in an electronic or other medium and is retrievable in perceivable form." [Rev] U.C.C. §3-103(a)(14). [51]

Additional amendment: In addition a new [Rev] U.C.C. §3-604(c) has been added that defines *signed*, with respect to a record that is not a writing, as including the attachment to, or logical association with, the record of an electronic symbol, sound, or process to or with the record with the present intent to adopt or accept the record. [51]

4. **Discharge of simple contract:** A party is discharged from liability on an instrument to another party by any act or agreement with such party that would discharge a simple contract for the payment of money. U.C.C. §3-601(a). Although not effective as a renunciation, an oral agreement supported by consideration is usually sufficient to discharge a party on a contract to pay money. [52]

VIII. ADMISSIBILITY OF EVIDENCE EXTRINSIC TO THE INSTRUMENT

A. **Effect of separate agreements:** Subject to the parol evidence rule, an obligor's duty to pay an instrument may be modified, supplemented, or nullified by a separate agreement (whether oral or written) between the obligor and a person entitled to enforce the instrument if the instrument was issued or, the obligation incurred, either: (1) in reliance on the agreement; or (2) as part of the same transaction giving rise to the agreement. U.C.C. §3-117. [52]

B. **Agreement as defense:** The agreement would be a defense available against any person other than a holder in due course without notice of the agreement. U.C.C. §3-117. [52]

C. **Same transaction:** An agreement can be part of the same transaction even if the agreement was neither executed contemporaneously with the instrument or obligation nor referred to in the instrument. [52]

D. **The parol evidence rule:** The parol evidence rule generally provides that no prior written agreement and no prior, or contemporaneous, oral agreement is admissible to vary, or contradict, the terms found in a writing intended by the parties to be the final expression of the parties' agreement as to those terms. A negotiable instrument, by its nature, is seldom intended to include the complete terms of the parties' agreement. Therefore, the parol evidence will seldom bar introduction of additional terms that do not contradict the terms of the instrument. Most courts hold that parol evidence is not admissible to prove a condition precedent to the obligation to pay. Courts differ as to whether evidence tending to show that the promise to pay is a sham or that the note would never be enforced against the obligor is admissible. Evidence that delivery of the instrument was for a special purpose or is conditional on some act or event may always be introduced. U.C.C. §3-305(a)(2). Evidence of any defense may always be introduced. Evidence to explain ambiguities contained in the instrument may always be introduced. [52-53]

IX. TRANSFER OF INSTRUMENT AND SHELTER PROVISION

A. **Rights of the transferee:** When an instrument is transferred, the transfer vests in the transferee all the rights of his transferor. U.C.C. §3-203(b). [53-54]

B. **Right to transferor's indorsement:** If the transferee does not become the holder of the instrument because the transferor failed to supply a necessary indorsement, absent a contrary agreement, if the transfer is for value, the transferee has the specifically enforceable right to obtain the transferor's unqualified indorsement. U.C.C. §3-203(c). [54]

C. **The shelter provision:** Under the *"shelter provision,"* a transferee may acquire the rights of a holder in due course through the transfer even if the transferee does not himself qualify as a holder in due course. U.C.C. §3-203(b). This includes the right to take free of all claims to the instrument, defenses, and claims in recoupment to the same extent as would his transferor/holder in due course. U.C.C. §3-305(b); U.C.C. §3-306. The transferee also is entitled to any rights the transferor inherited from his own transferor. Because the rights vested in the transferee are purely derivative, they can be no greater than those possessed by his transferor and are subject to the same limitations. The transferee takes subject to any claim of ownership, claim in recoupment, or defense to which his transferor/holder in due course would take subject. However, no transferee, who has engaged in any fraud or illegality affecting the instrument, can acquire the rights of a holder in due course through a transfer directly or indirectly from a holder in due course. U.C.C. §3-203(b). [54-55]

D. **Reacquisition by prior holder:** On reacquisition of an instrument, the reacquirer is given the right to cancel any indorsement not necessary to its chain of title, thereby enabling it to become the holder of the instrument and have the right to further negotiate the instrument. U.C.C. §3-207. The reacquirer's cancellation of intervening indorsements discharges any indorser whose indorsement has been canceled. By virtue of the cancellation, subsequent purchasers are deemed to have notice of the canceled indorser's discharge. U.C.C. §3-207. [55-56]

X. DEFENSES AND CLAIMS TO BANK CHECKS

A. **Right of bank to raise defenses:** The obligated bank retains the same right as a drawer of a personal check to raise defenses or third-party claims. However, certain penalties are assessed against the bank if it wrongfully refuses to pay a bank check. When a bank issues a cashier's check or teller's check to pay one of its own obligations, these special rules do not apply. For example, if a bank issues a cashier's check to pay its attorney, U.C.C. §3-411 does not apply. [56]

B. Penalty for wrongfully refusing to pay: An obligated bank that wrongfully refuses to pay a bank check is liable to the person asserting the right to enforce the check for any expenses, including attorneys' fees and loss of interest resulting from the nonpayment. U.C.C. §3-411(b); U.C.C. §3-411, Official Comment 2. The holder may recover consequential damages if the obligated bank refuses to pay the check after receiving notice of the particular circumstances giving rise to these damages. U.C.C. §3-411(b). [57]

C. Bank's defenses to liability for expenses and consequential damages: The obligated bank is not liable for expenses or consequential damages if its refusal to pay occurs in any one of four situations: (a) the obligated bank suspends payments (i.e., is insolvent); (b) the obligated bank has reasonable grounds to believe that the bank's claim or defense is available against the person entitled to enforce the instrument (If the bank has a defense of its own arising out of the issuance of the bank check and reasonably believes that this defense would be assertible against the holder, the bank is not liable for either consequential damages or expenses, whether or not it is successful in raising the defense. However, the bank is liable for the holder's loss of interest on the funds. In contrast, the obligated bank receives no protection against liability for expenses and consequential damages if it unsuccessfully attempts to raise a third-party's claim to the instrument.); (c) the obligated bank has a reasonable doubt that the person is entitled to payment; or (d) the obligated bank is prohibited by law from making payment. U.C.C. §3-411(c). [57]

XI. FEDERAL HOLDER-IN-DUE-COURSE STATUS

A. Introduction: Under the federal holder-in-due-course doctrine, federal common law, and not the Code, determines whether the FDIC or the RTC, in purchasing instruments, is a holder in due course. [58]

B. Federal holder-in-due-course doctrine: Under the federal holder-in-due-course doctrine, the FDIC and the RTC can qualify as a holder in due course even when they purchase, in bulk, a failed bank's instruments. Most courts seem to require that the FDIC and the RTC take the instrument in good faith and without actual knowledge of any defense to the instrument. Courts differ as to whether the FDIC or the RTC could be a holder in due course of an overdue instrument. The status of the federal holder-in-due-course doctrine has been put into question by the United States Supreme Court's decision in O'Melveny & Myers v. FDIC, 114 S. Ct. 2048 (1994). [58-59]

C. D'Oench, Duhme doctrine: Under the D'Oench, Duhme doctrine, defenses against the FDIC or the RTC have to be based on documents and not on secret agreements. The continued vitality of the D'Oench, Duhme doctrine was put into question by the enactment of FIRREA. Under 12 U.S.C. §1823(e), no agreement that had the result of diminishing the interests of the FDIC in any assets acquired by it (whether as a purchaser or as a receiver of an insured bank or savings and loan) was valid against the FDIC unless such agreement was (a) in a writing that was (b) executed by the bank contemporaneously with the acquisition of the note, (c) approved by the board of directors of the bank, and (d) reflected in the minutes of the board. [59]

CHAPTER 3

NATURE OF LIABILITY ON INSTRUMENTS

I. LIABILITY OF ISSUER, DRAWER, ACCEPTOR, AND INDORSER

A. **Introduction:** A party may sign a negotiable instrument in four basic capacities: an issuer of a note or cashier's check, a drawer of a draft, an acceptor of a draft, and an indorser. [67]

B. **Obligation of issuer of note or cashier's check:** There are no conditions to the issuer's obligation to pay a note or cashier's check. An issuer of a note or cashier's check is liable to pay the instrument when it is due. [68]

C. **Obligation of drawer:** Dishonor by the drawee must occur before a drawer is liable on a draft. U.C.C. §3-414(b). Liability as a drawer is not conditioned on notice of dishonor. U.C.C. §3-414(b); U.C.C. §3-414, Official Comment 2. When a draft is accepted by a nonbank, a drawer is treated as an indorser under U.C.C. §3-415(a) and (c). U.C.C. §3-414(d). In contrast, a drawer is completely discharged when a draft is accepted by a bank. U.C.C. §3-414(c). A drawer may disclaim liability on any draft (other than a check) by writing, on the draft, the words "without recourse." U.C.C. §3-414(e). [68]

D. **Drawee:** A check or other draft does not of itself operate as an assignment of any of the drawer's funds held by the drawee. A drawee is not liable to the holder unless the drawee accepts the draft. U.C.C. §3-408. [68]

E. **The obligation of an acceptor:** There are no conditions to an acceptor's obligation to make payment. Once a draft is due, the acceptor is obligated to make payment. An effective acceptance must be: (a) in writing; (b) on the instrument; (c) signed by the drawee; and (d) either delivered to the holder or the holder must be notified. The acceptance may consist of the drawee's signature alone. U.C.C. §3-409(a). [68-69]

F. **Obligation of indorser:** A signature is deemed to be an indorsement regardless of the signer's intent unless the accompanying words, terms of the instrument, place of signature, or other circumstances unambiguously indicate that the signature is made for a purpose other than as an indorsement. U.C.C. §3-204(a). A person may indorse an instrument to negotiate the instrument or to incur liability on the instrument. An anomalous indorser is an indorser who is not the holder of the instrument. An indorser's obligation to pay is owed to the person who is entitled to enforce the instrument or to a subsequent indorser who pays the instrument. U.C.C. §3-415(a). An indorser may disclaim liability on his indorser's contract by indorsing the instrument without recourse. U.C.C. §3-415(b). An indorser is not liable until the instrument has been dishonored and, unless excused, notice of dishonor is given. U.C.C. §3-415(a); U.C.C. §3-503. [69-70]

II. PRESENTMENT, DISHONOR, NOTICE OF DISHONOR

A. **Introduction:** Dishonor of an instrument is a condition to the liability of both a drawer and an indorser. U.C.C. §3-414(b); U.C.C.§3-415(a); U.C.C. §3-502, Official Comment 1. An instrument is dishonored when the drawee, acceptor, or maker refuses, or fails, to pay or accept the instrument on a proper presentment for payment or acceptance. When presentment is excused, dishonor occurs if the instrument is not duly accepted or paid. U.C.C. §3-502(e); U.C.C. §3-502, Official Comment 7. [71]

B. Presentment: *Presentment* is a demand for payment or acceptance made by, or on behalf of, the person entitled to enforce the instrument. U.C.C. §3-501(a). Presentment for payment must be made to the drawee or to a party obliged to pay the instrument (*e.g.*, the maker of a note or the acceptor of an accepted draft). U.C.C. §3-501(a). Presentment for acceptance must be made to the drawee. U.C.C. §3-501(a). [71]

1. **Manner and time of presentment:** Presentment may be made by any commercially reasonable means including orally, in writing, or by electronic communication. U.C.C. §3-501(b)(1). [71]

2. **Where presentment can be made:** In the absence of a Federal Reserve Regulation, clearing-house rule or contrary agreement, presentment can be made wherever the drawee, maker, or acceptor can be found, even if the instrument specifies a particular place of payment or acceptance. If the party expected to pay or accept cannot be found, the instrument may be presented at its place of payment. U.C.C. §3-501(b)(1). Regulation CC determines where a check may be presented. U.C.C. §3-111. [71]

3. **Rights of party to whom presentment is made:** Once a demand for payment or acceptance is made, the party to whom presentment is made has the right to demand, without thereby dishonoring the instrument, that the presenter exhibit the instrument, show reasonable identification, and give a signed receipt on the instrument or surrender the instrument on full payment. U.C.C. §3-501(b)(2). [71-72]

4. **Effect of delay in presentment:** The effect of a delay in presentment depends on the type of instrument as well as on whether the obligor is an indorser or the drawer. An indorser of a check is discharged from her indorser's liability if the check is not presented for payment or given to a depositary bank for collection within 30 days after her indorsement. U.C.C. §3-415(e). A drawer of a check is discharged only when the check is not presented for payment or given to a depositary bank for collection within 30 days of the check's stated date and only to the extent that she is deprived of funds maintained with the drawee bank because the drawee bank has suspended payment after the expiration of the 30-day period and failed to make payment on the check. U.C.C. §3-414(f); U.C.C. §3-414, Official Comment 6. A delay in presenting any instrument other than a check discharges neither the drawer nor an indorser. [72]

5. **When presentment excused:** When a presentment or a delay in presentment is excused, presentment is treated as having been made within the prescribed time limits. Presentment is excused if it cannot be made by the exercise of reasonable diligence. U.C.C. §3-504(a)(i). Presentment is also excused as to the drawer when the drawer has instructed the drawee not to pay or accept a draft. U.C.C. §3-504(a)(v). Presentment is not excused as to an indorser (assuming that he did not order payment stopped). In addition, presentment is excused when the drawer or an indorser has no reason to expect or right to require that the instrument be paid or accepted. U.C.C. §3-504(a)(iv). When presentment is waived under the terms of the instrument or otherwise, presentment is excused as to the drawer or indorser. U.C.C. §3-504(a)(iii). Presentment is also excused when the maker or acceptor repudiates the obligation to pay the instrument or is in insolvency proceedings or has died. U.C.C. §3-504(a)(ii). [72-73]

C. Dishonor: The manner in which an instrument is dishonored depends on the type of instrument. [73]

1. **Dishonor of demand note:** A note payable on demand is dishonored if the note is not paid on the day of presentment. U.C.C. §3-502(a)(1). [73]

2. **Dishonor of note not payable on demand:** A note that is not payable on demand is dishonored if it is not paid on the day it becomes payable. U.C.C. §3-502(a)(3). No presentment is required. [73]

3. **Dishonor of check:** There are two ways in which a check presented to the payor bank (other than for immediate payment over the counter) may be dishonored. [73]

   a. **Returns check:** A properly presented check is dishonored if the payor bank properly returns the check or sends notice of dishonor or nonpayment in compliance with U.C.C. §§4-301 and 4-302. U.C.C. §3-502(b)(1). [73]

   b. **Fails to return check or settle:** A payor bank that fails not only to promptly return the check (or send notice of nonpayment) but also to provisionally settle for the check, and, thus, becomes accountable for the check, dishonors the check. U.C.C. §3-502(b)(1); U.C.C. §3-502, Official Comment 4. [73]

4. **Dishonor of other demand draft:** A draft payable on demand is dishonored if presentment for payment is duly made to the drawee and the draft is not paid on the day of presentment. U.C.C. §3-502(b)(2). This applies to checks presented over the counter for immediate payment in cash. U.C.C. §3-502(b)(2); U.C.C. §3-502, Official Comment 4. [73]

5. **Dishonor of draft not payable on demand:** A draft not payable on demand is dishonored in two ways. [73]

   a. **Not paid on presentment:** If the draft is presented for payment and it is not paid on the day it is due or the day of presentment, whichever is later, it is dishonored. U.C.C. §3-502(b)(3)(i). However, payment or acceptance of an unaccepted documentary draft may be delayed without dishonor until no later than the close of the drawee's third business day following the day on which payment or acceptance is required under U.C.C. §3-502(b). U.C.C. §3-502(c). [73-74]

   b. **Presented for acceptance:** An unaccepted draft payable at a stated date, or a stated period after acceptance, is dishonored if the draft is presented for acceptance and acceptance is refused. U.C.C. §3-502(b)(3)(ii), (4); U.C.C. §3-502, Official Comment 4. [74]

6. **Dishonor of accepted draft:** Once a draft is accepted, the holder must present the draft to the acceptor for payment. [74]

   a. **Payable on demand:** An accepted draft payable on demand is dishonored if presentment for payment is duly made and the draft is not paid on the day of presentment. U.C.C. §3-502(d)(1); U.C.C. §3-502, Official Comment 6. [74]

   b. **Not payable on demand:** An accepted draft not payable on demand is dishonored if presentment for payment is duly made and payment is not made on the day it becomes payable or on the day of presentment, whichever is later. U.C.C.§3-502(d)(2);U.C.C.§3-503, Official Comment 6. [74]

D. **Notice of dishonor:** Notice of dishonor may be given by any commercially reasonable means. It may be oral, electronic, by telephone, or in writing. U.C.C. §3-503(b). Unless excused, a delay in giving notice of dishonor discharges an indorser on any type of instrument. U.C.C. §3-415(c). A delay in giving notice of dishonor does not discharge a drawer. U.C.C. §3-503, Official Comment 1. [74]

1. **Time within which notice of dishonor must be given:** When an instrument *is not* taken by a collecting bank for collection, notice of dishonor must be given within 30 days after the day on which the instrument is dishonored. U.C.C. §3-503(c). When an instrument is taken by a collecting bank for collection, the collecting bank must give notice of dishonor before midnight of the next banking day following the banking day on which the bank receives notice of dishonor. Persons, other than a collecting bank, must give notice of dishonor within 30 days following the day on which the person receives notice of dishonor. U.C.C. §3-503(c); U.C.C. §3-503, Official Comment 2. [74-75]

2. **When delay in notice of dishonor excused:** A delay in giving notice of dishonor is excused if the delay is caused by circumstances beyond the control of the person giving the notice and the person giving notice exercises reasonable diligence after the cause of the delay ceases to operate. U.C.C. §3-504(c). [75]

3. **When notice of dishonor excused:** Notice of dishonor is excused whenever it is waived in the instrument or otherwise. U.C.C. §3-504(b)(ii). [75]

III. TRANSFER WARRANTIES

A. **Introduction:** Any person who transfers an instrument for consideration makes the transfer warranties. U.C.C. §3-416(a). These warranties are made whether or not the transferor indorses the instrument and even when he indorses the instrument "without recourse." [75-76]

B. **To whom transfer warranties are made:** A transferor, who does not indorse the instrument, only makes the transfer warranties to his transferee. If he indorses the instrument, he makes the warranties to all subsequent transferees. If the instrument enters the bank collection process, any customer (whether or not indorsing the item) that transfers the item and receives a settlement, or other consideration, makes the warranties to its transferee and to any subsequent collecting bank. U.C.C. §4-207(a). [76]

C. **Content of transfer warranties:** A transferor makes five warranties:

1. **Transferor is a person entitled to enforce the instrument:** A transferor warrants that he is a person entitled to enforce the instrument. U.C.C. §4-207(a)(1); U.C.C. §3-416(a)(1). [76-77]

2. **All signatures are authentic and authorized:** A transferor warrants that all signatures are authentic and authorized. U.C.C. §4-207(a)(2); U.C.C. §3-416(a)(2). [77]

3. **No alteration:** A transferor warrants that the instrument has not been altered. U.C.C. §3-416(a)(3); U.C.C. §4-207(a)(3). An alteration includes the unauthorized addition of words or numbers to an incomplete instrument. [77]

4. **Transferor not subject to any defense or claim in recoupment:** A transferor warrants that the instrument is free from any defense or claim in recoupment of any party that can be asserted against the warrantor. U.C.C. §3-416(a)(4); U.C.C. §4-207(a)(4); U.C.C. §3-416, Official Comment 3. In essence, the transferor warrants that if he were to sue any party on the instrument, none of these parties would have a defense or claim in recoupment that could be asserted against him. The transferor breaches this warranty even if the transferee is a holder in

due course who would take the instrument free from the particular defense or claim in recoupment. U.C.C. §3-416, Official Comment 3. [77-78]

5. **No knowledge of insolvency proceedings:** A transferor warrants that it has no knowledge of insolvency proceedings with respect to the maker, acceptor, or drawer of an unaccepted item. U.C.C. §3-416(a)(5); U.C.C. §4-207(a)(5); U.C.C. §3-416, Official Comment 4. [78]

6. **2002 amendments:** The 2002 amendments to Articles 3 and 4 have added a new transfer warranty with respect to a remotely created consumer item. As to such items, the transferor warrants that the person on whose account the item is drawn has authorized the issuance of the item in the amount for which the item is drawn. [Rev] U.C.C. §3-416(a)(6) and [Rev] U.C.C. §4-207(a)(6). A *"remotely created consumer item"* is an item payable out of a consumer's account which is created by a merchant or telemarketer with the consumer's signature not appearing on the item. [Rev] U.C.C. §3-103(a)(16). [78]

IV. SURETIES AND ACCOMMODATION PARTIES

A. **What is an accommodation party?** If an instrument is issued for value given for the benefit of a party to the instrument ("the *accommodated party*") and another party to the instrument (the "accommodation party") signs the instrument for the purpose of incurring liability on the instrument without being a direct beneficiary of the value given for the instrument, the instrument is signed by the accommodation party "for accommodation." U.C.C. §3-419(a). [78]

1. **Both surety and debtor must sign instrument:** A person is an accommodation party only when both the surety and the debtor sign the same instrument. U.C.C. §3-419(a). [78]

2. **When both do not sign same instrument:** If the surety does not sign the same instrument as the debtor, he is not an accommodation party. He is still a surety with his rights, as a surety, being governed by the general law of suretyship. [78]

3. **Collection guaranteed:** When "collection guaranteed" or equivalent words are added to a signature that unambiguously indicate an intention to guarantee collection only, the signer undertakes only a guaranty of collection. U.C.C. §3-419(d). A guarantor of collection is obliged to pay the amount due only if the holder cannot collect from the accommodated party. U.C.C. §3-419(d); U.C.C. §3-419, Comment 4. [79]

   2002 amendments: Under [Rev] U.C.C. §3-419(d), a party who adds words like "collection guaranteed" to its signature is obligated to make payment only when the holder is unable to recover from the other party to the instrument. [Rev] U.C.C. §3-419(e) is simply intended to make it clear that, unless the person clearly indicates that he or she is guaranteeing collection, rather than payment, the creditor may proceed directly against the guarantor without first proceeding against the accommodated party. [79]

4. **Accommodation party cannot receive direct benefit from instrument:** A person is an accommodation party only if he has not received a direct benefit from the value given for the instrument. U.C.C. §3-419, Official Comment 1. Receiving an indirect benefit from the value given for the instrument will not deny that person accommodation party status. U.C.C. §3-419, Official Comment 1. [79]

5. **Accommodation party liable in capacity in which she signs:** An accommodation party is liable in whatever capacity she has signed, *i.e.,* indorser, maker, acceptor, or drawer. U.C.C. §3-419(b); U.C.C. §3-419, Official Comment 1. [79]

6. **2002 amendments:** Definitions of "principal obligor" and "secondary obligor" have been added. [79]

   a. **Principal obligor:** A "*principal obligor*" is the accommodated party or any other party to the instrument against whom a secondary obligor has recourse under [Rev] Article 3. [Rev] U.C.C. §3-103(a)(11). [79]

   Example: Mary makes a note payable to Joe. Joe indorses the note to Sally. Mary is a principal obligor because Joe has a right of recourse against her.

   b. **Secondary obligor:** A "*secondary obligor*" is any of the following:

      i. **Indorser:** An indorser is a secondary obligor because it has a right to recover from the maker, drawer, or prior indorser. [80]

      ii. **Accommodation party:** An accommodation party is a secondary obligor because it may recover from the accommodated party. [80]

      iii. **Drawer of an accepted draft:** Where a draft is accepted by a person (other than a bank), the drawer is treated as an indorser with the acceptor having the primary responsibility to pay the draft. As a result, the drawer is in the position of an indorser. [Rev] U.C.C. §3-414(d). Where the draft is accepted by a bank, the drawer is discharged. [Rev] U.C.C. §3-414(c). [80]

      iv. **Right to contribution:** Any other party to the instrument that has a right of recourse against another party to the instrument under [Rev] U.C.C. §3-116(b) is a secondary obligor to the extent of such a right. Under the latter section, a party having joint and several liability who pays the instrument is entitled to receive from another party having the same joint and several liability contribution in accordance with applicable law. [Rev] U.C.C. §3-103(a)(17). Because of the right of a party having joint and several liability who pays an instrument to receive contribution from his co-obligors, such a co-obligor is, in part, a secondary obligor and, also in part, a principal obligor. [Rev] U.C.C. §3-116, Revised Official Comment 1. [80]

      Example: John and Mary are co-makers of a note payable to Phil in the amount of $1,000. Upon Phil's demand, Mary pays the entire amount of the note. Mary, subject to an agreement to the contrary, has the right to recover $500 from John.

B. **Relationship between accommodation and accommodated parties:** An accommodation party is not liable on the instrument to the party accommodated, nor is he liable for contribution to the accommodated party in the event of payment by the accommodated party. U.C.C. §3-419(e). [80]

   1. **Right of reimbursement:** On payment, the accommodation party has a right to be reimbursed by the accommodated party. This promise is implied in the relationship whether or not the accommodated party makes an express promise to that effect. [80]

   2. **Right of subrogation:** The accommodation party, on full payment of the instrument, is entitled to enforce the instrument against the party accommodated. The accommodation party

obtains all the rights of the party he paid both on the instrument and to any collateral. U.C.C. §3-419(e); U.C.C. §3-419, Official Comment 5. [80]

3. **2002 amendments:** Under the 2002 amendments, the accommodation party may, in proper circumstances, have the court order the accommodated party to specifically perform its obligation to pay the instrument. [Rev] U.C.C. §3-419(e) [now subsection "(f)" under the 2002 amendments]. [81]

C. **Relationship between accommodation parties:** In the absence of an agreement to the contrary, two parties who sign in the same capacity in accommodation for another party are co-sureties. As co-sureties, they are jointly and severally liable. [81]

   1. **Right of contribution:** A co-surety who pays more than his proportional share of the obligation has a right of contribution from the other co-surety. U.C.C. §3-116(b). [81]

   2. **Subsuretyship:** An accommodation party may attempt to prove that he was the accommodation party not only for the original debtor but also for the other accommodation party (called "*subsuretyship*"). To do so, he must prove an express or implied understanding to that effect. [81]

D. **Defenses available to accommodation party**

   1. **May not raise lack of consideration:** As long as the instrument was issued for value for the benefit of the accommodated party, the accommodation party may not raise the defense of lack of consideration even though he has, in fact, received no benefit in any form. U.C.C. §3-303; U.C.C. §3-419. [81]

   2. **Right of accommodation party to raise accommodated party's defenses:** The accommodation party may raise any of the accommodated party's defenses or claims in recoupment. U.C.C. §3-305(d). However, the accommodation party may not raise, as a defense to his own obligation to pay, the accommodated party's discharge in insolvency proceedings, infancy, or lack of legal capacity. U.C.C. §3-305(d). [81-82]

E. **Discharge of indorsers and accommodation parties ("suretyship defenses")**

   1. **Limited to accommodation parties and indorsers:** The right to a discharge under U.C.C. §3-605 is limited to accommodation parties and indorsers. U.C.C. §3-605(a). An accommodation party is discharged only if the person entitled to enforce the instrument has actual knowledge of its status as an accommodation party or has notice of the accommodation from an indication on the instrument that the party has signed as "guarantor," "surety," or "accommodation party," or from the fact that the signature is an anomalous indorsement that is presumed to be made in the capacity of an accommodation party. U.C.C. §3-419(c); U.C.C. §3-605(h). [82]

      a. **2002 amendments:** The 2002 amendments to U.C.C. §3-605 have significantly changed the rules, as well as the terminology, for determining the effect on secondary obligors of an impairment of collateral, a release of the primary obligor, an extension granted to the primary obligor and a modification of the obligations of the primary obligor. [82]

         i. **Party to instrument:** [Rev] U.C.C. §3-605 only applies where the secondary obligor is a party to an instrument. Where the secondary obligor is not a party to the instrument, general suretyship law applies. [Rev] U.C.C. §3-605, Official Comment 1. [82]

ii. Terminology: Unlike original U.C.C. §3-605, which discusses these issues in terms of the effect that a discharge of a party under U.C.C. §3-604 has on the liability of an indorser or accommodation party having a right of recourse against the discharged party, [Rev] U.C.C. §3-605(a) speaks in terms of the effect that a "*release*" of the "principal obligor" has on the liability of a "secondary obligor." A "*principal obligor*" is the accommodated party or any other party to the instrument against whom a secondary obligor has recourse under Article 3. [Rev] U.C.C. §3-103(a)(11). [82-83]

iii. Secondary obligors: [Rev] U.C.C. §3-605 applies to the following five secondary obligors:

(1) An accommodation party;

(2) An indorser of a note who is not an accommodation party;

(3) A drawer of a draft that is accepted by a party that is not a bank;

(4) An indorser of a check; and

(5) A co-maker of an instrument, whether or not an accommodation party. [Rev] U.C.C. §3-103(a)(17). [83]

> **Note:** A co-maker's right of contribution under [Rev] U.C.C. §3-116(b) makes a co-maker a secondary obligor to the extent of its right of contribution. [Rev] U.C.C. §3-605, Official Comment 3.

2. Release of principal debtor: Release of the principal debtor (technically called "*discharge by cancellation or renunciation*") does not discharge the accommodation party or indorser under U.C.C. §3-605(b). Notwithstanding release of the principal debtor, the accommodation party or indorser retains both her right of recourse on the instrument and her right of reimbursement against the principal debtor. U.C.C. §3-419(e); U.C.C. §3-605, Official Comment 3. [83]

a. 2002 amendments: The 2002 amendments have complicated the rules as to the effect that a release of the principal obligor has on the liability of a secondary obligor. [83]

i. Liability of principal obligor to secondary obligor as to previous payments: Notwithstanding release of the principal obligor by the person entitled to enforce an instrument, the obligations of the principal obligor to the secondary obligor with respect to any previous payment made by the secondary obligor are not affected. [Rev] U.C.C. §3-605(a)(1). As a result, despite the release, the secondary obligor may recover from the principal obligor for any payments already made by the secondary obligor. [Rev] U.C.C. §3-605, Official Comment 4. [83]

ii. Liability of principal obligor to secondary obligor as to other obligations: Subject to the exception discussed below, the principal obligor is also discharged, to the extent of the release, from any unperformed obligations owed to the secondary obligor. [Rev] U.C.C. §3-605(a)(1). This includes not only the principal obligor's liability as an obligor on the instrument (e.g., as a maker, drawer, or indorser) but also as to any obligations under U.C.C. §§3-116 and 3-419. [Rev] U.C.C. §3-605, Official Comment 4. [83-84]

Rationale: Because the secondary obligor no longer faces liability on the instrument, the principal obligor can, likewise, have no liability to the secondary obligor. The secondary obligor's voluntary decision to pay the instrument, when not legally obligated to, should not impose an obligation on the principal obligor to reimburse him. [Rev] U.C.C. §3-605, Official Comment 4.

Exception: Where the terms of the release reserve the person entitled to enforce the instrument's recourse against the secondary obligor as well as the secondary obligor's recourse against the principal obligor, the principal obligor's obligation to the secondary obligor is not discharged. [Rev] U.C.C. §3-605(g).

Rationale: Where the person entitled to enforce the instrument's recourse against the secondary obligor is preserved, it would be unfair if the secondary obligor did not retain its rights against the principal obligor despite the principal obligor's release by the person entitled to enforce the instrument.

iii. **Liability of secondary obligor as to unperformed obligations:** Where a person entitled to enforce the instrument releases the obligation of the principal obligor in whole or in part, unless the terms of the release provide that the person entitled to enforce the instrument retains the right to enforce the instrument against the secondary obligor, the secondary obligor is discharged to the same extent as the principal obligor from any unperformed portion of its obligation on the instrument. [Rev] U.C.C. §3-605(a)(2) and Official Comment 4. [84]

(a) **Exception as to consideration given:** Even where the secondary obligor is not discharged under this section, the secondary obligor is discharged to the extent of the value of the consideration given for the release. [Rev] U.C.C. §3-605(a)(3) and Official Comment 4. [84]

(b) **Exception for harm caused to secondary obligor:** The secondary obligor is also discharged to the extent that the release would otherwise cause the secondary obligor a loss. [Rev] U.C.C. §3-605(a)(3) and Official Comment 4. The secondary obligor may be hurt by the release in that there is no longer the possibility that the primary obligor would make further payments that would reduce the remaining obligation of the secondary obligor. [Rev] U.C.C. §3-605, Official Comment 4. [84]

(c) **Effect of consent:** The secondary obligor is not discharged where it has consented to the release or is deemed to have consented to thereto under [Rev] U.C.C §3-605(f). [Rev] U.C.C. §3-605, Official Comment 4. [84]

(d) **Effect of failure to reserve recourse:** Unless the release reserves the secondary obligor's recourse against the principal obligor, the release eliminates the secondary obligor's claims against the principal obligor with respect to any future payment by the secondary obligor. [Rev] U.C.C. §3-605, Official Comment 4. [84]

Rationale: Permitting releases to be negotiated between the principal obligor and the person entitled to enforce the instrument without regard to the consequences to the secondary obligor would create an undue risk of opportunistic behavior by the obligee and principal obligor. [Rev] U.C.C. §3-605, Official Comment 4.

Exception for checks: Where a person entitled to enforce an instrument releases the obligation of a principal obligor on a check, in whole or in part, the secondary obligor whose liability is based upon its indorsement of the check is discharged without regard to the language or circumstances of the discharge or release. [Rev] U.C.C. §3-605(a)(2). The person entitled to enforce the instrument can avoid discharge of the indorser by contracting with the indorser for a different result at the time that she grants the release to the principal obligor. [Rev] U.C.C. §3-605, Official Comment 4.

3. **Extensions and modifications:** An accommodation party or indorser, having a right of recourse against a principal debtor, may be entitled to a discharge in the event that the person entitled to enforce the instrument modifies the obligation of, or grants an extension to, the principal debtor. U.C.C. §3-605(c), (d). [85]

4. **Extensions—extent of discharge:** An extension granted to the principal debtor only discharges the accommodation party or indorser to the extent that the extension causes the accommodation party or indorser a loss with respect to his right of recourse against the principal debtor. U.C.C. §3-605(c); U.C.C. §3-605, Official Comment 4. [85]

   a. **Form of agreement:** The extension must take the form of an agreement, whether or not binding, under which the person entitled to enforce the instrument gives more time to the principal debtor to pay the instrument. The mere failure to enforce the instrument when due or to foreclose on the collateral does not constitute an extension. [85]

   b. **Proof of loss:** The burden is placed on the accommodation party or indorser to prove that he suffered a loss by virtue of the extension. U.C.C. §3-605, Official Comment 4. [85]

   c. **2002 amendments**

      i. **Effect of extension on secondary obligor:** Where a person entitled to enforce an instrument grants the principal obligor an extension of time, the secondary obligor is discharged to the extent that the extension would otherwise cause the secondary obligor a loss. [Rev] U.C.C. §3-605(b)(2) and Official Comment 5. [85]

         Example: Principal obligor becomes insolvent during the extension. Had the extension not been granted, principal obligor would have been able to pay $1,000 of the $5,000 note. Assuming that secondary obligor can prove this, secondary obligor would be discharged to the extent of $1,000. [Rev] U.C.C. §3-605, Official Comment 5.

         Exception: An extension of time has no effect on the obligations of the principal obligor to the secondary obligor with respect to any previous payment made by the secondary obligor. [Rev] U.C.C. §3-605(b)(1). The rationale for this exception is that the secondary obligor, upon payment, has an independent right to recover the amount paid from the principal obligor.

      ii. **Effect on principal obligor's duty to secondary party:** Unless the terms of the extension preserve the secondary obligor's recourse against the principal obligor, any extension granted to the principal obligor extends the time for performance of any other duties owed to the secondary obligor by the principal obligor under Article 3. [Rev] U.C.C. §3-605(b)(1). As a result, if the secondary obligor pays the person entitled to enforce the instrument, the secondary obligor may not recover from the principal obligor during the time in which the time for payment was extended. [86]

iii. Secondary party's options: When the time for payment by the principal obligor has been extended by the person entitled to enforce payment, the secondary obligor has the following options:

(a) Perform as if no extension: Assuming that the secondary obligor is not discharged under [Rev] U.C.C. §3-605(b)(2), the secondary obligor may perform its obligations on the instrument as if the time for payment had not been extended. [Rev] U.C.C. §3-605(b)(3). [86]

(b) Treat time for performance as extended: Unless the terms of the extension provide that the person entitled to enforce the instrument retains the right to enforce the instrument against the secondary obligor as if the time for payment had not been extended, the secondary obligor may treat the time for performance of its obligations as having been extended to the same extent as that of the primary obligor. [Rev] U.C.C. §3-605(b)(3). [86]

(c) Reservation of rights: Where the terms of the extension provide that the person entitled to enforce the instrument retains its right to enforce the instrument against the secondary obligor on the original due date, the secondary obligor has the obligation to pay on the original due date. As a result, the secondary obligor may not delay payment until the extended due date. [Rev] U.C.C. §3-605, Official Comment 5. However, unless the extension agreement effects a reservation of the secondary obligor's right of recourse, the secondary obligor has no right to recover from the principal obligor until the extended due date. Because of the loss of its right to immediate recourse, the secondary obligor is discharged to the extent that this delay causes a loss to the secondary obligor. [Rev] U.C.C. §3-605(b)(2) and Official Comment 5. [86]

(d) Secondary obligor's option: Where the secondary obligor has the right, but not the duty, to pay the instrument on the original due date, the secondary obligor may assert its rights to discharge under [Rev] U.C.C. §3-605(b)(2) even if it does not exercise its option to pay on the original due date. [Rev] U.C.C. §3-605, Official Comment 5. In determining its loss, the fact that the secondary obligor did not exercise its option to pay on the original due date, and then recover from the principal obligor, may affect the loss resulting from the extension. [Rev] U.C.C. §3-605, Official Comment 5. [86]

Example: Holder grants extension to Maker by which the due date of the note is extended from January 15 to May 15. On February 15, Maker is solvent. Indorser has reason to know that Maker may not be solvent on May 15. Indorser's failure to make payment on January 15 and then demand reimbursement from Maker may diminish Indorser's right to a discharge. If Holder can prove that Maker would have paid Indorser some of the money had Indorser demanded payment on the original due date, Indorser's right to a discharge would be diminished to the extent that its failure to make payment and pursue Maker mitigated its loss. This is especially true if the secondary obligor has been given prompt notice of the extension and there is a preservation of rights so that the secondary obligor could have recovered from the principal obligor had it so done. [Rev] U.C.C. §3-605, Official Comment 5.

iv. **Reservation of rights:** A release or extension preserves a secondary obligor's recourse against the principal obligor if the terms of the release or extension provide both that: (1) the person entitled to enforce the instrument retains the right to enforce the instrument against the secondary obligor; and (2) recourse of the secondary obligor continues as though the release or extension had not been granted. [Rev] U.C.C. §3-605(g) and Official Comment 10. [87]

    (a) Manner of reservation: No particular language is necessary to preserve the secondary parties' recourse against the principal obligor. [Rev] U.C.C. §3-605, Official Comment 4. However, the reservation must be contained in the terms of the release. Parol evidence is not admissible to prove that the parties intended that the secondary obligor remain liable. [Rev] U.C.C. §3-605, Official Comment 4. [87]

    Examples: Statements such as the parties "intend to release the principal obligor but not the secondary obligor" or that the person entitled to enforce the instrument "reserves its rights" against the secondary obligor are sufficient. [Rev] U.C.C. §3-605, Official Comment 4.

5. **Modifications—extent of discharge:** When the person entitled to enforce the instrument agrees to materially modify the obligation of the principal debtor, with or without consideration, the accommodation party or indorser is discharged to the extent that the modification causes a loss with respect to her right of recourse against the principal debtor. U.C.C. §3-605(d); U.C.C. §3-605, Official Comment 5. [87]

a. **Burden of proof:** The loss suffered by the accommodation party or indorser is presumed to be equal to the amount of her right of recourse. As a result, unless the person entitled to enforce the instrument can prove that the loss is a lesser amount, the accommodation party or indorser is completely discharged. U.C.C. §3-605(d); U.C.C. §3-605, Official Comment 5. [87]

b. **Burden of proof where both modification and extension:** Because of the presumption of total loss in the case of a modification, if an agreement both materially modifies the obligation of the principal debtor and also grants an extension to him, the accommodation party or indorser will be completely discharged unless the person entitled to enforce the instrument can prove that the loss was in a lesser amount. U.C.C. §3-605, Official Comment 5. [87-88]

c. **2002 amendments** [88]

    i. **Discharge of secondary obligor:** If a person entitled to enforce an instrument agrees, with or without consideration, to a modification of the obligation of a principal obligor, the secondary obligor is discharged from any unperformed portion of its obligation to the extent that the modification would otherwise cause the secondary obligor a loss. [Rev] U.C.C. §3-605(c)(2). [88]

    ii. **Effect of modification on unperformed obligations:** The modification modifies any other duties owed to the secondary obligor by the principal obligor under Revised Article 3 to the same extent that the modification modifies the obligations of the principal obligor to the person entitled to enforce the instrument. [Rev] U.C.C. §3-605(c)(1) and Official Comment 6. [88]

      iii. Consideration irrelevant: Whether the modification was with or without consideration is irrelevant. [Rev] U.C.C. §3-605(c)(1). [88]

      iv. No effect on prior payments: Obligations of the principal obligor to the secondary obligor with respect to any previous payment by the secondary obligor are not affected by the modification. [Rev] U.C.C. §3-605(c)(1). [88]

      v. Secondary party's options where not discharged: To the extent that the secondary obligor is not discharged from performance under [Rev] U.C.C. §3-605(c)(2), the secondary obligor may satisfy its obligation on the instrument as if the modification had not occurred, or may treat its obligation on the instrument as having been correspondingly modified. [Rev] U.C.C. §3-605(c)(3) and Official Comment 6. [88]

    d. 2002 amendments as to burden of proof: With one exception, a secondary obligor asserting the right to a discharge has the burden of proof both with respect to the occurrence of the acts alleged to harm the secondary obligor and the loss or prejudice caused by those acts. [Rev] U.C.C. §3-605(h). [88]

    Exception: If the secondary obligor demonstrates prejudice caused by an impairment of its recourse, and the circumstances of the case indicate that the amount of loss is not reasonably susceptible of calculation or requires proof of facts that are not ascertainable, it is presumed that the act impairing the recourse caused a loss or impairment equal to the full liability of the secondary obligor on the instrument. [Rev] U.C.C. §3-605(i). In that event, the burden of proof as to any lesser amount of the loss shifts to the person entitled to enforce the instrument. [Rev] U.C.C. §3-605(i).

6. Consent and waiver: Any party who consents to a modification or to an extension is not discharged. U.C.C. §3-605(i); U.C.C. §3-305, Official Comment 8. [89]

    a. 2002 amendments: A secondary obligor is not discharged under [Rev] U.C.C. §3-605 if the secondary obligor either consents to the event or conduct or the instrument or a separate agreement of the party provides for a waiver of discharge. The waiver may, but does not have to, specifically mention [Rev] U.C.C. §3-605. [Rev] U.C.C. §3-605(f). To the extent that the circumstances indicate otherwise, consent by the principal obligor to an act that would lead to a discharge under [Rev] U.C.C. §3-605 constitutes consent to that act by the secondary obligor if the secondary obligor controls the principal obligor or deals with the person entitled to enforce the instrument on behalf of the principal obligor. [Rev] U.C.C. §3-605(f). [89]

7. Impairment of collateral: If the obligation to pay an instrument is secured by an interest in collateral and the person entitled to enforce the instrument impairs the value of the collateral, the obligation of an indorser or an accommodation party having a right of recourse against the obligor is discharged to the extent of the impairment. U.C.C. §3-605(e); U.C.C. §3-605, Official Comment 6. [89]

    a. Discharge of accommodation parties and indorsers: An accommodation party or indorser is discharged under U.C.C. §3-605(e) only if the person entitled to enforce the instrument knows of the accommodation or has notice of the accommodation under U.C.C. §3-419(c). U.C.C. §3-605(h). [89]

2002 amendments: A secondary obligor is not discharged under [Rev] U.C.C. §3-605 (a)-(d) unless the person entitled to enforce the instrument knows that the person is a secondary obligor or has notice under [Rev] U.C.C. §3-419(c) that the instrument was signed for accommodation. [Rev] U.C.C. §3-605(e). [89-90]

Rationale: A secondary obligor can, if it desires, always make its status clear to third parties. Unless the person entitled to enforce the instrument knows that he/she is hurting the right of recourse of the secondary obligor, he/she should not be punished for actions that will usually only benefit the primary obligor.

Example: Because Allen knows that his credit is suspect, Allen asks his friend Larry if Larry would act as the "borrower" in obtaining a loan from Bank. Larry makes a note to Bank evidencing a loan of $5,000. Allen signs the note as an anomalous indorser. When it is due, Bank accepts Allen's offer to pay Bank $1,000 in exchange for his release. Larry is not released by Bank's release of Allen because Bank had no way of knowing that it was hurting Larry by releasing Allen.

b. **Discharge of co-obligors:** If a person entitled to enforce the instrument impairs the value of the interest in the collateral, the obligation of any party who is jointly and severally liable with respect to the secured obligation is discharged to the extent that the impairment causes the party asserting the discharge to pay more than he would have been obliged to pay. U.C.C. §3-605(f); U.C.C. §3-605, Official Comment 7. [90]

8. **When is collateral impaired?** Impairment of collateral occurs when some unjustifiable act or omission on the part of the person entitled to enforce the instrument causes the collateral no longer to be available to satisfy the instrument. U.C.C. §3-605(g). [90]

a. **Duty of reasonable care:** Unless otherwise agreed, if the collateral is property in the possession of the person entitled to enforce the instrument, that person has the duty to use reasonable care in its custody and possession of the collateral. U.C.C. §3-605(g). [90]

b. **Acts constituting impairment:** Article 3 contains a nonexclusive list of acts that constitute impairment of collateral. [90]

   i. **Failure to perfect:** The failure to obtain or maintain perfection or recordation of the interest in collateral. [90-91]

   ii. **Release of collateral:** The release of collateral without substitution of collateral of equal value. [91]

   iii. **Duty to preserve:** The failure to perform a duty to preserve the value of the collateral owed to the debtor, accommodation party, or indorser. [91]

   iv. **Improper disposal:** The failure to comply with an applicable law (e.g., Article 9) in disposing of collateral. U.C.C. §3-605(g). [91]

c. **2002 amendments:** Although [Rev] U.C.C. §3-605(d) represents no substantive change from original [Rev] U.C.C. §3-605(e), there have been some changes of note. The 2002 amendments have substituted *"principal obligor"* for the party primarily liable and *"secondary obligor"* for accommodation party, "indorser," or "person who is secondarily liable." [Rev] U.C.C. §3-605(d). Similarly, in [Rev] U.C.C. §3-605(e)(i), the term *"secondary party"* has been substituted for "indorser or accommodation party having a right of recourse against the obligor." [Rev] U.C.C. §3-605(d). [91-92]

Note: The 2002 amendments have also added to the situations in which the value of collateral is impaired by including, as an act of impairment, the failure to comply with applicable law in otherwise enforcing an interest in collateral. [Rev] U.C.C. §3-605(d) and Official Comment 7.

Note: The 2002 amendments also make it clear that [Rev] U.C.C. §3-605(d) applies to collateral that is realty (and not just personal property) as long as the obligation in question is in the form of a negotiable instrument. [Rev] U.C.C. §3-605, Official Comment 7. As a result, this section would be applicable where the collateral is a note secured by a trust deed.

9. **Extent of discharge for impairment of collateral:** An accommodated party or indorser is discharged to the extent that he has been hurt by an impairment of the value of the collateral. The party seeking the discharge bears the burden of proof as to both the fact of impairment and the amount of the loss. U.C.C. §3-605(e); U.C.C. §3-605(f). The Code provides three alternative formulas for determining the extent of the impairment. [91]

   a. **Formula when debt fully secured:** When the debt is fully secured, the value of an interest in collateral is impaired to the extent that the value of the interest is reduced to an amount less than the amount of the right of recourse of the party asserting the discharge. U.C.C. §3-605(e)(i); U.C.C. §3-605, Official Comment 6. [91]

   b. **Formula when debt undersecured:** The value of an interest in collateral is impaired to the extent that the reduction in value of the interest causes an increase in the amount by which the amount of the right of recourse exceeds the value of the interest. U.C.C. §3-605(e)(ii). [91]

   c. **Formula where co-obligors:** Where the party seeking the discharge is jointly and severally liable with the person who gave the collateral to the person entitled to enforce the instrument, the co-obligor is discharged only to the extent that the impairment causes him to pay more than he would otherwise have been obliged to pay, taking into account his right of contribution. U.C.C. §3-605(f). [92]

10. **Consent to impairment of collateral:** A party is denied a discharge if he has consented to the act constituting the impairment. U.C.C. §3-605(i). [92]

V. LIABILITY OF AGENTS, PRINCIPALS, AND CO-OBLIGORS

A. **Liability of represented person:** A represented person is liable on an instrument if the representative is authorized to sign for the represented person. U.C.C. §3-402(a); U.C.C. §3-402, Official Comment 1. Any mark or symbol used by the representative that is intended to signify the represented person is sufficient to bind the represented person. U.C.C. §3-402(a); U.C.C. §3-401, Official Comment 1. [92]

   1. **In name of represented person:** The representative may sign the name of the represented person either with, or without, adding the agent's own name or capacity. U.C.C. §3-402(a); U.C.C. §3-401, Official Comment 1. [92-93]

2. **Undisclosed principal:** To the extent the representative is authorized to act on the represented person's behalf, an undisclosed principal is liable on the instrument even though neither his signature nor his identity appears on the instrument. U.C.C. §3-401(a); U.C.C. §3-401, Official Comment 1; U.C.C. §3-402, Official Comment 1. [93]

B. Liability of representative

1. **Unauthorized signature:** If the representative is not authorized to sign for the represented person or exceeds his authority in making the signature, the signature will operate as the signature of the representative personally. U.C.C. §3-403(a); U.C.C. §3-403, Official Comment 1. [93]

2. **Authorized signatures**
   a. **Not liable if agent signs represented person's name only:** If an authorized representative signs the represented person's name only, the representative is not personally liable. U.C.C. §3-401(a). [93]

   b. **Unambiguously signs in representative capacity:** An authorized representative who signs his own name to an instrument is not personally liable if the signature shows unambiguously that it is made on behalf of a represented person who is identified in the instrument. U.C.C. §3-402(b). [93]

      i. **Capacity and name of represented person:** When the representative signs his name together with his representative capacity and the represented person's name, it is clear that the representative is not personally liable. U.C.C. §3-402(b)(1). [93]

      ii. **Office not necessary:** It is not necessary for the representative to indicate the office he occupies as long as he clearly indicates that he is signing on behalf of the represented party. [93]

   c. **Ambiguous signature:** When the representative does not make it clear that he is signing on behalf of the represented person, the representative is personally liable to a holder in due course who takes the instrument without notice that the representative was not intended by the original parties to the instrument to be personally liable. U.C.C. §3-402(b); U.C.C. §3-402, Official Comment 2. [94]

      i. **As to other persons:** As to any other person, the representative is liable on the instrument unless he proves an actual agreement, whether express or implied, with the payee that he was not to be personally liable. U.C.C. §3-402(b)(2). [94]

      ii. **Exception for checks:** An authorized representative who signs as drawer on a check that is payable from an account of the represented person without indicating his representative status is not liable as long as the represented person is identified somewhere on the check. U.C.C. §3-402(c); U.C.C. §3-402, Official Comment 3. [94]

C. Liability of persons signing in the same capacity in the same transaction: Except as otherwise specified in the instrument, two or more persons who sign an instrument as makers, acceptors, or drawers are liable jointly and severally in the capacity in which they sign. U.C.C. §3-116(a). [94]

1. **Right of contribution:** Unless the parties otherwise agree, a party having joint and several liability is entitled to contribution from his joint and several obligors to the extent available

under applicable law. U.C.C. §3-116(b). Even if a party having joint and several liability is discharged by some act of the holder, his discharge does not affect the right of his joint and several obligor to receive contribution from the discharged party. U.C.C. §3-116(c); U.C.C. §3-116, Official Comment 1. [94-95]

2. **Liability of indorsers:** Subject to certain exceptions, indorsers are not jointly and severally liable. U.C.C. §3-116(a). Indorsers who are copayees and anomalous indorsers are jointly and severally liable unless one payee is accommodating the other payee or they agree to be liable otherwise than as jointly and severally. U.C.C. §3-116(a); U.C.C. §3-116, Official Comment 2. [95]

2002 amendments: U.C.C. §3-116(c) has been omitted:

(c) Discharge of one party having joint and several liability by a person entitled to enforce the instrument does not affect the right under subsection (b) of a party having the same joint and several liability to receive contribution from the party discharged.

Note: Parties that are jointly and severally liable are each, in part, a secondary obligor and, in part, a principal obligor. As a result, to the extent that each party is a secondary obligor, [Rev] U.C.C. §3-605 determines the effect of a release, an extension of time, or a modification of the obligation of one of the joint and several obligors, as well as the effect of an impairment of collateral provided by one of those obligors. [Rev] U.C.C. §3-116, Official Comment 1.

VI. EFFECT OF TAKING INSTRUMENT ON THE UNDERLYING OBLIGATION

A. Ordinary instruments

1. **Obligation suspended:** Unless the parties otherwise agree, when the person entitled to enforce the instrument takes an ordinary instrument for an underlying obligation, the obligation is suspended to the same extent that the obligation would be discharged if payment had been made in money. U.C.C. §3-310(b); U.C.C. §3-310(c). [96]

   a. **Checks:** When an uncertified check is taken, suspension of the obligation continues until the check is dishonored, paid, or certified. If the check is paid or certified, the obligation is discharged to the extent of the amount of the check. U.C.C. §3-310(b)(1). [96]

   b. **Notes:** When a note is taken, suspension of the obligation continues until dishonor or payment of the note. The obligation is discharged to the extent that the note is paid. U.C.C. §3-310(b)(2). [96]

2. **Effect of dishonor:** When the person entitled to enforce the instrument is also the person to whom the underlying obligation is owed, the person may enforce either the instrument or the obligation once the instrument is dishonored. U.C.C. §3-310(b)(3); U.C.C. §3-310, Official Comment 3. When the person entitled to enforce the instrument is not the person to whom the underlying obligation is owed, the person entitled to enforce the instrument may enforce only the instrument. U.C.C. §3-310(4). [96]

3. **Effect of discharge:** When the underlying obligor is discharged on the instrument, she is also discharged on the underlying obligation. U.C.C. §3-310(a), (b)(1), (2). [97]

B. Bank checks: Unless otherwise agreed, if a bank check (or any other instrument on which a bank is a maker or an acceptor) is taken for an obligation, the obligation is discharged to the same extent as had payment been made in cash. U.C.C. §3-310(a), (c); U.C.C. §3-310, Official Comments 2 and 5. If the debtor indorses the instrument, although the underlying obligation is discharged, his liability as an indorser on the instrument is not discharged. U.C.C. §3-310(a); U.C.C. §3-310, Official Comment 2. [97]

C. Taking instrument for underlying obligation: For an instrument to affect the underlying obligation, the instrument must be taken for the underlying obligation. U.C.C. §3-310(a), (b). Mere delivery of the instrument to the obligee by the obligor does not result in the obligee having taken the instrument for the underlying obligation. The obligee must, by her action or inaction, indicate that she has accepted the instrument in conditional or final payment of the obligation. [97]

VII. ACCORD AND SATISFACTION BY USE OF INSTRUMENT

A. Conditions for discharging of tendered instrument: Subject to two exceptions, tendering of an instrument discharges the underlying claim for which it was tendered if the following conditions are met:

- the debtor tenders the instrument in good faith and in full satisfaction of the claim;

- the claim is either unliquidated or subject to a bona fide dispute;

- the instrument is paid; and the instrument, or accompanying written communication, contains a conspicuous statement

- that the instrument is tendered in full satisfaction of the debt. U.C.C. §3-311(a), (b). [98]

B. Exception for lockbox accounts: If an organization informs a debtor that checks or other communications regarding disputed debts must be sent to a designated person, office, or place, the claim is not discharged if the instrument or communication was not received by the designated person, office, or place. U.C.C. §3-311(c)(1). [98]

C. Exception for returning payment: If a creditor does not require that claims be sent to a special address, the claim is not discharged if the creditor tenders repayment of the amount of the instrument within 90 days of its payment. U.C.C. §3-311(c)(2). [98]

D. Limitation on exceptions: Both exceptions are subject to a limitation. The claim is discharged if the debtor proves that, within a reasonable time before collection of the instrument was initiated, the creditor or its agent who had direct responsibility with respect to the disputed obligation knew that the instrument was tendered in full satisfaction. U.C.C. §3-311(d); U.C.C. §3-311, Official Comment 7. [98]

VIII. PROCEDURAL ISSUES INVOLVING NEGOTIABLE INSTRUMENTS

A. Persons entitled to enforce instrument: Persons entitled to enforce an instrument include the holder, a transferee of a holder, an accommodation party or indorser who pays the holder, the owner of a lost instrument under U.C.C. §3-309, and a person from whom payment has been recovered under U.C.C. §3-418(d). [99]

B. **Burden of proof in negotiable instruments cases:** A person entitled to enforce an instrument establishes a prima facie case for recovery by establishing that the obligor's signature is effective, producing the instrument, and proving that he is a person entitled to enforce the instrument. U.C.C. §3-308(a), (b). [99]

1. **Exception to producing instrument:** The plaintiff does not have to produce the instrument if the instrument has been lost, destroyed, or stolen, or if he is a person from whom a payment has been recovered pursuant to U.C.C. §3-418. [99]

2. **Proving signatures:** There are special rules regarding proof of the authenticity of a signature. Unless the defendant specifically denies that a signature is authentic, the signature is deemed to be authentic. Even if the defendant makes a specific denial, the plaintiff is entitled to a presumption that the signature is genuine and authorized. Once sufficient evidence is introduced to support a finding that the signature is either not genuine or is unauthorized, the presumption completely disappears. To rebut the presumption, the defendant need only testify that her signature is not genuine and submit a sample of her true signature. U.C.C. §3-308(a), U.C.C. §1-201(31); U.C.C. §3-308, Official Comment 1. [99]

3. **Burden on obligor to prove defense:** Once the plaintiff has established her prima facie case, she will recover against the obligor unless the obligor establishes a defense or a claim in recoupment. U.C.C. §3-308(b); U.C.C. §3-308, Official Comment 2. [100]

4. **After defense proved, duty of plaintiff to prove holder-in-due-course status:** Even if the obligor has established a defense or claim in recoupment, the plaintiff will recover if she proves that she is a holder in due course or has the rights of a holder in due course (unless the defense is one that is good against a holder in due course). U.C.C. §3-308(b); U.C.C. §3-308, Official Comment 2. [100]

IX. ENFORCEMENT OF LOST, DESTROYED, OR STOLEN INSTRUMENTS

A. **Lost, destroyed, or stolen ordinary instruments:** The person entitled to enforce an instrument that is lost by destruction, theft, or otherwise, may maintain an action as if he had produced the instrument. U.C.C. §3-309(b); U.C.C. §3-309, Official Comment. [100]

1. **Adequate protection:** To protect the obligor, a court can require the claimant to indemnify the obligor against any loss or expense. U.C.C. §3-309(b). [100]

2. **Right to recover on instrument only:** The claimant may recover on the instrument only. He may not enforce the obligation for which the instrument was given. U.C.C. §3-310(b)(4); U.C.C. §3-310, Official Comment 4. [100]

3. **What claimant must prove:** The claimant must prove that

   ■ he was either a holder or had the rights of a holder at the time he lost possession;

   ■ the loss of possession was not a result of his transfer of the instrument or of a lawful seizure of the instrument;

- he cannot reasonably obtain possession of the instrument because it was either destroyed, lost, or in the wrongful possession of an unknown person or a person that cannot be found or is not amenable to service of process; and

- the terms of the instrument include any terms necessary to make the instrument negotiable. U.C.C. §3-309(b). [100-101]

4. 2002 amendments: The 2002 amendments permit a person not in possession of an instrument to enforce the instrument if the person has directly or indirectly acquired ownership of the instrument from a person who was entitled to enforce the instrument when loss of possession occurred. [Rev] U.C.C. §3-309(a)(1)(B). [101]

Rationale: This permits a person who lost the instrument but has the right to enforce it under [Rev] U.C.C. §3-309 to transfer its right to enforce the instrument to another.

Required proof: A transferee of a lost instrument need only prove that its transferor was entitled to enforce the instrument. There is no need for the transferee to prove that it was in possession of the instrument at the time the instrument was lost. [Rev] U.C.C. §3-309, Official Comment 2.

Declaration of loss: The 2002 amendments substitute the term "***record***" for "writing." As a result, a declaration of loss may be made in a record that is not a writing. A "record" is "information that is inscribed on a tangible medium or that is stored in an electronic or other medium and is retrievable in perceivable form." [Rev] U.C.C. §3-103(a)(14).

B. Lost, destroyed, or stolen bank checks: A different set of rules applies when a bank check (i.e., a cashier's, teller's, or certified check) is lost, destroyed, or stolen. U.C.C. §3-312. [101]

1. Who may use U.C.C. §3-312: Only the drawer or payee of a certified check and the remitter or payee of a teller's or cashier's check (the "***claimant***") may proceed under U.C.C. §3-312. U.C.C. §3-312(a)(3)(ii). An indorsee of a bank check is denied the advantages of U.C.C. §3-312 and must proceed as if he were suing on an ordinary lost or stolen instrument. [101]

2. Manner of asserting claim: The claimant must send a communication to the issuing bank asserting the claim and be accompanied by a declaration of loss. U.C.C. §3-312(b). [101]

3. When claim is effective: The claim is not valid for 90 days. During this 90-day waiting period, the bank may, with impunity, pay the person entitled to enforce the check. U.C.C. §3-312(b)(2). After the 90-day period, the issuing bank becomes liable to the claimant if the bank has not already paid a person entitled to enforce the check. U.C.C. §3-312(b)(4); U.C.C. §3-312, Official Comment 4. [101-102]

4. Bank discharged by payment to claimant: Payment to the claimant discharges the bank's liability to a person entitled to enforce the check. U.C.C. §3-312(b)(4). If a holder in due course presents the bank check after the bank pays the claimant, the issuing bank may pay the holder in due course. The claimant is then obliged to repay the bank. If the bank refuses to pay the holder in due course, the claimant must pay the holder. U.C.C. §3-312(b); U.C.C. §3-312, Comment 3. [102]

CHAPTER 4

FORGERY, ALTERATION, AND OTHER FRAUDULENT ACTIVITY

I. UNAUTHORIZED SIGNATURES

A. Introduction: Subject to certain exceptions, an unauthorized signature is ineffective as the signature of the person whose name is signed. U.C.C. §3-403(a). An unauthorized signature may be an outright forgery or a signature by an agent in excess of her actual or apparent authority. U.C.C. §1-201(43); U.C.C. §3-403, Official Comment 1. An unauthorized signature is effective as the signature of the unauthorized signer in favor of a person who in good faith pays the instrument or takes it for value. U.C.C. §3-403(a). [107]

B. Two consequences of unauthorized signature: The fact that an unauthorized signature has no effect as the signature of the person whose name is signed has two distinct consequences. First, the person whose signature is signed is not liable on the instrument. Second, if the unauthorized signature is an indorsement in the chain of title, no person following the unauthorized indorsement can be a holder of the instrument. [107-108]

C. Transfer warranties: A transferor warrants that the transferor is the person entitled to enforce the instrument, U.C.C. §4-207(a)(1); U.C.C. §3-416(a)(1), and also that all signatures are authentic and authorized. U.C.C. §4-207(a)(2); U.C.C. §3-416(a)(2). [108]

2002 amendments: A new transfer warranty has been added as to remotely created consumer items. With respect to a remotely created consumer item, the transferor warrants that the person on whose account the item is drawn authorized the issuance of the item in the amount for which the item is drawn. [Rev] U.C.C. §3-416(a)(6) and [Rev] U.C.C. §4-208(a)(4). As a result, the risk of the item not being authorized by the person upon whose account it was drawn rests upon the person initially transferring the item. [108]

D. Presentment warranties: The person who obtains payment or acceptance, as well as any prior transferor, makes certain presentment warranties to any payor or acceptor who acts in good faith. U.C.C. §4-208(a), (d); U.C.C. §3-417(a), (d)(1). [108-109]

  1. Warranties made to drawee of unaccepted draft: The payor bank on a check (as well as any drawee of an unaccepted draft) is given three warranties: (1) that the warrantor is entitled to enforce the draft or authorized to obtain payment or acceptance on behalf of a person entitled to enforce the draft; (2) that the warrantor has no knowledge that the signature of the drawer is unauthorized; and (3) that the draft has not been altered. U.C.C. §4-208(a); U.C.C. §3-417(a). If the payor bank could have asserted the drawer's negligence against the drawer, the person against whom the payor bank is bringing the breach of presentment warranty action may assert the drawer's negligence as a defense to the payor bank's action. U.C.C. §4-208(c); U.C.C. §3-417(c). [109-110]

  2002 amendments: A new presentment warranty has been added as to remotely created consumer items under which the person obtaining the payment or acceptance and prior transferors warrant, as to remotely created consumer items, that the person on whose account the item is drawn authorized the issuance of the item in the amount for which the item is drawn. The effect of this warranty is to impose ultimate liability on the depositary bank that accepted the unauthorized remotely created item rather than on the payor bank, which had no means of determining whether it was authorized. This warranty applies not only when the item is unauthorized, but also when the consumer authorized the item in a different amount than that in which payment was made. [Rev] U.C.C. §3-417(a)(4); [Rev] U.C.C. §4-208(a)(4). [110]

2. **Warranties made to other payors:** All payors, other than drawees of unaccepted drafts, receive only the warranty that the warrantor is entitled to enforce the instrument or is authorized to obtain payment on behalf of a person entitled to enforce the instrument. U.C.C. §4-208(d); U.C.C. §3-417, Official Comment 4. No warranty is given that the presenter lacks knowledge of the unauthorized nature of the maker's or drawer's signature. U.C.C. §3-417, Official Comment 4. [110]

E. **Recovery by payor of payment made by mistake:** Even absent a presentment warranty, the payor may be able to recover the mistaken payment from its recipient under U.C.C. §3-418. A drawee can revoke its acceptance in the identical circumstances that it could recover the payment had payment been made instead. [111]

1. **Typical mistakes:** Typical mistaken payments by a drawee include payment over a forged drawer's signature, payment of a check drawn on insufficient funds, and payment over a valid stop payment order. [111]

2. **Protected persons under U.C.C. §3-418:** Payment may not be recovered from two classes of protected persons: any person who takes the instrument in good faith and for value, or any person who has, in good faith, changed position in reliance on the payment. U.C.C. §3-418(c). [111]

3. **Consequences when payment is recovered:** In the event that payment is recovered, the instrument is treated as having been dishonored. The person from whom payment is recovered can enforce the instrument against the drawer, maker, or indorser just as if the instrument had been dishonored on its initial presentment. U.C.C. §3-418(d); U.C.C. §3-418, Official Comment 2. [111]

2002 amendments: A new presentment warranty has been added as to remotely created consumer items under which the person obtaining the payment or acceptance and prior transferors warrant, as to remotely created consumer items, that the person on whose account the item is drawn authorized the issuance of the item in the amount for which the item is drawn. The effect of this warranty is to impose ultimate liability on the depositary bank that accepted the unauthorized remotely created item rather than on the payor bank, which had no means of determining whether it was authorized. This warranty applies not only when the item is unauthorized, but also when the consumer authorized the item in an amount different than that in which payment was made. [Rev] U.C.C. §3-416, Official Comment 8. As a result, the risk of the item not being authorized by the person upon whose account it was drawn rests upon the person initially transferring the item. [110]

F. **Conversion:** An instrument is converted if it is taken by transfer, other than by negotiation, from a person not entitled to enforce the instrument. An instrument is also converted if a payor bank or other payor makes payment with respect to the instrument to a person not entitled to enforce the instrument or to receive payment. U.C.C. §3-420(a). [111]

If an indorsement in the chain of title is unauthorized or missing, the instrument is converted. Because an instrument payable to bearer is negotiated by transfer of possession alone, there can be no conversion of an instrument payable to bearer.

1. **When taking instrument by agent is conversion:** A person who holds an instrument solely as a representative of another person (other than a depositary bank) who has, in good faith, dealt with an instrument or its proceeds on behalf of one who was not the person entitled to enforce the instrument is not liable in conversion or otherwise beyond the amount of any proceeds that it has not paid out. U.C.C. §3-420(c). A depositary bank is liable for conversion whether or not it acts in good faith or retains any of the proceeds from the check. U.C.C. §3-420(c). [111-112]

2. **Who may bring an action for conversion:** The proper party to bring an action for conversion of an instrument is the person who, before the theft or loss, was the person entitled to enforce the instrument. A payee may bring the action only if the instrument has been delivered to her. U.C.C. §3-420(a)(ii); U.C.C. §3-420, Official Comment 1. An action for conversion may not be brought by the drawer, acceptor, or other issuer of the instrument. U.C.C. §3-420(a)(i). [112-113]

3. **Defenses to conversion action:** The person sued for conversion may defend by proving that the owner is precluded from denying that the forged indorsement is effective as the owner's indorsement. [113]

G. **Application of rules when signature of maker or acceptor unauthorized:** In the absence of estoppel, ratification, or negligence, the maker or acceptor is not liable on an instrument on which his signature is forged or unauthorized because he did not sign the instrument. U.C.C. §3-401(a). If the maker or acceptor makes payment, the maker or acceptor will suffer the loss if the person to whom payment is made is a protected person under U.C.C. §3-418. Neither the maker nor the acceptor is given a presentment warranty as to the authenticity of his own signature. [113]

H. **Application of rules when signature of drawer unauthorized:** When the drawee makes payment of a check or other draft bearing the forged signature of the purported drawer, the drawee will usually suffer the loss. Neither the presenter nor prior transferors warrant to the drawee that the drawer's signature is genuine. The only warranty they make to the drawee is that they have no knowledge that the drawer's signature is unauthorized. U.C.C. §4-208(a)(3); U.C.C. §3-417(a)(3). The drawee or payor bank may not debit the drawer's account because, bearing his unauthorized signature, the draft is not properly payable. The drawee can only recover the mistaken payment from a person who is not a protected party. U.C.C. §3-418(c). If the drawee does not make payment, the loss will go back down the chain of title to the first solvent party after the forger (assuming that the forger is not solvent). The mechanism for passing the loss down the chain of title is the transfer warranty, given by each transferor, that all signatures are genuine and authorized. U.C.C. §3-416(a)(2); U.C.C. §4-207(a)(2). [114-115]

I. **Application of rules when indorsement is unauthorized**

1. **Allocation of loss when check not delivered to payee:** When the check or other draft has not been delivered to the payee, the payee has no right to sue for conversion. U.C.C. §3-420(a). She, however, retains whatever rights she had against the drawer on the underlying obligation for which the check was taken. The drawer has no right to sue the depositary or other collecting bank for either conversion, U.C.C. §3-420(a), or for breach of the presentment warranty

that she is a person entitled to enforce the instrument. U.C.C. §3-417, Official Comment 2. The drawer has not suffered a loss because the payor bank may not debit its account. The allocation of loss is the same whether or not the payor bank pays the check because, even if the check is paid, the payor bank may recover from the presenting bank and prior transferors for breach of their presentment warranty that they are a person entitled to enforce the instrument. U.C.C. §4-208 (a)(1); U.C.C. §3-417(a)(1). Whether or not the check is paid, the loss will flow back to the first solvent transferor following the forgery because each transferor warrants that it is a person entitled to enforce the instrument. U.C.C. §4-207(a)(1). [115]

2. **Allocation of loss after delivery to payee:** After delivery to the payee, the payee's rights depend on whether the instrument has been paid. [115]

    a. **Payee's rights if instrument not paid:** If the check is still missing, the payee may recover on the check from the drawer by complying with the requirements for the enforcement of lost, destroyed, or stolen instruments. U.C.C. §3-309. However, the payee may not recover from the drawer on the underlying obligation. U.C.C. §3-310(b)(4); U.C.C. §3-310, Official Comment 4. If the check is found prior to payment, the payee may recover possession of the check from the possessor. Once the payee recovers possession of the check, she may present the check for payment, and if it is not paid, she can recover from the drawer on her drawer's contract or on the underlying obligation. The party required to return the check can then recover from her transferor and any prior transferors for breach of their transfer warranty that they are a person entitled to enforce the instrument. U.C.C. §3-416(a)(1); U.C.C. §4-207(a)(1). [116]

    b. **Payee's rights if instrument paid:** If the check is paid, the payee may recover from the payor bank, the depositary bank, or any nonbank transferor for conversion. U.C.C. §3-420(a); U.C.C. §3-420, Official Comment 3. Ultimately, the first solvent party after the person who made the unauthorized indorsement bears the loss. The payor bank can recover from the presenter or prior transferors for breach of their presentment warranty that they are a person entitled to enforce the instrument. U.C.C. §4-208(a)(1). Each transferee can recover from prior transferors for breach of their transfer warranty that they are a person entitled to enforce the instrument. U.C.C. §3-416(a)(1); U.C.C. §4-207(a)(1). [116]

II. ALTERATIONS AND INCOMPLETE INSTRUMENTS

A. **What is an alteration?** An alteration is any unauthorized change in an instrument that attempts to modify, in any respect, the obligation of any party. This includes any unauthorized addition of words or numbers or other change to an incomplete instrument. U.C.C. §3407(a). [116]

B. **Allocation of loss in case of alteration:** In the absence of her own negligence, assent, or preclusion, a party who signs an instrument only promises to pay the instrument according to its terms at the time she signed the instrument. U.C.C. §3-412; U.C.C. §3-413(a); U.C.C. §3-414(b); U.C.C. §3-415(a). [117]

1. **Payment by drawee:** In the case of a check or other unaccepted draft, the allocation of loss does *not* depend on whether the drawee has paid or accepted the check or draft. If the drawee pays the check or draft, the drawee may debit the drawer's account only in the amount as originally drawn by the drawer unless the drawer is negligent or otherwise precluded from asserting the alteration. U.C.C. §4-401(d)(1). In the absence of grounds for precluding the drawer,

the drawee may recover from any person obtaining payment or acceptance or any previous transferor for breach of the presentment warranty that the draft has not been altered. U.C.C. §3-417(a)(2); U.C.C. §4-208(a)(2). The party from whom the drawee recovers can recover from his transferor and any prior transferors for breach of their transfer warranty that the draft had not been altered. U.C.C. §3-416(a)(3); U.C.C. §4-207(a)(3). [117]

2. **When drawer, maker, or acceptor pays:** When the drawer, maker, or acceptor makes payment, the party making payment will suffer the loss if payment has been made to a protected person under U.C.C. §3-418(c). This is because no warranty is given to the drawer, maker, or acceptor that the instrument has not been altered. U.C.C. §3-417, Comment 4. [117-118]

3. **When instrument not paid:** If an instrument is not paid, the person entitled to enforce the instrument may recover from any prior transferor for breach of its transfer warranty of no alteration. The person entitled to enforce the instrument may also recover, up to the amount for which the instrument was payable at the time of engagement, from prior indorsers, the maker, the drawer, or the acceptor on their respective obligations. U.C.C. §3-415(a); U.C.C. §3-412; U.C.C. §3-414(b); U.C.C. §3-413(a). [118]

C. **Discharge of party whose obligation is affected:** A fraudulently made alteration discharges a party whose obligation is affected by the alteration unless that party assents to the alteration or is precluded from asserting the alteration. Any transferee, other than one who takes the instrument for value, in good faith, and without notice of the alteration, also takes subject to the discharge. U.C.C. §3-407(c); U.C.C. §3-203(b). When an alteration is not fraudulent, the instrument may be enforced according to its original terms. U.C.C. §3-407(b). A payor bank, or other drawee, paying a fraudulently altered instrument or a person taking it for value, in good faith, and without notice of the alteration may enforce the instrument according to its original terms. U.C.C. §3-407(c); U.C.C. §3-407, Official Comment 2. [118]

D. **Incomplete instruments:** When the completion of an incomplete instrument is authorized, the instrument may be enforced as completed. U.C.C. §3-115(b). When the completion is unauthorized, a payor bank, acting in good faith, may enforce the instrument as completed. U.C.C. §3-407(c). Similarly, a person taking the instrument for value, in good faith, and without notice of the improper completion may enforce the instrument according to its terms as completed. U.C.C. §3-407(c). As to any other persons, the obligor is discharged and, therefore, is not liable on the instrument at all. U.C.C. §3-407(b). [118-119]

III. GROUNDS OF PRECLUSION

A. **Ratification:** An unauthorized signature may become effective as the signature of the person whose name is signed if ratified by that person. U.C.C. §3-403(a). [119]

B. **Estoppel:** A party may be estopped to deny the authenticity of a signature. U.C.C. §1-103 [Rev] U.C.C. 1-103(b). [119]

C. **Preclusion through negligence:** A person whose failure to exercise ordinary care substantially contributes to an alteration or to the making of a forged signature is precluded from asserting the alteration or forgery against a person who, in good faith, pays the instrument or takes it for value or for collection. U.C.C. §3-406(a). [119-120]

1. **Comparative negligence:** The negligent party may prove that the person asserting the preclusion failed to exercise ordinary care and that the failure substantially contributed to the loss. In this event, the loss is allocated according to principles of comparative negligence. U.C.C. §3-406(b). [120]

2. **Failure to exercise ordinary care:** The test as to whether a party has exercised ordinary care is the traditional tort test for negligence. [120]

   a. **Giving check to third party:** In some situations, the giving of a check to a third party for delivery to the payee so greatly increases the possibility of a forgery that the drawer will be precluded from asserting the subsequent forgery. [120]

   b. **Careless business practices:** Careless business practices can result in an increased possibility of forgery. [120]

   c. **Negligence in hiring or supervising employees:** An employer may also be precluded from denying the effectiveness of a signature forged by an employee if the employer has failed to exercise ordinary care in either hiring or supervising the employee. [120]

   d. **Guarding check forms:** It is unlikely that a court would hold a drawer to have failed to exercise ordinary care simply because he was not careful in guarding his blank check forms. [121]

   e. **Preventing alterations:** A party has a duty to use reasonable care in drawing or making an instrument such that it cannot be easily altered. U.C.C. §3-406, Official Comment 1. [121]

3. **Failure of payor bank to exercise ordinary care:** A drawer who is precluded from asserting that a signature is unauthorized may attempt to prove that the payor bank also failed to exercise ordinary care so as to cause the loss to be split between them under the principle of comparative negligence. [121]

   a. **Duty to discover forged indorsements:** When the payor bank is also the depositary bank or when the item is presented over the counter for payment, the bank fails to exercise ordinary care if it does not discover obvious irregularities in the identification of the person presenting the item for payment. Unless the payor bank is also the depositary bank, it is unlikely that it will be found to have failed to exercise ordinary care in failing to discover a forged indorsement. [121]

   b. **When drawer's signature forged:** When there is an obvious forgery of the drawer's signature and the bank does not discover it because it processes checks for payment by computer without visually inspecting the checks, the fact that the payor bank does not visually examine the check does not mean that the payor bank is negligent as long as its procedure is reasonable and commonly followed by other comparable banks in the area. U.C.C. §4-406, Revised Official Comment 4. [121-122]

   c. **Substantially contributes:** For the failure to exercise ordinary care to preclude the negligent party, the failure must substantially contribute to the making of the forgery or alteration. U.C.C. §3-406(a). This requires that the negligence must have been a contributing cause, and a significant factor, in enabling the forgery or alteration to have been made. U.C.C. §3-406, Official Comment 2. [122]

D. Impostors, fictitious payees, and employer's responsibility for unauthorized indorsements by employees

1. **The impostor rule:** An impostor is one who represents himself to be the named payee and by such representation induces the issuer to issue the instrument to him or to a person acting in concert with him. A person is also an impostor if she falsely represents herself to be the agent of the named payee. U.C.C. §3-404(a). The impostor rule applies whether the impostor acts in person, by mail, by telephone, or otherwise. U.C.C. §3-404(a). [122-123]

   a. **Need for indorsement:** An indorsement by any person in the name of the payee is effective in favor of a person who, in good faith, pays the instrument or takes it for value or for collection. U.C.C. §3-404(a). As long as the instrument is deposited in a depositary bank to an account in a name substantially similar to that of the payee, the depositary bank is the holder of the instrument regardless of whether the instrument is indorsed. U.C.C. §3-404(c)(ii). [123]

   b. **Who may assert that the indorsement is effective:** An indorsement by any person in the name of the payee is effective to negotiate the instrument, thus making the indorsee the holder. [123-124]

      i. **Good faith required:** A payor or taker who does not act in good faith may not assert that the indorsement is effective. U.C.C. §3-404(b)(2). [124]

      ii. **Comparative negligence:** When the taker or payor is negligent, the loss is allocated under comparative negligence principles between the drawer and the negligent party. U.C.C. §3-404(d); U.C.C. §3-404, Official Comment 3. [124]

2. **Fictitious payee rule:** There are three distinct situations in which a payee is regarded as a fictitious payee: [124]

   ▪ **Nonexistent payee:** The person identified as the payee does not, in fact, exist. U.C.C. §3-404(b)(ii). [124]

   ▪ **Payee intended to have no interest:** The maker or drawer issues an instrument intending that the named payee have no interest in the instrument. U.C.C. §3-404(b)(i). [124]

   ▪ **Employee signing instrument intends payee to have no interest:** An agent, employee, or officer signs on behalf of the drawer or maker intending the payee to have no interest in the instrument. [124]

   a. **Relevant intent is of party making signature:** In determining whether a payee is a fictitious payee, it is necessary to look at the intent of the person whose intent determines to whom an instrument is payable as determined under U.C.C. §3-110(a), (b). [124-125]

   b. **Form of required indorsement:** The same rules as to the need for an indorsement governing impostors also apply to fictitious payees except that because no person was the intended payee, any person in possession of the instrument is its holder. U.C.C. §3-404(b)(1). [125]

   c. **Who may assert that the indorsement is effective:** The same rule applies as in the case of impostors. [125]

d. Double forgeries: When a person who forges the drawer's name also intends that the payee have no interest in the check, the payee is a fictitious payee. U.C.C. §3-404, Official Comment 2, Case #4. As a result, the payor bank, rather than the depositary bank, suffers the loss when there is both a forged drawer's signature and a forged indorsement. [125]

3. Employer's responsibility for fraudulent indorsement by employee: When an employer hires an employee and gives the employee responsibility regarding instruments, the employer is liable when the employee makes a fraudulent indorsement. A *"fraudulent indorsement"* is either (1) an indorsement made in the name of the employer on an instrument payable to the employer; or (2) an indorsement in the name of the payee on an instrument issued by the employer. U.C.C. §3-405(a)(2). [125]

a. Rule: An indorsement in the name of the payee is effective in favor of any person who in good faith pays an instrument or takes it for value or for collection whenever an employer entrusts an employee with responsibility with respect to the instrument, and the employee, or a person acting in concert with him, makes a fraudulent indorsement. U.C.C. §3-405(b). [126]

b. Need for indorsement: The requirements are the same as in the case of impostors. U.C.C. §3-405(b), (c). [126]

c. Contributory negligence: If the person paying, or taking, the instrument fails to exercise ordinary care and the failure substantially contributes to the loss, the person bearing the loss may recover from the person failing to exercise ordinary care to the extent that her failure contributed to the loss. U.C.C. §3-405, Official Comments 2 and 4. [126]

d. Employee must have responsibility with respect to instruments: For the indorsement to be effective under this rule, the employer must entrust an employee with responsibility with respect to instruments. U.C.C. §3-405(a)(1); U.C.C. §3-405(b). Responsibility means authority to do any of the following:

- sign or indorse instruments on behalf of the employer;

- process instruments received by the employer for bookkeeping purposes, for deposit to an account, or for other disposition;

- prepare or process instruments for issue in the name of the employer;

- supply information for determining the names or addresses of payees;

- control the disposition of instruments issued in the name of the employer;

- act otherwise with respect to instruments in a responsible capacity. U.C.C. §3-405(a)(3).

An employee does not have responsibility with respect to an instrument just because he has access to instruments, or to blank or incomplete forms, as part of incoming or outgoing mail or otherwise. U.C.C. §3-405(3). [126-127]

E. Customer's duty to review bank statement: Certain duties are imposed on a customer if its bank sends, or makes available, to the customer a statement of account showing payment of items for her account. To trigger these duties, the bank must either return or make available to the customer the items paid or provide information in the statement of account sufficient to allow the customer to reasonably identify the items paid. U.C.C. §4-406(a). When neither the item nor its image is returned, the bank fulfills its duty to provide sufficient information if it gives to the customer the number of the item, its amount, and the date of payment. U.C.C. §4-406(a); U.C.C. §4-406, Revised Official Comment 1. [127]

1. **Customer's duty to examine bank statement:** Once the bank sends, or makes available, a statement of account or the items themselves, the customer has the duty to exercise reasonable promptness in examining the statement or the items to determine whether any payment was unauthorized due to an alteration or because a purported signature by, or on behalf of, the customer was unauthorized. If the customer should reasonably have discovered the unauthorized payment from the statement or items provided, the customer must promptly notify the bank of the relevant facts. U.C.C. §4-406(c); U.C.C. §4-406, Revised Official Comment 1. [127-128]

2. **Duty of bank to prove loss:** Even when a customer fails to reasonably discover or report a forgery or alteration, the customer is only precluded from asserting its unauthorized signature or alteration if the bank proves that it suffered a loss by reason of the failure. U.C.C. §4-406(d)(1); U.C.C. §4-406, Revised Official Comment 2. [128]

3. **Forgery or alteration by same wrongdoer:** The customer is also precluded from asserting an unauthorized signature or alteration by the same wrongdoer on any other item paid in good faith by the bank before it received notice from the customer of the unauthorized signature or alteration and after the customer had been afforded a reasonable period of time, not exceeding 30 days, in which to examine the item or statement of account and notify the bank. U.C.C. §4-406(d)(2); U.C.C. §4-406, Revised Official Comment 2. [128]

4. **Good faith and comparative negligence:** If the customer proves that the bank failed to act in good faith in paying an item, the loss falls completely on the bank. U.C.C. §4-406(e); U.C.C. §4-406, Revised Official Comment 2. In addition, the doctrine of comparative negligence applies to split the loss in the event that the bank has failed to exercise ordinary care in paying the item and that the failure substantially contributed to the loss. U.C.C. §4-406(e); U.C.C. §4-406, Revised Official Comment 2. [128]

5. **1-year preclusion:** If the customer does not discover and report the customer's unauthorized signature or any alteration on an item within 1 year after the statement or item is made available to the customer, the customer is precluded from asserting the alteration or unauthorized signature against the bank whether or not the bank exercised ordinary care. U.C.C. §4-406(f). [128-129]

6. **Duty of payor bank to raise defenses:** When a payor bank has the right to debit its customer's account because the customer is precluded under U.C.C. §3-406 or §4-406, the payor bank is not allowed to shift the loss from its customer to the presenting or depositary bank by re-crediting the customer's account and recovering from the presenting bank for breach of its presentment warranty. U.C.C. §4-406(f); U.C.C. §4-406, Official Comment 5; U.C.C. §4-208(c); U.C.C. §4-406, Revised Official Comment 5. [129]

IV. RESTRICTIVE INDORSEMENTS

A. **Introduction:** A "*restrictive indorsement*" is an indorsement written by, or on behalf of, the holder that limits negotiation of the instrument to a specific use. [129]

C
A
P
S
U
L
E

S
U
M
M
A
R
Y

B. Two types of restrictive indorsements:

1. **For deposit:** An indorsement that signifies a purpose of deposit or collection is a restrictive indorsement. U.C.C. §3-206(c). A *"for deposit"* indorsement indicates that the proceeds of the instrument can be credited only to the indorser's bank account. A blank *"for collection"* indorsement or a "for collection" indorsement that specifically designates a bank also similarly indicates an intention that the proceeds be deposited into the indorser's bank account. [129]

2. **Trust indorsement:** An indorsement that states that payment is to be made to the indorsee as agent, trustee, or other fiduciary for the benefit of the indorser or another person (*"trust indorsement"*) is a restrictive indorsement. U.C.C. §3-206(d). [129]

C. Effect of "for deposit" or "for collection" indorsement: Any bank in the bank collection process, except a depositary bank, may disregard a "for deposit" or similar indorsement. U.C.C. §3-206(c)(4). The depositary bank, whether it purchases the instrument or takes it for collection, converts the instrument unless it pays the indorser or applies the proceeds consistently with the indorsement by applying it to the indorser's account. U.C.C. §3-206(c)(2). The depositary bank can only become a holder in due course to the extent that it applies the funds for the indorser's benefit. U.C.C. §3-206(e). This even applies to a depositary bank that is also the payor bank. When a check is presented for immediate payment over the counter, the payor bank is liable for conversion unless the funds are received by the indorser. [130]

1. **Bank must credit proper account:** To be consistent with the terms of a "for deposit" indorsement, the depositary bank must credit the bank account designated by the indorser. [130]

2. **Nonbank:** Any person, other than a bank, who purchases an instrument restrictively indorsed for collection or deposit is treated just like the depositary bank. U.C.C. §3-206(c)(1); U.C.C. §3-206, Official Comment 3. [130]

D. Effect of trust indorsement: When the taker or payor deals directly with the indorsee, unless the taker has *notice* of the indorsee's breach of fiduciary duty, the payor can pay, or the taker can apply its value, without regard to whether the indorsee is violating a fiduciary duty to the indorser. U.C.C. §3-206(d)(1). A person who does not take the instrument directly from the indorsee is neither given notice nor otherwise affected by the restriction contained in the indorsement unless it *knows* that the fiduciary dealt with the instrument or its proceeds in breach of his fiduciary duty. U.C.C. §3-206(d)(2). A payor that makes payment of the check is only liable for conversion if it has actual knowledge that the indorsee has misused the funds. [130-131]

CHAPTER 5

PAYOR BANK/CUSTOMER RELATIONSHIP

I. WHEN ITEM PROPERLY PAYABLE

A. Introduction: A payor bank may charge against its customer's account only items that are *properly payable.* An item is properly payable if it is both authorized by the customer and complies with the bank/customer agreement. U.C.C. §4-401(a); U.C.C. §4-401, Official Comment 1. [141]

B. Items creating overdrafts: The bank may charge its customer's account for an item, even though it creates an overdraft, as long as the item is otherwise properly payable. U.C.C. §4-401(a); U.C.C. §4-401, Official Comment 1. Although having the right, the bank has no duty to pay an item that creates an overdraft, absent an agreement to the contrary. U.C.C. §4-402(a). [142]

C. Postdated checks: A payor bank may charge against its customer's account a check that is otherwise properly payable, even though payment was issued before the date of the check. U.C.C. §4-401(c). The payor bank may not properly pay a postdated check prior to its date if the customer has given notice to the bank of the postdating. The procedure for giving notice of postdating and the consequences of the bank paying a check contrary to a proper notice of postdating is the same as for placing a stop payment order on an item. U.C.C. §4-401(c), U.C.C. §4-401(c). [142]

D. Bank not obligated to pay check 6 months old: A bank is under no obligation to its customer to pay a check presented more than 6 months after its date (a ***stale check***). If in good faith, a bank may pay a stale check and charge its customer's account for the amount of the check. U.C.C. §4-404. [142-143]

E. Bank's right of set-off: The bank has the right to set off against its customer's account any matured debt the customer owes to the bank. Set-off is available only if both the debt the customer owes the bank and the debt the bank owes the customer have matured. There is no requirement that the bank give notice within any specified time before, or after, the set-off absent a statutory requirement. [143-144]

F. Death or incompetence of customer: A customer's death or incompetence does not revoke the bank's authority to pay or collect an item or account for proceeds of its collection until the bank knows of the death or the adjudication of incompetence and has a reasonable opportunity to act on it. U.C.C. §4-405(a). Even after the bank learns of its customer's death, the bank may, for 10 days after the date of death, pay a check, unless the bank is ordered to stop payment by a person claiming an interest in the account. U.C.C. §4-405(b). Although a bank can pay a check after the customer's death, the bank has no duty to pay the check. [144-145]

II. VARIATION BY AGREEMENT

A. Introduction: Because Article 4 is not a regulatory statute, it neither regulates the terms of, nor prescribes consumer protection constraints on, bank/customer agreements. U.C.C. §4-101, Official Comment 3. Although such an agreement may set the standards by which the bank's responsibility is to be measured, if those standards are not manifestly unreasonable, such an agreement may not disclaim a bank's liability for its own lack of good faith or failure to exercise ordinary care or limit the measure of damages resulting from its lack of good faith or failure to exercise ordinary care. U.C.C. §4-103(a). [145]

III. WRONGFUL DISHONOR

A. Bank's liability: A payor bank is liable to its customer for wrongful dishonor if it dishonors an item that is properly payable. However, a payor bank has no duty to pay an item that, although properly payable, would create an overdraft. U.C.C. §4-402(a). [146]

B. Pivotal issue is whether sufficient funds are in the account: In determining whether an item has been wrongfully dishonored, the pivotal question is whether there are adequate funds in the customer's account to cover payment of the dishonored item. The bank wrongfully dishonors a check if the reason that the customer's account did not contain sufficient funds was that the bank wrongfully debited the account as a result of, for example, a wrongful set-off, an improper honoring of a writ of garnishment, or the payment of a check bearing a forged signature. [146]

    1. Bank may pay checks in any order: The payor bank has the right to pay checks drawn on its customer's account in any order that it desires. U.C.C. §4-303(b). [146]

    2. Time for determining whether sufficient funds exist: A bank need only examine a customer's account once in deciding whether to dishonor an item for insufficient funds. U.C.C. §4-402(c). Any credits added to the customer's account after the bank has examined the account are not considered in determining whether the account contains sufficient funds. U.C.C. §4-402, Official Comment 4. [146]

C. Duty owed only to customer: A bank is liable only to its customer for wrongful dishonor of an item. U.C.C. §4-402(b). [146]

    1. Payee has no right: A payee or other holder of the item has no cause of action against the bank for wrongful dishonor of an item. [146]

    2. Corporate officers or partners not customers: Because "*customer*" is defined to include organizations, when a check drawn on a corporate, trust, or partnership account is dishonored, the person having the right to sue for the wrongful dishonor is the corporation, trust, or partnership and not the corporate officer, trustee, or partner who signed the check. However, nothing in Article 4 displaces any common law cause of action the officer, trustee, or partner may have against the bank. U.C.C. §4-402, Official Comment 5. [146-147]

D. Damages: A payor bank that wrongfully dishonors an item is liable to its customer for all damages proximately caused by the wrongful dishonor. U.C.C. §4-402(b). Damages may include loss of profits, damage to reputation, emotional distress damages, and punitive damages. U.C.C. §4-402, Official Comment 1. [147]

IV. CUSTOMER'S RIGHT TO STOP PAYMENT

A. Introduction: A customer has the right to stop payment of any item drawn on its account. U.C.C. §4-403(a). When there are two or more persons, each of whom is individually entitled to write items on an account, any of these persons may order payment stopped even if she is not the person who signed the item. U.C.C. §4-403, Official Comment 5. Neither a payee, an indorsee, nor a remitter has a right to stop payment on a check or other item. U.C.C. §4-403, Official Comments 2, 4. [147-148]

B. Requirements for stop payment order: To be effective, a stop payment order describing the item with reasonable certainty must be received at a time and in a manner that affords the bank a reasonable opportunity to act on the order before any of the actions described in U.C.C. §4-403(a) have been taken by the bank with respect to the item. The information that a bank may require a customer to supply is the information that the bank must have under current technology to identify the item with reasonable certainty. Most banks require that the customer supply either the precise amount of the check or the number of the check. U.C.C. §4-403, Official Comment 5.

A stop payment order may be either written or oral. A written stop payment order is effective for 6 months from the date that it is given, whereas an oral stop payment lapses after 14 calendar days. U.C.C. §4-403(b). [148-149]

2002 amendment: The 2002 amendments substitute the term "record" for "writing." A "*record*" is "information that is inscribed on a tangible medium or that is stored in an electronic or other medium and is retrievable in perceivable form." [Rev] U.C.C. §3-103(a)(14). [149]

C. **Timeliness of stop payment orders:** Under U.C.C. §4-303(a), a stop payment order arrives too late to terminate the bank's right or duty to pay an item if it comes after any of certain events. These events include:

- When the bank accepts or certifies an item.

- When the bank has paid the item (which includes payment in cash and as well as the bank's settlement for the item without having a right to revoke the settlement under statute, clearing-house rule, or agreement).

- When a bank becomes accountable for the amount of the item under U.C.C. §4-302.

- When, with respect to checks only, the stop payment order arrives after a cut-off hour established by the bank or, if no cut-off hour has been established, after the close of the next banking day after the banking day on which the bank receives the check. A bank may not establish a cut-off hour earlier than 1 hour after the opening of the next banking day following the banking day on which the bank received the check. U.C.C. §4-303(a). [149-150]

1. **Reasonable time to act:** Because a bank needs time to process stop payment orders and other legals (except for set-offs), the stop payment order must arrive early enough to give the bank a reasonable time to act on it prior to the time that the bank has done any of the specified acts. U.C.C. §4-303(a). Considering the pervasive presence of computers, "reasonable time" is probably a relatively short period. U.C.C. §4-303, Official Comment 6. Branches or separate offices of banks are treated as separate banks for most purposes, including for computing the time within which an action must be taken, in determining where an action may be taken or directed, or where notices or orders must be given. U.C.C. §4-107. [150]

2. **Effect of stop payment order arriving on time:** If the stop payment order arrives prior to any of the specified events, the payor bank has neither the right to pay the check nor a duty to the drawer to pay the check. The bank is liable to the drawer if, in spite of the timely stop payment order, it pays the check. [150-151]

3. **Effect of stop payment order arriving too late:** If a stop payment order comes too late, the payor bank has the right to pay the check or other item and incurs no liability to the drawer if it does so. However, the payor bank does not have to pay the check in that it may waive its right. The payor bank, thus, has the option as to whether or not to honor the stop payment order up until the point at which it would be liable to the holder under U.C.C. §4-215 or U.C.C. §4-302(a) for not paying or returning the check. [151]

4. **Same rules apply to other legals:** The same rules apply to the other legals. These other legals include:

- Legal process, such as writs of garnishment or execution.

- The payor bank acquiring knowledge that the drawer has filed a petition in bankruptcy, died, or become incompetent.

- The bank's right to set off against the customer's account a debt owed to it by the customer.

- When a writ of attachment, garnishment, execution, or set-off comes in time, the bank no longer has a duty to the customer to pay the check. If it refuses to pay the check, the bank is not liable to its customer for wrongful dishonor. [149]

5. **Differences in consequences of legal arriving too late:** There is a minor difference in the consequences between a legal arriving too late and a stop payment order arriving too late. The payor bank is liable to the drawer if it refuses to pay an item when the attachment, garnishment, or set-off occurs or knowledge of bankruptcy is obtained after one of the same events applicable in the case of a stop payment order. The reason for this different treatment is that, unlike in the case of a stop payment order, the customer will not have waived the duty the bank owes to the customer to pay the item. [151]

D. **Damages for payment in violation of stop payment order:** A payor bank is liable to its customer for any damages suffered by the customer when it pays an item over a valid stop payment order. The burden of proving the amount of loss is placed on the customer. U.C.C. §4-403(c). The measure of damages is the difference between the amount paid by the bank and the amount that the customer would have been obligated to pay on the item had payment been stopped. Losses from the payment of an item contrary to a stop payment order may also include damages for the wrongful dishonor of subsequent items. U.C.C. §4-403(c). [151-152]

E. **Payor bank's right of subrogation on improper payment:** When a payor bank makes a payment for which it cannot debit its customer's account, to prevent unjust enrichment, the bank is subrogated to the rights of any party who otherwise would be unjustly enriched. [152]

1. **What constitutes improper payment:** The bank's subrogation rights arise when a payor bank has paid a check or other item in any situation in which it cannot properly debit its customer's account. These situations include, among others, the following:

   - payment in violation of a valid stop payment order

   - early payment of a postdated check in violation of a proper notice of the postdating, U.C.C. §4-401(c)

   - payment, with knowledge of its customer's death, of a check more than 10 days after the death, U.C.C. §4-405(b) [152]

2. **Payor bank subrogated to other parties' rights against drawer:** To prevent the drawer from being unjustly enriched, the payor bank is subrogated to the rights of any holder in due course of the item against the drawer, U.C.C. §4-407(1), or of the payee or any other holder of the item against the drawer either on the item or from the transaction out of which the item arose. U.C.C. §4-407(2). [152-153]

3. **Payor bank subrogated to drawer's rights:** To prevent the payee or other holder from being unjustly enriched, the payor bank is also subrogated to the drawer's rights against the payee or any other holder of the item with respect to the transaction out of which the item arose. U.C.C. §4-407(3). [153]

V. FUNDS AVAILABILITY UNDER REGULATION CC

A. **Mandatory availability schedule:** Regulation CC provides mandatory availability schedules under which depositary banks must permit their depositors use of deposited funds within certain expedited deadlines. 12 C.F.R. §229.14(a). The mandatory availability schedule provides reasonable time periods within which a customer must be allowed use of the funds represented by a deposit corresponding with the likely time within which the bank would obtain notice of the item's nonpayment. [154]

   1. **Provide maximum hold time only:** A depositary bank may allow its customer immediate use of funds deposited even though it has the right to delay availability of the funds under the mandatory availability schedule. 12 C.F.R. §229.19(c), app. E at 493 (1995). [154]

   2. **Subject to chargeback:** The depositary bank's obligation to make funds available to its customer is subject to its right to charge back the customer's account in the event that the check is returned unpaid. [154]

B. **Funds subject to next-day availability:** The following types of deposits must be given next-day availability:

   ■ cash deposits made directly to a teller

   ■ deposits by electronic payment

   ■ deposit of a United States government check, e.g., Federal Reserve Bank or U.S. Treasury check

   ■ deposit of a state or local government check

   ■ deposit of a cashier's check, certified check, or teller's check in person

   ■ deposit of an on-us check

   ■ $100 of the aggregate amount of all checks deposited (not counting those that are otherwise entitled to next-day availability) in any one banking day. 12 C.F.R. §229.10. [154-155]

C. **Second-day and fifth-day availability:** When a check is not entitled to next-day availability, it is entitled to availability either on the second or fifth business day after its deposit depending on whether the check is a local or nonlocal check.

   1. Funds from a deposit of a local check must be made available on the second business day following the banking day of deposit. 12 C.F.R. §229.12(b)(1).

   2. Funds from a deposit of a nonlocal check must be made available on the fifth business day following the banking day of deposit. 12 C.F.R. §229.12(c)(1)(i). [155]

D. **Extensions of mandatory availability schedule:** There are several situations in which the mandatory availability schedule can be extended for a reasonable period of time, which is presumed to be 5 business days for local checks and 6 business days for nonlocal checks. 12 C.F.R. §229.13(h). [155]

   1. **Extension for cash withdrawal:** The time within which funds must be made available may be extended for 1 business day for funds represented by deposited checks if the depositor attempts to withdraw the funds in cash or by similar means. 12 C.F.R. §229.12(d). [155]

2. **New account exception:** The time within which funds must be made available can be extended when the funds are deposited in a new account. 12 C.F.R. §229.13(a). [155]

3. **Large deposit exception:** A bank may extend the hold for local and nonlocal checks to the extent that the aggregate deposit on any banking day is more than $5,000. The mandatory availability schedule still applies to the first $5,000 of deposits on that day. 12 C.F.R. §229.13(b). [156]

4. **Returned and redeposited check exception:** There is an exception for previously returned and redeposited checks because when a check has been dishonored once, there is a good chance that it will be dishonored again. 12 C.F.R. §229.13(c). [156]

5. **Repeatedly overdrawn exception:** This exception applies whenever any account or combination of accounts of a single customer has been repeatedly overdrawn. 12 C.F.R. §229.13(d). [156]

6. **Reasonable cause to doubt collectability exception:** This exception applies when the bank has reasonable cause to doubt that the check will be collected. 12 C.F.R. §229.13(e). [156]

7. **Emergency condition exception:** This exception is applicable in emergency conditions when there is an interruption of communications or computer or other equipment facilities, suspension of payments by another bank, war, or other emergency conditions beyond the control of the depositary bank. 12 C.F.R. §229.13(f). [156]

8. **Automated teller machines ("ATMs"):** Deposits of cash in a night depositary or at an ATM owned or controlled by the depositary bank are entitled to second-day availability. Deposits of cash or checks deposited in an ATM not owned or controlled by the depositary bank are entitled to fifth-day availability. 12 C.F.R. §229.12(f). [156]

E. **Availability under Article 4:** Article 4 or other state availability laws govern to the extent that they allow quicker availability of funds than allowed under Regulation CC. 12 C.F.R. §229.20(a). Because U.C.C. §4-214(f) makes a deposit of cash available at the opening of the bank's next banking day after receipt, it prevails over Regulation CC as to cash deposited by mail, in a night depositary, or in an ATM owned by the depositary bank. [156]

CHAPTER 6

THE BANK COLLECTION PROCESS

I. INTRODUCTION TO THE CHECK COLLECTION PROCESS

A. **Introduction:** The process by which the holder of a check converts the check into cash when he deposits the check into his bank account and his bank, acting as his agent, either directly or through one or more other banks, presents the check to, and obtains payment from, the bank on which the check is drawn is called the *"check collection process."* [161]

B. **Types of banks under Article 4:** Article 4 classifies banks into five categories.

1. **Payor bank:** A "payor bank" is "a bank that is a drawee of a draft." U.C.C. §4-105(3). [162]

2. **Depositary bank:** A "depositary bank" is "the first bank to take an item even though it is also the payor bank unless the item is presented for immediate payment over the counter." U.C.C. §4-105(2). [162]

3. **Collecting bank:** A "collecting bank" is "any bank handling an item for collection except the payor bank." U.C.C. §4-105(5). A depositary bank, as long as it is not also the payor bank, is a collecting bank. [162]

4. **Intermediary bank:** An "intermediary bank" is "any bank to which an item is transferred in the course of collection except the depositary or payor bank." U.C.C. §4-105(4). [162]

5. **Presenting bank:** A "presenting bank" is "any bank presenting an item except a payor bank." U.C.C. §4-105(6). [162-163]

C. **Types of banks under Regulation CC:** Regulation CC has created two classifications of banks.

1. **Paying bank:** Under Regulation CC, paying banks have duties above and beyond those imposed on payor banks under Article 4. "Paying bank" is a broader concept than "payor bank." The definition of a "paying bank" includes the bank whose routing number appears on a check even if it is not the true drawee bank. In addition, for bank collection functions, a bank through which a check is payable is a paying bank, even if the check is drawn on another bank. 12 C.F.R. §229.2(z). [163]

2. **Returning bank:** A "returning bank" is any bank other than the paying or depositary bank that handles the item on its return. 12 C.F.R. §229.2(cc). [163]

II. LAW GOVERNING THE CHECK COLLECTION PROCESS

A. **Introduction:** The bank collection aspects of Article 4 have been preempted to a fairly substantial extent by Congress's enactment of the Expedited Funds Availability Act, 12 U.S.C. §§4001 et seq., and by the Federal Reserve Board's promulgation of Regulation CC thereunder. To a lesser degree, Article 4 is preempted by Regulation J, which was promulgated under the authority granted to the Board of Governors of the Federal Reserve System by the Federal Reserve Act. 12 U.S.C. §§221 et seq. Regulation J's rules largely resemble Article 4's rules. When a check is sent for collection through a Federal Reserve Bank, both Regulations J and CC apply. When a check is not collected through a Federal Reserve Bank, only Regulation CC applies. When an item, other than a check, is collected through a Federal Reserve Bank, only Regulation J applies. When an item, other than a check, is not collected through a Federal Reserve Bank, neither Regulation J nor CC applies. [163-164]

III. VARIATION BY AGREEMENT

The rules set out in Article 4 and in Regulation CC can be varied by an agreement between the affected parties. U.C.C. §4-103(a); 12 C.F.R. §229.37. With rare exception, as long as the agreement is with respect to the item being handled, the bank's customer (usually the owner of the item) is bound by any agreement that is made by the bank in the process of collecting the item for him even though he is not a party to the agreement. U.C.C. §4-103, Official Comment 3. *Clearinghouse rules* have the effect of agreements varying the rules of Article 4 for items collected through the clearinghouse, whether or not specifically assented to by all parties interested in the items handled. U.C.C. §4-103(b); U.C.C. §4-103, Official Comment 3. [164]

IV. DUTIES OF PAYOR BANK

A. Duty to pay or settle on day of presentment: When a check is presented for payment, the payor bank can either pay or return the check on the day of presentment or defer posting of the check. When a payor bank defers posting of a check, the bank waits until the next banking day to decide whether to pay or return the check. To defer posting a check, the payor bank must settle with the presenting bank before midnight of the banking day of receipt or before any earlier time required by Regulation CC or J. This settlement can be revoked if the payor bank decides the next day to return the check. U.C.C. §4-301(a). [164-165]

1. **Exception for immediate payment over the counter:** When a demand item is presented for immediate payment over the counter, a payor bank has no right to defer its decision as to whether to pay the item. U.C.C. §4-301(a); U.C.C. §4-301, Official Comment 2. [165]

2. **Exception for "on-us" checks:** A payor bank does not need to provisionally settle for an *on-us* check on the day of receipt to have the right to defer the decision as to whether to pay or return the on-us item until the next banking day. U.C.C. §4-301(b); U.C.C. §4-301, Official Comment 4. [165]

3. **Failure to settle for demand item on day of receipt:** If the payor bank neither settles for the item nor returns the item by midnight of the banking day of receipt, the payor bank is penalized by being made accountable (liable) for the amount of the item. U.C.C. §4-302(a)(1). [165]

4. **Means of dishonoring item:** If the payor bank, after properly settling for the item on the day of its receipt, decides that it will not pay the item, it may revoke the settlement and recover the payment if it returns the item before it has finally paid the item and before its *midnight deadline*. U.C.C. §4-301(a)(1), (2). [165]

   a. **Cut-off hour:** A bank may fix 2:00 P.M. or later as a *cut-off hour* for the handling of money and items and the making of entries on its books. The bank may treat any item received after the cut-off hour as having been received on the next banking day. U.C.C. §4-108(a), (b). [165-166]

   b. **Extensions of midnight deadline for emergencies:** A payor bank may be excused from failing to meet the midnight deadline when:

      ■ unanticipated circumstances beyond the bank's control prevented it from doing so;

      ■ the circumstances could not be prevented by the bank through the exercise of reasonable care; and

      ■ the bank exercised such reasonable diligence as the circumstances required in both anticipating the effects of any foreseeable events and in dealing with the circumstances once they arose. U.C.C. §4-109(b); 12 C.F.R. §229.38(e). [166]

   c. **Special extensions under Regulation CC:** Regulation CC specifically provides for extensions of the midnight deadline in returning a check in two situations:

      i. **Rapid means of return:** The midnight deadline is extended by 1 day if the paying bank uses a means of delivery that would ordinarily result in the check being received by the bank to which it is sent on or before the next banking day following the midnight deadline. 12 C.F.R. §229.30(c)(1). [166]

    ii. **Highly expeditious means:** The midnight deadline is extended further if a paying bank uses a highly expeditious means of transportation, even if this means of transportation would ordinarily result in delivery after the receiving bank's next banking day. 12 C.F.R. §229.30(c)(1). [166-167]

5. **Manner of payment:** Because the payor bank has already settled for the item on the day of its receipt, once the midnight deadline (or any earlier deadline set by agreement, clearinghouse rule, Federal Reserve regulation, or circular) has passed, the check is deemed to be paid. U.C.C. §4-215(a)(3). At this point, the payor bank is precluded from revoking its settlement. U.C.C. §4-301(a). [167]

6. **Failure to settle or timely return item:** If the payor bank fails to settle for a demand item on the day of receipt or fails to pay or return the item by its midnight deadline, the bank becomes accountable for the item whether or not the item is properly payable. U.C.C. §4-302(a)(1). The payor bank may defend against its accountability for the item under the same conditions that it could recover, under U.C.C. §3-418(d), a payment made by mistake. In addition, the payor bank may defend by proving that the presenter breached one of the presentment warranties or by proving that the presenter presented or transferred the check intending to defraud the payor bank. U.C.C. §4-302(b); U.C.C. §4-302, Official Comment 3. [167]

2002 amendments: A new [Rev] U.C.C. §4-301(a)(2) has been added to encourage the electronic processing of checks. Under this new subsection, an image of the item, rather than the item itself, may be returned if the party to which the item is to be returned has entered into an agreement under which it will accept an image as return of the item and the image is returned in accordance with the agreement. As a result, the holder may not claim that because the item itself was not returned, the payor bank has missed its midnight deadline, thereby making the payment final as to all parties. [Rev] U.C.C. §4-301, Official Comment 8. Original [Rev] U.C.C. §4-301(a)(2) has been renumbered as (a)(3). In addition, the payor bank may, instead of sending a "written notice" of dishonor or nonpayment send a "record." [167-168]

Note: The 2002 amendments define "*record*" in [Rev] U.C.C. §3-103(a)(14) as "information that is inscribed on a tangible medium or that is stored in an electronic or other medium and is retrievable in perceivable form." [168]

7. **Payor bank's liability on documentary drafts and items not payable on demand:** A payor bank is accountable for the amount of a documentary draft (whether payable on demand or at a stated time) or other item not payable on demand only if the item is properly payable and the payor bank does not pay or accept the item or return it and any accompanying documents within the time limits allowed. U.C.C. §4-302(a)(2). [168]

8. **Final payment:** When the payor bank finally pays an item, the payment process has been completed. The payor bank may no longer revoke its settlement. The depositary bank becomes accountable to its customer for the amount of the item. U.C.C. §4-215(d). The drawer and indorsers are discharged from liability. U.C.C. §4-215, Comment 8. [168]

9. **Acts constituting final payment:** The payor bank finally pays an item when it has done any one of three acts:

    a. **Pays in cash:** A payor bank finally pays an item when it makes payment in cash. [168-169]

b. Settles for item without reserving right to revoke: A payor bank finally pays an item when the bank settles for the item without reserving a right to revoke the settlement under statute, clearinghouse rule, or agreement. Article 4 gives the payor bank an automatic right to revoke a settlement it has made if it meets the requirements specified in U.C.C. §4-301. U.C.C. §4-215, Official Comment 4. This does not apply to checks presented for payment over the counter. [169]

c. Fails to revoke provisional settlement by midnight deadline: A payor bank finally pays an item when the bank has made a provisional settlement for the item and fails to revoke the settlement by the midnight deadline (or an earlier time established by clearinghouse rule or agreement). U.C.C. §4-215(a). [169]

10. Duties of paying banks under Regulation CC in returning unpaid items: Regulation CC imposes two duties on a paying bank to ensure that the depositary bank quickly learns of a check's dishonor: the ***duty to expeditiously return*** unpaid items and the duty to give "prompt ***notice of the nonpayment*** of any item" in the amount of $2,500 or greater. [169]

a. Duty of expeditious return: A paying bank may meet either of two tests to satisfy its duty of expeditious return: the ***2-day/4-day test*** or the ***forward collection test.*** 12 C.F.R. §229.30(a). [170]

    i. 2-day/4-day test: The 2-day/4-day test requires that the paying bank return an item in a manner such that the item will normally be received by the depositary bank within certain time limits. 12 C.F.R. §229.30(a)(1). [170]

        ■ The time limit for the depositary bank to receive the return of a local check is not later than 4:00 P.M. on the second business day after the check was presented to the paying bank. 12 C.F.R. §229.30(a)(1)(i).

        ■ The time limit for the depositary bank to receive the return of a nonlocal check is not later than 4:00 P.M. on the fourth business day after presentment. 12 C.F.R. §229.30(a)(1)(ii).

    ii. The forward collection test: The forward collection test provides that a paying bank returns a check in an expeditious manner if it does so in a manner in which a similarly situated bank would normally handle a check drawn on the depositary bank and deposited for forward collection in that bank by noon on the banking day following the banking day on which the check was presented to the paying bank. 12 C.F.R. §229.30(a)(2)(iii). [170-171]

b. Duty to send notice of nonpayment: The paying bank has a duty to send notice of the nonpayment of any check in the amount of $2,500 or greater directly to the depositary bank. 12 C.F.R. §229.33(a). The notice may be communicated in any way as long as it is received by the depositary bank by 4:00 P.M. on the second business day following the banking day on which the check was presented to the paying bank. 12 C.F.R. §229.33(a). [171]

c. Liability for violation of paying bank's duties of expeditious return and notice of nonpayment: A paying bank is liable for damages for breach of its duties of expeditious return or of transmitting notice of nonpayment only if the bank fails to exercise ordinary care or to act in good faith. 12 C.F.R. §229.38(a). A paying bank that violates its duty of ordinary care is liable to the injured party for the amount of the check less the amount of loss that would have been incurred had ordinary care been exercised. 12 C.F.R. §229.38(a). [171]

V. DUTIES OF COLLECTING BANKS

A. Collecting bank's status as agent: When a customer deposits an item into her bank account, the depositary bank automatically becomes the customer's agent for the purpose of collecting the item. U.C.C. §4-201(a). Subsequent collecting banks become the subagent for the customer. The agency status of the depositary bank and other collecting banks terminates when they finally settle for the item. U.C.C. §4-201(a); U.C.C. §4-214(a); U.C.C. §4-214, Official Comment 3. [172]

B. Right of chargeback: The depositary bank may charge back its customer's account, or obtain a refund for the amount of any provisional settlement given to the customer, if, for any reason, the item is not finally paid by the payor bank. U.C.C. §4-214(a). The right to chargeback exists even if the depositary bank's failure to exercise ordinary care in sending the item for collection caused the dishonor. The bank remains liable to the customer for any damages caused by its failure to exercise ordinary care in collecting the deposited item. U.C.C. §4-214(d)(2); U.C.C. §4-214, Official Comment 6. [172-173]

  1. Requirements for chargeback: To exercise its right of chargeback or refund, the depositary bank must, by its midnight deadline (or within a longer reasonable time after it learns the facts), either return the item or send notification of the facts if the item is not available for return. U.C.C. §4-214(a). If the bank is both the depositary bank and the payor bank, it must act by its midnight deadline. U.C.C. §4-214(c); U.C.C. §4-301(a), (b). [173]

  2. Consequences of failing to meet requirements: Even if the depositary bank fails to act within the required time, it may still revoke its settlement, charge back its customer's account, or obtain a refund. The only consequence of the untimely act is that it is liable for any loss to the customer resulting from the delay. U.C.C. §4-214(a); U.C.C. §4-214, Official Comment 3. [173]

C. Duty of collecting bank to use ordinary care in collecting and returning items: Collecting banks owe a duty of ordinary care to their customers in performing their collection and return duties. U.C.C. §4-202(a). A collecting bank must take proper action before its midnight deadline following receipt of the item, notice, or settlement. Taking action within a longer time may be considered reasonable, but the burden of establishing the timeliness of the action is on the collecting bank. U.C.C. §4-202(b); U.C.C. §4-202, Official Comment 3. As in the case of a payor bank, a collecting bank is allowed additional time in the case of emergencies. U.C.C. §4-109(b). The measure of damages for a collecting bank's failure to exercise ordinary care in handling an item is the amount of the item reduced by an amount that could not have been realized by the use of ordinary care. On a showing of bad faith, damages may include any other damages the party has suffered as a proximate consequence. U.C.C. §4-103(e). [173-174]

D. Electronic presentment: *Electronic presentment* (or "*check truncation*") involves the transferring of the contents of the item through the information contained on the MICR-encoded line rather than transferring of the item itself. When an item is presented electronically, a "*presentment notice*" is sent in the place of the item itself. U.C.C. §4-110(a). [174]

E. Encoding warranties: To enable a check to be processed by computer, the depositary bank must encode the face amount of the check on the MICR line. The depositary bank may, by mistake, encode the check in a greater amount than it is actually payable ("*overencoding*") or encode the check in a lesser amount than actually payable ("*underencoding*"). To protect the payor bank and subsequent collecting banks from losses from the miscoding, any person who encodes information on an item warrants to any subsequent collecting bank and to the payor bank or other payor that the information is correctly encoded. U.C.C. §4-209(a). Under Regulation CC, any bank that handles a check or a returned check warrants that the encoded information is correct. 12 C.F.R. §229.34(c)(3). A person miscoding an item is liable to any person taking the item in good faith for the loss suffered, plus expenses and loss of interest incurred. U.C.C. §4-209(c); 12 C.F.R. §229.34(d). [174-175]

CHAPTER 7

WHOLESALE FUNDS TRANSFERS

I. WHAT IS A FUNDS TRANSFER?

A. Introduction: A "*funds transfer*" is "the series of transactions, beginning with the originator's payment order, made for the purpose of making payment to the beneficiary of the order." The term "funds transfer" includes all payment orders issued for the purpose of carrying out the originator's payment order. U.C.C. §4A-104(a). With certain exceptions, funds transfers are governed by Article 4A of the Uniform Commercial Code. U.C.C. §4A-102. [179]

B. Funds transfers must be between banks: A funds transfer is limited to payments made through the banking system. A transfer of funds by, or to, an entity other than a bank is excluded. U.C.C. §4A-104, Official Comment 2. [181]

C. Requirements for a payment order: To be a payment order, an instruction must meet the following three requirements:

   1. Unconditional: The instruction cannot state a condition to the obligation to pay the beneficiary other than as to the time of payment. U.C.C. §4A-103(a)(1)(i).

   2. Reimbursed by sender: The receiving bank must be paid or reimbursed by the sender. U.C.C. §4A-103(a)(1)(ii).

   3. Transmitted directly to receiving bank: The instruction must be transmitted by the sender directly to the receiving bank. U.C.C. §4-103(a)(1)(iii). This requirement eliminates credit cards and checks from coverage under Article 4A. U.C.C. §4A-104, Official Comment 5. [181-182]

D. Consumer transactions excluded: The Electronic Fund Transfer Act of 1978 (EFTA) covers most consumer funds transfers. Article 4A does not apply to any transaction if any part of the transaction is covered by EFTA. U.C.C. §4A-108. [182]

II. PAYMENT OBLIGATIONS IN CHAIN OF TITLE

A. Introduction: Acceptance of a payment order by a receiving bank, other than the beneficiary's bank, obligates the sender to pay the bank the amount of the sender's order. U.C.C. §4A-402(c).

The obligation of the sender is excused if the funds transfer is not completed because, for any reason, the beneficiary's bank does not accept the payment order. U.C.C. §4A-402(c). This is called a "***money-back guarantee***." U.C.C. §4A-402, Official Comment 2. When a payment order is issued to the beneficiary's bank, acceptance of the order by the beneficiary's bank obligates the sender to pay the beneficiary's bank the amount of the order. U.C.C. §4A-402(b); U.C.C. §4A-402, Official Comment 1. On acceptance by the beneficiary's bank, the obligation of the originator to pay the beneficiary on the underlying obligation is discharged and the obligation of the beneficiary's bank to pay the beneficiary is substituted for it. [182-183]

III. DUTIES AND LIABILITIES OF RECEIVING BANK

A. **Introduction:** A receiving bank is not obligated to accept a payment order. U.C.C. §4A-209, Official Comment 1. It has no duties until it accepts the order. U.C.C. §4A-212. The receiving bank (unless it is also the beneficiary's bank) accepts a payment order only when it executes the order. U.C.C. §4A-209(a). Because a receiving bank accepts the order only by executing it, notice of rejection is not necessary to avoid acceptance. [183]

B. **Duty to issue payment order:** A receiving bank, on the acceptance of a payment order, must issue a payment order on the execution date complying with the sender's order. U.C.C. §4A-302(a)(1). [183]

  1. **Time when payment order can be accepted:** The originator's bank cannot accept the originator's payment order until the execution date. If the receiving bank is also the beneficiary's bank, it cannot accept the payment order until the payment date. U.C.C. §4A-209(d). [183-184]

  2. **Damages for breach of duty by receiving bank:** If the receiving bank breaches its duty to properly execute an order, the receiving bank is liable for the sender's expenses in the funds transfer and for incidental expenses and interest lost as a result of its failure to properly execute the order. Absent an express written agreement to the contrary, consequential damages are not available to the sender. U.C.C. §4A-305(a), (b), (d). [184]

C. **Erroneous execution of payment order**

  1. **Duplicative order, order in greater amount than authorized, or order to wrong beneficiary:** When the receiving bank executes a payment order in an amount greater than the amount of sender's order, issues a duplicate order to the beneficiary, or issues an order to the wrong beneficiary, the sender, not having authorized these erroneous orders, is only obligated to reimburse the receiving bank for whatever payment was properly made according to the sender's original order. U.C.C. §4A-303(a), (c); U.C.C. §4A-402(c). [184]

    a. **Recovery from recipient:** Whether the receiving bank can recover the excess payment from the beneficiary or the improper payment from the recipient depends on the common law governing mistake and restitution. U.C.C. §4A-303(a). Courts apply two rules in determining whether the receiving bank may recover from the beneficiary. [184]

      i. **Mistake of fact rule:** Under the ***mistake of fact rule***, the receiving bank may recover from the beneficiary unless the beneficiary has detrimentally relied on the payment. [184]

ii. Discharge for value rule: Under the *discharge for value rule*, the beneficiary (or recipient) is entitled to retain the funds as long as it had given value to the sender (whether from this or some other transaction), had made no misrepresentations to the receiving bank, and had no notice of the bank's mistake. [185]

b. Right of subrogation: If, under the law of restitution, the beneficiary or recipient can retain the excess payment, the receiving bank becomes subrogated to any rights that the beneficiary had against the sender. U.C.C. §4A-303, Official Comment 2. [185]

2. **Payment in a lesser amount:** If the receiving bank issues a payment order in a lesser amount than authorized, it is entitled to payment from the sender in the lesser amount only unless the receiving bank issues an additional payment order for the remaining difference. U.C.C. §4A-303(b). [185]

IV. DUTIES OF BENEFICIARY'S BANK

A. **Overview:** A funds transfer is complete once the beneficiary's bank accepts the originator's bank's payment order. U.C.C. §4A-104(a); U.C.C. §4A-406(a). On its acceptance of the payment order, the beneficiary's bank becomes indebted to the beneficiary in the amount of the order on the payment date. U.C.C. §4A-404(a). Once this occurs, the originator's debt to the beneficiary on the underlying contract is discharged. [186]

B. **Manner in which beneficiary's bank accepts payment order:** Acceptance cannot take place before the payment date. U.C.C. §4A-209(d). Once the beneficiary's bank accepts the payment order, it may not later reject the order. U.C.C. §4A-210(d). Acceptance of a payment order by the beneficiary's bank occurs when the first of any of the following acts occur:

1. **Payment:** When the beneficiary's bank pays the beneficiary. U.C.C. §4A-209(b)(1)(i). [186]

2. **Acceptance by notification:** When the beneficiary's bank notifies the beneficiary of the receipt of the order or that its account has been credited for the order. U.C.C. §4A-209(b)(1)(ii). [186]

3. **Acceptance by receipt of payment:** When the beneficiary's bank receives payment of the entire amount of the order. U.C.C. §4A-209(b)(2). [186]

4. **By inaction:** Unless the beneficiary's bank rejects the order within 1 hour after the opening of the beneficiary's bank's next funds-transfer business day after the payment date, acceptance occurs automatically on the opening of the beneficiary's bank's next funds-transfer business day following the payment date of the order if either the amount of the order is covered by sufficient funds in an authorized account that the sender maintains with the beneficiary's bank or the beneficiary's bank has otherwise received full payment from the sender. U.C.C. §4A-209(b)(3). [186]

C. **Liability for failure to make prompt payment:** If the beneficiary's bank refuses to pay the beneficiary after proper demand by the beneficiary and receipt of notice of the particular circumstances giving rise to such damages, the beneficiary may recover consequential damages. U.C.C. §4A-404, Official Comment 2. However, the beneficiary's bank is not liable for consequential damages if it proves that it did not pay because of a reasonable doubt concerning the right of the beneficiary to payment. U.C.C. §4A-404(a). [187]

D. Duty to notify beneficiary: If the beneficiary's bank accepts a payment order that requires payment to an account of the beneficiary, it must give notice to the beneficiary of the receipt of the order before midnight of the next funds-transfer business day following the payment date. U.C.C. §4A-404(b). If the order does not instruct payment to an account of the beneficiary, the beneficiary's bank is required to notify the beneficiary only if the order requires notification. U.C.C. §4A-404(b). [187]

V. EFFECT OF ACCEPTANCE ON UNDERLYING OBLIGATION

A. Generally: Payment by the originator to the beneficiary occurs when the order is accepted by the beneficiary's bank. U.C.C. §4A-406(a). Payment by a funds transfer does not discharge the underlying obligation if all the following conditions are met:

■ the means of payment was prohibited under the contract governing the underlying obligation;

■ within a reasonable time after receiving notice of the order, the beneficiary notified the originator of its refusal to accept the means of payment;

■ the funds were neither withdrawn by the beneficiary nor applied to its debt; and

■ the beneficiary would suffer a loss that could have reasonably been avoided if payment had been made in a way that complied with the contract. U.C.C. §4A-406(b). [188]

VI. CANCELLATION (STOPPING PAYMENT) OF PAYMENT ORDER

A. Introduction: A cancelled payment order cannot be accepted. When an accepted order has been cancelled, the acceptance is nullified, and no person has any right or obligation based on the acceptance. U.C.C. §4A-211(e). [188]

B. Right to cancel unaccepted orders: Before the receiving bank has accepted the order, the sender has the absolute right to cancel the order if the sender gives timely notice of cancellation. U.C.C. §4A-211(b). [188-189]

1. Manner of cancellation: The sender may cancel its order orally, electronically, or in writing. U.C.C. §4A-211(a). Unless the receiving bank agrees otherwise, when there is a security procedure in effect between the sender and the receiving bank, the cancellation is not effective unless it is verified pursuant to the security procedure. U.C.C. §4A-211(a). [189]

2. Cancellation by operation of law: An unaccepted payment order is cancelled by operation of law at the close of the fifth funds-transfer business day of the receiving bank after the execution date or payment date of the order. U.C.C. §4A-211(d). [189]

C. Cancellation of order accepted by receiving bank: A receiving bank has no obligation to cancel an accepted order. U.C.C. §4A-211(c). Even if it chooses to do so, the cancellation is not effective unless the receiving bank cancels the payment order it sent in execution of the sender's order. U.C.C. §4A-211(c)(1); U.C.C. §4A-211, Official Comment 3. [189]

D. Cancellation of order after acceptance by beneficiary's bank: Once the beneficiary's bank has accepted an order, it has no obligation to agree to cancel the order. Although having no duty to agree to a cancellation, the beneficiary's bank may agree to a cancellation in four situations:

- if the payment order is unauthorized;

- if the payment order is duplicative of a payment order previously sent;

- if the payment order is mistakenly sent to a beneficiary who is not entitled to payment from the originator; or

- if a payment order is issued by mistake in an amount greater than the beneficiary is entitled to receive from the originator. U.C.C. §4A-211(c)(2). [189-190]

VII. LIABILITY FOR AUTHORIZED PAYMENT ORDERS

A. Introduction: The sender has the duty to reimburse the receiving bank for the amount of any authorized payment order. U.C.C. §4A-203, Official Comment 1. A payment order is authorized if the sender either actually or apparently authorized the order or is otherwise bound by the order under agency law. U.C.C. §4A-202(a). [190]

VIII. LIABILITY FOR UNAUTHORIZED PAYMENT ORDERS

A. Introduction: A sender is liable for an unauthorized order if it qualifies as a *"verified payment"* order. U.C.C. §4A-202(b). An order that passes on being properly tested according to a security procedure is called a *"verified payment order."* U.C.C. §4A-202(b). [190]

B. Requirements for sender's liability for verified payment orders: Determining whether the customer is liable to the receiving bank for an unauthorized but verified payment order is a two-step process.

    1. First step: The receiving bank must prove that the order is a verified payment order by proving the following:

        a. Agreement with customer: The bank had an agreement with its customer providing that orders would be verified pursuant to a security procedure.

        b. Commercially reasonable procedure: The security procedure is a commercially reasonable method of providing security against unauthorized payment orders.

        c. Bank complied with procedure: The bank accepted the payment order in good faith and in compliance with the security procedure and any written agreement or instructions of the customer. U.C.C. §4A-202(b). [191]

    2. Second step: If the bank proves that the order was a verified order, the order is effective as the order of the customer whether or not it was authorized by the customer. The customer is, therefore, liable to the receiving bank for the amount of the order. U.C.C. §4A-202(b). However, the customer can avoid liability by proving that the breach of security was not in any way attributable to the customer itself. To do so, the customer must prove that the order was not caused, directly or indirectly, by a person who falls into one of two categories.

a. Entrusted with duties as to payment orders: The first category includes any person who was entrusted, at any time, with duties to act for the customer with respect to payment orders or to the security procedure. U.C.C. §4A-203(a)(2)(i).

b. Access to source or facilities: The second category comprises any person who: (a) obtained access to the customer's transmitting facilities; or (b) obtained, from a source controlled by the customer and without authority of the receiving bank, information facilitating breach of the security procedure, regardless of how the information was obtained or whether the customer was at fault. Information includes any access device, computer software, or the like. U.C.C. §4A-203(a)(2). [191]

C. Summary of when loss falls on bank: The loss caused by an unauthorized payment order falls on the bank, and not on the customer, in four situations.

■ No commercially reasonable procedure was in effect.

■ The bank did not comply with the security procedure in place.

■ The customer can prove that the wrongdoer did not obtain the information from it.

■ The bank agreed to assume all or part of the loss. U.C.C. §4A-204, Official Comment 1. [192]

IX. ERRONEOUS PAYMENT ORDERS

A. Introduction: An erroneous payment occurs when the sender makes a mistake in the amount of the payment order it sends or in the identity of the beneficiary to whom the order is sent and the receiving bank accepts the order without noticing the error. [192]

B. Allocation of loss when no security procedure in place: The sender suffers the loss in the event that there is no established security procedure to determine the accuracy of the order. U.C.C. §4A-205, Official Comment 1. [192]

C. Allocation of loss when security procedure in place: When an established security procedure is in place to detect such errors, the loss shifts to the receiving bank if the sender proves that it had complied with the security procedure and that the error would have been detected if the receiving bank had also complied with the security procedure. U.C.C. §4A-205(a)(1). [192-193]

D. Duty of sender on receipt of notice of acceptance: On receipt of notice of the executed order or of the debiting of its account, the sender has the duty to exercise ordinary care to determine, on the basis of the information available to it, whether the order was erroneously executed or unauthorized or contained any other error and, if so, to notify the receiving bank of the relevant facts within a reasonable time not exceeding 90 days after the notification is received by the sender. With one exception, the only penalty for the sender's failure to perform this duty is that the receiving bank is not obligated to pay interest on any amount refundable to the sender for the period prior to the time before the bank learns of the execution error. U.C.C. §4A-304; U.C.C. §4A-204(a).

In the case of an erroneous payment order, the sender is also liable for any loss, not exceeding the amount of the order, which the receiving bank proves that it incurred as a result of the failure. U.C.C. §4A-205(b). However, the sender may be precluded from objecting to the receiving bank's retention of its payment for the order if the sender does not notify the receiving bank of its objection within 1 year after the sender received a notification reasonably identifying the order. U.C.C. §4A-505; U.C.C. §4A-505, Official Comment. [193]

X. MISDESCRIPTIONS

A. Nonexistent or unidentifiable person or account: If the name, bank account number, or other identification of the beneficiary refers to a nonexistent or unidentifiable person or account, no person has rights as the beneficiary of the order. U.C.C. §4A-207(a). As a result, the beneficiary's bank cannot accept the order and the funds transfer cannot be completed. U.C.C. §4A-207; U.C.C. §4A-207, Official Comment 1. Each sender in the funds transfer is relieved of liability and is entitled to a refund to the extent of any payment. U.C.C. §4A-207, Official Comment 1. [193]

B. When beneficiary identified by both name and number: When the beneficiary is identified by both a name and an identifying or bank account number and the name and number identify different persons, the beneficiary's bank may rely on the number as the proper identification of the beneficiary and credit the account number. U.C.C. §4A-207(b)(1). The loss will generally then fall on the bank sending the order. The customer is not obligated to pay the order unless the receiving bank proves that, before acceptance of the customer's order, the customer received notice from the receiving bank that payment might be made on the basis of the identifying number or bank account number even if it identifies a different person. U.C.C. §4A-207(c)(2). When the beneficiary's bank either pays the person identified by name or knows that the name and the number identify different persons, the beneficiary's bank assumes the risk that it has failed to pay the person intended by the sender. If it pays the proper person, the beneficiary's bank is entitled to payment. If it does not, no acceptance can occur and the originator's bank has no obligation to pay the beneficiary's bank. U.C.C. §4A-207(b)(2). [193-194]

C. Misdescription of intermediary bank or beneficiary's bank: Similar problems arise when the intermediary or beneficiary's bank is improperly described.

    1. Identification by number only: When a payment order identifies an intermediary bank or the beneficiary's bank by an identifying number only and that number is wrong, the bank sending the order will suffer any loss caused by the order being accepted by the wrong bank. U.C.C. §4A-208(a)(1). If the originator supplied only the number and not the name of the beneficiary's bank, the originator would be obligated to reimburse the originator's bank. U.C.C. §4A-208(a)(2). [194]

    2. Conflict between name and number: When there is a conflict between the name of the beneficiary's bank (or intermediary bank) and the identifying number, the receiving bank may rely on the number as the proper identification of the beneficiary's bank (or intermediary bank) if it does not know, at the time it executes the order, that the name and number identify different persons. U.C.C. §4A-208(b). The sending bank thus suffers the loss and may not recover from its customer. If a nonbank sender had included the conflicting description of the beneficiary's bank in its order to the sending bank, it would be obligated to reimburse the sending bank for any losses or expenses incurred in executing or attempting to execute the order if the sender received notice that the sending bank might rely on the identifying number only before its order was accepted by the sending bank. U.C.C. §4A-208(b)(2). If the receiving bank knows that the name and the number identify different banks, reliance on either the name or the number, if incorrect, is a breach of its duties in executing the sender's payment order. U.C.C. §4A-208(b)(4). [194-195]

XI. INJUNCTION

Availability of injunction: A creditor can obtain an injunction preventing the originator from issuing a payment order initiating a funds transfer to the beneficiary, the originator's bank from executing the originator's payment order, the beneficiary's bank from releasing funds to the beneficiary, or the beneficiary from withdrawing the funds. U.C.C. §4A-503. However, no intermediary bank can be enjoined from executing a payment order or a receiving bank from accepting the order or receiving payment from the sender. U.C.C. §4A-503, Official Comment. [195]

CHAPTER 8

CONSUMER ELECTRONIC FUND TRANSFERS

I. LAW GOVERNING CONSUMER ELECTRONIC FUND TRANSFERS

A. Governing law: Consumer electronic fund transfers are governed, for the most part, by the Electronic Fund Transfer Act ("EFTA"), 15 U.S.C. §1693, and Regulation E promulgated thereunder. [199]

II. WHAT IS AN ELECTRONIC FUND TRANSFER?

A. Introduction: An "*electronic fund transfer*" is any transfer of funds that is initiated through an electronic terminal, a telephone, or computer or magnetic tape for the purpose of instructing a financial institution to debit or credit a consumer asset account. 15 U.S.C. §1693a(6); 12 C.F.R. §205.3(b). The transfer must be initiated through an electronic terminal, a telephone, or computer or magnetic tape. A transfer from a consumer account initiated through use of a debit card is covered even though the transaction does not involve an electronic terminal, magnetic tape, or computer. 12 C.F.R. §205.3(b)(5). [199-200]

III. CONSUMER'S LIABILITY FOR UNAUTHORIZED TRANSFERS

A. Introduction: A consumer has only limited liability for unauthorized transfers out of her account. [201]

B. What is an unauthorized fund transfer? An electronic fund transfer is unauthorized if the transfer is initiated by a person without actual authority to initiate the transfer and the consumer did not receive a benefit from the transfer. 15 U.S.C. §1693a(11); 12 C.F.R. §205.2(k). An electronic fund transfer is not unauthorized if the consumer gave to the person initiating the transfer an access device unless the consumer has notified the financial institution involved that transfers by that person are no longer authorized. 15 U.S.C. §1693a(11); 12 C.F.R. §205.2(k)(1). [201]

1. **No longer authorized after notification:** Any transfer becomes an unauthorized transfer once the cardholder notifies the card issuer that the person having the card is no longer authorized to use the access device. [201]

2. **Obtained through robbery or fraud:** Any transfer is an unauthorized electronic fund transfer if it is made with an access device that was obtained either through robbery or through fraudulent inducement. 12 C.F.R. §205.2(k)(3), Official Staff Commentary. [201]

C. **Conditions to consumer's liability for unauthorized fund transfers:** Before a consumer is liable for an unauthorized fund transfer, three conditions must be met. 15 U.S.C. §1693g(a); 12 C.F.R. §205.6(a). [201]

1. **Transfer through accepted access device:** The unauthorized transfer must have been made by an accepted access device. [201]

2. **Means to identify consumer:** The financial institution must have provided some means by which the consumer can be identified when she uses the device. 12 C.F.R. §205.6(a). [201]

3. **Disclosures:** The financial institution must have provided the consumer with certain written disclosures as to her liability for unauthorized transfers. 12 C.F.R. §205.6(a). [201]

D. **Limitation of consumer liability:** If these conditions are met, the consumer is liable for the lesser of (a) the amount of any unauthorized fund transfers or (b) $50. 15 U.S.C. §1693g(a); 12 C.F.R. §205.6(b). The consumer is not liable for any unauthorized fund transfers that occur after the consumer has given notice to the financial institution that an unauthorized electronic fund transfer involving her account has been or may be made. 15 U.S.C. §1693g(a); 12 C.F.R. §205.6(b). The limitations on liability apply whether or not the consumer is negligent. 12 C.F.R. §205.6(b)-2, Official Staff Commentary. [202]

E. **Failure to report loss of device:** If the consumer does not notify its financial institution of the loss or theft of the access device within 2 business days after learning of the loss or theft, the consumer's liability increases to the lesser of (a) $500 or (b) the sum of (i) $50 or the amount of unauthorized electronic fund transfers that occur before the close of the 2 business days, whichever is less, and (ii) the amount of unauthorized electronic fund transfers that the financial institution establishes would not have occurred but for the consumer's failure to notify the institution within 2 business days after it learns of the loss or theft of the access device, and that occur after the close of the 2 business days and before notice to the financial institution. 12 C.F.R. §205.6(b)(2). [202]

F. **Failure to report unauthorized transfers on periodic statement:** In the event that the consumer fails to report within 60 days of a statement's transmittal any unauthorized electronic fund transfer that appears on the periodic statement, the consumer is liable to the financial institution for (a) up to $50 of any unauthorized transfer or transfers that appear on the statement, plus (b) the full amount of any unauthorized transfers that occur after the close of the 60 days after transmittal of the statement and before the consumer gives notice to the financial institution. 12 C.F.R. §205.6(b)(3). [202]

G. Combination of failure to report lost device and failure to report unauthorized transfers:
When there is a combination of a failure to report a lost or stolen access device and a failure to report the loss after the receipt of a periodic statement, the provisions that impose liability for the failure to report the lost or stolen access device govern the amount of liability for transfers that appear on the periodic statement and for transfers that occur before the close of 60 days after the consumer first received a periodic statement showing an unauthorized transfer. The provisions imposing liability for the failure to report the losses that appear on a periodic statement govern thereafter. 12 C.F.R. §205.6(b)(3). [202-203]

IV. STOPPING PAYMENT OF ELECTRONIC FUND TRANSFERS

A. No right to reverse ordinary fund transfers: The EFTA gives a consumer no right to reverse an electronic fund transfer (other than a preauthorized electronic fund transfer). A few states do allow an electronic fund transfer initiated by a consumer to be reversed under certain conditions. [203]

B. Stopping payment on preauthorized electronic fund transfers: There is a right to stop payment of any preauthorized electronic fund transfer from the consumer's account. A consumer can stop payment of a preauthorized electronic fund transfer by giving oral or written notice to its financial institution at any time up to 3 business days before the scheduled date of the transfer. 12 C.F.R. §205.10(c). If the notice is oral, the financial institution may require that written confirmation of the stop payment order be given within 14 days of the oral notification. 12 C.F.R. §205.10(c). Neither the EFTA nor Regulation E spell out clearly what type of damages may be available if the financial institution fails to stop a preauthorized transfer. [203-204]

V. CONSUMER LIABILITY TO THIRD PARTIES IN THE EVENT OF SYSTEM MALFUNCTION

A. Introduction: If there is a malfunction in the fund transfer system that prevents a preauthorized payment from being made, the consumer's obligation to make the payment is suspended until the system malfunction is corrected and the electronic fund transfer may be completed. 15 U.S.C. §1693j. The consumer must pay the bill if, at any time before the malfunction is corrected, the creditor demands in writing that payment be made by means other than an electronic fund transfer. 15 U.S.C. §1693j. [204-205]

VI. RESTRICTIONS ON ISSUANCE OF ACCESS DEVICES

A. Introduction: An access device not requested by the consumer may be issued only if it is not validated. 15 U.S.C. §1693i(b); 12 C.F.R. §205.5(b)(1). Issuance by the financial institution of an unrequested access device must be accompanied by a complete disclosure: (1) as to the consumer's rights and liabilities once the device is validated; (2) clearly explaining that the access device is not validated; and (3) instructing the consumer on how to dispose of the device in the event that the consumer does not wish to use the device. 12 C.F.R. §205.5(b). [205]

VII. SPECIAL RULES FOR PREAUTHORIZED TRANSFERS

A. Transfers to consumer's account: If the consumer's account is to be credited by a preauthorized electronic fund transfer from the same payor at least once every 60 days, the bank must give notice of the deposit by one of the following means:

1. **Notice that transfer made:** Oral or written notice within 2 business days after the transfer that the transfer has occurred.

2. **Notice that transfer not made:** Notice within 2 business days after a scheduled fund transfer that the transfer has not occurred.

3. **Readily available telephone line:** The bank may provide a readily available telephone line that the consumer may call to ascertain whether or not the preauthorized transfer occurred. 12 C.F.R. §205.10(a). [205]

B. Transfers from consumer's account: When the debit is in the same amount each month, no notification is required. If debits are in a varying amount, the consumer has the right to receive notice if a transfer varies in amount from the previous transfer or from the preauthorized amount. 12 C.F.R. §205.10(d). Notice must be given either by the bank or by the payee at least 10 days before the scheduled transfer date so as to enable the consumer not only to verify whether the amount is correct but also to deposit funds in the account to cover any deficit. 12 C.F.R. §205.10(d). [205-206]

VIII. DOCUMENTATION REQUIREMENTS

A. Receipts at electronic terminals: When the consumer initiates an electronic fund transfer at an electronic terminal, the financial institution itself, or through another party (for example, the merchant at a POS terminal), must provide a written receipt containing certain basic information as to the transaction. [206]

B. Periodic statements: The financial institution must provide periodic statements to the consumer providing certain basic information for each transfer occurring during the period covered for each account to, or from which, electronic fund transfers can be made. 15 U.S.C. §1693d(e); 12 C.F.R. §205.9(b). [206]

IX. ERROR RESOLUTION PROCEDURES

A. Introduction: The consumer must give oral or written notice of error to the financial institution no later than 60 days after the bank provided the consumer with the periodic statement indicating the error. 15 U.S.C. §1693f(a); 12 C.F.R. §205.11(b)(1)(i). [206]

B. Bank's duty to investigate: On receipt of the notice of error, the financial institution has the duty to promptly investigate and determine whether an error has occurred. 15 U.S.C. §1693f(a); 12 C.F.R. §205.11(c).

1. **Does not recredit:** If the financial institution does not provisionally recredit the consumer's account during the investigation, it must transmit the results of its investigation to the consumer within 10 business days. 15 U.S.C. §1693f(a); 12 C.F.R. §205.11(c)(1).

2. **Recredits:** If the bank provisionally recredits the account in the amount of the alleged error (including any applicable interest) within 10 business days after receipt of the notice of error, the financial institution may, as long as it acts promptly, take up to 45 calendar days to transmit the results of its investigation to the consumer. 15 U.S.C. §1693f(c); 12 C.F.R. §205.11(c)(2). [206-207]

C. **After the bank makes its determination:** If the bank determines that an error has occurred, it must promptly, and no later than 1 business day after this determination, correct the error and, whether or not the bank determines that an error has occurred, mail or deliver to the consumer a written explanation of its findings within 3 business days after concluding its investigation. 15 U.S.C. §1693f(b), (d); 12 C.F.R. §205.11(c)(2)(iii), (iv). [207]

X. LIABILITY FOR FAILING TO MAKE CORRECT FUND TRANSFER

A. **Introduction:** A financial institution is liable to its customer if it fails to make a fund transfer in the correct amount and in a timely manner. If the bank's failure was unintentional and occurred despite reasonable precautions established by the institution to guard against such failures, damages are limited to actual damages proved. This does not include consequential damages. 15 U.S.C. §1693h(c). [207]

XI. CIVIL LIABILITY

A. **Introduction:** The provisions of the EFTA may be enforced by administrative action. Besides administrative enforcement, the EFTA also provides for both individual and class civil actions by consumers. 15 U.S.C. §§1693m-1693n. [207]

■ Under certain conditions, damages may be trebled when: (1) the noncompliance is a failure to comply with the error resolution rules; or (2) the financial institution knowingly and willfully concluded that the consumer's account was not in error when such a conclusion could not reasonably have been drawn from the evidence available to the financial institution at the time of its investigation. 15 U.S.C. §1693f(e). [207-208]

■ A financial institution is not liable if its noncompliance resulted in an error that was properly resolved pursuant to the EFTA error resolution procedures. 15 U.S.C. §1693m(a). [208]

■ A financial institution is also not liable if it proves, by a preponderance of the evidence, that the noncompliance was not intentional and resulted from a bona fide error notwithstanding the maintenance of procedures reasonably adapted to avoid such noncompliance. 15 U.S.C. §1693m(c). [208]

■ A financial institution is likewise not liable if it both notifies the consumer of the noncompliance prior to the consumer bringing an action and pays to the consumer his actual damages. 15 U.S.C. §1693m(e). [208]

CHAPTER **9**

LENDER CREDIT CARDS

I. TERMINOLOGY IN CREDIT CARD TRANSACTIONS

The person who uses a credit card to make a purchase is the "cardholder." The bank that issued the card to the cardholder is the "issuing bank." The store or other party that takes the credit card in payment is the "merchant." The bank at which the merchant maintains its account is the "merchant's bank." [211]

II. LAW GOVERNING CREDIT CARD TRANSACTIONS

A. Introduction: The basic law of credit cards is federal law and can be found in the Truth in Lending Act, 15 U.S.C. §§1601 et seq., as amended both by the Fair Credit and Charge Card Disclosure Act and the Fair Credit Billing Act, and Regulation Z, 12 C.F.R. part 226, promulgated pursuant to the Truth in Lending Act. With two exceptions, these statutes and regulations cover only consumer use of credit cards. Business credit cards are also subject to the rules governing liability for unauthorized use and limitations on the right of the card issuer to issue unrequested cards. [211-212]

III. LIABILITY FOR UNAUTHORIZED USE

A. Introduction: A cardholder has very limited liability for an unauthorized use of her card. A cardholder is liable only for the lesser of (1) $50 or (2) the amount of money, property, labor, or services obtained by the unauthorized use. There is no liability for any unauthorized charges incurred after the consumer gives notice to the bank of the unauthorized use. 15 U.S.C. §1643(a)(1); 12 C.F.R. §226.12(b). With one exception, the rules governing liability for unauthorized use of a credit card apply to credit cards used for business purposes as well as for consumer purposes. 15 U.S.C. §1645. The one exception involves issuance by a card issuer of 10 or more credit cards for use by the employees of an organization. In this situation, the card issuer and the organization may contractually set liability for unauthorized use at an amount greater than otherwise permitted by law. However, an employee of the organization has the same limited liability as does a consumer as to both his employer and the card issuer. 15 U.S.C. §1645; 12 C.F.R. §226.12(b)(5). [212]

B. Conditions to liability: A cardholder has no liability whatsoever for an unauthorized use of her card unless three conditions are met.

    1. Accepted card: The card must be an accepted credit card. 12 C.F.R. §226.12(b)(2)(i). [212]

    2. Disclosures: The card issuer must have provided the cardholder with adequate notice of its maximum potential liability and of the means by which it can notify the card issuer of the loss or theft of its card. 12 C.F.R. §226.12(b)(2)(ii). [212]

    3. Merchant identification: The card issuer must have provided a means by which the merchant could have identified the cardholder as the authorized user of the card. 12 C.F.R. §226.12 (b)(2)(iii) and Official Staff Commentary. [212-213]

C. Unauthorized use: *"Unauthorized use"* is defined as the use of a credit card by a person, other than the cardholder, who does not have actual, implied, or apparent authority for such use, and from which the cardholder receives no benefit. 12 C.F.R. §226.12(b), n.22. The card issuer has the burden of proving that use of a card was authorized. 15 U.S.C. §1643(b). [213]

D. Authorized use: A use is *"authorized"* when the user has either actual or apparent authority to use the card.

    1. Actual authority: The user has actual authority to use a credit card when the cardholder either expressly or by implication gives the user authority to use the card. [213]

    2. Apparent authority: A user has apparent authority when the cardholder gives the impression to third parties that the user is authorized to use the card. [213]

        a. Knowingly giving card to user: Some courts find that if the cardholder voluntarily and knowingly gives the card to another person, the person to whom the card is given has apparent authority to use the card. [213-214]

        b. Informs card issuer: Courts are split as to whether the cardholder is liable for purchases made by the user after the cardholder informs the card issuer that the user no longer has actual authority to use the card. [214]

IV. RIGHT TO REFUSE PAYMENT

A. Consumer's right to refuse payment: If a consumer fails to satisfactorily resolve a dispute as to a product purchased with his credit card, the consumer can assert against the card issuer all claims (other than tort claims) and defenses arising out of the transaction and relating to the failure to resolve the dispute. 15 U.S.C. §1666i; 12 C.F.R. §226.12(c)(1). [214]

B. Conditions to right to withhold payment: There are three conditions to a consumer's right to withhold payment of her credit card bill for a purchase:

    1. Good-faith attempt to resolve dispute: The consumer must make a good-faith attempt to resolve the dispute with the merchant. 12 C.F.R. §226.12(c)(3)(i). [214]

    2. More than $50: The charge for the purchase must be more than $50. 12 C.F.R. §226.12(c)(3)(ii). [215]

    3. Purchase within same state or within 100 miles: The purchase must have occurred in the same state as the consumer's current designated address or, if not within the same state, within 100 miles of that address. 12 C.F.R. §226.12(c)(3)(ii). [215]

C. Exceptions: The geographical and monetary limitations do not apply when the merchant (a) is the same person as the card issuer; (b) is directly or indirectly controlled by or controls the card issuer; (c) is a franchised dealer of the card issuer's products or services; or (d) has obtained the order for the disputed transaction through a mail solicitation made or participated in by the card issuer. 12 C.F.R. §226.12(c)(3), n.26. [215]

D. Limited to amount of credit outstanding: The amount of the claim or defense that may be asserted cannot exceed the amount of credit outstanding for the disputed transaction at the time the cardholder first notifies the card issuer or the merchant of the existence of the claim or defense. 12 C.F.R. §226.12(c)(1); 12 C.F.R. §226.12(c)(1), n.25. [215]

V. ERROR RESOLUTION PROCEDURES

A. What cardholder must do on noticing billing error: If the cardholder wants to activate the error resolution procedure, the cardholder must send written notice of the billing error so that it is received by the card issuer no later than 60 days after the card issuer transmitted the statement that reflected the billing error. 12 C.F.R. §226.13(b)(1). [215-216]

B. What the card issuer must do on receipt of billing error notice: Within 30 days after receiving the billing error notice, the card issuer must either:

- mail or deliver to the cardholder a written acknowledgment of receipt of the notice, or

- comply with the appropriate resolution procedures. 12 C.F.R. §226.13(c)(1). [216]

   1. If error is found: If the card issuer determines that the billing error mentioned in the notice has occurred, the card issuer must, within two complete billing cycles (but in no event later than 90 days) after receiving the billing error notice, correct the billing error and credit the cardholder's account with any disputed amount and related finance or other charges, if any. The card issuer must also, during this period, mail or deliver to the cardholder a correction notice. 12 C.F.R. §226.13(e)(1), (2). [216]

   2. If no error found: Before the card issuer may determine that no billing error has occurred, it must conduct a reasonable investigation. 12 C.F.R. §226.13(f). If, after conducting a reasonable investigation, the card issuer determines that no billing error occurred, it must, within two complete billing cycles (but in no event later than 90 days) after receiving the billing error notice, mail or deliver to the cardholder an explanation that sets forth the reasons for its belief that the alleged billing error notice is incorrect in whole or in part. 12 C.F.R. §226.13(f)(1). It must also promptly notify the cardholder in writing of the time when payment is due and the portion of the disputed amount and related finance or other charges that are owed. 12 C.F.R. §226.13(g)(1). The cardholder has the same grace period within which to pay the amount due without incurring additional finance or other charges that it would have had had it just received the periodic statement showing the charge. 12 C.F.R. §226.13(g)(2). [216]

C. Remedy: Failure to comply with the requirements of the billing error resolution procedure results in the card issuer forfeiting the right to collect from the cardholder the amount of the alleged error together with any finance charges on that amount. The amount of the forfeiture, however, cannot exceed $50. 15 U.S.C. §1666(e). [216]

CHAPTER 1

WHAT IS A NEGOTIABLE INSTRUMENT?

ChapterScope ──────────────────────────────────

This chapter is an introduction to negotiable instruments. It examines how a negotiable instrument is different from an ordinary contract, the law governing negotiable instruments, the different types of negotiable instruments, and the requirements for negotiability. The key points in this chapter are:

- **Merger of debt into negotiable instrument:** Once a debt has been evidenced by a negotiable instrument, the negotiable instrument becomes the debt. As a result, payment or transfer of the negotiable instrument is payment or transfer of the debt.

- **Negotiable instrument as cash substitute:** A negotiable instrument differs from an ordinary contract in that a holder in due course obtains substantially greater rights and protections than does an assignee of an ordinary contract right.

- **U.C.C. Articles 3 and 4:** The basic law governing negotiable instruments is contained in Articles 3 and 4 of the Uniform Commercial Code, although some federal regulations also have an impact on the law of negotiable instruments.

- **Drafts and Notes:** The two basic types of negotiable instruments, drafts (primarily used as means of making payment) and notes (primarily used as a means of evidencing a debt), come in many different types.

- **Formal requirements for writing to qualify as a negotiable instrument:** Strict requirements must be met for a writing to qualify as a negotiable instrument. The primary requirements are that the writing be an unconditional promise or order to pay a fixed sum of money and that it contain certain key words indicating that the writing is payable to the order of an identified person or to the bearer.

I. WHAT IS A NEGOTIABLE INSTRUMENT?

A. **Introduction:** A negotiable instrument is a cross between a contract and money. On the one hand, a negotiable instrument is a simple contract by which a person either promises to make payment or orders someone to make payment on their behalf. On the other hand, the right sort of holder of a negotiable instrument (the person who has the right to collect on the instrument) is freed from many of the risks and burdens associated with being the assignee of an ordinary contract right.

B. **Primary difference from ordinary contract right:** An assignee of an ordinary contract right takes subject to all the defenses to which his assignor took subject. A holder in due course of a negotiable instrument takes the instrument free from virtually all defenses.

Example: Buyer purchases equipment from Equipment Dealer for $5,000 pursuant to an ordinary contract of sale. Equipment Dealer assigns the contract to Finance Company. The equipment is defective in breach of the warranty of merchantability. Finance Company takes subject to Buyer's breach of warranty claim. Restatement (Second) of Contracts §336(1) (1979). If, instead, Buyer executed a negotiable note that Equipment Dealer negotiated to Finance Company, Finance Company would take free of Buyer's breach of warranty claim if, and only if, Finance Company is a holder in due course. U.C.C. §3-305(b).

C. **Other differences:** The assignee of an ordinary contract right assumes the risk that the obligor has already paid the assignor. A holder in due course of a negotiable instrument who is without notice of the payment can recover from the obligor even if the obligor has previously paid the original creditor. U.C.C. §3-602(a). In addition, pleading and proving a case on a negotiable instrument is far simpler than on an ordinary contract. U.C.C. §3-308.

II. GOVERNING LAW

A. **Basic governing law:** The basic law governing negotiable instruments is contained in Articles 3 and 4 of the Uniform Commercial Code. The bank collection process is also governed by Federal Reserve Board Regulations CC and J. See Chapter 6. In 2002, the American Law Institute and the National Conference of Commissioners on Uniform State Laws proposed several amendments to Articles 3 and 4. Until enacted by the particular state, these amendments will not be the law in that state. However, in anticipation that these amendments could be enacted by many states, this book includes references to the new amendments throughout. The references are clearly identified as "2002 amendments" and include discussions on whatever impact the amendments will have on application of the law.

B. **Coverage of Article 3:** Subject to certain exclusions, Article 3 governs writings meeting the requirements of U.C.C. §3-104(a).

1. **Exclusions:** Section 3-102 specifically excludes from the scope of Article 3 the following writings that otherwise qualify as negotiable instruments: (1) investment securities governed by Article 8, (2) money, and (3) payment orders governed by Article 4A. U.C.C. §3-102(a).

C. **Coverage of Article 4:** Article 4 governs the bank collection process. The coverage of Article 4 is limited to items. An item is defined as "an instrument or other written promise or order to pay money handled by a bank for collection or payment." U.C.C. §4-104(a)(9).

1. **Item:** "Item" covers more than just Article 3 negotiable instruments. U.C.C. §4-104(c); U.C.C. §4-104, Official Comment 8.

a. **Any promise or order:** Any promise or order to pay money handled by a bank for collection or payment is an item whether or not the promise or order would qualify as a negotiable instrument under Article 3.

b. **Not negotiable items:** The following orders or promises are items even though not negotiable instruments under Article 3: a conditional promise or order, a savings account withdrawal slip, and certain bonds and other investment securities governed by Article 8.

2. **Exclusions:** "Item" does not include payment orders governed by Article 4A and debit and credit card slips. U.C.C. §4-104(a)(9).

D. **Article 4 prevails over Article 3:** When an instrument governed by Article 3 is handled by a bank for collection or payment, Article 3 and Article 4 both apply. Because Article 4 was specifically drafted to govern problems arising in the bank collection process, when the results reached under an applicable provision of Article 4 conflict with the results reached under a provision of Article 3, Article 4 controls. U.C.C. §3-102(b); U.C.C. §4-102(a).

E. Federal common law: In the absence of a federal statute or regulation, if the United States is a party to an instrument, its rights and duties are governed by federal common law and not by the Code. U.C.C. §4-102, Official Comment 1.

1. Basically same as Article 3: Generally, federal common law is virtually identical to Articles 3 and 4. U.C.C. §3-102, Official Comment 4.

2. Differences: Sometimes courts have been unwilling to apply the provisions of the Code.

Examples: Although put into question by a recent Supreme Court decision, courts had adopted the federal holder-in-due-course doctrine (see Chapter 2) instead of applying the standards found in U.C.C. §3-302. In addition, courts have refused to apply some of the doctrines precluding a drawer from claiming that an indorsement is forged. Compare United States v. Bank of Am. Natl. Trust & Sav. Assn., 438 F.2d 1213, 8 U.C.C. Rep. Serv. 962 (9th Cir. 1971) (§3-405 not applicable) with Bank of Am. Natl. Trust & Sav. Assn. v. United States, 552 F.2d 302, 21 U.C.C. Rep. Serv. 812 (9th Cir. 1977) (§3-405 applicable).

3. Not involving rights and duties of United States: If the dispute does not involve the rights or duties of the United States government but rather those of other parties to a U.S. government instrument, Articles 3 and 4 apply.

III. TYPES OF NEGOTIABLE INSTRUMENTS

A. Introduction: Article 3 negotiable instruments are classified into two basic categories: notes and drafts. A ***draft*** is any instrument that contains an order (a written instruction by one person to another to pay a third person). U.C.C. §3-104(e); U.C.C. §3-103(a)(6). [[Rev] U.C.C. §3-103(a)(8).] A ***note*** is any instrument that contains a promise (a written undertaking to pay money). U.C.C. §3-104(e); U.C.C. §3-103(a)(9). [[Rev] U.C.C. §3-103(a)(12).]

B. Notes: A note is a promise by one party (called the ***maker***) to pay to another party (called the ***payee***) a sum of money.

1. Purpose: The usual purpose of a note is to evidence a debt. Notes thus primarily serve a credit rather than a payment function.

2. Diversity of form: Notes may be as simple as a one-sentence writing that reads, "I promise to pay to the order of Aspen Publishers the sum of $20. (s) Law Student." Notes can, on the other hand, be several pages long and contain provisions, among others, for collateral securing the loan, conditions under which the note may be accelerated, the payment of attorneys' fees in the event of default, or interest before and after default.

3. Certificate of deposit: A certificate of deposit is a note issued by a bank. It is defined as "an acknowledgment by a bank of the receipt of money together with an engagement by the bank to repay the money." U.C.C. §3-104(j).

a. Purpose: Certificates of deposit are the means by which banks raise money and depositors assure themselves of a good return on their money.

b. Coverage under Article 3: Article 3, in fact, does not cover most certificates of deposit. Some certificates of deposit are not negotiable and therefore are not governed by Article 3. Other certificates of deposit qualify as investment securities under Article 8 and thus are excluded from the coverage of Article 3.

C. Drafts: A *draft*, sometimes known as a bill of exchange, is a three-party instrument by which a person called a *drawer* (the person who typically signs the draft in the lower right-hand corner) orders a person called a *drawee* (the person named in the draft to whom the order is directed) to pay the payee.

1. Purpose: Drafts are usually payment instruments by which the drawer makes payment to the payee.

2. Checks: The most common type of draft is a check. A *check* is a draft drawn on a bank (called either the *drawee bank* or the *payor bank*) and payable on demand. U.C.C. §3-104(f). A *bank* is "a person engaged in the business of banking, including a savings bank, savings and loan association, credit union and trust company." U.C.C. §4-105(1). [[Rev] U.C.C. §1-201(b)(4).] Because all checks are drafts, unless the Code specifically provides otherwise, checks are governed by the same rules that govern drafts.

3. Bank checks: There are three types of checks (cashier's, teller's, and certified checks) on which a bank makes a promise to pay (called *bank checks*). Bank checks are treated differently from ordinary checks for several purposes, including (1) the ability of the issuing bank to refuse payment, (2) the loss or destruction of the check, (3) the effect of taking a bank check on the underlying obligation, and (4) the statute of limitations on bringing an action against the issuing bank.

a. Cashier's checks: A cashier's check is a check for which the drawer and the drawee are the same bank or branches of the same bank. U.C.C. §3-104(g).

b. Teller's checks: A teller's check is a check drawn by one bank on another bank or "payable at" or "payable through" the other bank. U.C.C. §3-104(h).

c. Certified check: A certified check is a check drawn by the bank's customer and accepted by the drawee bank. Certification of the check constituted Chase's acceptance of the obligation to pay, and limited its right to refuse to honor the check. *See* Industrial Bank of Korea, N.Y. Branch v. JP Morgan and Chase Manhattan Corp., 3 Misc. 3d 128(A) (N.Y. Sup. App. Term Apr. 2004). Once a check is certified, a bank customer may not unilaterally stop payment by what is commonly referred to as a "stop-payment order." Dalessio v. Kressler, 6 A.D.3d 57 (N.Y.A.D. 2 Dept. 2004).

Example: Chris requests that First Interstate Bank certify his personal check drawn on First Interstate Bank. By certifying the check (the equivalent of "accepting" a draft), First Interstate Bank promises to pay the check.

4. Traveler's checks: A traveler's check is "an instrument that (i) is payable on demand, (ii) is drawn on or payable at or through a bank, (iii) is designated by the term "traveler's check" or by a substantially similar term, and (iv) requires, as a condition to payment, a countersignature by a person whose specimen signature appears on the instrument." U.C.C. §3-104(i).

a. Purpose: A traveler's check is purchased by a person for use as a substitute for cash virtually anywhere in the world.

b. Differences from ordinary checks: Unlike an ordinary check or draft, a traveler's check has two lines for the signature of the purchaser. The countersignature must be present before the check can be negotiated. To preserve the cash-like nature of traveler's checks, as long as the check is taken by a holder in due course, the countersignature need not be made by the purchaser. U.C.C. §3-106(c); U.C.C. §3-106, Official Comment 2. A holder in due course, as a result, does not take subject to the risk that the traveler's check was stolen and the countersignature forged.

5. **Personal money order:** A personal money order is a draft sold by the drawee to a person who typically does not have an account with the drawee. It is, in effect, a single-transaction checking account. If the drawee is a bank, the personal money order is a check; if a nonbank, a personal money order is a draft.

6. **Drafts (other than checks):** Many other types of drafts are used in various types of situations.

   a. Time and sight drafts: A time draft is a draft payable at a definite time. In contrast, a draft payable on demand is called a sight draft.

   b. Documentary drafts: A documentary draft is a draft, whether payable at a definite time or on demand, which is accompanied by a letter containing instructions that the draft is not to be paid unless the holder presents to the drawee certain designated documents.

   c. Banker's and trade acceptances: A banker's acceptance is a draft drawn on and accepted by a bank. By accepting the draft, the bank becomes liable to pay the draft. U.C.C. §3-413(a). A trade acceptance is a draft drawn on and accepted by a person other than a bank.

   Example: If Omaha State Bank accepted the draft drawn on it by Grain Broker, the resulting instrument would be a banker's acceptance. If Farmer drew a draft on Grain Broker and Grain Broker accepted the draft, the resulting instrument would be a trade acceptance.

7. **Payable through items:** A payable through item is a draft or note that names a specified bank as the person authorized to present the item to the drawer or maker. The bank through which the item is payable has no right to pay the item without the drawer's or maker's consent. U.C.C. §4-106(a); U.C.C. §4-106, Official Comment 1.

8. **Payable at items:** An instrument similar to a payable through item is a note or an acceptance "payable at" a bank. To be a payable at a bank, the note or acceptance must explicitly state that it is payable at a bank, for example, "Payable at Continental Bank."

   a. Two different treatments: Historically, banks in different states treated payable at items differently. To accommodate this difference in treatment, Article 4 provides two alternative provisions that a state may adopt as to the manner in which instruments payable at a bank are to be treated.

      i. First alternative: The first alternative provision treats a note or an acceptance payable at a bank as a draft drawn on that bank. U.C.C. §4-106(b), Alternative A; U.C.C. §4-106, Comment 2. The maker of the note (or the acceptor of the draft) is treated as the drawer of a draft and the bank at which the instrument is payable is treated as the drawee. Therefore, a note or an acceptance payable on demand is a check.

ii. **Second alternative:** Under the second alternative, a note or an acceptance payable at a bank is treated as though it is "payable through" the bank. U.C.C. §4-106(b), Alternative B. The maker of the note (or acceptor of the draft) is treated as both the drawer and the drawee of a draft, while the bank at which the instrument is payable is the only person who may present the instrument to the maker or acceptor for payment.

9. **Remotely created consumer item:** The 2002 Amendments have added a new type of negotiable instrument. A "remotely created consumer item" is "an item drawn on a consumer account, which is not created by the payor bank and does not bear a handwritten signature purporting to be the signature of the drawer." [Rev] U.C.C. §3-103(a)(16). A "consumer account" is an account established by an individual primarily for personal, family, or household purposes, including a joint account established by more than one individual. [Rev] U.C.C. §3-103(a)(2) and Official Comment 6.

Example: Consumer purchases vacation package over the telephone from Telemarketer. In payment for the package, Consumer authorizes Telemarketer to have Consumer's bank debit Consumer's bank account. In so ordering, Telemarketer warrants to Depositary Bank that Consumer authorized the debit. [Rev] U.C.C. §3-416(a)(6). Depositary Bank, in presenting the item to Payor Bank, also warrants that the consumer authorized issuance of the item in the amount for which it is drawn. [Rev] U.C.C. §3-417(a)(4). As a result, in the event the consumer did not in fact authorize the debit, the payor bank may recover the payment from the depositary bank who then may recover it from the telemarketer, assuming that it is solvent.

IV. REQUIREMENTS FOR NEGOTIABILITY

A. **Introduction:** Because the legal consequences of the use of a negotiable instrument are quite different from those attending the use of a simple contract to pay money, negotiable instruments law had to devise a clear means by which a person could distinguish a negotiable instrument from a simple contract. A person purchasing an instrument has to know with ease and certainty whether the instrument is negotiable or not. Similarly, a person signing an instrument has to know that she or he is thereby giving up certain very important rights. Negotiable instruments law chose to have the form of the writing be the distinguishing mark between negotiable writings and nonnegotiable writings. With rare exception, all writings that comply with the required form are negotiable, whereas all writings that do not comply are not negotiable.

B. **Compliance with U.C.C. §3-104(a):** Only a writing complying with the requirements of U.C.C. §3-104(a) is a negotiable instrument under Article 3. U.C.C. §3-104, Official Comment 1. A writing that does not meet these requirements can still be an enforceable obligation, although it is not governed by Article 3.

Examples: Typical assignments, sales agreements, guaranty agreements, and letters of credit often either include provisions not authorized by Article 3 or omit provisions required thereby and therefore do not qualify as negotiable instruments under Article 3.

C. **Requirements for negotiability:** Section 3-104(a) sets forth the requirements for negotiability:

- a signed writing;

- containing an unconditional promise or order;

■ payable in a fixed amount of money, with or without interest or other charges described in the promise or order;

■ payable to bearer or to order at the time it is issued or first comes into possession of a holder;

■ payable on demand or at a definite time; and

■ containing no other undertaking or instruction by the person promising or ordering payment to do any act in addition to the payment of money, except (a) an undertaking or a power to give, maintain, or protect collateral to secure payment; (b) an authorization or a power to the holder to confess judgment or realize on or dispose of collateral; or (c) a waiver of the benefit of any law intended for the advantage or protection of an obligor.

D. Instrument must be in writing: A negotiable instrument must take the form of a writing signed by the maker or drawer. U.C.C. §3-104, Official Comment 1.

Analysis: This requirement is not explicit. However, an instrument must contain a promise or an order. The definition of "promise" requires that the promise be in a writing signed by the person promising to pay (the maker), and the definition of "order" requires that the order be in a writing signed by the person giving the order (the drawer). U.C.C. §3-103(a)(9), (6). [[Rev] U.C.C. §3-103(a)(12), (a)(8).]

1. **What is a writing?** A writing is a "printing, typewriting or any other intentional reduction to tangible form." [[Rev] U.C.C. §1-201(b)(43).] Any form of marking on paper or similar material qualifies as a writing.

   Exception: Neither a phonograph record nor a tape recording, nor an electronic funds transfer that might take the form of impulses on tapes or computer disks is a writing.

   Rationale: The rules of Article 3, especially those for allocating losses for forgery and alteration, were formulated for more traditional "written" instruments and were not intended to be applied to recorded or computerized "instruments."

2. **Signed:** "Signed" includes "any symbol executed or adopted by a party with present intention to adopt or accept a writing." [[Rev.] U.C.C. §1-201(b)(37).]

   a. **Real name need not be used:** As long as the signer intends that the name, words, or mark be her signature, she may use any name, words, or mark as her signature, including a fictitious name, a trade name, or her first name. U.C.C. §3-401(b)(ii); U.C.C. §3-401, Official Comment 2.

   b. **Any form:** A signature may be in the form of printing, handwriting, typing, or even the imprint of a thumbprint. [Rev.] U.C.C. §1-201, Official Comment 37; U.C.C. §3-401(b); U.C.C. §3-401, Official Comment 2.

   c. **Any place on instrument:** The mark or symbol may appear anywhere on the instrument.

      Example: An instrument in handwriting stating "I, John Doe, promise to pay . . ." has been signed if no signature line is found on the bottom of the instrument. U.C.C. §3-401, Official Comment 2.

      Example: Although a signature may be typed, neither the name of the drawer (or maker) contained in a letterhead nor his typed name under the signature line is usually regarded as a signature.

E. Promise or order: To be negotiable, an instrument must contain a promise or an order. U.C.C. §3-104(a).

    1. Promise: A promise is an undertaking to pay money. U.C.C. §3-103(a)(9). [[Rev] U.C.C. §3-103(a)(12).] Although the word "promise" need not be used, the language must be promissory in nature.

    Example: The words "I owe you $500, which I hope to repay within a month" are not a promise because a mere acknowledgment of a debt is not sufficient to constitute a promise.

    2. Order: An order is an instruction to pay money. U.C.C. §3-103(a)(6). [[Rev] U.C.C. §3-103(a)(8).] Although the word "order" does not have to be used, the language must demand that the drawee make payment and not merely authorize or request her to make payment.

F. The promise or order must be unconditional: Unless a negotiable instrument is payable unconditionally, it cannot serve its functions. A check will not be accepted in lieu of cash if there are conditions attached to its payment. Similarly, a purchaser of a note will require a substantial discount from the note's face value if payment of the note is subject to a contingency.

    1. Express condition: A promise or an order that is expressly conditioned on the happening of a specified event is not unconditional. U.C.C. §3-106(a). Even if the condition is fulfilled, the instrument is still denied negotiability. The purchaser should not be required to refer to extrinsic facts to determine whether the condition has been fulfilled.

    Example: A check does not contain an unconditional order if the drawer has written that payment is conditioned on the delivery of a car whether or not the car has already been delivered. U.C.C. §3-106, Official Comment 1.

    2. Implied condition: The promise or order is regarded as unconditional where the promise or order is subject only to an implied or constructive condition. U.C.C. §3-106, Official Comment 1.

    Example: If the maker makes a note in payment for a car to be delivered, the note is deemed to be negotiable even though, under contract law, a court may imply that payment of the note is constructively conditioned on delivery of the car. The result would be the same even if the maker recited in the note that it was in payment for a "car to be delivered." In neither case does the note expressly state a condition to payment.

    3. Payment out of particular fund: A promise or an order is not made conditional merely because payment is to be made solely out of a particular fund or source. U.C.C. §3-106(b)(ii); U.C.C. §3-106, Official Comment 1.

    Rationale: If the purchaser does not like the source or fund out of which payment is to be made, he does not have to purchase the instrument. U.C.C. §3-106, Official Comment 1.

    Example: A negotiable note could read "This note is payable only out of the proceeds of a mortgage executed by Donald Buyer to Sam Seller dated January 15, 2002." In contrast, if the note read "This note is payable only if Donald Buyer makes payments to Sam Seller from the mortgage executed on January 15, 2002," it would not be unconditional because it is subject to an express condition.

4. **Reference to separate agreement:** The purchaser of a negotiable instrument is supposed to be able to determine its rights on the instrument, with certain exceptions, by looking at the instrument itself. Therefore, if the purchaser's rights are contained in a separate writing, the instrument is not negotiable.

   a. **Subject to or stated in another writing:** A promise or an order is not unconditional if it states that the promise or order is subject to, or governed by, another writing or stated in another writing. U.C.C. §3-106(a)(ii), (iii). [The 2002 amendments substitute the term "record" for "writing."]

   Rationale: The mere existence of the requirement that another writing be consulted is sufficient to destroy negotiability; it is irrelevant that examination of the other writing does not reveal a condition precedent to payment. U.C.C. §3-106, Official Comment 1.

   Example: A note that states "Payment of this note is subject to the terms of the Master Finance Agreement dated February 1, 2000" is not negotiable whether or not the agreement contains any conditions to payment because the holder must consult the Master Finance Agreement to determine her right to repayment of the note.

   b. **Reference to another writing:** An instrument that merely refers to the existence of another writing or record may be negotiable. U.C.C. §3-106(a).

   Example: A note stating that it is made "pursuant to" the Master Franchise Agreement dated February 1, 2000 is considered to contain an unconditional promise. The term "pursuant to" does not indicate that the note is controlled in any manner by the Master Franchise Agreement.

   c. **Distinction between "subject to" and "refers to":** In distinguishing between whether a promise or an order is subject to or merely refers to another writing, look to see whether the maker or drawer, by the language used in the instrument, is indicating an intention to make its rights and duties under the instrument conditional on terms found in the separate writing. If so, the instrument is subject to the other writing. If not, it is a permissible reference that will not destroy the negotiability of the writing.

   d. **Exceptions:** An instrument may retain its negotiability while referring to another writing for rights as to (a) collateral, (b) acceleration, or (c) prepayment. U.C.C. §3-106(b)(i).

   e. **2002 amendments:** To accommodate modern technology, the term "record" has been substituted for "writing." The 2002 amendments to Revised Article 3 define "record" in [Rev] U.C.C. §3-103(a)(14) as "information that is inscribed on a tangible medium or that is stored in an electronic or other medium and is retrievable in perceivable form."

G. **Fixed amount:** The principal sum must be payable in a fixed amount. U.C.C. §3-104(a).

1. **Determined by reference to instrument alone:** An instrument is not payable in a fixed amount if the terms used in the instrument to express the sum payable, or any component thereof, are ambiguous or if reference must be made to an outside source or writing to determine the principal amount.

   Rationale: Unless a purchaser can determine how much he will be paid under the instrument, he will be unable to determine a fair price to pay for it, thus defeating the basic purpose of negotiable instruments as a money substitute (in the case of drafts) or as a freely transferable promise of repayment (in the case of notes).

Example: A note is not negotiable when it guarantees "all indebtedness" or a "sum not to exceed."

2. **Exceptions:** Interest and other charges do not have to be payable in a fixed amount. U.C.C. §3-112, Official Comment 1.

   Rationale: Certain types of provisions may make the ultimate amount payable unascertainable at the time the instrument is issued, although the provision must be included for the parties to make the deal.

   a. **Provisions for interest:** Virtually any type of provision for the payment of interest is permissible. An instrument may state the obligation to pay interest as a fixed or variable amount of money or as a fixed or variable rate or rates. U.C.C. §3-112(b); U.C.C. §3-112, Official Comment 1.

      i. **Interest need not be determinable from instrument alone:** The amount or rate of interest may be stated or described in the instrument in any manner and may require reference to information not contained in the instrument. U.C.C. §3-112(b); U.C.C. §3-112, Official Comment 1.

          Example: A note payable with interest at the rate of "2% over the Bank of America prime rate" is negotiable. Similarly, interest can be stated as a described percentage of the profits of a specified business.

      ii. **Time from when interest payable:** When it is clear that the parties intended that interest be paid on the instrument but the instrument does not make clear the time from which interest is to be paid, interest on an interest-bearing instrument is payable from the date of the instrument. U.C.C. §3-112(a). Interest runs on an undated instrument from the date that the instrument was issued. U.C.C. §3-113(b).

      iii. **No means of determining interest:** When an instrument provides that it is payable "with interest" but the description in the instrument does not allow for its calculation, interest is payable at the judgment rate applicable at the place of payment and at the time interest first accrues. U.C.C. §3-112(b); U.C.C. §3-112, Official Comment 1.

   b. **Provisions for other charges:** An instrument is payable in a fixed amount even if it is payable with other charges that are not in a fixed amount.

      i. **Attorneys' fees and costs:** Provisions for attorneys' fees and costs of collection incurred in the collection of the instrument are permissible "other charges" even if they do not specify a particular sum.

          Example: A provision for attorneys' fees may provide for a percentage of the principal balance due, "reasonable attorneys' fees," or "attorneys' fees."

      ii. **Penalties and discounts:** Provisions for prepayment penalties, late payment penalties, or other penalties, discounts, or rebates are also permissible "other charges."

      iii. **Taxes and insurance not permissible:** A duty to pay taxes or to pay to insure collateral will probably not be found to be permissible other charges and therefore will defeat an instrument's negotiability.

H. Payable in money: An instrument is not negotiable unless it is payable in money. U.C.C. §3-104(a).

 1. **Money:** "Money" is defined as "a medium of exchange authorized or adopted by a domestic or foreign government and includes a monetary unit of account established by an intergovernmental organization or by agreement between two or more nations." [Rev] U.C.C. §1-201(b)(24).

    Example: A note payable in Euros issued by the European Union is payable in money.

    Example: An instrument payable in the United States in Swiss francs and an instrument payable in Canada in U.S. dollars are both payable in money. The instrument does not have to be payable in the country in whose currency the instrument is payable.

 2. **Payable in either currency:** Unless it otherwise provides, an instrument that states the amount payable in foreign currency may be paid either in that foreign currency or in an equivalent amount of U.S. dollars. U.C.C. §3-107.

I. Payable to order or to bearer: A negotiable instrument must either be "payable to order" or "payable to bearer." U.C.C. §3-104(a)(1).

 Rationale: For both a prospective purchaser and the obligor to know quickly and with certainty whether a writing is a negotiable instrument, Article 3 requires that certain key words be used for a writing to qualify as a negotiable instrument.

 Exception for checks: A check that meets all the requirements of U.C.C. §3-104(a) except for not being made payable to "order" or "bearer" is a negotiable instrument governed by Article 3. U.C.C. §3-104(c).

 Rationale: The transaction in which a check is taken is usually fairly quick. A taker of a check, including a depositary bank, would probably not notice if the check omitted the words "to the order of" and would likely believe that the check was negotiable. U.C.C. §3-104, Official Comment 2.

 1. **Payable to bearer:** An instrument that is payable to bearer may take one of several forms.

    a. **To bearer:** The instrument may simply state that it is payable "to bearer." U.C.C. §3-109(a)(1).

    b. **Words indicating to possessor:** The instrument may use language indicating that the person in possession of it is entitled to payment. U.C.C. §3-109(a)(1).

       Example: Instruments payable to "holder," to "cash," or to the "order of cash" are payable to bearer. U.C.C. §3-109(a)(3).

    c. **Blank:** An instrument that does not name a payee, e.g., "pay to order of _____," is payable to bearer. U.C.C. §3-109(a)(2).

       Note: The instrument, although negotiable, is also an incomplete instrument until the name of the payee is inserted. U.C.C. §3-109, Official Comment 2.

 2. **Payable to order:** An instrument is payable to order if it is payable to the "order of [an identified person]" or to an "[identified person] or order." U.C.C. §3-109(b).

Example: Instruments payable to "order of John Jones" or "John Jones or order" are payable to order.

3. **Payable to both order and bearer:** When an instrument is payable both to order and to bearer, the instrument is payable to bearer. U.C.C. §3-109(b); U.C.C. §3-109, Official Comment 2.

Example: Instruments containing the following designations are payable to bearer: (1) "bearer or order," (2) "order of bearer," (3) "John Doe or bearer," or (4) "order of cash." U.C.C. §3-109(a), Official Comment 2.

Rationale: Use of bearer words like "cash" or "bearer" more likely evidence the issuer's intention than does the word "order." This is especially likely where the drawer of a check clearly desired to make the check payable to cash but simply neglected to cross out the words "order of" on the check form. By treating these instruments as payable to bearer, subsequent transferees, who believe that the instrument is payable to bearer, and, thus, fail to obtain their transferor's indorsement, are protected. U.C.C. §3-109, Official Comment 2.

J. **Payable on demand or at a definite time:** An instrument is not negotiable unless it is payable either at a definite time or on demand. U.C.C. §3-104(a)(2).

1. **Payable on demand:** A promise or order is "payable on demand" if it states that it is payable on demand or at sight or otherwise indicates that it is payable at the will of the holder. U.C.C. §3-108(a).

Test: An instrument is payable on demand when the time payment is due is determined at the sole discretion of the holder.

Example: An instrument is not payable on demand if it is payable upon a contingency limiting the discretion of the holder to determine the time of payment, e.g., instruments payable "upon an acceptable permanent loan being secured" or "at the earliest convenience of the maker."

a. **Expressly payable on demand:** The following designations expressly indicate that the instrument is payable on demand: (a) "on demand," (b) "on presentation," or (c) "at sight."

b. **No date of payment:** An instrument that fails to state when payment is due is deemed to be payable on demand. U.C.C. §3-108(a)(ii).

Rationale: It is presumed that the failure of the parties to state the date on which payment is due means that the parties intended that the instrument be payable on demand.

Example: A note that states "I promise to pay to the order of Jill the sum of $200" is payable on demand.

c. **Fixed date and on demand:** An instrument that is payable both at a fixed date and also on demand before the fixed date is payable on demand.

Example: A note payable "on June 1, 2003 or earlier on demand of the holder" is payable on demand.

Note: An instrument otherwise payable on demand remains payable on demand even if it is postdated or antedated. U.C.C. §3-113(a).

2. **Payable at a definite time:** A promise or an order is "payable at a definite time" if it is payable at a time readily ascertainable when the promise or order is issued. U.C.C. §3-108(b).

The following instruments are payable at a definite time: at a fixed date ("on February 1, 2005"), a definite period after a stated date ("30 days after date"), or on "elapse of a definite period of time after sight or acceptance" ("45 days after acceptance").

a. Date readily ascertainable: An instrument is payable at a definite time as long as the date is readily ascertainable at the time the promise or order is issued even if the date is not specified in the instrument.

> **Example:** An instrument payable on "the day that the 2008 Summer Olympic Games commence" is payable at a definite time if the date the 2008 Summer Olympic Games begin has been set at the time that the instrument is issued.

b. Incomplete instrument: A note or draft payable a fixed period "after date" that does not state a date is an incomplete instrument. Once the note or draft is completed by the addition of a date, the instrument becomes payable at a definite time.

> **Example:** "30 days after date."

> **Exception:** A draft payable a fixed period "after sight" or "after acceptance" is a complete and negotiable instrument. U.C.C. §3-108(b). "After sight" means after the drawee has accepted the draft.

> **Rationale:** Even if no time for payment can be determined at the time of the instrument's issuance, the holder has it within her ability to set the date of payment by presenting the draft for acceptance.

c. Subject to acceleration: An instrument that is otherwise payable at a definite time remains so even if the time of payment is subject to acceleration. U.C.C. §3-108(b)(ii).

> **Definition:** The time of payment is subject to acceleration when a clause, either in the instrument or in another writing referred to in the instrument, allows the holder to demand, under specified conditions, payment prior to the time set in the instrument for payment.

> **Rationale:** Allowing the holder this right does not make the time of payment uncertain because it is usually within the holder's discretion to decide whether to accelerate the time of payment. Any type of acceleration clause is permissible. Great leeway is given for acceleration clauses because of the importance of these clauses to lenders. A lender, especially a bank, needs to have the ability to accelerate the time payment is due when any of numerous possible risks materialize.

> **Example:** An acceleration clause may provide for acceleration at the unrestricted option of the holder or limit acceleration to circumstances in which an installment has not been paid or the holder "deems himself insecure."

d. Subject to prepayment: An instrument that is subject to prepayment by the obligor remains payable at a definite time. U.C.C. §3-108(b)(i).

> **Rationale:** Despite the fact that the obligor reserves the right to make early payment of the instrument, the holder knows the latest date by which the instrument will be paid.

e. Subject to extension: An instrument is payable at a definite time even if it is subject to extension at the option of the holder, maker, or acceptor or automatically upon, or after, a specified act or event. U.C.C. §3-108(b)(iii), (iv).

    i. Right of holder to extend: An instrument remains negotiable even if the holder has the right to extend the time of payment indefinitely. U.C.C. §3-108(b)(iii); U.C.C. §3-108, Official Comment.

    Rationale: Like a demand instrument, the holder still retains control over when the instrument is due.

    ii. Right of maker or acceptor to extend: When the maker or the acceptor has the right to extend the time for payment, the instrument is payable at a definite time only if the right to extend is limited to extension to a further definite time. U.C.C. §3-108(b)(iv); U.C.C. §3-108, Official Comment. The same rule applies when the time for payment is automatically extended upon the occurrence of a specified event.

    Example: A clause providing that the maker may "extend the time of payment for a period of two additional years" will not destroy negotiability because the holder knows that he will receive payment no later than two years after the original due date. In contrast, a clause allowing the maker to "extend payment until the maker has sufficient cash to make payment" defeats the instrument's negotiability. When the maker or acceptor has the option to extend the time of payment or when the time is extended automatically upon a specified act or event, the holder has no power to determine when payment will be made. Thus, unless the option to extend is limited to an extension to a definite time, the holder will not know when he can expect payment.

K. No other promises or orders: To be negotiable an instrument can contain "no other undertaking or instruction by the person promising or ordering payment to do any act in addition to the payment of money." U.C.C. §3-104(a)(3); U.C.C. §3-104, Official Comment 1.

    1. Clauses defeating negotiability: Inclusion in an instrument of a promise, an obligation, an order, or a power not authorized by Article 3 defeats the instrument's negotiability.

    Example: A promise to pay taxes or to maintain a minimum working capital will defeat an instrument's negotiability.

    2. Permissible promises and instructions: The following promises or instructions are authorized by Article 3. U.C.C. §3-104(a)(3); U.C.C. §3-104, Official Comment 1.

      a. Collateral: An undertaking or a power to give, maintain, or protect collateral to secure payment will not defeat an instrument's negotiability. This would include provisions granting the holder a security interest in the collateral or securing both the obligation evidenced by the instrument itself and any other obligation of the obligor.

      b. Confession of judgment: An authorization or a power to the holder to confess judgment or realize on, or dispose of, collateral will not destroy negotiability.

      c. Waiver: A waiver of the benefit of any law intended for the advantage or protection of an obligor will not destroy negotiability.

    3. Limited to maker or drawer: The prohibition against additional terms is limited to undertakings and instructions given by the person promising or ordering payment. A promise by the holder does not violate this prohibition. U.C.C. §3-104(a)(3).

Example: Giving the holder the right to purchase, at the holder's own cost, a life insurance policy on the maker's life does not defeat negotiability. However, if the promise of the maker is made expressly conditional on the holder's purchase of the life insurance policy, the maker's promise is thereby made conditional.

4. **Conditional sales contracts:** Under a conditional sales contract, the buyer usually agrees to pay for goods in installments with the seller retaining title to the goods until payment in full has been made. Conditional sales contracts, being much more like Article 2 contracts for the sale of goods rather than negotiable instruments, are not the type of writing that should be governed by Article 3. Article 3 is not meant to apply to contracts for the sale of goods or services or for the sale or lease of real property or to similar writings that may contain a promise to pay money. U.C.C. §3-104, Official Comment 2. In most situations, these contracts will omit the required "order" or "bearer" language. However, even if these words are present, a court will more than likely find that a conditional sales contract is not covered by Article 3.

L. **Negotiability determined by writing itself:** Negotiability is determined solely by reference to the four corners of the instrument. A separate agreement cannot affect the negotiability of an instrument.

1. **Not negotiable by agreement alone:** A writing that fails to otherwise conform to the requirements of U.C.C. §3-104(a) does not become negotiable simply because the parties have agreed that it should be negotiable.

   Example: An instrument is not made negotiable merely by inclusion of phrases like "This instrument is negotiable," or "I will not raise any claim or defense."

2. **May be treated as negotiable:** However, even absent formal compliance with U.C.C. §3-104, a writing of the parties may be treated by a court as having the characteristics of a negotiable instrument.

   Example: A court could, by applying the doctrine of estoppel or ordinary principles of contract law, deny the obligor the right to raise any of her defenses against the assignee if the writing contains a provision denying the obligor a right to raise defenses against a subsequent assignee. U.C.C. §3-104, Official Comment 2.

3. **Writing "not negotiable" defeats negotiability:** By contrast, a legend such as "Not Negotiable" defeats an instrument's negotiability even if the instrument otherwise complies with U.C.C. §3-104(a). U.C.C. §3-104(d); U.C.C. §3-104, Official Comment 3.

   Exception: This latter rule does not apply to checks. U.C.C. §3-104(d); U.C.C. §3-104, Official Comment 3. Because of the cash-like nature of checks and the swiftness of their negotiation and payment, there is no justification for allowing a drawer to deny negotiability to a check.

Quiz Yourself on
WHAT IS A NEGOTIABLE INSTRUMENT?

1. Bank of America draws a check on itself. It is both the drawer and the drawee. What type of check is this? _____

2. Home Savings, as drawer, draws a check on Wells Fargo Bank, as drawee. What type of check is this? _____

3. Grain Broker agrees to purchase grain from Farmer to be delivered on February 1 with payment due on March 1. Grain Broker draws a draft on its bank, Omaha State Bank, payable to Farmer on March 1.

   a. What type of draft would this be? _____

   b. If it was payable on presentment or on demand, what type of draft would it be? _____

4. If Grain Broker does not want to make payment until it is assured of obtaining possession of the grain, what can Grain Broker do and how will he do it? _____

5. State Farm Insurance Company draws a draft on itself as drawee by which it orders itself to pay the insured who is named as the payee. The draft is made payable through Bank of America. For the insured to collect the draft, the insured or the insured's depositary bank must send the draft to Bank of America, which will present the draft to State Farm Insurance. What else could State Farm have done to reach the same result? _____

6. Answer the questions below as to the following instrument: _____

"To Bank of America
Pay to Mick Jagger the sum of $100.
/s/ Keith Richards"

   a. What type of instrument is it? _____

   b. Is the instrument negotiable? _____

   c. What are the Article 3 and 4 names of Bank of America, Mick Jagger, and Keith Richards? _____

7. Answer the questions below as to the following instrument:

"January 1, 2004

One year from this date, I promise to pay to cash the sum of $1,000 together with interest. This promise arises from the agreement I made with Lucy Sky Diamonds in which she promised to handle my personal injury case. In addition, in the event that this instrument is not paid when due, I promise to pay any attorneys' fees and costs incurred in the collection of this instrument.

/s/ Timothy Leary"

a. Is the instrument negotiable? _____

b. What type of instrument is it? _____

c. In what capacity did Timothy Leary sign? _____

Answers

1. **A cashier's check.** A check is a cashier's check where both the drawer and the drawee are the same bank or branches of the same bank.

2. **A teller's check.** A teller's check is a check drawn by one bank, here Home Savings, and "payable at" or "payable through" the other bank, here Wells Fargo Bank.

3. **a. A time draft.** A time draft is a draft payable at a definite time.

   b. A sight draft. A draft payable on demand is called a sight draft.

4. **Issue Farmer a documentary draft.** To do so, Grain Broker will issue to Farmer an ordinary draft accompanied by a letter containing instructions to Omaha State Bank, the drawee bank, that it should pay the draft only if Farmer delivers to Omaha State Bank a negotiable warehouse receipt for the requisite number of bushels of grain. By requiring delivery of a negotiable warehouse receipt before payment, Grain Broker is thereby guaranteed that it will be entitled to possession of the grain on the draft's payment.

5. **Issue a note.** Drafts drawn on the drawer and notes are treated the same way, so State Farm could have used a note made payable through Bank of America and avoided having to issue a draft.

6. **a. A check.** A check is a draft drawn on a bank payable on demand. U.C.C. §3-104(f). It is a draft because it is an order. U.C.C. §3-104(e). An order is a written instruction signed by the person giving the instruction. U.C.C. §3-103(a)(6). [[Rev] U.C.C. §3-103(a)(8).] It is drawn on a bank because it is directed to Bank of America. It is payable on demand because it is undated. U.C.C. §3-108(a).

   b. Yes. There is an unconditional order to pay a fixed amount of money. Although the writing does not include the word "order," it is still negotiable because a check does not need to be payable to order or bearer. U.C.C. §3-104(a)(1). An instrument can be negotiable even if it is not dated. U.C.C. §3-113(b).

   c. Bank of America is the drawee, U.C.C. §3-103(a)(2) [[Rev] U.C.C. §3-103(a)(4).], **and the payor bank**, U.C.C. §4-105(3). **Mick Jagger is the payee. Keith Richards is the drawer**. U.C.C. §3-103(a)(3). [[Rev] U.C.C. §3-103(a)(5).]

7. **a. Yes.** By being payable to "cash," it is payable to bearer. U.C.C. §3-109(a)(3). By being payable one year from a stated date, it is payable at a definite time. U.C.C. §3-108(b). An instrument may be payable with interest. If the rate of interest cannot be determined from the description, interest is payable at the judgment rate. U.C.C. §3-112. An instrument is payable in a fixed amount even if it is payable with other charges. U.C.C. §3-104(a). Other charges include attorneys' fees and costs of collection. Because the promise is not conditioned on the transaction with Lucy Sky Diamonds, the instrument contains an unconditional promise even though it refers to the transaction as the origins of the instrument. U.C.C. §3-106(b).

b. A note. It is a negotiable instrument that contains a promise. U.C.C §3-104(e).

c. Maker. The maker is the person who signs a note as the person undertaking to pay. U.C.C. §3-103(a)(5). [[Rev] U.C.C. §3-103(a)(7.]

Exam Tips on
WHAT IS A NEGOTIABLE INSTRUMENT?

☛ **Requirements for negotiability:** Always look to see whether the instrument is negotiable. If it fails in any way to meet the requirements for negotiability, none of the rules of Article 3 apply. However, because Article 4 applies to "items" and not just to negotiable instruments, Article 4 still applies.

☞ When determining negotiability, always ask:

  ☞ Is the instrument a signed writing?

  ☞ Does it contain an unconditional promise or order?

  ☞ Is it payable in a fixed amount of money, with or without interest or other charges described in the promise or order?

  ☞ Is it payable to bearer or to order at the time it is issued or first comes into possession of a holder?

  ☞ Is it payable on demand or at a definite time?

  ☞ Does it contain no other undertaking or instruction by the person promising or ordering payment to do any act in addition to the payment of money, except (a) an undertaking or a power to give, maintain, or protect collateral to secure payment; (b) an authorization or a power to the holder to confess judgment or realize on or dispose of collateral; or (c) a waiver of the benefit of any law intended for the advantage or protection of an obligor?

☛ **Exceptions to negotiability requirement:** Be aware, however, that there are exceptions to these rules.

  ☞ A check can be negotiable even if it is not payable to order or to bearer.

  ☞ An instrument that is subject to another writing in regard to rights as to collateral, acceleration, or prepayment can still be negotiable.

HOLDER-IN-DUE-COURSE STATUS AND AVAILABLE CLAIMS, DEFENSES, CLAIMS IN RECOUPMENT, AND DISCHARGES

ChapterScope

This chapter covers the requirements for obtaining holder-in-due-course status (the negotiable instrument equivalent to a good-faith purchaser for value) and the defenses, claims, claims in recoupment, and discharges to which a purchaser of an instrument takes subject. The key points in this chapter are:

- **Special rights of holder in due course:** A holder in due course is given special rights including the right to take free from virtually all claims to the instrument, defenses, and claims in recoupment as well as from any discharge of which she does not have notice.

- **Holder-in-due-course requirements:** There are strict requirements for obtaining holder-in-due-course status, including obtaining any necessary indorsement, taking for value, and being without notice of any claim, defense, or claim in recoupment.

- **Rights of persons denied holder-in-due-course status:** Certain purchasers, although meeting its requirements, are denied holder-in-due-course status. A person not qualifying as a holder in due course can still obtain the rights of a holder in due course if he takes the instrument through a transfer from a holder in due course.

- **Bank checks:** Special rules govern the right of a bank to raise defenses to its obligation to pay a bank check.

- **Federal negotiable instruments law:** Federal common law, not Uniform Commercial Code Articles 3 and 4, governs the rights of the United States on a negotiable instrument.

I. INTRODUCTION

A. **Holder-in-due-course status:** The primary value of a negotiable instrument is that it can free its possessor of many of the risks associated with cash or ordinary contract rights. However, in order not to be a vehicle for the perpetuation of injustice, the only type of possessor who obtains these protections is a holder in due course (the negotiable instrument's version of a good-faith purchaser for value). Because these protections are at the expense of another party, Article 3 imposes stringent requirements for obtaining holder-in-due-course status.

B. **General requirements for holder-in-due-course status:** To obtain holder-in-due-course status, the purchaser of an instrument must take the instrument:

   1. as a holder,
   2. for value,

3. in good faith, and

4. without notice of certain proscribed facts. U.C.C. §3-302(a).

> **Example:** Abe, the original holder of a note payable to bearer, loses the note. The note is found by Bill, who negotiates the note to Carl, who, paying value for the note in good faith and without notice of Bill's lack of title, qualifies as a holder in due course. Carl takes the note free from Abe's claim of ownership. U.C.C. §3-306. By protecting Carl, Abe (the innocent original owner of the note) loses the value of the note.

II. HOLDER STATUS

A. **Introduction:** Negotiable instruments law greatly reduces the risks of theft or loss associated with the use of cash by creating the status of holder, which ensures the person to whom an instrument is payable that the instrument cannot be paid without his signature (called an indorsement).

B. **Holder need not own instrument:** The status of holder is independent of that of the owner of the instrument. Although most holders are probably also the owner of the instrument, a holder does not have to be the owner. Holder status is acquired by meeting certain formalistic requirements apparent from the instrument itself, not by having any legal or equitable right to the instrument.

> **Rationale:** A person paying or purchasing the instrument must be able to determine immediately from the face of the instrument itself, together with the person's identification, whether she can safely deal with that person. The primary advantage of using a negotiable instrument—that is, the ease by which it can be sold or converted into cash—would be defeated if a person could not safely pay or purchase the instrument without investigating whether the person with whom she is dealing is truly the owner of the instrument.

C. **Requirements for holder status:** For a person to qualify as the holder of an instrument, the person must have possession of the instrument, and the obligation evidenced by the instrument must run to him.

D. **Ways of acquiring holder status:** There are two ways of acquiring holder status:

1. **Issuance of instrument:** An instrument is *issued* when it is first delivered by the maker or drawer to either a holder or nonholder for the purpose of giving rights on the instrument to any person (the latter called a "remitter"). U.C.C. §3-105(a).

    a. *Delivery* is "the voluntary transfer of possession." [Rev] U.C.C. §1-201(b)(15).

    b. *Remitter* is a person who purchases an instrument from its issuer if the instrument is payable to an identified person other than the purchaser. U.C.C. §3-103(a)(11). [[Rev] U.C.C. §3-103(a)(15).]

2. **Negotiation of instrument:** Negotiation is a transfer of possession of an instrument, whether voluntary or involuntary, by a person other than the issuer (i.e., maker or drawer) to another person who thereby becomes its holder. U.C.C. §3-201(a).

> **Note:** Negotiation can take place through involuntary transfer of possession. Although an actual transfer of possession is necessary for the transferee to become a holder, the transfer need not be voluntary. U.C.C. §3-201, Official Comment 1.

Example: A thief or finder of an instrument payable to bearer becomes the holder even though the transfer of possession was involuntary. U.C.C. §3-201, Official Comment 1. Of course, the thief, not qualifying as a holder in due course, would be subject to the true owner's claim of ownership. U.C.C. §3-305(a)(2).

E. Obligation must run to possessor: In addition to having possession of the instrument, the obligation contained in the instrument must run to that person if he is to be the holder. When an instrument is payable to bearer, transfer of possession alone is sufficient for its negotiation. To negotiate an instrument payable to order, the instrument must also be indorsed to that person or to bearer. U.C.C. §3-201(b).

F. Indorsement: An indorsement sufficient to negotiate an instrument must be written by or on behalf of the holder. U.C.C. §3-201(b).

Note: An indorsement written by one other than a holder is sufficient for the undertaking of the indorser's contract, but it is not sufficient to negotiate the instrument. U.C.C. §3-415(a); U.C.C. §3-204(a). A signature is an indorsement unless it unambiguously indicates otherwise. *Chicago Title Ins. Co. v. Allfirst Bank*, 394 Md. 270 (Md. 2006).

Note: A forged or unauthorized indorsement is not effective to negotiate the instrument. Thus, if an indorsement in the chain of title is forged or unauthorized, no transferee subsequent to the unauthorized or forged indorsement can become a holder. An unauthorized signature is not sufficient as an indorsement as to make the person possessing the instrument a holder thereof. *See Money Stop Financial Services v. AFT Trucking, LLC*, 2007 WL 702238 (N.J. Super. A.D. 2007).

Example: Dan, the payee, loses a check. Fred, the finder, forges Dan's indorsement on the check and transfers the check to Gina. Because Dan's indorsement was forged, neither Fred nor Gina is a holder of the check.

1. Types of indorsements: Two types of indorsements can be used to negotiate an instrument.

   a. Special indorsement: A special indorsement identifies the person to whom it is payable. U.C.C. §3-205(a).

   Example: If the check is payable to Bill, Bill specially indorses the check by making it payable to John and by signing his own name.

   Note: No words of negotiability, e.g., "order of," are required for a special indorsement. Both "Pay to the order of John Jones /s/ Bill," and "Pay to John Jones /s/ Bill" are special indorsements.

   b. Blank indorsement: A blank indorsement is an indorsement that is not payable to an identified person. An instrument indorsed in blank becomes payable to bearer and any person who possesses the instrument becomes its holder. A blank indorsement can consist of:

   - the unaccompanied signature of the holder;

   - the signature of the holder accompanied by such phrases as "pay to bearer," "pay to holder," "pay to bank," or "pay to cash"; or

   - use of the words "pay to _____" with no one's name filled in. U.C.C. §3-205(b).

    c. Conversion of blank indorsement to special indorsement: Any holder of an instrument indorsed in blank may convert the blank indorsement into a special indorsement by writing over the signature of the indorser the name of an indorsee. U.C.C. §3-205(c); U.C.C. §3-205, Official Comment 2.

2. Indorsement must be written on instrument: An indorsement must be written on the instrument itself.

    Exception: As long as the separate piece of paper, called an ***allonge,*** is affixed to the instrument, an indorsement on that separate piece of paper is sufficient to negotiate the instrument. U.C.C. §3-204(a).

    Example: When John attempts to indorse the check to Brian, John discovers that there is not sufficient room on the check to write the indorsement. As a result, John writes "Pay to Brian, /s/ John" on a separate piece of paper. John staples the piece of paper to the check. The separate piece of paper qualifies as an allonge and is sufficient to negotiate the check to Brian.

3. Manner of negotiation depends on last indorsement: An instrument becomes payable to order or payable to bearer depending on whether the last indorsement is a special or a blank indorsement. U.C.C. §3-205. If the last indorsement is a special indorsement, the instrument is payable to the order of the special indorsee and can be negotiated only by her indorsement. U.C.C. §3-109(c). An instrument originally payable to an identified person may be negotiated by delivery alone if the last indorsement is in blank. U.C.C. §3-109(c).

    Example: Assume that Shelan receives a check payable to "cash." Shelan may indorse the check "Pay to Gina, /s/Shelan" and deliver the check to Gina. The check is now payable to the order of Gina. For Gina to negotiate the check, she must indorse it. If Gina indorses the check by simply writing "Gina," the check is again payable to bearer and may be negotiated by delivery alone.

4. To whom an instrument is payable: The basic rule is that the person to whom an instrument is initially payable is determined by the intent of the person signing the instrument whether as the issuer (drawer or maker), in the name of the issuer, or on behalf of the issuer, whether or not that person is authorized. U.C.C. §3-110(a).

    Example: If the drawer of the check intends John Smith, the lawyer who used to teach at Loyola Law School, to be the person to whom the instrument is payable, an indorsement by another John Smith is not effective to negotiate the check. U.C.C. §3-110, Official Comment 1.

    a. Need not be real name of payee: An instrument is payable to the person intended by the signer even if the payee is identified by a name other than his real name or if her name is misspelled. U.C.C. §3-110(a).

        i. Indorsement in either name effective: When a payee is designated in a name other than her true name, an indorsement in either the payee's true name or the name appearing on the instrument (or in both) is effective to negotiate the instrument. U.C.C. §3-204(d); U.C.C. §3-204, Official Comment 3.

        Example: If the drawer mistakenly designates John Smith as Donald Dove, John Smith's indorsement in either the name of John Smith or Donald Dove would be effective to negotiate the instrument.

    ii. **Transferee or payor can require a signature for both names:** Subsequent transferees for value or collection or the payor can require the payee to sign in both names. U.C.C. §3-204(d); U.C.C. §3-204, Official Comment 3.

  b. **More than one person signing as issuer:** If an instrument is signed by more than one person as maker or drawer and each signer intends that a different person be the person designated as the payee, the instrument is payable to any person intended by any one of the signers. U.C.C. §3-110(a).

    Example: If a check made payable to "John Smith" is signed by two trustees of a trust, one of whom intends that the payee be John Smith, former law professor, and the other intends that the payee be John Smith, the former track star, the check is payable to either the former law professor or the former track star. The indorsement of either person will effectively negotiate the instrument. U.C.C. §3-110, Official Comment 1.

  c. **Intent of forger determinative:** When the drawer's signature on the check is forged, the payee is the person to whom the forger intended that payment be made.

    Example: If Henry forges the drawer's name, making the check payable to "John Smith" while intending the check to be payable to Henry himself, the check is payable to Henry.

  d. **Checkwriting machine:** When the signature of the issuer is made by automated means, such as by a checkwriting machine, the identity of the payee is determined by the intent of the person who supplied the name (or other identification) of the payee, whether or not the person was an authorized agent or even connected with the company. U.C.C. §3-110(b).

5. **When payable to account number:** When a check is made payable to a specific account number either with or without the name of the account owner, the following rules apply.

  a. **Account number only:** When only the account number is identified, the check is payable to the person who owns the bank account so numbered. U.C.C. §3-110(c)(1).

    Example: Even if the drawer intends that the check go to Mary Jones, if the check is made payable to account #1234 and that account belongs to John Smith, the check is payable to John Smith and not to Mary Jones.

  b. **Conflicting account number and name:** When an instrument states both a name and an account number, and the name and the account number refer to different persons, the instrument is payable to the named person whether or not the person in fact owns the account. U.C.C. §3-110(c)(1).

    Example: When a check is made payable to Jane Jones, account #5678, even if Jane Jones does not have an account #5678 (the account being owned by Fran George), the check is payable to Jane Jones.

6. **Payable to agent for identified person:** When an instrument is made payable to a named person with words describing her as an agent or a representative of a specified person, the instrument is payable to either the represented person, the representative, or a successor of the representative. U.C.C. §3-110(c)(2)(ii); U.C.C. §3-110, Official Comment 3.

  Example: When an instrument is payable to "Gary Williams, President of Blue Note Records," either (1) Blue Note Records through any authorized agent; (2) Gary Williams, whether or not he is, or ever was, the president of Blue Note; or (3) the current president of Blue Note Records may act as the holder of the instrument. U.C.C. §3-110(c)(2)(ii); U.C.C.§3-110, Official Comment 3.

7. **Payable to office or officer:** An instrument made payable to an office or officer is payable to the named person, the present officeholder, or the successor to the named person.

    Example: An instrument made payable to "Gloria Williams, Mayor of Los Angeles" is payable to either (1) Gloria Williams, whether she is, or ever was, mayor; (2) the present mayor; or (3) a successor to the mayor. U.C.C. §3-110(c)(2)(iv).

8. **Payable to fund or organization:** When an instrument is payable to a fund or an organization that is not a legal entity, including any informal organization or club, the instrument is payable to any representative of the members of the fund or organization. U.C.C. §3-110(c)(2)(iii).

9. **Payable to trust or estate:** When an instrument is payable to a trust, an estate, or a person described as trustee or representative of a trust or an estate, the instrument is payable to the trustee, the representative, or the successor of either, whether or not the instrument also names the beneficiary or estate. U.C.C. §3-110(c)(2)(i); U.C.C. §3-110, Official Comment 3. The person designated as the beneficiary has no right to negotiate, discharge, or enforce the instrument.

10. **Other words of description:** When a description does not fit into one of the categories of U.C.C. §3-110(c), the additional words can be ignored.

    Example: An instrument payable to "John Smith, Father of Jane Smith" is payable to John Smith whether or not he is the father of Jane Smith.

11. **Two or more payees:** When an instrument is payable to more than one person, whether one of the named payees alone may negotiate, enforce, or discharge the instrument or whether all the payees must act together depends on whether the instrument is payable to the payees jointly or in the alternative.

    a. **Jointly:** If an instrument is payable jointly, all payees must participate in any negotiation, discharge, or enforcement of the instrument. U.C.C. §3-110(d); U.C.C. §3-110, Official Comment 4.

        Example: An instrument payable to "John and Mary" may be negotiated only if John and Mary both indorse the instrument.

    b. **Alternative:** An instrument payable in the alternative may be negotiated, discharged, or enforced by any payee who is in possession of the instrument. U.C.C. §3-110(d); U.C.C. §3-110, Official Comment 4. Instruments payable "to P or R" or "to P and R in the alternative" or "to P/R" ("/" means either/or) are payable to P or R in the alternative.

        Example: An instrument made payable to "John or Mary" may be negotiated by either John's or Mary's indorsement. U.C.C. §3-110(d); U.C.C. §3-110, Official Comment 4.

    c. **Ambiguous:** When it is unclear whether an instrument is payable alternatively or jointly, e.g., "to P and/or R," the instrument is deemed to be payable in the alternative. U.C.C. §3-110(d).

G. Depositary bank's status as holder: If a customer delivers an item to a depositary bank for collection, the depositary bank becomes the holder of the item at the time it receives the item if the customer at the time of delivery was a holder of the item. U.C.C. §4-205(1); U.C.C. §4-205, Official Comment.

1. **No indorsement necessary:** It is irrelevant whether the customer or the depositary bank indorses the item. U.C.C. §4-205(1).

   Rationale: Often a customer may forget to indorse a check that she has deposited in her bank for collection. By depositing the check, the customer implicitly requests that the bank do whatever is necessary to collect the check for her. To require the depositary bank to indorse in the name of the customer would be a waste of the bank's resources. U.C.C. §4-205, Official Comment.

2. **Customer liable as indorser:** Whether or not her indorsement appears on the check, the customer is liable on the check in the event of its dishonor as though she had indorsed the check. U.C.C. §4-207(b).

3. **Depositary bank's warranty:** The depositary bank warrants to subsequent collecting banks, the payor, and the drawer that the amount of the item was paid to the customer or deposited in the customer's account. U.C.C. §4-205(2).

4. **Delivered for collection:** U.C.C. §4-205 applies only if the holder of the item delivers the item to the depositary bank for the purpose of engaging the bank to collect the item for her.

   Example: If a check is made payable jointly to a contractor and a subcontractor in payment for work performed jointly by them and the contractor deposits the check into its bank account, the bank does not become a holder of the check if the subcontractor did not authorize the contractor to deposit the check in its bank account. This is because the subcontractor did not, either by itself or through the contractor, deliver the check to the bank for the purpose of engaging the bank to collect the check for it.

III. VALUE

A. Issued or transferred for value: An instrument is issued or transferred for value if:

- the instrument is issued or transferred for a promise of performance, to the extent the promise has been performed;

- the transferee acquires a security interest or other lien in the instrument other than a lien obtained by judicial proceeding;

- the instrument is issued or transferred as payment of, or as security for, an antecedent claim against any person, whether or not the claim is due;

- the instrument is issued or transferred in exchange for a negotiable instrument; or

- the instrument is issued or transferred in exchange for the incurring of an irrevocable commitment to a third person by the person taking the instrument. U.C.C. §3-303(a).

B. Consideration vs. value: Value is related to, but not identical with, consideration. *Value* is viewed from the perspective of what the holder gave for the instrument. *Consideration* is viewed from the perspective of what the obligor received for his original issuance or transfer of the instrument.

C. Promise of performance as value: Any promise that would constitute consideration under the contract law of the applicable jurisdiction constitutes a "promise of performance" under Article 3.

D. Value to the extent performed: A promise of performance is only value to the extent that the promise has been performed. U.C.C. §3-303(a)(1).

Example: Assume that Sue issues a note for $1,000 to Car Dealer in payment for a car to be delivered. The car is not delivered. Car Dealer sells the note to Bank in exchange for which Bank promises to pay Car Dealer $800. Bank does not take the note for value until it pays Car Dealer the $800. Until Bank pays Car Dealer for the note, Bank loses nothing by not being allowed to recover from Sue on the note. Once Bank discovers that the note is subject to a claim, defense, or claim in recoupment, it has the right, under ordinary contract law, to suspend the remainder of its counterperformance. By refusing to make the payment, Bank can prevent the loss to Sue. Bank has the right to recover any loss from Car Dealer.

1. **Formula when partial performance by holder:** When a holder has only partially performed the agreed-on consideration, the holder has the rights of a holder in due course to the extent of the fraction of the amount payable under the instrument equal to the value of the partial performance divided by the value of the promised performance. U.C.C. §3-302(d).

   Example: Bank promises to pay Car Dealer in two installments of $400 each. If Bank learns of Sue's defense after paying the first installment, Bank can refuse to pay Car Dealer the second installment of $400. Because, prior to learning of Sue's defense, Bank had paid Car Dealer $400 of the promised $800, Bank is a holder in due course to the extent of half of the agreed consideration ($400/$800). Bank can therefore recover $500, which is one-half of the amount due ($1,000/2 = $500). U.C.C. §3-302, Official Comment 6.

E. Security interest in instrument as value: A holder who has a security interest in, or certain types of liens on, the instrument takes the instrument for value.

1. **Security interest in instrument:** The holder may acquire a security interest in, or a lien on, an instrument in two basic ways. The first is by means of a voluntary transfer by the debtor, usually an Article 9 security interest. U.C.C. §3-303(a)(2); U.C.C. §3-303, Official Comment 3. The second is the security interest that a collecting bank automatically acquires under U.C.C. §4-210(a).

   Example: Because Target needs additional cash to purchase new inventory, it borrows the money from Wedontcare Bank by negotiating Allen's note as security for repayment of the loan. Wedontcare Bank becomes a holder for value to the extent that it has acquired a security interest in the note.

2. **Lien on instrument:** A person who has a lien on the instrument by operation of law takes the instrument for value. The most typical type of lien is a common law or statutory banker's lien. U.C.C. §3-303(a)(2); U.C.C. §3-303, Official Comment 3. In contrast, a lien acquired by judicial process, e.g., attachment, garnishment, or execution, does not constitute value. U.C.C. §3-303(a)(2); U.C.C. §3-303, Official Comment 3.

Rationale: In contrast to a banker who may rely on the existence of its statutory or common law lien in the manner in which it conducts its business, a lien by judicial process is acquired after the debt to the creditor arose. The creditor does not rely on the lien in advancing the credit or in otherwise refraining from collecting the debt.

3. **Value only to extent of amount owed:** A lienholder or secured party takes the instrument for value only to the extent of the amount owed on the underlying debt. U.C.C. §3-302(e).

   Formula: If the person obliged to pay the instrument has a defense, claim in recoupment, or claim to the instrument that may be asserted against the person who granted the security interest, those rights may be asserted only to the amount payable under the instrument that exceeds the amount of the unpaid obligation secured at the time of enforcement. U.C.C. §3-302(e).

   Example: The above formula sounds more complex than it is. Assume that as security for a loan from Bank, Car Dealer grants to Bank a security interest in Sue's note in the amount of $5,000. The car is not delivered and Sue refuses to pay the note. At the time of enforcement, Car Dealer owes Bank $1,000. Bank acquires holder-in-due-course status only for the amount that is owed on the underlying obligation ($1,000). After Bank is paid the $1,000, it is made whole. The remainder of any funds recovered from Sue would, in any event, have to be refunded by Bank to Car Dealer. U.C.C. §3-302(e), Official Comment 6, Case # 6.

F. **Payment or security for antecedent debt as value:** The taking of the instrument in payment of, or as security for, an antecedent claim is value whether or not the claim is due. U.C.C. §3-303(a)(3).

   Rationale: If a person who takes a check or note for a debt could not be assured that she would take it free from any claims or defenses to the instrument, she would refuse to take the instrument in payment and would demand cash instead. Because most debts are paid by check or other negotiable instrument, chaos may ensue.

   Example: Assume that Target owes money to Sally Lawyer for legal services rendered. If Target negotiates Allen's note to Sally in payment for her services, Allen's note has been transferred for value.

   Note: The antecedent claim need not be against the transferor. A claim the holder has against any person is sufficient. U.C.C. §3-303, Official Comment 4.

   Example: If Robert, president of Target, makes a note payable to Sally in payment for Target's debt to Sally, Sally takes the note for value even though the debt was owed by Target and not by Robert.

G. **Negotiable instrument or irrevocable obligation as value:** When a negotiable instrument or an irrevocable obligation to a third person is given in exchange for an instrument, the holder takes the instrument for value. U.C.C. §3-303(a)(4), (5).

   Example: A bank that issues a letter of credit in exchange for a negotiable instrument transferred to it by the purchaser of the letter of credit takes the instrument for value even though it has yet to perform under the letter of credit. This is because, like a negotiable instrument, an ***irrevocable commitment to a third person*** is a commitment that cannot be rescinded in the event that the holder learns of a claim, defense, or claim in recoupment to the instrument in return for which the holder had given his commitment.

H. Taking for value by collecting bank: A collecting bank takes an item for value by acquiring a security interest in the item under Article 4. U.C.C. §4-211.

1. **Manner of acquiring a security interest:** A collecting bank acquires a security interest in an item and any accompanying documents or the proceeds of either the item or the documents:

   ■ in the case of an item deposited in an account to the extent to which credit given for the item has been withdrawn or applied;

   ■ in the case of an item for which it has been given credit available for withdrawal as of right, to the extent of the credit given whether or not the credit is drawn on or there is a right of charge-back; or

   ■ if it makes an advance on, or against, the item. U.C.C. §4-210(a).

   Rationale: U.C.C. §4-210 grants a security interest to a collecting bank specifically to encourage the bank to give its customers immediate use of funds represented by the deposited item. By allowing its customer to draw against the uncollected funds, the collecting bank may become a holder in due course and therefore recover from the drawer of the item despite any defense she may have against the customer.

2. **U.C.C. §4-210 not exclusive:** A collecting bank may also acquire a security interest under Article 9 or by other means.

3. **To extent credit given has been withdrawn or applied:** The collecting bank only acquires a security interest to the extent that the bank allows the customer to use the funds.

4. **Applies to debt of customer:** A collecting bank also acquires a security interest when it applies the item in part, or in full, payment of a debt owed to it by its customer. U.C.C. §4-210(a)(1).

   Example: Assume that at the time that a check in the amount of $5,000 is deposited in the customer's account, the account is overdrawn in the amount of $3,000. If the bank applies the check to the $3,000 overdraft, the collecting bank has a security interest in the check in the amount of $3,000.

5. **Withdrawal as a matter of right:** If the credit given for the item is available for withdrawal as a matter of right, the collecting bank has a security interest in the item whether or not the credit is drawn on or there is a right of charge-back. U.C.C. §4-210(a)(2).

   Example: The bank may have an arrangement with its customer under which the customer has the right to draw on funds that have not yet been collected by the bank or the bank may have a duty under U.C.C. §4-215(e) or under Regulation CC to allow the customer to draw on uncollected funds. Because the bank, whether or not the check is good, may be forced to allow its customer to withdraw the funds, the bank is at risk even though it has not yet actually released the funds.

6. **Makes advance against item:** When the bank makes an advance against the item, a security interest arises whether or not the item is deposited into the customer's account. U.C.C. §4-210(a).

7. **Simultaneous deposits:** When credits given for several items deposited at one time, or pursuant to a single agreement, are withdrawn or applied in part, the bank's security interest remains on all the items, any accompanying documents, or the proceeds of either. U.C.C. §4-210(b).

   Example: Assume that when the customer's account contains no funds, the customer simultaneously deposits five items in the amounts of $1,000, $2,000, $3,000, $4,000, and $5,000. The customer withdraws $3,000. The bank has a security interest on each of the five items to the extent of $3,000. As soon as $3,000 is collected from any of the items, the bank is made whole and the security interest in all the items is extinguished.

8. **Order withdrawn when deposits not simultaneous:** Credits first given are deemed to be first drawn on. U.C.C. §4-210(b). Thus, when items are not deposited simultaneously, the security interest attaches to the items in the order in which they were deposited.

   Example: Assume that the items in our last example were each deposited on different days in the order in which they are listed. Of the $3,000 withdrawn, the first $1,000 would be deemed to have been withdrawn against the $1,000 check. As a result, the bank would have a security interest in the check for its entire face amount of $1,000. The remaining $2,000 would be deemed to have been withdrawn against the second check deposited, the $2,000 check. The bank would then have a security interest in the $2,000 check for its entire face amount. The bank would have no security interest in the remaining three checks.

IV. GOOD FAITH

A. **Definition:** *Good faith* is defined as "honesty in fact and the observance of reasonable commercial standards of fair dealing." U.C.C. §3-103(a)(4). [[Rev] U.C.C. §3-103(a)(6); [Rev] U.C.C. §1-201(b)(20).] This standard is partially subjective and partially objective.

B. **Subjective element:** The subjective part of the standard is found in the requirement that the particular holder be honest in fact in the transaction.

   Example: Assume that a very naive person is approached on the street by a person who, in offering to sell him a $1,000 paycheck for $300 tells the naive prospective purchaser that his baby was sick and that the seller needed cash immediately to have the baby admitted into the hospital. If the naive person, in purchasing the check, truly believes the story, the purchase would be in good faith, despite the fact that no other person in the world may have believed the story.

   Note: Although the failure to inquire into suspicious circumstances does not, by itself, amount to a lack of good faith, the facts may be so suspicious that the trier of fact will not believe the holder's assertion that he was honest in fact.

   Example: Absent a plausible justification for such a large discount, when a $3,000 note is purchased by the holder for $500, the trier of fact may not believe the holder's assertion that he was unaware of any defect in the transaction.

   Note: When the trier of fact concludes that the holder desired to evade the knowledge that an investigation would disclose, the holder may be found to have lacked good faith.

C. **Objective element:** The objective element of good faith requires "the observance of reasonable commercial standards of fair dealing." U.C.C. §3-103(a)(4). [[Rev] U.C.C. §3-103(a)(6); [Rev]

U.C.C. §1-201(b)(20).] The duty of the holder to comply with reasonable commercial standards extends *only* to her obligation of fair dealing. The holder has no duty to exercise due care with respect to the purchase. U.C.C. §3-103, [Rev] Official Comment 4.

Example: A sinister-looking character named Simon asks a bank officer at Bank of Gotham to cash a $2,000 paycheck payable to, and indorsed by, one of the bank's own customers. Simon has no account at the bank and presents no identification to the officer. The officer, believing Simon's story that he had lost his wallet, cashes the check. Even though the officer was negligent, the officer was not attempting to obtain an unfair advantage for the bank and therefore acted in good faith. If, instead, the officer agreed to cash the check only at a substantial discount, the bank would have failed to observe reasonable commercial standards of fair dealing. By purchasing the check at a large discount, the bank officer would have attempted to profit at its customer's expense.

Note: A holder may lack good faith even though she has no notice of a claim or defense. Although the bank had no notice or knowledge that the instrument was stolen, it did not act in good faith.

V. NOTICE

A. **Notice of infirmities:** A holder cannot become a holder in due course if he has notice of the following infirmities in the instrument or in any underlying transaction in which the instrument was issued or negotiated:

- the instrument has been forged or altered;
- the instrument is irregular or incomplete;
- the instrument has been dishonored or is overdue;
- there is a claim to the instrument; or
- any party has a defense or claim in recoupment to the instrument.

B. **Notice need not relate to defense or claim raised:** A purchaser who has notice of a proscribed fact is completely denied holder-in-due-course status and, therefore, takes subject to all claims, defenses, and claims in recoupment whether or not related to the defense or claim of which she has notice.

Example: If the purchaser knows that there is a small breach of warranty claim in recoupment that could be asserted by the maker against the payee, she also takes subject to an unrelated third-party claim of ownership of the instrument.

C. **When notice effective:** For notice to be effective, it must be received at such time and manner as to give the purchaser a reasonable opportunity to act on it. U.C.C. §3-302(f).

D. **Effect of subsequent notice:** Once a purchaser becomes a holder in due course, notice subsequently obtained does not destroy his holder-in-due-course status.

E. **When notice imputed to organization:** Notice to an organization is effective for a particular transaction from the earlier of the time the notice either (a) is brought to the attention of the individual conducting the transaction or (b) should have been brought to his attention had the organization exercised due diligence. U.C.C. §1-201(27). [[Rev] U.C.C. §1-202(f).]

1. **Organization:** "Organization" is defined as including "a corporation, government or governmental subdivision or agency, business trust, estate, trust, partnership or association, two or more persons having a joint or common interest, or any other legal or commercial entity." U.C.C. §1-201(28). [[Rev] U.C.C. §1-201(b)(25).]

   Note: The same rules should also apply when the represented person is an individual.

2. **Due diligence:** Due diligence requires (1) that the organization maintain reasonable routines for the communication of significant information from individuals who have the duty to forward information to the person conducting the transaction and (2) reasonable compliance with the procedures established.

   a. **Duty to forward information:** Two groups of individuals are required to forward information that they have received.

      i. **Part of regular duties:** The first group are those individuals who have actual authority, as part of their regular duties, to receive and communicate such information. U.C.C. §1-201(27). [[Rev] U.C.C. §1-202(f).]

         Example: A bank teller, the bank president, or a receptionist, but not a janitor or a security guard, would seem to have, as part of his or her duties, the obligation to forward any type of mail or other notification he or she receives.

      ii. **Reason to know of importance:** The second group includes any person who has reason to know of the transaction and that the transaction would be materially affected by the information. U.C.C. §1-201(27). [[Rev] U.C.C. §1-202(f).]

   b. **Reasonable routines:** The organization must have reasonable routines established for the forwarding of relevant information.

      Example: If it is a reasonable business practice to deliver mail twice a day, the individual conducting the transaction, and thus the organization, is deemed to obtain notice when that individual receives the mail and has had a reasonable time to review the mail, and not when the mail was first delivered to the mail room.

      Example: If an officer of a bank learns that a person has just attempted to sell a stolen certificate of deposit to a neighboring bank, the officer should inform the tellers of this fact immediately rather than through interoffice mail the next day. In this case, the teller should be deemed to have notice of the theft shortly after the officer learned of it.

   c. **Reasonable compliance:** As long as the organization is in reasonable compliance with its established procedures, notice will not be imputed to the organization until the information actually reaches the party conducting the transaction. If there are no established procedures or if the established procedures are not generally followed, notice will be effective from the moment that the information would have reached the party conducting the transaction had reasonable procedures been in place at the time.

      Example: If the organization has a reasonable routine for distributing mail, notice will be effective only when a misplaced letter is actually delivered and not when it should have been delivered had it not been misplaced.

F. Manner of obtaining notice: A purchaser may obtain notice in three possible ways:

■ actual knowledge of the infirmity;

■ receipt of notification of the infirmity; or

■ from all the facts and circumstances known to him at the time in question he has reason to know that the infirmity exists. U.C.C. §1-201(25)(a)-(c). [[Rev] U.C.C. §1-202(a).]

1. **Actual knowledge:** A purchaser has actual knowledge of an infirmity when she is subjectively aware of the existence of the claim, defense, or claim in recoupment.

2. **Notification:** A person receives a notice or notification when (1) it comes to his attention or (2) it is duly delivered at the place of business through which the contract was made or at any other place held out by him as the place for receipt of such communications. U.C.C. §1-201(26). [[Rev] U.C.C. §1-202(e).]

    a. **Effective even if not read:** Notification is effective even if the holder did not actually read the notification and thereby acquire actual knowledge of the claim, defense, or claim in recoupment.

        Example: If a letter informing the purchaser of a defense is delivered to the purchaser's office, the purchaser is deemed to have notice of the defense even though he never reads the letter.

    b. **Notification on receipt:** A purchaser receives a notice or notification when it is duly delivered to either (a) the place of business through which the contract was made or (b) any other place held out by the purchaser as the place of receipt for such communications. U.C.C. §1-201(26)(b).

        Note: One's home address or post office box should be found to be a place held out by the purchaser as the place for receipt of such communications.

3. **Reason to know:** A purchaser may also have notice of an infirmity if, from all of the facts and circumstances known to the person at the time in question, he has reason to know that the infirmity exists. U.C.C. §1-201(25)(c). [[Rev] U.C.C. §1-202(a)(3).]

    a. **Subjective element:** There is a subjective element to the standard in that the test is whether "from all the facts and circumstances *known*" *to the person* [emphasis added], the purchaser has reason to know of the infirmity. These facts and circumstances include, among others, those comprising the claim, defense, or claim in recoupment; the reliability of the source of the information; the purchaser's knowledge of the business or type of transaction involved; and any facts the purchaser discovers from his own investigation.

        Example: An attorney may have reason to know of a defense under circumstances in which an elderly widow who has never engaged in a business transaction might not.

    b. **Two tests:** Two tests have been adopted by courts for determining whether a purchaser has *reason to know* of a claim, defense, or claim in recoupment.

        i. **Inferable knowledge test:** A majority of courts have adopted the "inferable knowledge" test. Under the inferable knowledge test, a person has reason to know of a claim, claim in recoupment, or defense only if the only reasonable conclusion she could reach from the facts known to her is that the claim, claim in recoupment, or defense exists. She has no duty to inquire into suspicious circumstances. The holder may assume an innocent explanation for a suspicious circumstance.

    ii. **Duty to inquire test:** The duty to inquire test is whether a reasonable person, considering all the facts and circumstances known to the purchaser, would have further investigated and thereby discovered the existence of the claim, defense, or claim in recoupment. This test is an objective test allowing the court to determine whether the holder, as a reasonable person, should have, through the exercise of reasonable diligence, discovered the defense, claim, or claim in recoupment. The purchaser must investigate to determine whether the suspicious circumstances indicate that some infirmity exists in the instrument or underlying transaction.

G. **Notice of claim or defense:** A purchaser cannot be a holder in due course if she has notice of any claim to the instrument as described in U.C.C. §3-306 or of any defense or claim in recoupment described in U.C.C. §3-305(a). U.C.C. §3-302(a)(2).

    1. **Notice not obtained from public filing:** Public filing or recording of a document does not, by itself, constitute notice of a defense, claim in recoupment, or claim to the instrument. U.C.C. §3-302(b).

    2. **Notice not obtained from executory promise:** Knowledge that an instrument was issued or negotiated in return for an executory promise (a promise to perform in the future) or accompanied by a separate agreement does not give a purchaser notice of a claim, defense, or claim in recoupment. Knowledge of an executory promise does not impose upon the purchaser the duty to inquire as to whether the promise has been performed. The purchaser has notice of a defense or claim in recoupment only if she has notice that a breach has already occurred.

    Example: Simply because Finance Company knows that Car Dealer has agreed to deliver a Mercedes 500SL to Maker does not impose on Finance Company an affirmative duty to determine whether the car has been delivered.

    3. **Notice from defenses from other transactions:** Whether the purchaser has notice of a defense to a particular instrument because she has dealt with the payee in the past and knows that many of payee's transactions are subject to defenses depends on which of the two tests the court adopts.

    4. **Purchase at a discount:** When an instrument is purchased at a substantial discount, whether the purchaser will be deemed to have notice of a claim or defense depends on which test the court adopts. Under the *inferable knowledge test*, the purchaser is not imputed with notice of a claim, defense, or claim in recoupment solely because of her knowledge of the discount alone. The holder has the right to assume, for example, that the large discount is a result of a substantial risk that the maker is insolvent or of the seller's urgent need for immediate cash. In contrast, under the *duty to inquire test*, a purchaser is required to investigate why the instrument is selling at such a large discount.

    5. **Notice of breach of fiduciary duty:** When a fiduciary in breach of her fiduciary duty negotiates an instrument for her own use, a question arises as to under what circumstances the purchaser is deemed to have notice of the breach and, therefore, takes subject to the claim of the represented person.

Examples: A treasurer of a corporation who writes a corporate check to American Express Company to pay her own personal credit card bill as well as a president of a small corporation who deposits a check payable to the corporation into his own personal bank account may be in breach of their fiduciary duties.

Example: Company that issued checks, on which the company's comptroller forged the signature, failed to allege that depository bank had knowledge of comptroller's breach of fiduciary duty, so as to support a claim for aiding and abetting the breach of fiduciary duty where the company merely asserted that bank knew of comptroller's fiduciary duty, but failed to allege that bank knew comptroller did not have company's authority to draw the checks to herself. Halifax Corp. v. Wachovia Bank, 268 Va. 641 (Va. 2004).

a. Definitions

i. Represented person: A represented person is the principal, beneficiary, partnership, corporation, or other person to whom the fiduciary owes a duty. U.C.C. §3-307(a)(2).

ii. Fiduciary: A fiduciary is "an agent, trustee, partner, corporate officer or director, or other representative owing a fiduciary duty with respect to an instrument." U.C.C. §3-307(a)(1). Fiduciaries include, among others, an executor of an estate; a guardian of a minor or an incompetent; any officer or other agent of a corporation, trust, or partnership; or an attorney.

b. Conditions to purchaser having notice: Certain conditions must be met before the purchaser will be deemed to have notice of a breach of fiduciary duty.

i. Represented person must make claim to instrument: If the fiduciary breaches her duty by negotiating the instrument for her own, or someone else's, benefit, the represented person has an equitable claim of ownership to the instrument or its proceeds. U.C.C. §3-307, Official Comment 2. A purchaser is deemed to have notice of a breach of fiduciary claim only if the represented person makes a claim to the instrument. Notice is not imputed to the purchaser if no such claim is made. U.C.C. §3-307(b)(iii).

ii. Taker must know that person with whom she is dealing is a fiduciary: The rules for determining whether the holder has *notice* of a breach of fiduciary duty only apply if the taker of the instrument from the fiduciary *knows* that the person with whom she is dealing is a fiduciary. U.C.C. §3-307(b)(ii).

Example: Assume that Jennifer Jones, the treasurer of Oasis Corporation, deposits a check payable to Oasis Corporation into her personal bank account at Bank of America. If Bank of America does not have actual knowledge that Jennifer Jones is the treasurer of Oasis Corporation, Bank of America does not have notice that Jennifer Jones breached her fiduciary duty to Oasis Corporation in depositing the check into her own bank account.

c. Three situations involving breach of fiduciary duty:

i. When instrument made payable to the represented party or to the fiduciary as such: A taker of an instrument payable to the represented party, or to the fiduciary as such, has notice of a breach of fiduciary duty if the instrument is (1) taken in payment of or as security for a debt known by the taker to be the personal debt of the fiduciary;

(2) taken in a transaction known by the taker to be for the personal benefit of the fiduciary; or (3) deposited in an account other than that of the fiduciary as such or of the represented person. U.C.C. §3-307(b)(2).

ii. **When instrument drawn or made by represented person or fiduciary as such to taker:** The same rules apply when an instrument is issued by the represented person, or the fiduciary as such, directly to the taker. U.C.C. §3-307(b)(4).

Example: If Jennifer as treasurer of Oasis Corporation writes a check payable to Mastercard in payment for her own personal credit card bill, the same rules apply as were applicable when the check was payable to Oasis Corporation itself.

Example: Steve Smith as guardian for Samantha Smith writes a check to Harry's Men's Store. If Steve attempts to pay for a suit with a check drawn on Samantha Smith's guardianship account, Harry's Men's Store should inquire as to whether this use of guardianship funds is proper.

iii. **When payable to fiduciary personally:** A different rule applies when the instrument is payable to the fiduciary personally, whether drawn by the represented person or by the fiduciary herself. In these cases, the taker has notice of a breach of fiduciary duty only if it has ***actual knowledge*** of the breach. U.C.C. §3-307(b)(3).

6. **Notice that an instrument is forged, altered, or otherwise irregular:** A purchaser cannot be a holder in due course if the instrument, when issued or negotiated to the holder, bears such apparent evidence of forgery or alteration or is otherwise so irregular or incomplete as to call into question its authenticity. U.C.C. §3-302(a)(1).

a. **Reasonable person standard:** Although the standard is whether the instrument on its face is so suspect that a reasonable person would question its authenticity, the purchaser's particular knowledge is relevant in determining whether the particular irregularity should have alerted the taker to the fact that something is wrong.

Example: Because a bank officer might know that the signature of a certain bank on a cashier's check is always printed, the bank officer will be deemed to have notice of a forgery if the signature is handwritten while most other purchasers will not be deemed to have such notice from the appearance of the check itself.

b. **Innocent alterations:** There will be times when even a clear alteration will not incite suspicion in a reasonable person.

Example: The crossing out of "1998" and the adding of "1999" on an instrument negotiated in January 1999 may indicate simply that the maker had forgotten that the year had changed.

7. **Notice that instrument is overdue or has been dishonored:** A purchaser is denied holder-in-due-course status if she has notice that an instrument is overdue or has been dishonored. U.C.C. §3-302(a)(2)(iii).

Rationale: Despite the fact that there may be many innocent explanations for why an instrument is overdue or has been dishonored, there is little commercial reason to encourage the purchase of overdue or dishonored instruments.

a. **When an instrument is overdue:**

    i. **Checks:** A check is *overdue* the day after the day demand for payment is duly made or 90 days after its stated date, whichever is earlier. U.C.C. §3-304(a)(1), (2).

       Example: If a check dated March 1 is presented for payment on April 1, the check is overdue if it is not paid by April 2. If presentment is not made by June 1 (90 days after the check's date), the check is overdue on that date.

    ii. **Other demand instruments:** Any other instrument payable on demand becomes overdue at the earlier of either (1) the day after the day demand for payment is duly made or (2) when the instrument has been outstanding for a period of time after its date that is unreasonably long. U.C.C. §3-304(a)(1) and (3). To determine if an unreasonably long period of time has passed, courts are instructed to look at the circumstances of the particular case in light of the nature of the instrument and usage of trade. U.C.C. §3-304(a)(3); U.C.C. §3-304, Official Comment 1.

    iii. **When date accelerated:** Once an instrument has been accelerated, causing the entire principal amount to be immediately due, the instrument becomes overdue on the day after the accelerated due date. U.C.C. §3-304(b)(3).

    iv. **Payable in installments:** Absent acceleration, an instrument payable in installments becomes overdue on default for nonpayment of an installment. The instrument remains overdue until the default is cured. U.C.C. §3-304(b)(1).

       Example: If a note is payable monthly in 10 installments on the first of every month and the first installment date passes without payment, the note becomes overdue. Once payment of that installment is made, the note is no longer overdue.

    v. **Not payable in installments:** Absent acceleration, an instrument not payable in installments is overdue on the day after its due date. U.C.C. §3-304(b)(2).

    vi. **Default in interest only:** As long as there is no default in the payment of the principal amount, the instrument is not overdue simply because there is a default in the payment of interest. U.C.C. §3-304(c).

       Rationale: This is because cash-flow problems often cause a maker to be late in the payment of interest and do not indicate that there is any problem in the underlying transaction.

b. **Purchaser must have notice that the instrument is overdue:** The purchaser must have notice that the instrument is overdue. For example, if the purchaser does not have notice that an installment was not paid, he does not have notice that the instrument is overdue.

8. **Notice of discharge:** Notice of the discharge of a party, other than a discharge in an insolvency proceeding, is not notice of a defense. As a result, a holder who has notice of a party's discharge can still qualify as a holder in due course. U.C.C. §3-302(b).

Rationale: In many situations a party is discharged from liability on an instrument under circumstances that do not cast doubt on the obligation of any other party.

Example: A co-maker may have been released by the holder and the release noted on the note. This has no effect on whether his co-maker is likewise discharged.

    a. Holder in due course takes subject to discharge of which he has knowledge: Despite the fact that he may qualify as a holder in due course, a holder who has notice of a discharge takes subject to the discharge of which he has notice. U.C.C. §3-302(b).

    b. Discharge in insolvency proceedings: If a taker knows that the maker, drawer, or acceptor (the people ultimately liable on an instrument) has been discharged in insolvency proceedings, the taker is denied holder-in-due-course status. U.C.C. §3-302, Official Comment 3.

VI. DENIAL OF HOLDER-IN-DUE-COURSE STATUS TO CERTAIN CLASSES OF PURCHASERS

A. Introduction: Four categories of holders, even after meeting all the requirements contained in U.C.C. §3-302(a) for holder-in-due-course status, do not thereby become holders in due course. Even though not qualifying as a holder in due course in his own right, such a purchaser is a transferee and therefore, under the shelter provision, is entitled to all of his transferor's rights. If his transferor was a holder in due course, the transferee is entitled to all of his transferor's rights as a holder in due course. U.C.C. §3-302, Official Comment 5.

B. Acquisition by taking over estate: A person who acquires an instrument by taking over an estate or other organization that previously held the instrument cannot by such acquisition become a holder in due course. U.C.C. §3-302(c)(iii).

Example: Assume that Jones made a note payable to Smith. Upon Smith's death, his executor takes subject to all the claims in recoupment and defenses to which Smith would have been subject. Smith's death should not deprive Jones of his right to raise his defenses or claims in recoupment.

C. Purchase in execution, bankruptcy, or creditor's sale: A purchaser of an instrument in an execution, a bankruptcy or creditor's sale or similar proceeding, or under legal process, cannot become a holder in due course. U.C.C. §3-302(c).

Example: When a state bank becomes insolvent, the state bank commissioner sells the bank's assets, including its negotiable instruments, at a judicial sale. Another bank or other financial institution may purchase all or some of these negotiable instruments. The purchasing institution realizes that, because of the bank's insolvency, it is quite possible that the obligors on the purchased instruments may have a claim or defense against the payee bank. For this reason, the purchasing institution does not deserve protection from these claims or defenses.

D. Purchase in bulk transaction: A person cannot become a holder in due course by purchase of an instrument as part of a bulk transaction not in the regular course of the transferor's business. U.C.C. §3-302(c)(ii). There are two types of bulk transactions:

    1. Liquidation sale: The first type of prohibited bulk transfer is a bulk sale of instruments for the purpose of liquidating the holder's assets in preparation for the termination of his business.

    Example: When Stereo Shack, a retailer of stereo equipment, decides to go out of business, it offers to sell to Finance Company all notes received from the purchasers of stereo equipment. The mere fact that Stereo Shack is going out of business should alert Finance Company that purchasers of stereos may have defenses to the notes being offered to it. Thus, there is no reason to encourage Finance Company to purchase these notes by offering it holder-in-due-course status.

Note: The purchaser is denied holder-in-due-course status regardless of whether it knows, or has reason to know, that its purchase is part of a bulk transaction not in the regular course of the seller's business.

Exception: A sale in the seller's ordinary course of business is not a bulk transfer.

Example: New Car Dealership, as part of its regular business practice, sells all notes obtained from the sale of its cars to a factor (a person who is engaged in the business of buying accounts, notes, or chattel paper at a discount) so as to acquire sufficient cash to purchase new inventory. Financing of this type is desirable and should be encouraged. For this reason, the factor, by its purchase, can acquire holder-in-due-course status as long as it meets all other requirements.

2. **Organizational change:** The second prohibited type of bulk transfer occurs when the organizational structure of the holder changes so that, even if the same actual entity retains the instruments, there has technically been a transfer from one entity to another. U.C.C. §3-302, Official Comment 5.

Example: When a partner is added to, or withdraws from, a partnership, the new partnership is deemed to be a different entity than the old partnership. For the new partnership to be the holder of the instrument, it is necessary that the instrument be indorsed from the old partnership to the new partnership. The new partnership should not, by the transfer, acquire holder-in-due-course status. Similar situations include the reorganization or merger of a corporation or the purchase by one bank of the assets of another bank facing insolvency.

Exception: An exception to these rules involves the purchase by the Federal Deposit Insurance Corporation (FDIC), the Federal Savings and Loan Insurance Corporation (FSLIC), or the Resolution Trust Corporation (RTC) of the assets of an insolvent bank. Under federal common law, the FDIC, the FSLIC, or the RTC may become a holder in due course of a note even if it purchased the note in a bulk transaction not in the regular course of the seller's business or acquired the note by taking over an insolvent bank. *See* Federal Sav. & Loan Ins. Corp. v. Murray, 853 F.2d 1251, 8 U.C.C. Rep. Serv. 2d 56 (5th Cir. 1988). U.C.C. §3-302, Official Comment 5. In light of O'Melveny & Myers v. FDIC, 114 S. Ct. 2048 (1994), the continued viability of this exception is questionable. *See* Calaska Partners Ltd. v. Corson, 672 A.2d 1099 (Me. 1996) (FDIC not a holder in due course when it takes notes in bulk transfer).

E. **Consumer notes:** The Federal Trade Commission (FTC), as well as most state legislatures, has enacted rules or statutes affecting the ability of a holder of an instrument, issued in a consumer transaction, to take free of the consumer's defenses. The following scenario illustrates the problem that the rule is intending to prevent. A thinly capitalized retailer or contractor, usually through sharp sales practices, convinces a consumer to pay for goods or services to be delivered or rendered in the future by executing a promissory note. The retailer or contractor immediately sells the note to a finance company. The services are never rendered nor the goods delivered. When the consumer attempts to raise failure of consideration as a defense, the finance company claims immunity from the defense by claiming to be a holder in due course. When the consumer attempts to recover from the retailer or contractor, the consumer discovers that the retailer or contractor either cannot be found or is insolvent.

1. **Definitions under FTC rule:**

    a. **Consumer transaction:** A consumer transaction is one in which a natural person uses a negotiable instrument (other than a check that is not postdated) to purchase goods or services to be used primarily for personal, family, or household purposes.

    b. **Consumer credit contract:** A consumer credit contract is an instrument that evidences a debt arising from either a loan by the seller to the consumer to purchase the goods or a loan from a creditor related to the seller to enable the consumer to purchase the goods. 16 C.F.R. §433.1. To be related to the seller, the creditor must have established a formal or informal relationship with the seller aimed at financing consumer purchases.

2. **FTC rule:** The Federal Trade Commission promulgated a rule aimed at preventing financiers of negotiable instruments from taking instruments free from consumers' defenses. A seller in the business of selling goods to consumers must include a legend in its consumer credit contracts that states: "Any holder of this Consumer Credit Contract is subject to all claims and defenses which the debtor could assert against the seller of goods or services obtained [pursuant hereto or] with the proceeds hereof. Recovery hereunder by the Debtor shall not exceed amounts paid by the Debtor hereunder." 16 C.F.R. §433.2(a), (b).

    a. **Where legend omitted:** A seller who fails to include such a legend commits an unfair or deceptive act or practice within the meaning of §5 of the Federal Trade Commission Act. The seller is subject to either a cease and desist order (an order forbidding it from engaging in such practices) or a civil action by the FTC. 15 U.S.C. §§45, 57b. Unless authorized by state law, a consumer has no private right of action for violation of this rule. *See* Holloway v. Bristol-Myers, 485 F.2d 986 (D.D.C. 1973).

    Note: Although a holder in due course takes free of the consumer's defenses, some courts may find that a person in the business of financing consumer sales has notice that the legend should have been included and, therefore, is not a holder in due course.

    b. **When legend included:** When the required language is included, the holder takes subject to the consumer's claims and defenses. The note remains negotiable, but there can be no holder in due course thereby enabling the consumer to assert any of his defenses against the holder. U.C.C. §3-106(d). Furthermore, the holder is liable to the consumer for damages up to, but no more than, the funds received by the holder from the consumer pursuant to the instrument.

    Example: Assume that Jean purchases home improvements from ABC Construction Co., in payment for which she executes a note for $3,000. The note is sold to House Finance. Jean has paid $1,000 on the note to House Finance and $1,000 to ABC Construction Co. If the note contains the FTC legend, House Finance takes subject to Jean's defense that the improvements were never made. Furthermore, Jean could assert her counterclaim against House Finance to the extent of $1,000 (the amount paid by her to House Finance), but not as to the $1,000 she paid to ABC Construction Co.

3. **State legislation:** Many states have also enacted legislation that preserves, to varying degrees, the ability of a consumer to raise defenses against a holder of the note. This legislation has taken diverse forms:

    a. **Uniform Consumer Credit Code:** The most influential legislation, which has been adopted by many states, is the 1969 version of the Uniform Consumer Credit Code

(UCCC), which provides that a seller or lessor in a consumer credit sale or consumer lease may not take, in payment, a negotiable instrument (other than a check). A holder is not in good faith, and, thus, cannot qualify as a holder in due course, if she takes a negotiable instrument with notice that the instrument is issued in violation of the UCCC. Regular financiers of negotiable instruments who know of this rule are, as a result, prevented from becoming holders in due course.

    b. All assignees take subject to consumers' claims and defenses: Some state legislation, including those states adopting the 1974 version of the UCCC, make an assignee of a consumer credit sale, whether or not a holder in due course, subject to all of the consumers' claims and defenses. Uniform Consumer Credit Code §3-404 (1974).

    c. Set time for consumer to raise defenses: Other states adopt statutory schemes that preserve the right of a consumer to raise defenses and claims against a holder in due course to the extent that the consumer gives notice of her claim or defense to the holder within a set period of time, either after her purchase or after notice of the negotiation to the holder. See, e.g., Ariz. Rev. Stat. Ann. §44-145 (1987) (a holder cannot be a holder in due course for a period of 90 days after receipt by the debtor of the goods or services).

4. 2002 amendments and consumer transactions: The 2002 amendments have added a new rule governing the ability of consumers to raise their claims or defenses in consumer transactions. A "consumer transaction" is "a transaction in which an individual incurs an obligation primarily for personal, family, or household purposes." [Rev] U.C.C. §3-103(a)(3).

    a. Instrument treated as if proper notice existed: In a consumer transaction, a negotiable instrument that omits the notice required by the Federal Trade Commission (or other similar legend required by any other applicable law) is to be treated as if the instrument had included the required notice. As a result, a consumer can raise the same claims and defenses that he could if the FTC language was included even though the instrument does not contain the proper notice requirement. [Rev] U.C.C. §3-305(e) and Official Comment 6.

    b. Nothing in [Rev] U.C.C. §3-305 limits right of consumer to raise claims: Thus, to the extent that a consumer protection statute gives the consumer the right to raise claims in recoupment or defenses, nothing in [Rev] U.C.C. §3-305 limits that right. In other words, [Rev] U.C.C. §3-305 is subject to any other law that establishes a different rule for consumer transactions. [Rev] U.C.C. §3-305(f) and Official Comment 7.

VII. DEFENSES, CLAIMS TO THE INSTRUMENT, CLAIMS IN RECOUPMENT, AND DISCHARGES

    A. Introduction: Any holder or person with the rights of a holder (collectively called a ***person entitled to enforce an instrument***) may recover from the obligor in the absence of a claim to the instrument, defense, claim in recoupment, or discharge. U.C.C. §3-308(b). In the event that the obligor has grounds to refuse payment, whether the person entitled to enforce the instrument may recover from the obligor depends on both whether the person entitled to enforce the instrument qualifies as a holder in due course and the ground on which the obligor seeks to refuse payment. Four categories of grounds may be asserted by the obligor in its attempt to defeat the person entitled to enforce the instrument's right to payment: defenses, claims in recoupment, claims to the instrument, and discharges.

- **Defenses:** A defense is any ground a party may have that is sufficient to permit him to avoid all or some of his liability on the instrument. For example, the duty of a buyer of goods to pay for the goods is usually conditioned on the seller delivering the goods. If the seller fails to deliver the goods, the buyer may raise failure of consideration as a defense to the note that he gave evidencing his obligation to pay for the goods.

- **Claim in recoupment:** A claim in recoupment is a set-off that arises from the same transaction out of which the instrument arose. In our example above, if the goods turn out to be defective and in breach of the seller's warranty that the goods are merchantable, the buyer cannot use breach of warranty as a defense to his obligation to pay for the goods. Once the goods are delivered, the buyer is obligated to pay for the goods notwithstanding a subsequent breach of warranty. U.C.C. §3-305, Official Comment 3. However, the buyer does have a claim for damages that can be asserted against the seller as a set-off against the buyer's duty to pay for the goods. This set-off is called, under Article 3, a "claim in recoupment."

- **Claim to the instrument:** A claim to the instrument is any claim of a property or possessory interest in the instrument or in its proceeds, including a claim to rescind a negotiation and to recover the instrument or its proceeds. When an instrument payable to bearer is stolen from the owner, the owner has a claim to the instrument.

- **Discharges:** Certain acts result in the obligor being excused from the duty to pay all, or a part, of his obligation to pay. These acts are called "discharges." For example, when the obligor makes payment of the instrument to the person entitled to enforce the instrument, he is discharged to the extent of his payment. U.C.C. §3-602(a).

B. Defenses and claims in recoupment to which all persons take subject: There are certain defenses to which any person takes subject whether or not the person qualifies as a holder in due course.

1. **Defenses and claims in recoupment assertible against holder itself:** The person entitled to enforce the instrument (sometimes called a "holder"), whether or not qualifying as a holder in due course, takes subject to any defense or claim in recoupment assertible against the holder himself. U.C.C. §3-305(a)(3), (b).

    Example: Assume that Bob issues a check to Carl's Auto in payment for a used car. The car has a defective transmission. Because it arose out of the transaction in which the check was issued, Bob may assert the breach of warranty as a claim in recoupment against Carl's Auto even if Carl's Auto is a holder in due course. However, if Carl's Auto negotiates the check to Don, who takes the check as a holder in due course, Bob may not raise his claim in recoupment as a defense to Don's action on the check because the claim in recoupment is not one assertible against Don himself.

2. **Real defenses:** Four defenses, called *real defenses,* are regarded as protecting such important interests that all holders, even ones acquiring the status of holder in due course, take subject.

    a. **Infancy:** To the extent that the obligor's infancy is a defense to a simple contract, it is also a defense available against any party (including a holder in due course). U.C.C. §3-305(a)(1)(i). The infant's right to raise infancy as a defense is subject to all the state's limitations on his right to defend against liability on a simple contract.

Example: If, in the applicable jurisdiction, a 16-year-old boy can defend against liability on an ordinary contract because he is under the age of majority, he may likewise defend against his liability on a negotiable instrument on the same basis.

b. **Incapacity, duress, or illegality:** Legal incapacity, duress, or illegality, to the extent that such defenses render the obligation of the obligor a nullity, are defenses assertible against any person. U.C.C. §3-305(a)(1)(ii).

Note: Unlike in the case of infancy, these defenses are real defenses *only if statutory or case law makes the transaction void.* A transaction is void when it has no effect whatsoever. In contrast, a transaction is voidable when a party has the option to either enforce or avoid the contract. If the transaction is merely voidable, the defense is a personal defense that is not available against a person having the rights of a holder in due course. U.C.C. §3-305, Official Comment 1.

i. **Incapacity:** Incapacity may include, among others, mental incompetency arising from the party's insanity or statutory incapacity to execute the instrument arising from a corporation's exceeding its corporate powers under its articles of incorporation or under state law. U.C.C. §3-305, Official Comment 1.

ii. **Duress:** In most states, the threat of physical injury makes an obligation void while a threat of economic injury (for example, to prosecute the obligor's son for theft) only makes the obligation voidable. U.C.C. §3-305, Official Comment 1.

iii. **Illegality:** Because the illegality must make the obligation obligor void, illegality will qualify as a real defense in few situations. In most situations, illegality will only make the obligation voidable. The type of illegality that most often constitutes a real defense is the use of the instrument to pay a gambling debt, as a bribe, or to purchase known stolen property.

c. **Fraud in the factum:** The obligor may raise as against any person the defense that he has been induced by fraud to sign the instrument with neither knowledge nor reasonable opportunity to learn of the instrument's character or its essential terms. U.C.C. §3-305(a)(1)(iii). This defense is almost never successful. To preserve the value of negotiable instruments and to encourage their purchase, an obligor is denied the right to raise fraud as a defense against a holder in due course if he intentionally or negligently signs a negotiable instrument. Where the obligor has been defrauded into believing that the writing that he signed is not a negotiable instrument, or at least does not contain the basic terms he believes it contains, he is relieved of liability if he has not acted carelessly in the transaction.

i. **Ignorance of instrument's character:** An obligor is ignorant of an instrument's character if she is under the impression that she is signing something other than a promise to pay money.

ii. **Ignorant of essential terms:** An obligor would be ignorant of the instrument's essential terms if she believes, for example, that she is signing a note payable in two years when, in fact, it is payable on demand. U.C.C. §3-305, Official Comment 1.

iii. **Knowledge:** In determining whether the obligor had either knowledge or a reasonable opportunity to learn of the character or essential terms of the instrument, the obligor's education, business experience, literacy, and intelligence are taken into consideration. U.C.C. §3-305, Official Comment 1.

    iv. Reasonable opportunity: The obligor cannot raise the defense if she, under the circumstances, should have discovered the character and essential terms of the instrument. If the obligor had the opportunity to, but did not, read the instrument, the defense will seldom be available.

    Example: If the obligor is illiterate and cannot read the instrument, he will not be able to raise this defense if a third person, such as a spouse or friend, was available to read the instrument to him. U.C.C. §3-305, Official Comment 1.

    Example: One of the hundreds of fans who, on any given day, ask Justin Timberlake for an autograph has Justin sign a piece of paper that, unknown to him, contains a promissory note. Because Justin cannot be expected to read the printing on every piece of paper he is handed for his autograph, Justin can assert the defense of fraud in the factum.

    v. Distinguished from fraud in the inducement: Fraud in the factum must be distinguished from fraud in the inducement. Fraud in the inducement occurs when the obligor, although knowing that he is signing a negotiable instrument, is defrauded into entering the transaction by misrepresentations concerning the nature of the transaction itself. Fraud in the inducement is not a defense against a person who has the rights of a holder in due course. It is, however, a defense against a person not having the rights of a holder in due course.

  d. Discharge in insolvency proceeding: The obligor's discharge in insolvency proceedings is a defense assertible against any person. U.C.C. §3-305(a)(1)(iv). An insolvency proceeding is defined as including bankruptcy regardless of whether the debtor is insolvent. U.C.C. §1-201(22). [[Rev] U.C.C. §1-201(b)(23).] The discharge is effective against all takers of the instrument because a discharge in bankruptcy or other insolvency proceeding is for the purpose of allowing the obligor to make a new start. However, the obligor has a defense only as to those debts that are actually discharged in the insolvency proceeding.

C. Defenses available only against a person without the rights of a holder in due course: The following defenses are available only against persons who do not have the rights of a holder in due course. All these defenses are cut off when the instrument is acquired by a holder in due course. U.C.C. §3-305(b).

  1. Ordinary defenses: A person not having the rights of a holder in due course takes subject to virtually any defense.

    a. Conditional issuance or nonissuance: A person without the rights of a holder in due course takes subject to the defenses that the instrument was not issued, conditionally issued, or issued for a special purpose. U.C.C. §3-105(b); U.C.C. §3-305(b)(1)-(3).

    Example: A note is delivered by John to Sam on the condition that Sam pay certain of John's bills. Sam fails to pay any of John's bills. Sam, despite failing to meet the condition, negotiates the note to Carol. If Carol does not have the rights of a holder in due course, she takes subject to the defense that the issuance of the note was conditional. U.C.C. §3-305(a)(2).

    b. Any contract defense: A person without the rights of a holder in due course takes subject to any defenses that would be available to him if the obligation arose out of an ordinary contract. U.C.C. §3-305(a)(2). These defenses include, among others: nonperformance of a condition precedent; want of consideration; partial or complete failure of consideration; and mistake, unconscionability, fraud, duress, illegality, infancy, incapacity, or usury. U.C.C. §3-303(b).

Exception: No consideration is necessary for an instrument given in payment of or as security for an antecedent obligation of any kind. U.C.C. §3-303(a)(3). The debt may be one owed by the obligor herself or it may be a debt owed by some third person (e.g., the obligor's husband, mother, brother, or a corporation of which the obligor is a shareholder). Because the instrument is, in effect, given in consideration for the debt, the obligor may raise any defense she has arising out of the antecedent obligation as a defense to her liability on the instrument.

Example: Assume that Karen has purchased goods from Sally pursuant to an oral contract under which Karen agrees to pay for the goods in 90 days. A week later, Karen sends Sally a check. Because the check was given in payment for an antecedent debt (the duty to pay for the goods), the promise contained in Karen's check is enforceable despite the absence of consideration. This conclusion is reached in a circuitous manner. U.C.C. §3-303(b) states that an instrument issued for value is also issued for consideration. U.C.C. §3-303(a)(3) then provides that an instrument is issued or transferred for value if it is issued or transferred as payment for, or as security for, an antecedent claim against any person, whether or not the claim is due. In our example, therefore, the promise to pay the check was supported by consideration even though Karen's debt was not due for 90 days.

2. **Claims in recoupment:** A claim in recoupment is assertible against any person not having the rights of a holder in due course.

Example: Assume that Buyer issues a note to Car Dealer for $10,000 in payment for a new car. Car Dealer transfers the note to Finance Company, which, having purchased the note after it is overdue, does not qualify as a holder in due course. The car has a defective transmission that would cost $1,500 to repair. Finance Company takes subject to the claim in recoupment that Buyer has against the payee Car Dealer because the claim arose from the transaction that gave rise to the instrument. U.C.C. §3-305(a)(3). If Finance Company had qualified as a holder in due course, it would have taken free of the claim of recoupment. U.C.C. §3-305(b).

Limitation: The claim of recoupment may be asserted against the transferee only to the extent that it reduces the amount owing on the instrument at the time the action is brought. U.C.C. §3-305(a)(3). There is no right to an affirmative recovery for amounts already paid. U.C.C. §3-305, Official Comment 3.

Example: Assume that Sally makes a note payable to Charley Contractor for work performed on her house. The note is payable $100 per month for 36 months. Charley negotiates the note to his cousin Vinny, who, knowing that Charley's work was faulty, does not qualify as a holder in due course. Sally pays $500 to Vinny. Sally now discovers that the work is faulty and has a breach of contract claim in recoupment for the entire $3,600. However, because there is no affirmative recovery for amounts already paid (the $500 paid to Vinny), Sally can defeat Vinny's action for the remaining $3,100 but can recover nothing from him. She would have to recover the $500 from Charley Contractor.

Limitation: As against the transferee, the obligor cannot raise a set-off from a transaction other than the one that gave rise to the instrument in that it is unfair to make the transferee bear the risk of wholly unrelated claims because the transferee was not a party to the unrelated transaction. U.C.C. §3-305, Official Comment 3.

Example: If Charley had also sold Sally a car that proved to be defective, Sally could not raise the claim arising from the sale of the car as a claim in recoupment in Vinny's action.

3. **Defenses and claims in recoupment of other persons:** With the exception of an accommodation party, an obligor may only raise her own defenses. She may not attempt to raise a defense or claim in recoupment of another party to the instrument, nor may the other party intervene in the action to raise the defense himself. U.C.C. §3-305(c); U.C.C. §3-305, Official Comment 4.

Example: Assume that David issues a check to Paul. Paul negotiates the check to Henry in payment for a car. Because the car has a defective transmission, Paul has a claim in recoupment against Henry for breach of the warranty of merchantability. David may not raise Paul's breach of warranty claim against Henry. Similarly, Paul may not intervene and raise his breach of warranty claim in Henry's action against David. If Henry sues Paul on his indorser's contract, Paul may raise the breach of warranty as a claim in recoupment. In this event, Paul is raising his own claim in recoupment to defend against his own liability.

4. **Claims to the instrument:** A person with the rights of a holder in due course takes free of all claims to the instrument. U.C.C. §3-306. A person who lacks the rights of a holder in due course takes the instrument subject to all valid claims of a property or possessory interest in the instrument or its proceeds, including a claim to rescind a negotiation and to recover the instrument or its proceeds. U.C.C. §3-306.

   a. **What is a claim?** Determining what constitutes a valid claim to an instrument is left to the subject jurisdiction's personal property law. In most jurisdictions, claims to an instrument include both equitable and legal claims of ownership as well as a secured party's right to possession of the instrument under her security agreement and the right of a lienholder to possession of the instrument. U.C.C. §3-306, Official Comment.

   b. **Legal claim of ownership:** A legal claim of ownership arises when the owner of an instrument claims that she has been wrongfully and involuntarily deprived of its possession.

      i. **Payable to order:** When an instrument payable to order lacks the owner's indorsement at the time it is lost or stolen, the owner will always have the right to recover the instrument because there can be no holder in due course of such an instrument.

      ii. **Payable to bearer:** When an instrument is payable to bearer or indorsed in blank, whether the owner of the lost or stolen instrument can recover it from the possessor depends on whether the instrument was acquired by a holder in due course.

   c. **Equitable claim:** An equitable claim of ownership arises when a prior owner claims that, although she voluntarily negotiated the instrument, she has the right to rescind the negotiation and regain title to the instrument. An equitable claim of ownership can arise from any ground that, under state law, gives the party a right to rescind the transaction in which she negotiated the instrument. U.C.C. §3-306, Official Comment. These grounds might include, among others, fraud, duress, mistake, illegality, breach of trust, infancy, incapacity, and nondelivery of the instrument.

    d. Third-party claims: When the party being sued on the instrument does not have a claim of her own, the obligor may not use the claim to defeat the holder's action unless the claimant is made a party to the action and asserts her own claim to the instrument. U.C.C. §3-305(c).

    Exception: A third-party claim may be asserted when the obligor knows that the holder is in wrongful possession of a stolen instrument. U.C.C. §3-602(b)(2). [[Rev] U.C.C. §3-602(e)(2).]

D. Discharges: An obligor may defend against her liability by contending that she has been partially or fully discharged from liability on the instrument. There are numerous grounds of discharge.

    1. Effect of discharge: A discharge is effective against any person except a holder in due course who was without notice of the discharge when she took the instrument. U.C.C. §3-601(b).

    Example: Assume that Joe makes a note payable to Paul who indorses the note to Hank. Hank releases Paul from liability on the instrument by a writing renouncing Paul's obligation to pay the instrument. Thereafter, Hank negotiates the note to Ralph. Paul's discharge is not effective against Ralph if Ralph qualifies as a holder in due course and does not have notice of the discharge when he takes the instrument. U.C.C. §3-601(b). In contrast, Paul's discharge would be effective against Ralph even if Ralph is a holder in due course if Ralph has notice of the discharge.

    2. Discharge by payment: An instrument is discharged (1) to the extent that payment is made (2) by or on behalf of a party obliged to pay the instrument and (3) to a person entitled to enforce the instrument. U.C.C. §3-602(a); U.C.C. §3-602, Official Comment 1.

        a. Discharge personal to party making payment: Discharge is personal to the person making payment. Only the person making payment is discharged.

        Example: Assume that Paul makes a note payable to Sam, who indorses the note to Sela. Sam pays Sela. Sam's payment to Sela provides him with a discharge of his indorser's liability. Paul is not discharged by Sam's payment. On payment, Sam may recover from Paul. U.C.C. §3-412.

        b. Payment must be made to person entitled to enforce instrument: Payment discharges the party obliged to pay only if payment is made to the person entitled to enforce the instrument. U.C.C. §3-602(a). As long as the person to whom payment is made is the person entitled to enforce the instrument, it is irrelevant whether the person entitled to enforce the instrument is the owner of the instrument. That is why payment to a thief of an instrument payable to bearer discharges the party making the payment. In contrast, the party making payment is not discharged if she pays someone who is not a person entitled to enforce the instrument.

        Example: Assume that because Paul does not know that Sam has negotiated the note to Sela, Paul pays Sam without first demanding to see the note. Paul is not discharged by his payment. Sam, not being in possession of the note, is not a person entitled to enforce the instrument, and therefore, payment to Sam does not discharge Paul. Paul remains liable to Sela, the person entitled to enforce the instrument.

        c. Discharge to extent of payment: The person making payment is discharged to the extent of the payment. U.C.C. §3-602(a).

Example: Payment of each installment of an installment note discharges the maker to the extent of the payment made. U.C.C. §3-602(a).

d. Adverse claim to instrument: Subject to certain exceptions, the obligor is also discharged to the extent of her payment to the person entitled to enforce the instrument even though payment is made with knowledge of a claim to the instrument by the true owner. U.C.C. §3-602(a).

Example: Sela defrauds Sam into indorsing a note to her. Sam calls up Paul and requests that he not pay Sela. Paul may ignore Sam's plea and pay Sela. Paul is not liable to Sam for conversion even if it turns out that Sam was the rightful owner of the instrument.

Rationale: It is not fair to the obligor to place him in the predicament of either being liable to the adverse claimant or facing a lawsuit by the person entitled to enforce the instrument.

i. Right of adverse claimant to prevent payment: The person claiming ownership of the instrument (also called the *adverse claimant*) has the ability to prevent payment. Payment to the person entitled to enforce the instrument does not discharge the person making payment if the adverse claimant's claim is valid and enforceable against the person entitled to enforce the instrument and either (1) the claimant obtains an injunction against payment and the obligor pays the person entitled to enforce the instrument even though he has knowledge of the injunction, or (2) the obligor accepts from the claimant indemnity against any loss resulting from the obligor's refusal to pay the person entitled to enforce the instrument.

ii. Injunction against payment: A court will not grant an injunction unless the person entitled to enforce the instrument, the claimant, and the party obliged to pay are all subject to the court's jurisdiction. In addition, the obligor is only denied a discharge if he has knowledge of the injunction.

Rationale: By requiring all parties to be present, the court's determination as to whether the person entitled to enforce the instrument or the adverse claimant is entitled to be paid will be binding on all of the parties concerned. This eliminates the possibility of inconsistent results that might occur if each person filed a separate lawsuit against the obligor.

Example: Assume that Sam obtains an injunction enjoining Paul from paying Sela. The injunction denies Paul a discharge only if he has knowledge of the injunction. Until Paul has knowledge of the injunction, Paul is discharged by his payment to Sela. However, once Paul has knowledge of the injunction, Paul will be liable to Sam if Sam ultimately proves that he is entitled to rescind the negotiation to Sela and, therefore, is the true owner of the instrument.

iii. Indemnification of obligor: If the obligor accepts indemnity from the claimant, the obligor is not discharged if she pays in spite of the indemnity. However, the obligor has no duty to accept indemnity from the claimant.

Example: Sam asks that Paul refuse to pay Sela. Sam offers to indemnify Paul against any losses and expenses incurred in defending against Sela's action. If Paul refuses the offer of indemnity, he is discharged by his payment to Sela. If, however, Paul accepts the indemnity but still pays Sela, Paul will be liable to Sam provided that Sam has a valid claim to the instrument enforceable against Sela.

Exception: Indemnification of the obligor is not effective to prevent the obligor's discharge if the instrument involved is a bank check.

Example: Assume that Norma acquires a cashier's check from Bank of America for the purpose of purchasing a car from Rick's Auto. Norma discovers, immediately upon handing over the cashier's check to Rick's Auto, that she has been defrauded. If Norma has sufficient time to obtain an injunction, she could prevent Bank of America from being discharged by its payment to Rick's Auto. U.C.C. §3-602, Official Comment 1. Not having time to obtain an injunction, however, Norma offers to indemnify Bank of America if it will refuse to pay Rick's Auto on the cashier's check. Bank of America agrees. Bank of America pays the cashier's check by mistake. Despite its agreement to accept the indemnity, Bank of America is discharged by its payment to Rick's Auto. Bank of America may, however, be liable to Norma for breach of the indemnity agreement. U.C.C. §3-602, Official Comment 1.

Rationale: The exception for cashier's and other bank checks is intended to discourage an obligated bank from refusing to pay a bank check.

iv. **Discharge if no valid claim:** The obligor is discharged even if she pays in violation of an injunction or after being indemnified if the claimant does not prove she has a valid claim of ownership.

Example: If Sam has no right to rescind the negotiation to Sela, he has no valid claim of ownership and Sela is, therefore, rightfully entitled to payment.

v. **Discharge where payment to subsequent holder in due course:** Because a holder in due course takes the instrument free from all claims to the instrument, payment to a holder in due course discharges the obligor.

Example: If Sela had negotiated the instrument to Gary, a holder in due course, payment to Gary would discharge Paul, the maker, from liability to Sam even if Sam had a valid claim to the instrument. U.C.C. §3-306.

vi. **Exception for stolen instruments:** Even if the claimant does not obtain an injunction or supply indemnity, the obligor is not discharged if she knows that the instrument is stolen and pays the person entitled to enforce the instrument knowing that he is in wrongful possession of the instrument. U.C.C. §3-602(b)(2). [[Rev] U.C.C. §3-602(e)(2).]

Example: If Sam informs Paul that Sela had stolen the instrument from him, Paul is not discharged even if Sam neither offers to indemnify Paul nor obtains an injunction against payment.

Rationale: An exception is made for stolen instruments for two reasons. First, by denying the obligor a discharge, she will be less likely to pay a thief or a person holding through a thief. This will make it more difficult for a thief to profit from his activity. Second, it is usually a fairly straightforward factual matter as to whether a theft has occurred. This limits the possibility of inconsistent results in the obligor's actions against the holder and against the owner.

e. 2002 amendments: A new subsection (b) has been added to [Rev] U.C.C. §3-602.

   i. When payment to former holder discharges note: Subject to [Rev] U.C.C. §3-602(e), a note is paid to the extent payment is made to a person who formerly was entitled to enforce the note only if, at the time of the payment, the party obliged to pay has not received adequate notification that the note has been transferred and that payment is to be made to the transferee. [Rev] U.C.C. §3-602(b) and Official Comment 2.

   Example: April makes a note payable to May. May immediately transfers the note to June. Neither May nor June inform April of the transfer. April is discharged by her payment to May even though May is no longer the person entitled to enforce the note. Had either May or June informed April of the transfer, April would be discharged only by her payment to June.

   ii. Adequacy of notification: For the notification to be adequate, it must:

   (a) be signed by either the transferor or the transferee;

   (b) reasonably identify the transferred note; and

   (c) provide an address at which subsequent payments are to be made. [Rev] U.C.C. §3-602(b).

   iii. Demand for proof of transfer: Upon request, a transferee is required to seasonably furnish reasonable proof that the note has been transferred.

   iv. Effect of failure to provide proof of transfer: Unless the transferee complies with the request, a payment to the person that formerly was entitled to enforce the note results in the obligor's discharge even if the obligor has received a notification of the transfer. [Rev] U.C.C. §3-602(b).

   v. Imputed notice of payment: [Rev] U.C.C. §3-602(d) provides that a transferee, or any party that has acquired rights in the instrument directly or indirectly from a transferee, is deemed to have notice of any payment that is made under [Rev] U.C.C. §3-602(b) between the date that the note is transferred to the transferee and before the party obliged to pay the note receives adequate notification of the transfer. It does not matter that the transferee is, or is not, a holder in due course.

   Example: In the example above, June is deemed to have notice of the payment to May because the payment was made before April was notified of the transfer. It does not matter that June purchased the note in a transaction by which June became a holder in due course. June should have notified April of the transfer. By failing to do so, June misled April into believing that May was still the person entitled to payment of the note.

3. Discharge by tender of payment: A tender of payment is an offer to make payment coupled with the willingness and ability to immediately transfer the money. There is no legitimate reason for the person entitled to enforce an instrument to refuse to accept a tender of payment of the instrument on its due date.

a. Tender discharges obligation to pay interest: An effective tender of payment discharges the obligation of the obligor to pay interest accruing after the due date on the amount tendered. U.C.C. §3-603(c).

Exception: The person entitled to enforce the instrument may refuse a tender of payment before the instrument is due if she is not paid the full interest due under the instrument.

Example: James makes a note in the principal sum of $10,000 with interest at 15 percent per annum payable in 6 years. The next year the rate of interest drops to 6 percent. James has no right to pay the note off unless he pays all of the agreed-on interest. The holder bargained for the right to be paid the full interest for the duration of the term of the instrument and is entitled to be paid such interest. U.C.C. §3-603(b).

b. **Indorsers and accommodation parties discharged:** Upon the holder's refusal of the obligor's tender, an indorser or an accommodation party who has a right of recourse with respect to the obligation to which the tender relates is discharged to the extent of the amount tendered. U.C.C. §3-603(b); U.C.C. §3-603, Official Comment.

Example: Assume that Jane's cousin had indorsed the note as a favor to Jane. Jane, as maker, tenders full payment on the due date of the note. The holder, for some reason, refuses the tender. Immediately thereafter, Jane runs into an economic reversal and can no longer pay the holder. The holder then demands that Jane's cousin pay the note. Jane's cousin is not liable to the holder. The holder should not be permitted to deny Jane's cousin (or any other indorser or accommodation party) a discharge by refusing to accept the tender. No legitimate reason existed for the holder's refusal to accept the tender.

c. **Co-obligors:** The law governing tender of payment under a simple contract determines whether a co-maker, co-acceptor, or co-indorser is discharged to the extent of her right of contribution. The law generally provides that a co-obligor is discharged to the extent of her right of recourse.

Example: Assume that Bill and Bruce were co-makers of a note. Bill offers to pay the entire amount of the note. The holder refuses the tender. Because Bruce would have a right to contribution in the amount of one-half of the note in the event that he had paid the note in full, Bruce would be discharged in the amount of one-half of the amount due under the note.

d. **Requirements for tender:** A tender of payment must be made to the person entitled to enforce the instrument. Other than that, the manner and effect of the tender is governed by the principles of law applicable to tender of payment under a simple contract. U.C.C. §3-603(a); U.C.C. §3-603, Official Comment. The obligor need not tender the full amount of the instrument.

Example: Assume that John made a note to Bill in the amount of $1,000 payable with interest. John tenders partial payment in the amount of $500. At the time of tender, John owed $100 in interest on the note. Between the time of tender and the time of trial, additional interest in the amount of $300 accrued. John is discharged for $150, which is the amount of interest accruing after his tender on the amount tendered. He is not discharged as to the principal amount ($1,000), interest accruing prior to the time payment was tendered ($100), interest on the principal amount that was not tendered ($150), or costs or attorneys' fees.

4. Discharge by cancellation or renunciation: The person entitled to enforce the instrument may, if she desires, discharge any party to the instrument even though she has received no payment or other consideration for the discharge. The manner of doing so will usually be by cancellation or renunciation.

   a. Discharge by cancellation: A person entitled to enforce an instrument may, without consideration, discharge any party to the instrument in any manner apparent on the face of the instrument or the indorsement. The holder may cancel the instrument by, for example, tearing it up; writing "void," "discharged," "paid," or other such language on the instrument; or by crossing out the party's signature. U.C.C. §3-604(a).

   b. Discharge by renunciation: A person entitled to enforce the instrument may, without consideration, discharge any party to the instrument by renouncing her rights in a signed writing. The writing must evidence a present intention to renounce the rights rather than merely a promise to renounce the rights in the future. U.C.C. §3-604(a).

   Example: I could discharge you from liability on a note by writing, "I release Reader from liability on the note executed on January 1, 2003."

   Exception: A renunciation is ineffective unless the party intends to renounce her rights. The requisite intent may be proven by delivery of the renunciation to the party sought to be discharged. However, as long as the party intends to renounce her rights, the renunciation need not be delivered to the person discharged thereby.

   2002 amendments: The 2002 amendments have changed the requirement of a "signed writing" to a "signed record." [Rev] U.C.C. §3-604(a). A "record" is "information that is inscribed on a tangible medium or that is stored in an electronic or other medium and is retrievable in perceivable form." [Rev] U.C.C. §3-103(a)(14).

   Additional amendment: In addition a new [Rev] U.C.C. §3-604(c) has been added that defines "signed," with respect to a record that is not a writing, as including the attachment to or logical association with the record of an electronic symbol, sound, or process to or with the record with the present intent to adopt or accept the record.

   c. Discharge by surrender: A party is discharged on surrender of the instrument to the party to be discharged. U.C.C. §3-604(a). To constitute a surrender, the instrument must be returned to the party with the intent to discharge her. Possession by the obligor raises a presumption of discharge in the absence of a satisfactory explanation for the obligor's possession of the instrument.

   d. Unintentional, mistaken, or fraudulently procured cancellation, renunciation, or surrender: A cancellation, renunciation, or surrender of an instrument is ineffective if it is unintentional, unauthorized, procured by fraud, or mistaken.

   Example: Accidentally tearing or mutilating an instrument does not discharge the affected parties. There is also no discharge if an instrument is mistakenly marked "Paid" either as a result of a clerical error or because the person entitled to enforce the instrument mistakenly believed that payment had been made in full. In determining whether a mistake vitiates the discharge, the rules of equity come into play.

   Example: Assume that Mary makes a note payable to Gail, who negotiates the note to Hank. Hank's secretary, believing that Hank had told her that the note had been paid, marked the note "Paid" and notified Gail that payment had been made. Believing the note to be paid, Gail makes a new loan to Mary. Because of the mistake by Hank's secretary, Gail was induced to make loans she would not have made had she known that she may be required to pay Hank on this note. Hank may not assert mistake as a grounds for denying Gail a discharge after Gail has relied on Hank's notification that the note had been paid by Mary.

5. **Discharge of simple contract:** A party is discharged from liability on an instrument to another party by any act or agreement with such party that would discharge a simple contract for the payment of money. U.C.C. §3-601(a).

   Example: Although not effective as a renunciation, an oral agreement supported by consideration is usually sufficient to discharge a party on a contract to pay money. Similarly, satisfaction by means other than the payment of money also provides a discharge under U.C.C. §3-601(a).

VIII. ADMISSIBILITY OF EVIDENCE EXTRINSIC TO THE INSTRUMENT

A. **Introduction:** Subject to the parol evidence rule, an obligor's duty to pay an instrument may be modified, supplemented, or nullified by a separate agreement (whether oral or written) between the obligor and a person entitled to enforce the instrument if the instrument was issued or the obligation incurred either (1) in reliance on the agreement or (2) as part of the same transaction giving rise to the agreement. U.C.C. §3-117.

   Example: Assume that Mary issues a note to Bret in the sum of $1,000 in payment for the purchase of a car. Mary can introduce evidence in Bret's action on the note that they had a separate oral agreement that she be entitled to a $200 deduction if the car does not pass a smog inspection if the evidence is admissible under the parol evidence rule.

B. **Agreement as defense:** The agreement would be a defense available against any person other than a holder in due course who is without notice of the agreement. U.C.C. §3-117.

   Example: If Bret negotiates the note to a bank, the agreement may be asserted as a defense against the bank if it either does not qualify as a holder in due course or has notice of the agreement.

C. **Same transaction:** An agreement can be part of the same transaction even if the agreement was neither executed contemporaneously with the instrument or obligation nor referred to in the instrument. The transaction can be any transaction in which a party undertakes liability on the instrument.

   Example: If, at the same time that Bob indorses a draft to Carl, Bob and Carl agree that Bob will not be called on to pay the draft unless Carl is unable to collect from Abe, Bob's liability is conditioned on Carl's inability to collect from Abe.

D. **The parol evidence rule:** The parol evidence rule generally provides that no prior written agreement and no prior or contemporaneous oral agreement is admissible to vary or contradict the terms found in a writing intended by the parties to be the final expression of the parties' agreement as to those terms. Evidence of a written agreement entered into contemporaneously with the instrument is always admissible.

1. **Consistent additional terms admissible:** A negotiable instrument, by its nature, is seldom intended to include the complete terms of the parties' agreement. Therefore, the parol evidence rule will seldom bar introduction of additional terms that do not contradict the terms of the instrument.

   Example: An agreement giving the holder a right to obtain attorneys' fees will not be barred by the parol evidence rule as long as the instrument does not specifically provide otherwise.

2. **Conditions precedent:** Most courts hold that parol evidence is not admissible to prove a condition precedent to the obligation to pay. *See* Akin v. Dahl, 661 S.W.2d 914 (Tex. 1983) (prior written agreement under which the maker and payee had agreed that any note would be payable only on death of maker was not admissible into evidence); Metro Natl. Bank v. Roe, 675 P.2d 331 (Colo. Ct. App. 1983) (holder will look to the other obligor first for payment).

3. **Sham:** Courts differ as to whether evidence tending to show that the promise to pay is a sham or that the note would never be enforced against the obligor is admissible. *Compare* Grossman v. Banco Industrial de Venezuela, C.A., 534 So. 2d 773 (Fla. Dist. Ct. App. 1988) (maker may not introduce evidence that payee told him that he would not have to pay note) *with* Herzog Contracting Corp. v. McGowen Corp., 976 F.2d 1062 (7th Cir. 1992) (maker may introduce evidence that note was not intended to create legal obligation).

   Rationale: The courts that allow evidence that a note is a sham reason that the obligor is not attempting to change the terms of the instrument when the obligor attempts to prove that the instrument was never intended to create a legal obligation.

4. **Special purpose or conditional delivery:** Evidence that delivery of the instrument was for a special purpose or is conditional on some act or event may always be introduced. U.C.C. §3-305(a)(2).

   Example: An indorser may show that his indorsement was not to be effective until four other indorsers/guarantors also signed. *See* Long Island Trust Co. v. International Inst. for Packaging Educ., Ltd., 38 N.Y.2d 493, 381 N.Y.S.2d 445, 344 N.E.2d 377 (1976).

5. **Defenses:** Evidence of any defense may also be introduced.

   Example: Proof that goods were not delivered and, therefore, that there was a failure of consideration, does not attempt to vary the terms of the agreement.

6. **Ambiguities:** Evidence offered to explain ambiguities in the instrument is always admissible.

IX. TRANSFER OF INSTRUMENT AND SHELTER PROVISION

A. **Introduction:** When an instrument is transferred, the transfer vests in the transferee all of the rights of his transferor. U.C.C. §3-203(b). In other words, the transferee steps into the shoes of his transferor.

Rationale: Vesting the rights of the transferor in the transferee makes sense. It makes no difference which particular person is attempting to enforce the instrument as long as the transferee has no more rights than the transferor.

B. **What is a transfer?** An instrument is transferred when it is delivered by a person other than its issuer (i.e., the maker or drawer), for the purpose of giving to the person receiving delivery the right to enforce the instrument. U.C.C. §3-203(a).

   1. **No transfer until delivery:** Until the instrument is delivered, the intended transferee obtains no rights in the instrument.

   2. **Intent to vest rights in transferee:** The transferor does not have to intend to vest rights of ownership in his transferee. The transferor must merely intend, by the delivery, to vest in the transferee the right to enforce the instrument so that, of the two of them, the transferee is the proper party to enforce the obligation. U.C.C. §3-203, Official Comment 1.

      Example: If Joe delivers an instrument to Tom for the purpose of having Tom collect the instrument for him, the requisite intent is present. In contrast, if Joe asks his attorney to safeguard the instrument for him, Joe does not transfer the instrument to his attorney because he does not intend for his attorney to have the right to enforce the instrument.

C. **Right to transferor's indorsement:** If the transferee does not become the holder of the instrument because the transferor failed to supply a necessary indorsement, absent a contrary agreement and if the transfer is for value, the transferee has the specifically enforceable right to obtain the transferor's unqualified indorsement. U.C.C. §3-203(c).

   Rationale: The presumption is that, unless otherwise agreed, whenever a transfer is for value, the parties intended that the transferee become the holder of the instrument.

   Exception: Absent a contrary agreement, the transferee has no right to require an indorsement of an instrument payable to bearer. U.C.C. §3-203, Official Comment 3.

   Rationale: Because there is no need to have the transferor's indorsement to make the transferee the holder, the only purpose would be for the transferor to undertake liability as an indorser. Absent an agreement to the contrary, the presumption is that no such liability was intended.

   Exception: Absent a contrary agreement, the transferee has no right to require an indorsement of an instrument payable to order that is not transferred for value. U.C.C. §3-203, Official Comment 3.

   Rationale: When a transfer is not for value, the transferee is lucky to get what he already received and should not have the right to impose anything further upon the transferor.

D. **The shelter provision:** The most important aspect of the rule that the transferee obtains the rights of his transferor is a corollary rule called the shelter provision.

   1. **Transferee acquires rights of holder in due course:** Under the shelter provision, a transferee may acquire the rights of a holder in due course through a transfer even though the transferee does not himself qualify as a holder in due course. U.C.C. §3-203(b).

   2. **Same rights as transferor:** A transferee of a holder in due course obtains all of the transferor's rights including the right to take free of all claims to the instrument, defenses, and claims in recoupment to the same extent as would his transferor/holder in due course. U.C.C. §3-305(b); U.C.C. §3-306.

   a. Includes inherited rights: The transferee also is entitled to any rights the transferor inherited from his own transferor.

     Example: If Joe, a holder in due course, gave a note as a gift to Mary, who subsequently gave the note to Jane, Jane acquires all of Joe's rights as a holder in due course.

   b. Transferee's rights no greater than transferor's: Because the rights vested in the transferee are purely derivative, they can be no greater than those possessed by his transferor and are subject to the same limitations. The transferee obtains only the rights of his transferor as a holder in due course; he does not obtain the status of a holder in due course. He can only obtain the status of a holder in due course by meeting its requirements himself. The transferee takes subject to any claim of ownership, claim in recoupment, or defense to which his transferor/holder in due course would take subject.

     Example: Ellen issues a note payable to Beth, who qualifies as a holder in due course. Beth gives the note as a gift to Charles. Not having taken the note for value, Charles does not become a holder in due course. He does, though, step into Beth's shoes and may recover from Ellen to the same extent as could Beth. If Ellen has a claim in recoupment that is assertible against Beth, Charles takes subject to this same claim in recoupment. If, however, Charles gave value for the note and, thus, independently met the requirements for holder-in-due-course status, he would take the note free of Ellen's claim in recoupment. U.C.C. §3-305(b).

3. Exceptions to shelter provision: No transferee who has himself engaged in any fraud or illegality affecting the instrument can acquire the rights of a holder in due course through transfer directly or indirectly from a holder in due course. U.C.C. §3-203(b).

   Example: Hank defrauds Linda into issuing a note. Hank negotiates the note to Marla, who not having notice of the fraud, takes the note as a holder in due course. Hank repurchases the note from Marla. Hank, despite his purchase from Marla, does not take free of Linda's defenses.

   Qualification: A person who has not engaged in fraud can acquire the rights of a holder in due course even though he had notice of the fraud.

   Example: Georgia, knowing of Hank's fraud, purchases the note from Marla. Georgia acquires Marla's rights as a holder in due course.

E. Reacquisition by prior holder: Some unique issues arise when an instrument is reacquired by a person who previously held the instrument.

1. Reacquisition by negotiation: If the reacquisition is by negotiation, the reacquiring party thereby becomes the holder of the instrument.

   Example: Janna makes a note payable to Ace Business Machines (ABM) in payment for the purchase of a computer. ABM sells the note to Crest Financial. When Janna begins missing payments, Crest Financial requests that ABM repurchase the note. Crest indorses the note to ABM. ABM is now the holder of the note. U.C.C. §3-207.

   Note: Although a few courts have held otherwise, most courts hold that reacquisition of an instrument does not give the reacquirer his prior status as a holder in due course. He only becomes a holder in due course in his own right if he fulfills the requirements for becoming a holder in due course at the time he reacquires the instrument.

2. **Reacquisition by transfer:** If the reacquisition is by transfer only, the reacquirer would not, by the transfer alone, become the holder of the instrument.

Example: If, in our example above, Crest Financial forgets to indorse the note to ABM, ABM cannot become the holder until Crest Financial indorses the note.

a. **Right to cancel intervening indorsements:** To relieve the reacquirer of the largely unnecessary act of obtaining missing prior indorsements, the reacquirer is given the right to cancel any indorsement not necessary to its chain of title, thereby enabling it to become the holder of the instrument and have the right to further negotiate the instrument. U.C.C. §3-207.

Example: Assume that Crest Financial had sold the note to Home Finance, which transferred the note back to ABM. ABM may cancel its own indorsement to Crest Financial and Crest Financial's indorsement to Home Finance. By canceling these indorsements, ABM is once again the holder.

b. **Intervening indorsers discharged:** The reacquirer's cancellation of intervening indorsements discharges any indorser whose indorsement has been cancelled. By the cancellation, subsequent purchasers are deemed to have notice of the cancelled indorser's discharge. U.C.C. §3-207.

X. DEFENSES AND CLAIMS TO BANK CHECKS

A. **Introduction:** When a customer makes payment by a bank check, the person receiving the bank check assumes that she has the same protections as she would have had had she received payment in cash. To protect this sense of security, special rules govern the bank's right to refuse payment on a bank check when used in a transaction by its customer. U.C.C. §3-411, Official Comment 1.

Example: Jamie wants to purchase a car from Nissan World. Nissan World demands a cashier's check in payment. Jamie buys the cashier's check from Wells Fargo Bank. Jamie negotiates the check to Nissan World. Nissan World gives possession of the car to Jamie.

B. **Rules not applicable if bank uses bank check:** A bank will issue a cashier's check or teller's check to pay one of its own obligations much in the same way that a customer uses a personal check. When a bank uses a cashier's or teller's check for its own purposes, these special rules do not apply.

Example: If Bank of America wants to pay its attorney, it will issue a cashier's check to its attorney. Bank of America is treated as though it was an ordinary drawer on a personal check.

C. **Terminology:** The drawer bank of a teller's or cashier's check and the accepting bank on a certified check are called the *obligated bank*. U.C.C. §3-411(a). Cashier's, teller's, and certified checks are called *bank checks*.

D. **Rules governing obligated bank's right to refuse payment on a bank check:** The rules found in U.C.C. §3-411 attempt to strike a balance between discouraging fraud and yet maintaining the cash-like nature of bank checks, thus retaining, for the holder of a bank check, its benefits. The obligated bank retains the same right as a drawer of a personal check to raise defenses or third-party claims. However, certain penalties are assessed against the bank if it wrongfully refuses to pay a bank check.

1. **Penalty for wrongfully refusing to pay:** An obligated bank that wrongfully refuses to pay a bank check is liable to the person asserting the right to enforce the check for any expenses, including attorneys' fees and loss of interest, resulting from the nonpayment. U.C.C. §3-411(b); U.C.C. §3-411, Official Comment 2.

   Example: In our example above, assume that, for some reason, Wells Fargo Bank refuses to pay Nissan World on the cashier's check that Jamie purchased from it. Wells Fargo Bank's right to raise any defense is governed by the same rules that would apply if Wells Fargo Bank was an ordinary drawer being sued on its personal check. If, however, Nissan World is successful in recovering from Wells Fargo Bank either because Nissan World qualified as a holder in due course or Wells Fargo Bank did not establish a defense, Nissan World could recover from Wells Fargo Bank its expenses, including attorneys' fees and interest.

2. **Consequential damages:** The holder may recover consequential damages if the obligated bank refuses to pay the check after receiving notice of the particular circumstances giving rise to such damages. U.C.C. §3-411(b).

   Example: If Nissan World needed the funds to purchase another car for sale to a subsequent purchaser, Nissan World's loss of profits on this sale could be recovered as damages if notice of this fact was communicated to Wells Fargo Bank in time enough for Wells Fargo Bank to make payment to Nissan World thereby avoiding the loss.

3. **Bank's defenses to liability for expenses and consequential damages:** The obligated bank is not liable for expenses or consequential damages if its refusal to pay occurs in any one of four situations:

   - the obligated bank suspends payments (i.e., is insolvent);

   - the obligated bank has reasonable grounds to believe that the bank's claim or defense is available against the person entitled to enforce the instrument;

   - the obligated bank has reasonable doubt that the person is entitled to payment; or

   - the obligated bank is prohibited by law from making payment. U.C.C. §3-411(c).

   Example: If Wells Fargo Bank has a defense of its own in that Jamie had paid for the cashier's check with a forged check, Wells Fargo Bank would be able to raise this defense against Nissan World if Nissan World does not qualify as a holder in due course. Wells Fargo Bank is not liable for either consequential damages or expenses, whether or not it is successful in raising the defense, as long as the bank reasonably believes both that it has such a defense and that Nissan World is subject to the defense. U.C.C. §3-411, Official Comment 3. This requires that Wells Fargo Bank have reasonable grounds to believe that Nissan World is not a holder in due course. Even if Wells Fargo Bank was reasonable in its belief, because Wells Fargo Bank had use of the funds during the delay, it is liable to Nissan World for interest on the funds.

4. **Third-party claims:** The obligated bank receives no protection against liability for expenses and consequential damages if it unsuccessfully attempts to raise a third-party claim to the instrument. However, the bank will, more than likely, be indemnified from liability either through an indemnity agreement or, if the claimant obtained an injunction, through the bond posted by the claimant in the injunctive action.

   Example: Jamie believes that Nissan World defrauded her into purchasing a defective car. If Jamie has the right to rescind the transaction because of Nissan World's fraud, Wells Fargo

Bank could raise Jamie's claim as a defense to Nissan World's action on the cashier's check. U.C.C. §3-202; U.C.C. §3-411, Official Comment 3. Under U.C.C. §3-305(c), Wells Fargo Bank may raise Jamie's claim as a defense to its liability to Nissan World if Jamie defends the action for the bank by successfully asserting her claim. If, however, Jamie cannot prove that she has the right to rescind, Jamie's mere breach of warranty defense cannot be used by Wells Fargo Bank as a defense. Even if Jamie does have a valid claim to the cashier's check, if the cashier's check has been negotiated by Nissan World to a holder in due course, the holder in due course will take free of Jamie's claim to the check. U.C.C. §3-306; U.C.C. §3-411, Official Comment 3. The reason for this result is that if Wells Fargo Bank could assert with impunity what turns out to be Jamie's invalid claim, the cash-like nature of bank checks would be defeated. Nissan World would have gained little by taking a cashier's check rather than Jamie's personal check. As a result, Wells Fargo Bank is given a choice. If Jamie's claim turns out to be valid, Wells Fargo Bank has no liability to Nissan World or any subsequent nonholder in due course. However, if the claim is invalid or if a subsequent holder in due course acquires the check, Wells Fargo Bank is liable to the person entitled to enforce the check for expenses and consequential damages, as appropriate. U.C.C. §3-207; U.C.C. §3-207, Official Comment.

XI. FEDERAL HOLDER-IN-DUE-COURSE STATUS

A. Introduction: One exception to the holder-in-due-course requirements set out in U.C.C. §3-302 is the *federal holder-in-due-course doctrine.* The federal holder-in-due-course doctrine was developed to govern the holder-in-due-course status of federal agencies that acquire negotiable instruments. In particular, the Federal Deposit Insurance Corporation (FDIC), and the Resolution Trust Company (RTC) acquire instruments in two different roles when a bank fails. The FDIC, as a *receiver* of the failed bank, may manage and protect the failed bank's assets. The FDIC, *in its corporate capacity,* insures the depositor's accounts. All of the powers that the FDIC has regarding banks, the RTC has regarding savings and loan associations.

B. Federal law governs: Under the federal holder-in-due-course doctrine, federal common law, and not the Code, determines whether the FDIC or the RTC in purchasing notes is a holder in due course. *See* Federal Deposit Ins. Corp. v. Wood, 758 F.2d 156 (6th Cir. 1985).

Note: The status of the federal holder-in-due-course doctrine has been put into question by the United States Supreme Court's decision in O'Melveny & Myers v. FDIC, 114 S. Ct. 2048 (1994). The court in *O'Melveny & Myers* held that California law, rather than federal law, governed the issue as to whether the FDIC, as receiver for a failed California bank, could recover from a law firm representing the bank for malpractice and breach of fiduciary duty. Since the decision in *O'Melveny & Myers,* several federal circuit courts have held that the federal holder-in-due-course doctrine has been preempted by 12 U.S.C. §1823(e), as amended in 1989 by the Financial Institutions Reform, Recovery, and Enforcement Act (FIRREA). *See* Divall Insured Income Fund Ltd. Partnership v. Boatmen's First Natl. Bank, 69 F.3d 1398 (8th Cir. 1995); RTC v. Maplewood Inv., 31 F.3d 1276 (4th Cir. 1994); and FDIC v. Massingill, 30 F.3d 601 (5th Cir. 1994). Some state courts are now holding that whether the RTC, FSLIC, or FDIC is a holder in due course is determined by state law. *See* Calaska Partners Ltd. v. Corson, 672 A.2d 1099 (Me. 1996).

C. Federal holder-in-due-course doctrine: Under the federal holder-in-due-course doctrine (at least as it existed before *O'Melveny & Myers*), notwithstanding U.C.C. §3-302(c), the FDIC and the RTC could qualify as a holder in due course even when they purchased in bulk a failed bank's instruments. However, courts differed as to the precise requirements that they must meet to qualify as a holder in due course. Most courts seemed to require that the FDIC and the RTC take the instrument in good faith and without actual knowledge of any defense to the instrument. *See* Federal Saving & Loan Ins. Corp. v. Mackie, 949 F.2d 818 (5th Cir. 1992). Courts differed as to whether the FDIC or the RTC could be a holder in due course of an overdue instrument. *Compare* Federal Deposit Ins. Corp. v. Wood, 758 F.2d 156 (6th Cir. 1985) (the FDIC qualified as a holder in due course even though it took the instrument with notice that it was overdue) *with* Federal Deposit Ins. Corp. v. Blue Rock Shopping Ctr., 849 F.2d 599 (3d Cir. 1988) (the FDIC was not a holder in due course when it acquired an instrument that was overdue).

Note: The federal holder-in-due-course doctrine applies only to negotiable instruments. *See* Resolution Trust Corp. v. 1601 Partners, Ltd., 796 F. Supp. 238 (N.D. Tex. 1992).

Note: A transferee from the FDIC or the RTC obtains all the rights that the FDIC or the RTC had as a holder in due course under the federal holder-in-due-course doctrine. *See* Federal Deposit Ins. Corp. v. Newhart, 892 F.2d 47 (8th Cir. 1989) (when FDIC is granted holder-in-due-course status under federal common law, its transferee obtains the rights of a holder in due course).

D. D'Oench, Duhme doctrine: Even when the FDIC or the RTC does not qualify as a holder in due course, proof of a defense against the FDIC or the RTC was made more difficult by the ***D'Oench, Duhme doctrine***. Under this doctrine, defenses had to be based on documents and not on secret agreements. *See* Resolution Trust Corp. v. Montross, 944 F.2d 227 (5th Cir. 1991). Many courts required not only that any defenses be proved through the failed bank's formal and board-approved records but that the FDIC or the RTC had to have actual knowledge of the defense. *See* Resolution Trust Corp. v. Juergens, 965 F.2d 149 (7th Cir. 1992).

Note: The continued vitality of the D'Oench, Duhme doctrine was put into question by the enactment of FIRREA. Under 12 U.S.C. §1823(e), no agreement that had the result of diminishing the interests of the FDIC in any assets acquired by it (whether as a purchaser or as a receiver of any insured bank or savings and loan) was valid against the FDIC unless such agreement (a) was in a writing that was (b) executed by the bank contemporaneously with the acquisition of the note, (c) was approved by the board of directors of the bank, and (d) was reflected in the minutes of the board. Many federal circuits have held that D'Oench, Duhme, other than as codified in 12 U.S.C. §1823(e), has been preempted by FIRREA. *See* Divall Insured Income Fund Ltd. Partnership v. Boatmen's First Natl. Bank, 69 F.3d 1398 (8th Cir. 1995).

Quiz Yourself on
HOLDER-IN-DUE-COURSE STATUS AND AVAILABLE CLAIMS, DEFENSES, CLAIMS IN RECOUPMENT, AND DISCHARGES

8. Joan buys a cashier's check from Bank of America payable to Southwest Auto to purchase a car.

a. Is Joan a remitter? _____

b. Is Joan a holder? _____

c. Bank of America issues the check when it delivers the check to Joan. What makes Bank of America the issuer? _____

d. Would Bank of America still be the issuer if the check was made payable to Joan directly? _____

9. Joan delivers a cashier's check made payable to Southwest Auto to them.

  a. Is this a negotiation of the check? _____

  b. If the check is payable to Joan, what else would Joan have to do for her transfer of possession to be a negotiation? _____

10. Bill indorses a check in blank and delivers the check to John.

  a. What can John do to avoid the risk of losing the check while indorsed in blank? _____

  b. Does allowing John to convert Bill's indorsement in blank into a special indorsement affect Bill's liability on the check? _____

11. Assume that Allen issues a note to Target in payment for a television set to be delivered to him by Target. Target immediately sells the note to Finance Company.

  a. If the television set is not delivered to Allen, what defense does Allen have? _____

  b. Has the finance company taken the note for value? _____

12. Assume that Wedontcare Bank purchases the note that Allen gave to Target in payment for the television set by issuing a check payable to Target. After receiving the check, Target negotiates the check to a holder in due course.

  a. Even though Wedontcare Bank discovers that Target never delivered the television set to Allen, is it still deemed to have taken the note for value? _____

  b. Would Wedontcare Bank have a right to refuse to pay the holder in due course on its check if, prior to payment of the check, Wedontcare Bank receives notice of Allen's defense? _____

13. Assume that a customer opens a checking account at her bank with the deposit of a check in the amount of $5,000. Before the deposited check is collected from the payor bank, the collecting bank pays a $4,000 check drawn by its customer.

  a. To what extent is the depositary bank a holder for value of the check? _____

  b. Why is the bank not a holder for value as to the remaining $1,000? _____

14. A purchaser receives her mail at 9:00 A.M. The day's mail includes a list of stolen certificates of deposit. The purchaser does not open her mail and read the list until after she purchases a certificate of deposit found on the list. She makes the purchase at 9:30 A.M.

  a. If she has not in fact read the list before her purchase, will she be deemed to have had notice of the theft? _____

b. If the purchaser of the certificate of deposit reads the list at 10:00 A.M. and discovers that the certificate was stolen, does this subsequently discovered knowledge destroy her holder-in-due-course status? _____

15. A finance company or bank that regularly purchases notes from the same retailer may know of defenses previously asserted by other customers of the retailer.

   a. Under the "inferable knowledge" test, will notice of a defense be imputed to the finance company or bank in this situation? _____

   b. Would your answer change under the "duty to inquire" test? _____

16. Assume that Jennifer Jones, treasurer of Oasis Corporation, negotiates a check made payable either to "Oasis Corporation" (the represented person) or to "Jennifer Jones, Treasurer of Oasis Corporation" (the fiduciary in her fiduciary capacity) in payment of a loan that Bank of America *knows,* from the loan application, to be for her personal benefit.

   a. Does Bank of America have notice of her breach of fiduciary duty? _____

   b. Assuming that Jennifer Jones negotiates a check payable to Oasis Corporation to Mastercard in payment of her personal credit card bill, under what circumstances would Mastercard be on notice that the transaction was for Jennifer Jones's personal benefit? _____

   c. Assume that a check issued by Oasis Corporation and payable to Jennifer Jones is negotiated by Jennifer Jones to Bank of America in payment for her personal bank loan. Under what circumstances does Bank of America have notice of a breach of fiduciary duty? _____

17. Assume that Bob issues a check to Carl's Auto in payment for a used car and that the car has a defective transmission.

   a. Can Bob assert a breach of warranty claim against Carl's Auto if Carl's Auto was unaware that the transmission was defective? _____

   b. If Carl's Auto negotiates the check to Don, who takes the check as a holder in due course, can Bob raise his claim in recoupment as a defense to Don's action on the check? _____

   c. In contrast, assume that Bob had done business with Carl's Auto before. A few months earlier, Bob had purchased a truck for his business. The truck has defective brakes in violation of the warranty that Carl's Auto gave to Bob on the truck. Can Bob raise the breach of warranty on the truck as a claim in recoupment in Carl's Auto's action on the check? _____

18. Gullible Gil is told by Lying Larry that the land that Gil is purchasing contains substantial oil reserves. Lying Larry knows that this is not true. Gil signs a note in payment for the land. Can Gil raise Lying Larry's fraud as a defense against a holder in due course? _____

19. Assume an instrument payable to Carla is stolen by Ted, who forges Carla's indorsement and then sells the instrument to Jane, who purchases the instrument in good faith and without notice of the forgery or of any other infirmity.

   a. Can Carla recover the instrument from Jane? _____

   b. If Carla had indorsed the instrument prior to Ted's theft, would Jane be a holder, and take free of Carla's claim of ownership? _____

   c. If Jane sues Sam, the maker of the note, can Sam raise Carla's claim of ownership to the instrument? _____

d. If Carla told Sam that Ted stole the instrument from her, can Sam raise Carla's claim of ownership against Jane even if Carla is not a party to the action? _____

20. Jane loses her paycheck. Fred finds the check, indorses the check in Jane's name, and negotiates the check to Check Cashing Service, which pays Fred the face amount of the check less a small fee. Check Cashing Service has no reason to believe that Jane's signature is forged or that Fred was not entitled to cash the check. Is Check Cashing Service a holder in due course? _____

21. On March 1, Bill issues a check to Hillary. On March 2, Hillary goes to the payor bank, which refuses to pay the check. On May 15, Hillary negotiates the check to Albert in payment for legal services to be rendered in the future. Is Albert a holder in due course? _____

22. Deleyla makes a note to Car Dealer payable in full on December 1. On November 1, Deleyla sends a check to Car Dealer in full payment for the car. Car Dealer sends Deleyla a receipt for the payment. On November 10, Finance Company purchases the note from Car Dealer. On December 1, Finance Company demands that Deleyla pay the note. Can Finance Company recover from Deleyla?

_____

23. John Jones is the treasurer of Orange Computer Company. Every Sunday night, John takes his family to Chasens Restaurant, where he has a charge account. Chasens sends John a bill for the $2,000 he charged the preceding month. John writes a check to Chasens on Orange Computer Company's checking account. Although authorized to write checks, John has no authority to use company funds to pay his personal expenses. When the check is presented for payment, it is dishonored. Can Chasens recover on the check from Orange Computer Company? _____

24. Susan purchases land from Max in exchange for which Susan executes a note in the sum of $30,000. Bank purchases the note from Max for $25,000. Unknown to Bank, Max did not own the land. After discovering the fraud, Bank decides that it wants to sell the note. It sells the note to Scott, a con artist, who sees a quick profit. Scott pays Bank $12,000 for the note. Scott demands payment from Susan. Can Susan raise her defense of fraud against Scott? _____

Answers

8. a. Yes. Joan is a remitter because the check is payable to someone other than herself.

b. Yes. Joan, being the payee, is a holder because she is in possession of an instrument payable to herself.

c. Delivery of the check to Joan. Bank of America is the issuer because it delivered the check to Joan, a nonholder, for the purpose of giving rights on the check to Southwest Auto.

d. Yes. If the check was payable to Joan herself, Bank of America would have issued the check when it delivered the check to her. The drawer has issued the instrument in that the drawer has delivered it to the holder (the payee) for the purpose of giving rights on the instrument to the holder (the payee).

9. a. Yes. It is a negotiation of the check because Southwest Auto, now having possession of a check made payable to itself, becomes the holder of the check.

b. Indorse the check. In addition to delivering the check, Joan would have to indorse the check to Southwest Auto.

10. a. John may write over Bill's indorsement the words "Pay to John." The check is now payable to John, and he must indorse the check before anyone else can become its holder.

   b. No. By indorsing the check in blank, Bill undertakes the indorser's obligation. This obligation is not changed by the addition of the words "Pay to John."

11. a. Failure of consideration. Allen has the defense of *failure of consideration* because he never received the television set.

   b. Depends on if finance company gave Target anything for the note. Whether Finance Company has taken the note *for value* depends not on whether Allen received consideration but on whether Finance Company has given anything to Target for the note.

12. a. Yes. Wedontcare Bank gives value simply by issuing a negotiable instrument. This is because Wedontcare Bank itself is exposed to personal liability in that, even if it has a defense, it will not be able to raise that defense against a subsequent holder in due course of the check.

   b. No. Wedontcare Bank has no right to refuse to pay the check. The possibility that a holder in due course might acquire the check and thereby deny Wedontcare Bank the right to refuse to pay the check is the reason why Wedontcare Bank is deemed to have given value.

13. a. $4,000. The depositary bank is a holder for value of the check to the extent of $4,000, the amount of the deposited check on which the customer drew.

   b. Because the bank can debit the account for remaining $1,000. The bank is not a holder for value as to the remaining $1,000 because if the $5,000 check is returned unpaid, the bank can debit (charge back) its customer's account for the remaining $1,000. As a result, it only needs holder-in-due-course protection for $4,000. U.C.C. §4-210(a)(1).

14. a. No. The purchaser will not be deemed to have had notice of the theft before the purchase. A purchaser is deemed to have notice only when she has had a reasonable opportunity to act on the notice. Because 30 minutes after receipt of the mail is probably not a reasonable time within which to require a person to open up and read all her mail, the purchaser will not be deemed to have notice simply because she had received the notification before she purchased the certificate of deposit.

   b. No. Once the holder has given value, it is too late for her to do anything about the notice when it is finally received. As a result, the holder is still deemed to be a holder in due course.

15. a. No. Notice of a defense to any specific note will not be imputed merely from the fact that the finance company or bank had notice of prior complaints. Even if the finance company or bank knew of many complaints from other customers, such complaints would not indicate that there is a defense to the specific instrument at issue.

   b. Maybe. Under the duty to inquire test, a court may find that the numerous prior complaints gave rise to a duty on the part of the finance company or bank to investigate the transaction at hand. If the investigation would have revealed a defense, the finance company or bank will be deemed to have notice of the defense.

16. a. Yes. However, if Bank of America does not know that the debt is Jennifer's personal debt, the fact that it has knowledge that Jennifer is a fiduciary neither gives notice to, nor imposes a duty on, it to inquire as to the use of the instrument.

b. Mastercard would only be put on notice if it had actual knowledge that Jennifer Jones is a fiduciary and that the credit card purchases were personal rather than business related. Otherwise, Mastercard does not have knowledge.

c. Bank of America only has notice of the breach of fiduciary duty if it knows both that the check was used for the benefit of Jennifer personally, and that the check was not intended by Oasis Corporation to be so used. The difference in rules is justified because it is not unusual for the represented party to pay or reimburse the fiduciary by issuing a check directly to her. U.C.C. §3-307, Official Comment 4.

17. a. Yes. Because it arose out of the transaction in which the check was issued, Bob may assert the breach of warranty as a claim in recoupment against Carl's Auto even if Carl's Auto qualifies as a holder in due course.

b. No. Bob may not raise his claim in recoupment as a defense to Don's action on the check because Don is a holder in due course and the claim in recoupment is not one that is assertible against Don himself.

c. No. Because the transaction in which Bob purchased the truck was a different one from the transaction out of which the check was issued, Bob may not raise the breach of warranty on the truck as a claim in recoupment in Carl's Auto's action on the check. U.C.C. §3-305(b).

18. No. Because Gil intentionally executed the note, Gil, rather than a holder in due course, should suffer the loss. Gil had knowledge of the character and essential terms of the note that he signed. As a result, the fraud cannot be asserted against a holder in due course.

19. a. Yes. Carla can recover from Jane because Jane, lacking a proper indorsement by Carla, is not a holder, and therefore not a holder in due course of the instrument. Not having the rights of a holder in due course, she takes subject to any valid claim to the instrument. Carla, being the true owner of the instrument, has a valid claim of ownership to it.

b. Yes. Although Carla would have a legal claim of ownership to the instrument, Jane would qualify as a holder in due course, and would, thus, take free of Carla's claim of ownership. If, however, Jane did not qualify as a holder in due course, Carla would be able to reclaim the instrument from Jane. For example, if Carla was defrauded into indorsing the instrument, and Jane had notice of that fact, then Jane would not qualify as a holder in due course, and would thus take subject to Carla's claim to the instrument. Under these circumstances, Carla could recover the instrument from Jane.

c. No. However, if Carla intervenes in the action, Carla may assert her own claim. If the claim is valid and if Jane is not a holder in due course, Sam will be required to pay Carla and not Jane.

d. Yes. If Sam pays Jane notwithstanding his knowledge of the claim of theft, Sam is not discharged and remains liable to Carla. Because of this risk of liability, the obligor (Sam) needs to be able to defend against the holder's (Jane's) action even when the true owner (Carla) is not a party to the action.

20. No. Even though Check Cashing Service took the check for value, in good faith, and without notice of the theft, it does not qualify as a holder in due course. Jane's indorsement, being unauthorized, did not negotiate the check. U.C.C. §3-201(b). As a result, Check Cashing Service, not being a holder, cannot be a holder in due course.

21. No. Despite the fact that the check was dishonored on presentment by Hillary, Albert is not denied holder-in-due-course status because Albert did not know of the dishonor. U.C.C. §3-302(a)(2)(iii).

Because he purchased the check within 90 days of its date, the date of the check did not give Albert notice that it was overdue. However, Albert did not give value for the check in that his promise to perform legal services was not yet performed. U.C.C. §3-303(a)(1).

22. **Yes.** Although Deleyla is discharged by her payment to Car Dealer, U.C.C. §3-602(a), Finance Company, being a holder in due course without notice of the discharge, takes free of the discharge. U.C.C. §3-601(b).

23. **Yes.** Orange has a claim that it is the equitable owner of the funds because the funds were used in violation of John's fiduciary duties. Chasens would take free of this claim to the funds if Chasens is a holder in due course. Chasens would be a holder in due course if it does not have notice that John was in breach of his fiduciary duty by using a company check to pay his personal restaurant bills. This situation is covered by U.C.C. §3-307(b)(4). For Chasens to have notice of the breach, it is necessary that Chasens both know that John is a fiduciary and that the transaction is for his personal benefit. Considering that the only person who may know that the transaction is for John's personal benefit is the waiter, while the person taking the check is the bookkeeper, it is unlikely that Chasens would be deemed to have such knowledge. Under [Rev] U.C.C. §1-202, the bookkeeper is the person whose knowledge or lack thereof is relevant. The knowledge of the waiter would not be imputed to the bookkeeper because the waiter neither had a duty to communicate such information nor knew that payment of the charge account bill would be materially affected by such knowledge. Furthermore, Chasens gave value for the check in that it applied the check to an antecedent claim. U.C.C. §3-303(a)(3). Therefore, Chasens would qualify as a holder in due course and take the check free of Orange's claim to the funds.

24. **No.** Although Scott, having notice of the defense, does not qualify as a holder in due course, he is the transferee of Bank and thereby obtains all of its rights. Not being a party to the fraud, Scott is not disqualified from acquiring Bank's rights. U.C.C. §3-203(b). As a holder in due course, Bank (and Scott, its transferee) can recover free from any of Susan's defenses except for real defenses. U.C.C. §3-305(a)(1), (b). Because Max's fraud was not fraud in the factum, it is not a real defense assertible against a person having the rights of a holder in due course.

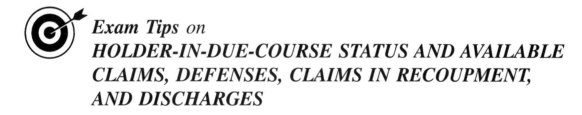

Exam Tips on
HOLDER-IN-DUE-COURSE STATUS AND AVAILABLE
CLAIMS, DEFENSES, CLAIMS IN RECOUPMENT,
AND DISCHARGES

☛ **Transferees:** Remember that even when the transferee takes an instrument (assuming it is payable to order) from the true owner, the transferee does not become a holder unless she acquires any necessary indorsement.

   ☞ Also note that if the transferee obtains notice of a claim or defense prior to obtaining the indorsement, the transferee can *never* qualify as a holder in due course.

☞ This does not mean that all is necessarily lost! Even though the transferee cannot become a holder in due course in her own right, she may acquire the rights of a holder in due course through the shelter provision. This would allow her to take free of any claim or defense as to which her transferor would take free.

☛ **Breach of fiduciary duty:** In determining whether a holder has notice of a breach of fiduciary duty, you should remember that the holder must have *actual knowledge* that the person is a fiduciary. In addition, the holder must, depending on the circumstance, *know* that the debt is the personal debt of the fiduciary or that the transaction is a breach of the person's fiduciary duty.

☛ **Breach and holder-in-due-course status:** Remember that it is possible for a payee to qualify as a holder in due course even though the payee has delivered defective goods or otherwise breached its contract with the maker or drawer. For example, a payee who sells a car to the maker may be a holder in due course even though she has breached the warranty of merchantability. Once the payee delivers the car, the payee has given value for the instrument. If the payee was without notice that the car is defective, the payee may qualify as a holder in due course. However, note that because the payee has dealt with the maker, the maker may raise the breach of warranty as a claim in recoupment in the payee's action on the note.

CHAPTER 3

NATURE OF LIABILITY ON INSTRUMENTS

ChapterScope _____

This chapter covers the nature of a party's liability on a negotiable instrument. It examines the liability of signers and transferors, the effect that taking a negotiable instrument has on the underlying obligation, accord and satisfaction, procedural issues, and the enforcement of lost or stolen instruments. The key points in this chapter are:

■ **Effect of signature on negotiable instrument:** The mere act of signing one's name to a negotiable instrument can obligate the signer to pay the instrument. However, there are differences in the conditions precedent to the signer's duty to pay depending on the capacity in which the person signs.

■ **Parties secondarily liable:** An indorser or a drawer is entitled to have the instrument dishonored by the maker or drawee before being obligated to pay the instrument. An indorser is discharged from liability when a necessary presentment or notice of dishonor is delayed.

■ **Transferor's warranties:** A person who transfers an instrument for consideration makes certain warranties as to the enforceability of the instrument whether or not the transferor indorses the instrument.

■ **Rights of surety:** A person who signs an instrument as a surety (called "an accommodation party" under Article 3) has certain special rights and defenses. Many of these same rights and defenses are available to an indorser.

■ **Effect of discharge:** Discharge of an instrument also discharges the underlying obligation for which the instrument was given.

■ **Procedure:** Several procedural advantages are available to a person maintaining an action on a negotiable instrument.

■ **Lost or stolen instruments:** Special rules enable the owner of a lost or stolen instrument to recover on the instrument.

I. LIABILITY OF ISSUER, DRAWER, ACCEPTOR, AND INDORSER

A. **Introduction:** The mere act of signing one's name anywhere on a negotiable instrument will, generally, obligate the signer to pay the instrument. However, the conditions precedent to a signer's liability vary depending on the capacity in which the party signs. A party may sign a negotiable instrument in four basic capacities: (1) an issuer of a note or cashier's check, (2) a drawer of a draft, (3) an acceptor of a draft, and (4) an indorser.

B. **Obligation of issuer of note or cashier's check:** The maker of a note or the drawer of a cashier's check (called the *issuer*) promises to pay the instrument according to its terms at the time the instrument was issued. U.C.C. §3-412. An issuer's liability is what may be called "primary." There are no conditions to the issuer's obligation to pay an instrument. He is liable to pay the instrument when it is due.

   Note: For that purpose, the obligation of an issuer of a cashier's check is identical to that of a maker of a note. Although a cashier's check seems like any other check, the issuing bank is both the drawer and the drawee of the check. This means that, just like the maker of a note, the holder will demand payment directly from the issuing bank.

C. **Obligation of drawer:** The drawer promises that if the draft is dishonored, she will pay the unaccepted draft according to its terms at the time it was issued. U.C.C. §3-414(b). Dishonor by the drawee must occur before the drawer is liable. U.C.C. §3-414(b). Liability as a drawer is not conditioned on notice of dishonor, as the drawer knows, or will find out soon from the drawee, if the draft is not paid. U.C.C. §3-414(b); U.C.C. §3-414, Official Comment 2.

   1. **Effect of acceptance:** When a draft is accepted by a nonbank, the drawer is treated as an indorser under U.C.C. §3-415(a), (c). U.C.C. §3-414(d). In contrast, the drawer is completely discharged when a draft is accepted by a bank. U.C.C. §3-414(c).

      Analysis: The drawer is discharged when a bank accepts the draft because the holder will look to the bank's assets instead of to the drawer's assets. If the holder wants both the drawer's and the bank's promise to pay the draft, the holder may achieve this goal by having the drawer indorse the accepted draft. In contrast, the drawer is not discharged if a draft is accepted by a nonbank because there is no reason to assume that the holder would be satisfied in looking to the acceptor's assets only rather than also to the drawer's assets. However, because the holder has, by presenting the draft for acceptance, impliedly agreed to look initially to the acceptor for payment, the drawer's obligation becomes the same as that of an indorser. U.C.C. §3-414(d); U.C.C. §3-414, Official Comment 4.

   2. **Disclaimer of liability:** A drawer may disclaim liability on any draft (other than a check) by writing, on the draft, the words *without recourse*. U.C.C. §3-414(e). A drawer is not permitted to draw a check without recourse because that would leave no one liable on the check. U.C.C. §3-414, Official Comment 5.

D. **Obligation of drawee:** The drawee is the person whom the drawer orders to pay the draft. The mere fact that a person is named as drawee of a draft does not, by itself, impose any obligation on that person to pay the holder of the draft.

   Analysis: A check or other draft does not, of itself, operate as an assignment of any of the drawer's funds held by the drawee. U.C.C. §3-408. The holder has no right to proceed directly against the drawee. The drawee is only liable to the drawer. The drawee is not liable to the holder unless the drawee accepts the draft. U.C.C. §3-408.

E. **The obligation of an acceptor:** When a draft is presented to the drawee for acceptance and the drawee accepts the draft, the drawee becomes liable as an acceptor. An acceptor promises to pay the draft according to its terms at the time of its acceptance. U.C.C. §3-413(a). Acceptance is the drawee's signed agreement to pay the draft as presented. U.C.C. §3-409(a). On acceptance, the acceptor becomes the primary party obligated to pay the draft. There are no conditions to the acceptor's obligation to make payment. Once the draft is due, the acceptor is obligated to make payment. If the acceptor fails to make payment on the date due, the person entitled to enforce the draft may immediately commence an action against the acceptor without giving notice to, or making a demand on, the acceptor to make payment.

1. **Acceptance vs. payment:** Acceptance of a draft must be distinguished from payment of a draft. When a draft is presented for payment, the drawee honors the draft by making payment to the person entitled to enforce the draft. Once payment is made, the drawee has no further obligation to that person. In contrast, when a draft is presented for acceptance, the person entitled to enforce the draft is not asking that the drawee pay the draft. Rather, she is asking that the drawee obligate itself to pay the draft in the future.

2. **Manner of acceptance:** An effective acceptance must be (1) in writing, (2) on the instrument, (3) signed by the drawee, and (4) either delivered to the holder or the holder must be notified. The acceptance may consist of the drawee's signature alone. Unlike the obligation of other parties to a negotiable instrument, an acceptance can become effective when the holder is notified of the acceptance even if the accepted draft has not yet been delivered to him. U.C.C. §3-409(a).

F. **Obligation of indorser:** An indorser promises that if the instrument is dishonored, he will pay the amount of the instrument according to its terms at the time of his indorsement. U.C.C. §3-415(a).

1. **What is an indorser?** "Indorser" is a catch-all category that covers anyone who signs an instrument in any capacity other than as a drawer, an acceptor, or a maker. A signature is deemed to be an indorsement regardless of the signer's intent unless the accompanying words, terms of the instrument, place of signature, or other circumstances unambiguously indicate that the signature is made for a purpose other than as an indorsement. U.C.C. §3-204(a).

2. **Two purposes of indorsement:** A person may indorse an instrument for two distinct purposes: (1) to negotiate an instrument and (2) to incur liability on the instrument. An indorsement can be made for any one or both of these purposes. An *anomalous indorser* is an indorser who is not the holder of the instrument. As a result, her indorsement, not being needed to negotiate the instrument, is simply for the purpose of incurring liability.

3. **To whom obligation owed:** An indorser's obligation to pay is owed to the person who is entitled to enforce the instrument or to a subsequent indorser who pays the instrument. U.C.C. §3-415(a).

   Example: Assume that a check drawn by Bob and payable to Jill is indorsed by Jill to Sally. Sally indorses the check to Grocer who indorses and deposits the check into his bank account at Crocker Bank. On presentment to Wells Bank, the check is dishonored. Because Crocker Bank is the person entitled to enforce the check, Crocker Bank may recover from any indorser, which includes Grocer, Sally, and Jill. If Sally pays Crocker Bank, Sally may recover from Jill. Jill's obligation runs to Sally because Sally is a subsequent indorser. However, Sally may not recover from Grocer because Grocer's obligation does not run to Sally; Sally is not a subsequent indorser. See Figure 3-1.

Figure 3-1

4. **Indorsement without recourse:** An indorser may disclaim liability on his indorser's contract by indorsing the instrument "without recourse." U.C.C. §3-415(b). An indorser may want to indorse without recourse when he is intending only to transfer title to the instrument and does not wish to incur any personal liability on the instrument.

Example: If a check is made payable jointly to an attorney and her client, the attorney may want to indorse the check so that her client can cash the check. However, because the attorney has no desire to become liable to subsequent purchasers of the check, she indorses the check "Attorney, without recourse."

Note: Despite indorsing without recourse, the indorser still faces the possibility of liability as a transferor of the check. A person who receives consideration for transferring an instrument makes certain warranties to subsequent parties.

5. **Dishonor and notice of dishonor required:** An indorser is not liable until the instrument has been dishonored and, unless excused, notice of dishonor is given. U.C.C. §3-415(a); U.C.C. §3-503. An indorser is discharged with respect to any instrument if a necessary notice of dishonor is not given. U.C.C. §3-415(c); U.C.C. §3-503(a).

Rationale: An indorser is not the primary party expected to make payment. Her contract requires payment only if the maker, drawee, or acceptor refuses to make payment. Thus, unless the instrument is dishonored by one of these parties, the indorser has no duty to pay. Because an indorser will not usually know that payment has not been made, notice of dishonor is made a condition to the indorser's liability.

6. **Discharge if presentment on check delayed:** An indorser is discharged if a check is not presented for payment or given to a depositary bank for collection within 30 days after her indorsement. U.C.C. §3-415(e).

Example: Assume that a check drawn by Bob is delivered to Jill on March 1. Jill indorses the check on March 5 and delivers it to Sally, who indorses the check on April 1 and delivers the check to Grocer. Grocer deposits the check in its account at Crocker Bank on April 27. The check is presented to Wells Bank for payment on May 3. Because the check was not deposited for collection or presented for payment within 30 days after her indorsement, Jill is discharged. However, Sally is not discharged. Although the check was not presented for payment within 30 days of her indorsement, it was deposited for collection within the 30-day period. See Figure 3-2.

Figure 3-2

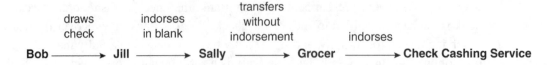

Limitation: This 30-day rule applies only to checks. A delay in presenting any instrument, other than a check, does not discharge an indorser.

7. **Liable in any order:** The person entitled to enforce the instrument may commence an action to recover from any of the indorsers, no matter in what order they signed.

Example: In our example above, Crocker Bank may recover from Jill without attempting to recover from Sally or Grocer.

II. PRESENTMENT, DISHONOR, NOTICE OF DISHONOR

A. Dishonor: Dishonor of an instrument is a condition to the liability of a drawer and an indorser. U.C.C. §3-414(b); U.C.C. §3-415(a); U.C.C. §3-502, Official Comment 1. An instrument is **_dishonored_** when the drawee, acceptor, or maker refuse or fail to pay or accept the instrument upon a proper presentment for payment or acceptance. When presentment is excused, dishonor occurs if the instrument is not duly accepted or paid. U.C.C. §3-502(e); U.C.C. §3-502, Official Comment 7.

B. Presentment: Presentment is a demand for payment or acceptance made by or on behalf of the person entitled to enforce the instrument. U.C.C. §3-501(a). A mere demand for payment or acceptance is sufficient to constitute presentment. Presentment for payment must be made to the drawee or to a party obliged to pay the instrument (the maker of a note or the acceptor of an accepted draft). U.C.C. §3-501(a). Presentment for acceptance must be made to the drawee. U.C.C. §3-501(a).

1. **Manner and time of presentment:** Presentment may be made by any commercially reasonable means including oral (telephone), written (mail), or electronic communication. U.C.C. §3-501(b)(1). Presentment is effective when the demand for payment or acceptance is received by the person to whom presentment is made. U.C.C. §3-501(b)(1). If the party to whom presentment is made has a cut-off hour for the receipt and processing of instruments and presentment is made after the cut-off hour, the party may treat the presentment as having occurred on the next business day. U.C.C. §3-501(b)(4).

   Example: If presentment is made at 3 P.M. on Friday and the bank has established a 2 P.M. cut-off hour, presentment is deemed to have been made on Monday because Saturday and Sunday are not business days.

2. **Where presentment can be made:** In the absence of a Federal Reserve Regulation, clearinghouse rule, or contrary agreement, presentment can be made wherever the drawee, maker, or acceptor can be found, even if the instrument specifies a particular place of payment or acceptance. If the party expected to pay or accept cannot be found, the instrument may be presented at its place of payment. U.C.C. §3-501(b)(1).

   Exception: Regulation CC determines where a check may be presented. U.C.C. §3-111.

3. **Rights of party to whom presentment is made:** Once the demand for payment or acceptance is made, the party to whom presentment is made has the right to demand, without thereby dishonoring the instrument, that the presenter do certain things. If the presenter fails within a reasonable time to comply with one of these authorized requests, the presentment is invalidated. Once all authorized demands have been satisfied, the time within which acceptance or payment must be made commences to run. The person to whom presentment is made may demand that the presenter do any of the following:

   a. **Exhibit the instrument:** This ensures that the presenter has actual possession of the instrument. U.C.C. §3-501(b)(2)(i).

   b. **Reasonable identification:** To be assured that the proper person is being paid, the person to whom presentment is made may demand reasonable identification from the presenter and, if presented on behalf of another, reasonable evidence of the agent's authority. U.C.C. §3-501(b)(2)(ii).

c. **Receipt or surrender:** To protect herself against the claim that payment was not made, a person who makes payment may demand a signed receipt on the instrument or surrender of the instrument if payment in full is made. U.C.C. §3-501(b)(2)(iii).

4. **Effect of delay in presentment:** An indorser and, under very limited circumstances, the drawer, is discharged when presentment for payment of a check is delayed beyond the required time. A delay in presenting any instrument, other than a check, discharges neither the drawer nor an indorser.

   a. **Discharge of indorser:** An indorser of a check is discharged from her indorser's liability if the check is not presented for payment or given to a depositary bank for collection within 30 days after her indorsement. U.C.C. §3-415(e).

   b. **Discharge of drawer:** A drawer of a check is discharged only when (a) the check is not presented for payment or given to a depositary bank for collection within 30 days from the check's stated date and (b) only to the extent that she is deprived of funds maintained with the drawee bank because the drawee bank has suspended payment after the expiration of the 30-day period and, thus, failed to make payment on the check. U.C.C. §3-414(f); U.C.C. §3-414, Official Comment 6.

      Rationale: The drawer is only hurt if the drawee bank has gone insolvent (suspends payment) during the delay in presentment, thereby depriving the drawer of funds otherwise available to pay the check.

      Example: Assume that a check dated July 1 was not given to a depositary bank for collection until August 15. If the payor bank went insolvent on August 8, the drawer would be entitled to a discharge. However, if the bank went insolvent on July 29, the drawer would not have been discharged. This is because, even if the check had been presented within the 30-day period (by July 30), the drawer would have still lost her funds.

5. **When presentment excused:** When a presentment or a delay in presentment is excused, presentment is treated as having been made within the prescribed time limits.

   a. **Reasonable diligence:** Presentment is excused if it cannot be made by the exercise of reasonable diligence. U.C.C. §3-504(a)(i).

      Example: The typical situation in which this excuse applies is when the presenter cannot locate the party to whom presentment must be made. When no place of payment is specified in the instrument, presentment is excused if the presenter cannot, with reasonable diligence, locate either the home or business address of the party to whom presentment is to be made.

   b. **Stop payment order:** Presentment is excused as to the drawer if the drawer has instructed the drawee not to pay or accept a draft. U.C.C. §3-504(a)(v).

      Note: Presentment is not excused as to an indorser (assuming that she did not order payment stopped).

   c. **No reason to expect payment:** Presentment is excused if the drawer or an indorser has no reason to expect or right to require that the instrument be paid or accepted. U.C.C. §3-504(a)(iv).

Examples: An indorser has no reason to expect that an instrument will be paid when she asserts an adverse claim upon the party obliged to pay. Presentment is also excused if a drawer knows that she has insufficient funds in her account to cover the check.

   d. **When excused or waived:** When presentment is waived under the terms of the instrument or otherwise, presentment is excused as to the drawer or indorser. U.C.C. §3-504(a)(iii).

   e. **When maker or acceptor dead, insolvent, or repudiates:** Presentment is excused when the maker or acceptor repudiates the obligation to pay the instrument, is in insolvency proceedings, or has died. U.C.C. §3-504(a)(ii).

C. **Dishonor:** The manner in which an instrument is dishonored depends on the type of instrument.

   1. **Dishonor of demand note:** A note payable on demand is dishonored if the note is not paid on the day of presentment. U.C.C. §3-502(a)(1).

   2. **Dishonor of note not payable on demand:** A note that is not payable on demand is dishonored if it is not paid on the day it becomes payable. U.C.C. §3-502(a)(3). No presentment is required for the note to be dishonored.

   Example: A note payable on January 1, 2004 is dishonored if it is not paid on that date. The holder can commence a lawsuit against the maker on January 2, even though payment was never demanded.

   3. **Dishonor of check:** A check presented to the payor bank (other than for immediate payment over the counter) may be dishonored in two ways.

      a. **Returns check:** A properly presented check is dishonored if the payor bank properly returns the check or sends notice of dishonor or nonpayment in compliance with U.C.C. §§4-301 and 4-302. U.C.C. §3-502(b)(1). U.C.C. §§4-301 and 4-302 set out the time and procedure that a payor bank must follow to make a proper dishonor of a check. Under this procedure, the payor bank must promptly return the check to the presenting bank with an indication that payment has been refused.

      b. **Fails to return check or settle:** A payor bank that fails not only to promptly return the check (or send notice of nonpayment) but also to provisionally settle for the check, and, thus, becomes accountable for the check, dishonors the check. U.C.C. §3-502(b)(1); U.C.C. §3-502, Official Comment 4.

   4. **Dishonor of other demand draft:** A draft payable on demand is dishonored if presentment for payment is duly made to the drawee and the draft is not paid on the day of presentment. U.C.C. §3-502(b)(2). This applies to checks presented over the counter for immediate payment in cash. Such checks are dishonored if they are not paid on the day of presentment. U.C.C. §3-502(b)(2); U.C.C. §3-502, Official Comment 4.

   5. **Dishonor of draft not payable on demand:** A draft that is not payable on demand is dishonored in two ways.

      a. **Not paid upon presentment:** If the draft is presented for payment and it is not paid on the day it is due or the day of presentment, whichever is later, it is dishonored. U.C.C. §3-502(b)(3)(i).

Exception: Payment or acceptance of an unaccepted documentary draft may be delayed without dishonor until no later than the close of the drawee's third business day following the day on which payment or acceptance is required under U.C.C. §3-502(b). U.C.C. §3-502(c).

Rationale: A drawee of a documentary draft is given a longer period to determine whether to pay a draft because of the time necessary to examine the accompanying documents. The period given coincides with the one prescribed under U.C.C. §5-112 for documentary drafts drawn under a letter of credit. U.C.C. §3-502, Official Comment 5.

   b. **Presented for acceptance:** An unaccepted draft payable at a stated date or a stated period after acceptance, e.g., 45 days after sight, is dishonored if the draft is presented for acceptance and acceptance is refused. U.C.C. §3-502(b)(3)(ii), (4); U.C.C. §3-502, Official Comment 4.

   Rationale: The holder has the right to know whether the drawee will honor the draft when it becomes due. Therefore, the holder has the right to present the draft for acceptance any time before the due date. If the drawee refuses to accept the draft on the day it is presented, the holder has an immediate cause of action against the drawer on the draft. When a draft is payable a fixed number of days after acceptance (called *after sight*), the exact date payment is due is not fixed until the draft has been accepted. A draft payable a fixed number of days after sight must therefore be presented for acceptance to determine when payment is due.

6. **Dishonor of accepted draft:** Once a draft is accepted, the holder must present the draft to the acceptor for payment.

   a. **Payable on demand:** An accepted draft payable on demand is dishonored if presentment for payment is duly made and the draft is not paid on the day of presentment. U.C.C. §3-502(d)(1); U.C.C. §3-502, Official Comment 6.

   b. **Not payable on demand:** An accepted draft not payable on demand is dishonored if presentment for payment is duly made and payment is not made on the day it becomes payable or on the day of presentment, whichever is later. U.C.C. §3-502(d)(2); U.C.C. §3-503, Official Comment 6.

   Example: An accepted draft payable on August 1 but presented for payment on July 25 is not dishonored until August 1.

D. **Notice of dishonor:** Notice of dishonor may be given by any person. Notice of dishonor may be given by any commercially reasonable means. It may be oral, electronic, or in writing. U.C.C. §3-503(b). Unless excused, a delay in giving notice of dishonor discharges an indorser on any type of instrument. U.C.C. §3-415(c).

Note: A delay in giving notice of dishonor does not discharge a drawer. U.C.C. §3-503, Official Comment 1.

1. **Time within which notice of dishonor must be given:**

   a. **Not taken by collecting bank for collection:** When an instrument is not taken by a collecting bank for collection, notice of dishonor must be given within 30 days after the day on which the instrument is dishonored. U.C.C. §3-503(c).

Example: Assume that Paul indorses a note to Kate, who indorses the note to Dan. The note is dishonored on April 1 by the maker. On April 23, Dan gives notice of dishonor to Kate only. Kate has until May 1 to give notice of dishonor to Paul. If Kate does not give notice to Paul by May 1, Paul is discharged from liability as an indorser. U.C.C. §3-415(c).

   b. Taken by collecting bank:

      i. Collecting bank: When an instrument is taken by a collecting bank for collection, the collecting bank must give notice of dishonor before midnight of the next banking day following the banking day on which the bank receives notice of dishonor. U.C.C. §3-503(c).

      Example: If a collecting bank receives notice of dishonor on Friday, it must give notice of dishonor by midnight on Monday, the next banking day.

      ii. Persons other than a collecting bank: Persons other than a collecting bank must give notice of dishonor within 30 days following the day on which the person receives notice of dishonor. U.C.C. §3-503(c); U.C.C. §3-503, Official Comment 2.

2. When delay in notice of dishonor excused: A delay in giving notice of dishonor is excused if the delay is caused by circumstances beyond the control of the person giving the notice and if the person giving notice exercises reasonable diligence after the cause of the delay ceases to operate. U.C.C. §3-504(c).

Example: The following are examples of some of the circumstances that might excuse a delay in the giving of notice of dishonor:

- illness

- suspension of communication facilities

- war

- suspension of commercial intercourse between countries

- unforeseen absenteeism of employees or strike

- inability to locate the party to whom notice must be given. U.C.C. §4-109(b).

3. When notice of dishonor excused: Notice of dishonor is excused whenever it is waived in the instrument or otherwise. U.C.C. §3-504(b)(ii). A waiver of presentment also waives notice of dishonor. U.C.C. §3-504(b).

III. TRANSFER WARRANTIES

A. Creating transfer warranties: A negotiable instrument is a type of personal property. A purchaser of an instrument expects the instrument to be authentic and to provide for legally enforceable obligations. When a person receives consideration for transferring an instrument, he makes certain warranties, called *transfer warranties*, as to the authenticity and the enforceability of the instrument.

B. Who makes the transfer warranties: Any person who transfers an instrument for consideration makes the transfer warranties. U.C.C. §3-416(a). The warranties are made whether or not the transferor indorses the instrument and even when he indorses the instrument without recourse.

Because these warranties are given only by transferors who receive consideration, neither anomalous indorsers nor transferors who have given the instrument as a gift make the transfer warranties.

C. To whom transfer warranties are made: Outside of the bank collection process, a transferor who does not indorse the instrument makes the transfer warranties to his transferee. If he indorses the instrument, he makes the warranties to all subsequent transferees.

Rationale: An indorser's warranties run to all subsequent transferees because these subsequent parties may have relied on his signature when purchasing the instrument.

Example: Assume that Jill receives a check from Bob and indorses it in blank. Jill then transfers the check to Sally who transfers it without indorsement to Grocer. Grocer indorses and transfers the check to Check Cashing Service. Because Sally did not indorse the check, she makes the transfer warranties only to Grocer. In the event of a breach of warranty, Check Cashing Service may sue Grocer or Jill, but not Sally. The inability of Grocer to sue Sally will probably not affect the ultimate allocation of the loss. In the first place, because Jill is liable to Sally, if Check Cashing Service recovers from Jill directly, the loss falls on the person who is ultimately liable for breach of the warranty (Jill). If Check Cashing Service sues Grocer, Grocer may recover from Sally. Because Grocer is Sally's immediate transferee, Sally makes the warranties to Grocer. Sally will then recover from Jill. See Figure 3-3.

Figure 3-3

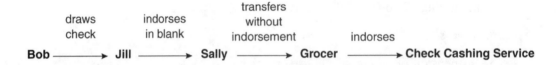

Exception: If the instrument enters the bank collection process, any customer (whether or not indorsing the item) of a collecting bank that transfers the item and receives a settlement or other consideration makes the warranties to its transferee and to any subsequent collecting bank. U.C.C. §4-207(a).

Example: Assume that Check Cashing Service deposits the check in its account in Crocker Bank and Crocker Bank transfers the check to Interstate Bank for presentment to Wells Bank. Even if Check Cashing Service does not indorse the check, it makes the transfer warranties to both Crocker Bank and Interstate Bank.

D. Content of transfer warranties: A transferor makes five warranties:

- that the transferor is a person entitled to enforce the instrument;

- that all signatures are authentic and authorized;

- that the instrument has not been altered;

- that the transferor is not subject to any defense or claim in recoupment; and

- that the transferor has no knowledge of insolvency proceedings instituted with respect to the maker, acceptor, or drawer of an unaccepted item.

1. **Warranty that transferor is a person entitled to enforce the instrument:** A transferor warrants that she is a person entitled to enforce the instrument. U.C.C. §4-207(a)(1); U.C.C.

§3-416(a)(1). This is basically a warranty that there are no unauthorized or missing indorsements that prevent the transferee from becoming a person entitled to enforce the instrument. U.C.C. §3-416, Official Comment 2.

Example: Bob draws a check payable to Jill, who indorses and transfers the check to Joan. Joan loses the check. Fred finds the check and forges an indorsement in Joan's name to Diane. Diane indorses the check to Dave. On presentment, the check is dishonored. Dave sues Diane, Fred, Joan, and Jill. Jill does not breach her warranty because she was a person entitled to enforce the instrument when she transferred the instrument. Because Joan did not voluntarily deliver the check to Fred, Joan did not transfer the check and therefore does not make the transfer warranties. Because Joan's indorsement is forged, Fred is not a person entitled to enforce the instrument. He therefore breaches his transfer warranty. Fred makes this warranty to Diane and to Dave. Under U.C.C. §3-403(a), Fred's unauthorized signing of Joan's name is effective as Fred's own signature. Even though Diane was unaware that the indorsement was forged, she nonetheless breaches this warranty because she is not a person entitled to enforce the instrument. See Figure 3-4.

Figure 3-4

2. **Warranty that all signatures are authentic and authorized:** A transferor warrants that all signatures are authentic and authorized. U.C.C. §4-207(a)(2); U.C.C. §3-416(a)(2). A forged or unauthorized signature of a drawer, a maker, an indorser, or an acceptor breaches this warranty.

3. **Warranty of no alteration:** A transferor warrants that the instrument has not been altered. U.C.C. §3-416(a)(3); U.C.C. §4-207(a)(3). Alteration includes the unauthorized addition of words or numbers to an incomplete instrument.

4. **Warranty that transferor not subject to any defense or claim in recoupment:** A transferor warrants that the instrument is free from any defense or claim in recoupment of any party that can be asserted against the warrantor. U.C.C. §3-416(a)(4); U.C.C. §4-207(a)(4); U.C.C. §3-416, Official Comment 3. In essence, the transferor warrants that if she were to sue any party on the instrument, none of these parties would have a defense or claim in recoupment that could be asserted against her. A transferor who is a holder in due course breaches this warranty only to the extent that she would be subject to a defense or claim in recoupment. The transferor breaches this warranty even if her transferee is a holder in due course who takes the instrument free from the particular defense or claim in recoupment. U.C.C. §3-416, Official Comment 3.

Example: Assume that Bob draws a check payable to Jill for the purchase of a car. Because the car has a defective transmission, Bob has a claim in recoupment against Jill. Jill has no notice of the defect in the transmission and therefore is a holder in due course. Jill negotiates the check to Sally, who takes the check as a holder in due course. Sally sues Jill for breach of the warranty that no defenses or claims in the check recoupment are good against Jill. Even though Jill is a holder in due course, because she dealt with Bob, she is subject to his claim in recoupment and, therefore, breaches this warranty. Furthermore, Jill breaches the warranty even though Sally, being a holder in due course, does not take subject to Bob's claim. If Sally negotiates the check to Wells Bank, she is not liable for breach of the warranty she made to Wells Bank because Bob's claim in recoupment is not good against her.

5. **Warranty of no knowledge of insolvency proceedings:** A transferor warrants that it has no knowledge of insolvency proceedings with respect to the maker, acceptor, or drawer of an unaccepted item U.C.C. §3-416(a)(5); U.C.C. §4-207(a)(5); U.C.C. §3-416, Official Comment 4. No warranty is made as to the transferor's lack of knowledge of any insolvency proceedings instituted against an indorser.

   Rationale: A transferor who knows that insolvency proceedings have been instituted against the drawer, maker, or acceptor commits a fraud by not informing her transferee of this fact because the transferee more than likely expects to recover from one of these parties. U.C.C. §3-416, Official Comment 4. In contrast, it is unlikely that the transferee expects to recover from prior indorsers.

6. **2002 amendments:** The 2002 official amendments to Articles 3 and 4 have added a new transfer warranty with respect to a remotely created consumer item. As to such items, the transferor warrants that the person on whose account the item is drawn has authorized the issuance of the item in the amount for which the item is drawn. [Rev] U.C.C. §3-416(a)(6) and [Rev] U.C.C. §4-207(a)(6). A remotely created consumer item is an item payable out of a consumer's account that is created by the merchant or telemarketer with the consumer's signature not appearing of the item. [Rev] U.C.C. §3-103(a)(16).

IV. SURETIES AND ACCOMMODATION PARTIES

A. **Introduction:** A surety is, in general terms, a person who guarantees the debt of another. If Son wants to purchase a car from Car Dealer, Car Dealer may require that Dad sign an agreement guaranteeing to repay the loan if Son fails to do so. Dad is a surety. Article 3 has its own rules regarding suretyship. Under Article 3, a surety is called an *accommodation party*. The debtor (the son) is called the *accommodated party*.

B. **What is an accommodation party?** If an instrument is issued for value given for the benefit of a party to the instrument (accommodated party) and another party to the instrument (accommodation party) signs the instrument for the purpose of incurring liability on the instrument without being a direct beneficiary of the value given for the instrument, the instrument is signed by the accommodation party *for accommodation*. U.C.C. §3-419(a).

   1. **Both surety and debtor must sign instrument:** A person is an accommodation party only when both the surety and the debtor sign the same instrument. U.C.C. §3-419(a).

      Example: If both Dad and Son sign the same promissory note, Dad is the accommodation party and Son is the accommodated party.

   2. **When both do not sign same instrument:** If the surety does not sign the same instrument as the debtor, he is not an accommodation party. He is still a surety but his rights as a surety are governed by the general law of suretyship. Under the general law of suretyship, Dad will be entitled to most of the same rights to which an accommodation party is entitled under Article 3.

      Example: If Dad signs a *separate* guaranty agreement or a separate note from the one signed by Son, Dad is not an accommodation party.

3. **Collection guaranteed:** When *collection guaranteed* or equivalent words are added to a signature and they unambiguously indicate an intention to guarantee collection only, the signer undertakes only a guaranty of collection. U.C.C. §3-419(d). A guarantor of collection is obliged to pay the amount due only if the holder cannot collect from the accommodated party. The holder must show that either execution of judgment against the accommodated party was returned unsatisfied or that it would be futile to attempt to recover from the accommodated party. U.C.C. §3-419(d); U.C.C. §3-419, Comment 4.

   2002 amendments: Under [Rev] U.C.C. §3-419(d), a party who adds words like "collection guaranteed" to its signature is obligated to make payment only when the holder is unable to recover from the other party to the instrument. [Rev] U.C.C. §3-419(e) is simply intended to make it clear that unless the person clearly indicates that he or she is guaranteeing collection, rather than payment, that the creditor may directly proceed against the guarantor without first proceeding against the accommodated party.

4. **Accommodation party cannot receive direct benefit from instrument:** The test to determine that a person is an accommodation party is whether he has received a direct benefit from the value given for the instrument. Only if he is not a direct beneficiary of the value given for the instrument can he be an accommodation party. U.C.C. §3-419, Official Comment 1.

   Example: Because the car went to Son and not Dad, Dad did not receive a direct benefit from the value given for the note. In contrast, if the car was to be used by both Dad and Son, Dad would be a direct beneficiary of the proceeds paid for the instrument and, therefore, would not be an accommodation party.

   Note: Receiving an indirect benefit from the value given for the instrument will not deny that person accommodation party status. U.C.C. §3-419, Official Comment 1.

   Example: Even if Dad benefited indirectly because he no longer had to drive Son to school, Dad would still be an accommodation party.

5. **Accommodation party liable in capacity in which she signs:** An accommodation party is liable in whatever capacity she has signed, i.e., indorser, maker, acceptor, or drawer. U.C.C. §3-419(b); U.C.C. §3-419, Official Comment 1.

   Example: An accommodation party who signs as an indorser undertakes the indorser's contract under which the accommodation party's promise to pay is conditioned on dishonor and notice of dishonor. U.C.C. §3-415. The liability of an accommodation party who signs as a maker or an acceptor is not conditioned on dishonor or notice of dishonor.

6. **2002 amendments:** New definitions of "principal obligor" and "secondary obligor" have been added.

   a. **Principal obligor:** *A principal obligor* is the accommodated party or any other party to the instrument against whom a secondary obligor has recourse under [Rev] Article 3. [Rev] U.C.C. §3-103(a)(11).

      Example: Mary makes a note payable to Joe. Joe indorses the note to Sally. Mary is a principal obligor because Joe has a right of recourse against her.

   b. **Secondary obligor:** A *secondary obligor* is any of the following:

   i. Indorser: An indorser is a secondary obligor because it has a right to recover from the maker, drawer, or prior indorser.

   ii. Accommodation party: An accommodation party is a secondary obligor because it may recover from the accommodated party.

   iii. Drawer of an accepted draft: Where a draft is accepted by a person (other than a bank), the drawer is treated as an indorser with the acceptor having the primary responsibility to pay the draft. As a result, the drawer is in the position of an indorser. [Rev] U.C.C. §3-414(d). Where the draft is accepted by a bank, the drawer is discharged. [Rev] U.C.C. §3-414(c).

   iv. Right to contribution: Any other party to the instrument that has a right of recourse against another party to the instrument pursuant to [Rev] U.C.C. §3-116(b) is a secondary obligor to the extent of such a right. Under the latter section, a party having joint and several liability who pays the instrument is entitled to receive from any party having the same joint and several liability contribution in accordance with applicable law. [Rev] U.C.C. §3-103(a)(17). Because of the right of a party having joint and several liability who pays an instrument to receive contribution from his co-obligors, such a co-obligor is, in part, a secondary obligor and, also in part, a principal obligor. [Rev] U.C.C. §3-116, Revised Official Comment 1.

   Example: John and Mary are co-makers of a note payable to Phil in the amount of $1,000. Upon Phil's demand, Mary pays the entire amount of the note. Mary, subject to an agreement to the contrary, has the right to recover $500 from John.

C. Relationship between accommodation and accommodated parties: An accommodation party is not liable on the instrument to the party accommodated, nor is he liable for contribution to the accommodated party in the event of payment by the accommodated party. U.C.C. §3-419(e). [[Rev] U.C.C. §3-419(f).]

Rationale: The accommodated party is the person who is benefiting from the accommodation party undertaking liability on the instrument and, therefore, should ultimately be the one to pay the instrument.

1. Right of reimbursement: On payment, the accommodation party has a right to be reimbursed by the accommodated party. This promise is implied in the relationship whether or not the accommodated party makes an express promise to that effect.

   Example: If Dad pays the car dealer $100 of the $2,000 loan balance, Dad can recover the $100 from Son.

2. Right of subrogation: The accommodation party, on full payment of the instrument, is entitled to enforce the instrument against the party accommodated. The accommodation party obtains all the rights of the party he paid both on the instrument and as to any collateral. U.C.C. §3-a419(e) [[Rev] U.C.C. §3-419(f)]; U.C.C. §3-419, Official Comment 5. In other words, on payment of the instrument, the accommodation party takes the place of the holder as regards the accommodated party.

   Example: On full payment of the loan, Dad, as the accommodation party, obtains the car dealer's rights as holder of the note. If the car dealer retained a security interest in the car to secure the note, Dad now has the security interest and becomes the secured party.

3. 2002 amendments: Under the 2002 amendments, the accommodation party may, in proper circumstances, go to court to have the accommodated party specifically perform its obligation to pay the instrument. [Rev] U.C.C. §3-419(e) [now subsection "(f)" under the 2002 amendments].

D. Relationship between accommodation parties: In the absence of an agreement to the contrary, two parties who sign in the same capacity in accommodation for another party are co-sureties. As co-sureties, they are jointly and severally liable.

Example: Assume that both Dad and Uncle sign as accommodation makers for Son. Because neither Dad nor Uncle received a direct benefit, both are accommodation parties. In addition, both are presumed to be co-sureties and, as such, are jointly and severally liable. U.C.C. §3-116(a).

1. Right of contribution: A co-surety who pays more than his proportional share of the obligation has the right of contribution from the other co-surety. U.C.C. §3-116(b).

Example: If Dad makes full payment, Dad can obtain half the amount he paid from Uncle.

2. Subsuretyship: An accommodation party may attempt to prove that he was not only the accommodation party for the original debtor but also for the other accommodation party. To do so, he must prove an express or implied understanding to that effect. This is called a *subsuretyship relationship*.

Example: Dad and Uncle may have an express (or implied) understanding that because Son is Dad's child, Dad, and not Uncle, will be ultimately liable in the event that Son does not pay. In this event, Uncle is an accommodation party for both Dad and Son. If Uncle makes payment, Uncle may recover fully from Dad. U.C.C. §3-116(b). If Dad makes payment, even though he may recover from Son, he may not recover from Uncle. U.C.C. §3-419(e). Although both Dad and Uncle are sureties for Son, Uncle is a subsurety for Dad.

E. Defenses available to accommodation party

1. May not raise lack of consideration: The obligation of an accommodation party may be enforced whether or not the accommodation party himself received any consideration. U.C.C. §3-419(b); U.C.C. §3-419, Official Comment 2. As long as the instrument was issued for value for the benefit of the accommodated party, the accommodation party may not raise the defense of lack of consideration even though he has, in fact, received no benefit in any form.

Rationale: Because an accommodation party incurs liability so that the accommodated party can receive the benefit, the accommodation party is deemed, for practically all purposes, to have bargained for whatever consideration is received by the accommodated party.

Example: Because Son received the car from Car Dealer in exchange for the note that he issued, Dad may not raise lack of consideration as a defense. U.C.C. §3-303; U.C.C. §3-419.

2. Right of accommodation party to raise accommodated party's defenses: With a few exceptions, the accommodation party may raise any of the accommodated party's defenses or claims in recoupment. U.C.C. §3-305(d).

Example: If the car is not delivered, Son has the defense of failure of consideration. If the car has defective brakes, Son has a claim in recoupment for breach of warranty. Dad may raise both the defense and the claim in recoupment.

Exception: The accommodation party may not raise, as a defense to his own obligation to pay, the accommodated party's discharge in insolvency proceedings, infancy, or lack of legal capacity. U.C.C. §3-305(d).

Rationale: These are the precise risks that the creditor was attempting to avoid by obtaining the signature of the accommodation party.

Example: Dad cannot raise Son's defense of infancy. If he could, Car Dealer never would have sold Son the car.

F. Discharge of indorsers and accommodation parties (suretyship defenses): Both an accommodation party and an indorser who pay an instrument step into the shoes of the person who was paid and acquire that person's rights through the doctrine of *subrogation*. These rights include any rights that person had on the instrument and to any collateral acquired from the primary obligor. Because indorsers and accommodation parties step into his shoes, they are hurt if the person entitled to enforce the instrument does anything to impair their right to recover against any prior parties.

1. **Suretyship defenses:** To the extent an indorser or accommodation party is injured by any unjustifiable action of the person entitled to enforce the instrument, the injured indorser or accommodation party may be discharged under U.C.C. §3-605. The various rules found in U.C.C. §3-605, by which an indorser or accommodation party may be discharged, are commonly referred to as *suretyship defenses.*

2. **Limited to accommodation parties and indorsers:** The right to a discharge under U.C.C. §3-605 is limited to accommodation parties and indorsers. U.C.C. §3-605(a). Other parties in the position of a surety and persons who sign separate guaranty agreements or other instruments that are not negotiable are not covered by U.C.C. §3-605.

   a. **Note:** An accommodation party is only discharged if the person entitled to enforce the instrument either (1) has actual knowledge of the accommodation or (2) has notice of the accommodation (a) from an indication on the instrument that the party has signed as "guarantor," "surety," or "accommodation party," or (b) from the fact that the signature is an anomalous indorsement that is presumed to be made in the capacity of an accommodation party. U.C.C. §3-419(c); U.C.C. §3-605(h).

   b. **2002 amendments:** The 2002 amendments to U.C.C. §3-605 have significantly changed the rules, as well as the terminology, for determining the effect upon secondary obligors of an impairment of collateral, a release of the primary obligor, an extension granted to the primary obligor and a modification of the obligations of the primary obligor.

      i. **Party to instrument:** [Rev] U.C.C. §3-605 only applies where the secondary obligor is a party to an instrument. Where the secondary obligor is not a party to the instrument, general suretyship law applies. [Rev] U.C.C. §3-605, Official Comment 1.

         (a) **Terminology:** Unlike original U.C.C. §3-605, which discusses these issues in terms of the effect that a discharge of a party under U.C.C. §3-604 has upon the liability of an indorser or accommodation party having a right of recourse against the discharged party, [Rev] U.C.C. §3-605(a) speaks in terms of the effect that a *release* of the "principal obligor" has on the liability of a "secondary obligor." A *principal obligor* is the accommodated party or any other party to the instrument against whom a secondary obligor has recourse under Article 3. [Rev] U.C.C.

§3-103(a)(11). A *secondary obligor* is either: (a) an indorser or an accommodation party; (b) a drawer on a draft that is accepted by a person other than a bank [Rev] U.C.C. §3-414(d); or (c) any other party to the instrument that has recourse against another party to the instrument pursuant to [Rev] U.C.C. §3-116(b). A party having joint and several liability who pays the instrument is entitled to receive from any party having the same joint and several liability contribution in accordance with applicable law. [Rev] U.C.C. §3-116(b).

(b) **Secondary obligors:** [Rev] U.C.C. §3-605 applies to the following five secondary obligors:

1. An accommodation party;
2. An indorser of a note who is not an accommodation party;
3. A drawer of a draft that is accepted by a party that is not a bank;
4. An indorser of a check; and
5. A co-maker of an instrument, whether or not an accommodation party. [Rev] U.C.C. §3-103(a)(17).

Note: A co-maker's right of contribution under [Rev] U.C.C. §3-116(b) makes a co-maker a secondary obligor to the extent of its right of contribution. [Rev] U.C.C. §3-605, Official Comment 3.

3. **Release of principal obligor:** Release of the principal obligor (technically called *discharge by cancellation or renunciation*) does not discharge the accommodation party or indorser under U.C.C. §3-605(b). Notwithstanding release of the principal debtor, the surety retains both her right of recourse on the instrument and her right of reimbursement against the principal debtor. U.C.C. §3-419(e); U.C.C. §3-605, Official Comment 3.

Example: Cindy, the person entitled to enforce the note, releases Alice, the maker of the note. Release of Alice does not release Betty, the accommodation party. After Betty pays Cindy, Betty may proceed against Alice.

a. **2002 amendments:** The 2002 amendments have complicated the rules as to the effect that a release of the principal obligor has on the liability of a secondary obligor.

   i. **Liability of principal obligor to secondary obligor as to previous payments:** Notwithstanding release of the principal obligor by the person entitled to enforce an instrument, the obligations of the principal obligor to the secondary obligor with respect to any previous payment made by the secondary obligor are not affected. [Rev] U.C.C. §3-605(a)(1). As a result, despite the release, the secondary obligor may recover from the principal obligor for any payments already made by the secondary obligor. [Rev] U.C.C. §3-605, Official Comment 4.

   ii. **Liability of principal obligor to secondary obligor as to other obligations:** Subject to the exception discussed below, the principal obligor is also discharged, to the extent of the release, from any unperformed obligations owed to the secondary obligor. [Rev] U.C.C. §3-605(a)(1). This includes not only the principal obligor's liability as an obligor on the instrument (e.g., as a maker, drawer, or indorser) but also any obligations under U.C.C. §§3-116 and 3-419. [Rev] U.C.C. §3-605, Official Comment 4.

   Rationale: Because the secondary obligor no longer faces liability on the instrument, the principal obligor can, likewise, have no liability to the secondary obligor. The secondary obligor's voluntary decision to pay the instrument, when not legally obligated to, should not impose an obligation on the principal obligor to reimburse him. [Rev] U.C.C. §3-605, Official Comment 4.

Exception: Where the terms of the release reserve the person entitled to enforce the instrument's recourse against the secondary obligor as well as the secondary obligor's recourse against the principal obligor, the principal obligor's obligation to the secondary obligor is not discharged. [Rev] U.C.C. §3-605(g).

Rationale: Where the person entitled to enforce the instrument's recourse against the secondary obligor is preserved, it would be unfair if the secondary obligor did not retain its rights against the principal obligor despite the principal obligor's release by the person entitled to enforce the instrument.

iii. **Liability of secondary obligor as to unperformed obligations:** Where a person entitled to enforce the instrument releases the obligation of the principal obligor in whole or in part, unless the terms of the release provide that the person entitled to enforce the instrument retains the right to enforce the instrument against the secondary obligor, the secondary obligor is discharged to the same extent as the principal obligor from any unperformed portion of its obligation on the instrument. [Rev] U.C.C. §3-605(a)(2) and Official Comment 4.

   (a) **Exception as to consideration given:** Even where the secondary obligor is not discharged under this section, the secondary obligor is discharged to the extent of the value of the consideration given for the release. [Rev] U.C.C. §3-605(a)(3) and Official Comment 4.

   (b) **Exception for harm caused to secondary obligor:** The secondary obligor is also discharged to the extent that the release would otherwise cause the secondary obligor a loss. [Rev] U.C.C. §3-605(a)(3) and Official Comment 4. The secondary obligor may be hurt by the release in that there is no longer the possibility that the primary obligor would make further payments that would reduce the remaining obligation of the secondary obligor. [Rev] U.C.C. §3-605, Official Comment 4.

   (c) **Effect of consent:** The secondary obligor is not discharged where it has consented to the release or is deemed to have consented to it under [Rev] U.C.C. §3-605(f). [Rev] U.C.C. §3-605, Official Comment 4.

   (d) **Effect of failure to reserve recourse:** Unless the release reserves the secondary obligor's recourse against the principal obligor, the release eliminates the secondary obligor's claims against the principal obligor with respect to any future payment by the secondary obligor. [Rev] U.C.C. §3-605, Official Comment 4.

   Rationale: Permitting releases to be negotiated between the principal obligor and the person entitled to enforce the instrument without regard to the consequences to the secondary obligor would create an undue risk of opportunistic behavior by the obligee and principal obligor. [Rev] U.C.C. §3-605, Official Comment 4.

   Exception for checks: Where a person entitled to enforce an instrument releases the obligation of a principal obligor on a check, in whole or in part, the secondary obligor whose liability is based on its indorsement of the check is discharged without regard to the language or circumstances of the discharge or release. [Rev]

U.C.C.§3-605(a)(2). The person entitled to enforce the instrument can avoid discharge of the indorser by contracting with the indorser for a different result at the time that she grants the release to the principal obligor. [Rev] U.C.C. §3-605, Official Comment 4.

4. **Extensions and modifications:** An accommodation party or indorser having a right of recourse against a principal obligor may be entitled to a discharge in the event that the person entitled to enforce the instrument modifies the obligation of, or grants an extension to, the principal debtor. U.C.C. §3-605(c), (d).

5. **Extensions—extent of discharge:** An extension granted to the principal debtor only discharges the secondary obligor to the extent that the extension causes the surety a loss with respect to her right of recourse against the principal obligor. U.C.C. §3-605(c); U.C.C. §3-605, Official Comment 4.

   a. **Form of agreement:** The extension must take the form of an agreement, whether or not binding, under which the person entitled to enforce the instrument gives more time to the principal debtor to pay the instrument. The mere failure to enforce the instrument when due, or to foreclose on the collateral, does not constitute an extension.

      Example: If the person entitled to enforce the instrument, whether intentionally or by neglect, fails for 2 years to attempt to collect from the principal debtor, the person entitled to enforce the instrument's failure is not an extension and does not discharge the accommodation party even if the principal debtor does not go insolvent until long after the due date. In contrast, the accommodation party will be discharged if the person entitled to enforce the instrument agrees that the principal debtor may delay payment for a week, and the delay causes a loss.

   b. **Proof of loss:** The burden is placed on the accommodation party or indorser to prove that she suffered a loss by virtue of the extension. U.C.C. §3-605, Official Comment 4.

      Example: Cindy agrees to extend the due date from January 1 to February 1. On January 16, Alice leaves the country with enough cash to pay the note. Betty is entitled to a discharge to the extent that she could prove that, had she paid the note on January 1, she could have recovered the money from Alice.

   c. **2002 amendments**

      i. **Effect of extension on secondary obligor:** Where a person entitled to enforce an instrument grants the principal obligor an extension of time, the secondary obligor is discharged to the extent that the extension would otherwise cause the secondary obligor a loss. [Rev] U.C.C. §3-605(b)(2) and Official Comment 5.

         Example: Principal obligor becomes insolvent during the period of the extension. Had the extension not been granted, principal obligor would have been able to pay $1,000 of the $5,000 note. Assuming that secondary obligor can prove this, secondary obligor would be discharged to the extent of $1,000. [Rev] U.C.C. §3-605, Official Comment 5.

         Exception: An extension of time has no effect on the obligations of the principal obligor to the secondary obligor with respect to any previous payment made by the secondary obligor. [Rev] U.C.C. §3-605(b)(1). The rationale for this exception is that the secondary obligor, upon payment, has an independent right to recover the amount paid from the principal obligor.

ii. **Effect on principal obligor's duty to secondary party:** Unless the terms of the extension preserve the secondary obligor's recourse against the principal obligor, any extension granted to the principal obligor extends the time for performance of any other duties owed to the secondary obligor by the principal obligor under Article 3. [Rev] U.C.C. §3-605(b)(1). As a result, if the secondary obligor pays the person entitled to enforce the instrument, the secondary obligor may not recover from the principal obligor during the time in which the time for payment was extended.

iii. **Secondary party's options:** When the time for payment by the principal obligor has been extended by the person entitled to enforce payment, the secondary obligor has the following options:

(a) **Perform as if no extension:** Assuming that the secondary obligor is not discharged under [Rev] U.C.C. §3-605(b)(2), the secondary obligor may perform its obligations on the instrument as if the time for payment had not been extended. [Rev] U.C.C. §3-605(b)(3).

(b) **Treat time for performance as extended:** Unless the terms of the extension provide that the person entitled to enforce the instrument retains the right to enforce the instrument against the secondary obligor as if the time for payment had not been extended, the secondary obligor may treat the time for performance of its obligations as having been extended to the same extent as that of the primary obligor. [Rev] U.C.C. §3-605(b)(3).

(c) **Reservation of rights:** Where the terms of the extension provide that the person entitled to enforce the instrument retains its right to enforce the instrument against the secondary obligor on the original due date, the secondary obligor has the obligation to pay on the original due date. As a result, the secondary obligor may not delay payment until the extended due date. [Rev] U.C.C. §3-605, Official Comment 5. However, unless the extension agreement affects a reservation of the secondary obligor's right of recourse, the secondary obligor has no right to recover from the principal obligor until the extended due date. Because of this loss of its right to immediate recourse, the secondary obligor is discharged to the extent that this delay causes a loss to the secondary obligor. [Rev] U.C.C. §3-605(b)(2) and Official Comment 5.

(d) **Secondary obligor's option:** Where the secondary obligor has the right, but not the duty, to pay the instrument on the original due date, the secondary obligor may assert its rights to discharge under [Rev] U.C.C. §3-605(b)(2) even if it does not exercise that option to pay on the original due date. [Rev] U.C.C. §3-605, Official Comment 5. In determining its loss, the fact that the secondary obligor did not exercise its option to pay on the original due date, and then recover from the principal obligor, may affect its loss resulting from the extension. [Rev] U.C.C. §3-605, Official Comment 5.

Example: Holder grants extension to Maker by which the due date of the note is extended from January 15 or May 15. On February 15, Maker is solvent. Indorser has reason to know that Maker may not be solvent on May 15. Indorser's failure to make payment on January 15 and then demand reimbursement from Maker may diminish Indorser's right to a discharge. If Holder can prove that Maker would have paid Indorser some of the money had Indorser demanded payment on the original due date, Indorser's right to a discharge would be diminished to the extent that its failure to make payment and pursue Maker would have mitigated its loss. This is especially true if the secondary obligor has been given prompt notice of the extension and there is a preservation of rights so that the secondary obligor could have recovered from the principal obligor had it so done. [Rev] U.C.C. §3-605, Official Comment 5.

   iv. Reservation of rights: A release or extension preserves a secondary obligor's recourse against the principal obligor if the terms of the release or extension provide both that: (1) the person entitled to enforce the instrument retains the right to enforce the instrument against the secondary obligor; and (2) recourse of the secondary obligor continues as though the release or extension had not been granted. [Rev] U.C.C. §3-605(g) and Official Comment 10.

      (a) Manner of reservation: No particular language is necessary to preserve the secondary parties' recourse against the principal obligor. [Rev] U.C.C. §3-605, Official Comment 4. However, the reservation must be contained in the terms of the release. Parol evidence is not admissible to prove that the parties intended that the secondary obligor remain liable. [Rev] U.C.C. §3-605, Official Comment 4.

      Example: Statements such as the parties "intend to release the principal obligor but not the secondary obligor" or that the person entitled to enforce the instrument "reserves its rights" against the secondary obligor are sufficient. [Rev] U.C.C. §3-605, Official Comment 4.

6. Modifications—extent of discharge: When the person entitled to enforce the instrument agrees to materially modify the obligation of the principal debtor, with or without consideration, an accommodation party or indorser is discharged to the extent that the modification causes a loss with respect to her right of recourse against the principal debtor. U.C.C. §3-605(d); U.C.C. §3-605, Official Comment 5.

   a. Burden of proof: The loss suffered by the accommodation party or indorser is presumed to be equal to the amount of her right of recourse. As a result, unless the person entitled to enforce the instrument can prove that the loss is a lesser amount, the accommodation party or indorser is completely discharged. U.C.C. §3-605(d); U.C.C. §3-605, Official Comment 5.

   Rationale: Modifications are treated differently than extensions because they are less common than extensions and are more likely to be detrimental to the accommodation party or indorser. U.C.C. §3-605, Official Comment 5.

   Example: Assume that the principal sum of the note is increased from $100,000 to $125,000. The accommodation party has the benefit of the presumption that the increase in principal caused her a loss in the entire amount of $100,000 (the amount for which she would otherwise be liable). In other words, it is presumed that had the note not been modified, the accommodated party would have been able to pay the entire $100,000. However, the person entitled to enforce the instrument may introduce evidence that, for example, the accommodated party's inability to pay was caused by a total collapse of her business and that the collapse would have occurred no matter what the amount of the principal was. In this case, the person entitled to enforce the instrument has rebutted the presumption that the modification caused the loss, thus denying the accommodation party a discharge.

b. 2002 amendments

    i. Discharge of secondary obligor: If a person entitled to enforce an instrument agrees, with or without consideration, to a modification of the obligation of a principal obligor, the secondary obligor is discharged from any unperformed portion of its obligation to the extent that the modification would otherwise cause the secondary obligor a loss. [Rev] U.C.C. §3-605(c)(2).

    ii. Effect of modification on unperformed obligations: The modification modifies any other duties owed to the secondary obligor by the principal obligor under Revised Article 3 to the same extent that the modification modifies the obligations of the principal obligor to the person entitled to enforce the instrument. [Rev] U.C.C. §3-605(c)(1) and Official Comment 6.

    iii. Consideration irrelevant: Whether the modification was with or without consideration is irrelevant. [Rev] U.C.C. §3-605(c)(1).

    iv. No effect on prior payments: Obligations of the principal obligor to the secondary obligor with respect to any previous payment by the secondary obligor are not affected by the modification. [Rev] U.C.C. §3-605(c)(1).

    v. Secondary party's options where not discharged: To the extent that the secondary obligor is not discharged from performance under [Rev] U.C.C. §3-605(c)(2), the secondary obligor may satisfy its obligation on the instrument as if the modification had not occurred, or may treat its obligation on the instrument as having been correspondingly modified. [Rev] U.C.C. §3-605(c)(3) and Official Comment 6.

c. 2002 amendments as to burden of proof: With one exception, a secondary obligor asserting discharge has the burden of proof both with respect to the occurrence of the acts alleged to harm the secondary obligor and the loss or prejudice caused by those acts. [Rev] U.C.C. §3-605(h).

Exception: If the secondary obligor demonstrates prejudice caused by an impairment of its recourse, and the circumstances of the case indicate that the amount of loss is not reasonably susceptible of calculation or requires proof of facts that are not ascertainable, it is presumed that the act impairing the recourse caused a loss or impairment equal to the full liability of the secondary obligor on the instrument. [Rev] U.C.C. §3-605(i). In that event, the burden of proof as to any lesser amount of the loss shifts to the person entitled to enforce the instrument. [Rev] U.C.C. §3-605(i).

d. Burden of proof where both modification and extension: Because of the presumption of total loss in the case of a modification, if an agreement both materially modifies the obligation of the principal debtor and also grants an extension to her, the accommodation party or indorser will be completely discharged unless the person entitled to enforce the instrument can prove that the loss was in a lesser amount. U.C.C. §3-605, Official Comment 5.

7. Consent and waiver: Any party who consents to a modification or to an extension is not discharged. U.C.C. §3-605(i); U.C.C. §3-605, Official Comment 8.

    a. 2002 amendments: A secondary obligor is not discharged under [Rev] U.C.C. §3-605 if the secondary obligor either consents to the event or conduct or the instrument or a separate agreement of the party provides for a waiver of discharge. The waiver may, but does not have to, specifically mention [Rev] U.C.C. §3-605. [Rev] U.C.C. §3-605(f). To the extent that the circumstances indicate otherwise, consent by the principal obligor to an act that would lead to a discharge under [Rev] U.C.C. §3-605 constitutes consent to that act by the secondary obligor if the secondary obligor controls the principal obligor or deals with the person entitled to enforce the instrument on behalf of the principal obligor. [Rev] U.C.C. §3-605(f).

8. Impairment of collateral: If the person entitled to enforce the instrument has impaired the collateral that the debtor gave to secure repayment of the instrument, a person having a right of recourse against the debtor may be discharged by the impairment. Separate rules apply to indorsers and accommodation parties, on the one hand, and to co-obligors on the other hand.

    a. Discharge of accommodation parties and indorsers: If the obligation to pay an instrument is secured by an interest in collateral and the person entitled to enforce the instrument impairs the value of the collateral, the obligation of an indorser or an accommodation party having a right of recourse against the obligor is discharged to the extent of the impairment. U.C.C. §3-605(e); U.C.C. §3-605, Official Comment 6.

        Example: If Betty acts as an accommodation party for Alice and is called on to pay Cindy, Betty acquires Cindy's rights on the instrument and to any collateral Alice may have given to secure the loan. Betty can, therefore, obtain repayment of the money she paid Cindy by selling the collateral Alice gave to secure the loan. Betty will suffer a loss only if the collateral is insufficient to repay the debt and Alice is unable to pay the deficiency. If Cindy causes harm to Betty's recourse against Alice or to the collateral, Betty is injured to the extent of the harm.

        Note: An accommodation party is discharged under U.C.C. §3-605(e) only if the person entitled to enforce the instrument knows of the accommodation or has notice of the accommodation under U.C.C. §3-419(c). U.C.C. §3-605(h).

        Rationale: Without notice of the party's accommodation status, the creditor may have no reason to suspect that her actions will harm the accommodation party.

        2002 amendments: A secondary obligor is not discharged under [Rev] U.C.C. §3-605(a)-(d) unless the person entitled to enforce the instrument knows that the person is a secondary obligor or has notice under [Rev] U.C.C. §3-419(c) that the instrument was signed for accommodation. [Rev] U.C.C. §3-605(e).

        Rationale: A secondary obligor can, if it desires, always make its status clear to third parties. Unless the person entitled to enforce the instrument knows that he or she is hurting the right of recourse of the secondary obligor, he or she should not be punished for actions that will usually only benefit the primary obligor.

        Example: Because Allen knows that his credit is suspect, Allen asks his friend Larry to act as the "borrower" in obtaining a loan from Bank. Larry makes a note to Bank evidencing a loan of $5,000. Allen signs the note as an anomalous indorser. When it is due, Bank accepts Allen's offer to pay Bank $1,000 in exchange for his release. Larry is not released by Bank's release of Allen because Bank had no way of knowing that it was hurting Larry by releasing Allen.

b. Discharge of co-obligors: If a person entitled to enforce the instrument impairs the value of an interest in the collateral, the obligation of any party who is jointly and severally liable with respect to the secured obligation is discharged to the extent that the impairment causes the party asserting the discharge to pay more than he would have otherwise been obliged to pay. U.C.C. §3-605(f); U.C.C. §3-605, Official Comment 7.

Example: Assume that you and your sister co-make a note to borrow money to start a business. Being jointly and severally liable, on your payment in full, you may recover one-half of your payment from your sister. Assume that your sister pledged certain stock certificates to secure this loan. The creditor impairs the collateral by returning the stock certificates to your sister. If you had made payment, the stock certificates could have been sold by you and the proceeds used to pay the debt. Your loss is not in the entire amount of the debt because had the entire amount been paid by the selling of the certificates, your sister could have recovered one-half of the amount from you. You are therefore only discharged to the extent that you are harmed by the impairment.

Note: An accommodation party who is denied a discharge because the person entitled to enforce the instrument does not know, or have notice, of his accommodation status may use this rule to achieve a partial discharge. U.C.C. §3-605, Official Comment 7.

Example: You may have co-made the note with your sister to enable her to start a business. You neither indicated on the note itself, nor told the holder, that you were acting as an accommodation party for your sister. However, as a co-maker, you are entitled to a discharge to the extent discussed above.

9. **When is collateral impaired?** Impairment of collateral occurs when some unjustifiable act or omission on the part of the person entitled to enforce the instrument causes the collateral to no longer be available to satisfy the instrument. The person entitled to enforce the instrument impairs the collateral only if he has breached some duty respecting the collateral. U.C.C. §3-605(g). This duty may arise from an agreement, a common law duty of due care, or some statutorily imposed duty.

Example: If the collateral is destroyed by fire or stolen, the creditor impairs the collateral only if he has breached a duty to insure against, or to use reasonable care to protect against, such loss. Contrast *Commerce Union Bank v. May*, 503 S.W.2d 112 (Tenn. 1973) (bank had no contractual duty) with *Arlington Bank & Trust v. Nowell Motors, Inc.*, 511 S.W.2d 415 (Tex. Ct. App. 1974) (bank had contractual duty to insure).

a. Duty of reasonable care: Unless otherwise agreed, if the collateral is property in the possession of the person entitled to enforce the instrument, that person has the duty to use reasonable care in its custody and possession of the collateral. If the collateral is personal property, the standard of reasonable care is governed by U.C.C. §9-207. U.C.C. §3-605(g).

b. Acts constituting impairment: Article 3 contains a nonexclusive list of certain acts that constitute impairment of collateral.

   i. Failure to perfect: The failure to obtain or maintain perfection or recordation of a security interest in the collateral.

Example: The person entitled to enforce the instrument's failure to file an Article 9 financing statement, which results in the creditor not acquiring a perfected security interest in the collateral, impairs the collateral.

ii. **Release of collateral:** The release of collateral without substitution of collateral of equal value impairs the collateral.

Example: If the person entitled to enforce the instrument obtains from the debtor a diamond ring as collateral for a loan, he has impaired the value of the collateral if he releases the diamond ring to the debtor without obtaining any substitute collateral of equal value.

iii. **Duty to preserve:** The failure to perform a duty to preserve the value of the collateral owed to the debtor, accommodation party, or indorser impairs the collateral.

Example: If the person entitled to enforce the instrument had the duty to insure the collateral and has failed to do so, he has impaired the value of the collateral.

iv. **Improper disposal:** The failure to comply with an applicable law in disposing of collateral impairs the value of the collateral. U.C.C. §3-605(g).

Example: If the person entitled to enforce the instrument has violated the rules contained in Article 9 for selling collateral on default, he impairs the value of the collateral.

10. **Extent of discharge for impairment of collateral:** An accommodated party or indorser is discharged to the extent that he has been hurt by an impairment of the value of the collateral. The party seeking the discharge bears the burden of proof as to both the fact of impairment and the amount of the loss. U.C.C. §3-605(e); U.C.C. §3-605(f). The Code provides two alternative formulas for determining the extent of the impairment.

a. **Formula when debt fully secured:** A debt is fully secured when the value of the collateral is equal to, or greater than, the amount owed on the obligation. When the debt is fully secured, the value of an interest in collateral is impaired to the extent that the value of the interest is reduced to an amount less than the amount of the right of recourse of the party asserting the discharge. U.C.C. §3-605(e)(i); U.C.C. §3-605, Official Comment 6.

b. **Formula when debt undersecured:** A debt is undersecured whenever the debt is greater than the value of the collateral. The measure of loss is, in this event, phrased in terms of how much greater the debt is undersecured because of the impairment. The value of an interest in collateral is impaired to the extent that the reduction in value of the interest causes an increase in the amount by which the amount of the right of recourse exceeds the value of the interest. U.C.C. §3-605(e)(ii). [[Rev] U.C.C. §3-605(d).]

2002 amendments: Although [Rev] U.C.C. §3-605(d) represents no substantive change from original [Rev] U.C.C. §3-605(e), there have been some changes of note. The 2002 amendments have substituted principal obligor for the party primarily liable and secondary obligor for "accommodation party," "indorser," or "person who is secondarily liable." [Rev] U.C.C. §3-605(d). Similarly, in [Rev] U.C.C. §3-605(e)(i), the term secondary party has been substituted for "indorser or accommodation party having a right of recourse against the obligor." [Rev] U.C.C. §3-605(d).

Note: The 2002 amendments have also added to the situations in which the value of collateral is impaired by including, as an act of impairment, the failure to comply with applicable law in otherwise enforcing an interest in collateral. [Rev] U.C.C. §3-605(d) and Official Comment 7.

Note: The 2002 amendments also make it clear that [Rev] U.C.C. §3-605(d) applies to collateral that is realty (rather than personal property) as long as the obligation in question is in the form of a negotiable instrument. [Rev] U.C.C. §3-605, Official Comment 7. As a result, this section would be applicable where the collateral is a note secured by a trust deed.

   c. **Formula where co-obligors:** When the party seeking the discharge is jointly and severally liable with the person who gave the collateral to the person entitled to enforce the instrument, the co-obligor is discharged only to the extent that the impairment causes him to pay more than he would otherwise have been obliged to pay, taking into account his right of contribution. U.C.C. §3-605(f) and Official Comment 3, paragraph 4.

11. **Consent to impairment of collateral:** A party is denied a discharge if he has consented to the act constituting the impairment. This consent may be given in advance, in the instrument itself, or after the act of impairment. U.C.C. §3-605(i). [[Rev] U.C.C. §3-605(f).] The consent may be express or implied. *See* McGhee v. First State Bank & Trust Co., 793 S.W.2d 133 (Ky. Ct. App. 1990) (when accommodation party actively negotiated renewal, question of fact whether accommodation party consented to extension).

V. LIABILITY OF AGENTS, PRINCIPALS, AND CO-OBLIGORS

A. **Represented person and representative:** For purposes of Article 3, a principal is referred to as the *represented person*. An agent is referred to as the *representative*. "Representative" includes an agent, an officer of a corporation or association, a trustee, an executor or administrator of an estate, or any other person empowered to act for another. U.C.C. §1-201(35). [[Rev] U.C.C. §1-201(b)(33).]

B. **Liability of represented person:** A represented person is liable on an instrument if the representative is authorized to sign for the represented person. An authorized signature by an agent or other representative is effective as the signature of the represented person. U.C.C. §3-402(a); U.C.C. §3-402, Official Comment 1.

   1. **Types of authority:** Under the law of agency, the authority of the representative may be actual authority, apparent authority, or inherent agency power. If the representative was, however, not authorized to sign for the represented person, the signature will not operate as the represented person's signature unless the represented person ratifies it or is otherwise precluded from contesting it. U.C.C. §3-403(a).

   2. **Manner of signing:** Any mark or symbol used by the representative that is intended to signify the represented person is sufficient to bind the represented person. U.C.C. §3-402(a); U.C.C. §3-401, Official Comment 1.

      a. **In name of represented person:** The representative may sign the name of the represented person either with, or without, adding the agent's own name or capacity. U.C.C. §3-402(a); U.C.C. §3-401, Official Comment 1.

Example: "Simon Industries," "Simon Industries, by Paul, President," or "Simon Industries, by Paul" are all sufficient to bind Simon Industries.

   b. Undisclosed principal: If a representative is authorized to sign on behalf of the represented person, the representative may sign his own name alone, e.g., "Paul." U.C.C. §3-402(a); U.C.C. §3-401, Official Comment 1. To the extent the representative is authorized to act on his behalf, the undisclosed principal is liable on the instrument even though neither his signature nor his identity appears thereon. U.C.C. §3-401(a); U.C.C. §3-401, Official Comment 1; U.C.C. §3-402, Official Comment 1.

C. Liability of representative: Whether the representative is liable depends both on whether he was authorized to sign for the represented person and the manner in which he signs the instrument.

   1. Unauthorized signature: If the representative is not authorized to sign for the represented person or exceeds his authority in making the signature, the signature operates as the signature of the representative personally. U.C.C. §3-403(a); U.C.C. §3-403, Official Comment 1. As a consequence, the representative will be personally liable in whatever capacity the signature was made. U.C.C. §3-403(a); U.C.C. §3-403, Official Comment 1.

   Example: If a purchasing agent for a buyer is authorized to negotiate the purchase but is not authorized to sign or issue negotiable instruments, the agent's unauthorized drawing of a check in the buyer's name will make the purchasing agent personally liable as drawer of the check.

   2. Authorized signature: Even when the representative is authorized to sign for the represented person, a failure to sign in the proper form may subject him to personal liability on the instrument.

   a. Not liable if agent signs represented person's name only: If the authorized agent signs the represented person's name only, the representative is not personally liable.

   Example: Paul, president of Simon Industries, is authorized to sign instruments on its behalf. If Paul signs the instrument "Simon Industries" without adding his own name, Paul is not personally liable on the instrument because his signature does not appear on the instrument. U.C.C. §3-401(a).

   b. Unambiguously signs in representative capacity: An authorized representative who signs his own name to an instrument is not personally liable if the signature unambiguously shows that it is made on behalf of a represented person who is identified in the instrument. U.C.C. §3-402(b).

      i. Capacity and name of represented person: When the representative signs his name together with his representative capacity and the represented person's name, it is clear that the representative is not personally liable. U.C.C. §3-402(b)(1).

      Example: A signature such as "Simon Industries, by Paul, President" unambiguously indicates that the representative is signing on behalf of the represented party. U.C.C. §3-402, Official Comment 2.

      ii. Office not necessary: It is not necessary for the representative to indicate the office he occupies as long as he clearly indicates that he is signing on behalf of the represented party, e.g., "Simon Industries by Paul" or "Simon Industries, Paul, Authorized Signer."

c. **Ambiguous signature:** When the representative does not make it clear that he is signing on behalf of the represented person, the representative is personally liable to a holder in due course who takes the instrument without notice that the representative was not intended, by the original parties to the instrument, to be personally liable. U.C.C. §3-402(b); U.C.C. §3-402, Official Comment 2.

Rationale: Subsequent purchasers of the instrument may be misled into believing that Paul is personally liable on the instrument. The expectations of these parties should be and, in fact, are protected. Even though Paul did not intend to be personally liable, his carelessness may have misled subsequent purchasers, and therefore he, rather than they, should suffer any loss.

Example: When the name "Simon Industries" does not directly precede or follow Paul's name and capacity, it may not be clear whether Paul is signing for himself personally or for Simon Industries. Similarly, if Paul signs a note "Simon Industries, Paul," it is unclear whether Paul is signing his name as an agent for Simon Industries or whether he is signing for the purpose of undertaking personal liability.

i. **As to other persons:** As to any other person, the representative is liable on the instrument unless he proves that the original parties to the instrument did not intend that he be personally liable. U.C.C. §3-402(b); U.C.C. §3-402, Official Comment 2.

Note: The representative must prove an actual agreement, whether express or implied, with the payee that he was not to be personally liable. U.C.C. §3-402(b)(2). The representative's undisclosed intention not to undertake personal liability is not sufficient.

ii. **Exception for checks:** An authorized representative who signs as drawer on a check that is payable from an account of the represented person without indicating his representative status is not liable as long as the represented person is identified on the check and the signature is an authorized signature of the represented person. U.C.C. §3-402(c); U.C.C. §3-402, Official Comment 3.

Example: If Paul, in signing a check on the account of Simon Industries and bearing its name, signs only "Paul" without any indication that he is acting on behalf of Simon Industries, Paul does not incur personal liability. The reason is simple. No one is going to assume that Paul, when signing a Simon Industries check, intends to incur personal liability.

D. **Liability of persons signing in the same capacity in the same transaction:** Except as otherwise specified in the instrument, two or more persons who sign an instrument as makers, acceptors, or drawers are liable jointly and severally in the capacity in which they sign. U.C.C. §3-116(a).

1. **Right of contribution:** Unless the parties otherwise agree, a party having joint and several liability is entitled to contribution from his joint and several obligors to the extent available under applicable law. U.C.C. §3-116(b).

Example: If Paul and Art are co-obligors, and Paul is forced to pay the note, he may recover half of the payment from Art. Of course, if the note was made by Paul, Art, and Carly, then each would be liable, as between each other, for one-third of the amount.

a. **Exception:** The presumption of equal liability may be overcome by evidence that the parties had agreed, between themselves, to a different allocation or had benefited in unequal portions.

b. **Not affected by discharge:** Even if a party (Paul) having joint and several liability is discharged by some act of the holder, his discharge does not affect the right of his joint and several obligor to receive contribution from the discharged party. U.C.C. §3-116(c); U.C.C. §3-116, Official Comment 1.

   2002 amendments: U.C.C. §3-116(c) has been omitted from [Rev.] U.C.C. §3-116:

   > (c) Discharge of one party having joint and several liability by a person entitled to enforce the instrument does not affect the right under subsection (b) of a party having the same joint and several liability to receive contribution from the party discharged.

   Note: Under the 2002 amendments, parties that are jointly and severally liable are each, in part, a secondary obligor and, in part, a principal obligor. As a result, to the extent that each party is a secondary obligor, [Rev] U.C.C. §3-605 determines the effect of a release, an extension of time, or a modification of the obligation of one of the joint and several obligors, as well as the effect of an impairment of collateral provided by one of those obligors. [Rev] U.C.C. §3-116, Official Comment 1.

2. **Liability of indorsers:** Subject to certain exceptions, indorsers are not jointly and severally liable. U.C.C. §3-116(a).

   Example: Assume that a note is made by Mick payable to Rod who indorses the note to Elton who indorses it to John, the holder. On default by Mick, John sues Rod and Elton. Although both Elton and Rod have indorsed the note, it is clear that Elton, being a subsequent indorser in the chain of title, has a right to recover in full from Rod. Elton was relying on Rod's indorsement when he purchased the note.

   Exception: Co-payees who indorse an instrument are jointly and severally liable unless one payee is accommodating the other payee or they agree to be liable otherwise than as jointly and severally. U.C.C. §3-116(a); U.C.C. §3-116, Official Comment 2.

   Example: If a note is made payable to Paul and Art and both indorse the note to Carly, it is presumed that upon payment by Paul, Paul can recover half of the payment from Art.

   Exception: Persons who sign as anomalous indorsers for the purpose of accommodating the maker are jointly and severally liable unless one anomalous indorser is acting as a subsurety for the other anomalous indorser. U.C.C. §3-116, Official Comment 2.

   Example: If Paul makes a note to Bank of Liverpool for the purpose of obtaining a loan and Ringo and George indorse the note as an accommodation to Paul, it is presumed that Ringo and George are, as between each other, agreeing to be equally liable. If, however, Ringo asks that George indorse the note as a favor to both him and Paul, George may be the surety for Paul and the subsurety for Ringo, in which case George, upon payment, may recover in full from Ringo.

VI. EFFECT OF TAKING INSTRUMENT ON THE UNDERLYING OBLIGATION

A. Introduction: The effect that the taking of an instrument has on the underlying obligation depends on whether the instrument is a bank instrument, such as a cashier's check or teller's check, or an instrument on which a bank is not the obligor.

B. Ordinary instruments

1. **Obligation suspended:** Unless the parties otherwise agree, when the person entitled to enforce the instrument takes an ordinary nonbank instrument (referred to as an *ordinary instrument*) for an underlying obligation, the obligation is suspended to the same extent that the obligation would be discharged if payment had been made in money. U.C.C. §3-310(b); U.C.C. §3-310(c).

   a. **No action to enforce:** While the underlying obligation is suspended, no action of any type, including lawsuits or set-offs, may be taken to enforce the obligation. The obligation is treated as not yet due.

      Example: When John gave his note to the car dealer, the car dealer could not, until dishonor, sue him on the underlying sales contract.

   b. **Checks:** When an uncertified check is taken, suspension of the obligation continues until the check is either dishonored, paid, or certified. If the check is paid or certified, the obligation is discharged to the extent of the amount of the check. U.C.C. §3-310(b)(1).

   c. **Notes:** When a note is taken, suspension of the obligation continues until dishonor of the note or until it is paid. The obligation is discharged to the extent that the note is paid. U.C.C. §3-310(b)(2).

2. **Effect of dishonor:** The effect of dishonor depends on whether the person who is enforcing the instrument is also the person to whom the underlying obligation is owed.

   a. **Person entitled to enforce instrument also underlying creditor:** When the person entitled to enforce the instrument is also the person to whom the underlying obligation is owed (the car dealer brings the action on the note), the person (the car dealer) may enforce either the instrument or the obligation once the instrument is dishonored. U.C.C. §3-310(b)(3); U.C.C. §3-310, Official Comment 3.

   b. **Not also underlying creditor:** When the person entitled to enforce the instrument is not the person to whom the underlying obligation is owed, the person entitled to enforce the instrument may enforce only the instrument. U.C.C. §3-310(4).

      Example: Assume that Car Dealer sells the note to Finance Company. In this case, because the person entitled to enforce the instrument (Finance Company) is not the person to whom the underlying obligation is owed (Car Dealer), it (Finance Company) may only enforce the instrument. Thus, for example, if the note does not contain a provision for attorneys' fees or interest, Finance Company, having neither the right to enforce the attorneys' fees provision nor the provision for interest found in the contract, has no right to interest or attorneys' fees.

3. Effect of discharge: When the underlying obligor is discharged on the instrument, she is also discharged on the underlying obligation. U.C.C. §3-310(a), (b)(1), and (2).

Example: When John pays the note, he is discharged on the note and on the underlying sales contract.

Note: Discharge is available even if the underlying obligor is not a party to the instrument. U.C.C. §3-310(b)(1), and (2).

Example: Assume that instead of borrowing money from Car Dealer, John had borrowed money directly from Finance Company. Finance Company makes a check payable to Car Dealer on John's behalf. Discharge of Finance Company on the check discharges John on the underlying sales contract. If the check is dishonored, Car Dealer may maintain an action against John on the underlying sales contract and against Finance Company on the check. Car Dealer, of course, can be paid only once. If the check had instead been made payable to John who indorsed it to Car Dealer, discharge of John on the check would also discharge John on the underlying sales contract. U.C.C. §3-310(b)(3); U.C.C. §3-310, Official Comment 3.

C. Bank checks: Unless otherwise agreed, if a certified check, cashier's check, teller's check, or any other instrument on which a bank is a maker or an acceptor is taken for an obligation, the obligation is discharged to the same extent as had payment been made in cash. U.C.C. §3-310(a), (c); U.C.C. §3-310, Official Comments 2, 5.

1. Only bank liable: The debt is discharged and the taker of the bank instrument is left with only his right to recover on the instrument against the bank.

2. Party liable if indorses: If the debtor indorses the instrument, although the underlying obligation is discharged, her liability as an indorser on the instrument is not discharged. U.C.C. §3-310(a); U.C.C. §3-310, Official Comment 2.

Rationale: The parties intended, by use of a bank instrument, to allocate the risk of the bank's insolvency to the taker, who could immediately present the bank instrument for payment. Any delay is her fault. If the taker does not want to assume the risk of the bank's insolvency, the parties may either expressly agree that the debtor remains liable on the underlying obligation despite payment by bank instrument, or the debtor may indorse the bank instrument.

D. Taking instrument for underlying obligation: For an instrument to affect the underlying obligation, the instrument must be "taken" for the underlying obligation. U.C.C. §3-310(a), (b). Mere delivery of the instrument to the obligee by the obligor does not result in the obligee having taken the instrument for the underlying obligation. The obligee must, by her action or inaction, indicate that she has accepted the instrument in conditional or final payment of the obligation. *See Savings & Loan Assn. v. Tear*, 435 A.2d 1083 (Me. 1981) (Bank teller accepted a money order in payment of an overdue installment on a mortgage. Although the bank immediately returned the money on review of its files by the appropriate employee, the bank was deemed to have taken the instrument in payment of the mortgage.).

Example: Unless previously authorized by Car Dealer as an acceptable form of payment, Car Dealer's receipt by mail of an instrument does not constitute taking of the instrument for the underlying obligation. Car Dealer can promptly return the instrument to John. John cannot unilaterally impose on Car Dealer payment by a negotiable instrument. However, if Car Dealer deposits or negotiates the instrument, Car Dealer will have taken the instrument for the obligation.

VII. ACCORD AND SATISFACTION BY USE OF INSTRUMENT

A. Introduction: Article 3 provides a procedure whereby a debtor can use a check for the purpose of reaching an accord and satisfaction with a creditor. Subject to two exceptions, tendering of an instrument discharges the underlying claim for which it was tendered if the following conditions are met:

- the debtor must tender the instrument in good faith and in full satisfaction of the claim;

- the claim must either be unliquidated or subject to a bona fide dispute;

- the instrument must be paid; and

- the instrument, or accompanying written communication, must contain a conspicuous statement that the instrument is tendered in full satisfaction of the debt. U.C.C. §3-311(a), (b).

B. Good faith required: An insurance company does not act in good faith when it sends a check in an unreasonably small amount knowing that the insured is destitute. U.C.C. §3-311, Official Comment 4.

C. Debtor discharged even if language stricken: The debtor is discharged even if the creditor strikes out the language indicating payment in full or otherwise indicates her protest.

D. Exception for lockbox accounts: If an organization informs a debtor that checks or other communications regarding disputed debts must be sent to a designated person, office, or place, the claim is not discharged if the instrument or communication was not received by the designated person, office, or place. U.C.C. §3-311(c)(1).

Rationale: Large companies often require customers to make payments directly to a lockbox located at its depositary bank or to one of its own post office boxes from which a clerk receives the checks, records the payment, and forwards the check to the depositary bank. Efficiency requires that the employee not read any accompanying correspondence or anything written on the back of the check. U.C.C. §3-311, Official Comment 5.

E. Exception for returning payment: If a creditor does not require that claims be sent to a special address, the claim is not discharged if the creditor tenders repayment of the amount of the instrument within 90 days of its payment. U.C.C. §3-311(c)(2).

F. Limitation on exceptions: Both exceptions are subject to a limitation. The debtor may prove that, within a reasonable time before collection of the instrument was initiated, the creditor or its agent who had direct responsibility with respect to the disputed obligation knew that the instrument was tendered in full satisfaction. U.C.C. §3-311(d); U.C.C. §3-311, Official Comment 7.

Example: Because a clerk processing checks sent to a lockbox account does not have authority to settle matters, the debt would not be discharged even if the clerk saw the full satisfaction language before depositing the check. U.C.C. §3-311, Official Comment 7.

VIII. PROCEDURAL ISSUES INVOLVING NEGOTIABLE INSTRUMENTS

A. Procedural differences for actions on negotiable instruments: There are several differences between the procedures applicable to actions on ordinary contracts and those applicable to actions on negotiable instruments.

B. Persons entitled to enforce instrument: A person who has the right to enforce an instrument is called a "person entitled to enforce the instrument." A "person entitled to enforce" an instrument includes, in addition to the holder of the instrument, three other groups of persons:

   1. Rights of a holder: A nonholder in possession of the instrument who has the rights of a holder. This category includes:

      a. Transferee: A transferee of a holder who, by the transfer, acquires the rights of a holder.

      b. Accommodation party: An accommodation party who pays the holder and thereby obtains the rights of the holder through subrogation.

      c. Indorser: An indorser who pays the holder and thereby acquires the right to enforce the instrument against prior parties.

   2. Owner of lost instrument: The owner of a lost instrument who brings an action under U.C.C. §3-309.

   3. Person from whom payment recovered: A person from whom payment has been recovered under U.C.C. §3-418(d). U.C.C. §3-418 allows a payor who made payment by mistake to recover its payment from certain recipients. In the event that payment is recovered, the instrument is treated as if it had originally been dishonored and the person from whom the payment has been recovered becomes the person entitled to enforce the instrument. U.C.C. §3-418(d).

C. Burden of proof in negotiable instruments cases: A person entitled to enforce an instrument establishes a prima facie case for recovery where he:

   ■ establishes that the obligor's signature is effective,

   ■ produces the instrument, and

   ■ proves that he is a person entitled to enforce the instrument. U.C.C. §3-308(a), (b).

   1. Exception to producing instrument: The plaintiff does not have to produce the instrument if the instrument has been lost, destroyed, or stolen, or if he is a person from whom a payment has been recovered pursuant to U.C.C. §3-418.

   2. Proving signatures: Unless the defendant specifically denies that a signature is authentic, the signature is deemed to be authentic. Even if the defendant makes a specific denial, the plaintiff is entitled to a presumption that the signature is genuine and authorized. U.C.C. §3-308(a). The presumption requires that the trier of fact find the signature to be genuine or authorized unless and until the obligor has introduced sufficient evidence to support a finding that the signature is either not genuine or unauthorized. U.C.C. §1-201(31) [[Rev] U.C.C. §1-206)]; U.C.C. §3-308, Official Comment 1. Once sufficient evidence is introduced, the presumption completely disappears. To rebut the presumption, the defendant need only testify that his signature is not genuine and submit a sample of his true signature.

3. **Burden on obligor to prove defense:** Once the plaintiff has established his prima facie case by (1) establishing that he is a person entitled to enforce the instrument, (2) producing the instrument, and (3) proving the authenticity of the obligor's signature, he will recover against the obligor unless the obligor establishes a defense or a claim in recoupment. U.C.C. §3-308(b); U.C.C. §3-308, Official Comment 2.

4. **After defense proved, duty of plaintiff to prove holder-in-due-course status:** Even if the obligor has established a defense or claim in recoupment, the plaintiff will still recover if he proves that he is a holder in due course or has the rights of a holder in due course. U.C.C. §3-308(b); U.C.C. §3-308, Official Comment 2. To accomplish this, he must prove that he satisfies every requirement for holder-in-due-course status. Even if the plaintiff succeeds in proving that he is a holder in due course, the plaintiff will be denied recovery if the defendant proves a defense effective against a person having the rights of a holder in due course such as a real defense, defenses or claims in recoupment that the defendant has against the plaintiff itself, or a discharge of which the plaintiff has notice. U.C.C. §3-305(b).

IX. ENFORCEMENT OF LOST, DESTROYED, OR STOLEN INSTRUMENTS

A. **Lost, destroyed, or stolen ordinary instruments:** The person entitled to enforce an instrument that is lost by destruction, theft, or otherwise, may maintain an action as if he had produced the instrument. To protect the obligor against the risk that the instrument had been indorsed in blank before being lost, a court cannot enter judgment in favor of the person entitled to enforce the instrument unless it finds that the obligor is adequately protected against any loss that might occur by reason of a claim by another person to enforce the instrument. U.C.C. §3-309(b); U.C.C. §3-309, Official Comment. The obligor cannot know whether the claimant had either previously negotiated the check or had indorsed it in blank before losing it. In either event, the obligor would be exposed to double liability if it was forced to pay the claimant and the instrument was subsequently presented by a holder in due course who would then take free of the obligor's claim of discharge by payment.

1. **Adequate protection:** To protect the obligor, a court can require the claimant to indemnify the obligor against any losses or expenses. U.C.C. §3-309(b). The amount should be sufficient to protect the obligor not only against liability in the face amount of the instrument but also for all expenses incurred to defend the action, including attorneys' fees and court costs.

2. **Right to recover on instrument only:** If the claimant proves certain facts, he may recover on the instrument as though he had produced the instrument itself. U.C.C. §3-309(b). However, the holder may not enforce the obligation for which the instrument was given. U.C.C. §3-310(b)(4); U.C.C. §3-310, Official Comment 4.

3. **What claimant must prove:** The claimant must prove that:

   a. **In possession and entitled to enforce:** He was in possession of the instrument and entitled to enforce it when the instrument was lost. This requires that he prove that he was either a holder or had the rights of a holder at the time he lost possession.

   b. **Neither transferred nor seized:** The loss of possession was not a result of his transfer of the instrument or of a lawful seizure of the instrument.

    c. Cannot obtain possession: He cannot reasonably obtain possession of the instrument because it was either destroyed, lost, or in the wrongful possession of an unknown person or a person who cannot be found or is not amenable to service of process. The claimant cannot maintain this type of action if he is able to reacquire possession of the instrument. U.C.C. §3-309(a).

    Rationale: When the person entitled to enforce the instrument knows who has possession of the instrument, he must bring an action against that person to recover the instrument. Similarly, the owner of an instrument who has been paid by a payor bank over a forged indorsement has no action under U.C.C. §3-309. His action is against the payor bank or the depositary bank for conversion.

    d. Terms: The terms of the instrument include any terms necessary to make the instrument negotiable. U.C.C. §3-309(b).

    e. 2002 amendments: The 2002 amendments permit a person not in possession of an instrument to enforce the instrument if the person has directly or indirectly acquired ownership of the instrument from a person who was entitled to enforce the instrument when loss of possession occurred. [Rev] U.C.C. §3-309(a)(1)(B).

    Rationale: This permits a person who lost the instrument but has the right to enforce it under [Rev] U.C.C. §3-309 to transfer its right to enforce the instrument to another.

    Required proof: A transferee of a lost instrument need only prove that its transferor was entitled to enforce the instrument. There is no need for the transferee to prove that it was in possession of the instrument at the time the instrument was lost. [Rev] U.C.C. §3-309, Official Comment 2.

    Declaration of loss: The 2002 amendments substitute the term *record* for "writing." As a result, a declaration of loss may be made in a record that is not a writing. A record is "information that is inscribed on a tangible medium or that is stored in an electronic or other medium and is retrievable in perceivable form." [Rev] U.C.C. §3-103(a)(14).

B. Lost, destroyed, or stolen bank checks: A different set of rules apply when a bank check (a cashier's, teller's, or certified check) is lost, destroyed, or stolen. The owner of a bank check who loses the bank check may not have the ability to post a bond in an amount sufficient to indemnify the obligated bank. To make it possible for the owner to recover from the bank, a procedure had to be devised to protect the bank against double liability while at the same time making it possible for the owner to recover from the bank. U.C.C. §3-312 provides such a procedure.

    1. Who may use U.C.C. §3-312: Only the drawer or payee of a certified check and the remitter or payee of a teller's or cashier's check (***claimant***) may proceed under U.C.C. §3-312. U.C.C. §3-312(a)(3)(ii). An indorsee of a bank check is denied the advantages of U.C.C. §3-312 and must proceed as if he were suing on an ordinary lost or stolen instrument.

    2. Manner of asserting claim: The claimant must send a communication to the bank issuing the bank check describing the check with reasonable certainty and requesting payment of the amount of the check. This communication must be accompanied by a declaration of loss. U.C.C. §3-312(b).

    3. When claim is effective: By complying with these simple requirements, the declarer has asserted a claim under U.C.C. §3-312. The claim, however, is not valid for 90 days. During this

90-day waiting period, the bank may, with impunity, pay the person entitled to enforce the check. U.C.C. §3-312(b)(2). After the 90-day period, the issuing bank becomes liable to the claimant if the bank had not already paid a person entitled to enforce the check. U.C.C. §3-312(b)(4); U.C.C. §3-312, Official Comment 4.

4. **Bank discharged by payment to claimant:** Payment to the claimant discharges the bank's liability to a person entitled to enforce the check. U.C.C. §3-312(b)(4). If a holder in due course presents the bank check after the bank pays the claimant, the issuing bank may pay the holder in due course. The claimant is then obliged to repay the bank. If the bank refuses to pay the holder in due course, the claimant must pay the holder. The declaration of loss made by the claimant is a warranty of the truth of the statements contained therein. U.C.C. §3-312(b); U.C.C. §3-312, Comment 3.

Quiz Yourself on
NATURE OF LIABILITY ON INSTRUMENTS

25. Bob draws a check payable to Jill. Jill indorses the check to Sally.

    a. What is the effect of Jill's indorsement of the check to Sally? _____

    b. If Sally refuses to purchase the check unless Jim, Jill's brother, also promises to pay the check, what is Jim's signature called? _____

26. Assume that Bank of America issues a cashier's check payable to Bill. When Bill wants to be paid, Bill will demand that Bank of America pay the check. Can Bank of America expect that anyone else will be called on to make payment? _____

27. When Bob draws a check payable to Jill for $300, Bob is ordering Wells Bank to pay $300 to Jill. What is Bob impliedly promising? _____

28. Assume that Son asks Dad to sign in accommodation so that he can purchase a car from Car Dealer. Car Dealer asks Dad to sign as maker and Son to indorse the note. Car Dealer takes a security interest in the car as collateral. Car Dealer sells the note, along with its security interest in the car, to Finance Company. Finance Company releases title of the car to Son. Is Dad discharged by the Finance Company releasing the title? _____ Would the result be any different under the 2002 amendments? _____

29. Assume that a person entitled to enforce an instrument released his security interest in his collateral, a car worth $20,000. The principal debtor then sells the car and loses the money. The remaining debt is $15,000. To what extent is the accommodation party discharged? _____ Would the result be different under the 2002 amendments? _____

30. The person entitled to enforce the instrument releases his security interest in the collateral, a car, when the car was worth $20,000 and the debt was $50,000. To what extent is the accommodation party discharged? _____ Would the result be different under the 2002 amendments? _____

31. Junior wants to purchase a car. From what Junior has heard from his college friends, he realizes that he will not be able to obtain a loan unless Father co-signs on the loan. Father and Junior go to Cal's

Cars. Father tells the salesman that they want to purchase a car. The salesman has Father and Junior sign the note as co-makers. The note is payable to Cal's Cars. Cal's Cars takes a security interest in the car to secure the note. Father asks that the car be put in Junior's name. Cal's Cars fails to properly perfect its security interest in the car. One of Junior's creditors executes on the car to satisfy a judgment he has against Junior. Immediately thereafter, Junior files for bankruptcy. To what extent can Cal's Cars recover from Father on the note? _____

32. Assume, instead, that Cal's Cars released Son from liability in payment of a portion of the amount due under the note. Can Cal's Cars sue Father for the remainder? If so, does Father have any recourse against Son? _____

33. On January 1, Charlie issues a check to Carmona. On January 10, Carmona indorses the check to Casey. On February 7, Payor Bank sets off a debt owed to it by Charlie against his bank account. No funds remain in the account when, on February 8, Casey presents the check to Payor Bank. Payor Bank therefore dishonors the check. May Casey recover from Charlie or Carmona? _____

34. Yonas issues a check in payment for a television set purchased from Jessee. The check is made payable to cash. Jessee, without indorsing the check, cashes it at Check Cashing Service. Discovering that the television set was stolen by Jessee, Yonas stops payment on the check. May Check Cashing Service recover from Jessee? _____

35. Hanook, as authorized agent for Masai Corporation, enters into a contract for the purchase by Masai of certain equipment from Tigist Machinery. In payment for the purchase, Hanook executes a promissory note payable to Tigist Machinery. The note states that "I (We) promise to pay. . . ." The note is signed "Masai Corporation, Hanook." Tigist Machinery sells the note to Genet Finance Company. Is Hanook personally liable on the note? _____

36. Danielle agreed to purchase a new Jaguar from Fisseha Automobile for $60,000 under a sales contract. Fisseha Automobile takes from Danielle a note for the purchase price payable in one year in 12 equal monthly installments. After 2 months, although Danielle is current in her payments, Fisseha Automobile demands payment of the entire purchase price under the sales contract. Is Danielle obligated to immediately pay the remainder of the purchase price? _____

37. In fact, Danielle does not make any additional payments on the note. Fisseha Automobile brings a legal action against Danielle for the remaining payments. In her answer, Danielle generally denies any liability on the note. Fisseha Automobile produces the note in court. Danielle introduces no evidence. Fisseha Automobile requests that the court enter a judgment for it as a matter of law. Is Fisseha Automobile entitled to such a judgment? _____

38. Assume that a check is indorsed by Paul to Kate to Dan. Assume that Dan receives notice of dishonor on August 1. Dan gives notice of dishonor to Kate on August 15.

a. Is the notice of dishonor timely as to Kate? _____

b. By what date does Kate have to give timely notice of dishonor to Paul? _____

39. Assume that Bob and Abe co-make a note in the amount of $5,000. As collateral, Abe grants to Carl, the payee, a security interest in property worth $1,000. Because Carl fails to perfect the security interest, the security interest is avoided by the trustee in Abe's bankruptcy. To what extent, if any, is Bob discharged? _____

40. Alice, as payee, gives, as a gift, the note to Beth but fails to indorse the note.

    a. Is Beth a holder of the note?   _____

    b. What rights does Beth have on the note?   _____

Answers

25. a. It makes Sally the holder of the check and obligates Jill to pay the check if dishonored. If Jill wants to avoid liability while still negotiating the check, Jill can indorse the check without recourse.

    b. An anomalous indorser. Jim's signature is anomalous because it was not necessary to make Sally the holder of the check. Jill's indorsement alone was sufficient.

26. No. Being a cashier's check, the check is drawn by Bank of America, as drawer, on itself as drawee. Bill will demand payment directly from Bank of America, and just like the maker of a note, they are obligated to make payment.

27. To make payment. By drawing the check, Bob is impliedly promising that if Wells Bank does not pay the check on presentment, Bob will pay Jill.

28. Dad is not discharged by the action of Finance Company unless Finance Company knew or had notice of his accommodation status. Without such notice, when Finance Company released the car to Son, Finance Company did not know that it was hurting Dad. Because Dad signed as maker of the note, Finance Company believed that Dad was to be ultimately liable and that on Dad's payment, he would have no recourse against Son who signed as an indorser. The result would be the same under the 2002 amendments. Unless the person entitled to enforce the instrument either knows or has notice under [Rev] U.C.C. §3-419(c) that the instrument was signed for accommodation, the accommodation party is not discharged by an impairment of the collateral. [Rev] U.C.C. §3-605(e).

29. $15,000. Had the security interest not been released, the accommodation party, on payment, could have looked to the car for repayment. Because the car is no longer subject to the security interest, the accommodation party has no way of recovering the $15,000 he has to pay to the person entitled to enforce the instrument. Using the terminology found in the Code, the value of the interest in the collateral has been reduced to $0, which is $15,000 less than the amount of the right of recourse. Therefore, the accommodation party would be discharged as to the entire $15,000. The result would be the same under the 2002 amendments. Under [Rev] U.C.C. §3-605(d), when collateral is impaired and the debt is oversecured, the secondary obligor is discharged to the extent that the impairment causes the value of the collateral to be reduced to an amount less than the amount of the secondary party's right of recourse, which is $15,000.

30. $20,000. The accommodation party loses $20,000 as a result of the release of the security interest. The right of recourse is $50,000 and the present value of the collateral is $0. Because of the impairment, the deficiency is now $50,000 rather than $30,000. Therefore, the increase in the amount by which the amount of the right of recourse exceeds the value of the interest is $20,000. The result would be the same under the 2002 amendments. Under [Rev] U.C.C. §3-605(d), collateral is impaired to the extent that the reduction in value of the interest causes an increase in the amount by which the amount of the recourse exceeds the value of the interest. Because the amount by which the amount of recourse exceeds the value of the interest has been increased from $30,000 to $50,000, the value has been impaired by $20,000.

31. An accommodation party is discharged when the person entitled to enforce the instrument impairs the collateral. Cal's Cars' failure to properly perfect its security interest in the car did impair the collateral. Even though Father is an accommodation party, Cal's Cars does not seem to have notice of his status. Therefore, Father is not discharged by its impairment. U.C.C. §3-605(h). [[Rev] U.C.C. §3-605(e).] However, Father would be treated as a person who is jointly and severally liable with Junior and therefore would be discharged up to the value of the car but for not more than half of the obligation. U.C.C. §3-605(f).

32. **Yes.** Discharge by renunciation or cancellation (in other words, a "release") of the accommodated party does not discharge the accommodation party. U.C.C. §3-605(b). Notwithstanding Son's release, once Father pays Cal's Cars, he is entitled to enforce the instrument against Son. U.C.C. §3-419(e).

33. **Yes.** Neither Charlie nor Carmona are discharged by Casey's delay in presenting the check for payment. Although the check was not presented within 30 days of its date, Charlie, as drawer, is not discharged because Payor Bank did not go insolvent. As a result, Charlie was not harmed by the delay. Carmona is not discharged because Casey presented the check within 30 days of his indorsement and therefore the presentment was timely as to Carmona.

34. **Yes.** Even though Jessee did not indorse the check, he still makes the transfer warranty to Check Cashing Service that the check is not subject to any defenses good against him. Because Jessee would take subject to Yonas's defense of failure of consideration, Jessee has breached the warranty he gave to Check Cashing Service. U.C.C. §3-416(a)(4).

35. **Yes.** A representative, even if authorized, who signs her name to an instrument may be personally liable unless the form of the signature unambiguously indicates that she is signing only as representative for the represented person. Because it is ambiguous as to whether Hanook is signing only in a representative capacity, he is liable to a holder in due course who takes the note without notice that he was not intended to be personally liable. U.C.C. §3-402(b)(2). As a result, only if Genet Finance Company has notice that Tigist Machinery and Hanook did not intend Hanook to be personally liable can Hanook avoid liability.

36. **No.** When Fisseha Automobile took the note in payment of Danielle's obligation under the sales contract, Danielle's obligation became suspended until dishonor of the note. Because Danielle is current in her payments, the note has not been dishonored, and, therefore, Fisseha Automobile cannot sue on the underlying obligation. U.C.C. §3-310(b)(2).

37. **Yes.** Danielle's signature as maker is admitted because Danielle did not specifically deny in the pleadings the validity of the signature. U.C.C. §3-308(a). Because Fisseha Automobile, the payee, produced the note, it is entitled to a judgment unless Danielle proves a defense or claim in recoupment. Because Danielle introduced no evidence of any possible defense or claim in recoupment, Fisseha Automobile is entitled to its judgment. U.C.C. §3-308(b).

38. **a. Yes.** Persons other than a collecting bank must give notice of dishonor within 30 days following the day on which the person receives notice of dishonor. U.C.C. §3-503(c); U.C.C. §3-503, Official Comment 2. Dan received notice on August 1 and gave notice 15 days later.

    b. September 14. Kate has until September 14 (30 days from the date she received notice of dishonor) to give notice of dishonor to Paul.

39. $500. Unless the parties otherwise agree, a party having joint and several liability is entitled to contribution from his joint and several obligors to the extent available under applicable law. U.C.C. §3-116(b). Even if a party having joint and several liability is discharged by some act of the holder, his discharge does not affect the right of his joint and several obligor to receive contribution from the discharged party. U.C.C. §3-116(c); U.C.C. §3-116, Official Comment 1. Although the result is the same, the analysis is different under the 2002 amendments. U.C.C. §3-116(c) has been omitted. Under the 2002 amendments, parties that are jointly and severally liable are each, in part, a secondary obligor and, in part, a principal obligor. As a result, to the extent that each party is a secondary obligor, [Rev] U.C.C. §3-605 determines the effect of a release, an extension of time, or a modification of the obligation of one of the joint and several obligors, as well as the effect of an impairment of collateral provided by one of those obligors. [Rev] U.C.C. §3-116, Official Comment 1. Under the 2002 amendments, Bob is also discharged to the extent of $500.

40. a. No. Beth is missing a necessary indorsement, and is, therefore, not a holder of the note.

    b. Because Alice transferred the note to her, Beth has all of Alice's rights as a holder and is, in her own right, a person entitled to enforce the instrument.

Exam Tips on
NATURE OF LIABILITY ON INSTRUMENTS

☛ **Raising suretyship defenses:** Always remember that the ability of an accommodation party to raise the suretyship defenses depends on whether the holder has notice of his status as an accommodation party.

☛ **Discharge of an indorser:** Notice that an indorser is only discharged if a check is not presented for payment or given to a depositary bank for collection within 30 days of *his indorsement*. The time for presentment does not run from the date of the check.

    ☞ Notice also that as long as the check is deposited for collection within 30 days of his indorsement, the indorser cannot claim a discharge even if the check is not presented for payment until after the 30-day period.

CHAPTER 4

FORGERY, ALTERATION, AND OTHER FRAUDULENT ACTIVITY

ChapterScope

This chapter examines the loss allocation in the event of a forged signature or alteration, the warranties made on presentment and transfer, conversion, the grounds precluding a party from claiming that a signature or an alteration is unauthorized, and the effect of restrictively indorsing an instrument. The key points in this chapter are:

- **Forgery ineffective:** A forged or unauthorized signature is wholly inoperative as the signature of the person whose name is signed.

- **Effect of unauthorized indorsement:** A person cannot be a holder of an instrument that contains an unauthorized indorsement in her chain of title.

- **Transfer warranty:** A person who transfers an instrument warrants that all signatures are authentic and that the instrument has not been altered.

- **Presentment warranty:** A person who presents a check for payment warrants that she is a person entitled to enforce the instrument and that the instrument has not been altered.

- **Conversion where indorsement forged:** A person who pays or purchases an instrument bearing a forged indorsement converts the instrument.

- **Preclusion through negligence:** A person may be precluded by her negligence from asserting the unauthorized nature of a signature or an alteration.

- **Preclusion of drawer to assert forged indorsement:** A drawer of a check, whether or not negligent, may be precluded by certain of her actions from claiming that an indorsement is forged.

- **Effect of restrictive indorsement:** The owner of a restrictively indorsed instrument may recover from the depositary bank or other taker of the instrument in the event that the instrument is transferred in violation of the restriction.

I. UNAUTHORIZED SIGNATURES

A. Introduction: Subject to certain exceptions, an unauthorized signature is ineffective as the signature of the person whose name is signed. U.C.C. §3-403(a). An unauthorized signature may be an outright forgery or a signature by an agent in excess of her actual or apparent authority. U.C.C. §1-201(43); U.C.C. §3-403, Official Comment 1.

B. Two consequences of unauthorized signature: The fact that an unauthorized signature has no effect as the signature of the person whose name is signed has two distinct consequences: (a) the person whose signature is signed is not liable on the instrument; and (b) if the unauthorized signature is an indorsement in the chain of title, no person following the unauthorized indorsement can be a holder of the instrument.

C. **Person whose name is signed not liable:** The person whose signature is unauthorized is not liable on the instrument whether the signature appears in the capacity of drawer, maker, acceptor, or indorser. U.C.C. §3-401(a).

   1. **Unauthorized signer liable:** An unauthorized signature is effective as the signature of the unauthorized signer in favor of a person who, in good faith, pays the instrument or takes it for value. U.C.C. §3-403(a).

   2. **Loss shifted:** The loss may be shifted to the person whose name is forged if that person is negligent or is otherwise precluded from claiming that the signature is not authorized.

D. **Effect of forged indorsement in chain of title:** When an indorsement in the chain of title is forged, no person following the forged indorsement can become a holder of the instrument.

   Note: This does not apply when the instrument is payable to bearer or indorsed in blank. In these cases, no indorsement is necessary to make the transferee a holder because the instrument is negotiated by delivery alone.

   1. **Person whose signature forged still owner:** Absent grounds for preclusion, the person whose indorsement is forged remains the owner of the instrument.

   2. **Different result if precluded:** When a person is precluded from claiming that her indorsement is forged, the forged indorsement is effective to negotiate the instrument.

E. **Transfer warranties:** Two transfer warranties are relevant in determining the allocation of loss when a signature is forged.

   1. **Person entitled to enforce instrument:** A transferor warrants that she is a person entitled to enforce the instrument. U.C.C. §4-207(a)(1); U.C.C. §3-416(a)(1). This is basically a warranty that there are no unauthorized or missing indorsements that prevent the transferee from becoming a person entitled to enforce the instrument. U.C.C. §3-416, Official Comment 2.

   2. **All signatures are authentic:** A transferor warrants that all signatures are authentic and authorized. U.C.C. §4-207(a)(2); U.C.C. §3-416(a)(2). A forged or unauthorized drawer's, maker's, indorser's, or acceptor's signature breaches this warranty.

   3. **2002 amendments:** A new transfer warranty has been added as to remotely created consumer items. With respect to a remotely created consumer item, the transferor warrants that "the person on whose account the item is drawn authorized the issuance of the item in the amount for which the item is drawn." [Rev] U.C.C. §3-416(a)(6) and [Rev] U.C.C. §4-208(a)(4). As a result, the risk of the item not being authorized by the person upon whose account it was drawn rests upon the person initially transferring the item.

F. **Presentment warranties:** Certain risks should not be borne by the person making payment. To protect the person making payment, she is given certain warranties when an instrument is presented for payment. These warranties are called the ***presentment warranties***. The same presentment warranties are contained in both Articles 3 and 4. The warranties under U.C.C. §3-417 are identical to those given under U.C.C. §4-208 except that U.C.C. §4-208 extends its coverage to items and not just to negotiable instruments.

1. **Persons who make presentment warranties:** The presentment warranties are made by the person who obtains payment or acceptance as well as by any prior transferor. U.C.C. §4-208(a), (d); U.C.C. §3-417(a), (d).

   Example: Assume that Jim draws a check payable to Don. Don loses the check. Don's indorsement is forged by Gil, who indorses the check in blank and gives the check as a present to his daughter Sally. Sally deposits the check in her bank account at Wells Bank, which sends the check for collection to Crocker Bank, which presents the check for payment to Bank of America. Bank of America pays the check. See Figure 4-1.

Figure 4-1

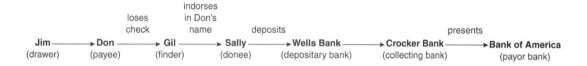

   Crocker Bank, as the entity that obtained payment, in addition to prior transferors Gil, Sally, and Wells Bank, all make the presentment warranties to Bank of America. Even though Gil did not receive consideration for the check, he still makes the presentment warranties. Even though Sally did not indorse the check, she still makes the presentment warranties. Furthermore, Wells Bank, although only an agent for collection, also makes the presentment warranties.

2. **To whom presentment warranties are made:** The presentment warranties are made to any payor or acceptor who acts in good faith. U.C.C. §4-208(a), (d); U.C.C. §3-417(a), (d)(1). The fact that the payor or acceptor was negligent in making payment or acceptance does not deny it the right to receive these warranties. U.C.C. §4-208(b); U.C.C. §3-417(b).

   Example: Even if an alteration is so obvious that it should have been noticed by the payor bank, the payor bank may still recover from the presenter for breach of the warranty that the check has not been altered.

3. **Warranties made to drawee of unaccepted draft:** The payor bank on a check (as well as any drawee of an unaccepted draft) is given three warranties:

   - the warrantor is entitled to enforce the draft or authorized to obtain payment or acceptance on behalf of a person entitled to enforce the draft;

   - the warrantor has no knowledge that the signature of the drawer is unauthorized;

   - the draft has not been altered. U.C.C. §4-208(a); U.C.C. §3-417(a).

     Example: The depository bank, rather than the drawer bank, was liable for payment made on altered check, even though the drawer bank destroyed the paper check, absent a showing that the check was forged, rather than altered, or that duplication of the entire check, rather than just physical alteration of the payee's name on the original check, was a common method of bank fraud. Wachovia Bank, N.A. v. Foster Bancshares, Inc., 457 F.3d 619 (7th Cir. Ill.) (2006).

   a. **Measure of damages:** The basic measure of damages for breach of a warranty made to the drawee is an amount equal to the amount paid less the amount that the drawee is entitled to receive from the drawer plus expenses and loss of interest arising from the breach.

U.C.C. §4-208(b); U.C.C. §3-417(b). Although no express provision authorizes them, attorneys' fees are not necessarily excluded. U.C.C. §3-417, Official Comment 5. The drawee may have the right to recover attorneys' fees under the phrase "expenses . . . resulting from the breach." U.C.C. §3-417, Official Comment 5.

   b. **Drawer's negligence may be asserted against payor bank:** If the payor bank could have asserted against the drawer that the drawer was negligent, the person against whom the payor bank is bringing the breach of presentment warranty action may assert the drawer's negligence as a defense to the payor bank's action. U.C.C. §4-208(c); U.C.C. §3-417(c).

4. **2002 amendments:** A new presentment warranty has been added as remotely created consumer items under which the person obtaining the payment or acceptance and prior transferors warrant, as to remotely created consumer items, that the person on whose account the item is drawn authorized the issuance of the item in the amount for which the item is drawn. The effect of this warranty is to impose ultimate liability on the depositary bank that accepted the unauthorized remotely created item rather than on the payor bank, which had no means of determining whether it was authorized. This warranty applies not only when the item is unauthorized, but also when the consumer authorized the item in a different amount than that in which payment was made. [Rev] U.C.C. §3-417(a)(4); [Rev] U.C.C. §4-208(a)(4).

5. **Warranties made to other payors:** Any payor, other than a drawee of an unaccepted draft, receives only the warranty that the warrantor is entitled to enforce the instrument or is authorized to obtain payment on behalf of a person entitled to enforce the instrument. U.C.C. §4-208(d); U.C.C. §3-417, Official Comment 4.

   a. **Persons entitled to warranty:** These payors include drawers or indorsers to whom a dishonored draft has been presented for payment, makers of notes, and acceptors of drafts. U.C.C. §4-208(d); U.C.C. §3-417(d).

   b. **No warranty as to unauthorized signature:** Neither the drawer nor the maker is given a warranty that the presenter lacks knowledge of the unauthorized nature of the maker's or drawer's signature. U.C.C. §3-417, Official Comment 4.

     Rationale: A drawer or maker should be able to determine whether her signature is authentic. U.C.C. §3-417, Official Comment 4.

     Note: Even absent a warranty, a drawer or maker could recover, under U.C.C. §3-418(a) or (b), any payment made to a presenter who had knowledge of the forgery at the time she took the instrument. Having such knowledge, the presenter would not have taken the instrument in good faith, and therefore, would not be protected under U.C.C. §3-418(c).

   c. **Warranty not given to acceptor:** No warranty is made to the acceptor of a draft that the warrantor lacked knowledge of the unauthorized nature of the drawer's signature.

     Note: The acceptor as the drawee of an unaccepted draft is given a warranty that the warrantor lacked knowledge as to the unauthorized nature of the drawer's signature. U.C.C. §3-417, Official Comment 4. As a result, the acceptor may recover both from the person presenting the draft for acceptance, if she knew of the unauthorized nature of the drawer's signature, and from persons who transferred the draft prior to its acceptance who had such knowledge. U.C.C. §3-417, Official Comment 4. The acceptor could also recover under U.C.C. §3-418(a) from any person, presenting the acceptance for payment, who had knowledge of the unauthorized nature of the drawer's signature when she took the acceptance.

    d. Accrual and notice of breach: A cause of action for breach of a presentment warranty accrues when the claimant has reason to know of the breach. U.C.C. §4-208(f); U.C.C. §3-417(f). The breach occurs when the item is paid or accepted. Notice of a claim for breach of a presentment warranty must be given to the warrantor within 30 days after the claimant had reason to know of the breach and could ascertain the warrantor's identity. Failure to give notice discharges the warrantor's liability to the extent of any loss caused by the delay in giving notice of the claim. U.C.C. §4-208(e); U.C.C. §3-417, Official Comment 7.

G. Recovery by payor of payment made by mistake: Even absent a presentment warranty, the payor may be able to recover the mistaken payment from its recipient under U.C.C. §3-418. A drawee who pays a draft on a mistaken belief may recover the amount of the draft from the person to whom payment was made or for whose benefit payment was made. U.C.C. §3-418(a); U.C.C. §3-418, Official Comment 1. The drawee can revoke its acceptance in the identical circumstances that it could recover the payment had payment been made instead.

    1. Typical mistakes: Typical mistaken payments by a drawee include payment over a forged drawer's signature, payment of a check drawn on insufficient funds, and payment over a valid stop payment order.

    2. Protected persons under U.C.C. §3-418: Payment may not be recovered from a ***protected person***. U.C.C. §3-418(c). There are two classes of protected persons.

        a. Good-faith takers for value: The first class includes any person who takes the instrument in good faith and for value. U.C.C. §3-418(c).

        b. Good-faith reliance: The second class includes any person who has, in good faith, changed position in reliance on the payment. U.C.C. §3-418(c).

        Note: The issue is not whether the person acted in good faith in the transaction in which he acquired the instrument, but whether his act of reliance on the payment is in good faith. A person who obtains payment with knowledge of the mistake does not act in good faith when he changes position in reliance on the payment.

    3. Consequences when payment is recovered: In the event that payment is recovered, the instrument is treated as having been dishonored. The person from whom payment is recovered is given the rights of a person entitled to enforce the dishonored instrument. U.C.C. §3-418(d); U.C.C. §3-418, Official Comment 2. As a result, this person can enforce the instrument against the drawer, maker, or indorser just as if the instrument had been dishonored on its initial presentment.

H. Conversion: Article 3 expressly states that the law of conversion of personal property applies to instruments. In addition, Article 3 specifically provides that certain acts constitute conversion. U.C.C. §3-420.

    1. When taking by transfer constitutes conversion: An instrument is converted if it is taken by transfer, other than by negotiation, from a person not entitled to enforce the instrument. U.C.C. §3-420(a). Because an instrument payable to bearer is negotiated by transfer of possession alone, there can be no conversion of an instrument payable to bearer. When an instrument is payable to the order of a specified person, that person must indorse the instrument for it to be negotiated. Therefore, if an instrument is transferred without the indorsement of the person to whom it is payable, it may be converted.

Exception: An instrument is not converted if the transferee is a person entitled to enforce the instrument because he is a transferee of a holder.

Example: If Jim had transferred the check to Don but had neglected to indorse the check, Don, being a transferee of a holder, would be a person entitled to enforce the check. Gene, therefore, would not be liable for conversion.

2. **When payment constitutes conversion:** An instrument is converted if a payor bank, or other payor, makes payment with respect to the instrument to a person not entitled to enforce the instrument or to receive payment. U.C.C. §3-420(a).

Example: If Bank of America makes payment of a check bearing Jim's unauthorized indorsement, Bank of America has converted the instrument. This would also be true if Gene was not a person entitled to enforce the instrument because Jim's indorsement was missing.

3. **When taking instrument by agent is conversion:** A person who holds an instrument solely as a representative of another person (other than a depositary bank) who has, in good faith, dealt with an instrument or its proceeds on behalf of one who was not the person entitled to enforce the instrument is not liable in conversion or otherwise beyond the amount of any proceeds that it has not paid out. U.C.C. §3-420(c).

Example: A messenger who was not aware that the person for whom he was acting was not entitled to enforce the instrument is not liable for conversion. If the messenger retains a portion of the proceeds, he is liable for the amount retained.

4. **Taking instrument for collection:** Although a depositary bank acts as its customer's agent in collecting the instrument, a depositary bank is liable for conversion whether or not it acts in good faith or retains any of the proceeds from the check. U.C.C. §3-420(c). An intermediary collecting bank is relieved of liability for conversion when it acts in good faith and retains none of the proceeds from the check.

Example: If Gene deposits the check in his account at Wells Bank, which transfers the check for collection to First Interstate Bank, Wells Bank, but not First Interstate Bank, would be liable for conversion.

Rationale: By having only the depositary bank, and not intermediary banks, liable for conversion, the loss falls on the person who would ultimately suffer the loss without having to involve intermediary banks (and possibly the payor bank) in the action. Had Jim sued the payor bank, the payor bank would have recovered from the intermediary bank for breach of its presentment warranty. The intermediary bank would recover from the depositary bank for breach of its transfer warranty that it is a person entitled to enforce the instrument. By allowing Jim, the owner, to directly sue the depositary bank, these other two banks are relieved of the burden of unnecessary litigation.

5. **Who may bring an action for conversion?** The proper party to bring an action for conversion of an instrument is the person who, before the theft or loss, was the person entitled to enforce the instrument.

   a. **Delivery required:** A payee may bring the action only if the instrument has been delivered to him. U.C.C. §3-420(a)(ii); U.C.C. §3-420, Official Comment 1.

Example: If the check had not been delivered to Jim, he would have no property rights in the check and, thus, may not bring an action for conversion. Until the instrument has been delivered, Jim still retains the right to sue the drawer on the underlying obligation. U.C.C. §3-420, Official Comment 1.

   b. **Issuer has no right to bring action for conversion:** An action for conversion may not be brought by the drawer, acceptor, or other issuer of the instrument. U.C.C. §3-420(a)(i).

Example: Assume, in our example above, that before the check was delivered to Jim, the check was stolen from the mail. The check is cashed by the thief. Bank of America debits the drawer's account and remits the funds to Wells Bank. The drawer may not sue Wells Bank for conversion. Because the indorsement was forged, Bank of America has no right to debit the drawer's account. The drawer's remedy is against Bank of America for recrediting of his account. The drawer, therefore, suffers no loss from the improper payment and cannot sue the depositary bank.

6. **Defenses to conversion action:** The person sued for conversion may defend by proving that the forged indorsement is effective as the indorsement of the owner. This may be accomplished by proving that the owner's negligence substantially contributed to the making of the forged indorsement (U.C.C. §3-406(a)), that the owner is precluded by estoppel or ratification from denying that the indorsement is authentic, that the owner has received the proceeds from the instrument, or that the indorsement is effective under U.C.C. §3-404 (Impostors and Fictitious Payees) or U.C.C. §3-405 (Employer's Responsibility for Indorsements by Employees).

7. **Measure of damages for conversion:** The measure of damages for conversion is presumed to be the amount payable including interest, but recovery may not exceed the amount of plaintiff's interest in the instrument. U.C.C. §3-420(b); U.C.C. §3-420, Official Comment 2. The defendant may prove liability in a lesser amount by introducing evidence of the insolvency of all of the obligors or proving a defense that is valid against the owner. Because conversion is a tort, punitive damages may be available in an appropriate case. *See* McAdam v. Dean Witter Reynolds, Inc., 896 F.2d 750 (3d Cir. 1990) (account executive of Dean Witter forged indorsements of checks payable to its customers. Depositary bank cashed checks for account executive in amounts as large as $475,000. Bank was in bad faith because it deliberately broke its own rules. Jury award of punitive damages affirmed.).

8. **Statute of limitations for conversion:** The statute of limitations on an action for conversion of an instrument expires 3 years after the cause of action accrues. The cause of action accrues when the act of conversion occurred. In the case of a payor, the cause of action accrues on the date of payment. In the case of a purchaser, the cause of action accrues on the date of his purchase. U.C.C. §3-118(g). The discovery rule, which provides that a cause of action accrues when the plaintiff knew or, in the exercise of ordinary diligence, could have discovered that an injury had been sustained as a result of the act of another, should not apply to claims for conversion of a negotiable instrument. Auto-Owners Ins. Co. v. Bank One, 852 N.E.2d 604 (Ind. App. 2006).

I. **Application of rules when signature of maker or acceptor unauthorized:** The allocation of loss when an instrument bears the unauthorized signature of the maker or acceptor depends, to a large degree, on whether the maker or acceptor pays the instrument. The same analysis applies when a draft is presented to the drawer itself for payment or acceptance.

1. **When payment not made:** In the absence of estoppel, ratification, or negligence, the maker or acceptor is not liable on an instrument on which his signature is forged or unauthorized because he did not sign the instrument. U.C.C. §3-401(a). Thus, the person presenting the note or acceptance for payment will suffer the loss unless that person can recover from a prior transferor on the warranty that all signatures are authentic or authorized.

2. **When payment made:** If the maker or acceptor makes payment, the maker or acceptor will suffer the loss if the person to whom payment is made is a protected person under U.C.C. §3-418. Neither the maker nor the acceptor is given a presentment warranty as to the authenticity of his own signature.

J. **Application of rules when signature of drawer unauthorized:** When the signature of the drawer is forged or otherwise unauthorized, which party suffers the loss depends in large part on whether the drawee (payor bank in the case of a check) pays the draft (or check).

1. **When drawee makes payment:** When the drawee makes payment of a check or other draft bearing the forged signature of the purported drawer, the drawee will usually suffer the loss. Neither the presenter nor prior transferors warrant that the drawer's signature is genuine. The only warranty they make is that they have no knowledge that the drawer's signature is unauthorized. U.C.C. §4-208(a)(3); U.C.C. §3-417(a)(3). The drawee or payor bank may not debit the account of the drawer because, bearing his unauthorized signature, the draft is not properly payable. The drawee can only recover the mistaken payment from a recipient of the payment who is not a protected party. U.C.C. §3-418(c).

   Rationale: Although it can be argued that a payor bank is in a better position than the holder to determine whether the drawer's signature is valid in that a payor bank may have a sample of its customer's signature, liability is imposed on the payor bank even if the forgery is perfect. The true explanation for imposing the loss on the payor bank lies in history. Lord Mansfield, in Price v. Neal, 97 Eng. Rep. 871 (K.B. 1752), first held that the drawee suffers the loss when it pays a draft over a forged drawer's signature. Thereafter, courts, without question, began following the holding. Banks, being the parties primarily affected by the rule, began obtaining insurance covering this risk. Once banks factored the cost of insurance into the price charged for checking accounts, there became no reason to change the rule.

   2002 amendments: A new presentment warranty has been added as remotely created consumer items under the person obtaining the payment or acceptance and prior transferors warrant, as to remotely created consumer items, that the person on whose account the item is drawn authorized the issuance of the item in the amount for which the item is drawn. The effect of this warranty is to impose ultimate liability on the depositary bank that accepted the unauthorized remotely created item rather than on the payor bank, which had no means of determining whether it was authorized. This warranty applies not only when the item is unauthorized, but also when the consumer authorized the item in a different amount than that in which payment was made. [Rev] U.C.C. §3-416, Official Comment 8. As a result, the risk of the item not being authorized by the person upon whose account it was drawn rests on the person initially transferring the item.

2. **When drawee does not make payment:** If the drawee does not make payment, the loss will go back down the chain of title to the first solvent party after the forger (assuming that the

forger is not solvent). The mechanism for passing down the loss is the transfer warranty, given by each transferor, that all signatures are genuine and authorized. U.C.C. §3-416(a)(2); U.C.C. §4-207(a)(2).

3. 2002 amendments: A new transfer warranty has been added as to remotely created consumer items. With respect to a remotely created consumer item, the transferor warrants that "the person on whose account the item is drawn authorized the issuance of the item in the amount for which the item is drawn." [Rev] U.C.C. §3-416(a)(6) and [Rev] U.C.C. §4-208(a)(4). As a result, the risk of the item not being authorized by the person upon whose account it was drawn rests on the person initially transferring the item.

K. Application of rules when indorsement is unauthorized: The rights of the parties when there is an unauthorized indorsement in the chain of title depend on whether the instrument has been delivered to the payee.

1. Allocation of loss when check not delivered to payee: When the check or other draft has not been delivered to the payee, the payee has no right to sue for conversion of the check. U.C.C. §3-420(a). The payee still retains whatever rights she had against the drawer on the underlying obligation for which the check was taken. Similarly, the drawer has no right to sue the depositary or other collecting bank for either conversion, U.C.C. §3-420(a), or for breach of the presentment warranty that it is a person entitled to enforce the instrument. U.C.C. §3-417, Official Comment 2. The drawer has not suffered a loss because the payor bank has no right to debit her account. The allocation of loss is the same whether or not payor bank pays the check. Upon payment of the check, the payor bank may recover the amount paid from the presenting bank and prior transferors for breach of their presentment warranty that they are a person entitled to enforce the instrument. U.C.C. §4-208(a)(1); U.C.C. §3-417(a)(1). The loss flows back to the first solvent transferor following the forgery because each transferor warrants that it is a person entitled to enforce the instrument. U.C.C. §4-207(a)(1).

Example: Assume a check payable to Paula is drawn by Dan on his account at Security Bank. Fred steals the check prior to its delivery to Paula. Fred forges Paula's indorsement and cashes the check with Local Grocer, who deposits the check in his checking account at Wells Bank, which sends the check for collection to Crocker Bank, which presents it for payment to Security Bank. Security Bank pays the check. Because the check was not delivered to Paula, Paula has no rights to, or on, the check. However, Paula retains whatever rights she had against Dan on the underlying obligation. Security Bank cannot debit Dan's account because the check was not properly payable. Security Bank's recourse is against Crocker Bank, Wells Bank, or Local Grocer for breach of their presentment warranty that they are a person entitled to enforce the instrument. Crocker Bank may recover from Wells Bank or Local Grocer on their transfer warranty that they are a person entitled to enforce the instrument. If Crocker Bank recovers from Wells Bank, Wells Bank, in turn, can recover from Local Grocer for breach of its transfer warranty.

Note: If the draft or check is dishonored, each transferee in turn will have the same right to recover from prior transferors on their transfer warranty that they are a person entitled to enforce the instrument. U.C.C. §3-416(a)(1); U.C.C. §4-207(a)(1).

2. Allocation of loss after delivery to payee: After delivery of the draft or check to the payee, the payee's rights depend on whether the instrument has been paid.

a. **Payee's rights if instrument not paid:** If the check is still missing, the payee may recover on the check from the drawer by complying with the requirements for the enforcement of lost, destroyed, or stolen instruments. U.C.C. §3-309. However, the payee may not recover from the drawer on the underlying obligation. U.C.C. §3-310(b)(4); U.C.C. §3-310, Official Comment 4. If the check is found prior to payment, the payee may recover possession of the check from the possessor. Because her indorsement is forged, no subsequent possessor can qualify as a holder in due course. As a result, any subsequent possessor would take subject to the payee's claim of ownership. Once the payee recovers possession of the check, she may present the check for payment, and, if it is not paid, she can recover from the drawer on either its drawer's contract or on the underlying obligation. The party required to return the check can then recover from her transferor and any prior transferors for breach of their transfer warranty that they are a person entitled to enforce the draft. U.C.C. §3-416(a)(1); U.C.C. §4-207(a)(1).

Example: Assume, in our example above, that Fred Forger steals the check from Paula Payee, forges Paula Payee's indorsement, and cashes the check with Local Grocer, which deposits the check in its own account at Wells Bank. Paula recovers possession of the check from Wells Bank. Wells Bank can recover from Local Grocer for breach of its transfer warranty that it is a person entitled to enforce the instrument. U.C.C. §4-207(a)(1).

b. **Payee's rights if instrument paid:** If the check is paid, the payee may recover from the payor bank, the depositary bank, or any nonbank transferor for conversion. U.C.C. §3-420(a); U.C.C. §3-420, Official Comment 3. Ultimately, the first solvent party after the person who made the unauthorized indorsement will bear the loss. The payor bank can recover from the presenter or prior transferors for breach of their presentment warranty that they are a person entitled to enforce the instrument. U.C.C. §4-208(a)(1). Each transferee can recover from prior transferors for breach of their transfer warranty that they are a person entitled to enforce the instrument. U.C.C. §3-416(a)(1); U.C.C. §4-207(a)(1).

II. ALTERATIONS AND INCOMPLETE INSTRUMENTS

A. **What is an alteration?** An alteration is any unauthorized change in an instrument that attempts to modify in any respect the obligation of any party. U.C.C. §3-407(a). Any change in the terms of an instrument that changes the contract of any party is an alteration. In addition, any unauthorized addition of words or numbers or other change to an incomplete instrument relating to the obligation of any party is also an alteration. U.C.C. §3-407(a).

Example: Polly draws a check in the amount of $50 payable to Jean. Jean alters the check by raising the amount to $500 and negotiates the check to Dentist in payment of her bill. By raising the amount of the check from $50 to $500, Jean has altered the check. It would also be an alteration if Jean changed the date of the check or the payee's name.

Note: Any change, no matter how small or benign, is an alteration. An increase in the amount payable by one penny is an alteration. Similarly, a reduction in the amount payable is also an alteration.

B. **Allocation of loss in case of alteration:** In the absence of his own negligence, assent, or preclusion, a party who signs an instrument only promises to pay the instrument according to its terms at the time he signed the instrument. U.C.C. §3-412; U.C.C. §3-413(a); U.C.C. §3-414(b); U.C.C. §3-415(a).

Example: Return to our example above. Assume that Dentist deposits the check in her account at Wells Bank, which presents the check to Bank of America. Bank of America pays the check and debits Polly's account. Because the check was payable for $50 when Polly signed it, Bank of America may only debit Polly's account in the amount of $50. In the event that Bank of America had refused to pay the check, Wells Bank could recover only $50 from Polly. However, because Jean and Dentist indorsed the check when it was payable in the amount of $500, Wells Bank could have recovered $500 from either of these parties.

1. **Preclusion to assert alteration:** A party whose failure to exercise ordinary care substantially contributes to an alteration is precluded from asserting the alteration as against a person who in good faith pays the instrument or takes it for value or collection. U.C.C. §3-406(a). In addition, a party who assents to the alteration or a party who is otherwise precluded from asserting the alteration may be liable on the instrument as altered. U.C.C. §3-407(b); U.C.C. §3-407, Official Comment 1.

2. **Payment by drawee:** In the case of a check or other unaccepted draft, the allocation of loss *does not* depend on whether the drawee has paid or accepted the draft. If the drawee pays the draft, the drawee may debit the drawer's account only in the amount for which the draft was originally drawn by the drawer unless the drawer is negligent or otherwise precluded from asserting the alteration. U.C.C. §4-401(d)(1). In the absence of grounds for precluding the drawer, the drawee may recover from any person obtaining payment or acceptance or any previous transferor for breach of the presentment warranty that the draft has not been altered. U.C.C. §3-417(a)(2); U.C.C. §4-208(a)(2). The party from whom the drawee recovers can recover from his transferor and any prior transferors for breach of their transfer warranty that the draft had not been altered. U.C.C. §3-416(a)(3); U.C.C. §4-207(a)(3).

   Example: In our example, Bank of America may only debit Polly's account in the amount of $50. Bank of America may recover the remaining $450 from Wells Bank, Dentist, or Jean. Wells Bank can recover from either Dentist or Jean.

3. **When drawer, maker, or acceptor pays:** When either the drawer, maker, or acceptor makes the payment, the party making payment will suffer the loss if payment has been made to a person protected under U.C.C. §3-418(c). This is because no warranty is given to the drawer, maker, or acceptor that the instrument has not been altered. U.C.C. §3-417, Comment 4.

   Rationale: These individuals should know what the terms of the instrument were at the time they signed it and should not pay the instrument if it has been altered. U.C.C. §3-417, Comment 4.

   Example: Assume that a note is made in the amount of $50 by Sam and payable to Gabriel. Gabriel raises the note to $500 and negotiates the note to Hank for value. Hank presents the note to Sam for payment. If Sam recognizes that the note has been altered and refuses to pay Hank, Hank can recover only $50 from Sam. Hank must recover the remaining money from Gabriel for breach of his transfer warranty that the note has not been altered. However, if Sam pays the note for the entire $500, he may have to suffer the loss unless he can recover from Gabriel. Hank does not warrant to Sam that the note has not been altered. Sam may have the right to recover the $450 from Hank under U.C.C. §3-418 if the law of restitution allows such recovery, but only if Hank does not qualify as a person who took the instrument in good faith and for value or has not, in good faith, changed position in reliance on the payment. U.C.C. §3-418(b), (c).

4. **When instrument not paid:** If an instrument is not paid, the person entitled to enforce the instrument may recover from any prior transferors for breach of their transfer warranty of no alteration and, in addition, may recover up to the amount for which the instrument was payable at the time of their engagement against prior indorsers, the maker, the drawer, or the acceptor. U.C.C. §3-415(a); U.C.C. §3-412; U.C.C. §3-414(b); U.C.C. §3-413(a).

   Example: In our earlier example, Wells Bank can recover $50 from Polly. It can recover $450 from Jean or Dentist on their transfer warranty that the instrument has not been altered. It can recover $500 from either Jean or Dentist on their indorser's contract.

C. **Discharge of party whose obligation is affected:** A fraudulently made alteration discharges a party whose obligation is affected by the alteration unless that party assents to the alteration or is precluded from asserting the alteration. When an alteration is not fraudulent, the instrument may be enforced according to its original terms. U.C.C. §3-407(b).

   Example: In our earlier example, Gabriel cannot enforce the instrument whatsoever against Sam.

   Rationale: The party affected is discharged as a means of discouraging the holder from attempting to alter the instrument. The holder is punished for his attempt to gain an advantage from the fraudulent alteration by being completely denied the right to enforce the instrument against the party whose contract has been changed. U.C.C. §3-407(b).

   1. **Against whom discharge effective:** Any transferee, other than one who takes the instrument for value, in good faith, and without notice of the alteration, also takes subject to the discharge. U.C.C. §3-407(c); U.C.C. §3-203(b). A payor bank or other drawee paying a fraudulently altered instrument or a person taking it for value, in good faith, and without notice of the alteration may enforce the instrument according to its original terms. U.C.C. §3-407(c); U.C.C. §3-407, Official Comment 2.

      Example: From our earlier example, if Hank took the instrument for value, in good faith, and without notice of the alteration, he could recover $50 from Sam. Otherwise, he would simply stand in Gabriel's shoes and recover nothing from Sam.

   2. **Alteration must be fraudulent:** An alteration does not discharge the party whose obligation is affected unless the alterer had a fraudulent intent in making the alteration. U.C.C. §3-407(b); U.C.C. §3-407, Official Comment 1. An alteration is fraudulent when the alterer intends to achieve an advantage for himself to which he has reason to know he is not entitled.

      Example: If the holder erroneously believes that the party has authorized or consented to the alteration or that he has the right to alter the instrument to reflect the true agreement of the parties, the fact that no such consent or authorization actually exists or that he has no such right does not make the alteration fraudulent U.C.C. §3-407, Official Comment 1.

D. **Incomplete instruments:** When the signer intends that the instrument as signed be completed by the addition of words or numbers, the instrument is called an incomplete instrument. For an instrument to be an incomplete instrument, it must contain a blank space for the missing term to be inserted. U.C.C. §3-115(a). The effect of completing an incomplete instrument depends on whether the completion was authorized.

1. **When completion authorized:** When the completion of an incomplete instrument is authorized, the instrument may be enforced as completed. U.C.C. §3-115(b).

   Example: Assume that you authorize your neighbor to write a check up to $500 for the repair of your furnace. If your neighbor fills in the sum of $400, the check may be enforced in the amount completed. The payor bank that pays the check may debit your account for $400. U.C.C. §4-401(d)(2); U.C.C. §4-401, Official Comment 4.

2. **When completion unauthorized:** When the completion is unauthorized, a payor bank acting in good faith may enforce the instrument as completed. U.C.C. §3-407(c). Similarly, a person taking the instrument for value, in good faith, and without notice of the improper completion may enforce the instrument according to its terms as completed. U.C.C. §3-407(c). As to any other persons, the obligor is discharged and, therefore, is not liable on the instrument at all. U.C.C. §3-407(b).

   Example: In our example above, assume that your neighbor filled in the check for $600. Even though the completion was unauthorized, the payor bank may debit your account for the entire $600. Assuming that the payor bank refused to pay the check, if the repair company is unaware of this limitation, it could enforce the check for the entire $600.

   Rationale: By leaving open a blank or space, the issuer has made it easy for the alterer to pass off the completion as authentic. For this reason, the issuer takes the risk that the instrument will be completed contrary to his authority.

III. GROUNDS OF PRECLUSION

A. **Introduction:** There are many grounds that can cause an unauthorized signature or alteration to be treated as though it was authorized: ratification (U.C.C. §3-403(a)), estoppel (U.C.C. §1-103), negligence (U.C.C. §3-406), failure of customer to examine her bank statement (U.C.C. §4-406), making instrument payable to impostor or fictitious payee (U.C.C. §3-404), and employer's responsibility for fraudulent indorsement by an employee (U.C.C. §3-405).

B. **Ratification:** An unauthorized signature may become effective as the signature of the person whose name is signed if ratified by that person. U.C.C. §3-403(a). *Ratification* is the election by the person whose name is signed to treat the unauthorized signature as though it were originally authorized by her. U.C.C. §3-403, Official Comment 3. The law of agency of the subject jurisdiction determines whether a person has ratified an unauthorized signature.

C. **Estoppel:** A party may be estopped to deny the authenticity of a signature. A party is estopped when she represents that the signature is authentic and the holder or payor relies to her detriment on such representation. U.C.C. §1-103.

D. **Preclusion through negligence:** A person whose failure to exercise ordinary care substantially contributes to an alteration or to the making of a forged signature is precluded from asserting the alteration or forgery against a person who, in good faith, pays the instrument or takes it for value or for collection. U.C.C. §3-406(a). The party claiming that the negligent party is precluded from asserting that the unauthorized signature or alteration is not effective must prove two separate elements: (a) that the party to be precluded failed to exercise ordinary care and (b) that the failure substantially contributed to the making of the forged signature or alteration.

1. **Who may assert the preclusion?** Three classes of persons may assert the preclusion:

   - any person who in good faith pays the instrument,

   - any person who in good faith takes the instrument for value, or

   - any person who in good faith takes the instrument for collection. U.C.C. §3-406(a); U.C.C. §3-406, Official Comment 1.

2. **Comparative negligence:** The party who is negligent may prove that the person asserting the preclusion, whether it be the payor bank, depositary bank, or holder itself, failed to exercise ordinary care and that the failure substantially contributed to the loss. In this event, the loss is allocated according to principles of comparative negligence. U.C.C. §3-406(b). The Code gives, however, absolutely no guidance as to how this split should take place.

3. **Failure to exercise ordinary care:** *Ordinary care* in the case of a person engaged in business means the observance of the reasonable commercial standards prevailing in the area in which the person is located with respect to the business in which the person is engaged. U.C.C. §3-103(a)(7).

   a. **Tort test of negligence:** The test as to whether a party has exercised ordinary care is the traditional tort test for negligence: whether the party's actions were reasonable considering the foreseeability of the loss, the magnitude of the potential loss, and the cost of the means required to eliminate the risk of loss. The following are some typical situations of negligence.

      i. **Giving check to third party:** In some situations, giving a check to a third party for delivery to the payee so greatly increases the possibility of a forgery that the drawer will be precluded from asserting the subsequent forgery. Whether the drawer has failed to exercise ordinary care depends on the likelihood that, under the circumstances, the third party would forge the payee's indorsement.

      ii. **Careless business practices:** Careless business practices can result in an increased possibility of forgery.

         Example: A company fails to exercise ordinary care when it allows a signature stamp to be accessible to nonauthorized personnel even though the stamp is not used by the drawer to sign checks. Use of the signature stamp by the nonauthorized personnel would give the appearance to third parties that the drawer had, in fact, signed the check.

      iii. **Negligence in hiring or supervising employees:** An employer may also be precluded from denying the effectiveness of a signature forged by an employee if the employer has failed to exercise ordinary care in either hiring or supervising the employee.

         Example: A company should not, without good reason, hire a bookkeeper who has a background of forgery or embezzlement or who has a gambling or drug problem. If such a bookkeeper is hired, she should be watched carefully.

         Example: When a bookkeeper is authorized both to write checks and to reconcile the books, a periodic audit by another person should be performed.

iv. **Guarding check forms:** It is unlikely that a court would hold a drawer to have failed to exercise ordinary care simply because she was not careful in guarding her blank check forms. This is because anyone can have checks printed up with another person's name and account number imprinted on them. Losing a checkbook without the loss of accompanying identification does not greatly increase the chance of a forgery.

v. **Preventing alterations:** A party has a duty to use reasonable care in drawing or making an instrument such that it cannot be easily altered. U.C.C. §3-406, Official Comment 1.

Example: When the numbers or words signifying the amount due on an instrument are written so as to leave space open for additional words or numbers to be inserted, the party drawing or making the instrument will usually be found to have failed to exercise ordinary care. U.C.C. §3-406, Official Comment 3, Case No. 3. If the instrument reads "in the amount of _____ two dollars," a subsequent party can add the words "two thousand and," thereby easily raising the amount to $2,002.

b. **Failure of payor bank to exercise ordinary care:** A drawer who is precluded from asserting that a signature is unauthorized may attempt to prove that the payor bank also failed to exercise ordinary care so as to cause the loss to be split between them under the principle of comparative negligence.

i. **When indorsement forged:** Whether the payor bank has failed to exercise ordinary care in discovering a forged indorsement depends, to a large extent, on whether the payor bank is also the depositary bank.

- When the payor bank is also the depositary bank or when the item is presented over the counter for payment, the bank fails to exercise ordinary care if it does not discover obvious irregularities in the identification of the person presenting the item for payment. *See* Consolidated Pub. Water Supply Dist. No. C-1 v. Farmers Bank, 686 S.W.2d 844 (Mo. Ct. App. 1985) (payor bank that cashes checks payable to corporation containing handwritten indorsements may be found to have not acted in accordance with reasonable commercial standards).

- Unless the payor bank is also the depositary bank, it is unlikely that it will be found to have failed to exercise ordinary care. The payor bank has no duty to determine whether every indorsement in the chain of title is present and authentic. A payor bank cannot know if an indorsement is forged and, thus, may rely on the presenting bank's guaranty of prior indorsements in paying the check.

ii. **When drawer's signature forged:** Because the payor bank has a copy of its customer's signature, there is at least some possibility that the payor bank may be able to detect a forgery of the drawer's signature. When payor banks used to visually examine a check in the process of deciding whether to pay the check, the payor bank had a duty to use ordinary care to discover any forgery or alteration. However, few banks now visually examine any checks other than extremely large ones. As a result, there is no way in which the bank will discover the forgery. To allow banks to achieve the efficiency available only by computer processing, the Code has provided a special rule when checks are processed by computer.

Even when there is an obvious forgery of the drawer's signature and the bank does not discover it because it processes checks for payment by computer without visually inspecting the checks, the bank still exercises ordinary care as long as "the failure to examine such instrument does not violate the bank's prescribed procedures and the bank's procedures do not vary unreasonably from general banking usage not disapproved by Article 3 or Article 4." U.C.C. §3-103(a)(7). [[Rev] U.C.C. §3-103(a)(9).]

4. **Substantially contributes:** For the failure to exercise ordinary care to preclude the negligent party, the failure must substantially contribute to the making of the forgery or alteration. U.C.C. §3-406(a).

   Example: The simplest case in which the failure to exercise ordinary care substantially contributes to a forgery is when the drawer is negligent in allowing unauthorized personnel access to a facsimile signature machine. By allowing such access, the forgery, looking identical to an authentic signature, is impossible to detect.

   a. **Test:** Although the negligence does not have to make detection of the forgery or alteration more difficult, as in the example of the facsimile signature machine, the negligence must have been a contributing cause and a significant factor in enabling the forgery or alteration to have been made. U.C.C. §3-406, Official Comment 2.

      Example: When Brother and Sister are in a bitter estate contest and Brother is in dire need of money, Drawer's negligence in handing a check to Brother for delivery to Sister would be a significant factor and a contributing cause in Brother's forging Sister's indorsement. Although Brother still has to convince a subsequent purchaser (or the payor) that Sister's indorsement is authentic, Drawer's negligence in delivering the check to a person of questionable integrity made the forgery more likely.

   b. **Does not significantly increase likelihood of loss:** If the negligence has no effect on the likelihood of the forgery or alteration being made or of its success, the negligence will not have substantially contributed to the making of the forgery or alteration.

      Example: Generally, the mailing of a check to a person other than the payee does not substantially contribute to the resultant forgery even though it may constitute the failure to exercise ordinary care. The forger must still convince the purchaser or payor that she is the payee. When the check is mailed to a different person having the same name as the intended payee, however, the ability of the forger to pass herself off as the payee is greatly increased. Thus, if the sender fails to exercise ordinary care in sending the check to a person bearing the same name as the payee, the sender's failure will be deemed to substantially contribute to the forged indorsement. U.C.C. §3-406, Official Comment 3, Case No. 2.

E. **Impostors, fictitious payees, and employer's responsibility for unauthorized indorsements by employees:** There are three situations in which, even absent proof of any specific negligence regarding the instrument, a forged indorsement is deemed to be effective to negotiate the instrument. In any of these three situations, if the person taking the instrument or paying the instrument is negligent, comparative negligence principles apply to split the loss.

   1. **The impostor rule:** *Impostor* is defined as a person who "by use of the mails or otherwise induces the issuer to issue the instrument to the impostor, or to a person acting in concert with the impostor, by impersonating the payee of the instrument or a person authorized to act for the payee." U.C.C. §3-404(a).

      Rationale: Impostors are subject to a separate rule because the drawer has made it extremely likely that the check will be cashed on a forged indorsement. The impostor chose the name either because she has already established a bank account under the chosen name or because she believes that she has other means of successfully cashing the check. The drawer's fault in not making sure that he was dealing with the real payee allowed the impostor to accomplish her fraud.

a. What is an impostor? An impostor is one who represents herself to be the named payee or a person authorized to act for the named payee and, by such representation, induces the issuer to issue the instrument to her or to a person acting in concert with her. U.C.C. §3-404, Official Comment 1. In essence, the drawer or maker is deemed to have made the instrument payable to the impostor under the assumed name of the named payee.

Example: Ivan Impostor is an impostor if he pretends to be Newt Gingrich and asks the drawer to give him a check for his upcoming Congressional campaign. Ivan Impostor would also be an impostor if he claimed that he was a member of Gingrich's campaign committee and asked for a check payable to Gingrich. In contrast, if Ivan steals a check intended for Gingrich from the drawer's mailbox and, thereafter in cashing the check, pretends to be Gingrich, the impostor rule would not apply.

b. Purports to be agent: A person is also an impostor when she falsely represents herself to be the agent of the named payee. U.C.C. §3-404(a).

c. Manner of impostor: The impostor rule applies whether the impostor acts in person, by mail, by telephone, or otherwise. U.C.C. §3-404(a). The manner of the imposture is irrelevant.

Example: If, on receipt of a campaign contribution solicitation letter from Ivan Impostor, signed by him under the name of Newt Gingrich, the drawer mails a check payable to Newt Gingrich to the designated address, any person's indorsement in the name of Newt Gingrich will be sufficient to negotiate the check.

Example: Courts differ as to whether the impostor rule applies when Wife, in filling out a loan application, forges Husband's signature and then forges Husband's indorsement on a check payable to Husband. Compare Broward Bank v. Commercial Bank, 547 So. 2d 687 (Fla. Dist. Ct. App. 1989) (impostor rule does not apply because husband took home papers for loan, brought them back with appearance of his wife's signature, and thereafter forged his wife's indorsement on check) with Franklin Natl. Bank v. Shapiro, 7 U.C.C. Rep. Serv. 317 (N.Y. Sup. Ct. 1970) (impostor rule applies because wife forged husband's signature on loan documents and on check).

d. Need for indorsement: An indorsement by any person in the name of the payee is effective in favor of a person who in good faith pays the instrument or takes it for value or for collection. U.C.C. §3-404(a). The indorsement need not be in the exact name of the payee as long as it is in a name substantially similar to that of the named payee. U.C.C. §3-404(c). As long as the instrument is deposited in a depositary bank to an account in a name substantially similar to that of the payee, the depositary bank is the holder of the instrument regardless of whether the instrument is indorsed. U.C.C. §3-404(c)(ii).

e. When indorsement effective: An indorsement by any person in the name of the payee is effective to negotiate the instrument, thus making the indorsee the holder.

Example: Assume, in our example above, that Ivan Impostor indorses the check to Local Grocer, who deposits the check into his bank account at Wells Bank, which presents the check for payment to Bank of America. Bank of America pays the check. Because Ivan's indorsement in the name of Newt Gingrich is effective, Local Grocer and Wells Bank are persons entitled to enforce the instrument. Neither Local Grocer nor Wells Bank breach their presentment warranty to Bank of America that they are persons entitled to enforce the check. Likewise, being persons entitled to enforce the check, their taking of the check is not conversion. On its payment to Wells Bank, Bank of America may charge the drawer's account.

    i. Good faith required: A payor or taker who does not act in good faith may not assert that the indorsement is effective. U.C.C. §3-404(b)(2).

    ii. Comparative negligence: When the taker or payor is negligent, the loss is allocated under comparative negligence principles between the drawer and the negligent party. U.C.C. §3-404(d); U.C.C. §3-404, Official Comment 3.

    Example: Assume that Ivan Impostor had deposited the check in an account under the name of Newt Gingrich that Ivan had opened at Wells Bank. If Wells Bank had allowed Ivan to establish a bank account in the name of Newt Gingrich without asking for any identification, Wells Bank's negligence would have contributed to Ivan Impostor's ability to accomplish his mischief. As a result, Drawer has a cause of action against Wells Bank to recover a portion of the loss. U.C.C. §3-404, Official Comment 3.

2. Fictitious payee rule: A *fictitious payee* is a person who is either not intended to have any interest in the instrument or is nonexistent. U.C.C. §3-404(b). When a drawer or maker issues an instrument payable to a fictitious payee, the maker or drawer will usually suffer any resulting loss.

    a. What is a fictitious payee: A payee is regarded as a fictitious payee in three distinct situations. In all these situations, the person signing as or on behalf of the drawer or the maker, intended that the payee have no interest in the instrument:

        i. Nonexistent payee: The person identified as the payee does not in fact exist. U.C.C. §3-404(b)(ii).

        Example: A check payable to Donald Duck does not designate any person who could possibly indorse the instrument.

        Rationale: The drawer is in the best position to determine whether the named payee exists.

        ii. Payee intended to have no interest: The maker or drawer issues an instrument intending that the named payee have no interest in the instrument. U.C.C. §3-404(b)(i).

        iii. Employee signing instrument intends payee to have no interest: When an agent, employee, or officer signs on behalf of the drawer or maker intending the payee to have no interest in the instrument, the actual signer is usually trying to defraud her employer. The agent, employee, or officer may attempt to hide her activity by padding the payroll or altering the records to show a debt owed to the named payee, or she may make no attempt at all to conceal her activity.

    b. Relevant intent is of party making signature: In determining whether a payee is a fictitious payee, it is necessary to look at the intent of the "person whose intent determines to whom an instrument is payable" as determined under U.C.C. §3-110(a) and (b). The intent of the signer of the instrument controls the identification of the person to whom the instrument is payable. It does not matter that the signer is acting on behalf of the maker or drawer or whether or not the person was authorized to make the instrument payable to the person identified by the signer. U.C.C. §3-110(a) and Official Comment 1. Where more than one person signs the instrument as maker or drawer and each signer intends by its designation to indicate a different person as the payee, the instrument is payable to any person intended by any one of the signers. U.C.C. §3-110(a).

c. **Form of required indorsement:** The same rules as to the need for an indorsement in the case of impostors also apply to fictitious payees except in one particular situation. In the case of a fictitious payee, because no person was the intended payee, any person in possession of the instrument is its holder. U.C.C. §3-404(b)(1).

Example: When Ivan Impostor pretends to be Newt Gingrich and asks the drawer to give him a check for his upcoming Congressional campaign, until an indorsement is made in the name "Newt Gingrich," no person, other than Newt Gingrich, can be its holder. U.C.C. §3-404(a).

d. **Who may assert that the indorsement is effective:** The same rule applies as in the case of impostors.

e. **Double forgeries:** When a person who forges the drawer's name also intends that the payee have no interest in the check, the payee is a fictitious payee. U.C.C. §3-404, Official Comment 2, Case No. 4. As a result, the payor bank, rather than the depositary bank, suffers the loss when there is both a forged drawer's signature and a forged indorsement.

Analysis: Because any indorsement in the name of the payee is effective to negotiate the instrument, the depositary bank is a person entitled to enforce the instrument. Therefore, the depositary bank does not breach its presentment warranty to that effect. The payor bank suffers the loss because the check is treated as bearing only a forged drawer's signature.

Example: Thief steals Drawer's checkbook and forges Drawer's signature on a check that Thief makes payable to his sister Agnes. Thief intends that Agnes have no interest in the check. Thus, any indorsement in Agnes's name is effective to negotiate the check. Thief, after signing Agnes's name, deposits the check in his bank account at Wells Bank. Bank of America pays the check. Because Drawer's signature is forged, Bank of America may not debit Drawer's account, nor may it recover from Wells Bank for breach of a presentment warranty. Bank of America therefore suffers the loss.

3. **Employer's responsibility for fraudulent indorsement by employee:** When an employer hires an employee and gives the employee responsibility regarding instruments, the employer is liable when the employee makes a fraudulent indorsement. A *fraudulent indorsement* is either (1) an indorsement made in the name of the employer on an instrument payable to the employer or (2) an indorsement in the name of the payee on an instrument issued by the employer. U.C.C. §3-405(a)(2).

Example: Sandra, bookkeeper for Diamonds-R-Forever, makes a fraudulent indorsement both when she forges Diamonds-R-Forever's indorsement on a check payable to Diamonds-R-Forever and when she takes a check issued by Diamonds-R-Forever, intended for Sapphire Gem Company, and indorses the check in the name of Sapphire Gem Company. Compare Mount Vernon Properties, LLC v. Branch Banking and Trust Co., 170 Md. App. 457 (Md. App. 2006) (question as to whether person who forged payee's indorsement on check was an employee of drawer of check, whether such person's authority was more than just having access to instruments being transported so as to make applicable the employer's responsibility for a fraudulent indorsement by its employee) with Schrier Brothers v. Golub, 123 Fed. Appx. 484 (3rd Cir. N.J. 2005) (wholesaler's former salesperson had "responsibility" for checks collected from his customers so as to make applicable the employer's responsibility for a fraudulent indorsement by its employee).

a. **Rule:** An indorsement in the name of the payee is effective in favor of any person who, in good faith, pays an instrument or takes it for value or for collection whenever an employer entrusts an employee with responsibility with respect to the instrument, and the employee or a person acting in concert with him, makes a fraudulent indorsement. U.C.C. §3-405(b).

Rationale: The loss is imposed on the employer for two reasons. First, she has a duty to prevent the loss by exercising care in hiring and supervising her employees. Second, even if the employer is not at fault in any manner, she is still in the best position to prevent the loss by purchasing a fidelity bond governing misappropriations by employees.

b. **Need for indorsement:** The requirements are the same as in the case of impostors. U.C.C. §3-405(b), (c).

c. **Contributory negligence:** If the person paying or taking the instrument fails to exercise ordinary care and the failure substantially contributes to the loss, the person bearing the loss may recover from the person failing to exercise ordinary care to the extent that her failure contributed to the loss. U.C.C. §3-405(b) and Official Comments 2 and 4.

d. **Employee must have responsibility with respect to instruments:** For an indorsement to be effective under this rule, the employer must entrust the employee with responsibility with respect to instruments. U.C.C. §3-405(a)(1); U.C.C. §3-405(b).

   i. **Employee:** "Employee" is broadly defined to include actual employees, independent contractors, and employees of an independent contractor retained by the employer.

   ii. **Responsibility:** "Responsibility" means authority (1) to sign or indorse instruments on behalf of the employer; (2) to process instruments received by the employer for bookkeeping purposes, for deposit to an account, or for other disposition; (3) to prepare or process instruments to be issued in the name of the employer; (4) to supply information for determining the names or addresses of payees; (5) to control the disposition of instruments issued in the name of the employer; or (6) to act otherwise with respect to instruments in a responsible capacity. U.C.C. §3-405(a)(3).

   Note: An employee does not have responsibility with respect to an instrument just because he has access to instruments, or to blank or incomplete forms, as part of incoming or outgoing mail or otherwise. U.C.C. §3-405(3). Therefore, an indorsement by a mail room attendant in the name of the payee is not effective when he steals the check from the mailroom. U.C.C. §3-405, Official Comment 3, Case No. 1.

   Example: A bookkeeper whose duties include the authority to process checks received by the employer for bookkeeping purposes has been entrusted with responsibility as to checks. U.C.C. §3-405(a)(3)(ii). Thus, when the bookkeeper deposits one of the checks into her personal bank account, the check is deemed to have been properly indorsed by the employer. U.C.C. §3-405, Official Comment 3, Case No. 3.

Example: An employee whose duties include entering addresses of suppliers into a computer has responsibility with regard to checks because she has responsibility to supply information determining the names or addresses of payees. U.C.C. §3-405(a)(3)(iv). When the employee adds a fraudulent address for a real supplier, her indorsement of the check in the name of the supplier is effective.

Example: Because Sandra, as treasurer, has authority to sign instruments on behalf of Diamonds-R-Forever, Sandra's indorsement in the name of Sapphire Gem Company, the payee, is effective even though she developed the intention to steal the check only after the check was issued to pay a bona fide debt owed to Sapphire Gem Company. U.C.C. §3-405(a)(3)(i); U.C.C. §3-405, Official Comment 2, Case No. 6.

F. Customer's duty to review bank statement: A customer has a duty to review its bank statement to determine whether any forgery of its own signature or any alteration has occurred. U.C.C. §4-406(c). U.C.C. §4-406 does not cover forged indorsements.

    1. Applies to items: Because the preclusion is found in Article 4, U.C.C. §4-406 applies to all items and not just to "instruments." However, it has been held that payee bank's encoding error was not encompassed within the 60-day limitations period in customer's account agreement in which to notify bank of alterations, forgeries, or "any other errors." *See* Douglas Companies, Inc. v. Commercial Nat. Bank of Texarkana, 419 F.3d 812 (8th Cir. Ark. 2005).

    2. No duty of bank to send statement of account to customer: Whether or not the bank has a duty to supply its customer with a statement of account or to return items to the customer depends solely on its agreement with its customer. U.C.C. §4-406, Revised Official Comment 1. In fact, most banks do send such statements. If items are not returned to the customer, the bank has the duty, for 7 years after receipt of the items, to retain either the items or legible copies thereof. U.C.C. §4-406(b).

    3. If bank sends statement of account: A bank that sends or makes available to a customer a statement of account showing payment of items on his account shall either return or make available to the customer the items paid or provide information in the statement of account sufficient to allow the customer to reasonably identify the items paid. U.C.C. §4-406(a).

        a. Check retention: In an attempt to decrease costs, banks have begun to institute the cost-saving practice of check retention. Under a check retention plan, the payor bank retains the check or other item instead of returning it to the customer along with the statement of account. U.C.C. §4-406, Revised Official Comment 3.

        b. Sufficient information: When neither the item nor its image is returned, the bank fulfills its duty to provide sufficient information if it gives to the customer the number of the item, its amount, and the date of payment. U.C.C. §4-406(a) and Revised Official Comment 1. This information is the information contained on the MICR-encoded line and thus is easily retrievable by the computer paying the item. U.C.C. §4-406, Revised Official Comment 1.

    4. Customer's duty to examine bank statement: Once the bank sends or makes available a statement of account or the items, the customer has the duty to exercise reasonable promptness in examining the statement or the items to determine whether any payment was unauthorized due to an alteration or because a purported signature, by or on behalf of the customer, was unauthorized. U.C.C. §4-406(c).

 a. Duty to notify bank: If the customer should reasonably have discovered the unauthorized payment from the statement or items provided, the customer must promptly notify the bank of the relevant facts. U.C.C. §4-406(c); U.C.C. §4-406, Revised Official Comment 1.

 b. Reasonable promptness: Courts have upheld bank/customer agreements giving the customer a period as short as 14 days to examine his bank statement and report his own unauthorized signature or alteration. In the absence of an agreement to the contrary and absent extenuating circumstances, however, it is unlikely that a delay of more than 30 days would be found to be reasonable.

5. **Duty of bank to prove loss:** Even when a customer fails to reasonably discover or report a forgery or an alteration, the customer is only precluded from asserting its unauthorized signature or alteration if the bank proves that it suffered a loss by reason of the failure. U.C.C. §4-406(d)(1); U.C.C. §4-406, Revised Official Comment 2.

 a. Difficulty of proof when single forgery or alteration involved: When a wrongdoer forges or alters only one check, he typically immediately withdraws the funds and either vanishes, becomes insolvent, or goes to jail by the time the statement is returned to the customer. As a result, the bank would suffer the loss whether or not the customer had promptly discovered and reported the forgery or alteration.

6. **Forgery or alteration by same wrongdoer:** The customer is also precluded from asserting an unauthorized signature or alteration by the same wrongdoer on any other item paid in good faith by the bank before it received notice from the customer of the unauthorized signature or alteration and after the customer had been afforded a reasonable period of time, not exceeding 30 days, in which to examine the item or statement of account and notify the bank. U.C.C. §4-406(d)(2); U.C.C. §4-406, Revised Official Comment 2.

 Note: The customer is not entitled to prove that a delay of more than 30 days was reasonable under the circumstances. U.C.C. §4-406, Revised Official Comment 2. If a customer fails to report the first forged item within 30 days, he is precluded from recovering for that transaction and for any additional items forged by the same wrongdoer. Spacemakers of America, Inc. v. SunTrust Bank, 271 Ga. App. 335 (Ga. App. 2005).

7. **Good faith and comparative negligence:** If the customer proves that the bank failed to act in good faith in paying an item, the loss falls completely on the bank. U.C.C. §4-406(e); U.C.C. §4-406, Revised Official Comment 2. Even if the bank acts in good faith, the customer may prove that the bank failed to exercise ordinary care in paying the item and that the failure substantially contributed to the loss. When the customer meets this burden, the loss is allocated between the customer and the bank according to the extent to which the customer failed to comply with his duties and the extent of the bank's failure to exercise ordinary care. U.C.C. §4-406(e); U.C.C. §4-406, Revised Official Comment 2.

8. **1-year preclusion:** A customer must discover and report the customer's unauthorized signature or any alteration on an item within 1 year after the statement or item is made available to the customer. The failure to so report precludes the customer from asserting the alteration or unauthorized signature against the bank whether or not the bank exercised ordinary care. U.C.C. §4-406(f).

 Note: Although the 1-year period does not cover forged indorsements, the general statute of limitations contained in Article 4 precludes a customer from having his account recredited for a debit resulting from the payment of an item bearing a forged indorsement if he delays more than 3 years after payment in filing the action. U.C.C. §4-111.

9. **Duty of payor bank to raise defense:** When a payor bank has the right to debit its customer's account because the customer is precluded under U.C.C. §4-406(c), (d), and (f), or U.C.C. §3-406 (customer's negligence substantially contributing to a forgery or an alteration) from asserting an unauthorized signature or alteration, the payor bank is not allowed to shift the loss from its customer to the presenting or depositary bank by recrediting the customer's account and recovering from the presenting bank for breach of its presentment warranty. U.C.C. §4-406(f); U.C.C. §4-406, Official Comment 5; U.C.C. §4-208(c); U.C.C. §4-406, Revised Official Comment 5.

IV. RESTRICTIVE INDORSEMENTS

A. **Definition: :** A *restrictive indorsement* is an indorsement written by or on behalf of the holder that limits negotiation of the instrument to a specific use.

B. **Types of restrictive indorsements:** There are two types of restrictive indorsements.

1. **For deposit:** An indorsement that signifies a purpose of deposit or collection is a restrictive indorsement. U.C.C. §3-206(c). A *for deposit* indorsement indicates that the proceeds of the instrument can only be credited to the indorser's bank account. A blank *for collection* indorsement or a "for collection" indorsement that specifically designates a bank, e.g., "To Bank of America, for collection, (s) James" also similarly indicates an intention that the proceeds be deposited into the indorser's bank account. *Pay any bank* is a blank indorsement that limits holder status to banks. U.C.C. §4-201(b). When an instrument is indorsed "Pay any bank," only a bank may acquire the rights of a holder until (1) the item is returned to the customer initiating collection or (2) the bank specially indorses the check to a nonbank. U.C.C. §4-201(b).

   Example: When James receives his paycheck, he may indorse it "for deposit only (signed) James." James indorses the check in this manner to ensure that the check's proceeds are deposited in his bank account.

2. **Trust indorsement:** An indorsement that states that payment is to be made to the indorsee as agent, trustee, or other fiduciary for the benefit of the indorser or another person (*trust indorsement*) is a restrictive indorsement. U.C.C. §3-206(d).

   Example: If Jim wants to negotiate a check for use by the estate of John Jones, Jim may indorse the check to Don, the executor of the estate, by stating "Don in trust for the estate of John Jones." By so doing, Jim indicates that Don is to use the funds only for the benefit of the estate of John Jones.

C. **Does not limit right to negotiate:** A restrictive indorsement deprives an indorsee neither of holder status nor of the right to further negotiate or transfer the instrument. U.C.C. §3-206(a).

   Example: Even if James, in the above example, loses his paycheck, Finder becomes the holder of the check because the check is payable in blank (James had not listed anyone as the special indorsee). Finder may further negotiate the check to Auto Loan Co. in payment of his own debt in violation of the restrictive indorsement. Auto Loan Co. by virtue of the indorsement becomes the holder of the check. It cannot, however, become a holder in due course of the check because it did not apply the value consistently with the indorsement.

D. Effect of "for deposit only" indorsement: A "for deposit only" indorsement limits the rights of the depositary bank and nonbank purchasers or payors, but not the rights of the payor bank or intermediary banks.

    1. Payor and intermediary banks exempted: Any bank in the bank collection process, except a depositary bank, may disregard a "for deposit" or similar indorsement. U.C.C. §3-206(c)(4).

    Exception: A payor bank that is also the depositary bank may not ignore a restrictive indorsement.

    Rationale: Because intermediary banks and the payor bank can ignore the restriction, they can efficiently process in bulk the vast number of checks they receive. Because the depositary bank is still bound by the restriction, at least one bank in the collection process is always bound by the restriction.

    2. Depositary bank liable for conversion: The depositary bank, whether it purchases the instrument or takes it for collection, converts the instrument unless it pays the indorser or applies the proceeds consistently with the indorsement by applying it to the indorser's account. U.C.C. §3-206(c)(2). The depositary bank can become a holder in due course only to the extent that it applies the funds for the indorser's benefit. U.C.C. §3-206(e).

    Note: This also applies to a depositary bank that is also the payor bank. When a check is presented for immediate payment over the counter, the payor bank is liable for conversion unless the funds are received by the indorser. To be consistent with the terms of a "for deposit" indorsement, the depositary bank must credit the bank account designated by the indorser.

    Example: If James indorses the check "For deposit in account number 1234, (signed) James," Wells Bank must credit account number 1234. If the indorsement does not specify a particular account, e.g., "for deposit, (signed) James," Wells Bank can deposit the proceeds into any of James's bank accounts. Bank of America (the payor bank) can also pay cash over the counter for the check as long as James receives the funds.

    3. Nonbank: Any person, other than a bank, who purchases an instrument restrictively indorsed for collection or deposit is treated just like the depositary bank and is deemed to have converted the instrument unless the amount paid for the instrument is received by the indorser or applied consistently with the indorsement. U.C.C. §3-206(c)(1); U.C.C. §3-206, Official Comment 3. Such a purchaser can become a holder in due course only to the extent that it applies the funds properly. U.C.C. §3-206(c)(1); U.C.C. §3-206(e).

    Example: In our earlier example, Auto Loan Co. cannot become a holder in due course because it applied the value inconsistently with the indorsement. Similarly, the payor bank has the right to refuse to pay Auto Loan Co. because such payment is inconsistent with the indorsement's effect. U.C.C. §3-206(f).

E. Effect of trust indorsement: The effect of a trust indorsement differs depending on whether the person deals directly with the fiduciary when he makes payment, takes the instrument for collection, or purchases the instrument.

    1. When taker deals directly with fiduciary: When the taker or payor deals directly with the fiduciary, unless the taker has *notice* of the fiduciary's breach of fiduciary duty, the payor can pay, or the taker can apply its value, without regard to whether the fiduciary is violating a fiduciary duty to the indorser. U.C.C. §3-206(d)(1).

Example: Let us return to our original example of Jim indorsing a check "payable to Don, in trust for the estate of John Jones." Don goes to Check Cashing Service and asks that it cash the check. Don uses the cash to buy himself a car. Unless Check Cashing Service has notice of Don's breach of fiduciary duty, Check Cashing Service, in purchasing the check from Don, can apply its value without regard to whether Don violated a fiduciary duty to Jim. Check Cashing Service would have notice of Don's breach of fiduciary duty only if it took the check in payment of, or as security for, a debt known by it to be Don's personal debt or in a transaction it knows to be for the personal benefit of Don. U.C.C. §3-307(b)(2). Unless Check Cashing Service knew that the proceeds would be used by Don personally, Check Cashing Service will qualify as a holder in due course and take free of the claim of ownership of the beneficiary (i.e., Estate of John Jones).

Example: If Don had deposited the check in his own personal bank account at Sunshine Bank, the bank would not be a holder in due course. Sunshine Bank, not being a holder in due course, would then take subject to the claim of ownership of the beneficiary (i.e., Estate of John Jones). U.C.C. §3-306.

2. **When taker does not deal directly with fiduciary:** A person who does not take the instrument directly from the fiduciary is neither given notice, nor otherwise affected, by the restriction contained in the indorsement unless it *knows* that the fiduciary dealt with the instrument or its proceeds in breach of his fiduciary duty. U.C.C. §3-206(d)(2).

Example: From the example above, assume instead that after Check Cashing Service took the check from Don, it deposited the check in its personal account at Moonlight Bank. In this case, Moonlight Bank did not take the check directly from Don (the fiduciary). Therefore, Moonlight Bank is neither given notice, nor otherwise affected by, the restriction contained in the indorsement unless it knows that the fiduciary (Don) dealt with the check or its proceeds in breach of his fiduciary duty. U.C.C. §3-206(d)(2). As a result, Moonlight Bank is a holder in due course and unaffected by the trust indorsement unless it knew that Don had used the funds for his own personal use. In the unlikely case that it had such knowledge, it would be denied holder-in-due-course status and would be subject to the claim of ownership of the beneficiary (Estate of John Jones). U.C.C. §3-206, Official Comment 4.

a. **Liability of payor:** A payor that makes payment of the check in this situation is liable for conversion only if it has actual knowledge that the fiduciary has misused the funds.

b. **Difference between direct and indirect takers or payors:** The difference between these two rules is that the first taker from the fiduciary, Check Cashing Service, is denied holder-in-due-course status if it has *notice* under U.C.C. §3-307 of Don's breach of fiduciary duty. Moonlight Bank, which did not take the check directly from Don, is only denied holder-in-due-course status if it had actual *knowledge* of Don's breach of fiduciary duty.

Quiz Yourself on
FORGERY, ALTERATION, AND OTHER FRAUDULENT ACTIVITY

41. Assume that Allen steals May's checkbook and forges May's signature as the drawer of the check.

    a. If the check is dishonored by payor bank, is May liable to the holder of the check?

    _____

    b. Similarly, in the event that payor bank pays the check, can payor bank charge May's account?

    _____

    c. Is Allen liable as the drawer of the check?   _____

    d. What result if May's negligence allowed Allen to commit the forgery?   _____

42. Assume that Fred forges Julia's indorsement on a check made payable to Julia. Fred then transfers the check to Raoul.

    a. Is Raoul the holder of the check?   _____

    b. If Payor Bank pays Raoul, is the drawer of the check discharged?   _____

43. Assume that Dan drew a check payable to Alice Faye. Carelessly looking up her address in a telephone book, he mails the check to the wrong Alice Faye. The wrong Alice Faye deposits the check in her account at Crocker Bank, which presents the check for payment to Union Bank. Union Bank pays the check. If Union Bank recredits Dan's account and sues Crocker Bank for breach of its presentment warranty, does Crocker Bank have a defense to the suit?   _____

44. Don sells a car to Sally, in payment for which Sally negotiates to Don a check supposedly drawn by Jim. Don presents the check to Bank of America and, immediately on payment, the teller, realizing that Jim's signature was forged, demands the payment back.

    a. Can payment be recovered from Don?   _____

    b. Assume that Don knew that the car he sold to Sally had defective brakes in breach of an express warranty. However, Don did not release the car to Sally until he cashed the check. Is Don protected?

    _____

45. Assume that Allen forges John's signature as maker of a note made payable to Peter. Peter indorses the note to Sally. John refuses to pay Sally.

    a. Will Sally suffer the loss?   _____

    b. Can Sally recover from Peter?   _____

    c. Can Sally or Peter recover from Allen?   _____

    d. If John fails to recognize that his signature on the note is forged and pays Sally, can John recover payment from Sally?   _____

46. Assume that Jane, the office manager of The Smoke Shop, having no authority to sign checks for her employer, forges the treasurer's signature on a check payable to David, Jane's husband. David, knowing of the forgery, deposits the check in his bank account at Security Bank, which allows him to withdraw the uncollected funds. Security Bank presents the check to Wells Bank, the payor bank. Wells Bank pays the check.

a. Can Wells Bank debit The Smoke Shop's account? _____

b. Can Wells Bank recover from Security Bank? _____

c. Can Wells Bank recover from David? _____

d. Can Wells Bank recover from Jane? _____

e. If Wells Bank does not pay the check, who could Security Bank recover from? _____

47. Don draws a check payable to Bill in the sum of $1,000. Without Don's fault, the check is stolen in the mail before it reaches Bill. The thief deposits the check in his own account at First Interstate Bank, which obtains payment from the payor bank, Bank of Oxnard. Does Don have any cause of action against First Interstate Bank? Against Bank of Oxnard? Does Bill have a cause of action against either bank? _____

48. Dean draws a check in the sum of $50 payable to Earl. Earl raises the amount of the check to $500 and transfers the check, without indorsement, to Frank for $500 cash. Frank presents the check to the payor bank, which refuses to make payment. To what extent may Frank recover from Dean? _____

49. After stealing Jane's checkbook, Thief forges her name as drawer and, so that no one can trace the check to him, makes the check payable in the name of his girlfriend, Doris. After indorsing the check in Doris's name, Thief cashes the check at Check Cashing Service. Check Cashing Service deposits the check in its account at Wells Bank, which obtains payment of the check from Bank of America. Can Bank of America debit Jane's account? Can Bank of America recover the payment from Wells Bank? _____

50. Emaye indorses her paycheck "For deposit only, /signed/ Emaye" and puts the check together with a deposit slip in an envelope addressed to her bank and places the envelope in her mailbox for the postman to pick up. The check is stolen from her mailbox. Thief deposits the check in his bank account at Crocker Bank, which obtains payment of the check from Far West Bank. Does Emaye have any recourse against either Crocker Bank or Far West Bank? _____

51. James Dean ("Dean") is a young aspiring agent who works in the mailroom of ICM, one of the bigger talent agencies in Los Angeles. Dean also has acquired a serious drug habit. To support his habit, he has devised a scheme to steal checks payable to ICM. He opens up a corporate bank account at Wells Bank in the name of Inter Circle Meditation. He makes friends with a person in ICM's bookkeeping department. He tells this person that his goal is to be a bookkeeper. The person agrees, during lunch breaks, to show Dean how the computerized bookkeeping system works. When alone at the computer, Dean examines the accounts receivables. He notices that MGM periodically makes substantial payments to ICM. While alone in the mailroom, he looks for envelopes bearing MGM's return address. He takes the checks out of the envelope and mails the checks for deposit to Wells Bank. He indorses the checks "ICM, Inter Circle Meditation." Wells Bank obtains payment of these checks from Bank of America, MGM's bank. Dean makes a bookkeeping entry in the ICM computer system crediting MGM's account for the payments. During the annual audit, the auditors discover the discrepancy between the amounts deposited in ICM's account and the amounts recorded on ICM's books. Dean confesses and goes to prison. Can ICM recover the money from Wells Bank? _____

52. Assume that David's car is damaged in an accident. David has the car towed to Ripoff Repair Shop. Loss Insurance Company, without telling David, issues a check for the repairs payable jointly to Ripoff Repair Shop and David. Ripoff Repair Shop forges David's indorsement on the check but never finishes the repairs. Can Loss Insurance Company be found negligent? _____

53. Assume that Steve, secretary for Alice, forges Alice's signature as drawer on a check. The forged signature bears no resemblance to Alice's true signature. Bank of America pays the check. Bank of America refuses Alice's demand to recredit her account on the grounds that Alice was negligent in supervising Steve. Alice raises comparative negligence as a defense. She contends that because the forgery was so obvious, Bank of America was negligent in not recognizing that her signature was a forgery. Bank of America claims that it did not notice the forgery because it never visually examines any checks under $5,000. Does the fact that Bank of America did not visually examine the check conclusively prove that Bank of America was negligent? _____

54. Assume that Fredda, representing herself to be an employee of Water Company, induces the drawer to issue a check payable to Water Company. Fredda indorses the check in the name of Water Company and deposits the check into her bank account.

    a. Is Fredda's indorsement effective to make the depositary bank a holder of the check?
    _____

    b. Who would suffer the loss? _____

55. Music Publishers submits a bill to Tune Corporation. Tommy Treasurer draws a check on behalf of Tune Corporation payable to Music Publishers intending to cash the check himself.

    a. Is Music Publishers a fictitious payee? _____

    b. Is Music Publishers a fictitious payee if Tommy Treasurer developed the intent to steal the instrument after he signed the instrument? _____

56. Assume that both Sally, the President, and Sandra, the Treasurer, must sign any corporate check. Sally draws up a check payable to Sapphire Gem Company intending to cash the check herself. Although Sandra intends that Sapphire Gem Company receive the proceeds, Sally does not.

    a. To whom is the check payable? _____

    b. Is Sapphire Gem Company a fictitious payee? _____

57. Sandra, treasurer of Diamonds-R-Forever, forges Sally's name, the president of the company, as drawer of checks payable to phony suppliers. Sandra forges $20,000 of these checks in February, cashes the checks, and spends the money on drugs. Although the statement from the bank containing the checks forged in February arrives on March 10, Diamonds-R-Forever does not examine the statement. The statement is finally examined on April 21 by Sally, who immediately notifies Bank of America of the forgeries.

    a. Assuming that Sandra has no reachable assets, can Bank of America prove that it could have prevented the loss if it had been promptly notified of the forgery? _____

    b. Assume that between March 10 and March 31, Sandra forges $40,000 more in checks. Between April 11 and April 15, Sandra forges $50,000 more in checks. On April 16, Sandra leaves the country. Diamonds-R-Forever receives its bank statement on March 10. To what extent is Diamonds-R-Forever precluded from asserting the forgeries? _____

    c. Assume that, in our example above, all the checks forged by Sandra were returned by Bank of America to Diamonds-R-Forever on March 10. If Diamonds-R-Forever does not report the forgeries by March 10 of the next year, will Diamonds-R-Forever be precluded from asserting the forgeries even if Bank of America had failed to exercise ordinary care in paying the checks?

_____

58. After indorsing a check in blank, Paul loses the check. The finder of the check cashes the check at his brother's bank by forging his brother's indorsement. What effect does the forged indorsement have?

_____

59. Automobile Dealer, in a plan to defraud Finance Company, submits to Finance Company loan applications and supporting loan agreements supposedly from prospective car buyers. Finance Company, without verifying any of the information on the loan applications, makes the loans and sends the checks to Automobile Dealer. Automobile Dealer forges the payees' indorsements on these checks. To what extent, if any, is Finance Company liable? _____

60. Tax Defrauder, in a scheme to defraud the IRS by claiming phony charitable deductions, sets up a bank account in the name of "ACS," makes checks payable to American Cancer Society and deposits the checks in the bank account that he set up. During one trip to the bank, Tax Defrauder loses one of these checks. Freddy Finder finds the check, forges the indorsement of American Cancer Society, and cashes the check at Check Cashing Service. Is Check Cashing Service the holder of the check?

_____

———————————

Answers

41. a. No. Unless there is a grounds for preclusion, May is not liable on the check because her signature does not appear on the check.

    b. No. Payor bank cannot charge May's account because May did not authorize payor bank to pay the check.

    c. Yes. When Allen signed May's name, it was as if Allen had signed the check in his own name. Allen is liable as the drawer of the check, and Payor Bank may recover from Allen.

    d. May may be precluded from denying that the signature on the check was her signature. In this event, if Payor Bank had refused to pay the check, the holder could recover from May on her drawer's obligation. If Payor Bank paid the check, Payor Bank could debit May's account just as if May's signature was authorized.

42. a. No. Raoul is not the holder of the check. Because only a holder can indorse an instrument for purposes of its negotiation, an unauthorized indorsement does not negotiate the check. U.C.C.§3-201(b). Until Julia indorses the check, no one, other than she, can become its holder.

    b. No. The drawer is still liable to Julia. Payor bank may not debit Drawer's account. U.C.C. §4-401(a).

43. Crocker Bank may defend the suit by proving that Dan's negligence caused the loss.

44. a. No. Because Don took the check in good faith and for value, the payment may not be recovered from him U.C.C. §3-418(c).

   b. Yes. Don is protected because he has changed position in good-faith reliance on the payment even though, because he knew of Sally's defense, he did not take the check in good faith. U.C.C. §3-418(c). However, if Don uses the money to pay his mortgage payment or gas bill, he would not be found to have changed position in reliance on the payment because he would have been required to have made these payments even if Bank of America had not paid the check.

45. a. Maybe. Sally will suffer the loss unless she can recover from Allen or Peter.

   b. Yes. Sally can recover from Peter for breach of his transfer warranty that all signatures on the instrument were authentic and authorized, U.C.C. §3-416(a)(2), and also on his indorser's contract. U.C.C. §3-415(a).

   c. Yes. Peter and Sally may recover from Allen because his unauthorized signature makes him liable as maker of the note. U.C.C. §3-403(a).

   d. Depends. John's chances of recovery depend on whether Sally is a protected person under U.C.C. §3-418. If Sally is a good-faith purchaser for value or has relied in good faith on the payment, Sally is protected from John's action in restitution, and, therefore, John suffers the loss. In the unlikely event that Allen is solvent and available for process, John can recover from him.

46. a. No. Wells Bank cannot debit The Smoke Shop's account because The Smoke Shop did not sign the check. U.C.C. §4-401(a).

   b. Maybe. Wells Bank may recover the proceeds from Security Bank if Security Bank is not a protected person.

   c. Yes. Wells Bank can recover from David not only because he is not a protected person under U.C.C. §3-418 and had knowledge of the forgery, but also because he has breached the presentment warranty of lack of knowledge that the drawer's signature is unauthorized.

   d. Yes. Wells Bank can recover from Jane because she was the actual forger. Remember, though, that if Jane and David are insolvent, Wells Bank ultimately suffers the loss.

   e. David and Jim. Security Bank can recover from David for breach of his transfer warranty that all signatures are authentic and authorized. If David had transferred by indorsement the check to Jim, who deposited the check in his checking account at Security Bank, Security Bank could recover from both David and Jim on their transfer warranty. Because the instrument was dishonored, the holder can also recover from any prior indorser on his indorser's contract. U.C.C. §3-415(a). The holder may also recover from Jane as drawer of the check because her unauthorized signing of the treasurer's name makes her liable in the capacity in which she signs. U.C.C. §3-403(a).

47. Don can sue the depositary bank (First Interstate Bank) neither for conversion, U.C.C. §3-420 (a)(i), nor for breach of the presentment warranties. U.C.C. §3-417, Official Comment 2. Don's recourse is to have Bank of Oxnard recredit his account. Bill, the payee, has no right to recover from either bank for conversion because the instrument was not delivered to him. U.C.C. §3-420(a).

48. $50. Because Earl fraudulently altered the check, Dean is discharged from liability. U.C.C. §3-407(b). However, because Frank took the check for value and in good faith and without notice of the alteration, he may enforce the check against Dean for its original amount of $50. U.C.C. §3-407(b).

49. No. Bank of America may not debit Jane's account because, bearing her forged drawer's signature, the check was not properly payable. Bank of America, likewise, cannot recover from Wells Bank. Because Thief did not intend for Doris to have an interest in the check, Doris is a fictitious payee. U.C.C. §3-404(b). Being a fictitious payee, Thief's indorsement in Doris's name is effective as against any person who in good faith pays the instrument or takes it for value or collection. Because Wells Bank qualifies as a good-faith taker for collection, the indorsement is effective. As a result, Wells Bank does not breach its presentment warranty that it is a person entitled to enforce the instrument. As in any case of payment over a forged drawer's signature, the loss falls on the payor bank unless it can recover the payment under U.C.C. §3-418. However, if Wells Bank has allowed Check Cashing Service to withdraw the funds, Bank of America would have no right to recover the payment from Wells Bank. U.C.C. §3-418(c).

50. Yes. Crocker Bank, being the depositary bank, is liable for conversion unless the proceeds are deposited in the indorser's bank account or paid to the indorser. Because the check was deposited in Thief's bank account, Crocker Bank is liable to Emaye for conversion. U.C.C. §3-206(c)(2). However, Emaye has no action against the payor bank. U.C.C. §3-206(c)(4).

51. Maybe. Wells Bank, being the depositary bank, is liable to ICM, the owner of the checks, for conversion unless ICM is precluded from claiming that the indorsement is unauthorized. U.C.C. §3-420(c). There are two possible grounds for preclusion. First, it can be argued that the indorsement is effective under U.C.C. §3-405 because Dean was an employee of ICM. However, ICM is not precluded because Dean is not a person who was entrusted with responsibility as to the instrument. U.C.C. §3-405. Second, it can be argued that ICM was negligent in the manner in which it handled its business such as to allow Dean access to the bookkeeping system. This is a question of fact. Even if ICM is precluded under one of these two theories, Wells Bank was probably negligent in allowing Dean to open a corporate bank account without requiring proper corporate resolutions. If this is the case, Wells Bank and ICM would share the loss under the principle of comparative negligence.

52. Yes. Loss Insurance Company may be found to be negligent in giving the check directly to Ripoff Repair Shop without telling David. In contrast, if Loss Insurance Company had dealt with Ripoff Repair Shop on many occasions in the past without any incidents, Loss Insurance Company may be found not to have been negligent.

53. No. However, as long as Bank of America's procedure is reasonable and commonly followed by other comparable banks in the area, failure to visually examine will not be conclusive proof of negligence. U.C.C. §4-406, Revised Official Comment 4. Because few banks visually inspect checks for forgeries or alterations, it is doubtful that Alice could successfully prove that Bank of America's failure to visually inspect the check was unreasonable and therefore negligent.

54. a. Yes. Fredda's indorsement is effective to make the depositary bank a holder of the check because, by falsely representing herself to be the agent of the named payee, Fredda is an impostor. U.C.C. §3-404(a). Being an impostor, an indorsement by any person is effective as to any person who takes the instrument for collection. U.C.C. §3-404(b)(2).

b. The depositary bank and the drawer. The loss would probably be split between the depositary bank and the drawer because the depositary bank probably failed to exercise ordinary care when it permitted Fredda to deposit the check into her own personal bank account. U.C.C. §3-404(d).

55. a. Yes. Even though the debt is actually owed to Music Publishers, the fact that Tommy Treasurer, the person signing the check on behalf of Tune Corporation, intends that Music Publishers not receive the proceeds makes Music Publishers a fictitious payee. U.C.C. §3-404(b)(i), (ii).

b. No. U.C.C. §3-405, Official Comment 2, Case No. 2. However, Tommy Treasurer's indorsement would be effective because Tune Corporation had entrusted him with responsibility as to instruments.

56. a. To either Sapphire Gem Company or to Sally. The check is payable to Sapphire Gem Company because Sandra intended that the check be payable to them, or to Sally personally, because Sally intended the check be payable to herself.

b. Yes. Because one of the signers for the drawer does not intend that Sapphire Gem Company be the person to whom the check is payable, Sapphire Gem Company is a fictitious payee. U.C.C. §3-404, Official Comment 2, Case No. 3.

57. a. No. Because the checks had already been cashed before the customer could have known of the forgeries, the bank could prove a loss only if it could prove that had it been promptly notified, it could have recovered the loss from Sandra. Because Sandra had no reachable assets, the bank is unable to prove a loss.

b. When Diamonds-R-Forever received its bank statement on March 10, it had a reasonable time, not exceeding 30 days, to examine the statement. The 30-day period expired on April 10. A court could find that less than 30 days was the extent of a reasonable time to examine the statement. If a court finds that 14 days was the extent of a reasonable time to examine the statement and report the forgeries, it will prohibit Diamonds-R-Forever from asserting the forgery of checks paid after March 24. Under any circumstances, Diamonds-R-Forever would be unable to assert the forgery on any check paid more than 30 days after it received the statement. The court must reach this result because any delay in excess of 30 days is deemed to be an unreasonable time for the customer to examine the statement of account and report any forgery or alteration. U.C.C. §4-406, Revised Official Comment 2.

c. Yes. U.C.C. §4-406(f) precludes the assertion of any forgery that is not reported within 1 year after the bank statement containing the item or its description, is made available to the customer whether or not the bank failed to exercise ordinary care in paying the item.

58. No. Because his brother's indorsement was not necessary to negotiate the check to the depositary bank, the depositary bank qualifies as a holder despite the forged indorsement.

59. Yes. Finance Company was negligent in failing to verify the applications' authenticity. U.C.C. §3-406. This was negligence in that Finance Company failed to observe the reasonable commercial standards in their business. U.C.C. §3-103(a)(9).

60. Yes. American Cancer Society is a fictitious payee because Tax Defrauder intended that American Cancer Society have no interest in the instrument. As a result, under U.C.C. §3-404(b)(1), any person in possession of the check is its holder.

Exam Tips on
FORGERY, ALTERATION, AND OTHER FRAUDULENT ACTIVITY

☞ **Diagram forgery questions:** When analyzing a question involving a forgery, it is essential that you diagram the transaction and carefully label each of the parties. Once you know the capacity of each party, the rules allocating the loss are simple.

> ☞ For example, assume that the issue is whether a check that has been paid over a forged indorsement has been converted.

>> ☞ First ask whether the instrument was delivered to the payee. If not, no conversion action lies. The drawer has no right to sue the depositary bank or the payor bank for conversion.

>> ☞ The drawer's remedy is to demand that the payor bank recredit his account.

>> ☞ If the instrument had been delivered to the payee prior to the forged indorsement, the payee may sue the depositary and payor banks for conversion.

>> ☞ The payee may not, however, sue an intermediary collecting bank.

> ☞ By properly labeling the parties, you need only to mechanically apply the allocation of loss rules.

CHAPTER 5

PAYOR BANK/CUSTOMER RELATIONSHIP

ChapterScope

This chapter covers the relationship between a payor bank and its customer. It examines when a payor bank may debit its customer's account, the enforceability of bank/customer agreements, a bank's liability for wrongful dishonor, a customer's right to stop payment, and the customer's right to availability of deposited funds under Regulation CC. The key points in this chapter are:

- **Properly payable items:** A bank may debit a customer's account when it pays any item that is properly payable.

- **Bank's right of set-off:** A bank has the right to set off against the customer's account any matured debts owed by the customer to the bank.

- **Variation by agreement:** An agreement between a customer and its bank may vary the provisions of Article 4 unless it attempts to disclaim the bank's obligation of good faith or duty to exercise reasonable care or is unconscionable.

- **Wrongful dishonor:** A bank is liable to its customer for any damages proximately caused when it wrongfully dishonors an item.

- **Bank's liability for payment over stop order payment:** A bank is liable to its customer only for the loss actually suffered by its customer when it pays an item in violation of a valid stop payment order.

- **Funds availability under Regulation CC:** Regulation CC requires a depositary bank to allow its customers use of the deposited funds according to a fairly strict Mandatory Availability Schedule.

I. WHEN ITEM PROPERLY PAYABLE

A. **Introduction:** A payor bank may charge against its customer's account only items that are properly payable. An item is properly payable if it is both authorized by the customer and complies with the bank/customer agreement. U.C.C. §4-401(a); U.C.C. §4-401, Official Comment 1. An instrument is not properly payable from a bank customer's account if it contains a forged drawer's signature or forged indorsement. *See* Lor-Mar/Toto, Inc. v. 1st Constitution Bank, 376 N.J. Super. 520 (N.J. Super. A.D. 2005).

Example: If a corporate account requires that any check drawn by the corporation be signed by two officers, a check signed by only one officer is not properly payable because the payment does not comply with the bank/customer agreement.

Example: If a necessary indorsement has been forged, the check is not properly payable because the customer did not authorize the bank to pay the person presenting the check for payment.

B. **Items creating overdrafts:** The bank may charge its customer's account for an item, even though it creates an overdraft, as long as the item is otherwise properly payable. U.C.C. §4-401(a); U.C.C. §4-401, Official Comment 1. Although having the right, the bank has no duty to pay an item that creates an overdraft, absent an agreement to the contrary. U.C.C. §4-402(a).

Rationale: By drawing an item in an amount greater than the balance in his bank account, a customer impliedly requests that the bank advance him funds by paying the item.

C. **Postdated checks:** A payor bank may charge against its customer's account a check that is otherwise properly payable, even though payment was made before the date of the check. U.C.C. §4-401(c).

Rationale: Most banks process checks by sending the check through a computer, which by reading the MICR-encoded line on the check determines whether to pay the check. Because the MICR-encoded line does not include the date of a check, the computer has no way of determining whether the check is postdated. U.C.C. §4-401, Official Comment 3. If banks were not permitted to debit their customer's account on a check paid before its date, banks would have to visually examine each check before paying it. The cost of this visual examination would be staggering.

Exception: The payor bank may not properly pay a postdated check prior to its date if the customer has given notice to the bank of the postdating. U.C.C. §4-401(c).

1. **Same procedure as stop payment order:** The procedure for giving notice of postdating is the same as for the placing of a stop payment order on an item. The postdating notice must describe the check with reasonable certainty and be given in enough time to allow the bank a reasonable opportunity to act on the notice before the check has been processed for payment or certified. U.C.C. §4-401(c).

2. **Same damages as for payment over stop payment order:** If, after proper notice of postdating has been given, the bank charges the check against the customer's account prior to the date of the check, the bank is liable for all damages resulting from the payment, including those damages resulting from the wrongful dishonor of subsequent items. U.C.C. §4-401(c). In the event of the bank's payment of a postdated check in violation of a properly given notice, the bank has the same subrogation rights as it does when it pays an item in violation of an effective stop payment order. *See* Siegel v. New England Merchants Natl. Bank, 386 Mass. 672, 437 N.E.2d 218 (1982).

   Example: Your bank paid a check you gave to Autos-R-Us as a deposit for the purchase of a new car, even though it was postdated and not supposed to be cashed for another two weeks. Autos-R-Us has never delivered the car and refuses to refund your deposit. The bank may debit your account because you did not give the bank proper notice of postdating.

D. **Bank not obligated to pay stale checks:** A bank is under no obligation to its customer to pay a check presented more than 6 months after its date (a stale check). U.C.C. §4-404.

Example: A payor bank does not wrongfully dishonor a check if it refuses to pay a check dated January 1 that is presented for payment on July 2.

Rationale: Because the staleness of a check may indicate that a problem exists, a bank is given discretion as to whether to pay a stale check. U.C.C. §4-404, Official Comment.

1. **Bank has option to pay:** If acting in good faith, a bank may pay a stale check and charge its customer's account for the amount of the check. U.C.C. §4-404. This gives the bank an option

as to whether to pay a stale check. U.C.C. §4-404, Official Comment. The bank needs this discretion because, at times, it may know that the drawer wants the check to be paid. U.C.C. §4-404, Official Comment.

2. **Drawer remains liable:** Notwithstanding the bank's dishonor of a stale check, the drawer remains liable to the person entitled to enforce the check. The drawer's liability is terminated only when the statute of limitations has run. U.C.C. §3-118.

E. **Bank's right of set-off:** The bank has the right to set off against its customer's account any matured debt the customer owes to the bank.

1. **Account must belong to customer:** Subject to a few exceptions, the bank may set off a debt owed to it by its customer only against an account belonging to the customer himself.

   a. **Bank must not have knowledge or reason to know that the account belongs to another:** A bank may not exercise its right of set-off if the bank has actual knowledge, or reason to know, that the funds in an account belong to a person other than the customer or that the funds are held in trust by the customer for another. *See* Universal C.I.T. Credit Corp. v. Farmers Bank of Portageville, 358 F. Supp. 317 (E.D. Mo. 1973) (bank had enough facts to put it on inquiry as to the third party's interest).

   b. **No right when account shows third-party interest:** A bank has no right to make a set-off against an account when the designation of the account indicates that a third party has an interest in the account. *See* Energetics, Inc. v. Allied Bank, 784 F.2d 1300 (5th Cir. 1986) (bank not permitted to set off a debt of its customer Republic Drilling against an account entitled "Well Account—Energetics," which contained prepayments by Energetics of drilling expenses).

   c. **Equitable rule:** Some courts adopt the "equitable rule" that when a third party has an interest in an account (e.g., a secured party claiming proceeds in an account), a bank, even without notice of the third party's interest, cannot exercise its right of set-off unless the bank has changed its position in reliance on the reasonable belief that the account belongs solely to its depositor. *See* National Indem. Co. v. Spring Branch State Bank, 162 Tex. 521, 348 S.W.2d 528 (1961) (even though the bank had no notice that funds in an insurance agent's account were premiums he received in trust for his employer, the set-off was improper because the bank had not changed its position).

   d. **Joint accounts:** Authority is split as to whether a bank can set off a debt of one account holder against an account jointly held. Some courts permit the bank to set off the debt against the entire account regardless of the respective interests of the account holders. *See* Burgess v. First Natl. Bank, 31 Colo. App. 67, 497 P.2d 1035 (1972). Other courts hold that the set-off may be exercised only to the extent of the respective interests of the account holders. *See* Peoples Bank v. Turner, 169 Md. 430, 182 A. 314 (1936).

2. **Debts must be matured:** Set-off is available only if both the debt the customer owes the bank and the debt the bank owes the customer have matured. *See* Bottrell v. American Bank, 773 P.2d 694 (Mont. 1989) (set-off not available where debt not matured).

Example: You have borrowed money from your bank to purchase a car. You have agreed to make monthly payments of $400 payable on the first of every month. You send your landlord a check on the first of the month. The bank sets off the car payment against your account on the second of the month. The landlord presents the check to the bank on the third of the month.

After the set-off, your account contained insufficient funds to pay your rent check. Because your car payment was due on the first, the debt had matured, and the bank could set it off against your account. If the car payment was not due until the fifth of the month, the set-off would have been improper.

3. **Notice not required:** The bank is not required to give notice within any specified time before, or after, the set-off absent a statutory requirement.

Example: California requires that a consumer depositor be given notice no later than the day following the set-off so that the consumer can claim an exemption or that the debt is not due. Cal. Fin. Code §864(c).

4. **Limitations on consumer debts:** Both state and federal law limit to some extent a bank's right of set-off as to debts arising out of a consumer credit transaction.

Example: Under §169 of the Fair Credit Billing Act of 1974, 15 U.S.C. §1666h, a bank credit card issuer (absent consent in writing) may not set off a debt arising from the use of the credit card against a deposit account of the credit card holder.

F. **Death or incompetence of customer:** Under traditional agency law, the death or incompetence of the principal terminates the agent's authority. Application of this rule to the payment of checks would be disastrous to the banking system because a bank, when paying or collecting a check, has no way of knowing whether one of its customers is incompetent or has died. As a result, the Code gives banks the right to pay or collect items even after a customer's death or incompetency.

1. **Effect of incompetence:** A customer's incompetence does not revoke the bank's authority to pay or collect an item or account for proceeds of its collection until the bank knows of the adjudication of incompetence and has a reasonable opportunity to act on it. U.C.C. §4-405(a). Even after the bank knows that its customer is incompetent, the bank remains authorized to act on behalf of the customer in the collection or payment of an item until the judicial appointment or qualification of a personal representative for the customer.

2. **Effect of death:** Until the bank knows of the customer's death and has had a reasonable opportunity to act on the knowledge, the bank has the right to pay, collect, account, accept, or certify an item. U.C.C. §4-405(a).

   a. **May pay checks for 10 days:** Even after the bank learns of its customer's death, the bank may, for 10 days after the date of death, pay a check, unless the bank is ordered to stop payment by a person claiming an interest in the account. U.C.C. §4-405(b).

   Rationale: The bank is allowed to pay checks (but not other items) presented in the 10-day period after the date of death because most of these checks represent bona fide debts. Many of the checks are in payment of ordinary bills. Rather than making these creditors file a claim against the estate, it is simpler for the bank to pay the checks and have the executor or administrator of the estate recover any improper payment. U.C.C. §4-405, Official Comment 2.

   b. **No duty to pay:** Although a bank can pay a check after the customer's death, the bank has no duty to pay the check. The bank is not liable for wrongful dishonor if it refuses to pay a check after its customer has died. *See* Bank Leumi Trust Co. v. Bally's Park Place, Inc., 528 F. Supp. 349 (S.D.N.Y. 1981).

c. **Right to stop payment:** To ensure that the drawer has not been pressured shortly before his death to write checks, a bank may not pay a check with knowledge of its customer's death if ordered to stop payment by any person claiming an interest in the account. U.C.C. §4-405(b). The stop payment order has the same requirements and effects as an ordinary stop payment order except that any surviving relative, creditor, or other person who claims an interest in the account may order the bank not to pay the check. The bank is not required to determine whether the person's claim to the account has merit. U.C.C. §4-405, Official Comment 3.

II. VARIATION BY AGREEMENT

A. **Introduction:** Because Article 4 is not a regulatory statute, it neither regulates the terms of the bank/customer agreement nor prescribes consumer protection constraints on bank/customer agreements. Article 4 leaves the protection of bank customers to the individual state legislatures to enact legislation and to the courts to regulate abuse through normal contract doctrines such as unconscionability, public policy, and contracts of adhesion. U.C.C. §4-101, Official Comment 3.

B. **Limitations on agreements:** Article 4 does place two limitations on any agreement that varies the provisions of Article 4: (a) such an agreement may not disclaim a bank's liability for its own lack of good faith or failure to exercise ordinary care, nor (b) may it limit the measure of damages resulting from its lack of good faith or failure to exercise ordinary care. U.C.C. §4-103(a).

C. **Contracts of adhesion:** Even when an agreement does not violate either of the two limitations imposed by Article 4, bank/customer agreements are virtually always contracts of adhesion. Consequently, courts carefully scrutinize a bank's attempt to limit its customer's rights or disclaim the bank's own duties. Courts often refuse to enforce provisions found in a bank/customer agreement or on a deposit slip that cause hardship to the customer or result in unfair surprise.

Example: Courts have refused to enforce a requirement found on a stop payment order form that the bank is obligated to stop payment of a check only if all of the information is accurate, including the amount to the penny. *See* Staff Serv. Assocs. v. Midatlantic Natl. Bank, 207 N.J. Super. 327, 504 A.2d 148 (1985).

1. **Customer's actual knowledge relevant:** The extent to which the customer has actual knowledge, or had a clear opportunity to acquire knowledge, is instrumental in the court's decision as to whether it will enforce the provision. *See* Rapp v. Dime Savings Bank of New York, 164 A.D.2d 964, 408 N.Y.S.2d 540 (1978), *aff'd*, 48 N.Y.2d 658, 421 N.Y.S.2d 347, 396 N.E.2d 740 (1979) (court enforced an agreement giving the bank the right to place a reasonable hold on uncollected funds when the agreement was printed on the reverse side of the deposit slip, posted in all branch offices, and explained to individual checking account customers on the opening of their accounts).

2. **Against public policy:** A court may refuse to enforce a provision of a bank/customer agreement that it finds to be in violation of public policy. One ground of public policy may be Article 4 itself. Article 4 establishes certain basic rights that bank customers assume are guaranteed them when they open their checking account.

Example: A court probably would not permit a bank to completely eliminate any of the basic rights that Article 4 has granted to bank customers: the right to stop payment, the right to sue for wrongful dishonor, or the right to object to the payment of items not properly payable.

3. **Agreements may limit customers' rights:** Courts often enforce bank/customer agreements that greatly limit the time within which a customer may claim that a signature or alteration is unauthorized. *See* Simcoe & Erie Gen. Ins. Co. v. Chemical Bank, 770 F. Supp. 149 (S.D.N.Y. 1991) (14 days).

III. WRONGFUL DISHONOR

A. **Introduction:** Subject to one exception, a payor bank is liable to its customer for wrongful dishonor if it dishonors an item that is properly payable. U.C.C. §4-402(a). A payor bank has no duty to pay an item that, although properly payable, would create an overdraft. U.C.C. §4-402(a).

Example: The definition of "properly payable" was not intended to require that the bank pay items drawn on insufficient funds. If the drawer draws a check for $1,000,000 on an account containing only $5, the bank cannot be liable for wrongful dishonor if it refuses to pay the check. The bank would be liable only if it breaches an agreement with its customer to honor overdrafts, e.g., a ready reserve agreement or check overdraft protection.

B. **Pivotal issue is whether sufficient funds in account:** In determining whether an item has been wrongfully dishonored, the pivotal question is whether the customer's account has adequate funds to cover payment of the dishonored item. This almost always depends on whether a prior debit or credit by the bank was proper.

1. **Bank may pay checks in any order:** The payor bank has the right to pay checks drawn on its customer's account in any order that it desires. U.C.C. §4-303(b). This discretion allows banks to process checks by computer without concern that a subsequently dated check had been paid while an earlier dated check was dishonored.

2. **Time for determining whether sufficient funds exist:** A bank need only examine a customer's account once when deciding whether to dishonor an item for insufficient funds. This examination may be made at any time during the period between the time when the bank received the item and when it returned the item. U.C.C. §4-402(c).

C. **Duty owed only to customer:** A bank is liable only to its customer for wrongful dishonor of an item. U.C.C. §4-402(b). Customer is defined as "any person either having an account with the bank or for whom the bank has agreed to collect the item." U.C.C. §4-104(a)(5). Person includes both individuals and organizations. [Rev] U.C.C. §1-201(b)(27).

1. **Payee and other holders:** A payee or other holder of the item has no cause of action against the bank for wrongful dishonor of an item. Thus, your landlord has no cause of action against your bank for wrongful dishonor. The bank's duty was owed only to you.

2. **Corporate officers or partners not customers:** Because "customer" is defined to include organizations, when a check drawn on a corporate, trust, or partnership account is dishonored, the person having the right to sue for the wrongful dishonor is the corporation, trust, or partnership and not the corporate officer, trustee, or partner who signed the check. However, nothing in Article 4 displaces any common law cause of action the officer, trustee, or partner may have against the bank. U.C.C. §4-402, Official Comment 5. *See* Agostino v. Monticello Greenhouses, Inc., 166 A.D.2d 471, 560 N.Y.S.2d 690 (1990) (although corporate officer may

not maintain cause of action for wrongful dishonor where checks drawn on corporate account, he may bring a negligence action against the bank under U.C.C. §1-103 if the dishonor causes his arrest).

D. Damages: A payor bank that wrongfully dishonors an item is liable to its customer for all damages proximately caused by the wrongful dishonor. U.C.C. §4-402(b). The test for determining the liability of a payor bank for damages caused by a wrongful dishonor is the tort test of proximate causation.

1. **Loss of profits:** If a transaction fails to go through because the check was wrongfully dishonored, damages may include any resultant loss of profits. *See* Murdaugh Volkswagen, Inc. v. First Natl. Bank, 801 F.2d 719 (4th Cir. 1986) (damages may include injury to credit of corporation including the value of assets when bankruptcy caused by loss of credit); Skov v. Chase Manhattan Bank, 407 F.2d 1318 (3d Cir. 1969) (awarded three years of lost profits when supplier stopped doing business with customer); Twin City Bank v. Isaacs, 283 Ark. 127, 672 S.W.2d 651 (1984) (damages included losses from inability to purchase house when deposit check wrongfully dishonored).

2. **Damage to reputation:** If the customer's reputation was harmed because checks sent in payment of its bills were wrongfully dishonored, the customer can recover damages for the loss to her reputation. *See* Morse v. Mutual Fed. Sav. & Loan Assn., 536 F. Supp. 1271 (D. Mass. 1982) (loss of reputation damages available).

3. **Emotional distress damages:** Although one clearly foreseeable consequence of a wrongful dishonor is the embarrassment, emotional distress, and mental anguish that a customer suffers as a result of the dishonor, courts are reluctant to award a customer damages for these injuries because of the ease of fabricating such injuries. Many courts require that the bank's behavior be reckless or outrageous before such damages are awarded. *See* Morse v. Mutual Fed. Sav. & Loan Assn., 536 F. Supp. 1271 (D. Mass. 1987) (mental suffering and loss of reputation damages available); Twin City v. Isaacs, 283 Ark. 127, 672 S.W.2d 651 (1984) (damages for mental anguish available on intentional dishonor).

4. **Punitive damages:** Whether a bank is liable for punitive or other noncompensatory damages is left to the court's determination under [Rev.] U.C.C. §1-103(b) or [Rev] U.C.C. §1-305(a). U.C.C. §4-402, Official Comment 1. However, when the dishonor is willful and wanton, courts have allowed punitive damages for wrongful dishonor. *See* In re Brandywine Assocs., 30 U.C.C. Rep. Serv. 1369 (Bankr. E.D. Pa. 1980) (available only when malicious, oppressive, or reckless); Alaska State Bank v. Fairco, 674 P.2d 288, 37 U.C.C. Rep. Serv. 1782 (Alaska 1983) (punitive damages available when willful and wanton).

IV. CUSTOMER'S RIGHT TO STOP PAYMENT

A. Introduction: A customer has the right to stop payment of any item drawn on its account. U.C.C. §4-403(a).

B. Closed accounts: The same basic rules apply when a check is paid after the customer has closed her account as apply when the customer stops payment of an item. U.C.C. §4-403(a).

C. More than one customer: When there are two or more persons, each of whom is individually entitled to write items on an account, any of these persons may order payment stopped even if she is not the person who signed the item. U.C.C. §4-403, Official Comment 5.

Example: If you and your spouse have a joint checking account, your spouse may stop payment on a check written by you.

D. Payable from customer's account: A customer may stop payment only on an item payable from its account. A payee or an indorsee has no right to stop payment on a check or other item. U.C.C. §4-403, Official Comment 2.

Example: You cannot stop payment on a cashier's check you purchased from your bank because it is not payable from your account. U.C.C. §4-403, Official Comment 4. Because it is your bank's credit that is at stake and not yours, you should not have the right to impugn the bank's credit by stopping payment on one of its obligations.

E. Effect of stop payment order: The only effect of a stop payment order is to prevent the holder from immediately obtaining possession of the funds represented by the item. Stop payment orders do not change who ultimately gets the funds. This is because issuance of a stop payment order has no effect on a party's liability as drawer of the item. U.C.C. §4-403, Official Comment 7.

Example: After you stop payment on a check given in payment for a defective television set, you will be sued by the holder. U.C.C. §3-414(b). You will be obligated to pay the check unless you have a defense or claim in recoupment that is assertible against the holder. U.C.C. §3-305(a), (b).

F. Requirements for stop payment order: To be effective, a stop payment order describing the item with reasonable certainty must be received at a time and in a manner that affords the bank a reasonable opportunity to act on the order before the bank has completed any of the actions with respect to the item described in U.C.C. §4-303 and discussed in subsection G, *infra* U.C.C. §4-403(a).

1. **Adequate description of item:** A check or other item is identified with reasonable certainty when the bank is given sufficient information to enable it to identify the item on which payment is to be stopped. U.C.C. §4-403(a), Official Comment 5.

   a. **Technological capabilities:** The information that a bank may require a customer to supply is the information that the bank must have, under current technology, to identify the item with reasonable certainty. U.C.C. §4-403, Official Comment 5.

   b. **Precise information:** Most banks require that the customer supply either the precise amount of the instrument or the number of the check.

      Rationale: The state of current technology is such that the computers that banks find economically feasible can be programmed to read only the information contained on the MICR-encoded line. The only information encoded on the MICR line that would enable the computer to identify an individual check is either the check number or the amount payable. Because most current computers used for processing checks can be programmed to identify checks only by either the precise amount payable or the precise check number, a mistake in one digit results in the computer failing to stop payment of the item.

      Example: If you indicated on the stop payment order that your check to Target was in the amount of $1,001 instead of its actual amount of $1,000, your stop payment order would not be effective.

2. Oral or written: A stop payment order may be either written or oral. U.C.C. §4-403(b). A written stop payment order is effective for 6 months from the date that it is given, whereas an oral stop payment order lapses after 14 calendar days. U.C.C. §4-403(b). If a written confirmation of the oral order is given within the 14-day period, the oral order is effective for 6 months beginning at the time the oral order was given. U.C.C. §4-403(b); U.C.C. §4-403, Official Comment 6.

    a. Renewal: Stop payment orders may be renewed as often as desired for the same respective periods.

    b. Effect of expiration: When a stop payment order expires, it is as if the order had never been given, and the payor bank may, in good faith, pay the item (even though the item had at one time been subject to the stop payment order). U.C.C. §4-403, Official Comment 6.

    Example: Assume that you originally issued a stop payment order on January 2 and that you attempted to renew the order on August 1. Because the renewal was not within the 6-month period, it is effective only from August 1, the date the renewal is received. Your stop payment order would have been ineffective between July 2 and July 31. If the bank had paid the item any time between July 2 and July 31, the bank's payment would have been proper.

    2002 amendments: The 2002 amendments substitute the term "record" for "writing." A "record" is "information that is inscribed on a tangible medium or that is stored in an electronic or other medium and is retrievable in perceivable form." [Rev] U.C.C. §3-103(a)(14).

G. Timeliness of stop payment order, legal process, notice, and set-off: An important question arises as to when a stop payment order is in time to require the payor bank to refuse to pay the item. This same question arises as to other events (called the legals) that contend for priority as to the funds in the customer's account. These other legals are (a) legal process, such as writs of garnishment or execution; (b) the payor bank learning that the drawer has filed a petition in bankruptcy, died, or become incompetent; or (c) the bank's right to set off against the customer's account a debt owed to it by the customer. Needless to say, the customer's self-interest differs when the issue involves stop payment orders as contrasted with the other legals. In the case of a stop payment order, the customer wants the order to be effective to prevent the bank from paying the check. In the case of the other legals, the issue cannot arise if the customer has sufficient funds in her account to pay the check and the bank or her other creditors. When the issue does arise, the customer will almost always prefer that the check be paid out of her account rather than have the money go to her bank or other creditors.

1. Test for determining when stop payment order or other legals come too late: Under U.C.C. §4-303(a), a stop payment order or other legal arrives too late to terminate the bank's right or duty to pay an item if it comes after any of the following events.

    a. Bank certifies item: When the bank accepts or certifies an item, the bank becomes liable to the holder. At this point, the item is effectively paid and the stop payment order or other legal is too late. U.C.C. §4-303(a)(1).

    b. Pays or becomes accountable for the item: When the bank has already paid the item, the funds are gone and, therefore, there is no payment to be stopped or funds to be garnished or set off against. Payment can be in cash or occur where the bank settles for the item without having a right to revoke the settlement under statute, clearinghouse rule, or agreement. Likewise, when a bank becomes accountable for the amount of the item under U.C.C. §4-302, the bank has in effect made payment. U.C.C. §4-303(a)(2), (3), (4). The issue as to when and under what circumstances a bank pays, or becomes accountable for, an item is discussed in Chapter 6.

c. **Arrives after cut-off hour:** When, with respect to checks only, the stop payment order or other legal arrives after a cut-off hour established by the bank or, if no cut-off hour has been established, after the close of the next banking day after the banking day on which the bank receives the check, the stop payment order or other legal is too late. A bank may not establish a cut-off hour earlier than one hour after the opening of the next banking day following the banking day on which the bank received the item. U.C.C. §4-303(a)(5).

Example: Assume that the bank had a cut-off hour of 10:00 a.m. The check is presented on Tuesday. A stop payment order or other legal is too late if it arrives after 10:00 a.m. on Wednesday.

Rationale: Although the bank is not yet liable for the item by the time the stop payment order or other legal is deemed to be too late, the bank needs to know at what point in time it can safely pay an item without worrying about a subsequent stop payment order or other legal. Because a bank needs time to process stop payment orders and other legals (except for set-offs), the stop payment order or other legal must arrive early enough to give the bank a reasonable time to act on it prior to the time that the bank has done any of the specified events. U.C.C. §4-303(a). Considering the pervasive presence of computers, "reasonable time" is probably a relatively short period. U.C.C. §4-303, Official Comment 6; *see* Chute v. Bank One, N.A., 10 Ohio App. 3d 122, 460 N.E.2d 720 (1983) (bank can place stop payment order in computer within very short time).

Note: Because each branch of a bank is considered, for most purposes, to be a separate bank, a stop payment order or other legal given to a branch other than the one at which the drawer keeps her account is not effective. U.C.C. §4-107, Official Comment 2. However, because the branch to which notice is given is part of the same organization as the payor bank, it has a duty to forward the stop payment order or other legal to the payor branch. [Rev] U.C.C. §1-202(f); U.C.C. §4-107, Official Comment 4. The stop payment order or other legal will be effective when it is (or should have been) received by the payor branch. [Rev] U.C.C. §1-202(f); U.C.C. §4-107, Official Comment 4.

2. **Effect of stop payment order or other legal arriving on time:** If the stop payment order or other legal arrives prior to any of the specified events, the payor bank has neither the right to pay the check nor a duty to its customer to pay the check. Thus, when a stop payment order comes in time to terminate the bank's right and duty to pay the check, the bank is liable to the drawer if, in spite of the timely stop payment order, it pays the check. When a writ of attachment, a garnishment, an execution, or the like comes in time, the bank no longer has a duty to the customer to pay the check. As a result, if it refuses to pay the check, the bank is not liable to its customer for wrongful dishonor. Similarly, when a set-off is exercised by the bank in time, the bank has no duty to the customer to pay the check and, thus, may properly debit the customer's account.

Note: U.C.C. §4-303 does not answer the question as to whether the bank is liable to the creditor if it pays the check despite the fact that the legal is timely. Whether the payor bank is liable to the creditor is answered, not by Article 4, but by the debtor-creditor law of the particular state. *See, e.g.,* Wilton Enter., Inc. v. Cook's Pantry, Inc., 230 N.J. Super. 126, 552 A.2d 1031 (1988) (bank liable to creditor because levy came in time).

3. **Effect of stop payment order or other legal arriving too late:** If a stop payment order comes too late, the payor bank has the right to pay the check or other item and incurs no liability to the drawer if it does so. However, the payor bank does not have to pay the check in that it may waive that right. Although it has a duty to the drawer to pay the check, by issuing the stop payment order the drawer has, in effect, waived the bank's duty to pay the item. As a result, the bank is not liable to the drawer if it honors the stop payment order. The payor bank thus has the option as to whether to honor the stop payment order up until the point at which it would be liable to the holder if it fails to pay the check. The bank is liable to the holder when it has made final payment under U.C.C. §4-215 or is accountable for the item under U.C.C. §4-302(a). The payor bank is liable to the drawer if it refuses to pay an item when the attachment, garnishment, or set-off occurs or knowledge of bankruptcy is obtained after one of the same events applicable in the case of a stop payment order. The reason for this different treatment is that, unlike in the case of a stop payment order, the customer will not have waived the duty the bank owes to the customer to pay the item.

   Example: Assume that your bank has established a cut-off hour of 10:00 A.M. Your check to Target arrived at the bank on Tuesday. You call your bank at noon on Wednesday and ask that it stop payment on the check. If the bank has not already incurred liability to Target, the bank may agree to stop payment of the check.

   Note: If the bank, prior to obtaining knowledge of the drawer's bankruptcy, pays the check, the bank is not liable to the trustee in bankruptcy. Although at the moment that the petition is filed all assets belong to the bankruptcy estate, the Bankruptcy Reform Act of 1978 is consistent with Article 4 in providing that the bank is not liable to the trustee for paying an item after the bankruptcy petition is filed as long as the bank does not have actual knowledge of the bankruptcy. 11 U.S.C. §542(c).

H. **Damages for payment in violation of stop payment order:** A payor bank is liable to its customer for any damages suffered by the customer when it pays an item over a valid stop payment order. The burden of proving the amount of loss resulting from payment contrary to the stop payment order is placed on the customer. U.C.C. §4-403(c).

1. **Measure of damages:** The measure of damages is the difference between the amount paid by the bank and the amount that the customer would have been obligated to pay on the check had payment been stopped. When a bank pays an item in violation of a valid stop payment order, the customer may contend that damages should be in the full amount of the item. The customer's argument is, "But for the bank not honoring my stop payment order, I would have had the amount of the item back in my account." However, this argument ignores the fact that the customer would have been sued on the item or on the underlying obligation had payment been stopped. As a result, ultimately she may have to pay some or all of the amount of the item to the holder or to the original obligee. For this reason, the measure of damages is the actual loss the customer suffered, taking into account any liability she avoided by having the check paid.

   Example: Ralph writes a check in the amount of $1,000 to Target for the purchase of a television set. The television set had a defective screen that cost $400 to repair. The payor bank pays the check over Ralph's stop payment order. Ralph's loss depends on whether the check is still retained by Target or whether it was acquired by a holder in due course. If Target still retains the check, had payment been stopped Target could have recovered $600 from Ralph ($1,000 contract price less $400 breach of warranty damages). Therefore, Ralph's damages arising from the bank's failure to stop payment of the check is the $400 that Ralph could have avoided paying Target had payment been stopped. If Target, however, negotiated the check to a holder in due course, the holder in due course would have taken the check free of Ralph's breach of warranty claim in recoupment and, therefore, could have recovered the entire $1,000 from Ralph. As a result, Ralph suffered no loss by virtue of the bank's failure to honor the stop payment order.

Example: Drawer did not show a "loss" from its bank's failure to honor a stop payment request on check to payee in that drawer's alleged loss from contracting for other delivery services arose from payee's breach of delivery and logistics agreement rather than from bank's act in honoring the check. NCS Healthcare, Inc. v. Fifth Third Bank, 2005 WL 1484025 (Ohio App. 8 Dist. 2005).

2. **Damages also include wrongful dishonor of subsequent items:** Losses from the payment of an item contrary to a stop payment order may also include damages for the wrongful dishonor of subsequent items. U.C.C. §4-403(c).

I. **Payor bank's right of subrogation on improper payment:** When a payor bank makes a payment for which it cannot debit its customer's account, some party will be unjustly enriched by the payment. This party will be either the customer, who has received a benefit for which it has not paid, or the person with whom the customer dealt, who has received full payment despite being subject to the customer's defense or claim in recoupment. To protect the payor bank against unfairly being saddled with this loss, the payor bank is subrogated to the rights of any person who has been unjustly enriched by the payment.

1. **What constitutes improper payment:** The bank's subrogation rights arise not only when a payor bank has paid a check over a valid stop payment order but also in any situation in which the payor bank cannot charge its customer's account for the payment. These situations include, among others, a bank that makes an early payment of a postdated check in violation of a proper notice of the postdating issued by the drawer, U.C.C. §4-401(c), and a bank that, with knowledge of its customer's death, pays a check more than 10 days after the death. U.C.C. §4-405(b).

2. **Payor bank subrogated to other parties' rights against drawer:** To prevent the drawer from being unjustly enriched, the payor bank is subrogated to the rights of (1) any holder in due course of the item against the drawer or maker and (2) the payee or any other holder of the item against the drawer or maker either on the item or from the transaction out of which the item arose. U.C.C. §4-407(1), (2).

Example: When the payor bank paid the Target check over Ralph's valid stop payment order, the bank lost its right to charge the payment to Ralph's account. However, denying the bank the right to charge Ralph's account will result in Ralph being unjustly enriched. If the bank had to recredit Ralph's account for the entire $1,000, he will have received a free television set worth $600. As a result, assuming that the bank paid Target, the bank is subrogated to Target's rights against Ralph on the check and on the underlying obligation. Because Target could recover $600 ($1,000 purchase price minus the $400 breach of warranty damages) from Ralph, so can the bank. The bank needs to recredit Ralph's account only for the $400 difference between the amount of the item and the amount to which it is subrogated to Target's rights against Ralph. If Target had negotiated the check to a holder in due course, because the holder in due course could recover the entire $1,000 from Ralph on the check, so can the payor bank. As a result, it has no obligation to recredit Ralph's account at all.

3. **Payor bank subrogated to drawer's rights:** To prevent the payee or other holder from being unjustly enriched, the payor bank is subrogated to the drawer's rights against the payee or any other holder of the item with respect to the transaction out of which the item arose. U.C.C. §4-407(3).

   Example: Even if the bank has to recredit Ralph's account for $400 only, it still is out of pocket that amount. Target has the entire $1,000 even though Ralph had a breach of warranty action against it for $400. To prevent Target from being unjustly enriched, the payor bank is subrogated to Ralph's rights as drawer against Target with respect to the transaction out of which the item arose. Because Ralph had a $400 breach of warranty action against Target, so does the payor bank.

   The payor bank usually has the right to recover only from the payee. Because subsequent holders are not liable to the drawer for the payee's breach of contract, there will probably be no rights under which the payor bank is subrogated against these subsequent parties.

   The payor bank's subrogation rights ensure that the loss resulting from the improper payment is imposed on the party ultimately responsible for the loss. Assuming Target is solvent, the same party suffers the loss whether or not the bank honored the stop payment order. However, if Target is insolvent, whether Ralph or the payor bank suffers the loss depends on whether the check has been acquired by a holder in due course. Ralph suffers the loss only if he would have suffered the loss had payment been properly stopped. If payment had been stopped and Target sued Ralph, Ralph could have asserted his claim in recoupment. Because the payor bank's failure to honor the stop payment order denied Ralph the ability to recover from the insolvent Target, the payor bank must suffer the resultant loss. However, if the check had been acquired by a holder in due course, even if the payor bank honored the stop payment order, the holder in due course would have recovered the entire amount from Ralph. Ralph would have been left with a worthless claim in recoupment action against the insolvent Target. Because the payor bank's failure to stop payment of the check did not cause Ralph's loss, Ralph must suffer the loss occasioned thereby.

V. FUNDS AVAILABILITY UNDER REGULATION CC

A. **Introduction:** Prior to the promulgation of Regulation CC, when a customer deposited a check, banks would place a substantial hold on the funds represented by the check to protect themselves from their customer using the funds on a check that is subsequently returned unpaid. However, the hold not only protected the bank against loss from returned checks but also gave the bank a windfall whenever the check was, in fact, paid prior to the expiration of the hold period. In these cases, the bank had the interest-free use of the customer's money (called float). In most cases, the holds, being far longer than the time it actually took to collect the funds, resulted in the creation of an exorbitant amount of float. The extent of the float generated thereby created such a serious problem that Congress enacted the Expedited Funds Availability Act (EFAA), 12 U.S.C. §4001.

B. Regulation CC: Regulation CC was promulgated by the Federal Reserve Board pursuant to the authority delegated to it by Congress in the EFAA. Regulation CC has two substantive subparts. Subpart B provides mandatory availability schedules under which depositary banks must permit their depositors use of deposited funds within certain expedited deadlines. In addition, depositary banks are required to pay interest on interest-bearing accounts no later than the business day on which the bank receives credit for the funds from its transferee bank. 12 C.F.R. §229.14(a). To protect depositary banks from potential losses that would be caused by being required to allow their customers use of the funds prior to the time that they would normally receive notice that the check is being returned unpaid, subpart C provides rules that impose on payor banks the duty to expedite the check return process so that depositary banks quickly learn of a check's dishonor.

1. **Mandatory funds availability schedule:** The mandatory availability schedules provide reasonable time periods within which a customer must be allowed use of the funds represented by a deposit corresponding with the likely time within which the bank would obtain notice of the item's nonpayment. The mandatory availability schedules are written into the EFAA itself and fleshed out in Regulation CC, subpart B. Banks must disclose their availability policy to their customers in a clear and conspicuous manner. 12 C.F.R. §229.16.

   a. **Provide maximum time only:** The mandatory availability schedule provides only the maximum time within which funds must be made available to the customer. A depositary bank may allow its customer immediate use of funds deposited even though it has the right to delay availability of the funds under the mandatory availability schedule. 12 C.F.R. §229.19(c), Commentary 1.

   b. **Subject to chargeback:** The depositary bank's obligation to make funds available to its customer is subject to its right to charge back the customer's account in the event that the check is returned unpaid.

2. **Next-day availability:** Some types of deposits are so likely to be paid that the depositary bank is required to allow the depositor next-day availability of the funds, which means that the funds must be made available at the start of business on the business day after the banking day on which the deposit was made. 12 C.F.R. §229.10.

   a. **Definitions:** A business day is any day other than a Saturday, Sunday, or holiday. 12 C.F.R. §229.2(g). A banking day is any *business day* on which an office of a bank is open to the public for substantially all of its banking functions. 12 C.F.R. §229.2(f).

   Example: Funds deposited on Tuesday must be made available on Wednesday (the next business day). Wednesday need not be a banking day for the depositary bank as long as it is a business day.

   b. **Funds subject to next-day availability:** The following types of deposits must be given next-day availability: (a) cash deposits made directly to a teller; (b) deposits by electronic payment; (c) deposit of a United States government check, e.g., Federal Reserve Bank or U.S. Treasury check; (d) deposit of a state or local government check; (e) deposit of a cashier's check, certified check, or tellers' check in person; (f) deposit of an on-us check; and (g) $100 of the aggregate amount of all checks deposited (not counting those that are otherwise entitled to next-day availability) in any one banking day. 12 C.F.R. §229.10.

Example: When there is a $1,000 deposit of a cashier's check and a $500 deposit of ordinary checks, the bank must make $1,100 available on the next business day. 12 C.F.R. §229.10, Commentary 5b.

3. **Second-day and fifth-day availability:** When a check is not entitled to next-day availability, it is entitled to availability either on the second or fifth business day after its deposit depending on whether the check is a local or nonlocal check.

   a. **Definitions:** A local check is a check drawn on or payable through or at a local paying bank. 12 C.F.R. §229.2(r). A local paying bank is a paying bank that is located in the same Federal Reserve Bank check processing region as the depositary bank. 12 C.F.R. §229.2(s). A nonlocal check is a check drawn on or payable through or at a bank not located in the same check processing region as the depositary bank. 12 C.F.R. §229.2(v).

   b. **Local checks:** Funds from a deposit of a local check must be made available on the second business day following the banking day of deposit. 12 C.F.R. §229.12(b)(1).

   Example: Assume that Wells Bank and Bank of America are both located in the same check processing region because both banks are in the Southern California area. If you deposit your paycheck in your account at Bank of America on Thursday, Bank of America must make the funds available to you at the beginning of business on the following Monday. 12 C.F.R. §229.12(b), Commentary 1.

   c. **Nonlocal checks:** Funds from a deposit of a nonlocal check must be made available on the fifth business day after the banking day of deposit. 12 C.F.R. §229.12(c)(1)(i).

   Example: If Wells Bank was located in Portland and Bank of America was located in Los Angeles, your paycheck would be a nonlocal check. If you deposited your paycheck on Tuesday, Bank of America would have to make the funds available for withdrawal on the following Tuesday. 12 C.F.R. §229.12(c), Commentary.

4. **Extensions of mandatory availability schedule:** The mandatory availability schedule can be extended when a substantially increased risk of loss would be imposed on the depositary bank if it were required to honor the mandatory availability schedule. Generally, the depositary bank must give notice to its depositor when it invokes one of these exceptions. 12 C.F.R. §229.13(g). When a bank uses one of these exceptions to extend the time for withdrawal, the time may only be extended for a reasonable period, which is presumed to be 5 business days for local checks and 6 business days for nonlocal checks. 12 C.F.R. §229.13(h).

   a. **Extension for cash withdrawal:** The time within which funds must be made available may be extended for one business day for funds represented by deposited checks if the depositor attempts to withdraw the funds in cash or by similar means. 12 C.F.R. §229.12(d). Thus, the depositor may write a check on the funds on the day of availability but not withdraw the funds in cash.

   b. **New account exception:** The time within which funds must be made available can be extended when the funds are deposited in a new account. An account is new during its first 30 days if the customer did not have another account at the bank for at least 30 days prior to the opening of the account. 12 C.F.R. §229.13(a).

c. **Large deposit exception:** A bank may extend the hold for local and nonlocal checks to the extent that the aggregate deposit on any banking day is more than $5,000. The mandatory availability schedule still applies to the first $5,000 of deposits on that day. 12 C.F.R. §229.13(b).

d. **Returned and redeposited check exception:** There is an exception for previously returned and redeposited checks because when a check has been dishonored once, the chance is good that it will be dishonored again. 12 C.F.R. §229.13(c).

e. **Repeatedly overdrawn exception:** This exception applies whenever any account or combination of accounts of a single customer has been repeatedly overdrawn. 12 C.F.R. §229.13(d).

f. **Reasonable cause to doubt collectability exception:** This exception applies when the bank has reasonable cause to doubt collectability of a check. 12 C.F.R. §229.13(e). Examples of reasonable cause may be if the depositary bank receives notice from the paying bank that the check is being returned or if the check is more than 6 months old.

g. **Emergency condition exception:** This exception is applicable in emergency conditions in which there is an interruption of communications or computer or other equipment facilities, suspension of payments by another bank, war, or other emergency conditions beyond the control of the depositary bank. 12 C.F.R. §229.13(f).

h. **ATMs:** Deposits of cash in a night depositary or at an ATM owned or controlled by the depositary bank are entitled to second-day availability. Deposits of cash or checks deposited in an automated teller machine not owned or controlled by the depositary bank are entitled to fifth-day availability. 12 C.F.R. §229.12(f).

C. **Availability under Article 4:** Article 4 or other state availability laws govern to the extent that they allow quicker availability of funds than allowed under Regulation CC. 12 C.F.R. §229.20(a). In most cases, Regulation CC allows as quick or quicker availability than does Article 4. For example, under U.C.C. §4-215(e)(1), a depositary bank does not have to allow use of funds represented by a deposited item until it has had a reasonable time to receive return of the item. Because of the vagueness of this standard, banks were able to impose holds far longer than now allowed under Regulation CC.

Exception: Under U.C.C. §4-214(f), a deposit of cash becomes available at the opening of the bank's next banking day after receipt. Because Regulation CC provides that a state law allowing earlier availability of funds than allowed under Regulation CC governs, U.C.C. §4-214(f) prevails over Regulation CC as to cash deposited by mail, in a night depositary, or in an ATM owned by the depositary bank.

Quiz Yourself on PAYOR BANK/CUSTOMER RELATIONSHIP

61. The day after you deposit your paycheck, you write a check to your landlord. Without the funds represented by your paycheck, you do not have sufficient funds in your account to cover your rent check.

The landlord goes to your bank and presents the check for payment over the counter. Your bank refuses to pay the check. Has your bank wrongfully dishonored the rent check? _____

62. Assume that a check you wrote to the American Red Cross was issued after your rent check. You did this deliberately to ensure that your account would have adequate funds to pay the rent check. You were not concerned with whether the American Red Cross check was paid as it was a charitable donation. However, the bank processed and paid the American Red Cross check first. This left insufficient funds to pay your rent check. Had the American Red Cross check not been paid, there would have been sufficient funds to pay your rent check. Was the bank justified in dishonoring your rent check?

_____

63. Assume that your rent check was received by your bank at 9:00 A.M. Your bank examines your account at 10:00 A.M. and determines that there are insufficient funds to cover the check. At 11:00 A.M., the bank credits your account with the amount of your paycheck.

a. If you needed your paycheck credited to your account to cover your rent check, could the bank have properly dishonored your rent check? _____

b. If, instead, the bank examined your account at noon, at which time there were adequate funds, would the bank be liable if it dishonored the check? _____

64. If your landlord has you arrested and prosecuted for writing a check on insufficient funds, when there were, in fact, sufficient funds in your account to cover the check, what are your remedies against the bank? _____

65. To make sure that the car is delivered before he is obligated to make payment, Vlade postdates the check he gives in payment for a new Hornet he is purchasing from Kobe. Kobe cashes the check before its stated date and never delivers the car. Can the payor bank debit Vlade's account on payment of the check? _____

66. In addition to having a checking account at Utah State Bank, Carol has also taken out a business loan in the amount of $50,000 from the bank due on March 1. On February 28, Carol writes a $30,000 check to her major business supplier. At the time, Carol's bank account contained $70,000. On March 2, the check is presented for payment. Instead of paying the check, Utah State Bank sets off her $50,000 loan against her checking account and dishonors the check. Is Utah State Bank liable to Carol for wrongful dishonor? _____

67. Assume that the set-off was exercised at 11:30 A.M. on March 2. Utah State Bank had established a cut-off hour of 10:00 A.M. Because of the dishonor, the supplier stops doing business with Carol, who, unable to find another supplier, goes out of business. Has Utah State Bank now wrongfully dishonored the check? If so, to what damages would Carol be entitled? _____

68. Nick issues a check in the amount of $2,000 to Van Exel Sounds for the purchase of a stereo system. Immediately upon taking the system home, Nick discovers that the system does not work. It would cost $500 to repair the system. Nick calls up Payor Bank, telling it the amount of the check and the check number, and orders payment stopped. On presentment the next day by Van Exel Sounds, Payor Bank pays the check. Was the stop payment order effective? If so, to what extent, if any, must Payor Bank recredit Nick's account? If it recredits Nick's account, can it recover from Van Exel Sounds?

_____

69. On Monday, Alainis deposits in her Los Angeles bank account a $10,000 royalty check she receives from her recording company drawn on a New York bank. When is her bank required under Regulation CC to make the funds available to her? _____

70. Assume that you are the president of a small family-owned corporation. You are the only person authorized to sign checks for the corporation. Furthermore, everyone that does business with your corporation does so because of their faith in you personally. A check that you write to your major supplier is dishonored because of the bank's mistake. However, before the bank recognizes the mistake, the supplier has filed a criminal complaint against you for writing a check on insufficient funds. You are arrested. The members of your country club no longer talk to you and you are banished from the Rotary Club. Do you have a cause of action against the bank for wrongful dishonor? _____

Answers

61. No. The issue is at what point in time did your bank have to allow you to draw upon the funds represented by your paycheck. Under Regulation CC, because your check was a local check, the bank need only make the funds available on the second day following the banking day of deposit. 12 C.F.R. §229.12(b)(1). Under U.C.C. §4-215(e)(1), your bank has no obligation to allow you use of the funds represented by your paycheck until it has had a reasonable time to receive return of the paycheck in the event that it is dishonored. Under no circumstances would this result in your having use of the funds in time to cover your rent check.

62. Yes. The bank was justified in dishonoring your rent check and is not liable for wrongful dishonor. A bank has the right to pay checks in any order. U.C.C. §4-303(b). Your belief that the rent check would be paid before the American Red Cross check does not negate the fact that there were insufficient funds in your account when the rent check was to be paid.

63. a. Yes. Any credits added to the customer's account after the bank has examined the account are not considered in determining whether the account contains sufficient funds. U.C.C. §4-402, Official Comment 4.

   b. Yes. The balance at the time of that later examination is used to determine whether there were adequate funds to pay the rent check, regardless of the fact that adequate funds did not exist in the account until three hours after the rent check was actually presented for payment. U.C.C. §4-402, Official Comment 4. Because there were sufficient funds to cover the rent check at the time the bank examined the account, the bank would be liable for wrongful dishonor if it dishonored the check.

64. You can recover from your bank any damages suffered on account of the arrest and prosecution. These damages may include your costs of defense and any harm done to your reputation. If you are evicted because of the dishonor, you could recover any damages resulting from the eviction. U.C.C. §4-402(b); U.C.C. §4-402, Official Comment 3.

65. Yes. A check is properly payable and may be charged against a customer's account even though payment is made before its date unless the customer gives the bank proper notice of postdating. U.C.C. §4-401(c).

66. No. The bank has a right to set off against Carol's checking account any matured debt. Because the debt was due on March 1, the debt was matured on March 2. No notice is required before a set-off can be exercised. Because the set-off was exercised before any of the events listed in U.C.C. §4-303(a), the set-off had priority over the check. U.C.C. §4-303(a).

67. **Because the set-off was not exercised until after the cut-off hour of the next banking day after the banking day on which Utah State Bank received the check, the set-off was too late.** U.C.C. §4-303(a)(5). As a result, it is liable to Carol for wrongful dishonor. She is entitled to any damages proximately caused by the dishonor, including loss of profits resulting from the termination of her business.

68. **Yes.** The stop payment order was timely and contained sufficient information to allow Payor Bank to identify the check. U.C.C. §4-403(a). Nick has the burden of proving a loss. Had payment been stopped, Van Exel Sounds could have recovered $1,500 from Nick: $2,000 (purchase price) minus $500 (breach of warranty damages). As a result, Nick's loss caused by the bank's failure to honor the stop payment order was $500. When Nick demands that the bank recredit his account, Payor Bank will claim that it is subrogated to Van Exel Sounds's right to recover the $1,500 from Nick. U.C.C. §4-407(2). Payor Bank can use its right to be subrogated to Nick's rights to recover the remaining $500 from Van Exel Sounds. U.C.C. §4-407(3).

69. Generally, a depositary bank must make funds available on a nonlocal check on the fifth business day after the banking day of deposit. 12 C.F.R. §229.12(c)(1)(i). This would mean that the funds have to be made available to her on the following Monday. **However, because this is a deposit of over $5,000, the bank may extend the hold on the amount exceeding $5,000 for a reasonable period not exceeding 6 days. 12 C.F.R. §229.13(h).**

70. **No.** Not being the bank's customer, you have no cause of action against the bank for wrongful dishonor. U.C.C. §4-402, Official Comment 5. Because "customer" is defined to include organizations, when a check drawn on a corporate, trust, or partnership account is dishonored, the person having the right to sue for the wrongful dishonor is the corporation, trust, or partnership and not the corporate officer, trustee, or partner who signed the check.

Exam Tips on
PAYOR BANK/CUSTOMER RELATIONSHIP

☛ **Determining the extent of a bank's liability:** Remember that a bank that fails to honor a proper stop payment order is not necessarily liable to its customer for the amount of the check.

   ☞ To determine to what damages the payor bank is liable, you must ask how much the drawer would have had to pay the holder had payment been stopped.

   ☞ If the check has been acquired by a holder in due course, the drawer would have had to pay the full amount of the check and therefore appears to have suffered no damages on account of the bank's failure to honor his stop payment order.

   ☞ However, beware that even in this event, the drawer may have suffered a loss if a subsequent check is wrongfully dishonored because payment had not been properly stopped on the earlier check.

THE BANK COLLECTION PROCESS

ChapterScope ━━━━━━━━━━━━━━━━━━━━━━━━━━━━━━━━━━━━

This chapter covers the process by which a check or other item deposited by a customer is ultimately paid by the payor bank. It examines the types of banks involved in the process, the law governing the bank collection process, the ability of banks to agree among themselves to vary the provisions of Article 4 and Regulation CC, and the duties of payor and collecting banks under both Article 4 and Regulation CC. The key points in this chapter are:

- ■ **Effect of Regulation CC:** The bank collection aspects of Article 4 have been preempted to a large extent by Regulation CC.

- ■ **Payor bank's accountability on presented items:** A payor bank that does not settle for a demand item or return the item on the day of presentment is liable for the amount of the item. Even if the payor bank settles for the item on the day of presentment, it is liable for the item if it does not pay or return the item by its midnight deadline.

- ■ **Payor bank's duties under Regulation CC:** A payor bank has a duty under Regulation CC to expeditiously return a check and to give prompt notice of the nonpayment of any check in excess of $2,500.

- ■ **Role of collecting bank:** A collecting bank is the customer's agent in collecting an item. Its agency status terminates when the item is paid. As agent, it has a duty of ordinary care in all of its actions.

- ■ **Collecting bank's right of chargeback:** In the event that a collecting bank does not, for any reason, obtain payment of an item, it may charge back its customer's account for the amount of the item.

I. INTRODUCTION TO THE CHECK COLLECTION PROCESS

- A. **Introduction:** When a check is given in payment of an obligation, the holder of the check needs to convert the check into cash. To do so, the holder can either present the check himself to the bank on which the check is drawn or he can deposit the check into his own bank account. His bank, acting as his agent, will then, either directly or through one or more other banks, present the check to and obtain payment from the bank on which the check is drawn. This process is called the ***check collection process.***

- B. **Bank:** A bank is "any person engaged in the business of banking." This includes, among others, commercial banks, savings banks, savings and loan associations, credit unions, and trust companies. U.C.C. §4-105(1).

- C. **Branch banking:** Branches or separate offices of banks are treated as separate banks for most purposes including for computing the time within which an action must be taken, in determining where an action may be taken or directed, or where notices or orders must be given. U.C.C.

§4-107. For example, presentment to the Beverly Hills branch of Wells Bank would not be proper if the check was drawn on the Santa Monica branch of Wells Bank. U.C.C. §4-107, Official Comment 2.

D. Types of banks under Article 4: Article 4 classifies banks into five categories.

   1. Payor bank: A *payor bank* is "a bank that is a drawee of a draft." U.C.C. §4-105(3).

     Example: Assume that your employer drew your paycheck on Wells Bank. You deposited the check in your account at Bank of America, which sent the check to Crocker Bank for collection. Crocker Bank then presented the check to Wells Bank for payment. Because your employer drew the check on Wells Bank, Wells Bank is the drawee of the draft. Because it is also a bank, it is the payor bank. See Figure 6-1.

   2. Depositary bank: A *depositary bank* is "the first bank to take an item even though it is also the payor bank unless the item is presented for immediate payment over the counter." U.C.C. §4-105(2).

Figure 6-1

     Example: Bank of America is the depositary bank. When you deposit the check into your bank account at Bank of America, Bank of America becomes the depositary bank. Bank of America would still be the depositary bank had the check also been drawn on Bank of America, making it also the payor bank. U.C.C. §4-105(2); U.C.C. §4-105, Official Comment 3. However, Bank of America would be the payor bank only (and not a depositary bank) if you demanded payment for the check from Bank of America by presenting the check for immediate payment over the counter.

   3. Collecting bank: A *collecting bank* is "any bank handling an item for collection except the payor bank." U.C.C. §4-105(5). A depositary bank, as long as it is not also the payor bank, is a collecting bank.

     Example: When Bank of America, the depositary bank, sends your paycheck to Crocker Bank for presentment to Wells Bank, both Bank of America and Crocker Bank are collecting banks.

     Note: One of the most common ways of collecting checks is through the *Federal Reserve System*, which is the central bank of the United States. The Federal Reserve System is a network of 12 Federal Reserve District Banks spread throughout the country and 25 additional branches of these banks.

   4. Intermediary bank: An *intermediary bank* is "any bank to which an item is transferred in the course of collection except the depositary or payor bank." U.C.C. §4-105(4).

     Example: Only Crocker Bank is an intermediary bank. Wells Bank, being the payor bank, is not an intermediary bank. As the depositary bank, Bank of America is also not an intermediary bank.

   5. Presenting bank: A *presenting bank* is "any bank presenting an item except a payor bank." U.C.C. §4-105(6).

Example: Because Crocker Bank is the bank that presented the check to Wells Bank, Crocker Bank is the presenting bank.

E. Types of banks under Regulation CC: Regulation CC has created two classifications of banks.

    1. Paying bank: Under Regulation CC, paying banks have duties above and beyond those imposed on payor banks under Article 4. *Paying bank* is a broader concept than "payor bank." The definition of a paying bank includes the bank whose routing number appears on a check even if it is not the true drawee bank. In addition, for bank collection functions, a bank through which a check is payable is a paying bank, even if the check is drawn on another bank. 12 C.F.R. §229.2(z).

    2. Returning bank: A *returning bank* is any bank other than the paying or depositary bank that handles the item on its return. 12 C.F.R. §229.2(cc).

    Example: If Wells Bank decides not to pay your paycheck, it must return the paycheck to Bank of America, the depositary bank. Wells Bank may decide to return the check, not through Crocker Bank (the bank that presented the check), but rather through Interstate Bank. Interstate Bank would be a returning bank. Had Wells Bank returned the check through Crocker Bank, Crocker Bank would likewise be a returning bank. 12 C.F.R. §229.31.

F. Clearinghouses: A common method of collecting checks when the check is deposited in a bank in the same city or county as the bank on which the check is drawn is through a clearinghouse. A *clearinghouse* is an association of banks or nonbank payors such as express companies or governmental agencies regularly clearing items. U.C.C. §4-104(a)(4).

Example: First Bank of Arkansas and Little Rock State Bank are both members of the Little Rock Clearing House. Every morning at 10:00 A.M., on the premises of the clearinghouse, First Bank of Arkansas will present to Little Rock State Bank all the checks drawn on that bank. At the same time, Little Rock State Bank will present to First Bank of Arkansas all the checks drawn on that bank. On this particular day, First Bank of Arkansas presents four checks to Little Rock State Bank in the sum total of $1,500. Little Rock State Bank presents eight checks to First Bank of Arkansas in the sum total of $2,000. The banks will settle their mutual obligations on a net basis, which means that First Bank of Arkansas will pay Little Rock State Bank the $500 difference between the total amount of the checks presented to each other.

II. LAW GOVERNING THE CHECK COLLECTION PROCESS

A. Introduction: Although Article 4 is the basic law governing the bank collection process, federal statutory and regulatory law preempts any conflicting provisions of Article 4. The bank collection aspects of Article 4 have been preempted by Congress's enactment of the Expedited Funds Availability Act, 12 U.S.C. §4001, and by the Federal Reserve Board's promulgation of Regulation CC thereunder. Regulation CC governs the collection of checks through any banking channel. To a lesser degree, Article 4 is preempted by Regulation J, which was promulgated under the authority granted to the Board of Governors of the Federal Reserve System by the Federal Reserve Act. 12 U.S.C. §221. Regulation J, which governs the collection of items through the Federal Reserve System, binds any bank that sends an item for collection through a Federal Reserve Bank. 12 C.F.R. §210.3. Regulation J's rules largely resemble Article 4's rules.

Note: When a check is sent for collection through a Federal Reserve Bank, both Regulations J and CC apply. When a check is not collected through a Federal Reserve Bank, only Regulation CC applies. When an item, other than a check, is collected through a Federal Reserve Bank, only Regulation J applies. When an item, other than a check, is not collected through a Federal Reserve Bank, neither Regulation J nor CC applies.

III. VARIATION BY AGREEMENT

A. **Introduction:** The rules set out in Article 4 and in Regulation CC regulating the bank collection process can be varied by agreement between the affected parties. U.C.C. §4-103(a); 12 C.F.R. §229.37.

B. **Limitations:** Parties can agree to vary the provisions of Article 4 or Regulation CC subject to two limitations: (a) such an agreement may not disclaim a bank's liability for its own lack of good faith or failure to exercise ordinary care, nor (b) may it limit the measure of damages resulting from its lack of good faith or failure to exercise ordinary care. U.C.C. §4-103(a); 12 C.F.R. §229.37. The parties may, however, determine by agreement the standards by which the bank's responsibility is to be measured if those standards are not manifestly unreasonable. U.C.C. §4-103(a).

   Example: An agreement between a depositary bank and a payor bank may reduce the time that the payor bank has to determine whether it will pay or dishonor a check.

C. **Binding on customer:** With rare exception, as long as the agreement is with respect to the item being handled, the bank's customer (usually the owner of the item) is bound by any agreement that is made by the bank in the process of collecting the item for him even though he is not a party to the agreement. U.C.C. §4-103, Official Comment 3.

D. **Clearinghouse rules:** *Clearinghouse rules* have the effect of agreements varying the rules of Article 4 for items collected through the clearinghouse, whether or not specifically assented to by all parties interested in the items handled. U.C.C. §4-103(b); U.C.C. §4-103, Official Comment 3.

IV. DUTIES OF PAYOR BANK

A. **Introduction:** Article 4 and Regulation CC impose certain duties and time restrictions on a payor bank when an item is presented for payment.

B. **Duty to pay or settle on day of presentment:** When a check is presented for payment, the payor bank has a choice. One choice is to either pay or return the check on the day of presentment. The second choice is to *defer posting* of the check. When a payor bank defers posting of a check, the bank waits until the next banking day to decide whether to pay or return the check. This second choice is at a cost. To defer posting a check, the payor bank must settle with the presenting bank before midnight of the banking day of receipt or before any earlier time established by Regulations CC or J. This settlement can be revoked if the payor bank decides the next day to return the check. U.C.C. §4-301(a).

   Example: Crocker Bank presents your paycheck to Wells Bank on Friday morning. If Wells Bank wants to defer posting of your paycheck, it must settle with Crocker Bank for the amount of the check by midnight on Friday. It will settle by crediting Crocker Bank's account either with Wells Bank or with a Federal Reserve Bank. If Wells Bank decides to return the check unpaid the next day, it will revoke the settlement by either debiting the credit it gave Crocker Bank or instructing the Federal Reserve Bank to debit Crocker Bank's account and credit Wells Bank's account.

1. **Exception for immediate payment over the counter:** When a demand item is presented for immediate payment over the counter, a payor bank has no right to defer its decision as to whether to pay the item. U.C.C. §4-301(a); U.C.C. §4-301, Official Comment 2.

   Example: If you go to the branch of Wells Bank on which the check was drawn and demand that it make payment of the check, Wells Bank would have to either pay the check or dishonor it on the day of presentment. U.C.C. §3-502(b)(2).

2. **Exception for on-us checks:** A payor bank does not need to provisionally settle for an "on-us" check on the day of receipt to have the right to defer the decision as to whether to pay or return the on-us item until the next banking day. An *on-us* is an item on which the payor bank and depositary bank are the same bank. U.C.C. §4-301(b); U.C.C. §4-301, Official Comment 4.

   Example: If both you and your employer bank with Wells Bank, the deposit of your paycheck in Wells Bank makes your paycheck an on-us item. Wells Bank does not need to provisionally settle with you on the day of receipt to have the right to defer the decision as to whether to pay or return the paycheck until the next banking day. Unlike when one bank settles with another bank, the payor bank has no assurance that you will have the capacity to repay the funds in the event that the check is returned to you the next day.

3. **Failure to settle for demand item on day of receipt:** If the payor bank neither settles for the item, nor returns the item, by midnight of the banking day of receipt, the payor bank is penalized by being ***accountable*** (liable) for the amount of the item. U.C.C. §4-302(a)(1). *See* NBT Bank, Nat. Ass'n v. First Nat. Community Bank, 393 F.3d 404 (3rd Cir. Pa. 2004) (U.C.C. §4-302 imposes strict accountability on a payor bank that fails to revoke its provisional settlement on a dishonored check prior to the midnight deadline).

   Extension: The midnight deadline for payor bank to return a check to depositary bank after maker stopped payment was extended by placing the check in possession of a courier for transport to the Federal Reserve Bank; the courier was a highly expeditious means of delivery that would ordinarily result in delivery of the check to the Federal Reserve Bank on the next banking day. *See* U.S. Bank Nat. Ass'n v. HMA, L.C., 169 P.3d 433 (Utah 2007).

4. **Means of dishonoring item:** If the payor bank, after properly settling for the item on the day of its receipt, decides that it will not pay the item, it may revoke and recover the settlement if it returns the item (1) before it has finally paid the item and (2) before its midnight deadline. U.C.C. §4-301(a)(1), (2). [[Rev] U.C.C. §4-301(a)(1),(3).] The ***midnight deadline*** is midnight on the bank's next banking day following the banking day on which the item was received. U.C.C. §4-104(a)(10).

   Example: Your paycheck was received by Wells Bank on Friday. Because Saturday and Sunday are not banking days, the next banking day is Monday. Thus, Wells Bank has to return the check by midnight on Monday.

   a. **Cut-off hour:** A bank may fix an afternoon hour of 2:00 P.M. or later as a ***cut-off hour*** for the handling of money and items and the making of entries on its books. The bank may treat any item received after the cut-off hour as having been received on the next banking day. U.C.C. §4-108(a), (b).

Example: Wells Bank has established a cut-off hour of 2:00 P.M. If the check arrives after that hour on Friday, it will be deemed to have been received on Monday, the next banking day. In this event, the midnight deadline would be midnight on Tuesday.

b. Extensions of midnight deadline for emergencies: A payor bank may be excused from failing to meet the midnight deadline when an unanticipated emergency prevents it from doing so if certain conditions are met. U.C.C. §4-109(b); 12 C.F.R. §229.38(e).

   i. Circumstances beyond bank's control: The delay must be caused by circumstances beyond the bank's control.

   Example: A blackout of electricity may prevent the bank from using its computer for processing checks.

   ii. Could not have been prevented: The bank must prove that those circumstances not only caused the delay, but that the circumstances could not be prevented by the bank through the exercise of reasonable care.

   Example: If a computer broke down because the bank failed to regularly service the computer, the delay is not excused because the breakdown was within the bank's control.

   iii. Diligence before and after circumstance: The bank must also prove that it exercised such reasonable diligence as the circumstances required in both anticipating the effects of any foreseeable events and in dealing with the circumstance once it arose.

   Example: If a bank has reason to know that computers occasionally break down, the bank should have access to a backup computer or other processing equipment in the event of a computer breakdown. If it does not have such access, the delay is not excused. *Compare* Port City State Bank v. American State Natl. Bank, 486 F.2d 196 (10th Cir. 1973) (bank's delay excused because of computer failure) *with* Blake v. Woodford Bank & Trust Co., 555 S.W.2d 589 (Ky. App. 1977) (court refused to excuse the bank's failure to return the checks by its midnight deadline because the responsible employees had left the bank prior to midnight without leaving any instructions for the bookkeepers and because the checks could have been returned on time had the employees placed the checks in the mail).

c. Special extensions under Regulation CC: Regulation CC specifically provides for extensions of the midnight deadline in returning a check in two situations.

   i. Rapid means of return: The midnight deadline is extended by one day if the paying bank uses a means of delivery that would ordinarily result in the check being received by the bank to which it is sent on or before the next banking day following the midnight deadline. 12 C.F.R. §229.30(c)(1).

   Example: If instead of mailing a check before the midnight deadline, the payor bank sends the check by a courier who picks up the check at 3:00 A.M. (3 hours after the midnight deadline), the midnight deadline is extended one day if the check would normally be delivered by the courier on the next banking day.

ii. **Highly expeditious means:** The midnight deadline is extended further if a paying bank uses a highly expeditious means of transportation, even if this means of transportation would ordinarily result in delivery after the receiving bank's next banking day. 12 C.F.R. §229.30(c)(1).

Example: If a paying bank in Los Angeles ships a returned check by air courier directly to the New York depositary bank, the midnight deadline is extended even if the check would normally be received by the New York depositary bank after its next banking day following the Los Angeles bank's midnight deadline. 12 C.F.R. §229.30(c)(1), App. E. Commentary. This is because shipment by air courier would result in the depositary bank receiving the returned check sooner than had the check been mailed before the midnight deadline.

5. **Manner of payment:** Because the payor bank has already settled for the item on the day of its receipt, the bank has nothing more to do if it decides to pay the item. Once the midnight deadline (or any earlier deadline set by agreement, clearinghouse rule, Federal Reserve regulation, or circular) has passed, the check is deemed to be paid. U.C.C. §4-215(a)(3). At this point, the payor bank is precluded from revoking its settlement. U.C.C. §4-301(a).

6. **Failure to settle or timely return of item:** If the payor bank fails to settle for a demand item on the day of receipt or fails to pay or return the item by its midnight deadline, the bank becomes accountable for the item. U.C.C. §4-302(a)(1). This means that the bank is liable for the face amount of the item. U.C.C. §4-302, Official Comment 3.

Rationale: The bank is penalized for its untimely actions by being liable in the face amount of the item whether or not the holder suffers any loss.

a. **Liable whether or not properly payable:** Because accountability is a punishment for the payor bank's tardiness, the payor bank is accountable for the item whether or not the item is properly payable. U.C.C. §4-302(a)(1).

Example: Even if the account does not contain sufficient funds or the item bears a forged drawer's signature, the bank nonetheless is liable for the amount of the item.

b. **Payor bank's defenses against accountability:** The payor bank may defend against its accountability for an item under the same conditions that it could recover a payment made by mistake under U.C.C. §3-418(d). In addition, the payor bank may defend by proving that the presenter breached one of the presentment warranties or by proving that the presenter presented or transferred the check intending to defraud the payor bank. U.C.C. §4-302(b); U.C.C. §4-302, Official Comment 3.

Example: Assume that Wells Bank is accountable for your paycheck because it did not give a settlement on the day it received the paycheck. Wells Bank may defend against its duty to account by showing that the item contained a forged indorsement or has been altered or that the check was presented by you pursuant to a scheme to defraud it.

c. **2002 amendments:** A new [Rev] U.C.C. §4-301(a)(2) has been added to encourage the electronic processing of checks. Under this new subsection, an image of the item, rather than the item itself, may be returned if the party to which the item is to be returned has entered into an agreement under which it will accept an image as return of the item and the image is returned in accordance with the agreement. As a result, the holder may not claim that because the item itself was not returned, the payor bank has missed its midnight deadline, thereby making the payment final as to all parties. [Rev] U.C.C. §4-301, Official Comment 8. Original [Rev] U.C.C. §4-301(a)(2) has been renumbered as (a)(3). In addition, the payor bank may, instead of sending a "written notice" of dishonor or nonpayment sends a "record."

Note: The 2002 amendments define record in [Rev] U.C.C. §3-103(a)(14) as "information that is inscribed on a tangible medium or that is stored in an electronic or other medium and is retrievable in perceivable form."

7. **Payor bank's liability on documentary drafts and items not payable on demand:** A payor bank is accountable for the amount of a documentary draft (whether payable on demand or at a stated time) or other item not payable on demand only if (1) the item is properly payable and (2) the payor bank does not pay or accept the item or return it and any accompanying documents within the time limits allowed. U.C.C. §4-302(a)(2).

   a. **Must be properly payable:** Unlike demand items, the payor bank is liable for these types of items only if they are properly payable.

   b. **Time within which bank must act:** Article 4 does not determine the time within which a bank must act to avoid accountability for these items. This is left to U.C.C. §3-502.

      i. **Documentary drafts:** A bank has until the close of business on the third business day following presentment to determine whether to pay a documentary draft. U.C.C. §3-502 (c).

         Example: If a documentary draft presented to the bank is payable on February 1, the bank has until the close of business on February 4 to pay or return the draft. If the draft is properly payable, the bank is accountable for the draft if it does not return it by that time. However, if there are insufficient funds to cover the draft, the bank is not liable despite its delay.

      ii. **Drafts payable on stated date:** When a draft is payable on a stated date, a payor bank must make payment on the day of presentment or on the stated date, whichever is later. U.C.C. §3-502(b)(3).

8. **Final payment:** When the payor bank finally pays an item, the payment process has been completed. The payor bank may no longer revoke its settlement. In addition, the depositary bank becomes accountable to its customer for the amount of the item. U.C.C. §4-215(d). At this point the drawer and indorsers are discharged from liability. U.C.C. §4-215, Comment 8. The payor bank finally pays an item when it has done any one of the following three acts. U.C.C. §4-215(a).

   a. **Pays in cash:** A payor bank finally pays an item when it makes payment in cash. An item is paid in cash when, on presentment over the counter to a teller, the teller pays cash for the item.

      Example: When you take your paycheck to Wells Bank and demand that the teller give you cash for the check, the teller's act of handing you the cash is final payment of the check. However, when both the customer and the drawer of the check have an account at the same bank, whether payment is made when the teller gives cash to the customer depends on whether and how the customer fills out the deposit slip and whether there is a provision in the bank/depositor contract that provides otherwise.

- **Less cash:** When the customer fills out a deposit slip listing first the check and then listing some amount in the column reading "less cash," the bank has not finally paid the check. Rather, the customer has deposited the check into its bank account and the bank, in its role as depositary bank, has advanced funds against the check.

- **No deposit slip:** Even if no deposit slip is filled out, the handing over of cash to the depositor is not final payment if the depositor's contract provides otherwise.

b. **Settles for item without reserving right to revoke:** A payor bank finally pays an item when the bank settles for the item without reserving a right to revoke the settlement under statute, clearinghouse rule, or agreement. U.C.C. §4-215(a)(2); U.C.C. §4-215, Official Comment 4. The reservation must be specifically authorized by statute, clearinghouse rule, or other agreement. However, Article 4 gives a payor bank an automatic right to revoke a settlement it has made if it meets the requirements specified in U.C.C. §4-301. U.C.C. §4-215, Official Comment 4. This does not apply to checks presented for payment over the counter.

Example: When the presenting bank presents an item to the payor bank, the payor bank's settlement on the day of presentment does not constitute payment of the item because U.C.C. §4-301 specifically allows the payor bank to revoke the settlement if it meets the conditions contained in the section.

c. **Fails to revoke provisional settlement by midnight deadline:** The payor bank finally pays an item when the bank has made a provisional settlement for the item and fails to revoke the settlement by the midnight deadline, or an earlier time established by clearinghouse rule or agreement. U.C.C. §4-215(a)(3). The payor bank must provisionally settle for an item. If the payor bank fails to make a provisional settlement, the bank has not finally paid the item although the bank is accountable for the item. By not having finally paid the item, the drawer and indorser are still liable thereon.

Example: Assume that Wells Bank not only fails to settle for your paycheck on the day of presentment but also fails to return or pay your paycheck by its midnight deadline. Wells Bank is accountable to you for the amount of your paycheck. U.C.C. §4-302(a)(1). However, because you do not yet have the funds represented by the paycheck, payment of the check is not final. As a result, your employer, being the drawer, is still liable to you on the check.

9. **Duties of paying banks under Regulation CC in returning unpaid items:** To protect depositary banks that are required to make funds represented by deposited items available according to the expedited Mandatory Availability Schedule under Regulation CC, Regulation CC imposes two duties on the paying bank to ensure that the depositary bank quickly learns of a check's dishonor: (1) the duty to expeditiously return unpaid items and (2) the duty to give prompt notice of nonpayment of any item in the amount of $2,500 or greater.

Note: The paying bank's duties to expeditiously return unpaid items and to give prompt notice of nonpayment do not affect whether the bank has paid or dishonored the check under Article 4. A breach of either of these duties does not result in the bank having paid the check. The check is still dishonored. However, the paying bank is liable for any damages caused by its breach.

a. **Duty of expeditious return:** A paying bank has a duty to expeditiously return unpaid items. A paying bank may meet either of two tests to satisfy its duty of expeditious return: the *2-day/4-day test* or the *forward collection test.* 12 C.F.R. §229.30(a).

   i. **2-day/4-day test:** The 2-day/4-day test requires that the paying bank return an item in a manner such that it will normally be received by the depositary bank within certain time limits. 12 C.F.R. §229.30(a)(1).

       ■ **Local checks:** The time limit for the depositary bank to receive the return of a local check is no later than 4:00 P.M. on the second business day after the check was presented to the paying bank. 12 C.F.R. §229.30(a)(1)(i).

       Example: Assume that your local paycheck was presented to Wells Bank on Friday. Wells Bank must return the check to Bank of America so that it would normally be received by Bank of America by 4:00 P.M. on Tuesday. (Saturday and Sunday are not business days and therefore are not included in the calculation.) Wells Bank may mail the check to Bank of America if, under normal circumstances, the check would be received by Bank of America no later than Tuesday at 4:00 P.M.

       ■ **Nonlocal checks:** The time limit for the depositary bank to receive the return of a nonlocal check is no later than 4:00 P.M. on the fourth business day after presentment. 12 C.F.R. §229.30(a)(1)(ii).

       Example: In the case of a nonlocal check that is received by Wells Bank on Friday, it must be sent in a manner as to be received by Bank of America by 4:00 P.M. on Thursday of the following week.

   ii. **The forward collection test:** The forward collection test provides that a paying bank returns a check in an expeditious manner if it does so in a manner that a similarly situated bank would normally handle a check drawn on the depositary bank and deposited for forward collection in that bank by noon on the banking day following the banking day on which the check was presented to the paying bank. 12 C.F.R. §229.30(a)(2)(iii). The payor bank has to act as though the check had been deposited for collection. This means that the payor bank must act as though its customer deposited the check by noon on the next banking day following the banking day that the check was in fact presented to the payor bank. The forward collection test rests on the assumption that in sending a check for collection, a depositary bank has an incentive to use a means of collection that is reasonably prompt so that it will have use of the funds represented by the check. 12 C.F.R. §229.30(a)(2). If the payor bank uses similar means, it acts expeditiously.

       Example: If your paycheck was presented for payment on Friday, Wells Bank must treat the paycheck as if it were a check drawn by you on Bank of America and deposited by your employer in its account at Wells Bank by noon on Monday. The issue would thus be whether Wells Bank handled the check in the same way in which it would have handled a check for collection deposited in your employer's account by noon on Monday.

       The standard is based on how similarly situated banks would collect such a check. Thus, if similarly situated banks would use an intermediary collecting bank or a Federal Reserve Bank to present the check to the payor bank, the paying bank must use an intermediary collecting bank or a Federal Reserve Bank to return the check. 12 C.F.R. §229.30(a), Commentary, Examples b, (iii), (iv).

Example: A midnight deadline for the payor bank to return a check to the depositary bank after maker stopped payment was extended by placing the check in possession of a courier for transport to the Federal Reserve Bank; the courier was a highly expeditious means of delivery that would ordinarily result in delivery of the check to the Federal Reserve Bank on the next banking day. *See* U.S. Bank Nat. Ass'n v. HMA, L.C., 169 P.3d 433 (Utah 2007).

b. **Duty to send notice of nonpayment:** The paying bank has a duty to send notice of the nonpayment of any check in the amount of $2,500 or greater directly to the depositary bank. 12 C.F.R. §229.33(a). This ensures that the depositary bank quickly learns of the dishonor of any large items in time enough to prevent having to allow its customer use of the funds under Regulation CC. The notice may be communicated in any way, as long as it is received by the depositary bank by 4:00 P.M. on the second business day following the banking day on which the check was presented to the paying bank. 12 C.F.R. §229.33(a).

Example: If the check was presented on Wednesday to Wells Bank, the notice must be received by Bank of America by 4:00 P.M. on Friday.

Warranty: To protect depositary banks from erroneous notices, a paying bank that sends a notice of nonpayment warrants to its transferee bank, any subsequent transferee bank, the depositary bank, and the owner of the item that it was authorized to send notice of nonpayment. 12 C.F.R. §229.34(b)(2). The paying bank does not warrant that the notice of nonpayment is accurate and timely. 12 C.F.R. §229.34(b), Commentary.

Note: Depositary banks receive little protection from the warranty of notice of nonpayment because damages are limited to the consideration received. Therefore, the paying bank is not liable for any liability incurred by the depositary bank to its customer for wrongful dishonor of subsequent items.

c. **Liability for violation of paying bank's duties of expeditious return and notice of nonpayment:** A bank is liable for damages for breach of its duties of expeditious return or of transmitting notice of nonpayment only if the bank fails to exercise ordinary care or to act in good faith. 12 C.F.R. §229.38(a). A paying bank that violates its duty of ordinary care is liable to the injured party for the amount of the check less the amount of loss that would have been incurred had ordinary care been used. 12 C.F.R. §229.38(a). The bank's failure to act in good faith gives rise to liability for all damages proximately caused. 12 C.F.R. §229.38(a). The bank is not liable for costs or attorneys' fees incurred by the injured party.

d. **Warranties given by paying bank on return of item:** Under Regulation CC, the payor bank warrants to the returning bank, the depositary bank, and the owner of the check that (a) it returned the check by its midnight deadline (or any earlier time required by Article 4, Regulation J, or Regulation CC), (b) it is authorized to return the check, (c) the check has not been materially altered, and (d) in the case of a notice in lieu of return, the original check has not and will not be returned. 12 C.F.R. §229.34(a).

Note: Although the payor bank is already accountable for the amount of the check under Article 4 because the bank was late in returning the check, U.C.C. §4-302(a), the depositary bank may choose to recover for breach of the warranty on returned checks because the damages available to it under Regulation CC may include finance charges, attorneys' fees, and other expenses related to the returned check. 12 C.F.R. §229.34(d).

V. DUTIES OF COLLECTING BANKS

A. **Introduction:** Collecting banks—including depositary, intermediary, and presenting banks— have certain duties in the bank collection process.

B. **Collecting bank's status as agent:** When a customer deposits an item into her bank account, the depositary bank automatically becomes the customer's agent for the purpose of collecting the item. U.C.C. §4-201(a).

   Example: When you, as the holder of your paycheck, deposit the paycheck in your bank account, you are asking your bank to undertake the job of collecting the check from the payor bank.

   1. **Intermediary and presenting banks:** Subsequent collecting banks, including any intermediary and presenting banks, become the subagent for the customer.

      Example: When Bank of America sends the check for collection to Crocker Bank, a subsequent collecting bank, Crocker Bank, as a collecting bank, becomes your subagent. U.C.C. §4-201(a). Crocker Bank is responsible directly to you. Despite the fact that Crocker Bank was chosen by Bank of America, it is not the agent of Bank of America. U.C.C. §4-201(a).

   2. **Termination of agency status:** The agency status of the depositary bank and other collecting banks terminates when they finally settle for the item. U.C.C. §4-201(a); U.C.C. §4-214(a); U.C.C. §4-214, Official Comment 3. Final settlement occurs in most situations when the payor bank has made final payment. At this point, the depositary bank becomes indebted to the customer in the amount of the item, and the customer's relationship with the depositary bank is transformed from principal and agent to creditor and debtor. U.C.C. §4-201, Official Comment 4.

C. **Right of chargeback:** A depositary bank will provisionally credit its customer's account on deposit of an item. However, subject to funds availability rules, the customer has no right to use the funds until the item is paid by the payor bank. The depositary bank may charge back its customer's account or obtain a refund for the amount of any provisional settlement given to the customer if, for any reason, the item is not finally paid by the payor bank. U.C.C. §4-214(a). *See* Call v. Ellenville National Bank, 5 A.D.3d 521 (N.Y.A.D. 2 Dept. 2004) (When final settlement was not made on check by payor bank due to discovery that check was counterfeit, collecting bank was entitled to revoke provisional settlement made on check and charge back customer's account or obtain refund from him for funds drawn on the check even though the bank represented to the customer that check had cleared.).

   Example: Whether your paycheck was dishonored because your employer had insufficient funds in its account, because it stopped payment on the check, or because the payor bank may have gone insolvent, Bank of America may charge back your account for the full amount of the check.

   1. **Right to refund:** The depositary bank retains its right of chargeback (or can obtain a refund) when it allows its customer to draw on the uncollected funds or was required to do so under Regulation CC. U.C.C. §4-214(d)(1); U.C.C. §4-201(a); 12 C.F.R. §229.32(b), Commentary b.

2. **Even if collecting bank negligent:** Even if the depositary bank's failure to exercise ordinary care in sending the item for collection caused the dishonor, it may charge back its customer's account. U.C.C. §4-214, Official Comment 5. Of course, the bank remains liable to the customer for any damages caused by its failure to exercise ordinary care in collecting the deposited item. U.C.C. §4-214(d)(2); U.C.C. §4-214, Official Comment 6.

3. **Requirements for chargeback:** To exercise its right of chargeback or refund, the depositary bank must, by its midnight deadline (or within a longer reasonable time after it learns the facts), either (a) return the item or (b) send notification of the facts if the item is not available for return. U.C.C. §4-214(a).

   Note: If the bank is both the depositary bank and the payor bank, it must act by its midnight deadline. U.C.C. §4-214(c); U.C.C. §4-301(a), (b).

4. **Consequences of failing to meet requirements:** Even if the depositary bank fails to act within the required time, it may still revoke its settlement, charge back its customer's account, or obtain a refund. The only consequence of the untimely act is that it is liable for any loss to the customer resulting from the delay. U.C.C. §4-214(a); U.C.C. §4-214, Official Comment 3.

   Note: It may be very difficult for the customer to prove a loss. Unless the drawer and all indorsers become insolvent or leave the jurisdiction in the period between the time the item should have been returned and the time the item was in fact returned, the customer will be unable to prove a loss.

D. **Duty of collecting bank to use ordinary care in collecting and returning items:** Collecting banks owe a duty of ordinary care to their customer when performing their collection and return duties. U.C.C. §4-202(a). These duties include, among others, presenting or sending an item for presentment, choosing a route to forward an item for collection, sending notice of dishonor or nonpayment, returning the item, or settling for an item. U.C.C. §4-202(a).

   1. **Acting reasonably:** Part of a collecting bank's duty to exercise ordinary care is to act reasonably. A collecting bank must take proper action before its midnight deadline following receipt of the item, notice, or settlement. Taking action within a longer time may be considered reasonable, but the burden of establishing the timeliness of the action is on the collecting bank. U.C.C. §4-202(b); U.C.C. §4-202, Official Comment 3.

      Example: If you deposit a check on Monday, Bank of America must send the check for collection by midnight on Tuesday. If the check was mutilated, and, therefore, Bank of America's computer could not read the MICR-encoded line, the fact that it was required to hand-process the check may justify it in missing the midnight deadline in sending the check for collection.

   2. **Delay excused:** As in the case of a payor bank, a collecting bank is allowed additional time in the case of emergencies. U.C.C. §4-109(b).

      Example: If a blackout of electricity in its area prevented Bank of America from processing the check by computer, Bank of America's delay in forwarding the check for collection may be excused.

   3. **Liable only for own negligence:** A collecting bank is liable only for its own failure to exercise ordinary care. It is not liable for the actions of another bank unless it failed to exercise ordinary care in choosing that bank. U.C.C. §4-202(c).

4. **Measure of damages for failure to exercise ordinary care:** The measure of damages for a collecting bank's failure to exercise ordinary care in handling an item is the amount of the item reduced by an amount that could not have been realized by the use of ordinary care. Upon a showing of bad faith, damages may include any other damages the party has suffered as a proximate consequence. U.C.C. §4-103(e).

It may be hard for the customer to prove a loss. If the drawer withdrew the funds after a reasonable time for presentment had expired but prior to the time that the check was ultimately presented, the customer will be able to prove a loss. Had the collecting bank presented the check within a reasonable time, the check would have been paid. The customer may also successfully establish a loss if he proves that he has parted with money or property after the time that notice of dishonor should have been received. In contrast, if the funds were withdrawn during the reasonable time allowed for the bank to present the check, the customer cannot prove that he suffered any loss by virtue of the delay.

Example: Assume that Customer agreed to sell to Buyer a diamond ring. Although Buyer pays by check, Customer and Buyer agree that Customer does not have to deliver the diamond ring until the check clears. After 2 weeks Customer, noticing that his bank had taken the hold off his account for the amount of the check (and thus assuming that the check had been paid), sends the diamond ring to Buyer. In reality, his bank had misplaced the check and did not forward the check for collection for 3 weeks. On presentment, the check was dishonored. Buyer has vanished. Customer has suffered a loss in the amount of the diamond ring's value because of his bank's negligence in collecting the check.

5. **Electronic presentment:** A new way of presenting checks or other items is through electronic presentment. *Electronic presentment (or check truncation)* involves the transfer of the content of the item through the information contained on the MICR-encoded line rather than transfer of the item itself. In development now is a second means of electronic presentment called *imaging technology* that will allow the check's image to be electronically transmitted to the payor bank. U.C.C. §4-110, Official Comment 1. When an item is presented electronically, a presentment notice is sent in the place of the item itself. U.C.C. §4-110(a). The item is deemed presented when the presentment notice is received. U.C.C. §4-110(b).

E. **Encoding warranties:** To be processed by computer, the depositary bank will encode the face amount of the check on the MICR line. The depositary bank may make a mistake in its encoding. It may encode the check in a greater amount than it is actually payable (*overencoding*) or encode the check in a lesser amount than actually payable (*underencoding*). To protect the payor bank and subsequent collecting banks from losses from the misencoding, any person who encodes information on an item warrants to any subsequent collecting bank and to the payor bank or other payor that the information is correctly encoded. U.C.C. §4-209(a). Under Regulation CC, any bank that handles a check or a returned check warrants that the encoded information is correct. 12 C.F.R. §229.34(c)(3).

1. **Liability for misencoding:** A person misencoding an item is liable to any person taking the item in good faith for the loss suffered, plus expenses and loss of interest incurred. U.C.C. §4-209(c); 12 C.F.R. §229.34(d).

Overencoding example: Your paycheck, drawn in the amount of $1,000, is wrongly encoded by the depositary bank in the amount of $10,000. When the check reaches the payor bank, the payor bank's computer automatically treats the check as being drawn in the overencoded amount of $10,000. The payor bank pays the check. The payor bank, however, can debit your employer's account for only $1,000, the amount for which the check was drawn. The payor bank can recover the difference from the depositary bank that made the encoding mistake. If the item was dishonored because it was overencoded, the depositary bank is liable to the payor bank for any damages for which the payor bank is liable to its customer for wrongful dishonor.

Underencoding example: Conversely, your paycheck may have been underencoded in the amount of $100. The payor bank's computer will debit the drawer's account for $100 and order payment to the depositary bank in that amount. Because the check was in reality payable in the amount of $1,000, the payor bank, having failed to return the check by its midnight deadline, is accountable for the full amount of the check under U.C.C. §4-302(a). As a result, the presenting bank can recover the remaining $900 from the payor bank. Because your employer wrote the check for $1,000, the payor bank may debit its account for the remaining $900. U.C.C. §4-209, Official Comment 2. However, if your employer's account does not contain sufficient funds, the payor bank will suffer a loss because of the erroneous underencoding of the check. The depositary bank will be liable to the payor bank for this loss.

Quiz Yourself on
THE BANK COLLECTION PROCESS

71. On Thursday, Joey writes a check to Lucky for $50,000. Joey has $50,000 in his bank account. Lucky deposits the check in his bank account at Roma Savings and Loan. At noon on Friday, Roma Savings and Loan presents the check to Sicily Bank. Because of its size, the check is given to the bank manager for processing. The bank manager notices that Joey has a $30,000 loan that is due on Tuesday, May 4. Realizing that paying the check may make it unlikely that the bank will obtain repayment for the loan, the manager decides to hold the check until Tuesday. At 9:00 A.M. on Tuesday, the manager sets off, against the account, the money that Joey owes the bank. Because Joey's account now contains only $20,000, the bank dishonors the check. Is Sicily Bank liable to Lucky? If so, for what damages?

_____

72. Assume in the preceding example that Sicily Bank did not settle for the check with Roma Savings and Loan on the day of presentment. If Sicily Bank becomes insolvent, may Lucky recover from Joey?

_____

73. Assume that Presenting Bank presents a $3,000 nonlocal check to Payor Bank on Tuesday and that Payor Bank decides on Wednesday to dishonor the check. What are Payor Bank's duties under Regulation CC and by what deadlines must it act to fulfill these duties? _____

74. Sally deposits a check in her account at Wells Bank on March 1. Wells Bank credits Sally's account for the amount of the check. Sally withdraws the funds. Wells Bank misplaces the check. It finds the check on March 20. The check is dishonored on presentment to the payor bank. Wells Bank gets notice of the nonpayment on March 22. Wells Bank returns the check to Sally on March 29. May Wells Bank charge back Sally's account for the amount of the check? _____

Answers

71. Yes. Sicily is liable to Lucky for the face amount of the check because it did not pay or return the check or send notice of dishonor until after its midnight deadline. U.C.C. §4-302. The check was presented on Friday and therefore Monday at midnight is the midnight deadline.

72. Yes. Because Sicily Bank did not settle for the check on the day of receipt, payment does not become final merely by the passage of time. U.C.C. §4-215(a)(3). Although Sicily Bank has become accountable for the check, Joey is not discharged until Sicily Bank pays the check. As a result, Lucky can still recover from Joey.

73. Payor Bank has both the duty to expeditiously return the check and to give notice of nonpayment. There are two ways in which it can meet the duty of expeditious return. First, it can comply with the *2-day/4-day test*. Under this test, it must return the check by a means such that Depositary Bank would receive the check by 4:00 P.M. on the following Monday (the fourth business day after presentment). 12 C.F.R. §229.30(a)(1). Second, it can meet the *forward collection test*, which just requires that it return the check in a manner similar to that which it would send a check for collection. 12 C.F.R. §229.30(a)(2). It meets its duty to give notice of nonpayment if the notice is received by Depositary Bank by Thursday at 4:00 P.M. (the second business day following the banking day on which the check was presented to the paying bank). 12 C.F.R. §229.33(a).

74. Yes. Although Wells Bank was required to give notice of the chargeback by its midnight deadline or a longer reasonable time after it learns that the check will be returned, U.C.C. §4-214(a), it still retains the right to charge back Sally's account. The only consequence of its delay is that it is liable to Sally for any loss caused by the delay. In addition, it may charge back her account even if its failure to exercise ordinary care caused the loss and even if Sally has drawn on the funds. U.C.C. §4-214(d).

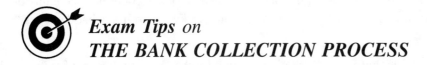

Exam Tips on
THE BANK COLLECTION PROCESS

☞ **Keep separate the duties under Article 4 and Regulation CC:** Be careful not to confuse the consequences of a payor bank failing to meet its duties under Article 4 and its duties under Regulation CC.

   ☞ If, for example, a payor bank meets the midnight deadline imposed by U.C.C. §4-302 in returning a check presented for payment, the payor bank is not accountable for the check.

   ☞ This is true even though the bank has failed to expeditiously return the check or give proper notice of nonpayment under Regulation CC.

   ☞ The paying bank is only liable for violation of its Regulation CC duties if it has failed to exercise ordinary care.

☞ Even if it is in violation of Regulation CC, a paying bank is liable only for the amount of the check less the amount of the loss that would have been incurred had ordinary care been exercised.

☛ **Consequences of each branch being a separate bank:** Remember that each branch of a bank is a separate bank. As a result, an attempted presentment of a check to a branch other than the payor branch does not commence the running of the time within which the payor bank must act.

☞ Similarly, the giving of a stop payment order to the nonpayor branch is not effective until that branch has had a reasonable time to forward the stop payment order to the payor branch.

CHAPTER 7

WHOLESALE FUNDS TRANSFERS

ChapterScope ───────────────────────────────

This chapter examines the different aspects of a funds transfer including the respective parties and their payment obligations, the duties of the different banks, cancellation of a funds transfer, liability for unauthorized transfers, erroneous payment orders, and misdescriptions. The key points in this chapter are:

- **Definition of funds transfer:** A funds transfer is a transfer of funds (often communicated electronically) between two banks.

- **Sender's obligation to pay:** A sender of a funds transfer is obligated to pay the payment order only if the funds reach the beneficiary's bank, in which event the sender's obligation on the underlying transaction is discharged.

- **Sender's obligation to reimburse:** The sender is obligated to reimburse the receiving bank only according to the terms of its payment order. If the receiving bank issues an order in a greater amount than the payment order or to the wrong beneficiary, the receiving bank must recover the payment from the recipient.

- **Sender's liability for unauthorized orders:** Subject to certain qualifications, a sender is liable for unauthorized orders if the order has been verified according to a commercially reasonable security procedure.

- **Sender's liability for mistakes in a payment order:** A sender is liable for any mistake it makes in a payment order unless the sender sent the order in compliance with a security procedure and the error would have been detected if the receiving bank had complied with the security procedure.

I. WHAT IS A FUNDS TRANSFER?

A. Definition of funds transfer: A *funds transfer* (also sometimes known as a *wire transfer* or a *wholesale wire transfer*) is a transfer of funds (often transmitted electronically) between two banks. With certain exceptions, funds transfers are governed by Article 4A of the Uniform Commercial Code. U.C.C. §4A-102.

Example: General Motors (GM) agrees to purchase computers from International Business Machines (IBM) for a price of $5 million. GM instructs its bank, Bank of America, by telephone, to pay $5 million to IBM's account at Chase Manhattan Bank. Bank of America debits GM's account and wires instructions to IBM's bank, Chase Manhattan Bank, to credit IBM's account in that amount. Chase Manhattan Bank credits IBM's account and, as a means of obtaining payment, debits the account that Bank of America maintains with it. U.C.C. §4A-104, Official Comment 1, Case #2. See Figure 7-1.

B. Terminology of funds transfers:

1. **Sender:** A *sender* is the person giving the instruction to the receiving bank. U.C.C. §4A-103(a)(5). GM, in our example above, is the sender.

2. **Customer:** A *customer* is a person (including a bank) having an account with a bank or from whom a bank has agreed to receive payment orders. U.C.C. §4A-105(a)(3). GM is the customer of Bank of America. If Bank of America issues a payment order to Bank of Missouri, Bank of America is the customer of Bank of Missouri.

3. **Receiving bank:** A *receiving bank* is the bank to which the sender's instruction is addressed. U.C.C. §4A-103(a)(4). Bank of America is a receiving bank because GM has instructed Bank of America to pay IBM.

4. **Beneficiary:** A *beneficiary* is the person to be paid by the beneficiary's bank. U.C.C. §4A-103(a)(2). IBM is a beneficiary because GM has instructed Bank of America to cause Chase Manhattan Bank to pay IBM.

5. **Beneficiary's bank:** A *beneficiary's bank* is the bank identified in a payment order to make payment to the beneficiary. U.C.C. §4A-103(a)(3). Chase Manhattan Bank is the beneficiary's bank because GM's payment order instructed Chase Manhattan Bank to credit IBM's account.

6. **Payment order:** A *payment order* is defined, in part, as "an instruction of a sender to a receiving bank, transmitted orally, electronically, or in writing, to pay, or to cause another bank to pay, a fixed or determinable amount of money to a beneficiary." U.C.C. §4A-103(a)(1).

Figure 7-1

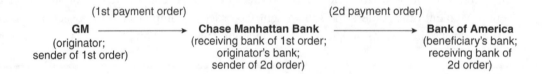

Example: The instruction from GM to Bank of America is a payment order. GM (the sender) gave an instruction orally, by telephone, to Bank of America (the receiving bank) to cause Chase Manhattan Bank to pay a fixed amount, $5 million, to IBM (the beneficiary). Bank of America's wire to Chase Manhattan Bank is also a payment order in that Bank of America (the sender) instructs Chase Manhattan Bank (the receiving bank) to pay IBM (the beneficiary).

7. **Originator:** The sender of the first payment order is the *originator* of the funds transfer. U.C.C. §4A-104(c). GM is the originator.

8. **Originator's bank:** The *originator's bank* is the receiving bank to which the payment order of the originator is issued if the originator is not a bank. U.C.C. §4A-104(d). Bank of America is the originator's bank.

C. **What is a funds transfer:** A *funds transfer* is "the series of transactions, beginning with the originator's payment order, made for the purpose of making payment to the beneficiary of the order." U.C.C. §4A-104(a).

Example: In our example, a series of transactions—the two payment orders—began with GM's (the originator) payment order, which was made for the purpose of making payment to IBM (the beneficiary).

1. **Includes all payment orders:** The term "funds transfer" includes all payment orders issued for the purpose of carrying out the originator's payment order. U.C.C. §4A-104(a).

    Example: Bank of America's wire and Chase Manhattan Bank's subsequent payment to IBM are part of the funds transfer originated by GM.

2. **One-bank funds transfer:** The same bank can be both the sending bank and the receiving bank. This type of transaction is called a ***book transfer*** because the payment is accomplished by the receiving bank both crediting the account of the beneficiary and debiting the account of the sender. U.C.C. §4A-104, Official Comment 1, Case #1.

    Example: If both IBM and GM have an account with Bank of America, GM could instruct Bank of America to credit IBM's account. In this instance, Bank of America would be both the receiving bank and the beneficiary's bank.

3. **Intermediary bank:** If the sending bank does not have an account with the receiving bank, the order may be sent through a third bank that has an account with both the sending and the receiving bank. This bank is called an ***intermediary bank.***

Figure 7-2

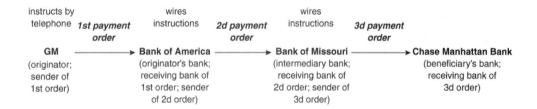

Example: Bank of America may instruct Bank of Missouri, with which it has an account and which has an account with Chase Manhattan Bank, to pay $5 million to IBM's account at Chase Manhattan Bank. Bank of Missouri will debit Bank of America's account and then send a payment order to Chase Manhattan Bank, which then will credit IBM's account and debit the account of Bank of Missouri. U.C.C. §4A-104, Official Comment 1, Case #3. This funds transfer has three payment orders: one from GM to Bank of America, a second from Bank of America to Bank of Missouri, and a third from Bank of Missouri to Chase Manhattan Bank. See Figure 7-2.

D. **Funds transfers must be between banks:** A *funds transfer* is limited to payments made through the banking system. A transfer of funds by an entity other than a bank is excluded. U.C.C. §4A-104, Official Comment 2. Because the definition of "payment order" requires that the instruction must be sent to a receiving bank requesting it to pay or to cause another bank to pay money to the beneficiary, only an interbank transfer can be a funds transfer. Transfers of funds through Western Union or similar companies, therefore, are not covered by Article 4A.

E. **Requirements for a payment order:** To be a payment order, an instruction must meet the following three requirements.

1. **Unconditional:** The instruction cannot state a condition to the obligation to pay the beneficiary other than as to the time of payment. U.C.C. §4A-103(a)(1)(i).

   Example: An instruction that states that Chase Manhattan Bank is to pay IBM only on delivery of bills of lading covering 400 IBM PC computers is not a payment order.

2. **Reimbursed by sender:** The receiving bank must be paid or reimbursed by the sender. U.C.C. §4A-103(a)(1)(ii). In other words, the instruction must be sent by the person who is going to make the payment.

   Example: When GM orders Bank of America to pay IBM, GM is both the sender and the person who will make payment to Bank of America. Therefore, the order is a payment order. If, on the other hand, GM has a preexisting arrangement with its California distributor giving the distributor the right to order Bank of America to transfer funds from GM's account to the distributor's account in payment for expenses incurred by the distributor, the distributor's order to Bank of America would not be a payment order. This is because the distributor would be the sender, but it is GM's account which is to be debited.

3. **Transmitted directly to receiving bank:** The instruction must be transmitted by the sender directly to the receiving bank. U.C.C. §4-103(a)(1)(iii). This requirement eliminates credit cards and checks from coverage under Article 4A. U.C.C. §4A-104, Official Comment 5.

   Example: If GM sends a check to IBM, IBM presents the check for payment to Bank of America. This is not a payment order because GM does not send the check directly to Bank of America. U.C.C. §4A-104, Official Comment 5.

F. **Consumer transactions excluded:** The Electronic Fund Transfer Act of 1978 (EFTA) covers most consumer funds transfers. Article 4A does not apply to any transaction if any part of the transaction is covered by EFTA. U.C.C. §4A-108. This means that most consumer transfers are excluded from coverage under Article 4A.

II. PAYMENT OBLIGATIONS IN CHAIN OF TITLE

A. **Introduction:** Acceptance of a payment order by a receiving bank, other than the beneficiary's bank, obligates the sender to pay the bank the amount of the sender's order. U.C.C. §4A-402(c). The obligation of the sender is excused if the funds transfer is not completed because, for any reason, the beneficiary's bank does not accept the payment order. U.C.C. §4A-402(c). This is called a ***money-back guarantee***. U.C.C. §4A-402, Official Comment 2. When a payment order is issued to the beneficiary's bank, acceptance of the order by the beneficiary's bank obligates the sender to pay the beneficiary's bank the amount of the order. U.C.C. §4A-402(b); U.C.C. §4A-402, Official Comment 1. On acceptance by the beneficiary's bank, the obligation of the originator to pay the beneficiary on the underlying obligation is discharged and the obligation of the beneficiary's bank to pay the beneficiary is substituted for it.

Example: GM issues a payment order to Bank of America, which then issues a payment order to an intermediary bank, Bank of Missouri, which in turn issues a payment order to Chase Manhattan Bank, the beneficiary's (IBM) bank. On acceptance by Bank of America, GM becomes obligated to pay Bank of America the amount of the order. Similarly, on acceptance of the payment order it sent to Bank of Missouri, Bank of America becomes obligated to pay Bank of Missouri the amount of the order. Bank of Missouri, which sent the order, is obligated to pay Chase Manhattan

Bank on Chase Manhattan Bank's acceptance of the order. On acceptance by Chase Manhattan Bank, the obligation of GM to pay IBM for the computers is discharged and the obligation of Chase Manhattan Bank to pay IBM is substituted for it.

III. DUTIES AND LIABILITIES OF RECEIVING BANK

A. Introduction: A receiving bank is not obligated to accept a payment order. U.C.C. §4A-209, Official Comment 1. A receiving bank has no duties until it accepts the order. U.C.C. §4A-212. The receiving bank (unless it is also the beneficiary's bank) accepts a payment order only when it executes the order. U.C.C. §4A-209(a).

B. Rejection: Because a receiving bank accepts the order only by executing it, notice of rejection is not necessary to avoid acceptance. The receiving bank, however, may decide to give notice of rejection so as to allow the sender to correct the order or seek other means of payment. U.C.C. §4A-210, Official Comment 1. A receiving bank can reject the payment order by giving notice of rejection to the sender orally, electronically, or in writing. U.C.C. §4A-210(a).

C. Execution of order: By executing the order, the receiving bank promises to issue a payment order complying with the sender's order. U.C.C. §4A-302(a)(1). Execution occurs when the receiving bank issues a payment order intending to carry out the sender's order. U.C.C. §4A-301(a).

1. **Execution date:** The receiving bank is obligated to issue the payment order on the execution date. *Execution date* is the day on which the receiving bank may properly issue a payment order executing the sender's order. U.C.C. §4A-301(b). The execution date refers to the day that the payment order should be executed rather than the day that it is actually executed. U.C.C. §4A-301, Official Comment 2. The sender may, in its instructions, set the execution date. U.C.C. §4A-301(b). Where only a payment date is stated, the execution date is the payment date if the order can be transmitted by a means allowing payment on the same date. *Id*. If not, the execution date is an earlier date on which execution is reasonably necessary to allow payment to the beneficiary on the payment date. *Id*.

2. **Payment date:** The *payment date* is the day on which the amount of the order is payable to the beneficiary by the beneficiary's bank. U.C.C. §4A-401. In other words, the payment date indicates the day the beneficiary is to receive payment. U.C.C. §4A-401, Official Comment. The originator in its order usually indicates a payment date rather than an execution date because the originator is more concerned as to when the beneficiary receives the payment than when the originator's bank sends the payment order.

3. **Duty to issue payment order:** A receiving bank, on the acceptance of a payment order, must issue a payment order on the execution date complying with the sender's order. U.C.C. §4A-302(a)(1). If the sender's instruction states a payment date, the receiving bank is obligated to transmit the order at a time and by a means reasonably necessary to allow payment to the beneficiary on the payment date or as soon thereafter as is feasible. U.C.C. §4A-302(a)(2). If the sender's instructions specify the means by which the payment order is to be transmitted, the receiving bank must use those means. U.C.C. §4A-302(a)(1).

4. **Time when payment order can be accepted:** To protect the originator against early execution of its payment order, the originator's bank cannot accept the originator's payment order until the execution date. U.C.C. §4A-209(d). If the receiving bank is also the beneficiary's bank, it could not accept the order until the payment date. U.C.C. §4A-209(d).

Example: Assume that on April 1, GM instructs Bank of America to make a payment on April 15 to IBM's account at Chase Manhattan Bank. Bank of America's payment order to Chase Manhattan Bank mistakenly provides for immediate payment. Chase Manhattan Bank immediately releases the funds to IBM. Because Chase Manhattan Bank complied with Bank of America's order, Bank of America is required to pay Chase Manhattan Bank on Chase Manhattan Bank's acceptance of the order. However, GM is not obligated to pay Bank of America until Bank of America has itself accepted the order. Bank of America cannot accept the order until the execution date, which is deemed to be the date prior to the payment date on which execution must take place to enable the order to be received by Chase Manhattan Bank in time for it to make payment on the payment date. Therefore, no acceptance can occur by Bank of America until shortly before April 15. Early payment has not injured GM because it is not required to pay Bank of America until the execution date.

5. **Damages for breach of duty by receiving bank:** If the receiving bank breaches its duty by, for example, breaching an express agreement to execute an order, failing to complete an order it has accepted, or issuing an order that does not comply with the terms of sender's payment order, the receiving bank is liable for the sender's expenses in the funds transfer and for incidental expenses and interest lost as a result of its failure to properly execute the order. U.C.C. §4A-305(b). Absent an express written agreement to the contrary, consequential damages are not available to the sender. U.C.C. §4A-305(a), (b), (d).

   Rationale: Exposing a receiving bank to the possibility of consequential damages is inconsistent with the low cost and high speed of wire transfers. U.C.C. §4A-305, Official Comment 2.

D. **Erroneous execution of payment order:** An erroneous execution of a payment order refers to mistakes made by the receiving bank in its execution of the sender's order.

   1. **Duplicative order, order in greater amount than authorized, or to wrong beneficiary:** When the receiving bank executes a payment order in an amount greater than the amount of sender's order, issues a duplicate order to the beneficiary, or issues an order to the wrong beneficiary, the sender, not having authorized these erroneous orders, is only obligated to reimburse the receiving bank for whatever payment was to be made according to the sender's original order. U.C.C. §4A-303(a), (c); U.C.C. §4A-402(c).

      Example: If GM issues an order to pay IBM $5 million but Bank of America issues an order in the amount of $7 million, GM is liable to Bank of America for $5 million only. U.C.C. §4A-303, Official Comment 2. Bank of America must seek the remaining $2 million from IBM. If Bank of America issues a payment order to Xerox as the beneficiary instead of properly issuing an order to IBM, GM is not obliged to pay Bank of America on the payment order. U.C.C. §4A-303(c).

      a. **Recovery from recipient:** Whether the receiving bank can recover the excess payment from the beneficiary or the improper payment from the recipient depends on the common law governing mistake and restitution. U.C.C. §4A-303(a). A court may apply either of two rules in determining whether the receiving bank may recover from the beneficiary.

         i. **Mistake of fact rule:** Under the *mistake of fact rule*, the receiving bank may recover from the beneficiary unless the beneficiary has detrimentally relied on the payment.

Example: Because GM's payment was in excess of the amount owed under the contract, IBM may have shipped additional computers under a subsequent order. However, unless IBM relied on the payment, Bank of America can recover the mistaken payment.

ii. **Discharge for value rule:** Under the ***discharge for value rule***, the beneficiary (or recipient) is entitled to retain the funds as long as it had given value to the sender (whether from this or some other transaction), had made no misrepresentations to the receiving bank, and had no notice of the bank's mistake. *See* Banque Worms v. Bank America International, 13 U.C.C. Rep. Serv. 2d 657 (N.Y. 1991); In re Calumet Farm, Inc., 398 F.3d 555 (6th Cir. Ky. 2005); *In re* Calumet Farm, Inc., 398 F. 3d 555 (6th Cir. 2005).

Example: Assume that GM had owed IBM other debts totaling $2 million. IBM could retain the payment even though IBM did not change position in reliance on the payment.

b. **Right of subrogation:** If, under the law of restitution, the beneficiary or recipient can retain the excess payment, the receiving bank becomes subrogated to any rights that the beneficiary had against the sender. U.C.C. §4A-303, Official Comment 2.

Example: Bank of America could recover from GM on the debts it owed to IBM, which were discharged by the mistaken payment.

2. **Payment in a lesser amount:** If the receiving bank issues a payment order in a lesser amount than authorized, it is entitled to payment from the sender in the lesser amount only unless the receiving bank issues an additional payment order for the remaining difference. U.C.C. §4A-303(b).

Example: Bank of America issues a payment order in the amount of $3 million, but GM's payment order to it was in the amount of $5 million. In this event, Bank of America is entitled to payment from GM for only $3 million unless Bank of America issues an additional payment order for the remaining $2 million difference. U.C.C. §4A-303(b). Bank of America would also be liable to GM for failing to properly execute the payment order.

3. **Duty of sender on receipt of notification of error:** On receipt of notice of the order as executed or of the debiting of its account, the sender has the duty to exercise ordinary care to determine, on the basis of the information available to it, whether the order was erroneously executed and, if so, to notify the receiving bank of the relevant facts within a reasonable time not exceeding 90 days after the notification is received by the sender (GM in our example). U.C.C. §4A-304. The only penalty for the sender's failure to perform this duty is that the receiving bank is not obligated to pay interest on any amount refundable to the sender for the period prior to the time the bank learns of the execution error. U.C.C. §4A-304. However, the sender may be precluded from objecting to the receiving bank's retention of its payment for the order if the sender does not notify the receiving bank of its objection within 1 year after the sender received a notification reasonably identifying the order. U.C.C. §4A-505; U.C.C. §4A-505, Official Comment. *See* Regatos v. North Fork Bank, 5 N.Y.3d 395 (N.Y. 2005) (Both the one-year period of repose in U.C.C. §4-A-505, governing a bank customer's time in which to notify the bank of an unauthorized transfer of funds, and the "reasonable time" referred to in U.C.C. §4-A-204 (1), which determines the customer's ability to recover interest on the misallocated money, begin to run when the customer receives actual notice of the improper transfer.).

IV. DUTIES OF BENEFICIARY'S BANK

A. Overview: A funds transfer is complete once the beneficiary's bank accepts the originator's bank's payment order. U.C.C. §4A-104(a); U.C.C. §4A-406(a). On its acceptance of the payment order, the beneficiary's bank becomes indebted to the beneficiary in the amount of the order on the payment date. U.C.C. §4A-404(a). Once this occurs, the originator's debt to the beneficiary on the underlying contract is discharged.

B. Manner in which beneficiary's bank accepts payment order: Acceptance of a payment order by the beneficiary's bank occurs when the first of any of the following acts occurs. However, acceptance cannot take place before the payment date. U.C.C. §4A-209(d).

1. **Payment:** The beneficiary's bank accepts the payment order when it pays the beneficiary. U.C.C. §4A-209(b)(1)(i). The beneficiary's bank will usually make payment by crediting the beneficiary's account. In this event, payment occurs when the beneficiary's bank has either (1) notified the beneficiary of its right to withdraw the credit, (2) properly applied the credit to a debt owed to it by the beneficiary, or (3) otherwise made the funds available to the beneficiary. U.C.C. §4A-405(a).

2. **Acceptance by notification:** The beneficiary's bank accepts the payment order when it notifies the beneficiary of the receipt of the order or that its account has been credited for the order. U.C.C. §4A-209(b)(1)(ii). However, notification does not operate as acceptance if the notice informs the beneficiary that the beneficiary's bank is rejecting the order or that funds with respect to the order may not be withdrawn or used until receipt of payment from the sender of the order. U.C.C. §4A-209(b)(1)(ii).

3. **Acceptance by receipt of payment:** Acceptance of the payment order occurs when the beneficiary's bank receives payment of the entire amount of the order. U.C.C. §4A-209(b)(2).

4. **By inaction:** The beneficiary's bank may accept a payment order by its inaction. U.C.C. §4A-209(b)(3). Unless the beneficiary's bank rejects the order, acceptance occurs automatically on the opening of the beneficiary's bank's next funds-transfer business day following the payment date of the order if either the amount of the order is covered by sufficient funds in an authorized account that the sender maintains with the beneficiary's bank or the beneficiary's bank has otherwise received full payment from the sender. U.C.C. §4A-209(b)(3). A *funds-transfer business day* is that part of a day during which the bank is open for the receipt, processing, and transmittal of payment orders and cancellations and amendments of payment orders. U.C.C. §4A-105(a)(4).

C. Rejection of payment order: Acceptance can be prevented from occurring by the beneficiary's bank's inaction if the beneficiary's bank gives timely notice of its rejection of the order. U.C.C. §4A-209, Official Comment 8.

1. **Time within which rejection must occur:** Rejection must occur within 1 hour after the opening of the beneficiary's bank's next funds-transfer business day after the payment date. U.C.C. §4A-209(b)(3).

   Example: If the payment date is Friday, assuming that its funds-transfer business day begins at 9:00 A.M., Chase Manhattan Bank must give notice of rejection before 10:00 A.M. on Monday.

2. **No rejection after acceptance:** Once the beneficiary's bank accepts the payment order, it may not later reject the order. U.C.C. §4A-210(d).

D. **Liability for failure to make prompt payment:** If the beneficiary's bank refuses to pay the beneficiary after proper demand by the beneficiary and receipt of notice of the particular circumstances giving rise to such damages, the beneficiary may recover consequential damages. If the damages are extraordinary, the beneficiary also must give notice of this fact. U.C.C. §4A-404, Official Comment 2. *See* Evra Corp. v. Swiss Bank Corp., 673 F.2d 951 (7th Cir. 1982) (the failure of the beneficiary's bank to complete a wire transfer for $27,000 caused the beneficiary to lose a valuable ship charter with resultant damages in the amount of $2 million; the court held that such damages were not foreseeable and therefore could not be recovered).

Example: Assume that IBM needs $5 million to exercise an option to purchase land to build a new factory. If Chase Manhattan Bank fails to make timely payment to IBM, Chase Manhattan Bank is liable for the damages that IBM will suffer in not being able to exercise the option only if IBM not only demands payment from Chase Manhattan Bank but also gives notice, at the time of demand, of the general type or nature of the damages that it will suffer. U.C.C. §4A-404, Official Comment 2. If IBM's inability to exercise the option will cause it to lose $100 million due to the rapid rate of appreciation of real estate, IBM must inform Chase Manhattan Bank of this fact. Because Chase Manhattan Bank normally would not be aware that a $100 million loss would result from a $5 million transfer, IBM is not permitted to recover these extraordinary damages unless it informs Chase Manhattan Bank that the damages may be of such a magnitude. U.C.C. §4A-404(a); U.C.C. §4A-404, Official Comment 2.

Exception: The beneficiary's bank is not liable for consequential damages if it proves that it did not pay because of a reasonable doubt concerning the right of the beneficiary to the payment. U.C.C. §4A-404(a). The beneficiary's bank could avoid liability by, for example, proving that it did not know whether it, in fact, had received the payment and, therefore, whether acceptance had really occurred or that it questioned whether the person demanding payment was authorized to act for the beneficiary. U.C.C. §4A-404, Official Comment 3.

E. **Duty to notify beneficiary:** The beneficiary's bank has the duty, under certain circumstances, to notify the beneficiary of receipt of the order. If the beneficiary's bank accepts a payment order that requires *payment to an account* of the beneficiary, it must give notice to the beneficiary of the receipt of the order before midnight of the next funds-transfer business day following the payment date. U.C.C. §4A-404(b). Without this notice, the beneficiary may be unaware that the funds have been received.

Exception: If the order does not instruct payment to an account of the beneficiary, however, the beneficiary's bank is required to notify the beneficiary only if the order requires notification. U.C.C. §4A-404(b). For example, when the order is to pay IBM rather than to credit one of its accounts, Chase Manhattan Bank's act of payment by itself gives IBM notice that the funds have been received.

V. EFFECT OF ACCEPTANCE ON UNDERLYING OBLIGATION

A. **When payment is accomplished:** Payment by the originator to the beneficiary occurs when the order is accepted by the beneficiary's bank. U.C.C. §4A-406(a). Payment is accomplished by substituting the obligation of the beneficiary's bank for that of the originator. U.C.C. §4A-406, Official Comments 1, 2.

Example: When GM makes payment by a funds transfer to IBM, its obligation to IBM on the underlying contract is discharged not when Bank of America sends the payment order to Chase Manhattan Bank but only when Chase Manhattan Bank accepts the payment order. Once Chase Manhattan Bank accepts Bank of America's payment order, the obligation of GM to IBM is discharged.

Exception: Payment by a funds transfer does not discharge the underlying obligation if all of the following conditions are met: (1) the means of payment was prohibited under the contract governing the underlying obligation; (2) within a reasonable time after receiving notice of the order, the beneficiary notified the originator of its refusal to accept the means of payment; (3) the funds were neither withdrawn by the beneficiary nor applied to its debt; and (4) the beneficiary would suffer a loss that could have reasonably been avoided if payment had been made in a way that complied with the contract. U.C.C. §4A-406(b).

Example: Assume that GM promised to pay IBM by a cashier's check drawn on Bank of America. Instead, GM issued a payment order to Bank of America, which in turn issued a payment order that was accepted by Chase Manhattan Bank. Before IBM withdraws the credit, Chase Manhattan Bank becomes insolvent. IBM has the right to refuse the payment, thereby denying GM a discharge. GM cannot shift the risk of Chase Manhattan Bank's insolvency to IBM when the required means of payment did not provide for such an allocation of risk. If the contract between GM and IBM does not prohibit the use of a funds transfer as a means of payment, GM would be discharged when the transfer is completed. U.C.C. §4A-406, Official Comment 2.

VI. CANCELLATION (STOPPING PAYMENT) OF PAYMENT ORDER

A. **Introduction:** The sender may want to stop payment of a payment order. In our example, GM (the sender) may have a defense arising out of the underlying transaction with IBM, or the order may be unauthorized, in a greater amount than intended, a duplicate of an earlier order, or sent to Xerox instead of IBM. U.C.C. §4A-211, Official Comment 1. Under Article 4A, stop payment is called cancellation.

B. **Effect of cancellation:** A cancelled payment order cannot be accepted. When an accepted order has been cancelled, the acceptance is nullified, and no person has any right or obligation based on the acceptance. U.C.C. §4A-211(e).

Example: If GM issues a cancellation to Bank of America that is timely and proper, it is as if GM never issued the original payment order. If GM's attempt at cancellation is not effective, it is liable on its payment order as if there had been no attempt at cancellation.

C. **Right to cancel unaccepted orders:** Before the receiving bank has accepted the order, the sender has the absolute right to cancel the order if the sender gives timely notice of cancellation. U.C.C. §4A-211(b).

Rationale: The receiving bank is not hurt because, by not yet accepting the order, it incurred no obligation to make payment. U.C.C. §4A-211, Official Comment 3.

1. **Manner of cancellation:** The sender may cancel its order orally, electronically, or in writing. U.C.C. §4A-211(a). Unless the receiving bank agrees otherwise, when there is a security procedure in effect between the sender and the receiving bank, the cancellation is not effective unless it is verified pursuant to the security procedure. U.C.C. §4A-211(a). Notice of cancellation must be given at a time and in a manner that affords the receiving bank a reasonable opportunity to act on the communication before acceptance of the payment order. U.C.C. §4A-211(b). Because execution of an order is acceptance of the order, the cancellation must be received in sufficient time to ensure that the appropriate bank employee can prevent execution of the order. U.C.C. §4A-211, Official Comment 3.

2. **Cancellation by operation of law:** An unaccepted payment order is cancelled by operation of law at the close of the fifth funds-transfer business day of the receiving bank after the execution date or payment date of the order. U.C.C.§4A-211(d).

   Example: If GM, in its payment order, instructed that payment be made to IBM on Monday, February 4, the order, if not yet accepted by Chase Manhattan Bank, is cancelled by operation of law at the close of business on Monday, February 11.

   Rationale: When the payment order is not executed within a few days of its execution date or accepted within a few days of its payment date, the order probably has a problem. Although the sender probably regards the unaccepted payment order as dead, he may have neglected to cancel the order. This rule protects the sender from an unexpected delayed acceptance. U.C.C. §4A-211, Official Comment 7.

D. **Cancellation of order accepted by receiving bank:** A receiving bank has no obligation to cancel an accepted order. U.C.C. §4A-211(c). Even if it chooses to do so, the cancellation is not effective unless the receiving bank cancels the payment order it sent in execution of the sender's order. U.C.C. §4A-211(c)(1); U.C.C. §4A-211, Official Comment 3.

   Example: Bank of America becomes liable to Bank of Missouri (the intermediary bank) once Bank of Missouri accepts the order. If Bank of America is unable to cancel its order to Bank of Missouri, it will be obligated to reimburse Bank of Missouri. GM has no right to cancel its order if Bank of America cannot cancel its order to Bank of Missouri. U.C.C. §4A-211, Official Comment 3.

E. **Cancellation of order after acceptance by beneficiary's bank:** Once the beneficiary's bank accepts the order, the funds transfer is complete. The beneficiary has been paid and the originator's debt to the beneficiary discharged. As a result, cancellation of an order accepted by the beneficiary's bank can occur only in rare situations. Once the beneficiary's bank has accepted an order, it has no obligation to agree to cancel the order. Although having no duty to agree to a cancellation, the beneficiary's bank may agree to a cancellation in four situations:

   ■ if the payment order is unauthorized;

   ■ if the payment order is duplicative of a payment order previously sent;

   ■ if the payment order is mistakenly sent to a beneficiary who is not entitled to payment from the originator; or

■ if a payment order is issued by mistake in an amount greater than the beneficiary is entitled to receive from the originator. U.C.C. §4A-211(c)(2).

Example: An unauthorized employee of GM sends a payment order to Bank of America payable to IBM. Being unauthorized, Chase Manhattan Bank, the beneficiary's bank, exercises its right to agree to the cancellation. Bank of America then may cancel its order to Bank of Missouri, which in turn may cancel its order to Chase Manhattan Bank. On cancellation, the acceptance is nullified and Chase Manhattan Bank is entitled to recover the payment from IBM to the extent permitted by the law of mistake and restitution. U.C.C. §4A-211, Official Comment 4, Case #1. *See* Khawaja v. J.P. Morgan Chase Bank, 10 Misc. 3d 862 (N.Y. City Civ. Ct. 2005) (Senders of transfer advices, whereby one bank customer transferred funds to the account of another customer of same bank, had the right to cancel the transfers with the bank's consent where the advices constituted unauthorized payment orders. Upon cancellation, the bank was entitled to recover from beneficiary any amount that it initially credited his account to extent allowed by law governing mistake and restitution.

VII. LIABILITY FOR AUTHORIZED PAYMENT ORDERS

A. **Introduction:** The sender has the duty to reimburse the receiving bank for the amount of any authorized payment order. U.C.C. §4A-203, Official Comment 1. A payment order is authorized if the sender either actually or apparently authorized the order or is otherwise bound by the order under the law of agency. U.C.C. §4A-202(a).

VIII. LIABILITY FOR UNAUTHORIZED PAYMENT ORDERS

A. **Introduction:** A sender is liable for an unauthorized order if it qualifies as a *verified order*. An order that passes on being properly tested according to a security procedure is called a *verified payment order*. U.C.C. §4A-202(b).

Rationale: Because most payment orders are transmitted through electronic means, the receiving bank has no way to determine the identity or authority of the person sending the message unless it has established some type of security procedure that can be employed to determine whether the order is authorized and accurate. If the receiving bank establishes such a security procedure and verifies the order pursuant to that procedure, it must be able to rely on the order and know that it will get reimbursed once it executes the order. Thus, the sender is liable for any order, whether authorized or not, that is verified according to a proper security procedure.

B. **Security procedure:** A security procedure is a procedure by which the bank may test the authenticity and/or accuracy of an order. A *security procedure* is defined as "a procedure established by agreement of a customer and a receiving bank for the purpose of (i) verifying that a payment order or communication amending or canceling a payment order is that of the customer, or (ii) detecting error in the transmission or content of the order, amendment or cancellation." U.C.C. §4A-201. A security procedure may take any number of forms, including a code or an algorithm, identifying words or numbers, encryption, or callback procedures. U.C.C. §4A-201. However, because of the ease of forging a signature, the comparison of a signature on a payment order (or other communication) with an authorized specimen is not, by itself, a security procedure. U.C.C. §4A-201.

C. Requirements for sender's liability for verified payment orders: Determining whether the customer is liable to the receiving bank for an unauthorized but verified payment order is a two-step process.

    1. First step: The receiving bank must prove that the order is a verified payment order. The bank proves that it is a verified payment order by proving the following:

        a. Agreement with customer: The bank had an agreement with its customer providing that orders would be verified pursuant to a security procedure.

        b. Commercially reasonable procedure: The security procedure is a commercially reasonable method of providing security against unauthorized payment orders.

        c. Bank complied with procedure: The bank accepted the payment order in good faith and in compliance with the security procedure and any written agreement or instruction of the customer. U.C.C. §4A-202(b).

        Rationale: The loss is thrust on the customer because it is the customer's burden to supervise its own employees and to ensure that confidential information and access to transmitting facilities are kept secure. Once the bank proves that the order is a verified order, it is likely that the leak came from the customer's side. U.C.C. §4A-203, Official Comment 3.

        Note: The burden of making a commercially reasonable security procedure available is on the bank because it knows what procedures are possible and how well they will work. If the bank fails to offer a commercially reasonable security procedure or fails to comply with the security procedure adopted, the bank suffers the loss. U.C.C. §4A-203, Official Comments 2, 3.

    2. Second step: If the bank proves that the order was a verified order, the order is effective as the order of the customer whether or not it was authorized by the customer. The customer is therefore liable to the receiving bank for the amount of the order. U.C.C. §4A-202(b). However, the customer can avoid liability by proving (indirectly) that the security breach was the responsibility of the bank. The customer does so by proving that the breach of security was not in any way attributable to the customer itself. To do so, the customer must prove a negative. It must prove that the order was not caused, directly or indirectly, by a person who falls into one of two categories.

        a. Entrusted with duties as to payment orders: The first category includes any person who was entrusted at any time with duties to act for the customer with respect to payment orders or to the security procedure. U.C.C. §4A-203(a)(2)(i).

        b. Access to source or facilities: The second category comprises any person who (a) obtained access to the customer's transmitting facilities or (b) obtained, from a source controlled by the customer and without authority of the receiving bank, information facilitating breach of the security procedure, regardless of how the information was obtained or whether the customer was at fault. Information includes any access device, computer software, or the like. U.C.C. §4A-203(a)(2).

        Note: It would be extremely difficult for a customer to bear this burden of proof unless the customer can affirmatively show that the leak came from a source controlled by the bank.

D. Summary of when loss falls on bank: There are, thus, four situations in which the loss caused by an unauthorized payment order falls on the bank and not on the customer:

- no commercially reasonable procedure was in effect;

- the bank did not comply with the security procedure in place;

- the customer can prove that the wrongdoer did not obtain the information from it; or

- the bank agreed to assume all or part of the loss. U.C.C. §4A-204, Official Comment 1.

E. Contrary agreement prohibited: The customer cannot agree to take more of the loss than provided for in Article 4A. U.C.C. §4A-202(f).

F. Duty of customer on receipt of notification of error: On being notified of the relevant facts, the customer has the duty to exercise ordinary care to determine whether the order was unauthorized and, if so, to notify the receiving bank of the relevant facts within a reasonable time not exceeding 90 days after the notification is received by the sender that her account was debited or the order accepted. U.C.C. §4A-204(a). The only penalty for the sender's failure to perform this duty is that the receiving bank is not obligated to pay interest on any amount refundable to the sender. However, the sender may be precluded from objecting to the receiving bank's retention of its payment for the order if the sender does not notify the receiving bank of its objection within 1 year after the sender received a notification reasonably identifying the order. U.C.C. §4A-505; U.C.C. §4A-505, Official Comment.

IX. ERRONEOUS PAYMENT ORDERS

A. Introduction: An erroneous payment occurs when the sender makes a mistake in the payment order it sends and the receiving bank accepts the order without noticing the error. The mistake may be in the amount of the order or in the identity of the beneficiary. Whether the sender or the receiving bank suffers the loss depends, to a large extent, on whether a security procedure was in place to detect such errors.

Example: GM may have mistakenly instructed that payment be made to Xerox, instead of to IBM, or GM may have sent an order duplicative of an order previously sent to IBM or in an amount greater than it had intended.

B. Allocation of loss when no security procedure in place: The sender suffers the loss in the event that there is no established security procedure to determine the accuracy of the order. U.C.C. §4A-205, Official Comment 1.

Rationale: Without an established security procedure, the receiving bank has no way of determining that an error has been made. Because only GM could have prevented the error, the loss falls on GM. GM's remedy is to recover from Xerox, in the first case, and from IBM in the last two cases. U.C.C. §4A-205, Official Comment 1.

C. Allocation of loss when security procedure in place: When an established security procedure is in place to detect such errors, the loss shifts to the receiving bank if the sender proves that it had complied with the security procedure and that the error would have been detected if the receiving bank had also complied with the security procedure. U.C.C. §4A-205(a)(1).

Example: If GM had intended to send an order for $5 million but had erroneously sent an order for $7 million, GM would be obligated to pay Bank of America only $5 million if GM proves that it complied with the security procedure and that the error would have been detected if Bank of America also complied with the security procedure. Bank of America could recover the remaining $2 million from IBM (the beneficiary of the order) to the extent allowed by the law governing mistake and restitution. U.C.C. §4A-205(a)(3); U.C.C. §4A-205, Official Comment 1.

D. Sender's duty on receipt of notice of acceptance: Once the sender receives notification from the receiving bank that the order has been accepted by the bank or that the sender's account has been debited in the amount of the order, the sender has a duty of ordinary care to discover (on the basis of the information that it has) any error concerning the order and to advise the receiving bank of the relevant facts within a reasonable time (not exceeding 90 days) after notification is received by the sender. U.C.C. §4A-205(b); U.C.C. §4A-205, Official Comment 2. If the receiving bank proves that the sender failed to perform this duty, the sender is liable to the receiving bank for any loss, not exceeding the amount of the order, that the receiving bank proves it incurred as a result of the failure. U.C.C. §4A-205(b); U.C.C. §4A-205, Official Comment 2.

X. MISDESCRIPTIONS

A. Introduction: In different situations, the originator (or other sender) may have improperly described the beneficiary. In these situations, the question arises as to whether the originator (or other sender), the originator's bank, an intermediary bank, or the beneficiary's bank suffers any loss caused by the misdescription.

B. Nonexistent or unidentifiable person or account: If the name, bank account number, or other identification of the beneficiary refers to a nonexistent or unidentifiable person or account, no person has rights as the beneficiary of the order. U.C.C. §4A-207(a). As a result, the beneficiary's bank cannot accept the order and the funds transfer cannot be completed. U.C.C. §4A-207; U.C.C. §4A-207, Official Comment 1. Each sender in the funds transfer is relieved of liability and is entitled to a refund to the extent of any payment. U.C.C. §4A-207, Official Comment 1.

Example: Assume that one of GM's creditors is Ace Welding Company. In sending a payment order to Bank of America, GM misdescribes the beneficiary as "Acme Welding Company." Unfortunately, accounts exist at Chase Manhattan Bank not only under the name of "Ace Welding Company" but also under the name of "Acme Hardware Company." Chase Manhattan Bank must reject the order. Bank of America has no obligation to pay its payment order and GM has no obligation to pay Bank of America. U.C.C. §4A-402(c).

C. When beneficiary identified by both name and number: When the beneficiary is identified by both a name and an identifying or bank account number and the name and number identify different persons, the beneficiary's bank may rely on the number as the proper identification of the beneficiary and credit the account number. U.C.C. §4A-207(b)(1). The loss will generally then fall on the bank sending the order. The customer is not obligated to pay the order unless the receiving bank proves that before acceptance of the customer's order, the customer received notice from the receiving bank that payment might be made on the basis of the identifying number or bank account number even if it identifies a different person. U.C.C. §4A-207(c)(2).

Example: Assume that GM's order identified the supplier as "Ace Welding Company, Acct. No. 1234." Chase Manhattan Bank credits the order to account number 1234. Although GM has properly identified the beneficiary by name, the account number is the number of Avis Rent-a-Car. As a result, the money is paid to Avis and not to Ace. Chase Manhattan Bank is nonetheless entitled to payment from Bank of America. However, Bank of America is not entitled to payment from GM unless it supplied GM with notice that payment may be made by identifying number rather than by name. U.C.C. §4A-207(c)(1).

Rationale: Payment orders received by beneficiary's banks from other banks are processed by an automated device that processes the order by reading the identifying number or the bank account number and not the name of the beneficiary. As a result, the beneficiary's bank will not generally even notice the name of the intended beneficiary. U.C.C. §4A-207, Official Comment 2. However, when the beneficiary's bank either pays the person identified by name or knows that the name and the number identify different persons, the beneficiary's bank assumes the risk that it has failed to pay the person intended by the sender. If it pays the proper person, the beneficiary's bank is entitled to payment. If it does not, no acceptance can occur and the originator's bank has no obligation to pay the beneficiary's bank. U.C.C. §4A-207(b)(2).

D. **Misdescription of intermediary bank or beneficiary's bank:** Similar problems arise when the intermediary or beneficiary's bank is improperly described.

   1. **Identification by number only:** When a payment order identifies an intermediary bank or the beneficiary's bank by an identifying number only and that number is wrong, the bank sending the order will suffer any loss caused by the order being accepted by the wrong bank. U.C.C. §4A-208(a)(1).

   Example: Assume that GM issues a payment order to Bank of America identifying the beneficiary's bank as Chase Manhattan Bank. Bank of America issues a payment order to Bank of Missouri (the intermediary bank) describing the beneficiary's bank as "Bank No. 156234." However, the number actually describes Bank of Connecticut. Bank of Missouri sends the order to Bank of Connecticut, which accepts the order. Bank of Missouri is entitled to reimbursement from Bank of America. U.C.C. §4A-208, Official Comment 1, Case #1. Not only is Bank of America not entitled to reimbursement from GM, but it is liable for damages to GM as provided for under U.C.C. §4A-305(b). U.C.C. §4A-208, Official Comment 1, Case #1. However, if the originator (GM) supplied only the number and not the name of the beneficiary's bank, the originator would be obligated to reimburse the originator's bank. U.C.C. §4A-208(a)(2).

   2. **Conflict between name and number:** When there is a conflict between the name of the beneficiary's bank (or intermediary bank) and the identifying number, the receiving bank may rely on the number as the proper identification of the beneficiary's bank (or intermediary bank) if it does not know at the time it executes the order that the name and number identify different persons. U.C.C. §4A-208(b). In this event, the sending bank suffers the loss and may not recover from its customer. *See* TME Enterprises, Inc. v. Norwest Corp., 124 Cal. App. 4th 1021 (Cal. App. 2 Dist. 2004) (The fact that a bank accepted an incoming wire transfer of funds that specified both an account number and a named beneficiary did not mean that it had actual knowledge that the holder of the account number specified and the name designated as the beneficiary were inconsistent. As a result, the bank did not violate Federal Reserve Board's Regulation J when it accepted the transfer.).

Example: Assume that Bank of America, in its order to Bank of Missouri, describes the beneficiary's bank as "Chase Manhattan Bank, No. 156234." Unfortunately, No. 156234 describes Bank of Connecticut. The loss falls on Bank of America.

Exceptions: If a nonbank sender had included the conflicting description of the beneficiary's bank in its order to the sending bank, it would be obligated to reimburse the sending bank for any losses or expenses incurred in executing or attempting to execute the order if the sender received notice that the sending bank might rely on the identifying number only in accepting the order. U.C.C. §4A-208(b)(2).

If the receiving bank knows that the name and the number identify different banks, reliance on either the name or the number, if incorrect, is a breach of its duties in executing the sender's payment order. U.C.C. §4A-208(b)(4).

XI. INJUNCTION

A. **Generally:** A creditor can obtain an injunction preventing the originator from issuing a payment order initiating a funds transfer to the beneficiary, the originator's bank from executing the originator's payment order, the beneficiary's bank from releasing funds to the beneficiary, or the beneficiary from withdrawing the funds. U.C.C. §4A-503. However, no intermediary bank can be enjoined from executing a payment order or a receiving bank from accepting the order or receiving payment from the sender. U.C.C. §4A-503, Official Comment.

Quiz Yourself on
WHOLESALE FUNDS TRANSFERS

75. Assume that Xerox instructs Bank of California to transfer funds to Ford Motor Company's account at Detroit State Bank. Assuming that Bank of California will send a payment order directly to Detroit State Bank, how many payment orders are involved in the transaction and what are the capacities in which each of the parties act? _____

76. True or False: A receiving bank is liable for wrongful dishonor if it fails to accept a payment order when the sender has sufficient funds in its account to cover the payment order. _____

77. True or False: A receiving bank must send notice of rejection if it does not want to accept an order. _____

78. True or False: If a receiving bank accepts a payment order prior to the execution date, it may debit the sender's account even though it remains liable for any losses caused by the early execution. _____

79. True or False: A receiving bank is not liable for consequential damages when it fails to execute an order even if those damages are foreseeable. _____

80. True or False: Assuming that the contract does not forbid payment by funds transfer, once the beneficiary's bank accepts the payment order sent by the originator's bank, the originator is discharged from liability on the underlying transaction even if the beneficiary's bank becomes insolvent.

———————————————

81. True or False: As long as the beneficiary's bank has not yet accepted the payment order, the originator has an absolute right to cancel its payment order. ———————————————

82. An order is sent to Bank of California allegedly from Xerox instructing the bank to transfer $1 million to Laundered Money, Inc. at Swiss Bank. Bank of California tests the payment order against the security procedure that Bank of California and Xerox have agreed should be used to test orders of this type. The payment order passes. Xerox proves that no authorized person sent the order. Can Bank of California charge Xerox's account for the amount of the order? ———————————————

Answers

75. There are two payment orders: the order from Xerox to Bank of California and the order from Bank of California to Detroit State Bank. Xerox is the sender of first payment order, U.C.C. §4A-103(a)(5), the originator, U.C.C. §4A-104(c), and the customer of Bank of California, U.C.C. §4A-105(a)(3). Bank of California is the receiving bank on the first payment order, U.C.C. §4A-103(a)(4), the originator's bank, U.C.C. §4A-104(d), the sender of the second payment order, U.C.C. §4A-103(a)(5), and the customer of Detroit State Bank, U.C.C. §4A-105(a)(3). Detroit State Bank is the receiving bank of the second payment order, U.C.C. §4A-103(a)(4), and the beneficiary's bank, U.C.C. §4A-103(a)(3). Ford Motor Company is the beneficiary, U.C.C. §4A-103(a)(2).

76. False. A receiving bank has no duty to accept a payment order. U.C.C. §4A-209, Official Comment 1.

77. False. Until it accepts the order, it has no duties regarding the order. U.C.C. §4A-212.

78. False. A payment order cannot be accepted before its execution date. U.C.C. §4A-209(d). Consequently, the sender has no obligation to reimburse the receiving bank for the payment order.

79. True. Absent an express written agreement to the contrary, a receiving bank is not liable to the sender for consequential damages. U.C.C. §4A-305(a)-(c).

80. True. The originator's obligation to the beneficiary is discharged the moment that the beneficiary's bank accepts the payment order. U.C.C. §4A-406(a).

81. False. Once the originator's bank accepts the payment order, the originator has no right to cancel the order unless the originator's bank not only consents to the cancellation but also is able to cancel the payment order it sent pursuant to the originator's instructions. U.C.C. §4A-211(c).

82. Yes. A sender is liable for an unauthorized order if it qualifies as a verified order. Because the order passed on being properly tested according to a security procedure, it is a verified order. U.C.C. §4A-202(b). Xerox can avoid liability only by proving that the order was not caused, directly or indirectly, by a person entrusted with duties as to payment orders or a person who had access to

Xerox's transmitting facilities or from information facilitating breach of the security procedure obtained from a source controlled by Xerox. U.C.C. §4A-203(a).

Exam Tips on *WHOLESALE FUNDS TRANSFERS*

☛ **A customer's liability and burden of proof:** Remember that, as a general matter, the customer and not the receiving bank is liable for a verified payment order even though it is unauthorized.

    ☞ Once the receiving bank proves that the order is a verified payment order, the customer has the substantial burden of proving that the breach of the security procedure was not its fault.

    ☞ Note that it is almost impossible for the customer to prove that no unauthorized person had access to its transmitting facilities or to information as to the security procedure.

    ☞ The customer can avoid liability only by affirmatively proving that it was the receiving bank's fault that the security procedure was breached.

CHAPTER 8

CONSUMER ELECTRONIC FUND TRANSFERS

ChapterScope

This chapter examines what constitutes an electronic fund transfer governed by Regulation E, a consumer's liability for an unauthorized fund transfer, stopping payment of a fund transfer, special rules for preauthorized transfers, documentation requirements, error resolution procedures, and a financial institution's liability for failing to make a correct fund transfer. The key points in this chapter are:

- **Electronic fund transfers covered by Regulation E:** An electronic fund transfer covered by Regulation E is a transfer of funds that is initiated through an electronic terminal, a telephone, or computer or magnetic tape for the purpose of instructing a financial institution to debit or credit a consumer asset account.

- **Types of electronic fund transfers:** Typical electronic fund transfers include point-of-sale transactions and automated teller machine transactions.

- **Consumer liability:** A consumer is liable only up to $50 for an unauthorized transfer from his account. However, this liability can be increased if the consumer either fails to report the loss of his access device or to report unauthorized transfers appearing on a periodic statement.

- **Stop payment:** A consumer, although having no right to stop payment on an ordinary electronic fund transfer, may stop payment on a preauthorized fund transfer from his account.

- **Notification of error:** A financial institution must follow established procedures once the consumer notifies it of an error.

I. LAW GOVERNING CONSUMER ELECTRONIC FUND TRANSFERS

A. **Introduction:** Consumer electronic fund transfers are governed, for the most part, by the Electronic Fund Transfer Act (EFTA), 15 U.S.C. §1693, and Regulation E promulgated thereunder. The EFTA preempts state law to the extent that the state law is inconsistent with the EFTA. State laws that provide greater protection for consumers than the protection afforded by the EFTA are not preempted. 15 U.S.C. §1693q; 12 C.F.R. §205.12(b).

II. WHAT IS AN ELECTRONIC FUND TRANSFER?

A. **Introduction:** An electronic fund transfer is any transfer of funds that is initiated through an electronic terminal, a telephone, a computer, or magnetic tape for the purpose of instructing a financial institution to debit or credit a consumer asset account. 15 U.S.C. §1693a(6); 12 C.F.R.

§205.3(b). A ***consumer asset account*** is one that contains a consumer's assets. 15 U.S.C. §1693a(2); 12 C.F.R. §205.2(b)(1). Electronic fund transfers resulting in an extension of credit on a credit line are not covered by the EFTA.

Example: Article 4 did not apply to a cause of action against a bank, for approval of unauthorized electronic fund transfers with an automatic teller machine card. Rather, EFTA applied Hospicomm, Inc. v. Fleet Bank, N.A., 338 F. Supp. 2d 578 (E.D. Pa. 2004).

Example: Bank's transfer of funds from account holders' checking account to debt collector was not an electronic fund transfer subject to requirements of the EFTA where the debt collector personally presented a paper draft on the holders' account to a teller at its bank. Vigneri v. U.S. Bank Nat'l Assn., 437 F. Supp. 2d 1063 (D. Neb. 2006).

B. Typical electronic fund transfers: The most common types of electronic fund transfers are:

- **Point-of-sale transfers:** Point-of-sale transfers (***POS transfers***) use a debit card at a terminal located at the merchant's business location that, through a computer linkup, determines whether the consumer's bank account contains sufficient funds and, if it does, immediately debits the consumer's bank account and credits the merchant's bank account.

- **Automated teller machine (*ATM*) transfers**

- **Direct deposits or automatic payments**

C. How initiated: The transfer must be initiated through an electronic terminal, a telephone, or computer or magnetic tape.

Example: When a consumer preauthorizes a creditor to initiate a debit to the consumer's account, the transaction is governed by the EFTA if the bank debits the consumer's account according to information provided to the bank by the creditor on computer or magnetic tape. 12 C.F.R. §205.3(b)(1), Official Staff Commentary.

Example: Transfers through POS terminals, ATMs, and cash dispensing machines are covered because these are electronic terminals. 12 C.F.R. §205.2(f). The EFTA also covers home banking services in which a consumer initiates transfers to, or from, an account (a) by a computer or a television set linked to the financial institution's computer system or (b) under a pay-by-phone plan by which the consumer telephonically instructs her financial institution to make a payment to a creditor. 12 C.F.R. §205.2(f)(1), Official Staff Commentary.

Exception: A transfer from a consumer account initiated through use of a debit card is covered even though the transaction does not involve an electronic terminal, magnetic tape, or computer. 12 C.F.R. §205.3(b)(5). A ***debit card*** is an access device that has the capability to transfer funds by debiting the consumer's bank account.

Example: A consumer may be able to use a debit card almost like a check to purchase goods or services. In this type of transaction, the merchant makes a copy of the information contained on the card and asks the consumer to sign the debit slip. The debit slip is then forwarded for payment through the merchant's bank to the consumer's bank.

Rationale: Although no electronic terminal is used, the transaction is nonetheless governed by the EFTA to protect consumers who may naturally assume that because the transaction is initiated by a debit card, they have the same protections whether the merchant makes a copy of the debit card or has the consumer run the debit card through an electronic terminal.

III. CONSUMER'S LIABILITY FOR UNAUTHORIZED TRANSFERS

A. Introduction: A consumer has only limited liability for unauthorized transfers out of his account.

B. What is an unauthorized fund transfer? An electronic fund transfer is unauthorized if the transfer is initiated by a person without actual authority to initiate the transfer and the consumer did not receive a benefit from the transfer. 15 U.S.C. §1693a(11); 12 C.F.R. §205.2(k).

Exception: An electronic fund transfer is not unauthorized if the consumer gave to the person initiating the transfer an access device unless the consumer has notified the financial institution involved that transfers by that person are no longer authorized. 15 U.S.C. §1693a(11); 12 C.F.R. §205.2(k)(1). An *access device* is a "card, code, or other means of access to a consumer's account, or any combination thereof, that may be used by the consumer for the purpose of initiating electronic fund transfers." 12 C.F.R. §205.2(a)(1).

1. **No longer authorized after notification:** Any transfer becomes an unauthorized transfer once the cardholder notifies the card issuer that the person having the card is no longer authorized to use the access device. After being notified, the card issuer can prevent any further transfers by blocking the ability of the device to access the account.

2. **Obtained through robbery or fraud:** Any transfer is an unauthorized electronic fund transfer if it is made with an access device that was obtained either through robbery or through fraudulent inducement. 12 C.F.R. §205.2(k)(3), Official Staff Commentary.

   Example: Assume that Grandfather's wallet, which contained his ATM card, is stolen. A subsequent transfer initiated by the thief's use of the card would be unauthorized. The same would be true if Nurse, without Grandfather's consent, took the card out of his wallet. If Grandfather was forced at gunpoint to withdraw funds from an ATM, his withdrawal also would be treated as an unauthorized transfer. 12 C.F.R. §205.2(k)(4), Official Staff Commentary.

C. Conditions to consumer's liability for unauthorized fund transfers: Before a consumer is liable for an unauthorized fund transfer, three conditions must be met. 15 U.S.C. §1693g(a); 12 C.F.R. §205.6(a).

1. **Transfer through accepted access device:** The unauthorized transfer must have been made by an accepted access device. An access is *accepted* (1) on receipt of the device if the consumer requested the financial institution to issue the device to her; (2) if the consumer did not request that the access device be issued to her, when the consumer signs the access device, uses, or authorizes another person to use the device for the purpose of transferring funds or obtaining money, property, or services; (3) when the consumer requests validation of the device; or (4) if it is issued in substitution for, or in renewal of, a previously accepted access device. 12 C.F.R. §205.2(a)(2)(ii). *Validation* occurs when the financial institution has taken all steps necessary to enable the consumer to use the access device to initiate an electronic fund transfer. 12 C.F.R. §205.5(b)(4).

2. **Means to identify consumer:** The financial institution must have provided some means by which the consumer can be identified when she uses the device. 12 C.F.R. §205.6(a). The means will often be a PIN, but it may also be a signature, photograph, or fingerprint.

3. **Disclosures:** The financial institution must have provided the consumer with certain written disclosures as to her liability for unauthorized transfers. 12 C.F.R. §205.6(a).

D. Limitation of consumer liability: If these conditions are met, the consumer is liable for the lesser of (a) the amount of any unauthorized fund transfers or (b) $50. 15 U.S.C. §1693g(a); 12 C.F.R. §205.6(b). The consumer is not liable for any unauthorized fund transfers that occur after the consumer has given notice to the financial institution that an unauthorized electronic fund transfer involving her account has been or may be made. 15 U.S.C. §1693g(a); 12 C.F.R. §205.6(b). The limitations on liability apply whether or not the consumer is negligent. 12 C.F.R. §205.6(b)-2, Official Staff Commentary.

Example: On March 1, Jane loses her ATM card. She had written her PIN on the card. On March 10, the finder withdraws $400 in cash from her account. On March 15, she realizes that the card is gone. On March 19, she notifies the bank of the loss. The finder withdraws another $600 on March 20. Jane owes $50. Jane's liability is not increased because she wrote her PIN on the card thus enabling the thief to have access to her account.

E. Failure to report loss of device: If the consumer does not notify its financial institution of the loss or theft of the access device within 2 business days after learning of the loss or theft, the consumer's liability increases to the lesser of (a) $500 or (b) the sum of (i) $50 or the amount of unauthorized electronic fund transfers that occur before the close of the 2 business days, whichever is less, and (ii) the amount of unauthorized electronic fund transfers that the financial institution establishes would not have occurred but for the consumer's failure to notify the institution within 2 business days after it learns of the loss or theft of the access device, and that occur after the close of the 2 business days and before notice to the financial institution. 12 C.F.R. §205.6(b)(2).

Example: On March 1, Jane loses her ATM card. On March 10, the finder withdraws $400 in cash from her account. On March 15, she realizes that the card is gone. The finder withdraws another $600 on March 19. On March 20, she notifies the bank of the loss. Under the second alternative in (b)(i), the amount of loss that occurred *before* 2 days after she learned of the loss is $400. Because that amount is larger than $50, she is liable under (b)(i) for only $50 of the original $400 loss. The $600 withdrawal, however, occurred *more* than 2 days after she learned of the loss of her ATM card. Her failure to notify the bank caused the entire $600 loss because the bank would have deactivated the card had she notified the bank of the loss. Therefore, her total liability under (b)(i) and (b)(ii) is $650. However, under (a), her liability is only $500. Because she is liable only for the lesser of (a) and (b), her liability is in the amount of $500.

F. Failure to report unauthorized transfers on periodic statement: In the event that the consumer fails to report within 60 days of a statement's transmittal any unauthorized electronic fund transfer that appears on the periodic statement, the consumer is liable to the financial institution for (a) up to $50 of any unauthorized transfer or transfers that appear on the statement, plus (b) the full amount of any unauthorized transfers that occur after the close of the 60 days after transmittal of the statement and before the consumer gives notice to the financial institution. 12 C.F.R. §205.6(b)(3).

Example: In Kruser v. Bank of America, 230 Cal. App. 3d 741, 281 Cal. Rptr. 463 (1991), a consumer's failure to report a $20 unauthorized transfer shown on his periodic statement made the consumer liable for $9,020 of unauthorized transfers occurring 9 months later, even though he promptly reported these later transfers.

G. Combination of failure to report lost device and failure to report unauthorized transfers: When there is a combination of a failure to report a lost or stolen access device and a failure to report the loss after the receipt of a periodic statement, the provisions that impose liability for the failure to report the lost or stolen access device govern the amount of liability for transfers that appear on the periodic statement and before the close of 60 days after the consumer first received a periodic statement showing an unauthorized transfer. The provisions imposing liability for the failure to report the losses that appear on a periodic statement govern thereafter. 12 C.F.R. §205.6(b)(3).

Example: Assume, in our original example, that Jane did not notice and, therefore, did not report to her bank the unauthorized transfers occurring in March and appearing on the periodic statement arriving on April 1. In April, $2,000 in additional unauthorized transfers took place. In May, $3,000 in additional unauthorized transfers took place. In June $4,000 in additional unauthorized transfers took place. She finally notifies her bank of these unauthorized transfers on July 1. The provisions governing the failure to report a lost or stolen access device determine her liability for unauthorized transfers up to June 1, which is 60 days after transmittal of the statement showing an unauthorized transfer. Her liability is limited to $500 for the transfers up until June 1 even though the total of these unauthorized transfers was $6,000. However, there is no such limit to her liability for unauthorized transfers occurring between June 1 and the time she notified her bank. She is therefore liable for the entire $4,000 of unauthorized transfers occurring during that period. Her total liability is therefore $4,500 ($500 up to June 1 and $4,000 thereafter).

IV. STOPPING PAYMENT OF ELECTRONIC FUND TRANSFERS

A. **Introduction:** Whether an electronic fund transfer can be stopped depends on whether it is an ordinary electronic fund transfer or a preauthorized electronic fund transfer.

B. **No right to reverse ordinary fund transfer:** An electronic fund transfer such as a POS transaction takes place instantaneously. As a result, there is no way to stop payment on the fund transfer in the event that the consumer decides afterward that he is dissatisfied with the purchase. A separate question is whether the consumer has a right to reverse a previously made transfer.

1. **EFTA:** Congress, in enacting the EFTA, determined that a consumer should have no right to reverse an electronic fund transfer (other than a preauthorized electronic fund transfer).

   Note: Payment by electronic fund transfer should be the equivalent of payment in cash. If a consumer wants to retain the ability to prevent a merchant from receiving payment for the goods, the consumer can pay by check or credit card. Once the electronic fund transfer is completed, the consumer's only recourse is to recover the payment from the merchant.

2. **State law:** A few states do allow an electronic fund transfer initiated by a consumer to be reversed under certain conditions. Under Michigan law, for example, a consumer may reverse a fund transfer if the following conditions are met: (1) the consumer makes a good-faith effort to seek redress from the merchant and return the goods or services, (2) the transaction is for more than $50, and (3) the request for reversal is made within 4 calendar days of the transaction. Mich. Comp. Laws §488.16.

C. **Stopping payment on preauthorized electronic fund transfers:** There is a right to stop payment of any preauthorized electronic fund transfer from the consumer's account. A *preauthorized electronic fund transfer* is any transfer that is authorized in advance and that recurs at substantially regular intervals. 15 U.S.C. §1693a(9); 12 C.F.R. §205.2(i). A consumer can stop payment of a preauthorized electronic fund transfer by giving oral or written notice to its financial institution at any time up to 3 business days before the scheduled date of the transfer. 12 C.F.R. §205.10(c).

Example: If the preauthorized transfer is scheduled to take place on Monday, February 1, the consumer can stop payment of the transfer by giving notice any time up to Wednesday, January 27. (Saturday and Sunday do not count because they are not business days.)

Rationale: Preauthorized electronic fund transfers serve a very different purpose than do POS or other similar transfers. The primary purpose of a POS transfer is as a substitute for payment in cash. Allowing reversibility would defeat this purpose. In contrast, the primary purpose of a preauthorized electronic fund transfer is to eliminate the expense and inconvenience of paying by check. The consumer is relieved of the burden and expense of writing out and mailing checks. The creditor is saved the time and expense of opening the mail containing the checks and of depositing the checks into its account. Allowing the consumer the right to stop payment of a preauthorized debit does not undercut the advantages either party obtains through the arrangement.

1. **Manner of stopping payment:** A preauthorized transfer may be stopped orally or in writing. If the notice is oral, the financial institution may require that written confirmation of the stop payment order be given within 14 days of the oral notification. 12 C.F.R. §205.10(c). Reconfirmation in writing is a practical necessity. If, on request, the consumer fails to confirm the stop payment order in writing, the oral stop payment order ceases to be binding 14 days after it has been made. 12 C.F.R. §205.10(c). When the creditor resubmits the bill after the 14-day period, it will be paid.

2. **Damages for failing to stop preauthorized fund transfer:** A financial institution is liable to its customer for damages if, once a proper stop payment order is given, the institution fails to stop payment of a preauthorized fund transfer. 15 U.S.C. §1693h(a)(3).

   Example: You stop payment on a preauthorized electronic fund transfer to your cable television supplier because you are not satisfied with the service. Your bank ignores your stop payment order. You are required to file a lawsuit to recover the funds. Absent a defense, your bank would be liable to you for failing to stop payment of your preauthorized fund transfer to your cable television supplier.

   a. **Damages if failure unintentional:** Neither the EFTA nor Regulation E spell out clearly what type of damages may be available if the financial institution fails to stop a preauthorized transfer. It is likely that when the bank's failure was not intentional, a court would adopt the measure of recovery found in Article 4 governing the failure of a bank to honor a stop payment order on a check.

   b. **Damages if failure intentional:** If the bank's failure was intentional, the bank may be obligated to pay as consequential damages the consumer's legal expenses in recovering the payment from the recipient together with interest for the loss of the use of the funds.

V. CONSUMER LIABILITY TO THIRD PARTIES IN THE EVENT OF SYSTEM MALFUNCTION

A. **Introduction:** If there is a malfunction in the fund transfer system that prevents a preauthorized payment from being made, the consumer's obligation to make the payment is suspended until the system malfunction is corrected and the electronic fund transfer may be completed. 15 U.S.C. §1693j. The consumer must pay the bill if, at any time before the malfunction is corrected, the creditor demands in writing that payment be made by means other than an electronic fund transfer. 15 U.S.C. §1693j.

Example: The mortgagee could not foreclose on the mortgagor when the failure to make payment by an electronic fund transfer resulted from a "system malfunction" or technical problem in the payment process. *See* Household Finance Realty Corp. of New York v. Dunlap, 15 Misc. 3d 659 (N.Y. Sup. 2007).

VI. RESTRICTIONS ON ISSUANCE OF ACCESS DEVICES

A. **Introduction:** An access device not requested by the consumer may be issued only if it is not validated. 15 U.S.C. §1693i(b); 12 C.F.R. §205.5(b)(1). Issuance by the financial institution of an unrequested access device must be accompanied by a complete disclosure (1) as to the consumer's rights and liabilities once the device is validated, (2) clearly explaining that the access device is not validated, and (3) instructing the consumer on how to dispose of the device in the event that the consumer does not wish to use the device. 12 C.F.R. §205.5(b).

Rationale: To protect consumers against unexpected liabilities, the EFTA places restrictions on the ability of financial institutions to issue access devices to consumers who have not requested the device. 15 U.S.C. §1693i(a); 12 C.F.R. §205.5(b).

Example: Because a debit card cannot access a consumer's account without a PIN, an access device is not validated unless a PIN has been assigned to it. Thus, a financial institution cannot send an unsolicited debit card to a consumer if a PIN has been assigned to the card.

VII. SPECIAL RULES FOR PREAUTHORIZED TRANSFERS

A. **Introduction:** Because preauthorized fund transfers serve different purposes than do ordinary fund transfers, e.g., POS or ATM transactions, special rules apply to preauthorized fund transfers.

B. **Transfers to consumer's account:** If the consumer's account is to be credited by a preauthorized electronic fund transfer from the same payor at least once every 60 days, the bank must give notice of the deposit by one of the following.

   1. **Notice that transfer made:** Oral or written notice within 2 business days after the transfer that the transfer has occurred.

   2. **Notice that transfer not made:** Notice within 2 business days after a scheduled fund transfer that the transfer has *not* occurred.

   3. **Readily available telephone line:** The bank may provide a readily available telephone line that the consumer may call to ascertain whether or not the preauthorized transfer occurred. 12 C.F.R. §205.10(a).

C. **Transfers from consumer's account:** When the debit is in the same amount each month, no notification is required. Because the consumer knows that the debit will occur, any notification would be superfluous. If debits are in a varying amount, the consumer has the right to receive notice if a transfer varies in amount from the previous transfer or from the preauthorized amount.

12 C.F.R. §205.10(d). Notice must be given either by the bank or by the payee at least 10 days before the scheduled transfer date so as to enable the consumer not only to verify whether the amount is correct but also to deposit funds in the account to cover any deficit. 12 C.F.R. §205.10(d).

VIII. DOCUMENTATION REQUIREMENTS

A. **Introduction:** One of the disadvantages of making payment or withdrawing funds by electronic fund transfer, rather than by check, is the absence of a returned check to evidence the payment or the withdrawal. To remedy this deficiency, the EFTA and Regulation E contain various documentation requirements for electronic fund transfers.

B. **Receipts at electronic terminals:** When the consumer initiates an electronic fund transfer at an electronic terminal, the financial institution itself, or through another party (for example, the merchant at a POS terminal), the consumer must be provided with a written receipt containing certain basic information as to the transaction.

C. **Periodic statements:** The financial institution must provide periodic statements to the consumer providing certain basic information for each transfer occurring during the period covered for each account to, or from which, electronic fund transfers can be made. 15 U.S.C. §1693d(e); 12 C.F.R. §205.9(b).

IX. ERROR RESOLUTION PROCEDURES

A. **Introduction:** To protect consumers, the financial institution must follow an established procedure in the event that the consumer claims an error has occurred.

B. **What is an "error"?** *Errors* include unauthorized and incorrect electronic fund transfers, omissions from a periodic statement, computational or bookkeeping errors, receipt of an incorrect amount of money from an electronic terminal, improper identification of an electronic fund transfer, and a consumer's request for any documentation required by Regulation E or for additional information or clarification regarding an electronic fund transfer. 15 U.S.C. §1693f(f); 12 C.F.R. §205.11(a)(1). *See* Gale v. Hyde Park Bank, 384 F.3d 451 (7th Cir. Ill. 2004) (Checking account holder stated a claim against its bank under the EFTA for the bank's failure to comply with error resolution requirements when he alleged that he did not receive a timely report of the results of his complaint that a debit card transaction did not post to his account until four months after the transaction and that he did not receive information about the bank's error-resolution procedures.

C. **Notice of error:** The consumer must give oral or written notice of error to the financial institution no later than 60 days after the bank provided the consumer with the periodic statement indicating the error. 15 U.S.C. §1693f(a); 12 C.F.R. §205.11(b)(1)(i). If the consumer fails to give notice within the 60-day period, the consumer has no right to require that the bank go through the error resolution procedure. However, the consumer may still bring an action against the bank to recredit its account because of the error.

D. **Bank's duty to investigate:** On receipt of the notice of error, the financial institution has the duty to promptly investigate and determine whether an error has occurred. 15 U.S.C. §1693f(a); 12 C.F.R. §205.11(c). How long it has to make a determination depends on whether it has recredited the consumer's account.

1. **Does not recredit:** If the financial institution does not provisionally recredit the consumer's account during the investigation, it must transmit the result of its investigation to the consumer within 10 business days. 15 U.S.C. §1693f(a); 12 C.F.R. §205.11(c)(1).

2. **Recredits:** If the bank provisionally recredits the account in the amount of the alleged error (including any applicable interest) within 10 business days after receipt of the notice of error, the financial institution may, as long as it acts promptly, take up to 45 calendar days to transmit the results of its investigation to the consumer. 15 U.S.C. §1693f(c); 12 C.F.R. §205.11(c)(2).

E. **After the bank makes its determination:** If the bank determines that an error has occurred, it must promptly, and no later than 1 business day after this determination, correct the error and, whether or not the bank determines that an error has occurred, mail or deliver to the consumer a written explanation of its findings within 3 business days after concluding its investigation. 15 U.S.C. §1693f(b), (d); 12 C.F.R. §205.11(c)(2)(iii), (iv).

X. LIABILITY FOR FAILING TO MAKE CORRECT FUND TRANSFER

A. **Introduction:** A financial institution is liable to its customer if it fails to make a fund transfer in the correct amount and in a timely manner.

Note: If the bank's failure was unintentional and occurred despite reasonable precautions established by the institution to guard against such failures, damages are limited to actual damages proved. This does not include consequential damages. 15 U.S.C. §1693h(c).

XI. CIVIL LIABILITY

A. **Enforcement actions provided by EFTA:** The provisions of the EFTA may be enforced by administrative action. Besides administrative enforcement, the EFTA also provides for civil actions by consumers. 15 U.S.C. §1693m-n.

B. **Individual consumers:** An institution that fails to comply with the provisions of the EFTA is liable to the injured consumer for any actual damage sustained by the consumer because of the noncompliance, together with an amount not less than $100 nor greater than $1,000, plus the costs of a successful action to enforce the liability, including reasonable attorneys' fees. 15 U.S.C. §1693m(a).

Example: Borrower was not entitled to recover damages as result of mortgage lender's violation of the EFTA where there were no unauthorized or erroneous electronic transfers as the failure was a result of a technical malfunction of which the borrower was unaware. *See* Household Finance Realty Corp. of New York v. Dunlap, 15 Misc. 3d 659 (N.Y. Sup. 2007).

C. **Class actions:** In the event of a class action, instead of the $100 and $1,000 limitations, the total recovery for the class arising out of the same failure to comply is limited to the lesser of $500,000 or 1 percent of the net worth of the defendant plus actual damages, costs, and reasonable attorneys' fees. 15 U.S.C. §1693m(a)(2)(B).

D. **Treble damages:** Damages may be trebled where: (a) the noncompliance is a failure to comply with the error resolution rules, or (b) the financial institution knowingly and willfully concluded that the consumer's account was not in error when such a conclusion could not reasonably have been drawn from the evidence available to the financial institution at the time of its investigation. 15 U.S.C. §1693f(e).

E. **Defenses to liability:** A financial institution is not liable if its noncompliance resulted in an error that was properly resolved pursuant to the EFTA error resolution procedures. 15 U.S.C. §1693m(a). For example, if your bank improperly charged your account for an electronic fund transfer that did not take place, your bank is not liable to you if it, in a timely manner, investigated your claim and recredited your account.

1. **Bona fide error:** A financial institution is also not liable if it proves, by a preponderance of the evidence, that the noncompliance was not intentional and resulted from a bona fide error notwithstanding the maintenance of procedures reasonably adapted to avoid such noncompliance. 15 U.S.C. §1693m(c).

2. **Offers to pay damages:** A financial institution is likewise not liable if it both notifies the consumer of the noncompliance prior to the consumer bringing an action and pays to the consumer his actual damages. 15 U.S.C. §1693m(e).

Quiz Yourself on CONSUMER ELECTRONIC FUND TRANSFERS

83. On February 1, while hiking in the Sierra Mountains, Gerry loses his wallet containing his ATM card. Gerry does not notice that his wallet is gone until February 3, when he stops for gas on his return trip home. On his arrival home on February 4, he telephones his bank to inform it of the loss of his card. Five hundred dollars were withdrawn from his account on February 3. For how much of the $500 is Gerry liable? _____

84. Assume that Gerry did not report the loss of the card until February 9 and that an additional $1,000 was withdrawn from his account between February 6 and 9. How much of the total $1,500 will Gerry be liable for? _____

85. True or False: Under the EFTA, a consumer has 3 days to order her bank to reverse any point-of-sale transfer from her account. _____

86. True or False: A financial institution may issue a validated access device if it is requested by the consumer. _____

87. Although Grandfather has authorized Nurse to write checks on his account, he has not authorized her to initiate electronic fund transfers. However, because of the frequency with which she has been writing checks, Grandfather's bank reasonably believes that she has full authority to conduct financial transactions for him. Although Nurse may have apparent authority to initiate electronic fund transfers, are transfers initiated by her authorized? _____

88. What if Nurse secretly learns Grandfather's *personal identification number (PIN)* and makes his mortgage payment by an electronic fund transfer. Is the transfer unauthorized? _____

89. If Grandfather gave his ATM card and his PIN to Nurse, and told her not to use the card until he authorized her to do so, are her withdrawals unauthorized if she makes them before Grandfather gives her permission? _____

90. You just purchased a television set from Radio Shack. You paid for the set by an electronic fund transfer through the POS terminal located at the store. You took the television set home and discovered that the set did not work. Radio Shack refuses to take the set back. What options for recourse do you have? What rights does your bank have? _____

91. You instruct your bank to transfer funds by August 1 to the seller of the house you want to purchase. The bank fails to do so. Because of the bank's failure, you lose the right to purchase the house. The house appreciates in value. Is your bank liable? _____

92. In the preceding example, if the bank's failure to transfer the funds was unintentional, what would you be allowed to recover? _____

Answers

83. $50. A consumer is liable for the lesser of the actual unauthorized transfers or $50. 15 U.S.C. §1693(g)(a); 12 C.F.R. §205.6(b).

84. $500. By not notifying the bank within 2 business days after learning of the loss, Gerry is liable for the lesser of (1) $500 or (2) $50 or any lesser amount charged between February 3 and February 5 plus the amount charged between February 6 and 9 that the bank can prove would not have occurred but for Gerry's failure to notify the bank of the loss. Because if Gerry had notified the bank of the loss within 2 days, none of the $1,000 loss would have occurred, the total amount under (2) is $1,050. As $500 is less, Gerry's liability is limited to $500. 12 C.F.R. §205.6(b)(2).

85. False. A consumer has no right under the EFTA to stop or reverse any electronic fund transfer except a preauthorized electronic fund transfer.

86. True. A financial institution is prevented from issuing a validated device unless it is requested by the consumer. 15 U.S.C. §1693(i)(b); 12 C.F.R. §205.5(b)(1).

87. No. Regardless of her apparent authority, any transfer initiated by Nurse is unauthorized because she has no actual authority to do so.

88. No. The transfer is not unauthorized because Grandfather received a benefit from it.

89. No. Nurse's withdrawal of funds through the use of the card is not regarded as unauthorized even though Nurse used the card before Grandfather authorized her to do so. By giving Nurse his ATM card and his PIN, Grandfather gave Nurse the means to make the transfer without the financial institution or a merchant (if the transfer is at a POS terminal) knowing that her use was unauthorized.

90. None. You can neither prevent your bank from paying Radio Shack nor order your bank to reverse the transfer. Likewise, your bank has no right to demand the payment back from Radio Shack or its bank.

91. Yes. Absent a defense, your bank would be liable to you for failing to make the funds transfer to the seller of the house by August 1.

92. You would be limited to your costs in making the transfer and any loss of interest. You would not be allowed to recover your lost profits on the purchase of the house if your bank's failure was unintentional and your bank employed reasonable precautions to avoid such a failure. If your bank's failure was intentional or your bank did not employ reasonable precautions, you would then be entitled to your lost profits.

Exam Tips on
CONSUMER ELECTRONIC FUND TRANSFERS

☛ **Consumer liability for fund transfers:** Remember that a consumer is liable for a transfer **only if** she either actually authorized the person to make the transfer or benefited from the transfer.

    ☞ The only time that a consumer is liable for an unauthorized transfer is if she gave the access device and the PIN to the unauthorized user.

    ☞ A consumer is not liable for an unauthorized transfer simply because she was negligent.

    ☞ However, always remember that a consumer's exposure to liability increases if she fails to report a lost or stolen access device or an unauthorized transfer on a periodic statement.

CHAPTER 9

LENDER CREDIT CARDS

ChapterScope

This chapter examines the law governing credit card transactions, a consumer's liability for the unauthorized use of a credit card, the right to refuse payment of a credit card charge, and error resolution procedures. The key points in this chapter are:

- **Truth in Lending Act and Regulation Z:** Consumer use of credit cards is governed by the Truth in Lending Act and Regulation Z. Business credit cards are subject only to the rules governing unauthorized use and the issuance of unrequested cards.

- **Liability for unauthorized use of credit card:** A cardholder is liable for only up to $50 of charges from the unauthorized use of her card. However, use of a card by a person to whom the cardholder has given possession is not unauthorized despite any instructions to the contrary.

- **Cardholder's right to refuse payment:** A cardholder has the right to assert against the card issuer any defense or claim arising from the underlying transaction as long as the cardholder has attempted to settle the dispute with the merchant and the transaction meets certain geographical limitations.

- **Billing error procedure:** The card issuer must comply with a fairly strict billing error procedure when a cardholder gives notice that a billing error has occurred.

I. TERMINOLOGY IN CREDIT CARD TRANSACTIONS

A. **Introduction:** If a person purchases a television set from Radio Shack by use of a Mastercard, that person is called the *cardholder*. Bank of America, which issued the card to the cardholder, is called the *issuing bank* or the *card issuer*. Radio Shack is called the *merchant*. Wells Bank, the bank at which Radio Shack maintains its account, is called the *merchant bank*.

II. LAW GOVERNING CREDIT CARD TRANSACTIONS

A. **Introduction:** Credit cards are not governed by a comprehensive set of statutes or regulations. Rather, they are governed by an assortment of diverse federal and state consumer protection laws.

B. **Federal law:** The basic law governing credit cards is federal law and can be found in the Truth in Lending Act, 15 U.S.C. §1601, as amended by the Fair Credit and Charge Card Disclosure Act, the Fair Credit Billing Act, and Regulation Z, 12 C.F.R. part 226, promulgated pursuant to the Truth in Lending Act. These statutes and regulations cover only the relationship between the card issuer and the cardholder. Even as to this relationship, it covers only certain issues: disclosure requirements, error resolution, the right of a cardholder to raise defenses, and the liability of a cardholder for unauthorized transactions.

1. **Primarily consumer protection:** With two exceptions, these statutes and regulations cover only consumer use of credit cards. Business credit cards are also subject to the rules governing liability for unauthorized use and the right of the card issuer to issue unrequested cards. Business credit cards are governed, in all other respects, by the agreement entered into between the business and the card issuer.

2. **Other law:** Although some state consumer protection laws govern credit cards, much of the cardholder/card issuer relationship is left to the cardholder agreement. The remaining relationships (i.e., merchant/merchant bank and card issuer/merchant bank) are governed by the agreements establishing their respective relationships. The law governing the agreements between the various parties to a credit card transaction is ordinary contract law.

III. LIABILITY FOR UNAUTHORIZED USE

A. **Introduction:** A cardholder has very limited liability for an unauthorized use of her card. A cardholder is liable only for the lesser of (1) $50 or (2) the amount of money, property, labor, or services obtained by the unauthorized use. There is no liability for any unauthorized charges incurred after the consumer gives notice to the bank of the unauthorized use. 15 U.S.C. §1643(a)(1); 12 C.F.R. §226.12(b). It has been held that a commercial bank has a duty to verify the authenticity and accuracy of a credit account application before issuing a credit card. *See* Wolfe v. MBNA America Bank, 485 F. Supp. 2d 874 (W.D. Tenn. 2007).

   Example: On March 1, Jane loses her Mastercard. She does not notice that the Mastercard is gone until April 10 when she gets her Mastercard bill showing charges in the amount of $5,000. She immediately notifies the card issuer. Jane is liable for $50.

   Exception: With one exception, the rules governing liability for unauthorized use of a credit card apply to credit cards used for business purposes as well as for consumer purposes. 15 U.S.C. §1645. The one exception involves issuance by a card issuer of 10 or more credit cards for use by the employees of an organization. In this situation, the card issuer and the organization may contractually set liability for unauthorized use at an amount greater than otherwise permitted by law. However, an employee of the organization has the same limited liability as does a consumer as to both his employer and the card issuer. 15 U.S.C. §1645; 12 C.F.R. §226.12(b)(5).

B. **Conditions to liability:** A cardholder has no liability whatsoever for an unauthorized use of her card unless three conditions are met.

   1. **Accepted card:** The card must be an accepted credit card. 12 C.F.R. §226.12(b)(2)(i). An *accepted credit card* is any credit card that a cardholder has (1) requested or applied for and received, (2) signed, or (3) used or authorized another person to use to obtain credit. Any credit card issued as a renewal or substitute becomes an accepted credit card when received by the cardholder. 12 C.F.R. §226.12(a)(2), n.21.

   2. **Disclosures:** The card issuer must have provided the cardholder with adequate notice of its maximum potential liability and of the means by which it can notify the card issuer of the loss or theft of its card. 12 C.F.R. §226.12(b)(2)(ii).

   3. **Merchant identification:** The card issuer must have provided a means by which the merchant could have identified the cardholder as the authorized user of the card. Two of the more common ways for a card issuer to provide a means of identification are by (1) including tape

on the back of the credit card where the cardholder may provide a sample of his signature and (2) including a photograph of the cardholder on the face of the credit card. 12 C.F.R. §226.12(b)(2)(iii) and Official Staff Commentary.

C. Unauthorized use: *Unauthorized use* is defined as the use of a credit card by a person other than the cardholder, who does not have actual, implied, or apparent authority for such use, and from which the cardholder receives no benefit. 12 C.F.R. §226.12(b), n.22. The card issuer has the burden of proving that use of a card was authorized. 15 U.S.C. §1643(b).

D. Authorized use: A use is *authorized* when the user has either actual or apparent authority to use the card.

  1. Actual authority: The user has actual authority to use a credit card when the cardholder either expressly or by implication gives the user authority to use the card.

  Example: Assume that your brother asks you for money to fill his car with gas. Without saying a word, you hand him your credit card. You have impliedly authorized him to use the card to purchase gas. (Had you told your brother that he could use your card to purchase gas, he would have express actual authority.) However, you did not give him actual authority to use the card to purchase a television set when you loaned him the card to buy gas.

  Example: Debtor had no defense in the debtor's action to collect the outstanding balance of the account credit card debt from unauthorized purchases made by the debtor's housemate when the unauthorized purchases were possible through debtor's intentional, careless, or negligent conduct as provided in the Truth in Lending Act. *See* New Century Financial Services, Inc. v. Dennegar, 394 N.J. Super. 595 (N.J. Super. A.D. 2007).

  2. Apparent authority: A user has apparent authority when the cardholder gives the impression to third parties that the user is authorized to use the card.

  Example: From the example above, assume that the gas station owner called to ask you whether your brother was authorized to use your card and you told him that your brother could charge the purchase of gas. You, however, forget to get the card back from your brother. The next week, your brother charges another purchase of gas on your credit card. Your telephone confirmation of your brother's authority to use your card gave the gas station owner the impression that your brother was authorized to use the card. Even though your brother was not, in fact, authorized to make the second purchase of gas, your brother had apparent authority to do so. Therefore, his use of the card was authorized and you are liable for the second purchase as well as for the first.

  Example: A corporate credit cardholder's failure to inspect its monthly billing statements sacrificed any Truth in Lending Act protections from liability for unauthorized use by repeatedly paying without protest all of the employee's charges on the account after receiving notice of them from card issuer. DBI Architects, P.C. v. American Express Travel-Related Services Co., Inc., 388 F.3d 886 (D.C. Cir. 2004).

   a. Knowingly giving card to user: The specific characteristics of a credit card transaction have encouraged courts to adopt a very expansive definition of what constitutes apparent authority. Some courts find that if the cardholder voluntarily and knowingly gives the card to another person, the person to whom the card is given has apparent authority to use the card.

Example: If your brother went to Radio Shack and purchased a television set, the fact that you gave him the card to purchase gas gives him apparent authority to purchase the television set even though you made no representations to Radio Shack that led it to believe that your brother was authorized to use your card. *See* Martin v. American Express, 361 So. 2d 597 (Ala. Civ. App. 1978) (cardholder gave his business associate his American Express Card with express authority to charge up to $500. The cardholder instructed American Express not to allow the total charges on his American Express Card to exceed $1,000. The business associate charged $5,300 on the card. The court found that the business associate had apparent authority to charge the entire $5,300 on the card and, therefore, held that the cardholder was liable for the entire amount).

    b. Informs card issuer: Courts are split as to whether the cardholder is liable for purchases made by the user after the cardholder informs the card issuer that the user no longer has actual authority to use the card. *Compare* Standard Oil Co. v. Steele, 489 N.E.2d 842 (Ohio Mun. Ct. 1985) (not liable) *with* Walker Bank & Trust v. Jones, 672 P.2d 73 (Utah, 1983) (use of a credit card by a spouse continues to be apparently authorized until the card is returned to the card issuer even though the cardholder had notified the card issuer that the spouse's use of the card was no longer authorized).

IV. RIGHT TO REFUSE PAYMENT

    A. Introduction: If a consumer fails to satisfactorily resolve a dispute as to a product purchased with his credit card, the consumer can assert against the card issuer all claims (other than tort claims) and defenses arising out of the transaction and relating to the failure to resolve the dispute. 15 U.S.C. §1666i; 12 C.F.R. §226.12(c)(1).

    Example: Jane purchases a television set from Radio Shack on her Mastercard. It turns out that the set is defective. Jane goes back to Radio Shack and demands that it either fix the television set or give back her money. Radio Shack refuses to do either. Jane may have a right to raise her breach of warranty claim against Radio Shack as a defense to her obligation to pay Mastercard for the amount charged for the television set. If Bank of America recredits her account, Bank of America would pass the loss back down the line to Wells Bank (the merchant's bank) and Wells Bank would charge back Radio Shack's account. If Radio Shack believes that her claim is not well founded, it would then have to attempt to recover the payment from her.

    B. Conditions to right to withhold payment: There are three conditions to a consumer's right to withhold payment of her credit card bill for a purchase.

    1. Good-faith attempt to resolve dispute: The consumer must make a good-faith attempt to resolve the dispute with the merchant. 12 C.F.R. §226.12(c)(3)(i).

    Example: The fact that Jane went to Radio Shack and asked it to fix the set or return her money is probably sufficient to constitute a good-faith attempt to resolve the dispute. 12 C.F.R. §226.12, Official Staff Commentary, Comment 12(c)(3)(i).

    Example: The fact that the transaction for which the issuing bank was attempting to collect charges was for a business or commercial purpose did not preclude the cardholder from asserting the nondelivery defense under the Truth in Lending Act, in issuing bank's action to collect charges on credit card for merchandise that was never delivered. *See* Citibank (South Dakota), N.A. v. Mincks, 135 S.W.3d 545 (Mo. App. S.D. 2004).

2. **More than $50:** The charge for the purchase must be more than $50. 12 C.F.R. §226.12(c)(3)(ii).

3. **Purchase within same state or within 100 miles:** The purchase must have occurred in the same state as the consumer's current designated address or, if not within the same state, within 100 miles of that address. 12 C.F.R. §226.12(c)(3)(ii).

   Note: By issuing a credit card to the cardholder, the card issuer undertakes the obligation of monitoring merchants in the cardholder's area but not in an area outside her state or more than 100 miles from her residence. If no geographical limitation were placed on the cardholder's right to refuse payment, merchants distant from the cardholder's residence would be leery of allowing her to pay by credit card. This is because if the cardholder refuses to pay the credit card charge, the merchant would have to undertake the costly task of attempting to recover from her in her state of residence.

   Regulation Z: Regulation Z does not determine where a transaction takes place. The Official Staff Commentary to Regulation Z simply states that "[T]he question of where a transaction occurs (as in the case of mail or telephone orders, for example) is to be determined under state or other applicable law." 12 C.F.R. §226.12, Official Staff Commentary, Comment 12(c)(3)(ii)(1). There is no helpful case law on the question of where a purchase takes place when the merchant is in one state and the consumer is in another state.

C. **Exceptions:** The geographical and monetary limitations do not apply when the merchant (a) and the card issuer are the same person, (b) is directly or indirectly controlled by, or controls, the card issuer, (c) is a franchised dealer of the card issuer's products or services, or (d) has obtained the order for the disputed transaction through a mail solicitation made, or participated in, by the card issuer. 12 C.F.R. §226.12(c)(3), n.26.

D. **Limited to amount of credit outstanding:** The amount of the claim or defense that may be asserted cannot exceed the amount of credit outstanding for the disputed transaction at the time the cardholder first notifies the card issuer or the merchant of the existence of the claim or defense. 12 C.F.R. §226.12(c)(1); 12 C.F.R. §226.12(c)(1), n.25.

V. ERROR RESOLUTION PROCEDURES

A. **Introduction:** Cardholders are given substantial protections in the event that they claim the card issuer has made a billing error. *Billing errors* are basically mistakes found in the credit card statement that the card issuer sends to the cardholder. Among others, billing errors include (1) billing for an extension of credit that was not made to the cardholder, (2) billing for property or services that were neither accepted nor delivered to the cardholder, (3) improper identification of an extension of credit, (4) failing to properly credit a payment or other credit, or (5) making a computational or accounting error. 12 C.F.R. §226.13(a).

   Example: When Jane receives her credit card statement, she notices that she was charged not only for the television set that she purchased from Radio Shack but also for a VCR that she looked at but did not purchase. The charge for the VCR is a billing error because it was a billing for an extension of credit that was not made to Jane.

B. **What cardholder must do on noticing billing error:** If the cardholder wants to activate the error resolution procedure, the cardholder must send written notice of the billing error so that it is received by the card issuer no later than 60 days after the card issuer transmitted the statement that reflected the billing error. 12 C.F.R. §226.13(b)(1). Although failing to do so results in the cardholder losing the protections accorded to her under the error resolution procedure, her failure does not prevent her from bringing a breach of contract, or other action, against the card issuer for recrediting of her account.

Example: If the statement reflecting Radio Shack's erroneous billing of the VCR to Jane's account was sent to Jane on March 1, Bank of America would have to receive her billing error notice by May 1.

C. **What the card issuer must do on receipt of billing error notice:** Within 30 days after receiving the billing error notice, the card issuer must either (a) mail or deliver to the cardholder a written acknowledgment of receipt of the notice or (b) comply with the appropriate resolution procedures. 12 C.F.R. §226.13(c)(1).

   1. **If error is found:** If the card issuer determines that the billing error mentioned in the notice has occurred, the card issuer must, within two complete billing cycles (but in no event later than 90 days) after receiving the billing error notice, correct the billing error and credit the cardholder's account with any disputed amount and related finance or other charges, if any. The card issuer must also, during this period, mail or deliver to the cardholder a correction notice. 12 C.F.R. §226.13(e)(1), (2).

   2. **If no error found:** Before the card issuer may determine that no billing error has occurred, it must conduct a reasonable investigation. 12 C.F.R. §226.13(f). If, after conducting a reasonable investigation, the card issuer determines that no billing error occurred, it must, within two complete billing cycles (but in no event later than 90 days) after receiving the billing error notice, mail or deliver to the cardholder an explanation that sets forth the reasons for its belief that the alleged billing error is incorrect in whole or in part. 12 C.F.R. §226.13(f)(1). It must also promptly notify the cardholder in writing of the time when payment is due and the portion of the disputed amount and related finance or other charges that is owed. 12 C.F.R. §226.13(g)(1). The cardholder has the same grace period within which to pay the amount due without incurring additional finance or other charges that it would have had had it just received the periodic statement showing the charge. 12 C.F.R. §226.13(g)(2).

      Example: Assume that Bank of America allows a 21-day grace period to make payment without incurring a finance charge. If on March 1 Bank of America notifies Jane that she owes the charge for the VCR, she has until March 22 to pay, without a finance charge, the amount found not to be in error.

D. **Remedy:** Failure to comply with the requirements of the billing error resolution procedure results in the card issuer forfeiting the right to collect from the cardholder the amount of the alleged error together with any finance charges on that amount. The amount of the forfeiture, however, cannot exceed $50. 15 U.S.C. §1666(e).

Quiz Yourself on
LENDER CREDIT CARDS

93. Although Rene realizes that she has lost her Visa card, she does not inform the card issuer for 2 weeks. In these 2 weeks, $1,000 is charged on the card. For how much of this amount is Rene liable? _____

94. Assume that Rene orders take-out food from a local restaurant. Rene asks her neighbor, Don, who is going to pick up the order for her, to charge the order on her Visa card. On the way to the restaurant, Don stops off at Target Department Store and charges, on Rene's card, the purchase of a television set for $600. To what extent is Rene liable for the purchase? _____

95. Simone, who lives in Los Angeles, purchases an expensive watch while on vacation in New York. She charges the purchase on her American Express card. When the watch turns out to be a phony, she demands that the merchant give her money back. The merchant refuses. Can Simone refuse to pay the portion of her American Express bill that represents the purchase price of the watch? _____

96. If Bank of America issues to IBM 1,000 cards to be used by its employees, what are IBM's and the employee cardholders' limitations on liability? _____

97. Assume that in the preceding example, Bank of America and IBM agree that IBM is liable for up to $1,000 of any unauthorized charges. Is the employee cardholder also liable for up to $1,000? _____

98. Adam gives his daughter his credit card, instructing her to buy groceries for dinner that night. The manager at the grocery store calls Adam and asks whether his daughter was authorized to use his card. Adam responds affirmatively. He forgets, though, to get the card back from his daughter. The next week, his daughter charges another purchase of groceries on Adam's credit card. Was this second use of the card authorized? _____

99. Jane lives in New York City, and purchased a new couch in Newark, New Jersey (which is within 100 miles of New York City). If the couch was severely damaged during the store's guaranteed-safe delivery, can she withhold payment? _____

100. Assume the same facts as above, except that Jane bought her couch in Los Angeles, California. Can she refuse payment on the charge? _____

Answers

93. $50. A cardholder is liable for a maximum of $50 of any unauthorized charges. 15 U.S.C. §1643(a)(1); 12 C.F.R. §226.12(b). Rene's liability is not increased even though, had she notified the card issuer, the loss may have been prevented.

94. Possibly $600. Use of a credit card is not unauthorized if the user has apparent authority. 12 C.F.R. §226.12(b), n.22. Some courts hold that if the cardholder voluntarily gives the card to a third person, that person has apparent authority to use the card. If the court finds that Rene's giving of the card to Don gave him apparent authority, Rene would be liable for the entire purchase.

95. **No.** A cardholder may only refuse to pay for a purchase that was made within the same state as the consumer's designated address or within 100 miles of that address. 12 C.F.R. §226.12(c)(3)(ii). Because Simone's purchase meets neither of these conditions, she must pay her full American Express bill.

96. **Same as for consumers.** The limitations on liability applicable to consumers are also applicable to IBM's and its employees' liability on the credit cards, absent an agreement to the contrary.

97. **No.** Regardless of the agreement between IBM and the bank, the employee cardholder is not liable to either Bank of America or IBM beyond the $50 limit imposed by the Truth in Lending Act.

98. **Yes.** Adam's telephone confirmation of his daughter's authority to use his card gave the grocery store manager the impression that his daughter was authorized to use the card. Even though the daughter was not, in fact, authorized to make the second purchase of groceries, the daughter had apparent authority to do so. Therefore, her use of the card was authorized and Adam is liable for the second purchase as well as for the first.

99. **Yes.** Jane may withhold payment on a purchase made in any location in the state of New York as well as on any purchase made within 100 miles of her residence. She can, therefore, refuse to pay the charge for the couch bought in Newark, New Jersey, to the extent that the couch was damaged.

100. **No.** She may not refuse payment on a charge made in Los Angeles because Los Angeles is outside of the 100-mile range of her residence in New York City.

Essay Exam Questions

QUESTION 1: Virginia has wanted for years to make a movie about her idol, Brittany Spears. Virginia has the option to buy the exclusive film rights to Brittany's autobiography entitled "As Bland as I Want to Be" for $10,000 from Brittany's manager, who happens to be her father. Unfortunately, Virginia does not have the funds to purchase the option and the option is set to expire on November 4. As luck would have it, on October 20, Rihanna, Virginia's best friend, after hearing of Virginia's problem, writes a check to Virginia for the $10,000 as a surprise gift for Virginia's 30th birthday. On November 3, Virginia indorses the check to Brittany's father in payment for the rights.

On November 5, Virginia discovers that Brittany's father does not own the film rights to the book. Virginia immediately informs Rihanna, who issues a proper stop payment order to her bank, Hollywood State Bank. Virginia writes a letter to Brittany's father demanding return of the check and telling him that payment has been stopped. Brittany's father does not respond to the letter.

On January 13, desperately needing money, Brittany's father goes to Quick and Easy Check Cashing Service ("Quick and Easy"). Quick and Easy tells Brittany's father that it can only give him $3,000 for the $10,000 check. Quick and Easy explains that it does not know Rihanna or Virginia and fears that if the check is dishonored, neither of them will have the money to make it good. Brittany's father indorses the check to Quick and Easy and takes the $3,000.

On January 24, Quick and Easy, without indorsing the check, deposits it at its account at Not-So-Fast Bank, which account is overdrawn to the extent of $8,000. Not-So-Fast Bank applies the check to the overdraft and then sends the check for payment to Hollywood State Bank, which refuses to pay the check. What rights does Not-So-Fast Bank have against the various parties?

QUESTION 2: Rosemary was Milt's bookkeeper. Rosemary had no authority to draw or indorse checks in Milt's name. Rosemary did have authority, however, to reconcile the returned checks and bank statement with the check ledger. Rosemary had a gambling problem. Rosemary had to find cash to pay her bookies. In June 2008, Rosemary took a check payable to Milt and drawn by John Denver on Wells Fargo Bank, indorsed the check in Milt's name, and cashed the check at Bank of America, the bank at which Milt had his account. Because the teller knew that Rosemary was Milt's bookkeeper, the teller gladly cashed the check. In July 2008, Rosemary took a check drawn by Milt and payable to Placido Domingo and indorsed the check in Placido Domingo's name and deposited the check in an account at Bank of California that she established under the name of "P. Domingo Inc." In establishing the account, Rosemary showed the bank a phony certificate of incorporation and a phony corporate resolution authorizing her to open the account. The check is returned in the August 2008 bank statement. In June 2009, Rosemary signed as drawer a check on Milt's account payable to Placido Domingo and deposited the check in the account she established at Bank of California. The check is paid by Bank of America and returned to Milt on August 8 with his July, 2009 bank statement.

At the end of June 2009, Rosemary withdrew all of the money from the account she established at Bank of California, went on vacation, and never returned. Milt, being too busy, did not reconcile his July and August bank statements until September 30, 2009.

a. As to the John Denver check, discuss the following:
  1. May John Denver demand that Wells Fargo Bank recredit his account?

2. May Milt recover from John Denver on the check or on the underlying obligation for which it was given?

3. May Milt recover from Wells Fargo Bank or from Bank of America?

   b. As to the July 2008 check, may Milt demand that Bank of America recredit his account? May Milt recover from Bank of California?

   c. As to the June 2009 check, may Milt demand that Bank of America recredit his account? If Bank of America chooses to recredit Milt's account, may it recover from Bank of California?

QUESTION 3:   On January 15, the option that Sam [the drawer/customer] has to purchase a large plot of prime commercial real estate (the "Factory") is set to expire. Because the option price is $500,000 and the Factory has a present market value of $800,000, Sam wants to ensure that he properly exercises the option. For this purpose, on January 12, Sam writes and delivers a check, drawn upon Bank of Santa Monica, to Bob, the seller of the Factory, in the amount of $10,000, the amount required to exercise the option.

On January 13, Bob deposits the check in his account at Wells Fargo Bank. On January 14 at 7:00 A.M., Wells Fargo Bank, through the Los Angeles Clearing House, presents the check to Bank of Santa Monica. Upon presentment of the check, Bank of Santa Monica settles with Wells Fargo Bank for the check. Bank of Santa Monica has established a cut-off hour of 10:00 A.M. On January 14 at 3:00 P.M., the check is stamped paid, Sam's account is debited, and the check is placed in Sam's folder to be returned to him with his monthly statement. A loan that Sam has from the bank is set to become due on January 15.

At 11:00 A.M. on January 15, the bank sets off the amount due under the loan against Sam's account. Because there are insufficient funds in the account to cover the setoff, Bank of Santa Monica takes the check out of the folder, cancels the word "paid" stamped on the check, revokes the settlement it gave to Wells Fargo Bank, recredits Sam's account, and then exercises its setoff. At 5:00 P.M. on January 15, Bank of Santa Monica mails the check back to Wells Fargo Bank. It arrives on January 17 at 9:00 A.M. On January 17, Bank of Santa Monica sends notice to Sam that the check had bounced. Bob tells Sam that the option is now expired.

   a. Bob sues Bank of Santa Monica for the amount of the check. Discuss whether he will be successful.

   b. Sam sues Bank of Santa Monica for wrongful dishonor. Discuss whether he will be successful and if so, what his damages would be.

QUESTION 4:   Frank borrows $100,000 from his friend Sam. Frank executes a note to Sam promising to repay the loan in 1 year with 10 percent interest. The note is secured by a mortgage on Frank's house. Sam hears of an investment in a new company called Fortune Gems that sounds great. Sam has no cash to invest. Fortune Gems, however, agrees to accept Frank's note in payment for 5,000 shares of Fortune Gems stock. Each share of stock is supposed to pay $10 in dividends every 6 months. Sam indorses the note to Fortune Gems. The president of Fortune Gems runs into financial difficulties. His personal loan from Finance Company for $50,000 is past due. The president negotiates Frank's note to Finance Company in full payment for the debt. Fortune Gems fails to pay any dividends.

When the note becomes due, Finance Company sues Frank. At Sam's request, Frank refuses to pay the note. Sam requests that Frank raise Sam's defense that Fortune Gems breached its agreement to pay the dividends, and that Sam was defrauded into purchasing the stock. In the alternative, Sam wants to intervene in the action and raise his contentions. May he do either?

QUESTION 5:   David and Sarah Marsh are having marital problems. They have little cash left, but they have a piece of valuable property in Beverly Hills. David Marsh devises a scheme to convert the property into cash for himself. He applies for a second mortgage in the sum of $200,000 from Far East Savings and Loan. He forges Sarah's name on the mortgage application, the mortgage itself, and the promissory note evidencing the mortgage. His forgery is quite good. On the two occasions on which he needs the documents notarized, he tells the notary at work that Sarah is sick and cannot come in but that he needs these documents notarized that day. Although the notary knows that he should not be notarizing the documents without actually seeing Sarah sign them, he thinks that he recognizes her signature and owes David a favor. Far East Savings and Loan issues a check on its account at Bank of Newport payable jointly to David and Sarah. David forges Sarah's indorsement on the check and deposits the check in his account at First Interstate Bank, which obtains payment from Bank of Newport. David withdraws the $200,000 and leaves the country. May Far East Savings and Loan recover the funds from First Interstate Bank? May Bank of Newport charge the account of Far East Savings and Loan? If not, may Bank of Newport recover from First Interstate Bank?

QUESTION 6: On May 1, 2004, Anna purchases a Van Gogh drawing from Wealthy Collector ("Wealthy") for $2 million in payment for which Anna writes a check payable to Wealthy. Wealthy indorses the check as a gift to his spoiled son, Rupert. Anna discovers that the drawing, unbeknownst to Wealthy, is a copy and not an original Van Gogh. Anna issues a proper written stop payment order to Dupes National Bank. Rupert, being a heavy gambler, owes his bookie, Killer, $3 million. He indorses the check to Killer in payment for a portion of the debt. On September 15, 2004, Killer deposits the check in his checking account at Folsom State Bank. Folsom State Bank applies the check to a debt owed it by Killer. On presentment, Dupes National Bank, overlooking the stop payment order, pays the check. Anna demands that Dupes National Bank recredit her account. Discuss whether Dupes National Bank must recredit Anna's account. If Dupes National Bank is required to recredit Anna's account, what rights does Dupes National Bank have against Folsom State Bank or Wealthy?

QUESTION 7: Wally Cox has been the faithful and honest bookkeeper for Mr. Peeper's Smoke Shop for 20 years. Wally's mother, with whom Wally lives, is in need of a serious medical operation. Despite having medical insurance, it will cost Wally $100,000 to pay for the operation. Having only $92,000, Wally is $8,000 short. Being too embarrassed to ask anyone for help, Wally decides to "borrow" money from Mr. Peeper's Smoke Shop without telling his boss. Wally prints out a phony invoice from a real supplier of cigars, Fidel Jones. He writes a check out to Fidel Jones in the amount of $8,000 and forges the name of his boss, the only person authorized to sign for Mr. Peeper's Smoke Shop. He indorses the check in the name of Fidel Jones and deposits the check in his account at Wells Bank. On presentment, the check is paid by Bank of America. The operation is unsuccessful; Wally's mother passes away. Because of the shock, Wally has a heart attack and also passes away. When the bank statement containing the forged check is received, no one notices the forgery. Three months later, when the books of Mr. Peeper's Smoke Shop are audited, the accountant notices the discrepancy. Mr. Peeper's Smoke Shop, immediately after the discovery by the accountant, tells Bank of America of the forgery. Must Bank of America recredit Mr. Peeper's Smoke Shop's account for the $8,000? Does Bank of America have a right to recover the $8,000 from Wells Bank?

Essay Exam Answers

SAMPLE ANSWER TO QUESTION 1:   A depositary bank can become a holder even though it does not obtain the indorsement of its customer. Although Not-So-Fast Bank gave value for the check when it applied the check to an antecedent debt, it does not qualify as a holder in due course because it took the check with notice that the check was overdue. Not-So-Fast Bank took the check on January 24 while the check was written on October 20. Assuming that the check was dated, the check was overdue because it was taken more than 90 days after its date.

Assuming that it gave notice of the chargeback, it may charge back Quick and Easy's account. In addition, it may recover under UCC §4-207(b)'s transfer warranty, which presumes a transferor indorsed the instrument. Not-So-Fast Bank can also recover from Brittany's father. He has no defense to his liability because Quick and Easy did nothing wrong regarding him. A nonholder in due course can recover on a check when there is no defense that can be asserted against it. Not-So-Fast Bank cannot recover against Virginia or Rihanna in its own right because Rihanna has the defense that she did not receive any consideration for the check and Virginia has the defense of fraud. However, if Quick and Easy qualifies as a holder in due course, Not-So-Fast Bank obtains all of its rights, and therefore, can recover even if these parties have a defense. However, a question arises as to whether Quick and Easy is a holder in due course. Even though it only gave $3,000 for the check, this would constitute value. Quick and Easy's failure to inquire probably would not constitute a lack of good faith. Considering that it was fearful that the drawer and indorser were not solvent, under the inferable knowledge test, an argument can be made that it had an innocent explanation for its large discount and therefore did not have notice. Under the duty to inquire test, a 70 percent discount on a check may be suspicious enough to impose a duty on Quick and Easy to inquire of Brittany's father. Because Virginia has asserted an adverse claim to the check, Brittany's father cannot be a holder in due course because he had notice of Virginia's claim to the check.

However, Virginia's liability as an indorser is discharged because the check was not presented for payment or given to a depositary bank for collection within 30 days of her indorsement. Virginia indorsed the check on November 3. The check was not deposited until January 24. As a result, Virginia is discharged. The discharge would not be effective against a holder in due course who did not have notice of the defense. Because Virginia probably did not date her indorsement, Virginia would not be discharged if any of the parties qualify as a subsequent holder in due course. Although Not-So-Fast Bank cannot so qualify, an argument can be made that if Quick and Easy is a holder in due course, it would take free of the discharge and, if Not-So-Fast Bank obtains all of its rights under the shelter provision, it should also take free of the discharge.

SAMPLE ANSWER TO QUESTION 2:

  a. John Denver check
    1. Because Rosemary has authority to reconcile bank statements, she more than likely has responsibility with regard to instruments for purposes of U.C.C. §3-405. As a result, an indorsement by Rosemary on a check payable to her employer Milt is effective under U.C.C. §3-405(b) as to a person who pays the check in good faith. Because Wells Fargo Bank paid the instrument in good faith, the indorsement was good and the instrument was properly payable. Therefore John Denver may not have his account recredited.

   2. Milt may not recover from John Denver. Because the indorsement was good as to Wells Fargo Bank, the check was properly paid. This discharges Denver's liability on the check. Once the check is paid, Denver's liability on the underlying obligation is also discharged under U.C.C. §3-310(b)(1).

   3. Milt may not recover from Wells Fargo Bank, because the indorsement was effective. However, if Bank of America was deemed to have failed to exercise ordinary care, Milt may recover from Bank of America to the extent of its failure. However, it is unlikely that Bank of America has failed to properly act. At least if one argues by analogy, Bank of America had no notice of any breach of fiduciary duty merely because it cashed the check for Rosemary because Bank of America may believe that Milt asked that Rosemary get the check cashed for him.

b. Under U.C.C. §3-405, because Rosemary was entrusted with responsibility as to checks, her indorsement of a check drawn by Milt and payable to Placido Domingo is effective as to Bank of America, which paid the check in good faith. Therefore, Milt may not recover from Bank of America. However, as to Bank of California, Milt may partially recover if a court finds that Bank of California failed to exercise ordinary care and its failure contributed to the loss. It is unclear to what extent Bank of California exercised ordinary care in allowing Rosemary to establish the bank account in the corporate name. In addition, a question arises as to whether the fact that the check was payable to an individual and deposited in a corporate account should have alerted Bank of California to the problem.

c. Because Rosemary had no authority to write checks for Milt, her signing of Milt's name was not effective unless Milt was negligent in hiring or supervising her. There is no evidence of such negligence. Milt may require Bank of America to recredit his account. Because Rosemary only forged one check in Milt's name as drawer, the repeat forgery rule does not apply. As a result, Milt is not precluded under U.C.C. §4-406 from asserting the forgery unless Bank of America proves that Milt failed to promptly review his bank statement and notify Bank of America of the forgery and that, as a result, it suffered a loss because of the failure. Even though Milt may have failed to be prompt in reviewing his bank statement, Bank of America suffered no loss on account of the delay because Rosemary had already withdrawn all of the money and had fled before the check was even returned to Milt.

Bank of America cannot recover from Bank of California because there was no breach of any presenter's warranty. Because Rosemary was the person whose intent determines the person to whom the check is payable, and Rosemary did not intend Placido Domingo to be the payee, then, under U.C.C. §3-404(b), any indorsement is sufficient to negotiate the check. However, Bank of America can recover under U.C.C. §3-404(d) to the extent that Bank of California was negligent in allowing the account to be established or the check to be deposited in the account.

SAMPLE ANSWER TO QUESTION 3:   In determining whether Bob has any rights against Bank of Santa Monica, the question is whether the check has been finally paid. If it has been finally paid, then the money belongs to Bob. If not, then it does not. Because the setoff took place after the cut-off hour, the setoff is deemed to have been taken place on the next business day, which is January 16. As a result, the account, being that the setoff should not have taken place and the account should not have been debited contained sufficient funds to pay the check. As a result, Sam's check should have been paid. Because it was not paid, Sam has a cause of action for wrongful dishonor. The damages available for wrongful dishonor include all damages [U.C.C. §4-402(b)] proximately caused by the wrongful dishonor. The measure of damages is those in tort and not in contract. Damages can include loss of reputation, emotional distress damages, and punitive damages.

SAMPLE ANSWER TO QUESTION 4: It would appear that Finance Company does not qualify as a holder in due course. Finance Company knew, when it took the note, that the president of Fortune Gems was negotiating the note for his own benefit. If Finance Company also knew that he was the president of the company, Finance Company would have notice of his breach of fiduciary duty. U.C.C. §3-307(b)(2). If it had notice of a breach of fiduciary duty, Finance Company could not qualify as a holder in due course. However, a taker does not have notice of a breach of fiduciary duty unless the represented person makes a claim to the instrument. If Fortune Gems makes no claim to the instrument, Finance Company may still qualify as a holder in due course.

Finance Company may also fail to qualify as a holder in due course if the fact that it purchased the note at such a substantial discount is found to give it notice of a claim or defense. Whether it would be imputed with such notice would depend on whether the court adopts the duty to inquire test or the inferable knowledge test. Under the duty to inquire test, Finance Company would have the duty to investigate why a $100,000 secured note would be sold for $50,000. However, under the inferable knowledge test, in the absence of any other suspicious circumstances, Finance Company could assume an innocent explanation for the substantial discount.

Finance Company may also fail to qualify as a holder in due course in that it may have failed to act in good faith. The fact that it purchased the note at a substantial discount coupled with the fact that it took a note payable to the corporation in payment for the personal debt of its president may be found to indicate that Finance Company has failed to observe reasonable commercial standards of fair dealing.

Assuming that Finance Company fails to qualify as a holder in due course, the question arises as to whether Frank can raise Sam's defense of breach of contract or of fraud. An obligor may not raise a third-party defense or claim. However, a third party may intervene (or otherwise become part of the action) and raise his own claim to the instrument. Because the failure to pay dividends is a mere defense and not a claim to the instrument, Sam may not raise this defense in Finance Company's action against Frank.

However, if Sam could have rescinded the stock purchase on account of Fortune Gems' fraud, then Sam would have a claim to the instrument that could be asserted against Finance Company as long as it does not qualify as a holder in due course.

SAMPLE ANSWER TO QUESTION 5: As the drawer, Far East Savings and Loan has no right to bring an action for conversion against First Interstate Bank. U.C.C. §3-420(a)(i). Not being the party making payment, Far East Savings and Loan also has no right to sue First Interstate Bank on the presentment warranty that it is a person entitled to enforce the instrument. U.C.C. §3-417, Official Comment 2.

Far East Savings and Loan's proper action is against Bank of Newport for recrediting of its account. If Sarah's indorsement is regarded as unauthorized, Bank of Newport has no right to debit Far East Savings and Loan's account. Initially, it seems that the indorsement is unauthorized. Bank of Newport could argue, however, that the indorsement is authorized in that David was an impostor. By forging Sarah's name to the mortgage application, he was pretending to be his wife, thereby inducing Far East Savings and Loan to issue the check. If this is the case, then any indorsement in Sarah's name is sufficient to negotiate the check. U.C.C. §3-404(b)(2). If so, Bank of Newport properly paid the check. On the other hand, it can be argued that David merely forged Sarah's name and did not at any time claim to be her. If so, David would not be an impostor. Sarah's indorsement would not be effective and therefore Bank of Newport could not debit Far East Savings and Loan's account. Bank of Newport could also argue that Far East Savings and Loan was negligent in issuing the check without seeing Sarah sign the mortgage. However, it was probably reasonable for Far East Savings and Loan to rely on the notarization of her signatures.

If Far East Savings and Loan is not precluded under U.C.C. §3-404 or U.C.C. §3-406 from contending that Sarah's indorsement was unauthorized, First Interstate Bank would not be a person entitled to enforce the instrument. As a result, First Interstate Bank would have breached the presentment warranty that it gave to Bank of Newport that it was a person entitled to enforce the instrument. U.C.C. §4-208(a)(i). In this event, the loss would fall on First Interstate Bank. However, if Far East Savings and Loan is precluded under either of these provisions, the indorsement is good and therefore it did not breach its warranty that it is a person entitled to enforce the instrument.

SAMPLE ANSWER TO QUESTION 6:   Whether Dupes National Bank must recredit Anna's account depends on whether Anna has suffered a loss by virtue of Dupes National Bank's failure to properly honor the stop payment order. Although Anna can initially show that she suffered a loss by her account being debited for the amount of the check, Dupes National Bank may assert its subrogation rights as a set-off. Under U.C.C. §4-407, upon its improper payment, Dupes National Bank becomes subrogated to the rights of any holder in due course and of the payee or any other holder of the instrument. Dupes National Bank will claim that Folsom State Bank is a holder in due course. The fact that Folsom State Bank applied the check to an antecedent debt does constitute value. However, Folsom State Bank is not a holder in due course because it had notice that the check was overdue. A check is deemed to be overdue 90 days after its date. U.C.C. §3-304(a)(2). As a result, Anna could have raised her breach of contract claim against Folsom State Bank. U.C.C. §3-305(a)(2), (3). Because Wealthy sold the painting to Anna, Wealthy would likewise take subject to this defense. U.C.C. §3-305(a)(3), (b). As a result, because any rights to which Dupes National Bank would be subrogated are subject to Anna's defense or claim in recoupment, Dupes National Bank has no right to debit Anna's account.

Dupes National Bank cannot recover from Folsom State Bank. Folsom State Bank took the check in good faith and for value. As a result, payment is final as to Folsom State Bank. U.C.C. §3-418(c). Although Dupes National Bank is subrogated to Anna's rights against any party, Anna had no rights against Folsom State Bank. As a result, there are no rights to which Dupes National Bank could be subrogated. However, because Anna has a right to recover from Wealthy under the underlying contract for sale, Dupes National Bank, being subrogated to Anna's rights against Wealthy on the underlying contract, can recover from Wealthy. U.C.C. §4-407(3).

SAMPLE ANSWER TO QUESTION 7:   Initially, the check was not properly payable because the check bore a forged drawer's signature. As a result, unless Mr. Peeper's Smoke Shop is precluded from asserting the forgery, Bank of America may not debit its account for the amount of the check. Wally was a trusted and honest employee for 20 years. For this reason, Mr. Peeper's Smoke Shop was probably not negligent in the authority and autonomy that it gave to Wally and, therefore, it would not be precluded under U.C.C. §3-406 from asserting that its signature as drawer was unauthorized.

However, Mr. Peeper's Smoke Shop did have the responsibility to examine its returned bank statements and items to discover its unauthorized signature on any check. U.C.C. §4-406(c). By not examining the statement for 3 months, Mr. Peeper's Smoke Shop failed in its duty to exercise reasonable promptness in examining the statement. As a result, it will be liable for any loss suffered by the bank. U.C.C. §4-406(d)(1). However, because Wally immediately passed away, it is unlikely that the bank would have been able to collect from him even if Mr. Peeper's Smoke Shop would have promptly informed it of the forgery. For these reasons, Bank of America must recredit Mr. Peeper's Smoke Shop's account.

Bank of America may not recover the money from Wells Bank. Because Wally was the bookkeeper for the drawer, Mr. Peeper's Smoke Shop, Wally was entrusted with responsibility with regard to instruments. As a result, his indorsing of the check in the name of Fidel Jones was effective to negotiate the check. U.C.C. §3-405(b). Because the indorsement was effective, Bank of America has no right to recover from Wells Bank for the loss. Bank of America may have the right to recover some of the funds from Wells Bank if a court finds that Wells Bank was negligent in allowing Wally to deposit the check in his account. This would be a question of fact. U.C.C. §3-405(b).

Glossary

Acceleration clause: The time of payment is subject to acceleration when a clause, either in the instrument, or in another writing referred to in the instrument, allows the holder to demand, under specified conditions, payment prior to the time set in the instrument for payment.

Acceptance of a draft: The drawee's signed agreement to pay the draft as presented. U.C.C. §3-409(a).

Accepted access device: An access device is accepted: (1) on receipt of the device if the consumer requested the financial institution to issue the device to her; (2) if the consumer did not request that the access device be issued to her, when the consumer signs the access device, uses, or authorizes another person to use the device for the purpose of transferring funds or obtaining money, property, or services; (3) when the consumer requests validation of the device; or (4) if it is issued in substitution for, or in renewal of, a previously accepted access device. 12 C.F.R. §205.2(a)(2)(ii).

Accepted credit card: Any credit card that a cardholder has: (1) requested or applied for and received; (2) signed, or (3) used or authorized another person to use to obtain credit. Any credit card issued as a renewal or substitute becomes an accepted credit card when received by the cardholder. 12 C.F.R. §226.12(a)(2), n.21.

Acceptor: When a draft is presented to the drawee for acceptance and the drawee accepts the draft, the drawee becomes liable as an acceptor.

Access device: A card, a code, or other means of access to a consumer's account, or any combination thereof, that may be used by the consumer for the purpose of initiating electronic fund transfers. 12 C.F.R. §205.2(a)(1).

Accommodated party: If an instrument is issued for value given for the benefit of a party to the instrument and another party to the instrument signs the instrument for the purpose of incurring liability on the instrument without being a direct beneficiary of the value given for the instrument, the party for whose direct benefit the value is given is an accommodated party. U.C.C. §3-419(a).

Accommodation party: If an instrument is issued for value given for the benefit of a party to the instrument and another party to the instrument signs the instrument for the purpose of incurring liability on the instrument without being a direct beneficiary of the value given for the instrument, the party who does not receive the direct benefit is an accommodation party. U.C.C. §3-419(a).

Accountable: The payor bank is liable for the amount of the item. U.C.C. §4-302, Official Comment 2.

Actual knowledge: A purchaser's subjective awareness of the existence of a claim, defense, or claim in recoupment.

Adequate protection: When an instrument is lost, destroyed, or stolen, a court may not enter judgment against the obligor and in favor of the person entitled to enforce the instrument unless it determines that the obligor is adequately protected against loss resulting from a claim of another person to enforce the instrument. Adequate protection is a flexible concept. When there is no real risk of loss, a court could find that the obligor is already adequately protected. On the other hand, when there is a real risk of loss, the court can require the claimant to obtain a bond indemnifying the obligor against any losses or expenses. U.C.C. §3-309(b).

Adverse claimant: A person, other than the person entitled to enforce the instrument, who asserts a claim of ownership to an instrument.

After sight: After the drawee has accepted the draft.

Allonge: A separate piece of paper affixed to an instrument that contains an indorsement of the instrument. U.C.C. §3-204(a).

Alteration: Any unauthorized change in an instrument that attempts to modify, in any respect, the obligation of any party; also, any unauthorized addition of words or numbers or other change to an incomplete instrument which addition or change relates to the obligation of any party. U.C.C. §3-407(a).

Anomalous indorser: An indorser who is not the holder of the instrument. U.C.C. §3-205(d).

Bank: Any person engaged in the business of banking, including, among others, commercial banks, savings banks, savings and loan associations, credit unions, and trust companies. U.C.C. §4-105(1).

Bank checks: A check on which a bank makes a promise to pay. There are three types of bank checks: cashier's, teller's, and certified checks.

Banker's acceptance: A draft drawn on, and accepted by, a bank. By accepting the draft, the bank becomes liable to pay the draft. U.C.C. §3-413(a).

Banking day: Under Article 4, "the part of a day on which a bank is open to the public for carrying on substantially all of its banking functions." U.C.C. §4-104(a)(3). Under Regulation CC, any business day on which an office of a bank is open to the public for substantially all of its banking functions. 12 C.F.R. §229.2(f).

Beneficiary: The person to be paid by the beneficiary's bank. U.C.C. §4A-103(a)(2).

Beneficiary's bank: The bank identified in a payment order that is to make payment to the beneficiary. U.C.C. §4A-103(a)(3).

Billing error: A mistake found in the credit card statement that the card issuer sends to the cardholder. Among others, billing errors include: (1) billing for an extension of credit that was not made to the cardholder; (2) billing for property or services that were neither accepted by, nor delivered to, the cardholder; (3) improper identification of an extension of credit; (4) failing to properly credit a payment or other credit; or (5) making a computational or accounting error. 12 C.F.R. §226.13(a).

Blank indorsement: An indorsement that is not payable to an identified person. U.C.C. §3-205(b).

Book transfer: A funds transfer in which the same bank is both the sending bank and the receiving bank; so called because the payment is accomplished by the receiving bank both crediting the account of the beneficiary and debiting the account of the sender. U.C.C. §4A-104, Official Comment 1, Case #1.

Business day: Under Regulation CC, any day other than a Saturday, Sunday, or holiday. 12 C.F.R. §229.2(g).

Cancellation: Stopping payment of a payment order under Article 4A.

Cashier's check: A check with respect to which the drawer and the drawee are the same bank or branches of the same bank. U.C.C. §3-104(g).

Certificate of deposit: An acknowledgment by a bank of the receipt of money together with an engagement by the bank to repay the money. U.C.C. §3-104(j).

Certified check: A check accepted by the bank on which it is drawn. U.C.C. §3-409(d).

Chain of title: An indorsement necessary to negotiate an instrument.

Chargeback: The right of a depositary bank to debit its customer's account when an item, which it is collecting for its customer, is returned by the payor bank unpaid. U.C.C. §4-214(a).

Check: A draft drawn on a bank and payable on demand. U.C.C. §3-104(f).

Check collection process: The process by which a check that is deposited in the depositary bank is either directly, or through one or more other banks, presented for payment to the payor bank.

Check truncation: The transferring of the contents of an item through the information contained on the MICR-encoded line rather than transferring the item itself.

Claimant: For purposes of recovering on a lost, destroyed, or stolen bank check, the drawer or payee of a certified check and the remitter or payee of a teller's or cashier's check. U.C.C. §3-312(2).

Claim in recoupment: A set-off that arises from the same transaction out of which the instrument arose. U.C.C. §3-305, Official Comment 3.

Claim to instrument: Any claim of a property or possessory interest in the instrument or in its proceeds, including a claim to rescind a negotiation and to recover the instrument or its proceeds. U.C.C. §3-306.

Clearinghouse: An association of banks or nonbank payors (for example, express companies or government agencies) regularly clearing items. U.C.C. §4-104(a)(4).

Collecting bank: Any bank handling an item for collection except the payor bank. U.C.C. §4-105(5).

Consumer credit contract: An instrument that evidences a debt arising from either a loan by the seller to the buyer to purchase the goods or a loan from a creditor, who is related to the seller, to enable the consumer to purchase the goods. 16 C.F.R. §433.1.

Consumer transaction: A transaction in which a natural person uses a negotiable instrument (other than a check that is not postdated) to purchase goods or services to be used primarily for personal, family, or household purposes.

Contribution: The amount that a person must pay to her co-obligor who pays more than his proportional share of the obligation. U.C.C. §3-116(b).

Conversion: The tort cause of action belonging to the owner of an instrument when his ownership rights in the instrument have been interfered with. U.C.C. §3-420(a).

Co-sureties: Two or more parties who sign in the same capacity in accommodation for another party.

Customer: Under Article 4, any person either having an account with the bank or for whom the bank has agreed to collect the item. U.C.C. §4-104(a)(5). Under Article 4A, a person (including a bank) having an account with a bank or from whom a bank has agreed to receive payment orders. U.C.C. §4A-105(a)(3).

Cut-off hour: The hour established by a bank after which items may be treated as having been received on the next banking day. U.C.C. §4-108.

Debit card: An access device that has the capability to transfer funds by debiting the consumer's bank account.

Defense: Any ground a party may have that is sufficient to permit her to avoid all or some of her liability on an instrument.

Defer posting: A payor bank's right to wait until the next banking day to decide whether to pay or return an item. U.C.C. §4-301, Official Comment 1.

Delivery: Voluntary transfer of possession. U.C.C. §1-201(14).

Depositary bank: The first bank to take an item even though it is also the payor bank unless the item is presented for immediate payment over the counter. U.C.C. §4-105(2).

Discharge: An act that results in an obligor being excused from the duty to pay all or a part of his obligation.

Dishonor: The refusal, or failure, to pay or accept an instrument upon a proper presentment for payment or acceptance. When presentment is excused, dishonor occurs if the instrument is not duly accepted or paid. U.C.C. §3-502(e); U.C.C. §3-502, Official Comment 7.

Documentary draft: A draft to be presented for acceptance or payment if specified documents, securities, certificates, or the like are to be received by the drawee before acceptance or payment of the draft. U.C.C. §4-104(a)(6).

Draft: Any instrument that contains an order (a written instruction by one person to another to pay a third person). U.C.C. §3-104(e); U.C.C. §3-103(a)(6).

Drawee: The person ordered in a draft to make payment. U.C.C. §4-104(a)(8).

Drawer: The person who signs, or is identified in a draft, as the person ordering payment. U.C.C. §3-103(3).

Due diligence: As used in determining whether an organization has notice of a fact, requires (1) that the organization maintain reasonable routines for the communication of significant information from individuals who have the duty to forward information to the person conducting the transaction; and (2) reasonable compliance with the procedures established. U.C.C. §1-201(27).

EFTA: Electronic Fund Transfer Act.

Electronic fund transfer: Any transfer of funds that is initiated through an electronic terminal, telephone, or computer or magnetic tape for the purpose of instructing a financial institution to debit or credit a consumer asset account. 15 U.S.C. §1693a(6); 12 C.F.R. §205.3(b).

Electronic presentment: A means of presenting an item for payment by transference of the contents of the item through the information contained on the MICR-encoded line rather than transferring the item itself. There is also a second means of electronic presentment called "imaging technology" that allows the check's image to be electronically transmitted to the payor bank. U.C.C. §4-110, Official Comment 1.

Employee: Actual employees, independent contractors, and employees of an independent contractor retained by the employer.

Encoding: The encoding in magnetic numerical characters ("MICR") of certain information, usually its amount, on an instrument.

Equitable claim of ownership: A prior owner's claim that although she voluntarily negotiated the instrument, she has the right to rescind the negotiation and regain title to the instrument. U.C.C. §3-306, Official Comment.

Erroneous execution of payment order: Mistake made by the receiving bank in its execution of the sender's order. U.C.C. §4A-303.

Error: Unauthorized and incorrect electronic fund transfer, omission from a periodic statement, computational or bookkeeping error, receipt of an incorrect amount of money from an electronic terminal, improper identification of an electronic fund transfer, or a consumer's request for any documentation required by Regulation E or for additional information or clarification regarding an electronic fund transfer. 15 U.S.C. §1693f(f).

Execution date: The day on which the receiving bank may properly issue a payment order executing the sender's order. U.C.C. §4A-301(b).

Fictitious payee: A person who is not intended to have any interest in the instrument; also, a nonexistent person. U.C.C. §3-404(b).

Fiduciary: An agent, trustee, partner, corporate officer or director, or other representative owing a fiduciary duty with respect to an instrument. U.C.C. §3-307(a)(1).

Final payment: The end of the payment process, after which the payor bank may no longer revoke its settlement.

Float: A bank's interest-free use of its customer's money that occurs when the bank has collected the funds but not yet allowed its customer to use the funds.

For collection: A restrictive indorsement that limits application of the proceeds of the instrument to deposit into the indorser's bank account or otherwise for collection for the benefit of the indorser.

For deposit: A restrictive indorsement that indicates that the proceeds of the instrument can be credited only to the indorser's bank account. U.C.C. §3-206(c).

Fraud in the factum: The assertion that the obligor has been induced by fraud to sign the instrument with neither knowledge nor reasonable opportunity to learn of the instrument's character or its essential terms. U.C.C. §3-305(a)(1)(iii).

Fraud in the inducement: A situation in which the obligor, although knowing that he is signing a negotiable instrument, is defrauded into entering the transaction by misrepresentations concerning the transaction itself.

Fraudulent indorsement: (1) An indorsement made in the name of the employer on an instrument payable to the employer; (2) an indorsement made in the name of the payee on an instrument issued by the employer. U.C.C. §3-405(a)(2).

Funds transfer: The series of transactions, beginning with the originator's payment order, made for the purpose of making payment to the beneficiary of the order. U.C.C. §4A-104(a).

Funds-transfer business day: That part of a day during which the bank is open for the receipt, processing, and transmittal of payment orders and cancellations and amendments of payment orders. U.C.C. §4A-105(a)(4).

Good faith: Honesty in fact and the observance of reasonable commercial standards of fair dealing. U.C.C. §3-103(a)(4); U.C.C. §4A-105(a)(6).

Holder: The person in possession if the negotiable instrument is payable to bearer or, in the case of an instrument payable to an identified person, if the identified person is in possession. U.C.C. §1-201(20).

Holder in due course: The negotiable instrument's version of a good-faith purchaser for value. To obtain holder-in-due-course status, a purchaser must take the instrument as a holder, for value, in good faith, and without notice of certain proscribed facts. U.C.C. §3-302(a).

Impairment of collateral: An unjustifiable act or omission on the part of the person entitled to enforce the instrument that causes the collateral no longer to be available to satisfy the instrument. U.C.C. §3-605(g).

Impostor: A person who represents herself to be the named payee or an agent of the named payee and, by such representation, induces the issuer to issue the instrument to her or to a person acting in concert with her. U.C.C. §3-404, Official Comment.

Incomplete instruments: A signed instrument the contents of which show that it is incomplete but that the signer intended to complete it by the addition of words or numbers. U.C.C. §3-115(a).

Indorsement: A signature, other than that as maker, drawer, or acceptor, that alone or accompanied by other words is made on an instrument for the purpose of: (1) negotiating the instrument; (2) restricting payment of the instrument; or (3) incurring indorser's liability on the instrument. U.C.C. §3-204(a).

Indorser: A catch-all category that covers anyone who signs an instrument in any capacity other than as a drawer, an acceptor, or a maker. U.C.C. §3-204(a).

Insolvency proceedings: Assignment for the benefit of creditors or other proceedings intended to liquidate or rehabilitate the estate of the person involved. U.C.C. §1-201(22).

Intermediary bank: Under Article 4, any bank to which an item is transferred in the course of collection except the depositary or payor bank. U.C.C. §4-105(4). Under Article 4A, a bank through which a sending bank sends a payment order to the receiving bank. U.C.C. §4A-104(b).

Issuance: An instrument that is first delivered by the maker or drawer to either a holder or nonholder for the purpose of giving rights on the instrument to any person. U.C.C. §3-105(a).

Issuer: The drawer or maker of an instrument. U.C.C. §3-105(c).

Item: An instrument or other written promise or order to pay money handled by a bank for collection or payment. U.C.C. §4-104(a)(9).

Legal claim of ownership: The claim of an owner of an instrument that he has been wrongfully and involuntarily deprived of its possession.

Legals: Legal process in the context of whether a bank has the right or duty to pay an item, such as writs of garnishment or execution, the payor bank acquiring knowledge that the drawer has filed a petition in bankruptcy, died, or become incompetent, and the bank's right to set off against the customer's account a debt owed to it by the customer. U.C.C. §4-303(a).

Local check: A check drawn on or payable through or at a paying bank located in the same check processing region as the depositary bank. 12 C.F.R. §229.2(r).

Midnight deadline: Midnight on the bank's next banking day following the banking day on which the item was received. U.C.C. §4-104(a)(10).

Money: A medium of exchange authorized or adopted by a domestic or foreign government including a monetary unit of account established by an intergovernmental organization or by agreement between two or more nations. U.C.C. §1-201(24).

Money-back guarantee: The excuse of the obligation of the sender if the funds transfer is not completed because the beneficiary's bank does not accept the payment order. U.C.C. §4A-402(c), Official Comment 2.

Negotiable instrument: A writing that meets the requirements for negotiability found in U.C.C. §3-104(a).

Negotiation: A transfer of possession of an instrument, whether voluntary or involuntary, by a person, other than the issuer (i.e., maker or drawer), to another person who thereby becomes its holder. U.C.C. §3-201(a).

Next-day availability: The required availability of funds at the start of business on the business day after the banking day on which the deposit was made. 12 C.F.R. §229.10.

Nonlocal check: A check drawn on, or payable through or at, a bank not located in the same check processing region as the depositary bank. 12 C.F.R. §229.2(v).

Note: Any instrument that contains a promise. U.C.C. §3-104(e).

Notice: Actual knowledge of an infirmity; receipt of notification of an infirmity; or from all the facts and circumstances known to a purchaser at the time in question having reason to know that the infirmity exists. U.C.C. §1-201(25)(a)-(c); [[Rev]1-202]

Notice of dishonor: The notice that must be given of the dishonor of an instrument so as to fulfill a condition precedent to the obligation of an indorser. U.C.C. §3-503(a).

Notification: A person receives a notice or notification when: (1) it comes to his attention or (2) it is duly delivered at the place of business through which the contract was made or at any other place held out by him as the place for receipt of such communications. U.C.C. §1-201(26); [[Rev]1-202](e).

Obligated bank: The drawer bank of a teller's or cashier's check and the accepting bank on a certified check. U.C.C. §3-411(a).

On-us item: An item on which the payor bank and depositary bank are the same bank. U.C.C. §4-301(b); U.C.C. §4-301, Official Comment 4.

Order: An instruction to pay money. U.C.C. §3-103(a)(6).

Ordinary care: The observance of the reasonable commercial standards prevailing in the area in which the person is located, with respect to the business in which the person is engaged. U.C.C. §3-103(a)(9). There is a separate definition of ordinary care in the case of a bank that takes an instrument for processing for collection or payment by automated means. U.C.C. §3-103(a)(9).

Organization: A corporation, government or governmental subdivision or agency, business trust, estate, trust, partnership or association, two or more persons having a joint or common interest, or any other legal or commercial entity. U.C.C. §1-201(28).

Originator: The sender of the first payment order in a funds transfer. U.C.C. §4A-104(c).

Originator's bank: The receiving bank to which the payment order of the originator is issued if the originator is not a bank. U.C.C. §4A-104(d).

Overdue: An instrument that has not been paid although the time for its payment has passed. A check is overdue the day after the day demand for payment is duly made or 90 days after its stated date, whichever is earlier. U.C.C. §3-304(a)(1), (2).

Pay any bank: A blank indorsement that limits holder status to banks. U.C.C. §4-201(b).

Payable on demand: A promise or an order stating that it is payable on demand or at sight or otherwise indicates that it is payable at the will of the holder. U.C.C. §3-108(a).

Payable through item: A draft or note that names a specified bank as the person authorized to present the item to the drawer or maker. The bank through which the item is payable has no right to pay the item without the drawer's or maker's consent. U.C.C. §4-106(a); U.C.C. §4-106, Official Comment 1.

Paying bank: Regulation CC's term for a payor bank. It is, however, broader in that it includes, among other entities that do not qualify as payor banks, the bank whose routing number appears on a check even if it is not the true drawee bank. 12 C.F.R. §229.2(z).

Payment date: The day on which the amount of a payment order is payable to the beneficiary by the beneficiary's bank. U.C.C. §4A-401.

Payment order: An instruction of a sender to a receiving bank, transmitted orally, electronically, or in writing, to pay, or to cause another bank to pay, a fixed or determinable amount of money to a beneficiary. U.C.C. §4A-103(a)(1).

Payor bank: The bank that is the drawee of a draft. U.C.C. §4-105(3).

Person: An individual or an organization. U.C.C. §1-201(30).

Person entitled to enforce instrument: The holder of an instrument, a person who has the rights of a holder, or a person who is entitled to enforce the instrument under U.C.C. §3-309 or §3-418(d). U.C.C. §3-301.

Personal money order: A draft sold by the drawee to a person who, typically, does not have an account with the drawee.

PIN: A personal identification number for purposes of electronic fund transfers.

Point-of-sale transfer ("POS transfer"):   A transfer of funds through a terminal located at the merchant's business location that, through a computer link, immediately debits the consumer's bank account and credits the merchant's bank account.

Postdated check: A check issued before its date. U.C.C. §4-401(c).

Preauthorized electronic fund transfer: Any electronic fund transfer that is authorized in advance and that recurs at substantially regular intervals. 15 U.S.C. §1693a(9); 12 C.F.R. §205.2(i).

Presenting bank: Any bank presenting an item except a payor bank. U.C.C. §4-105(6).

Presentment: A demand for payment or acceptance made by, or on behalf of, the person entitled to enforce the instrument. U.C.C. §3-501(a).

Presentment warranties: Warranties given to the person paying or accepting an instrument or item. U.C.C. §3-417; U.C.C. §4-208.

Principal obligor: The accommodated party or any other party to the instrument against whom a secondary obligor has recourse under [Rev] Article 3. [Rev] U.C.C. §3-103(a)(11).

Promise: An undertaking to pay money. U.C.C. §3-103(a)(9).

Properly payable: An item both authorized by the customer and complying with the bank/customer agreement. U.C.C. §4-401(a); U.C.C. §4-401, Official Comment 1.

Ratification: The election by the person whose name is signed to treat the unauthorized signature as though it were originally authorized by him. U.C.C. §3-403, Official Comment 3.

Receiving bank: The bank to which the sender's instruction is addressed. U.C.C. §4A-103(a)(4).

Record: Information that is inscribed on a tangible medium or that is stored in an electronic or other medium and is retrievable in a perceivable form. U.C.C. §3-103(a)(14).

Rejection of payment order: Notice given by the receiving bank to the sender that it will not accept the payment order. U.C.C. §4A-210.

Remitter: A person who purchases an instrument from its issuer if the instrument is payable to an identified person other than the purchaser. U.C.C. §3-103(a)(11).

Remotely created consumer item: An item payable out of a consumer's account that is created by the merchant or telemarketer with the consumer's signature not appearing on the item. U.C.C. §3-103(a)(16).

Representative: An agent, an officer of a corporation or association, a trustee, an executor or administrator of an estate, or any other person empowered to act for another. [Rev] U.C.C. §1-201(b)(33).

Represented person: The principal, beneficiary, partnership, corporation, or other person to whom the fiduciary owes a duty. U.C.C. §3-307(a)(2).

Responsibility: For purposes of determining whether an employer is liable for a fraudulent indorsement by its employee, authority: (1) to sign or indorse instruments on behalf of the employer; (2) to process instruments received by the employer for bookkeeping purposes, for deposit to an account, or for other disposition; (3) to prepare or process instruments for issue in the name of the employer; (4) to supply information for determining the names or addresses of payees; (5) to control the disposition of instruments issued in the name of the employer; or (6) to act otherwise with respect to instruments in a responsible capacity. U.C.C. §3-405(a)(3).

Restrictive indorsement: An indorsement written by, or on behalf of, the holder that limits negotiation of the instrument to a specific use. U.C.C. §3-206.

Returning bank: Any bank, other than the paying or depositary bank, that handles the item on its return. 12 C.F.R. §229.2(cc).

Secondary obligor: Any of the following: (a) an indorser; (b) an accommodation party; (c) the drawer of an accepted draft; or (d) any other party to the instrument that has recourse against another party to the instrument pursuant to [Rev] U.C.C.§3-116(b). [Rev] U.C.C. §3-103(a)(17).

Security procedure: A procedure established by agreement between a customer and a receiving bank for the purpose of: (1) verifying that a payment order or communication amending or canceling a payment order is that of the customer or; (2) detecting an error in the transmission or content of the order, amendment, or cancellation. U.C.C. §4A-201.

Sender: The person giving the instruction to the receiving bank. U.C.C. §4A-103(a)(5).

Settle: To pay in cash, by clearinghouse settlement, in a charge or credit or by remittance, or otherwise as agreed. A settlement may be either provisional or final. U.C.C. §4-104(a)(11).

Shelter provision: The provision that allows a transferee, even though not qualifying as a holder in due course, to acquire all of the rights of her holder in due course/transferor. U.C.C. §3-203(b).

Sight draft: A draft payable on demand.

Signature: Any symbol executed or adopted by a party with the present intention to adopt or accept a writing. [Rev] U.C.C. §1-201(37); [Rev] U.C.C. §1-201(b)(37).

Special indorsement: An indorsement that identifies the person to whom it is payable. U.C.C. §3-205(a).

Stale check: A check that is presented more than 6 months after its date. U.C.C. §4-404.

Subrogation: The right of a person making payment to step into the shoes of the party paid, thereby acquiring the latter party's rights against any third party who was obligated to pay the same debt.

Subsurety: An accommodation party that is not only the accommodation party for the original debtor but also for another accommodation party.

Surety: A person who guarantees the debt of another. The Article 3 version of a surety is an "accommodation party."

Teller's check: A check drawn by one bank on another bank or payable at or payable through the other bank. U.C.C. §3-104(h).

Tender of payment: An offer to make payment coupled with the willingness and ability to immediately transfer the money. U.C.C. §3-603.

Time draft: A draft payable at a definite time.

Trade acceptance: A draft drawn on, and accepted by, a person other than a bank.

Transfer: An instrument delivered by a person other than its issuer (i.e., the maker or drawer) so as to give to the person receiving delivery the right to enforce the instrument. U.C.C. §3-203(a).

Transfer warranties: When a person receives consideration for transferring an instrument, she makes certain warranties, called "transfer warranties," as to the authenticity and the enforceability of the instrument. U.C.C. §3-416; U.C.C. §4-207.

Traveler's check: An instrument that (1) is payable on demand, (2) is drawn on or payable at or through a bank, (3) is designated by the term "traveler's check" or by a substantially similar term, and (4) requires, as a condition to payment, a countersignature by a person whose specimen signature appears on the instrument. U.C.C. §3-104(i).

Trust indorsement: A restrictive indorsement that states that payment is to be made to the indorsee as agent, trustee, or other fiduciary for the benefit of the indorser or another person. U.C.C. §3-206(d).

Unauthorized signature: An outright forgery or a signature by an agent in excess of his actual or apparent authority. U.C.C. §1-201(43); U.C.C. §3-403, Official Comment 1.

Unauthorized use: The use of a credit card by a person, other than the cardholder, who does not have actual, implied, or apparent authority for such use, and from which the cardholder receives no benefit. 12 C.F.R. §226.12(b), n.22.

Validation: The financial institution's completion of all steps necessary to enable the consumer to use an access device to initiate an electronic fund transfer. 12 C.F.R. §205.5(b)(4).

Verified payment order: An order that passes on being properly tested according to a security procedure. U.C.C. §4A-202(b).

Writing: A printing, typewriting, or any other intentional reduction to tangible form. U.C.C. §1-201(46); [Rev] U.C.C. §1-201(b)(43).

Table of Cases

Agostino v. Monticello Greenhouses 146

Akin v. Dahl 53

Alaska State Bank v. Fairco 147

Arlington Bank & Trust v. Nowell
    Motors, Inc. 90

Auto-Owners Ins. Co. v. Bank One 113

Bank of Am. Natl. Trust & Sav. Assn. v. United
    States 3

Bank Leumi Trust Co. v. Bally's Park
    Place, Inc. 144

Banque Worms v. Bank America
    International 185

Blake v. Woodford Bank & Trust Co. 166

Bottrell v. American Bank 143

Brandywine Assocs., In re, ... 147

Broward Bank v. Commercial Bank 123

Burgess v. First Natl. Bank 143

Calaska Partners Ltd. v. Corson 38, 58

Call v. Ellenville National Bank 172

Calumet Farm, In re, ... 185

Chicago Title Ins. Co. v. Allfirst Bank 21

Chute v. Bank One, N.A. 150

Citibank (South Dakota), N.A. v. Mincks 214

Commerce Union Bank v. May 90

Consolidated Pub. Water Supply Dist. No.
    C-1 v. Farmers Bank 121

Dalessio v. Kressler 4

DBI Architects, P.C. v. American Express
    Travel-Related Services Co., Inc. 213

Divall Insured Income Fund Ltd.
    Partnership v. Boatmen's First
    Natl. Bank 58, 59

Douglas Companies, Inc. v. Commercial
    Natl. Bank of Texarkana 127

Energetics, Inc. v. Allied Bank 143

Evra Corp. v. Swiss Bank Corp. 187

FDIC v. Massingill 58

Federal Deposit Ins. Corp. v. Blue Rock
    Shopping Ctr. 59

Federal Deposit Ins. Corp. v. Newhart 59

Federal Deposit Ins. Corp. v. Wood 58, 59

Federal Sav. & Loan Ins. Corp. v. Mackie 59

Federal Sav. & Loan Ins. Corp. v. Murray 38

Franklin Natl. Bank v. Shapiro 123

Gale v. Hyde Park Bank 206

Grossman v. Banco Industrial de
    Venezuela, C.A. 53

Halifax Corp. v. Wachovia Bank 34

Herzog Contracting Corp. v. McGowen
    Corp. 53

Holloway v. Bristol-Myers 39

Hospicomm, Inc. v. Fleet Bank 200

Household Finance Realty Corp. of
    New York v. Dunlap 205, 207

Industrial Bank of Korea, N.Y. Branch v.
    JP Morgan and Chase Manhattan
    Corp. 4

Khawaja v. J.P. Morgan Chase Bank 190

Kruser v. Bank of America 202

Long Island Trust Co. v. International Inst. for
    Pkg. Educ., Ltd. 53

Lor-Mar/Toto, Inc. v. 1st Constitution Bank 141

Martin v. American Express 214

McAdam v. Dean Witter Reynolds, Inc. 113

McGhee v. First State Bank & Trust Co 92

Metro Natl. Bank v. Roe 53

Money Stop Financial Services v. AFT
    Trucking 21

Morse v. Mutual Fed. Sav. & Loan Assn. 147

Mount Vernon Properties, LLC v. Branch
    Banking and Trust Co. 125

Murdaugh Volkswagen, Inc. v. First
    Natl. Bank 147

National Indem. Co. v. Spring Branch
    State Bank 143

NBT Bank, Natl. Ass'n v. First Natl.
    Community Bank 165

NCS Healthcare, Inc. v. Fifth Third Bank 152

New Century Financial Services, Inc. v.
    Dennegar 213

O'Melveny & Myers v. FDIC 38, 58

Peoples Bank v. Turner 143

Port City State Bank v. American State
    Natl. Bank 166

Price v. Neal 114

Rapp v. Dime Sav. Bank of N.Y. 145

Regatos v. North Fork Bank 185

Resolution Trust Corp. v. 1601Partners Ltd. 59

Resolution Trust Corp. v. Juergens 59

Resolution Trust Corp. v. Montross 59

RTC v. Maplewood Inv. 58

Savings & Loan Assn. v. Tear 97

Schrier Brothers v. Golub 126

Siegel v. New England Merchants Natl. Bank ... 142

Simcoe & Erie Gen. Ins. Co. v. Chemical
    Bank 146

Skov v. Chase Manhattan Bank 147

Spacemakers of America, Inc. v. SunTrust
    Bank 128

Staff Serv. Assocs. v. Midatlantic Natl. Bank 145

Standard Oil Co. v. Steele 214

TME Enterprises, Inc. v. Norwest Corp. 194

Twin City Bank v. Isaacs 147

United States v. Bank of Am. Natl. Trust & Sav.
    Assn. 3

Universal C.I.T. Credit Corp. v. Farmers
    Bank of Portageville 143

U.S. Bank Natl. Assn v. HMA, L.C. 165, 171

Vigneri v. U.S. Bank Natl. Assn. 200

Wachovia Bank, N.A. v. Foster
    Bancshares, Inc. 109

Walker Bank & Trust v. Jones 214

Wilton Enter., Inc. v. Cook's Pantry, Inc. 151

Wolfe v. MBNA America Bank 212

Table of Statutes

United States Code

11 U.S.C.
§542(c) 151

12 U.S.C.
§221 163
§1823(e) 58, 59
§4001 .... 153, 163

15 U.S.C.
§45 39
§57b 39
§1601 211
§1643(a)(1) 212, 217
§1643(b) 213
§1645 212
§1666(e) 216
§1666h 144
§1666i 214
§1693 199
§1693(g)(a) 209
§1693(i)(b) 209
§1693a(2) 200
§1693a(6) 199
§1693a(9) 203
§1693a(11) 201
§1693d(e) 206
§1693f(a) 206, 207
§1693f(b) 207
§1693f(c) 207
§1693f(e) 208
§1693f(f) 206
§1693g(a) 201, 202
§1693h(a)(3) 204
§1693h(c) 207
§1693i(a) 205
§1693i(b) 205
§1693j 205
§1693m 207
§1693m(a) 207, 208
§1693m(a)(2)(B) 207
§1693m(c) 208
§1693m(e) 208
§1693n 207
§1693q 199

Code of Federal Regulations

12 C.F.R.
part 226 211
§205.2(a)(1) 201
§205.2(a)(2)(ii) 201
§205.2(b)(1) 200
§205.2(f) 200
§205.2(f)(1), Staff Comm. 200
§205.2(i) 203
§205.2(k) 201
§205.2(k)(1) 201
§205.2(k)(3), Staff Comm. 201
§205.2(k)(4), Staff Comm. 201
§205.3(b) 199–200
§205.3(b)(1), Staff Comm. 200
§205.3(b)(5) 200
§205.5(b) 205
§205.5(b)(1) 205, 209
§205.5(b)(4) 201
§205.6(a) 201
§205.6(b) 202, 209
§205.6(b)-2, Staff Comm. 202
§205.6(b)(2) 202, 209
§205.6(b)(3) 202, 203
§205.9(b) 206
§205.10(a) 205
§205.10(c) 204
§205.10(d) 206
§205.11(a)(1) 206
§205.11(b)(1)(i) 206
§205.11(c) 206
§205.11(c)(1) 207
§205.11(c)(2) 207
§205.11(c)(2)(iii) 207
§205.11(c)(2)(iv) 207
§205.12(b) 199
§210.3 163
§226.12, Staff Comm. 214, 215
§226.12(a)(2), n.21 212
§226.12(b) 212, 217
§226.12(b), n.22 .... 213, 217
§226.12(b)(2)(i) 212
§226.12(b)(2)(ii) 212

§226.12(b)(2)(iii) 213
§226.12(b)(2)(iii), Staff Comm. 213
§226.12(b)(5) 212
§226.12(c)(1) 214, 215
§226.12(c)(1), n.25 215
§226.12(c)(3), n.26 215
§226.12(c)(3)(i) 214
§226.12(c)(3)(ii) 215, 217
§226.12(c)(3)(ii)(1) 215
§226.13(a) 215
§226.13(b)(1) 216
§226.13(c)(1) 216
§226.13(e)(1) 216
§226.13(e)(2), Comment 216
§226.13(f) 216
§226.13(f)(1) 216
§226.13(g)(1) 216
§226.13(g)(2) 216
§229.2(cc) 163
§229.2(f) 154
§229.2(g) 154
§229.2(r) 155
§229.2(s) 155
§229.2(v) 155
§229.2(z) 163
§229.10 154
§229.10, Comment 5b 155
§229.12(b), Comment 1 155
§229.12(b)(1) 155, 158
§229.12(c), Comment 155
§229.12(c)(1)(i) 155, 159
§229.12(d) 155
§229.12(f) 156
§229.13(a) 155
§229.13(b) 156
§229.13(c) 156
§229.13(d) 156
§229.13(e) 156
§229.13(f) 156
§229.13(g) 155
§229.13(h) 155, 159
§229.14(a) 154
§229.16 154
§229.19(c), Comment 1 154
§229.20(a) 156
§229.30(a) 170
§229.30(a), Comment, Ex. b, (iii), (iv) 171
§229.30(a)(1) 170, 176
§229.30(a)(1)(i) 170
§229.30(a)(1)(ii) 170
§229.30(a)(2) 170, 176

§229.30(a)(2)(iii) 170
§229.30(c)(1) 166, 167
§229.30(c)(1), App. E. Comment 167
§229.31 163
§229.32(b), Comment b 172
§229.33(a) 171, 176
§229.34(a) 171
§229.34(b), Comment 171
§229.34(b)(2) 171
§229.34(c)(3) 174
§229.34(d) 172, 174
§229.37 164
§229.38(a) 171
§229.38(e) 166
part 226 211

16 C.F.R.
§433.1 39
§433.2(a) 39
§433.2(b) 39

Arizona Rev. Stat. Ann.

§44-145 (1987) 40

Cal. Fin. Code

§864(c) 144

Mich. Comp Laws

§488.16 203

Restatement (Second) of Contracts

§336(1) (1979) 2

Uniform Commercial Code

§1-103 .... 119, 147
§1-103(b) 147
§1-201, Comment 37 7
§1-201(22) 43
§1-201(25)(a) 32
§1-201(25)(b) 32
§1-201(25)(c) 32
§1-201(26) 32
§1-201(26)(b) 32
§1-201(27) 30, 31
§1-201(28) 31
§1-201(31) 99
§1-201(35) 92

§1-201(43) 107
§1-201(b)(4) 4
§1-201(b)(15) 20
§1-201(b)(20) 29, 30
§1-201(b)(23) 43
§1-201(b)(24) 11
§1-201(b)(25) 31
§1-201(b)(27) 146
§1-201(b)(33) 92
§1-201(b)(37) 7
§1-201(b)(43) 7
§1-202 . . . . 58, 65
§1-202(a) 32
§1-202(a)(3) 32
§1-202(e) 32
§1-202(f) 30, 31, 150
§1-206 99
§1-305(a) 147
§3-30(b)(3) 35
§3-102 2
§3-102, Comment 4 3
§3-102(a) 2
§3-102(b) 3
§3-103, Comment 4 30
§3-103(a)(2) 6, 17
§3-103(a)(2), Comment 6 6
§3-103(a)(3) 17, 40
§3-103(a)(4) 17, 29
§3-103(a)(5) 17, 18
§3-103(a)(6) 7, 8, 17, 29
§3-103(a)(7) 18, 120, 122
§3-103(a)(8) 3, 7, 8, 17
§3-103(a)(9) 3, 7, 8, 122, 138
§3-103(a)(11) 20, 79, 83
§3-103(a)(12) 3, 7, 8
§3-103(a)(14) 9, 51, 101, 149, 168
§3-103(a)(15) 20
§3-103(a)(16) 6, 78
§3-103(a)(17) 80, 83
§3-104 15
§3-104, Comment 1 . . . . 6, 7, 14
§3-104, Comment 2 . . . . 11, 15
§3-104, Comment 3 15
§3-104(a) 2, 6, 8, 9, 11, 15, 17
§3-104(a)(1) 11, 17
§3-104(a)(2) 12
§3-104(a)(3) 14
§3-104(c) 11
§3-104(d) 15
§3-104(e) 3, 17, 18
§3-104(f) 4, 17

§3-104(g) 4
§3-104(h) 4
§3-104(i) 4
§3-104(j) 3
§3-105(a) 20
§3-105(b) 43
§3-106, Comment 1 . . . . 8, 9
§3-106, Comment 2 5
§3-106(a) 8, 9
§3-106(a)(ii) 9
§3-106(a)(iii) 9
§3-106(b) 17
§3-106(b)(i) 9
§3-106(b)(ii) 8
§3-106(c) 5
§3-106(d) 39
§3-107 11
§3-108, Comment 14
§3-108(a) 12, 17
§3-108(a)(ii) 12
§3-108(b) 12, 13, 17
§3-108(b)(i) 13
§3-108(b)(ii) 13
§3-108(b)(iii) 13, 14
§3-108(b)(iv) 13, 14
§3-109, Comment 2 . . . . 11, 12
§3-109(a), Comment 2 12
§3-109(a)(1) 11
§3-109(a)(2) 11
§3-109(a)(3) 11, 17
§3-109(b) 11, 12
§3-109(c) 22
§3-110, Comment 1 . . . . 22, 23, 125
§3-110, Comment 3 . . . . 23, 24
§3-110, Comment 4 24
§3-110(a) 22, 23, 124, 125
§3-110(b) 23, 124
§3-110(c) 24
§3-110(c)(1) 23
§3-110(c)(2)(i) 24
§3-110(c)(2)(ii) 23, 24
§3-110(c)(2)(iii) 24
§3-110(c)(2)(iv) 24
§3-110(d) 24
§3-111 71
§3-112 17
§3-112, Comment 1 10
§3-112(a) 10
§3-112(b) 10
§3-113(a) 12
§3-113(b) 10, 17

§3-115(a) 119
§3-115(b) 119
§3-116 .... 83, 95
§3-116, Comment 1 .... 80, 95, 106
§3-116, Comment 2 95
§3-116(a) 81, 94, 95
§3-116(b) 80, 81, 83, 94, 106
§3-116(c) 95, 106
§3-117 52
§3-118 143
§3-118(g) 113
§3-201, Comment 1 .... 20, 21
§3-201(31) 99
§3-201(a) 20
§3-201(b) 21, 64, 135
§3-202 58
§3-203, Comment 1 54
§3-203, Comment 3 54
§3-203(a) 54
§3-203(b) 53, 54, 55, 65, 118
§3-203(c) 54
§3-204, Comment 3 .... 22, 23
§3-204(a) 21, 22, 69
§3-204(d) 22, 23
§3-205 22
§3-205, Comment 2 22
§3-205(a) 21
§3-205(b) 21
§3-205(c) 22
§3-206, Comment 3 130
§3-206, Comment 4 131
§3-206(a) 129
§3-206(c) 129
§3-206(c)(1) 130
§3-206(c)(2) 130, 137
§3-206(c)(4) 130, 137
§3-206(d) 129
§3-206(d)(1) 131
§3-206(d)(2) 131
§3-206(e) 130
§3-206(f) 130
§3-207 .... 55, 56, 58
§3-207, Comment 58
§3-302 .... 3, 58
§3-302, Comment 3 37
§3-302, Comment 5 .... 37, 38
§3-302, Comment 6 26
§3-302(a) 20, 37
§3-302(a)(1) 35
§3-302(a)(2) 33
§3-302(a)(2)(iii) 35, 64

§3-302(b) 33, 36, 37
§3-302(c) 37, 58
§3-302(c)(ii) 37
§3-302(c)(iii) 37
§3-302(d) 26
§3-302(e) 27
§3-302(e), Comment 6, Case 6 27
§3-302(f) 30
§3-303 81
§3-303, Comment 3 26
§3-303, Comment 4 27
§3-303(a) 25
§3-303(a)(1) 26, 65
§3-303(a)(2) 26
§3-303(a)(3) 27, 44, 65
§3-303(a)(4) 27
§3-303(a)(5) 27
§3-303(b) 44
§3-304, Comment 1 36
§3-304(a)(1) 36
§3-304(a)(2) 36
§3-304(a)(3) 36
§3-304(b)(1) 36
§3-304(b)(2) 36
§3-304(b)(3) 36
§3-304(c) 36
§3-305 40
§3-305, Comment 1 .... 42, 43
§3-305, Comment 3 .... 41, 44, 45
§3-305, Comment 4 45
§3-305, Comment 6 40
§3-305, Comment 7 40
§3-305(a) 33, 148
§3-305(a)(1) 65
§3-305(a)(1)(i) 41
§3-305(a)(1)(ii) 42
§3-305(a)(1)(iii) 42
§3-305(a)(1)(iv) 43
§3-305(a)(2) 21, 43, 53
§3-305(a)(3) 41, 44
§3-305(b) 2, 41, 43, 44, 54, 55,
                                 64, 65, 100, 148
§3-305(b)(1) 43
§3-305(b)(2) 43
§3-305(b)(3) 43
§3-305(c) 45, 46, 58
§3-305(d) 81, 82
§3-305(e) 40
§3-305(f) 40
§3-306 .... 20, 33, 45, 48,
                                    54, 58, 131

§3-306, Comment 45
§3-307 131
§3-307, Comment 2 34
§3-307, Comment 4 64
§3-307(a)(1) 34
§3-307(a)(2) 34
§3-307(b)(2) 35, 131
§3-307(b)(4) 35, 65
§3-307(b)(ii) 34
§3-307(b)(iii) 34
§3-308 2
§3-308, Comment 1 99
§3-308, Comment 2 100
§3-308(a) 99, 105
§3-308(b) 40, 99, 100, 105
§3-309 . . . . 99, 101, 116
§3-309, Comment 100
§3-309, Comment 2 101
§3-309(a) 101
§3-309(a)(1)(B) 101
§3-309(b) 100, 101
§3-310, Comment 2 97
§3-310, Comment 3 . . . . 96, 97
§3-310, Comment 4 . . . . 100, 116
§3-310, Comment 5 97
§3-310(a) 97
§3-310(b) 96, 97
§3-310(b)(1) 96, 97
§3-310(b)(2) 96, 97, 105
§3-310(b)(3) 96, 97
§3-310(b)(4) 96, 100, 116
§3-310(c) 96
§3-311, Comment 4 98
§3-311, Comment 5 98
§3-311, Comment 7 98
§3-311(a) 98
§3-311(b) 98
§3-311(c)(1) 98
§3-311(c)(2) 98
§3-311(d) 98
§3-312 101
§3-312, Comment 3 102
§3-312, Comment 4 102
§3-312(a)(3)(ii) 101
§3-312(b) 101, 102
§3-312(b)(2) 102
§3-312(b)(4) 102
§3-401, Comment 1 . . . . 92, 93
§3-401, Comment 2 7
§3-401(a) 93, 108, 114
§3-401(b) 7

§3-401(b)(ii) 7
§3-402, Comment 1 . . . . 92, 93
§3-402, Comment 2 . . . . 93, 94
§3-402, Comment 3 94
§3-402(a) 92, 93
§3-402(b) 93, 94
§3-402(b)(1) 93
§3-402(b)(2) 94, 105
§3-402(c) 94
§3-403, Comment 1 . . . . 93, 107
§3-403, Comment 3 119
§3-403(a) 77, 92, 93, 107,
                                          108, 119, 136
§3-404 . . . . 113, 119
§3-404, Comment 1 123
§3-404, Comment 2 . . . . Case 3, 138
§3-404, Comment 2, Case 4 125
§3-404, Comment 3 124
§3-404(a) 122, 123, 125, 137
§3-404(b) 124, 137
§3-404(b)(i) 124, 137
§3-404(b)(ii) 124, 137
§3-404(b)(1) 125, 138
§3-404(b)(2) 124, 137
§3-404(c) 123
§3-404(c)(ii) 123
§3-404(d) 124, 137
§3-405 . . . . 3, 113, 119, 137
§3-405, Comment 2 126
§3-405, Comment 2, Case 2 138
§3-405, Comment 2, Case 6 127
§3-405, Comment 3, Case 1 126
§3-405, Comment 3, Case 3 126
§3-405, Comment 4 126
§3-405(3) 126
§3-405(a)(1) 126
§3-405(a)(2) 125
§3-405(a)(3) 126
§3-405(a)(3)(i) 127
§3-405(a)(3)(ii) 126
§3-405(a)(3)(iv) 127
§3-405(b) 126
§3-405(c) 126
§3-406 . . . . 119, 129, 138
§3-406, Comment 1 . . . . 120, 121
§3-406, Comment 2 122
§3-406, Comment 3, Case 2 122
§3-406, Comment 3, Case 3 121
§3-406(a) 113, 117, 119,
                                          120, 122
§3-406(b) 120

§3-407, Comment 1 . . . . 117, 118
§3-407, Comment 2 118
§3-407(a) 116
§3-407(b) 117, 118, 119, 136
§3-407(c) 118, 119
§3-408 68
§3-409(a) 68, 69
§3-411 . . . . 56, 57
§3-411, Comment 1 56
§3-411, Comment 2 57
§3-411, Comment 3 58
§3-411(a) 56
§3-411(b) 57
§3-411(c) 57
§3-412 . . . . 46, 68, 117, 118
§3-413(a) 5, 68, 117, 118
§3-414, Comment 2 68
§3-414, Comment 4 68
§3-414, Comment 5 68
§3-414, Comment 6 72
§3-414(b) 68, 71, 117, 118, 148
§3-414(c) 68, 80, 83
§3-414(d) 68, 80, 83
§3-414(e) 68
§3-414(f) 72
§3-415 79
§3-415(a) 21, 68, 69, 70, 71,
                                          117, 118, 136
§3-415(b) 70
§3-415(c) 68, 70, 74, 75
§3-415(e) 70, 72
§3-416, Comment 2 . . . . 77, 108
§3-416, Comment 3 77
§3-416, Comment 4 78
§3-416, Comment 8 114
§3-416(a) 75
§3-416(a)(1) 77, 108, 115, 116
§3-416(a)(2) 77, 108, 115, 136
§3-416(a)(3) 77, 117
§3-416(a)(4) 77, 105
§3-416(a)(5) 78
§3-416(a)(6) 6, 78, 108, 115
§3-417 108
§3-417, Comment 2 . . . . 115, 136
§3-417, Comment 4 . . . . 110, 117
§3-417, Comment 5 110
§3-417, Comment 7 111
§3-417(a) 109
§3-417(a)(1) 115
§3-417(a)(2) 117
§3-417(a)(3) 114

§3-417(a)(4) 6, 110
§3-417(b) 109, 110
§3-417(c) 110
§3-417(d) 109, 110
§3-417(d)(1) 109
§3-417(f) 111
§3-418 . . . . 99, 111, 114, 118,
                                                       136, 137
§3-418, Comment 1 111
§3-418, Comment 2 111
§3-418(a) 110, 111
§3-418(b) 110, 118
§3-418(c) 110, 111, 114, 117, 118, 136, 137
§3-418(d) 99, 111, 167
§3-419 . . . . 81, 83
§3-419, Comment 1 79
§3-419, Comment 2 81
§3-419, Comment 4 79
§3-419, Comment 5 80
§3-419(a) 78
§3-419(b) 79, 81
§3-419(c) 82, 89, 104
§3-419(d) 79
§3-419(e) 79, 80, 81, 83, 105
§3-a419(e) 80
§3-419(f) 80
§3-420 111
§3-420, Comment 1 . . . . 112, 113
§3-420, Comment 2 113
§3-420, Comment 3 116
§3-420(a) 111, 112, 115,
                                                       116, 136
§3-420(a)(i) 113, 136
§3-420(a)(ii) 112
§3-420(b) 113
§3-420(c) 112, 137
§3-501(a) 71
§3-501(b)(1) 71
§3-501(b)(2)(i) 71
§3-501(b)(2)(ii) 71
§3-501(b)(2)(iii) 72
§3-501(b)(4) 71
§3-502 168
§3-502, Comment 1 71
§3-502, Comment 4 . . . . 73, 74
§3-502, Comment 5 74
§3-502, Comment 6 74
§3-502, Comment 7 71
§3-502(a)(1) 73
§3-502(a)(3) 73
§3-502(b) 74

§3-502(b)(1) 73
§3-502(b)(2) 73, 165
§3-502(b)(3) 168
§3-502(b)(3)(i) 73
§3-502(b)(3)(ii) 74
§3-502(c) 74, 168
§3-502(d)(1) 74
§3-502(d)(2) 74
§3-502(e) 71
§3-503 70
§3-503, Comment 1 74
§3-503, Comment 2 . . . . 75, 105
§3-503, Comment 6 74
§3-503(a) 70
§3-503(b) 74
§3-503(c) 74, 75, 105
§3-504(a)(i) 72
§3-504(a)(ii) 73
§3-504(a)(iii) 73
§3-504(a)(iv) 72
§3-504(a)(v) 72
§3-504(b) 75
§3-504(b)(ii) 75
§3-504(c) 75
§3-601(a) 51, 52
§3-601(b) 46, 65
§3-602 49
§3-602, Comment 1 . . . . 46, 48
§3-602, Comment 2 49
§3-602(a) 2, 41, 46, 47, 65
§3-602(b) 49
§3-602(b)(2) 46, 48
§3-602(d) 49
§3-602(e) 49
§3-602(e)(2) 46, 48
§3-603, Comment 50
§3-603(a) 50
§3-603(b) 50
§3-603(c) 49
§3-604 82
§3-604(a) 51
§3-604(c) 51
§3-605 . . . . 82, 83, 89, 95, 106
§3-605, Comment 1 82
§3-605, Comment 3 . . . . 83, 92
§3-605, Comment 4 . . . . 83, 84, 85, 87
§3-605, Comment 5 . . . . 85, 86, 87, 88
§3-605, Comment 6 . . . . 88, 89, 91
§3-605, Comment 7 . . . . 89, 90, 92
§3-605, Comment 8 89
§3-605, Comment 10 87

§3-605(a) 82, 89
§3-605(a)(1) 83
§3-605(a)(2) 84, 85
§3-605(a)(3) 84
§3-605(b) 83, 89, 105
§3-605(b)(1) 86
§3-605(b)(2) 85, 86
§3-605(b)(3) 86
§3-605(c) 85, 89
§3-605(c)(1) 88
§3-605(c)(2) 88
§3-605(c)(3) 88
§3-605(d) 85, 87, 89, 91, 92, 104
§3-605(e) 89, 91, 104, 105
§3-605(e)(i) 91
§3-605(e)(ii) 91
§3-605(f) 84, 89, 90, 91, 92, 105
§3-605(g) 84, 87, 90, 91
§3-605(h) 82, 88, 89, 105
§3-605(i) 88, 89, 92
§4-101, Comment 3 145
§4-102, Comment 1 3
§4-102(a) 3
§4-103, Comment 3 164
§4-103(a) 145, 164
§4-103(b) 164
§4-103(e) 174
§4-104, Comment 8 2
§4-104(a)(4) 163
§4-104(a)(5) 146
§4-104(a)(9) 2
§4-104(a)(10) 165
§4-104(c) 2
§4-105, Comment 3 162
§4-105(1) 4, 161
§4-105(2) 162
§4-105(3) 17, 162
§4-105(4) 162
§4-105(5) 162
§4-105(6) 162
§4-106, Comment 1 5
§4-106, Comment 2 5
§4-106(a) 5
§4-106(b), Alt. A 5
§4-106(b), Alt. B 6
§4-107 161–162
§4-107, Comment 2 . . . . 150, 162
§4-107, Comment 4 150
§4-108(a) 165
§4-108(b) 165
§4-109(b) 75, 166, 173

§4-110, Comment 1 174
§4-110(a) 174
§4-110(b) 174
§4-111 129
§4-201, Comment 4 172
§4-201(a) 172
§4-201(b) 129
§4-202, Comment 3 173
§4-202(a) 173
§4-202(b) 173
§4-202(c) 173
§4-205 25
§4-205, Comment 25
§4-205(1) 25
§4-205(2) 25
§4-207(a) 76
§4-207(a)(1) 76, 108, 115, 116
§4-207(a)(2) 77, 108, 115
§4-207(a)(3) 77, 117
§4-207(a)(4) 77
§4-207(a)(5) 78
§4-207(a)(6) 78
§4-207(b) 25
§4-208 108
§4-208(a) 109
§4-208(a)(1) 115, 116
§4-208(a)(2) 117
§4-208(a)(3) 114
§4-208(a)(4) 108, 110, 115
§4-208(b) 109, 110
§4-208(c) 110, 129
§4-208(d) 109, 110
§4-208(e) 111
§4-208(f) 111
§4-209, Comment 2 175
§4-209(a) 174
§4-209(c) 174
§4-210 28
§4-210(a) 26, 28
§4-210(a)(1) 28, 63
§4-210(a)(2) 28
§4-210(b) 29
§4-211 28
§4-214, Comment 3 .... 172, 173
§4-214, Comment 5 173
§4-214, Comment 6 173
§4-214(a) 172, 173, 176
§4-214(c) 173
§4-214(d) 176
§4-214(d)(1) 172
§4-214(d)(2) 173

§4-214(f) 156
§4-215 151
§4-215, Comment 4 169
§4-215, Comment 8 168
§4-215(a) 168
§4-215(a)(2) 169
§4-215(a)(3) 167, 169, 176
§4-215(d) 168
§4-215(e) 28
§4-215(e)(1) 156, 158
§4-301 .... 73, 169
§4-301, Comment 2 165
§4-301, Comment 4 165
§4-301, Comment 8 168
§4-301(a) 164, 165, 167, 173
§4-301(a)(1) 165
§4-301(a)(2) 165, 167, 168
§4-301(a)(3) 165, 168
§4-301(b) 165, 173
§4-302 .... 73, 150, 165, 176
§4-302, Comment 3 167
§4-302(a) 151, 171, 175
§4-302(a)(1) 165, 167, 169
§4-302(a)(2) 168
§4-302(b) 167
§4-303 .... 148, 150
§4-303, Comment 6 150
§4-303(a) 149, 150, 159
§4-303(a)(1) 149
§4-303(a)(2) 150
§4-303(a)(3) 150
§4-303(a)(4) 150
§4-303(a)(5) 150, 159
§4-303(b) 146, 158
§4-401, Comment 1 .... 141, 142
§4-401, Comment 3 142
§4-401, Comment 4 119
§4-401(a) 125, 136, 141, 142
§4-401(c) 142, 152, 158
§4-401(d)(1) 117
§4-401(d)(2) 119
§4-402, Comment 1 147
§4-402, Comment 3 158
§4-402, Comment 4 158
§4-402, Comment 5 .... 146, 159
§4-402(a) 142, 146
§4-402(b) 146, 147, 158
§4-402(c) 146
§4-403, Comment 2 148
§4-403, Comment 4 148
§4-403, Comment 5 148

§4-403, Comment 6 149
§4-403, Comment 7 148
§4-403(a) 147, 148
§4-403(a), Comment 5 148
§4-403(b) 149
§4-403(c) 151, 152
§4-404 . . . . 142, 143
§4-404, Comment 143
§4-405, Comment 2 144
§4-405, Comment 3 145
§4-405(a) 144
§4-405(b) 144, 145, 152
§4-406 . . . . 119, 127
§4-406, Comment 5 129
§4-406, Rev'd Comment 1 . . . . 127, 128
§4-406, Rev'd Comment 2 . . . . 128, 138
§4-406, Rev'd Comment 3 127
§4-406, Rev'd Comment 4 137
§4-406, Rev'd Comment 5 129
§4-406(a) 127
§4-406(a), Rev'd Comment 1 127
§4-406(b) 127
§4-406(c) 127, 128, 129
§4-406(d) 129
§4-406(d)(1) 128
§4-406(d)(2) 128
§4-406(e) 128
§4-406(f) 128, 129, 138
§4-407(1) 152
§4-407(2) 152, 159
§4-407(3) 153, 159
§4A-102 179
§4A-103(a)(1) 180
§4A-103(a)(1)(i) 182
§4A-103(a)(1)(ii) 182
§4A-103(a)(1)(iii) 182
§4A-103(a)(2) 180, 196
§4A-103(a)(3) 180, 196
§4A-103(a)(4) 180, 196
§4A-103(a)(5) 180, 196
§4A-104, Comment 1, Case 1 181
§4A-104, Comment 1, Case 2 179
§4A-104, Comment 1, Case 3 181
§4A-104, Comment 2 181
§4A-104, Comment 5 182
§4A-104(a) 180, 181, 186
§4A-104(c) 180, 196
§4A-104(d) 180, 196
§4A-105(a)(3) 180, 196
§4A-105(a)(4) 186
§4A-108 182

§4A-201 190
§4A-202(a) 190
§4A-202(b) 190, 191, 196
§4A-202(f) 192
§4A-203, Comment 1 190
§4A-203, Comment 2 191
§4A-203, Comment 3 191
§4A-203(a) 197
§4A-203(a)(2) 191
§4A-203(a)(2)(i) 191
§4A-204, Comment 1 192
§4A-204(1) 185
§4A-204(a) 192
§4A-205, Comment 1 . . . . 192, 193
§4A-205, Comment 2 193
§4A-205(a)(1) 192
§4A-205(a)(3) 193
§4A-205(b) 193
§4A-207 193
§4A-207, Comment 1 193
§4A-207, Comment 2 194
§4A-207(a) 193
§4A-207(b)(1) 193
§4A-207(b)(2) 194
§4A-207(c)(1) 194
§4A-207(c)(2) 193
§4A-208, Comment 1, Case 1 194
§4A-208(a)(1) 194
§4A-208(a)(2) 194
§4A-208(b) 194
§4A-208(b)(2) 195
§4A-208(b)(4) 195
§4A-209, Comment 1 . . . . 183, 196
§4A-209, Comment 8 186
§4A-209(a) 183
§4A-209(b)(1)(i) 186
§4A-209(b)(1)(ii) 186
§4A-209(b)(2) 186
§4A-209(b)(3) 186
§4A-209(d) 183, 186, 196
§4A-210, Comment 1 183
§4A-210(a) 183
§4A-210(d) 187
§4A-211, Comment 1 188
§4A-211, Comment 3 189
§4A-211, Comment 4, Case 1 190
§4A-211, Comment 7 189
§4A-211(a) 189
§4A-211(b) 188, 189
§4A-211(c) 189, 196
§4A-211(c)(1) 189

250   PAYMENT SYSTEMS

§4A-211(c)(2) 190
§4A-211(d) 189
§4A-211(e) 188
§4A-212 .... 183, 196
§4A-301, Comment 2 183
§4A-301(a) 183
§4A-301(b) 183
§4A-302(a)(1) 183
§4A-302(a)(2) 183
§4A-303, Comment 2 .... 184, 185
§4A-303(a) 184
§4A-303(b) 185
§4A-303(c) 184
§4A-304 185
§4A-305, Comment 2 184
§4A-305(a) 184, 196
§4A-305(b) 184, 194, 196
§4A-305(c) 184, 196
§4A-305(d) 184
§4A-401 183
§4A-401, Comment 183
§4A-402, Comment 1 182

§4A-402, Comment 2 182
§4A-402(b) 182
§4A-402(c) 182, 184, 193
§4A-404, Comment 2 187
§4A-404, Comment 3 187
§4A-404(a) 186, 187
§4A-404(b) 187
§4A-405(a) 186
§4A-406, Comment 1 188
§4A-406, Comment 2 188
§4A-406(a) 186, 188, 196
§4A-406(b) 188
§4A-503 195
§4A-503, Comment 195
§4A-505 .... 185, 192
§4A-505, Comment 185, 192
§5-112 74
§9-207 90

Uniform Consumer Credit Code

§3-404 (1974) 40

Subject Matter Index

ACCELERATION CLAUSE, 13

ACCEPTANCE, 68, 69

ACCEPTED CREDIT CARD, 212

ACCOMMODATION PARTIES
accommodated party, and, 81
contribution, 81, 92, 94
defenses, 81–82
discharge, 82–92
extensions/modifications, 85–89
generally, 78–92
impairment of collateral, 89–92
reimbursement, 80, 83–84, 87
subrogation, 80, 82, 99
subsuretyship, 81
suretyship defenses, 82
who are they, 78–80

ACCORD AND SATISFACTION, 98

AFTER ACCEPTANCE, 13

AFTER DATE, 13

AFTER SIGHT, 13

ALTERATIONS, 30, 35, 116–119.
See also UNAUTHORIZED
SIGNATURES

ANOMALOUS INDORSER, 69

ANTECEDENT DEBT, 27

ATM TRANSFERS. *See* CONSUMER
ELECTRONIC FUND TRANSFERS

AVAILABILITY OF FUNDS, 153–156

BANK, 4

BANK CHECKS
defenses/claims, 56–58
lost/destroyed/stolen, 101–102
payment by instrument, 97
types, 4

BANK COLLECTION PROCESS
branch banking, 161–162
chargeback, 172–173
collecting banks, duties of, 172–175
cut-off hour, 165
documentary drafts, 168
electronic presentment, 174
failure to settle/return item, 167–168
final payment, 168–169
generally, 161
governing law, 163–164
manner of dishonoring item, 165–167
manner of payment, 167
midnight deadline, 165–167, 169, 171, 173
on-us checks, 165
overview/terminology, 161–163
payor bank, duties of, 164–172
pay/settle on day of presentment, 164–165
returning unpaid items, 169–172
variation by agreement, 164

BANK STATEMENT, 127–128

BANK/CUSTOMER AGREEMENT, 145–146

BANK/CUSTOMER RELATIONSHIP. *See*
PAYOR BANK/CUSTOMER
RELATIONSHIP

BANKER'S ACCEPTANCE, 5

BANKING DAY, 154

BENEFICIARY, 180

BENEFICIARY'S BANK, 180

BILL OF EXCHANGE, 4

BILLING ERRORS (CREDIT CARDS), 215–216

BLANK FOR COLLECTION INDORSEMENT,
129

BLANK INDORSEMENT, 21

BREACH OF FIDUCIARY DUTY, 33–35

BULK TRANSACTIONS, 37–38

BURDEN OF PROOF, 99–100

BUSINESS DAY, 154

CANCELLATION, 51–52

CARD ISSUER, 211

CARDHOLDER, 211

CARELESS BUSINESS PRACTICES, 120

CASHIER'S CHECKS, 4

CERTIFICATE OF DEPOSIT, 3–4

CERTIFIED CHECK, 4

CHARGEBACK, 172–173

CHECK COLLECTION PROCESS. *See* BANK COLLECTION PROCESS

CHECK TRUNCATION, 174

CHECKS, 4

CHECKWRITING MACHINE, 23

CLAIM IN RECOUPMENT, 41, 44–45

CLAIM TO THE INSTRUMENT, 41, 45

CLEARING HOUSE, 163

CLEARING-HOUSE RULES, 164

COLLATERAL, 14

COLLECTING BANK, 162

COLLECTION GUARANTEED, 79

COMPARATIVE NEGLIGENCE, 120, 124
  bank's failure to exercise ordinary care in paying
    item, 128

CONDITIONAL SALES CONTRACTS, 15

CONFESSION OF JUDGMENT, 14

CONSUMER CREDIT CONTRACT, 39

**CONSUMER ELECTRONIC FUND
    TRANSFERS**
  accepted access device, 201
  bona fide error, 208
  civil liability, 207–208
  class actions, 207
  consumer liability for unauthorized transfers,
    201–203
  documentation requirements, 206
  error resolution procedures, 206–207
  generally, 199
  governing law, 199
  how initiated, 200
  liability for failure to make correct transfer, 207
  loss/theft of access device, 202–203
  periodic statements, 206
  preauthorized fund transfers, 203–206
  receipts, 206
  stop payment, 203–204

  system malfunction (consumer liability),
    204–205
  unrequested access devices, 205

CONSUMER NOTES, 38–40

CONSUMER TRANSACTION, 39

CONTRIBUTION, 81, 95

CONVERSION, 111–113

CREDIT CARDS
  billing errors, 215–216
  generally, 211
  governing law, 211–212
  liability for unauthorized use, 212–214
  refusal of payment, 214–215
  terminology, 211

CUSTOMER/BANK RELATIONS. *See* BANK
    COLLECTION PROCESS; PAYOR
    BANK/CUSTOMER RELATIONSHIP

CUT-OFF HOUR, 165

DAMAGES. *See* MEASURE OF DAMAGES

DEATH, 144–145

DEFENSES
  accommodation parties, 81–82
  consumer electronic fund transfers, 208
  conversion action, 113
  holder in due course, 41–46

DEFER POSTING, 164–165

DELIVERY, 20

DEPOSITORY BANK, 162

DISCHARGE
  accommodation parties, of, 82–92
  cancellation, 51–52
  effect of, 46
  fraudulent alteration, 118
  insolvency proceeding, in, 43
  notice of, 36–37
  payment, 46–50
  renunciation, 51–52
  simple contract, 52
  surrender, 51
  tender of payment, 49–50

DISCHARGE FOR VALUE RULE, 185

DISCOVERY RULE, 113

DISHONOR, 70, 71, 73–75, 96

DOCUMENTARY DRAFTS, 5, 168

D'OENCH, DUHME DOCTRINE, 59

DOUBLE FORGERIES, 125

DRAFTS, 5

DRAWEE, 4

DRAWEE BANK, 4

DRAWER, 4

DUE DILIGENCE, 31–32

DURESS, 42

DUTY TO FORWARD INFORMATION, 31

DUTY TO INQUIRE TEST, 33

EFTA, 199–200

ELECTRONIC FUND TRANSFER, 199 et seq.
  See also CONSUMER ELECTRONIC
  FUND TRANSFERS, WHOLESALE
  FUNDS TRANSFERS

ELECTRONIC FUND TRANSFER ACT (EFTA),
  199–200

ELECTRONIC PRESENTMENT, 174

EMPLOYER RESPONSIBILITY FOR
  FRAUDULENT INDORSEMENT BY
  EMPLOYEE, 125–127

ENCODING WARRANTIES, 174–175

EQUITABLE CLAIM OF OWNERSHIP, 45

ERRONEOUS EXECUTION OF PAYMENT
  ORDER, 184–185

ERRONEOUS PAYMENT ORDERS, 192–193

ERRORS (CONSUMER ELECTRONIC FUND
  TRANSFERS), 206–207

ESTOPPEL, 119

EXPRESS CONDITION, 8

EXTENSIONS/MODIFICATIONS, 85–89

EXTRINSIC EVIDENCE, 52–53

FEDERAL DEPOSIT INSURANCE
  CORPORATION (FDIC), 58–59

FEDERAL HOLDER-IN-DUE-COURSE
  DOCTRINE, 58–59

FEDERAL RESERVE SYSTEM, 162

FICTITIOUS PAYEE, 124–125

FIDUCIARY, 34

FIFTH-DAY AVAILABILITY, 155

FIXED AMOUNT, 9–10

FOR COLLECTION INDORSEMENT, 129

FOR DEPOSIT, 129

FOR DEPOSIT ONLY INDORSEMENT, 129–130

FORGERY. *See* ALTERATIONS;
  UNAUTHORIZED SIGNATURES

FORWARD COLLECTION TEST, 170

FORWARDING OF RELEVANT
  INFORMATION, 31

FRAUD IN THE FACTUM, 42–43

FRAUD IN THE INDUCEMENT, 43

FRAUDULENT ACTIVITY. *See* ALTERATIONS,
  UNAUTHORIZED SIGNATURES

FRAUDULENT INDORSEMENT, 125

FUND TRANSFERS. *See* CONSUMER
  ELECTRONIC FUND TRANSFERS,
  WHOLESALE FUNDS TRANSFERS

FUNDS AVAILABILITY, 153–156

GOOD FAITH, 29–30

HOLDER IN DUE COURSE
  admissibility of extrinsic evidence, 52–53
  bank checks, defenses/claims, 56–58
  claim in recoupment, 41, 44–45
  claims to instruments, 41, 45
  defenses, 41–46
  denial of, to certain purchasers, 37–40
  discharge, 46–52.
    See also DISCHARGE
  federal holder-in-due-course doctrine,
    58–59
  generally, 19–20
  good faith, 29–30
  holder status, 20–25
  indorsement, 21–24

HOLDER IN DUE COURSE (*cont.*)
  notice, 30–37.
    See also NOTICE
  refusal payment, 40–52
  shelter provision, 53–56
  transfer of instrument, 53–56
  value, 25–29

HOLDER STATUS, 20–25

ILLEGALITY, 42

IMAGING TECHNOLOGY, 174

IMPAIRMENT OF COLLATERAL, 89–92

IMPLIED CONDITION, 8

IMPOSTORS, 122–124

INCAPACITY, 42

INCOMPETENCE, 144

INCOMPLETE INSTRUMENTS, 118–119

INDORSEMENT, 21–24

INDORSEMENT WITHOUT RECOURSE, 70

INFANCY, 41–42

INFERABLE KNOWLEDGE TEST, 32–33

INJUNCTION
  negotiable instrument, 47
  wholesale funds transfer, 195

INNOCENT ALTERATIONS, 35

INTERMEDIARY BANK, 162

ISSUANCE OF INSTRUMENT, 20

ISSUING BANK, 211

ITEM, 2

ITEM PROPERLY PAYABLE, 141–145

LEGAL CLAIM OF OWNERSHIP, 45

LEGALS, 149–151

LIABILITY ON NEGOTIABLE INSTRUMENTS
  acceptor, 68–69
  accord and satisfaction, 98
  agents (representative), 93–94
  burden of proof, 99–100
  co-obligors, 94–95

  dishonor, 71, 73–75
  drawee, 68
  drawer, 68
  generally, 67–70
  indorsers, 69–70, 95
  issuer, 68
  lost/destroyed/stolen instruments, 100–102
  payment by instrument, 96–98
  principal (represented person), 92–93
  procedural issues, 99–100
  sureties/accommodation parties, 78–92.
    See also ACCOMMODATION
    PARTIES
  transfer warranty, 75–78

LIEN ON INSTRUMENT, 26–27

LIQUIDATION SALE, 37–38

LOCAL CHECKS, 155

LOCKBOX ACCOUNTS, 98

LOST/DESTROYED/STOLEN INSTRUMENTS,
  100–102

MAKER, 3

MANDATORY AVAILABILITY SCHEDULE,
  154

MEASURE OF DAMAGES
  breach of duty by receiving bank, 184
  breach of warranty, 109–110
  collecting bank's failure to exercise ordinary care,
    173–174
  consumer electronic fund transfers, 207–208
  conversion, 113
  failure to stop preauthorized fund transfer, 204
  stop payment order, 151–152
  wrongful dishonor, 147

MERCHANT, 211

MERCHANT BANK, 211

MIDNIGHT DEADLINE, 165–167, 171

MISTAKE OF FACT RULE, 184–185

MISTAKEN PAYMENT, 111

MODIFICATIONS/EXTENSIONS, 85–89

MONEY, 11

MONEY-BACK GUARANTEE, 182–183

NEGLIGENCE, 119–122

NEGOTIABLE INSTRUMENT
alterations, 35, 116–119
forgery. *See* UNAUTHORIZED SIGNATURES
holder in due course. *See* HOLDER IN DUE COURSE
liability. *See* LIABILITY ON NEGOTIABLE INSTRUMENTS
ordinary contract right, compared, 1–2
procedural issues, 99–100
requirements for negotiability. *See* REQUIREMENTS FOR NEGOTIABILITY
restrictive indorsement, 129–131
types, 3–6
what is it, 1

NEXT DAY AVAILABILITY, 154–155

NONLOCAL CHECKS, 155

NOT NEGOTIABLE, 15

NOTES, 3–4

NOTICE, 30–37
actual knowledge, 32
breach of fiduciary duty, 33–35
claim/defense, 33–37
discharge, 36–37
duty to inquire test, 33
forgery/alteration, 35
inferable knowledge test, 32–33
manner of obtaining, 32
notification, 32
organization, to, 30–31
overdue/dishonored, 35–36
purchase at discount, 33
reason to know, 32–33
subsequent, 30
when effective, 30

NOTICE OF DISCHARGE, 36–37

ON-US CHECKS, 165

ORDINARY CARE, 120–122

ORGANIZATIONAL CHANGE, 38

ORIGINATOR, 180

ORIGINATOR'S BANK, 180

OVERDRAFTS, 142

OVERDUE, 35–36

OVERENCODING, 174–175

PAROL EVIDENCE RULE, 52–53

PARTIAL PERFORMANCE, 26

PAY ANY BANK, 129

PAYABLE AT DEFINITE TIME, 12–14

PAYABLE AT ITEMS, 5–6

PAYABLE ON DEMAND, 12

PAYABLE THROUGH ITEM, 5

PAYABLE TO ACCOUNT NUMBER, 23

PAYABLE TO AGENT FOR IDENTIFIED PERSON, 23–24

PAYABLE TO BEARER, 11–12

PAYABLE TO FUND/ORGANIZATION, 24

PAYABLE TO OFFICE/OFFICER, 24

PAYABLE TO ORDER, 11–12

PAYABLE TO TRUST/ESTATE, 24

PAYEE, 3

PAYING BANK, 163

PAYMENT, 46–50

PAYMENT BY INSTRUMENT, 96–98

PAYMENT ORDER, 180

PAYOR BANK, 4, 162

PAYOR BANK/CUSTOMER RELATIONSHIP
bank statement, 127–128
bank/customer agreement, 145–146
customer's death, 144–145
customer's incompetence, 144
funds availability, 153–156
generally, 141
item properly payable, 141–145
postdated checks, 142
setoff, 143–144
stale checks, 142–143
stop payment, 147–153
subrogation, 152–153
wrongful dishonor, 146–147

PERSONAL MONEY ORDER, 5

POINT OF SALE (POS) TRANSFERS, 200.
    See also CONSUMER ELECTRONIC
    FUND TRANSFERS

POSTDATED CHECKS, 142

**PREAUTHORIZED ELECTRONIC FUND
    TRANSFERS**, 203–204

PRESENTING BANK, 162–163

PRESENTMENT, 71–73

PRESENTMENT WARRANTIES, 108–111

PRINCIPAL OBLIGOR, 79

PROMISE OR ORDER, 8

PROPERLY PAYABLE, 141–145

PROVISIONS FOR INTEREST, 10

PURCHASE AT DISCOUNT, 33

RATIFICATION, 119

REAL DEFENSES, 41–43

REACQUISITION BY PRIOR HOLDER,
    55–56

REASON TO KNOW, 32–33

RECEIVING BANK, 180

RECORD, 51

REFERS TO/SUBJECT TO, 9

REFUSAL OF PAYMENT
    credit cards, 214–215
    negotiable instrument, 40–52

REGULATION CC, 153–156, 163–164,
    166–167

REGULATION J, 163–164

REIMBURSEMENT, 80

REMITTER, 20

REMOTELY CREATED CONSUMER ITEM, 6

RENUNCIATION, 51–52

REPRESENTATIVE, 93–94

REPRESENTED PERSON, 92–93

REQUIREMENTS FOR NEGOTIABILITY
    compliance with U.C.C., 6
    fixed amount, 9–10
    generally, 6–15
    negotiability determined by writing itself, 15
    no other promises or orders, 14–15
    payable at definite time, 12–14
    payable in money, 11
    payable on demand, 12
    payable to order/bearer, 11–12
    promise or order, 8
    unconditionality, 8–9
    writing, 7

RESOLUTION TRUST COMPANY (RTC), 58–59

RESTRICTIVE INDORSEMENTS, 129–131

RETURNING BANK, 163

RTC, 58–59

SECONDARY OBLIGOR, 79–80

SECOND-DAY AVAILABILITY, 155

SECURITY INTEREST IN INSTRUMENT, 26–27

SECURITY PROCEDURE, 190

SETOFF, 143–144

SHELTER PROVISION, 53–56

SIGHT DRAFT, 5

SIGNATURE, 7

SIMULTANEOUS DEPOSITS, 29

SPECIAL INDORSEMENT, 21

STALE CHECKS, 142–143

STOLEN INSTRUMENTS, 100–102

STOP PAYMENT
    electronic fund transfers, 203–204
    negotiable instruments, 147–153
    payment order, 188–190
    preauthorized electronic fund transfers, 203–204

SUBJECT TO ACCELERATION, 13

SUBJECT TO EXTENSION, 13–14

SUBJECT TO PREPAYMENT, 13

SUBJECT TO/REFERS TO, 9

SUBROGATION
accommodation parties, 80
payor bank (improper payment), 152–153
wholesale fund transfer, 185

SUBSEQUENT NOTICE, 30

SUBSURETYSHIP, 81

SURETIES. *See* ACCOMMODATION PARTIES

SURETYSHIP DEFENSES, 82

SURRENDER, 51

TAKING OVER AN ESTATE, 37

TELLER'S CHECKS, 4

TENDER OF PAYMENT, 49–50

THIRD-PARTY CLAIMS, 57–58

TIME DRAFT, 5

TRADE ACCEPTANCE, 5

TRANSFER OF INSTRUMENT, 53–56

TRANSFER WARRANTIES, 75–78

TRAVELER'S CHECKS, 4–5

TRUST INDORSEMENT, 129, 130–131

TRUTH IN LENDING ACT, 211

TWO OR MORE PAYEES, 24

TWO-DAY/FOUR-DAY TEST, 170

UNAUTHORIZED FUND TRANSFERS, 201–203

UNAUTHORIZED SIGNATURES
bank statement, 127–128
consequences, 107–108
conversion, 111–113
employer responsibility for employee, 125–127
estoppel, 119
fictitious payee, 124–125
forged indorsement in chain of title, 108
generally, 107
impostors, 122–124
liability of person whose name is signed, 108
mistaken payment, 111
negligence, 119–122
preclusion, 117, 119–129
presentment warranties, 108–111

ratification, 119
transfer warranties, 108
when indorsement unauthorized, 115–116
when signature of drawer unauthorized, 114–115

UNAUTHORIZED USE OF CREDIT CARD, 212–214

UNCONDITIONALITY, 8–9

UNDERENCODING, 174–175

UNIFORM COMMERCIAL CODE (U.C.C.), 2–3

UNIFORM CONSUMER CREDIT CODE, 39–40

VALUE, 25–29

VERIFIED PAYMENT ORDER, 191

WAIVER, 14

WARRANTIES
encoding, 174–175
presentment, 108–111
return of unpaid items, 171
transfer, 75–78, 108

WHOLESALE FUNDS TRANSFERS
cancellation of payment order, 188–190
duties of beneficiary's bank, 186–187
duties/liabilities of receiving bank, 183–184
effect of acceptance of underlying obligation, 188
erroneous execution of payment order, 184–185
erroneous payment orders, 192–193
execution of order, 183–184
generally, 179
injunction, 195
liability for authorized payment orders, 191
liability for unauthorized payment orders, 192
misdescriptions, 193–195
payment obligations in chain of title, 182–183
payment order, 180–182
security procedure, 190
terminology, 180
verified payment orders, 191

WIRE TRANSFERS. *See* WHOLESALE FUNDS TRANSFERS

WITHOUT RECOURSE, 70

WRITING, 7

WRONGFUL DISHONOR, 146–147